BOOK ILLUSTRATORS OF THE TWENTIETH CENTURY

BOOK
ILLUSTRATORS
of the
Twentieth Century

Brigid Peppin
Lucy Micklethwait

ARCO PUBLISHING, INC.
New York

To David Curtis and David Micklethwait.

Published 1984 by Arco Publishing, Inc.
215 Park Avenue South, New York, NY 10003

Produced by Ian Cameron and Jill Hollis
for Cameron Books Ltd, 2a Roman Way, London N7

Editorial consultant: Simon Heneage

Library of Congress Cataloging in Publication Data

Peppin, Brigid.
  Book illustrators of the twentieth century.

  1. Illustrators—Biography.   2. Illustration
  of books—20th century.   I. Micklethwait, Lucy.
  II. Title.
NC961.6.P45 1983   741.64'092'2 [B]   83-3745
ISBN 0-668-05670-3

Printed in Great Britain

FOREWORD

This is the first reference book to attempt a comprehensive coverage of British book illustrators working in the twentieth century. The coverage is primarily of fiction and poetry illustrators, whose work was first published in Britain between 1900 and 1975.

The biographical section of each entry gives a brief outline of the artist's life and career. As there are few published sources of information on twentieth-century illustrators (particularly those working after World War II), the entries have been compiled from a combination of standard reference works on artists, monographs, general studies of book illustration and previously unpublished information supplied by the illustrators themselves, or their families, in answer to questionnaires (indicated at the end of the entry by [Q]).

In most cases, book lists are based on the British Library catalogue, supplemented by information gleaned from second-hand and antiquarian booksellers and private book collectors. Where an illustrator's output was or has been particularly prolific and is comprehensively documented in an existing work of reference (indicated in the References section of the entry), or the illustrator has particularly requested that a selected list should appear, a shortened list has been provided. The Periodicals section lists periodicals to which an illustrator has contributed. The References section is intended to acknowledge sources of information used in the compilation of the entry and to facilitate further research. Standard works have been abbreviated to avoid lengthy repetition, as have the names of societies that appear in the biographical sections of the entries. These abbreviations are listed before the alphabetical sequence of entries.

The illustrations are reproduced with permission of the publishers, where they or their successors can be traced, or of the illustrators themselves. The names of the publishers are given in the captions. In some cases, where the artist has contributed only one or two pictures to an anthology, the title listed in the caption may not appear in the book list. Where the date given in the caption is later than that in the book list, we do not have firm evidence as to whether the book is a late impression or a new and differently illustrated version.

During our six years' work on this book, we have been conscious of the lack of reliable documentation in the field. This has inevitably led to

some of the entries being incomplete. We would welcome any additional information from readers.

We would like to thank the many illustrators or their families who have responded to our queries, and all those listed below who have contributed expert assistance or given us access to their collections.

Helen Binyon
John Buchanan Brown
Victoria Burgess
Mr & Mrs Cawthorne
Laura Cecil
R.J. Cleevely
John Clute
Nicola Cross
Paul Delaney
William Feaver
Peter Firmin
Henry Ford
Albert Garrett
Clare Rangdale Green
Len Hawkey
Pamela Hidaka
Raymond Lister
Ruari McLean
Alice Macnab
Dodie Masterman
Graham Ovenden
Helen Peppin
Portman Books
Charlotte Robinson
Bertram Rota Ltd
Joanna Selborne
Norman Shaw
Peyton Skipwith
Paul Smith
Bettina Tayleur
Donna Thynne
Gabriel White

We would particularly like to thank Simon Heneage for the sustained support he has given us over the many years it has taken to complete the book, and the publishers on both sides of the Atlantic for their unending patience in waiting for it.

ABBREVIATIONS

A	Associate
AIA	Artists International Association
BI	British Institution
EWE	English Wood-Engraving Society (amalgamated with SWE, 1932)
FAS	Fine Art Society
GI	Glasgow Institute of Fine Arts
ICA	Institute of Contemporary Arts
IS	International Society of Sculptors, Painters and Gravers
NEAC	New English Art Club
NS	National Society of Painters Sculptors and Printmakers
NSA	Nottingham Society of Artists
OWS	Old Watercolour Society (became RWS)
PS	Pastel Society
RA	Royal Academy
RBA	Royal Society of British Artists
RBSA	Royal Birmingham Society of Artists
RCA	Royal College of Art
RCamA	Royal Cambrian Academy
RDS	Royal Drawing Society
RE	Royal Society of Painter-Etchers and Engravers
RHA	Royal Hibernian Academy
RI	Royal Institute of Painters in Watercolours
RIBA	Royal Institute of British Architects
RMS	Royal Society of Miniature Painters Sculptors and Gravers
ROI	Royal Institute of Oil Painters
RP	Royal Society of Portrait Painters
RSA	Royal Scottish Academy
RSMA	Royal Society of Marine Artists
RSW	Royal Scottish Society of Painters in Water-Colours
RUA	Royal Ulster Academy of Painting, Sculpture and Architecture
RWA	Royal West of England Academy
RWS	Royal Society of Painters in Water-Colours (previously OWS)
SA	Society of Antiquaries
SGA	Society of Graphic Artists
SIA	Society of Industrial Artists and Designers
SPCK	Society for Promoting Christian Knowledge
SWA	Society of Women Artists
SWE	Society of Wood Engravers
WAG	Walker Art Gallery, Liverpool
WIAC	Women's International Art Club

REFERENCES

Baker	Charles Baker *Bibliography of British Book Illustrators 1860-1900* Birmingham Bookshop, 1978.
Balston EWE	Thomas Balston *English Wood Engraving 1900-1950* Art & Technics, 1951.
Balston WEMEB	Thomas Balston *Wood Engraving in Modern English Books* OUP/National Book League, 1949
Bénézit	E. Bénézit *Dictionnaire critique et documentaire des Peintres, Sculpteurs, Dessinateurs et Graveurs* (first published 1911-23) 10 vols, Librairie Grund, 1976.
Bland	David Bland *A History of Book Illustration* (first published, 1911-23) Faber & Faber, 1969
Bliss	Douglas Percy Bliss *A History of Wood-Engraving* Dent, 1928
Bradshaw	Percy V. Bradshaw *The Art of the Illustrator* 20 parts, Press Art School, 1918.
Bryan	M. Bryan *Dictionary of Painters and Engravers* 5 vols, G. Bell, 1904-05.
Chamot, Farr & Butlin	Mary Chamot, Dennis Farr and Martin Butlin *The Modern British Paintings, Drawings and Sculpture* 2 vols, Tate Gallery/Oldbourne Press, 1964.
Contemporary Artists	Colin Naylor and Genesis P-Orridge *Contemporary Artists* St James Press, 1977.
Contemporary Authors	*Contemporary Authors* vols 1-102, Gale Research Co., Detroit, 1962-81.
Cope	Dawn and Peter Cope *Illustrators of Postcards from the Nursery* East West Publications, 1978.
Crane	Walter Crane *Of the Decorative Illustration of Books Old and New* (first published G. Bell, 1896) Bell & Hyman, 1979.
Crouch	Marcus Crouch *Treasure Seekers and Borrowers: Children's Books in Britain 1900-1960* London Library Association, 1962.
Cuppleditch	David Cuppleditch *London Sketch Club* Dilke Press, 1978.
DNB	Dictionary of National Biography 63 vols plus supplements: I (1901), II (1912), *1901-11* (1912), *1912-21* (1927), *1922-30* (1937), *1931-40* (1949), *1941-50* (1959), *1951-60* (1971) published by Smith Elder & Co. 1885-1912, OUP 1927-71.
Doyle BWI	Brian Doyle *The Who's Who of Children's Literature* Hugh Evelyn, 1968.
Doyle CL	Brian Doyle *The Who's Who of Boys' Writers and Illustrators* Brian Doyle, 1964.
Driver	David Driver *The Art of the Radio Times* BBC/European Illustration, 1981.
Everitt	Graham Everitt *English Caricaturists and Graphic Humorists of the 19th Century* (first published 1886) S. Sonnenschein, 1893.
Eyre	F. Eyre *British Children's Books in the 20th Century* Longmans, 1971.
Fisher	Margery Fisher *Who's Who in Children's Books* Weidenfeld & Nicolson, 1975.
Garrett BWE	Albert Garrett *British Wood Engraving of the 20th Century* Scolar Press, 1980.
Garrett HBWE	Albert Garrett *A History of British Wood Engraving* Midas Books, 1978.
Gilmour	Pat Gilmour *Artists at Curwen* Tate Gallery, 1977.
Guichard	Kenneth M. Guichard *British Etchers 1850-1940* Robin Garton, 1977.
Hammerton	J.A. Hammerton *Humorists of the Pencil* Hurst & Blackett, 1905.
Harper	Charles G. Harper *English Pen Artist of To-Day* Percival, 1892.
Hillier	Bevis Hillier *Cartoons and Caricatures* Studio Vista, 1970.
Hofer	Philip Hofer (introduction) and Eleanor M. Garvey (catalogue) *The Artist and the Book 1860-1960 in Western Europe and the United States* Museum of Fine Arts Boston/Harvard College Library, 1961.

Houfe	Simon Houfe *The Dictionary of British Book Illustrators and Caricaturists 1800-1914* Antique Collectors' Club, 1978.
Hürlimann	Bettina Hürlimann *Picture Book World* Oxford University Press, 1968.
ICB	*Illustrators of Children's Books* vol 1 1744-1945 compiled by Bertha E. Mahoney, Louise Payson Latimer and Beulah Folmsbee; vol 2 1946-56 compiled by Bertha Mahoney Miller, Ruth Hill Viguers and Marcia Dalphin; vol 3 1957-66 compiled by Lee Kingman, Grace Allen Hogarth and Harriet Quimby. Published by Horn Book Inc., Boston 1947-78.
Jacques	Robin Jacques *Illustrators at Work* Studio Books, 1963.
Johnson	Diana Johnson *Fantastic Illustration and Design in Britain 1850-1930* Antique Collector's Club, 1976.
Lewis	John Lewis *The 20th Century Book: its illustration and design* Studio Vista, 1967.
Low	David Low *British Cartoonists, Caricaturists and Comic Artist* Collins, 1942.
McLean	Ruari McLean *Victorian Book Design and Colour Printing* (first published 1963) revised edition Faber & Faber, 1972.
Mallalieu	Huon Mallalieu *Dictionary of British Watercolour Artists* Antique Collectors' Club, 1976.
Muir	Percy Muir *Victorian Illustrated Books* Batsford, 1971.
Pennell MI	Joseph Pennell *Modern Illustration* G. Bell, 1895.
Pennell PD	Joseph Pennell *Pen Drawing and Pen Draughtsmen: their work and their methods* (first published 1889) Macmillan, 1920.
Peppin	Brigid Peppin *Fantasy, Book Illustration 1860-1920* Studio Vista, 1975.
Price	R.G.G. Price *A History of Punch* Collins, 1957.
Ray	Gordon N. Ray *The Illustrator and the Book in England* Pierpont Morgan Library/OUP, 1976.
Rothenstein	John Rothenstein *Modern English Painters* 3 vols (first published Eyre & Spottiswoode, 1952), revised editions Macdonald & Jane's 1974-76.
Ryder	John Ryder *Artists of a Certain Line* Bodley Head, 1960.
Shone	Richard Shone *The Century of Change* Phaidon, 1977.
Sketchley	R.E.D. Sketchley *English Book Illustrations of Today* Kegan Paul, 1903.
Spielmann	M.H. Spielmann *The History of 'Punch'* Cassell, 1895.
Taylor	John Russell Taylor *The Art Nouveau Book in Britain* (first published 1966) Paul Harris, 1979.
Thieme & Becker	Dr Ulrich Thieme and Dr Felix Becker *Allgemeines Lexikon der Bildenden Künstler von der Antike bis zur Gegenwart* 37 vols, Wilhelm Engelman, Leipzig 1907-50; later vols, E.A. Seeman, Leipzig.
Thorpe	James Thorpe *English Illustration: the 'Nineties* Faber, 1935.
Usherwood	R.D. Usherwood *Drawing for the Radio Times* Bodley Head/Radio Times, 1961.
Veth	Cornelius Veth *Comic Art in England* Edward Goldston, 1930.
Vollmer	Hans Vollmer *Allgemeines Lexikon der Bildenden Künstler des XX Jahrhunderts* 6 vols including supplement, E.A Seeman, Leipzig 1953-62.
Waters	Grant M. Waters *Dictionary of British Artists Working 1900-1950* 2 vols, Eastbourne Fine Art, 1975.
Wa	*Who's Who in Art* 19 vols, Art Trade Press, 1927-80.
WaG	Walter Amstutz *Who's Who in Graphic Art. An illustrated book of reference to the world's leading graphic designers, illustrators, typographers and cartoonists* Amstutz & Herdeg Graphis Press, Zurich 1962.
C. Wood	Christopher Wood *The Dictionary of Victorian Painters* (first published 1971) Antique Collectors' Club, 1978.

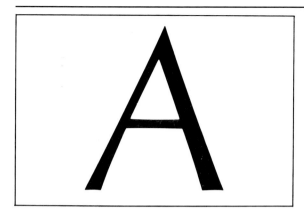

Joseph Abbey (b. 1889)

Born in Amsterdam, Holland, but lived in England from the age of three. Brother of S. Van Abbé*. Joseph Abbey worked, mainly in black and white, for newspapers, magazines, children's books and annuals. His most successful subjects were animals, birds and plants. He was editor of *Chums* during the 1930s and exhibited flower paintings at several London galleries, including the Royal Academy. [Q]

Books illustrated include:
Joseph Abbey Birds and their Eggs (1949)
Enid Blyton The Mystery of the Burnt Cottage (1943), The Mystery of the Disappearing Cat (1944), The Mystery of the Hidden House (1948)
W.E. Johns Biggles in Spain (with Howard Leigh, 1939)
Harold J. Massingham Birds of the Seashore (with others, 1931)
Arthur Mee's Hero Book (with others, nd)

Periodicals: Chums, Tom Merry's Own Annual

References: Doyle; BWI; Johnson & Greutzner

Hilary Ruth Abrahams (b. 1938)

Usually works as Hilary Abrahams. Born in London. Studied at St Martin's School of Art and at the Royal College of Art. Freelance illustrator of children's and educational books and part-time teacher since 1962. Works mainly in black and white, using a pen and Indian ink, and sometimes in watercolour. Principally published by Dennis Dobson (1960s) and by André Deutsch (1970s and 1980s).

Books illustrated include:
A. Abrahams Polonius Penguin Comes to Town (1963), Polonius Penguin Learns to Swim (1963), Polonius Penguin and the Flying Doctor (1964)
Molly Burkett Look for the Buzzards (1981)
Estelle Corney Pa's Top Hat (1980)
John Cunliffe Sara's Giant and the Upside Down House (1980)
John Harris Sam and the Dragon (1968)
Angus MacVicar The Cave of the Hammers (1968)
George Sand (trans Philippa Pearce) Wings of Courage (1982)
Margery Sharp The Children Next Door (1974)
Noel Streatfeild Enjoying Opera (1966)
Leo Tolstoy How Varnika Grew Up in a Single Night (1966)
Barbara Willard Jubilee! (1973)
Helen Young Magic Balloon, Sleeping Chair (1975)

References: ICB 3, 4

Laszlo Bela Acs (b. 1931)

Usually works as Laszlo Acs. Born in Budapest, Hungary. Studied at the Academy of Fine Art, Budapest, and Hornsey College of Art, London. Worked for three years in advertising, then for 18 months as Head of Graphic Design for Independent Television. He then turned to children's book illustration, working mainly in black and white in a style with affinities to the work of his compatriot, Victor Ambrus*. Lecturer in graphic design at Exeter College of Art (1978). Elected MSIA.

Books illustrated include:
Laszlo Acs Boys' Choice (1965)
Allan Aldous Bushfire (1967)
Peggy Appiah Ring of Gold (1976)
Gillian Avery Call of the Valley (1976)
Norman Coats Energy and Power (1968)
Penelope Farmer Emma in Winter (1966)
Winifred Finlay Tales of Sorcery and Witchcraft (1980)
Christina Green Beetle Bay (1976)
Leonard R. Gribble Famous Stories of the Wild West (1967)
Nina Warner Hooke A Donkey Called Paloma (1981)
Brian Jackson Our Living World (with Gaynor Chapman*, 1964)
William Mayne Max's Dream (1977)
Naomi Mitchison Don't Look Back (1969)
James Muirden The Earth's Neighbours (1975)
C. Everard Palmer Baba and Mr Big (1976)
David Stacey Fire in My Bones (1975)
Joan Tate Picture Charlie (1964)
Elizabeth Taylor Mossy Trotter (1967)
Geoffrey Trease When the Drums Beat and Other Stories (1979)
R.J. Unstead Living in Pompeii (1976)

Reference: ICB 4

Frank Adams (active 1903-44)

Book illustrator and landscape artist, about whom little seems to have been recorded except that he exhibited watercolours in London between 1923 and 1935. He illustrated books for children in the brightly coloured 'nursery' tradition of John Hassall*, with touches of Cecil Aldin's* style. Most of his illustrations for adult books consist of landscape sketches. In the lavishly produced

Frank Adams. 'Is it you, my prince?' for The Sleeping Beauty from The Golden Budget of Nursery Stories (Blackie, c.1929).

The Scholar Gipsy, tipped-in watercolour plates are surmounted by detailed pastoral festoons in pen and ink.

Books illustrated include:
Matthew Arnold The Scholar Gipsy (1933)
Lewis Carroll Alice's Adventures in Wonderland (1912)
Patrick R. Chalmers Rhymes of Flood and Field (1931)
Edgar Dickle Psammyforshort (1929), The Paper Boat (1944)
Alexandre Dumas The Three Musketeers (c.1925)
Evelyn Everett-Green The Lord of Dynevor (c.1910)
E.A. Gillie Barbara in Brittany (with A.A. Dixon*, 1905)
Thomas Gray Elegy Written in a Country Churchyard (1931)
Charles Kingsley The Water Babies (1907)
Mabel Marlowe Wotta Woppa and Other Stories (1932)
Frances Pitt Tommy White-Tag the Fox (1912)
Jessie Pope Three Jolly Huntsmen (1912)
Isaak Walton The Compleat Angler (1930)
Boys' and Girls' Story Book (with others, nd)
Favourite Nursery Tales (c.1920)
The Golden Budget of Nursery Stories (with John Hassall*, c.1929)
My New Big Book (with others, 1938)
Nursery Rhymes and Tales (1904)
The Story of Jack and Jill (1930)

Periodicals: Blackie's Annuals, Cassell's Children's Annuals, Little Folks

Reference: Johnson & Greutzner

George Worsley Adamson (b. 1913)

Works as George Adamson. Born in New York City and son of a master car-builder. He began his education there. Later studied at Wigan Mining and Technical College, Lancashire, at Wigan School of Art and at Liverpool School of Art.

George Adamson. 'Colonel Dedshott of the Catapult Cavaliers' from *Professor Branestawm's Treasure Hunt* by Norman Hunter (The Bodley Head, 1966).

Served in the Royal Air Force during World War II and worked as an official war artist for several months. Lecturer in engraving and illustration at Exeter School of Art (1946-53). Has subsequently worked as a freelance designer, illustrator and humourist; also a printmaker (drypoint and aquatint), designer of posters and animated films, and children's author. Adamson has contributed to *Punch* since 1939, including coloured covers, and has illustrated over 85 books in many fields—BBC publications, poetry, humour, and educational and children's books. Devoting much time and attention to the initial design of his work, he then draws rapidly with a characteristically economical and elegant line. Passages of closely observed detail (based on memory, drawings from nature, or photographs) are frequently balanced with blank or sparsely drawn areas. Elected ARE (1981); MSIAD. [Q]

Books illustrated include:
G.W. Adamson A Finding Alphabet (1965), Widdecombe Fair (1966), Finding 1 to 10 (1968), Rome Done Lightly (1972)
Aesop Fabulae Aesopi (1965)
George Barker Runes and Rhymes and Tunes and Chimes (1969), To Aylsham Fair (1970)
Margaret Stuart Barry Boffy and the Teacher Eater (1971), Boffy and the Momford Ghosts (1974)
Irene Byers Silka the Seal (1962)
A. Elliott Cannon A Question of Identity (1960), Silver City (1960)
Richard Carpenter Catweazle Books (1970-71)
J.L. Carr Red Windcheater (1969)
Mary Cockett Tufty (1968), Armful of Sparrows (1969)
David Scott Daniell Golden Pomegranate (1960)
G.P.W. Earle Foundations of English (1962)
L.H. Evers Danny's Wonderful Uncle (1963)
Alison Farthing The Queen's Flowerpot (1968)
Roger Lancelyn Green (ed) Strange Adventures in Time (1973)
Trevor Griffiths Tip's Lot (1972)
Willis Hall The Royal Astrologer (1960)
Roy Herbert Rufus Tractor (1961), Rufus Rolls On (1964)
Ted Hughes Meet My Folks! (1961), How the Whale Became (1963), The Iron Man (1968)
Norman Hunter Professor Branestawm Books (1966-77)
Richard Ingrams and John Wells The Collected Letters of Dennis Thatcher: Dear Bill (1980), The Other Half (1981), One for the Road (1982), My Round (1983)
Barbara Ireson (ed) Nursery Nonsense (1956), The Faber Book of Nursery Verse (1958), Verse That Is Fun (1962)
Geoffrey Jackson The Oven Bird (1972)
Clarence Jonk Yami and his Unicycle (1962)
Geraldine Kaye Bonfire Night (1968)
Charles Kingsley Westward Ho! (1957)
Kenneth Lillington Conjuror's Alibi (1960)
Stewart Love The Great Marco Scandal (1980)
Margaret Lovett Sir Halmanac and the Crimson Star (1965)
Kenneth Methold Vital English (1963)
Piet Niemand Jan Domm (1962)
Richard Parker Me and My Boots (1971)
Pandora Pollen Henry and Henrietta (1969)
Ronald Ridout Word Perfect (1957-60)
Gladys Staines Twelve Little Plays (1957)
Boswell Taylor Running Dog (1965), The Door That Would Not Open (1971)
Marjorie Vasey The Day is Over (1954)
Frank Waters The Day the Village Blushed (1978)
Benjamin Winterborn One Step Enough (1979) *retitled* Changing Scenes (1980)
W.H. Wood Perils of Pacifico (1959)
People and Leisure (World Today Series, 1969)
Second Stages in Welsh (BBC Schools, 1959)
Singing Together (BBC Schools, 1960)

Periodicals: British Airports World, Country Fair, The Countryman,

The Daily Telegraph, The Illustrated London News, The Listener, Nursing Times, Private Eye, Punch, Radio Times, The Sketch, The Tatler

References: Fisher p.143; ICB 2, 3, 4; Johnson and Greutzner; Wa (1980)

Mary Adshead (b. 1904)

Born Bloomsbury, London. Daughter of Professor S.D. Adshead, architect and town planner. Studied at the Slade School of Fine Art (1922-25). Her work has included murals, house portraits, collages, shell grottoes and postage stamp designs. In 1929, she married Stephen Bone* and they collaborated on several children's books. Her illustrations are bold and lively, with clear compositions and vigorous outlines. [Q]

Books illustrated include:
Stephen Bone and Mary Adshead The Little Boy and His House (1936), The Silly Snail (1942), The Little Boys and Their Boats (1953)
Eva Erleigh In The Beginning (1926)
Mary Norton Bonfires and Broomsticks (1947)
J. Supervielle Souls of the Soulless (1933)

References: Crouch; ICB 2; Johnson & Greutzner; Vollmer; Wa (1970); Waters; Mary Adshead *Travelling with a Sketchbook* (A. & C. Black 1966)

Janet Ahlberg (active from 1975)

Illustrator of children's books written by her husband Allan Ahlberg. She won the Kate Greenaway medal for 1978 with *Each Peach Pear Plum.*

Books illustrated include:
Allan Ahlberg A Place to Play (1975), Sam the Referee (1975), Fred's Dream (1976), The Great Marathon Football Match (1976), Burglar Bill (1977), Here Are the Brick Street Boys (1977), The Vanishment of Thomas Tull (1977), Cops and Robbers (1978), Each Peach Pear Plum (1978), The Old Joke Book (1979), The One and Only Two Heads (1979), Son of a Gun (1979), Two Wheels, Two Heads (1979), Funnybones (1980), Jeremiah in the Dark Woods (1980), Mr Biff the Boxer (1980), Mrs Wobble the Waitress (1980), Peepo! (1981)
Felicia Law Card (1977), Junk (1977)

Kathleen Ainslie (active 1903-10)

Author and illustrator of curious little (Christmas stocking-sized) children's books, which, with their hand-written texts and Dutch doll characters, show the influence of the Uptons'* slightly earlier 'Golliwogg' series. The drawings are obviously the work of an amateur, but there are several delightful endpaper designs. *Votes for C.S. and Me* satirises the female emancipation movement.

Books illustrated include:
Kathleen Ainslie Lady Tabitha and Us (1903), At Great-Aunt Martha's (1905), Oh! Poor Amelia Jane! (1905), What I Did (1905), Catharine Susan's Little Holiday (1905), Catharine Susan's Calendar (1906), Catharine Susan in Hot Water (1910), Catharine Susan and Me's Coming Out (1910), Votes for Catharine Susan and Me (1910)

Periodicals: Little Folks

Alastair

See Hans Henning Voight

Cecil Charles Windsor Aldin (1870-1935)

Worked as Cecil Aldin. Born in Slough, son of a successful speculative builder. After a month in the studio of the 'classical-aesthetic' painter Albert Moore, he studied animal anatomy at the South Kensington School of Art, and later worked under the animal painter Frank Calderon. He achieved early success as a comic illustrator, contributing to numerous periodicals during the 1890s, and designing posters (for Cadburys, in particular). He lived in Chelsea, then at Bedford Park, where a flourishing artists' colony included his friends Dudley Hardy* and Lance Thackeray*, then moved to Henley-on-Thames where he became Master of Foxhounds in 1914. He retired to Mallorca in 1930. In his autobiography, *Time I was Dead*, Aldin acknowledged 'I may as well state here and have done with it that I have no pretensions to Art. Art for the true artist should have a capital A. For me, I am ashamed to say, it has had rather a small one for my painting has always been founded on substrata of hunting possibilities, that is to say, it has had to provided me with the wherewithal to enable me to hunt, and has been tainted with this aftermath of sporting commercialism.' Sharing the values and aspirations

Cecil Aldin. 'Catch him, Dad!' from *Jerry, the Story of an Exmoor Pony* by Eleanor E. Helme and Nance Paul (Eyre & Spottiswoode, c.1932).

of a wide audience, he achieved immense popularity, evoking the English dream of Life in the Country in a relaxed and easy graphic style. As well as hunting scenes (in which he largely avoided the suggestion of mud and raw weather so insistently present in the work of his sporting-artist contemporary G.D. Armour*), he specialised in delicately shaded drawings of country inns, in cheerful olde worlde scenes and canine subjects, particularly dog-portraits, the best of which are the humorous ones.

Books illustrated include:

Cecil Aldin A Sporting Garland (c.1900), The Black Puppy Book, The Bobtail Puppy Book, Ten Little Puppy Dogs, Pickles, A Puppy Dog's Tale, Rough and Tumble, The Twins, The Mongrel Puppy Dog, The White Puppy Book, A Gay Dog, Sleeping Partners (1904-14), Old Inns (1921), Old Manor Houses (1923), Cathedral and Abbey Churches of England (1924), Ratcatcher to Scarlet (1926), Romance of the Road (1928), An Artist's Models (1930), Mrs Tickler's Caravan (1931), Time I Was Dead (1934), Just Among Friends, Pages From My Sketch Book (1934), Exmoor (1935), Hunting Scenes (1936)

Marion Ashmore Lost, Stolen or Strayed (1931)

James Buckland Two Little Runaways (1898)

May Byron Cecil Aldin's Happy Family (c.1912), Cecil Aldin's Merry Party (1913), Jack and Jill (c.1914)

Patrick R. Chalmers A Dozen Dogs or So (1928), Forty Fine Ladies (1930), Dogs of Every Day (1933), The Last Muster (1939)

Charles Dickens The Posthumous Papers of the Pickwick Club (2 vols, 1910)

Walter Emanuel Dog Day (1902), The Snob (1904), Dogs of War (1906), The Dog Who Wasn't What He Thought He Was (1914)

Duncan Fife Scarlet Blue and Green (1932)

Svend Fleuron Flax, Police Dog (c.1931), Wild Horses of Iceland (1933)

Kenneth Hare Road and Vagabonds (c.1930)

Eleanor E. Helme and Nance Paul Jerry, The Story of an Exmoor Pony (c.1932)

Henry Hutchinson Prehistoric Man and Beast (1896)

Washington Irving Old Christmas (1908), Bachelors and Bachelors' Confessions (1909)

Rudyard Kipling His Apologies (1932)

Maurice Maeterlinck My Dog (1913)

John Masefield Right Royal (1922)

J.B. Morton Who's Who in the Zoo (1933)

Winifred H. Nurse Berkshire Vale (1927)

Ouida Mouflou (c.1915)

Winthrop M. Praed Everyday Characters (1896)

Anna Sewell Black Beauty (1912)

Harry A. Spurr A Cockney in Arcadia (with John Hassall*, 1899)

Sir R. Steele The Perverse Widow (1909), The Henpecked Man (1909)

R.S. Surtees Jorrocks on 'unting (1909), Handley Cross (1912)

John Vickerman Hotspur the Beagle (1934)

Richard Waylett Jock and Some Others (c.1916)

Periodicals: Animal World, Black and White, The Boy's Own Paper, The Captain, Cassell's Family Magazine, The English Illustrated Magazine, The Gentlewoman, Good Words, The Graphic, Happy Annual, The Illustrated London News, Illustrated Sporting and Dramatic News, The Lady's Pictorial, Land and Water Illustrated, The Ludgate Monthly, The Pall Mall Budget, The Pall Mall Magazine, Pearson's Magazine, The Poster, Printer's Pie, Punch, The Queen, The Royal Magazine, The Sketch, The Sphere, The Windsor Magazine

References: Bénézit; Crouch; Cuppleditch; Guichard; Hammerton; Houfe; ICB 1; Johnson & Greutzner; Mallalieu; Thieme & Becker; Thorpe; Vollmer; Wa (1934); Waters; J.C. Wood; *Pearson's Magazine* (November 1906); *The Studio* 102 (1931); Cecil Aldin *Time I Was Dead* (Eyre & Spottiswoode 1934); Gwen Aldin (foreword) *Hunting Scenes* (Eyre & Spottiswoode 1936); Roy Heron *Cecil Aldin: The Story of a Sporting Artist* (Webb & Bower 1981)

Alan Aldridge. 'Punchinello' from his *The Butterfly Ball and the Grasshopper's Feast*, with verses by William Plomer (Cape, 1973).

Alan Aldridge (active from c.1967)

Born in Aylesbury, Buckinghamshire. Attended Romford Technical College but left at 15 and supported himself with an assortment of jobs including insurance clerk, repertory actor, dock hand and barrow boy. In 1963, he took a short evening course in commercial graphics. Soon he had achieved spectacular success with designs for posters, book covers, record sleeves, car, furniture and body painting, as well as magazine and book illustration. In 1966, he was appointed art director of Penguin Books, but left in 1968 to set up his own studio, Ink, which received commissions from many of the leading pop groups and glossy magazines of the day, including the Beatles' ill-fated *Apple Corps*. As Aldridge's career embodied many of the aspirations of the 'swinging sixties', so his drawing epitomised the graphic idiom of the decade. His use of brilliant 'psychedelic' colours in combination with ebulliently decorative draughtsmanship gave his work the vigorous popular appeal of fairground art; but he used this apparently unsophisticated language to convey ideas of almost surrealist complexity, abounding in visual ambiguities, allusions and jokes. Stylistically his most influential innovation was his use of the airbrush for fine colour gradation and shading over much of the picture surface, giving the illusion of undulating movement within the crisp contours. As his draughtsmanship developed, he increasingly incorporated graphic references to cultural traditions as diverse as oriental painting and pre-Columbian art, while his imagery continued to invite closer and more intense scrutiny. After disbanding Ink, Aldridge continued to work freelance, finding a regular publisher in Jonathan Cape. In 1974, he won the Children's Book of the Year Award with *Butterfly Ball*; more recently he has designed animated films.

Books illustrated include:
Richard Adams The Ship's Cat (1977)
Alan Aldridge The Beatles Illustrated Lyrics (with others, 1969), Phantasia, of Dockland, Rockland and Dodos (with Harry Willock, 1981)
Alan Aldridge & George Perry The Penguin Book of Comics (1967)
Alan Aldridge and William Plomer The Butterfly Ball and the Grasshopper's Feast (1973)
George E. Ryder The Peacock Party (1979)
Ted Walker The Lion's Cavalcade (with Harry Willock, 1980), Ann in the Moon

Periodicals: Harper's, Nova, The Queen, The Sunday Times, Vogue, Woman's Mirror

References: Student (Autumn 1969); Alan Aldridge *Phantasia* (Jonathan Cape 1981)

Elizabeth Alldridge (active 1930-50)

Illustrator in black and white, known mainly for her simplified but evocative illustrations of the Worzel Gummidge books published by Frederick Warne.

Books illustrated include:
Elizabeth Alldridge The Blue Feather Club (1940)
Richard Morse A Book of Common Trees (1942)
Barbara Euphan Todd Worzel Gummidge (1936), Worzel Gummidge Again (1937)

References: Fisher p.386; *After Alice* (Museum of Childhood catalogue, London 1977)

Marian Allen (active 1917-48)

Marian Allen, in common with many of her contemporaries, specialised in mannered drawings of long-legged children, using solid areas of black to contrast with dotted-line effects. F.J. Harvey Darton refers to her as 'Marion', Johnson & Greutzner refer to a Marion Allen who worked in Birmingham 1905-21, who may be the same artist.

Books illustrated include:
Marian Allen The Wind on the Downs (1918), The Wind in the Chimney (1931), Some of Christ's Children (1946), Anemone Pearl, The Tale of a Mermaid's Tail (1948), The Hobgoblin of Great Mummers (1948)
W.M. Dawson and M. Allen A Peep into Nursery Rhyme Land (1917)
Rose Fyleman Joy Street Poems (1927)
Laurence Housman Turn Again Tales (1930)
Compton Mackenzie Santa Claus in Summer (nd)

Periodical: Number Five Joy Street

Reference: Darton

Marian Allen. For *Candlelight Cottage* by Compton Mackenzie from *Number Five Joy Street* (Basil Blackwell, nd).

Olive Allen (active 1900-11)

Studied at Liverpool School of Art and exhibited at the Walker Art Gallery in 1900. She re-wrote several titles in the 'Grandmother's Favourites' series of children's classics (published by T.C. & E.C. Jack), illustrating them in a simple style with heavy outlines. Her colour work was on the whole more successful than the black and white.

Books illustrated include:
F.H. Burnett Little Saint Elizabeth (with others, nd)
Lewis Carroll Alice's Adventures in Wonderland (1910)
Maria Edgeworth Holiday House (1908), (retold by Olive Allen) Simple Susan (1908)
J.A. Henderson Gardens Shown to the Children (1911)
Catherine Sinclair (retold by Olive Allen) Holiday House (1908)

References: Houfe; The Studio 20 (1900), special (1900-01)

Christopher Gifford Ambler (b. 1886)

Worked as Christopher Ambler. Animal painter and illustrator. He drew in pen and ink, pencil or brush, often with added colour or halftone washes, in a bold, cheerfully sketchy style. Recorded by Brian Doyle as having briefly illustrated the boys' paper *Nelson Lee*, in 1929.

Books illustrated include:

Cecil R. Acton Exmoor River (1938)
C.G. Ambler Maxims of Marquis (1937), Smiler (1945), Working Dogs (1949), Ten Little Foxhounds (1950), Zoolyricks (1950)
Joseph Chipperfield Storm of Dancerwood (1948), Greatheart (1950), Grey Chieftain (1952), Silver Star (1953), Greeka (1953), Rooloo (1955), Wolf of Badenoch (1958), Ghost Horse (1959), Grasson (1960), Seokoo of the Black Wind (1961), Sabre of the Storm Valley (1962), Checoba (1964), Boru (1965)
William Cowper The Diverting History of John Gilpin (1947)
James Gilroy Furred and Feathered Heroes of World War II (1946)
Herbert Strang (ed) The Big Book for Boys (with others, n.d.)

Periodicals: The Boy's Own Paper, Nelson Lee, Oxford Annual

References: Doyle BWI; ICB 2; Johnson & Greutzner

Victor Gyozo Lazlo Ambrus (b. 1935)

Works as Victor Ambrus. Born in Budapest, Hungary. Studied at the Academy of Fine Art in Budapest. Arrived in England after the Hungarian uprising of 1956, and studied at the Royal College of Art (1957-60). Visiting lecturer at West Surrey College of Art (formerly Farnham School of Art) from 1964 to 1975. Etcher, graphic designer and illustrator of some 250 books for publishers in Britain and abroad. For black and white illustrations, he uses a fine pen and indian ink; for colour work, he uses watercolour, coloured inks, crayons, and felt-tip pens. His line is delicate, and he uses varied textures to enhance the pictorial message, rather than merely as a decorative embellishment. His favourite subjects are historical and military scenes. In 1965, he won the Kate Greenaway medal for *The Three Poor Tailors* and his work in general, and in 1975 *Mishka* and *Horses in Battle* won him the prize a second time. Elected RE (1966), FRSA (1977). [Q]

Books illustrated include:

E.M. Almedingen Little Katia (1966), Young Mark (1967)
Victor Ambrus The Three Poor Tailors (1965), Brave Soldier Janosh (1967), Hot Water for Boris (1967), Seven Skinny Goats (1969), The Sultan's Bath (1971), Country Wedding (1975), Horses in Battle (1975), Mishka (1975), Under the Double Eagle (1979), The Valiant Little Tailor (1980), Dracula (1980), Dracula's Bedtime Storybook (1981), Blackbeard (1982)
Margaret Balderson When Jays Fly to Barbmo (1969)
Edward Blishen (ed) Miscellany One (Oxford University Press 1964)
Hesba F. Brimstead A Sapphire for September (1967)
Hester Burton Castors Away! (1962), Time of Trial (1963), A Seaman at the Time of Trafalgar (1963), No Beat of Drum (1966), In Spite of All Terror (1968), Thomas (1969), The Rebel (1971), Riders of the Storm (1972), Kate Rider (1974)
Peter Carter Madatan (1974)
Arthur Catherall Prisoners in the Snow (1967), Kidnapped by Accident (1968), Red Sea Rescue (1969)
Nan Chauncy High and Haunted Island (1964), Marthinna's People (1967), The Lighthouse Keeper's Son (1969)
Joseph Chipperfield Hunter of Harter Fell (1977)
Alexander Cordell The Traitor Within (1971)
Peter Dawlish The Royal Navy (1963), The Merchant Navy (1966)
Daniel Defoe Robinson Crusoe (1968)
Eleanor Farjeon and William J.C. Mayne The Hamish Hamilton Book of Kings (1964), The Hamish Hamilton Book of Queens (1965)
Kathleen Fidler Haki the Shetland Pony (1968)
Winifred Finlay Folk Tales from the North (1968), Folk Tales from Moor and Mountain (1969), Cap O' Rushes (1974)
Edward Fitzgerald The British Army (1964)
J.G. Fyson The Three Brothers of Ur (1964), The Journey of the Eldest Son (1965)

Victor Ambrus. For *Joe Smith, or the Day the World Went Mad* from *Miscellany One* edited by Edward Blishen (Oxford University Press, 1964).

Mary Gough A Turkish Village (1965)
Roger Lancelyn Green The Hamish Hamilton Book of Other Worlds (1976)
Frederick Grice The Courage of Andy Robson (1969)
Helen Griffiths The Wild Heart (1963), The Greyhound (1964), The Wild Horse of Santander (1966), Leon (1967), Stallion of the Sands (1968), Russian Blue (1973), Just a Dog (1974), Witch Fear (1975), Pablo (1977)
Frank Knight True Stories of the Sea (1973), True Stories of Exploration (1973), True Stories of Spying (1975)
Rosemary Manning Arripay (1963)
Ruth Manning-Sanders The Glass Man and the Golden Bird (1968), The Red King and the Witch (1964)
William Mayne The Changeling (1961)
Bernard Miles Shakespeare's Tales (1976)
Elyne Mitchell Light Horse to Damascus (1971), Silver Brumby Whirlwind (1973), The Colt at Taparoo (1976), Son of the Whirlwind (1977), The Colt from Snowy River (1980)
Diana Moorhead The Green and the White (1974)
Richard Parker Private Beach (1964)
K.M. Peyton Windfall (1962), The Maplin Bird (1964), The Plan for Birdsmarsh (1965), Thunder in the Sky (1966), Flambards (1967), The Edge of the Cloud (1969), Flambards in Summer (1969)
Barbara Léonie Picard One is One (1965), The Young Pretenders (1966), Twice Seven Tales (1968), Tales of Ancient Persia (1972)
Madeleine Polland Stranger in the Hills (1969)
Sheena Porter Hills and Hollows (1962), Jacob's Ladder (1963), Deerfold (1966)
James Riordan The Legend of King Arthur (1982), Arabian Nights (1982)
Ruth M. Sanders Jonnikin and the Flying Basket (1969)
Ian Serraillier The Challenge of the Green Knight (1966), Robin in the Greenwood (1967), Robin and his Merry Men (1969), Marko's Wedding (1972)
Rosemary Sutcliff The Hound of Ulster (1963), The Chief's Daughter (1967), The Circlet of Oak Leaves (1968), The Truce of the Games (1971), Tristan and Iseult (1971), The Changeling (1974)
Mary Treadgold The Heron Ride (1962), Return to the Heron (1963)
R.K. Unstead The Story of Britain (1969)
Peter Webster Pasang the Sherpa (1964)
Ronald Welch Ferdinand Magellan (1955), The Galleon (1971), Tank Commander (1972), Ensign Carey (1976)

References: Contemporary Authors; Doyle CL; Eyre; Fisher pp. 60, 70; Hürlimann; ICB 3, 4; Wa (1980); *The Junior Bookshelf* vol 28, no 2 (1964); Diana Klemin *The Illustrated Book* (Clarkson N. Potter, New York, 1970).

John Henry Amschewitz (1882-1942)

Born in Ramsgate. Studied at the Royal Academy Schools. Worked as a muralist (commissions included paintings in Liverpool Town Hall), painter, etcher and cartoonist. His compositions were characterised by strong diagonal emphasis and his figures by exaggerated gesture. He worked in full colour and halftone. He visited South Africa (1916-22) and settled there in 1939. Elected RBA (1914).

Books illustrated include:
Angelo S. Rappoport Myths and Legends of Ancient Israel (3 vols 1928)
Everyman (Medici Society 1911)

Periodicals: The Graphic, The Illustrated London News, The Sphere

References: Bénézit; Guichard; Johnson & Greutzner; Vollmer and supp; Wa (1934); Waters; S.B. Amschewitz *The Paintings of John Henry Amschewitz* (Batsford 1951)

Anne Anderson (b. 1874)

Born of Scottish Lowland parents; childhood spent in the Argentine, but later lived in Berkshire. She married Alan Wright* with whom she collaborated on several children's books. Her decorative illustrations, in black and white line or delicately coloured, show appealingly-clothed children with innocent pear-shaped faces. Her work was highly characteristic of the period and echoed the languid Art Nouveau charm of the work of Jessie M. King*; it enjoyed a considerable vogue during the 1920s. Also an etcher, watercolourist and designer of greetings cards.

Books illustrated include:
Anne Anderson Aucassin and Nicolette (1911), The Funny Bunny ABC (1912), The Patsy Book (1919), The Cosy Corner Book (1943), The Gilly Flower Garden Book (nd), The Rosie-Posie Book (nd)
Madeleine Barnes Fireside Stories (1922)
Louey Chisholm (ed) A Staircase of Stories (with others, nd)
John R. Crossland and J.M. Parrish (ed) The Children's Wonder Book (with others, 1933)
Ethel C. Eliot The House Above the Trees (1921)
E.W. Garrett Rip (1919), Wanda and the Garden of the Red House (1924)
Agnes G. Herbertson Sing-Song Stories (1922)
Constance Howard Mr Pickles and the Party (1926)
Natalie Joan Cosy-Time Tales (1922)
Charles Kingsley The Water Babies (1924)
Peggy Morrison Cosy Chair Stories (1924)
J. Spyri Heidi (1924)
'Mrs Herbert Strang' (ed) The Golden Book for Girls (with others, nd), My Big Picture Book (with others, nd), The Violet Book for Children (with others, nd)
Alan Wright and Anne Anderson The Busy Bunny Book (1916), Two Bold Sportsmen (1918), The Cuddly-Kitty and the Busy Bunny (1926), The Podgy-Puppy (1927), The Naughty Neddy Book (1918)
The Children's Wonder Book (with others, Odhams 1933)
Fairy Tales (Collins, 3 parts 1929)
Fairy Tales (Nelson, 6 parts 1928)
Grimm's Fairy Tales

Anne Anderson. Headpiece to introduction from *The Children's Wonder Book* (Odhams, 1933).

Hans Andersen's Fairy Tales (1924)
My Big New Book (Blackie, with others, 1938)
Old French Nursery Songs (nd)
The Old Mother Goose Nursery Rhyme Book (1926)
The Sleepy Song Book (nd)

Periodicals: Blackie's Children's Annual, Cassell's Children's Annual, Mrs Strang's Annuals, Playbox Annual, Watkin's Annual, Wonder Annual.

References: Johnson & Greutzner; *The Book Collector* vol 28 no 4 (1979); *The Lady* (1st December 1977)

Florence Mary Anderson (active 1914-30)

Worked as Florence Anderson until around 1920 when she reverted to her maiden name—Molly MacArthur (except for the 1930 edition of *The Cradle Ship* for which she re-drew the illustrations but under her married name). Book illustrator in colour and black and white; also a watercolour painter and wood engraver. Her early illustrations consisted mainly of delicate fairy pictures, but during the 1920s her work became bolder, with experiments in linear pattern.

Books illustrated include:
F.M. Anderson The Rainbow Twins (1919), Woodcuts and Verses (1922), Tribute (c.1925)

Florence Anderson. 'The Three Jolly Batchelors' from *Little Folks* (1930-31).

Dorothy Black Adventures in Magic Land (1917)
Trevor Blakemore China Clay (1922)
Chrysanthème (pseud) The Black Princess (1966)
Edith Howes The Cradle Ship (1916), The Cradle Ship (adapted and with new illustrations, 1930)
Lady Margaret Sackville The Dream Pedlar (1914), The Travelling Companions (1915)
Helen de G. Simpson Mumbudget (1928)
May Wynne The Adventures of Dolly Dingle (1920)

Periodicals: Cassell's Family Magazine, Little Folks

References: Johnson & Greutzner

Marie Felicity Angel (b. 1923)

Usually works as Marie Angel. Born in London. Studied at Croydon School of Art (1940-45) and the Royal College of Art (1945-48). Freelance calligrapher and illustrator, working mainly for American publishers. Her watercolour drawings are detailed and descriptive, reflecting her fondness for birds and small animals, flint and thatched buildings, and gardening. [Q]

Books illustrated include:
Marie Angel The Art of Calligraphy (1978), Bird, Beast and Flower (1980), Painting for Calligraphers (1983)
James Dickey Tucky the Hunter (1979)
Beatrix Potter The Tale of the Faithful Dove (1970), The Tale of Tuppeny (1973)
Also many titles published in America.

References: ICB 4; Wa (1980)

Bruce Angrave (b. 1920s)

Born in Leicester, son of a graphic designer and photographer. Studied at Chiswick Art School, Ealing School of Art and at the Central School of Art, London. Freelance illustrator and designer, specialising in paper sculpture for exhibitions (e.g. the Festival of Britain in 1951, Expo 70 in Japan); for the Festival of Britain he also designed

Bruce Angrave. 'Pustle and Mortar' from *TripliCAT* (Collins, 1978).

the carved wood and steel sculptures for the celebrated Tree Walk at the Battersea Fun Fair. He sometimes works as a television designer, and has won a British Academy of Film and Television Arts award. His illustrations, mainly drawn in black ink with rapidograph-type pens are humorous, decorative and formalised, and in a graphic style initially influenced by R. Taylor of *The New Yorker*. Several of his early books (e.g. *The Other Passenger*, illustrated with striking surrealist pastiches) have poster-like illustrations in full colour. He was influenced in poster design by Eckersley*, Lewitt-Him* and Abram Games (designer of the Festival of Britain symbol). He also works as a TV designer and has received a BAFTA award. [Q]

Books illustrated include:
Bruce Angrave Lord Dragline the Dragon (1944), The New English Fictionary (1953), Sculpture into Paper (1957), CATalogue (1976), MagnifiCAT (1977), TripliCAT (1978), Angrave's Amazing Autos (1980), Paper into Sculpture (1981), The Mechanical Emperor (nd), Mr Bosanko (nd)
John Keir Cross The Other Passenger (1944)
Ann Huxley Caught in the Act (1953)
Stephen MacFarlane Lucy Maroon (1944)
Catherine Munnion Budget and Buy (1975)

Periodicals: Aeronautics, Radio Times, Time and Tide, Woman, Woman's Realm

References: Wa (1972); Mary Banham & Bevis Hillier (ed) *A Tonic to the Nation* (Thames & Hudson 1976)

Mabel Marguerite Annesley (1881-1959)

Worked as Lady Mabel Annesley. Born in Ireland, daughter of the 5th Earl of Annesley. Soon after the death of her husband in World War I, she inherited the impoverished family estate in Ireland from her father and brother, and took over its management and farming. At the same time she studied wood engraving at the Central School under Noel Rooke*. Later she travelled to Egypt, Australia and New Zealand, and finally emigrated to New Zealand in 1945. Her wood engravings were mostly on a small scale; she used strong black/white contrasts with some hatching to create simplified, direct images.

Books illustrated include:
Mabel Annesley As the Sight is Bent (1964)
A.E. Coppard (ed) Robert Burns (1925)
Richard Rowley County Down Songs (1924), Apollo in Mourne (1926)

References: Balston WEMEB; Garret HBWE; Johnson & Greutzner; *The Studio* special (Spring 1927, Spring 1930); *The Times* (obituary 6th June 1950); Lady Mabel Annesley *As the Sight is Bent* (Museum Press 1964)

Peter Frederick Anson (1889-1975)

Worked as Peter Anson. Born in Portsmouth. Studied at the Architectural Association School (1908-10) and later under F.L.M. Griggs*. Also a landscape and portrait painter and a writer.

He became a Cistercian monk, attached to Caldey Abbey in Wales, and Nunraw Abbey in Scotland. His illustrations mainly consisted of straightforward, functional pen and ink drawings of buildings or fishing subjects. He spent a year touring Britain in a horse-drawn caravan visiting and drawing Roman Catholic churches for a series published in *The Universe*. He died in Edinburgh.

Books illustrated include:
Peter F. Anson A Pilgrim's Guide to Franciscan Italy (1927), A Medley of Memoirs (1929), Fishing Boats and Fishing Folk (1930), A Pilgrim Artist in Palestine (1932), The Quest for Solitude (1932), Fishermen and Fishing Ways (1932), The Caravan Pilgrim (1938), The Benedictines of Caldey (1940), How to Draw Ships (1941), British Sea Fishermen (1944), Harbour Head: maritime memories (1945), A Roving Recluse: more memories (1946), Churches: their Plan and Furnishing (1948), Scots Fisherfolk (1950), Banff and Macduff: an official guide (1956), Fashions in Church Furniture (1965), Building up the Waste Places (1973)
Sir David D.H. Blair A Last Medley of Memories (1936)

References: Contemporary Authors; Johnson & Greutzner; Vollmer; Wa (1972); Waters 1, 2

Anton

See Beryl Antonia Botterill

Honor C. Appleton (active 1900-40)

Watercolour painter and children's illustrator. Best known for her illustrations to Mrs H.C. Cradock's *Josephine* books, published between 1916 and 1940. These appealing outline drawings and watercolour plates were probably largely responsible for the stories' enduring popularity.

Honor C. Appleton. 'Do look at that ditch' from *Josephine's Christmas Party* by Mrs H.C. Cradock (Blackie, 1927).

Josephine and her battered entourage were usually depicted from a 'toy-level' viewpoint a few inches above the floor, with the skirting board as an obvious indication of scale.

Books illustrated include:
Honor C. Appleton The Bad Mrs Ginger (1902), Dumpy Proverbs (1903), Babies Three (1921), Me and My Pussies (1924)
Lewis Carroll Alice's Adventures in Wonderland (1936)
Mrs H.C. Cradock Josephine and her Dolls (1916), Josephine's Happy Family (1917), Josephine is Busy (1918), Where the Dolls Lived (1919), Josephine's Birthday (1920), Josephine, John and the Puppy (1920), Peggy's Twins (1920), The House of Fancy (1922), Peggy and Joan (1922), Josephine Keeps School (1925), The Best Teddy Bear in the World (1926), Josephine Goes Shopping (1926), Josephine's Christmas Party (1927), Pamela's Teddy Bears (1927), The World's Best Stories for Children (1930), Josephine Keeps House (1931), Josephine's Pantomime (1939), Josephine Goes Travelling (1940)
Charles Dickens A Christmas Carol (1920)
F.H. Lee Children's Book of Heroines (1929)
F.H. Pritchard The Children's Ali Baba (with M.S. Orr 1938)

Periodicals: Blackie's Annuals, Pictorial Education Quarterly

References: Bénézit; Johnson & Greutzner

Edward Jeffrey Irving Ardizzone (1900-79)

Worked as Edward Ardizzone. Born in Haiphong, China, the son of an employee of the Eastern Telegraph Company. He attended evening classes in life drawing given by Bernard Meninsky at Westminster School of Art, while employed as a statistical clerk in London (1919-26). He worked freelance as an illustrator from 1926, achieving widespread recognition with his first children's book *Little Tim and the Brave Sea Captain* (1936). Served in the Royal Artillery (1939-40); Official War Artist (1940-45), noted for his war diaries. Taught illustration at Camberwell School of Art (1948-52). Worked for UNESCO in India (1952-53). Part-time tutor at the Royal College of Art School of Etching (1953-61).

Ardizzone worked in watercolour, pen and ink, pencil and lithograph as a painter, printmaker, greetings card designer and illustrator of over 170 books, many of them his own. He was awarded the Kate Greenaway Medal (1956) for *Tim All Alone* and the Carnegie Medal (1955) and Hans Christian Andersen Medal (1956) with *The Little Bookroom*. He particularly enjoyed illustrating poetry. He worked mainly from memory, early developing a freely drawn and unmistakable style that changed very little during the course of his long career. He acknowledged the influence of Bernard Meninsky on his work, and also the 19th-century draughtsmen Daumier, Doré and Caldecott. His brother-in-law Gabriel White considered that 'perhaps no artist since Randolph Caldecott has captured so easily the qualities essential in successful illustration for a child. Ardizzone's are bold and clear and tell the tale in the simplest lines and colours.' [Q]

Books illustrated include:

Aingelda Ardizzone The Night Ride (1973)

Aingelda and Edward Ardizzone The Little Girl and the Tiny Doll (1966)

Edward Ardizzone Little Tim and the Brave Sea Captain (1936), Lucy Brown and Mr Grimes (1937), Tim and Lucy Go to Sea (1938), Baggage to the Enemy (1941), Nicholas the Fast-Moving Diesel (1947), Paul, the Hero of the Fire (1948), Tim to the Rescue (1949), Tim and Charlotte (1951), Tim in Danger (1953), Tim All Alone (1956), Johnny the Clockmaker (1956), Tim's Friend Towser (1962), Peter the Wanderer (1963), Diana and her Rhinoceros (1964), Sarah and Simon and No Red Paint (1965), Tim and Ginger (1965), Tim to the Lighthouse (1968), The Young Ardizzone (1970), Tim's Last Voyage (1972), Diary of a War Artist (1974), Ardizzone's Kilvert (1976), Ship's Cook Ginger (1977), Ardizzone's Hans Andersen (1978)

Joan Ballantyne Holiday Trench (1959), Kidnappers at Coombe (1960)

H.E. Bates My Uncle Silas (1939), Sugar for the House (1957)

John Betjeman A Ring of Bells (1962)

Margaret Black Three Brothers and a Lady (1947)

Paul Bloomfield (ed) The Mediterranean (1935)

Christianna Brand Naughty Children (1962), Nurse Matilda (1964), Nurse Matilda Goes to Town (1967), Nurse Matilda Goes to Hospital (1974)

John Buchan The Thirty-Nine Steps (1964)

John Bunyan The Pilgrim's Progress (1947)

Henry Cecil Brief to Counsel (1958), Know About English Law (1965) Learn About English Law (1974)

Jean Chapman Do You Remember What Happened? (1969)

G.K. Chesterton Father Brown Stories (1959)

Leonard Clark The Year Round (1965)

Dorothy Clewes Upside Down Willie (1968), Special Branch Willie (1969), Fire-brigade Willie (1970)

William Cole Folk Songs of England, Ireland, Scotland and Wales (1961)

Stephen Corrin The Fantastic Tale of the Plucky Sailor and the Postage Stamp (1954)

George Crabbe The Library (1930)

Eric Crozier The Story of Let's Make an Opera (1962)

Daniel Defoe Robinson Crusoe (1968)

Walter de la Mare Peacock Pie (1946), The Story of Joseph (1958), The Story of Moses (1959), The Story of Samuel (1960), Stories from the Bible (1962)

Charles Dickens Great Expectations (1939), Bleak House (1955), David Copperfield (1955), Short Stories (1971)

Eleanor Estes Pinkie-Pie (1958), The Witch Family (1960), The Alley (1964), Miranda the Great (1967), The Tunnel of Hugsy Goode (1972)

Dana Faralla The Singing Cupboard (1962), Swanhilda-of-the-Swans (1964)

Eleanor Farjeon The Little Bookroom (1955), Jim at the Corner (1958), Italian Peepshow (1960), Eleanor Farjeon's Book (1960), Kaleidoscope (1963), The Old Nurse's Shopping Basket (1965)

Hallam Fordham (ed) Hey Nonny Yes (1947)

Pamela Fox A Likely Place (1967)

C. Denis Freeman and Douglas Cooper The Road to Bordeaux (1940)

John N. Goldman The School in our Village (1957)

Maurice Gorham The Local (1939), Back to the Local (1949), The Londoners (1951), Showmen and Suckers (1951)

Catherine Gough Boyhoods of the Great Composers (2 vols 1960, 1963)

Robert Graves The Penny Fiddle (1961), Ann at Highwood Hall (1964)

Nicholas S. Gray Down in the Cellar (1961)

Graham Greene The Little Fire Engine (1973)

Enid Dickens Hawksley (ed) Charles Dickens' Birthday Book (1948)

John T. Hayes London since 1912 (1962)

H.J. Kaeser Mimff (1939), Mimff in Charge (1949), Mimff Takes Over (1954), Mimff-Robinson (1958)

James Kenward The Suburban Child (1955)

Clive King Stig of the Dump (1963)

Noel Langley The True and Pathetic History of Desbarollda (1947), The Land of Green Ginger (1966)

William J. Lederer Timothy's Song (1965)

Sheridan Le Fanu In a Glass Darkly (1929)

Mary Levin The Second-Best Children in the World (1972)

C. Day Lewis The Otterbury Incident (1948)

Kathleen Lines Dick Whittington (1970)

Albert N. Lyons Tom, Dick and Harriet (1937)

H.B. McCaskie (trans) The Poems of François Villon (1946)

J.C. Mardrus and E. Powys (trans) The Tale of Ali Baba (1949)

André Maurois The Battle of France (1940)

Edward Ardizzone. From *Merry England* by Cyril Ray (Vista Books, 1960).

Naomi Mitchison The Rib of the Green Umbrella (1960)

Shirley Morgan Rain, Rain Don't Go Away (1972)

E. Nesbit Long Ago When I Was Young (1966)

Claire Newberry Marshmallow (1956)

Freda P. Nichols The Milldale Riot (1965)

Zarah Nuber The Modern Prometheus (1952)

A. Philippa Pearce Minnow on the Say (1955)

J.B. Phillips (trans) St Luke's Life of Christ (1956)

Cyril Ray Merry England (1960)

James Reeves The Blackbird in the Lilac (1952), Pigeons and Princesses (1956), Wandering Moon (1956), Prefabulous Animiles (1957), Exploits of Don Quixote (1959), Titus in Trouble (1959), Hurdy-Gurdy (1961), Sailor Rumbelow and Britannia (1962), Three Tall Tales (1964), The Story of Jackie Thimble (1965), The Secret Shoemakers and Other Stories (1966), Rhyming Will (1967), The Angel and the Donkey (1969), How the Moon Began (1971), Complete Poems for Children (1973), The Lion that Flew (1974), More Prefabulous Animiles (1975)

Diana Ross Old Perisher (1965)

George Scurfield A Stickful of Nonpareil (1956)

William Shakespeare Comedies (1959)

Virginia Sicotte A Riot of Quiet (1969)

R.L. Stevenson Travels with a Donkey (1967), Home from the Sea (1970)

Noel Streatfeild The Growing Summer (1966)

G.W. Stonier Pictures on the Pavement (1955)

Robert S. Surtees Hunting with Mr Jorrocks (1956)

John Symonds Lottie (1956), Elfrida and the Pig (1959), The Stuffed Dog (1967)

W.M. Thackeray The Newcomers (1954), The History of Henry Esmond (1956)

Dylan Thomas A Child's Christmas (1978)

Meriol Trevor Sun Slower, Sun Faster (1955)

Anthony Trollope The Warden (1952), Barchester Towers (1953)

Mark Twain The Adventures of Huckleberry Finn (1961), The Adventures of Tom Sawyer (1961)
John Walsh The Truants and Other Poems for Children (1965)
Jean Webster Daddy-Long-Legs (1966)
T.H. White The Godstone and the Blackymor (1959)
Ursula Moray Williams The Nine Lives of Island Mackenzie (1959)
Eva-Lis Wuorio The Island of Fish in the Trees (1962), The Land of Right Up and Down (1964), Kali and the Golden Mirror (1967)
Peter Young Ding Dong Bell (1957)

References: Bland; Chamot, Farr & Butlin; *Contemporary Artists*; Crouch; Doyle CL; Driver; Eyre; Gilmour; Hürlimann; ICB 1, 2, 3, 4; Jacques; Johnson & Greutzner; Kirkpatrick; Lewis; Ryder; Usherwood; Vollmer; Wa (1980); Waters; *Apollo* 16 (1932); *Image* 6 (Spring 1951); *OWS Club Volume* 55; *Signature* 14 (May 1940); *The Studio* 102 (1931), 149 (1955), special (Winter 1931); Brian Alderson *Edward Ardizzone, a preliminary hand-list of his illustrated books (1929-70)* (The Private Library 2nd series vol 5 no 1 Spring 1972); Edward Ardizzone *Diary of a War Artist* (Bodley Head 1974), *The Young Ardizzone: an autobiographical fragment* (Studio Vista 1970); Miriam Hoffman and Eva Samuels *Authors and Illustrators of Children's Books* (R.R. Bowker 1972); Lynton Lamb *Drawing for Illustration* (Oxford University Press 1962); John Lewis *A Handbook Type and Illustration* (Faber 1956); Gabriel White *Edward Ardizzone* (Bodley Head 1979); Justin Whintle and Emma Fisher *The Pied Pipers* (Paddington Press 1974)

Ernest Alfred Aris (1882-1963)

Studied at Bradford School of Art and the Royal College of Art. Prolific animal illustrator who worked during the post-Beatrix Potter era when the children's market was inundated with stories about small animals. Aris's work reveals an assured graphic technique with considerable textural variety, combined with evident affection for rabbits and birds; he was a highly popular illustrator of his time. In later life he lived in Hornsey, North London. Elected member SGA 1943.

Book illustrated include:
E.A. Aris The Log Books (3 parts 1912), Pirates Three (1914), The Twins of Bunnyville (1914), That Little Brown Bunny (5 parts 1915-16), Bunnikin Brighteyes the Indian (1916), Little Sinbad the Sailor (1916), Playtime Tales and Pictures of Wee Things (1916), Sir Timothy Tapertail (1916), Woodfolk Market (1916), The Three Bad Ducklings (1917), A Toy-Town Tale (1917), The Toy-Town Tiger (1917), The Treasure Seekers (1917), The Wee Babes in the Wood (1918), A Bold Bad Bunny (1920), The House that Jack Built (1920), A Hole in the Curtain (1922), The Story of Roger Quack (1922), Bunny-Go-Lucky (1923), The Betsy Trot series (1924), The Mystery of Cabbage Patch House (1928), Mrs Beak-Duck and her Friends in the Wood (1933), A Tale of Bold Bad Mouse (1933), Twinkle Mouse of Cornstalk Cottage (1933), Betty o' the Barn (1935), Famous Animal Tales (1935), The Uncle Toby Books (4 parts c.1937), The Brambledown Tales (4 parts 1947), Fishing—A Comprehensive Guide to Freshwater Angling (1947), The Ernest Aris Nature Series (4 parts, 1948), A Bad Little Bear (nd), Chiseltooth the Beaver (nd), Just a Tiny Mite (nd), Little Toddler Tail (nd), Mrs Flutter-Hen and her Troublesome Chicks (nd), The Story of Ebenezer Bristles (nd)
E.A. Aris and C.S. Bayne Charlecote Series (4 parts 1927)
E.A. Aris and Madeleine Collier The Book of Delightful Nonsense (1948)
E.A. Aris and May C. Gillington Hide-Away Stories (1929)
Rodney Bennet The Adventures of Spot (1933)
Enid Blyton The Book of Brownies (nd)
Madeleine Collier Books for Children (1926)
John R. Crossland and J.M. Parrish The Children's Wonder Book (with others, 1933)
May C. Gillington The Hole in the Bank (1918)
Jan MacDonald Najla, the Sheikh's Daughter (1944)
Hermon Ould New Plays from Old Stories (1924)
F. Saint Mars The Trail of the Wind (1923)
Stephen Southwold Yesterday and Long Ago (1928)
Mrs Herbert Strang (ed) The Violet Book for Children (with others, nd)
Jane Thorneycroft Dawn the Faun (1948)

Lorna Wood The Smiling Rabbit and Other Stories (1939), The Travelling Tree and Other Stories (1943)
A Story Book for Me (with others, Blackie nd)

Periodicals: Blackie's Girl's Annual, Cassell's Children's Annual, The Graphic, Little Folks, Playbox Annual, Printer's Pie

References: Houfe; Wa (1972); Waters; *The Artist* 16 (1938); E.A. Aris *The Art of the Pen* (Pen-in-Hand Publishing Co. 1948)

Maxwell Ashby Armfield (1881-1972)

Worked as Maxwell Armfield. Born Ringwood, Hampshire. Studied at Birmingham School of Art under Arthur Gaskin, in Paris where he shared a studio with Norman Wilkinson of Four Oaks* and Keith Henderson*, and in Italy. Lived in America 1915-22. He was co-director, with his wife Constance Smedley, of the Greenleaf Theatre Drama School, and lectured on stage design in America and Mexico. He was also a painter, etcher, poet, composer, and writer of theosophical works under the pseudonym 'Mayananda'. A leading member of the Tempera Society; his work in the medium was influenced by early Netherlandish and Italian Quattrocento painting. His book illustrations, in black and white, partial colour and full colour, were decorative rather than spatial in approach and

Maxwell Armfield. 'The Spotted Stag' from *Modern Book Illustrators and their Work* edited by C. Geoffrey Holme and Ernest G. Halton (The Studio, 1914).

executed with care and refinement. Elected ARWS (1937), RWS (1941).

Books illustrated include:
Hans Andersen Fairy Tales (1910), The Ugly Duckling and Other Fairy Tales (1913)
Maxwell Armfield The Hanging Garden and Other Verse (1914), The Syntax of Art. Book 4. Rhythmic Shape (1920), White Horses (1923), An Artist in America (1925), An Artist in Italy (1926), Stencil Printing (1927), Tempera Painting Today (1946), The Confessions of Saint Augustine (1909), Aucassin and Nicolette (1910)
Arthur Gray Cambridge and its Story (1912)
Edward Hutton Rome (1909), Venice and Venetia (1911), The Cities of Lombardy (1912)
Vernon Lee (pseud) The Ballet of Nations (1915)
Frederic Lees A Summer in Touraine (1909)
Donald Mackenzie Indian Fairy Stories (1915)
William Morris The Life and Death of Jason (1915)
Helen M. Rossetti Shelley and his Friends in Italy (1911)
William Shakespeare The Winter's Tale (1922)
Constance Smedley (later Armfield) The Flower Book (1910), Sylvia's Travels (1911), Commoners' Rights (1912), Wonder Tales of the World (1920), The Armfield's Animal Book (1922), Tales from Timbuktu (1923)

Periodicals: The Christian Science Monitor, Holly Leaves

References: Bénézit; Houfe; ICB 1; Johnson & Greutzner; Phaidon; Thieme & Becker; Vollmer; Wa (1970); Waters; *Drawing & Design* 18 (October 1921), 23 (March 1922); *The Studio* 70 (1917), 86 (1923), 88 (1924), 105 (1933), special (Autumn 1914, Winter 1923-24); *Homage to Maxwell Armfield* (Fine Art Society catalogue 1970); *Maxwell Armfield 1881-1972* (Southampton Art Gallery catalogue 1978); Constance Armfield *Crusaders* (Duckworth 1929)

Joshua Charles Armitage (b. 1913)

Has often worked as 'Ionicus'. Born in Hoylake, Cheshire, son of a fisherman. Studied at Liverpool School of Art (1929-35). His career as a teacher (1936-50) was interrupted by service in the Royal Navy as an instructor during World War II. Book and magazine illustrator since 1950

G.D. Armour. 'The Little Bay Horse Would Have No More Of It' from *The Sport of Our Ancestors* edited by Lord Willoughby de Broke (Constable, 1925).

working in black and white and colour. Also a painter in oil and watercolour. Contributor to *Punch* from 1944. Designer of book jackets for Penguin Books since 1968. Early in his career, he developed a simplified pen and ink style of unusual clarity, using firm outlines and varied yet precise hatching. His contributions to *Punch* had a discernible influence on humorous draughtsmanship during the late 1950s and 1960s.[Q]

Books illustrated include:
Edward Blishen Town Story (1964)
Dr David Carrick Executive Health (1978)
Carlo Collodi The Adventures of Pinocchio (1960)
Ann Lawrence Tom Ass (1972), The Half-Brothers (1973), The Good Little Devil (1978)
Irmelin Lilius Gold Crown Lane (1976), The Goldmaker's House (1977), Horses of the Night (1979)
Ogden Nash A Boy and His Room (1964), The Untold Adventures of Santa Claus (1965)
R.G.G. Price How to Become Headmaster (1960), Survive With Me (1962)
Gerald Sparrow How to Become a Millionaire (1960)
Geoffrey Trease The Claws of the Eagle (1977)
Barbara Willard and Frances Howell Junior Motorist (1969)
P.G. Wodehouse Sunset at Blandings (1977) and over 50 other Wodehouse titles

Periodicals: Amateur Gardening, Daily Mirror, The Dalesman, Evening Standard, Lilliput, Punch, The Tatler

References: Fisher p.357; Wa 18

George Denholm Armour (1864-1949)

Usually worked as G.D. Armour. Born Waterside, Lanarkshire, son of a cotton broker. Studied at St Andrew's University, Edinburgh School of Art, and the Royal Scottish Academy Schools. Sporting artist in black and white and watercolour. Introduced to *Punch* (1894) by Phil May* with whom he shared a studio in the Fulham Road, London, he soon established himself as a popular humorous illustrator of huntin', shootin' and fishin' scenes. He contributed to *Country Life* from 1912. His penmanship, although clearly influenced by Phil May, lacked his linear flexibility and animation. While his horse drawings were graceful and spirited, he depicted the riders as raw-boned individuals decidedly lacking in charm; he excelled at depicting the discomforts of a wet winter afternoon in the saddle. His work offers an interesting contrast with the more romantic and idealised view of sport presented by his close contemporary, Cecil Aldin*. After leaving London, he lived in Wiltshire, Somerset and Dorset. He was awarded the OBE (1919) for service in the Army Remount Service in Salonica during World War I.

Books illustrated include:
Thomas Scott Anderson Hulloas from the Hills (1899), Hound and Horn in Jed Forest (1900)
G.D. Armour Pastime with Good Company (1914), Humour in the Hunting Field (1928), A Hunting Alphabet (1929), Sport, and there's the humour of it' (1935), Bridle and Brush (1937)

2

ATTWELL

'B.B.' The Sportsman's Bedside Book (1937)
Richard Ball Broncho (1930), Penny Farthing (1931)
Peter Beckford Thoughts on Hunting (1911)
Isaac Bell Foxiana (1929)
John A. Budden Charlie the Fox (1932)
Moyra Charlton Patch (1931)
Crascredo No Joke (1929)
Edward W.D. Cuming British Sport Past and Present (1909), The British Sport Series (1913)
Lord Willoughby de Broke (ed) The Sport of our Ancestors (1925)
John W. Fortescue The Story of a Red Deer (1925)
Homer Hawkins Hoof-Beats (1932)
Thomas B. Marson Scarlet and Khaki (1930)
John Masefield Reynard the Fox (1921)
William H. Ogilvie and G.D. Armour Horse Laughter (1938)
Charles W.G. Saint John Wild Sports and Natural History of the Highlands (1919)
Richard C. Simpson Fish—and Find Out (1937)
Robert S. Surtees Hunts with Jorrocks (1908), Mr Jorrock's Lectors (1910), Thoughts on Hunting (1925), Young Tom Hall (1926), The Hunting Tours of Surtees (1927), Town and Country Capers (1929)
Richard G. Verney The Sport of our Ancestors (1921)

Periodicals: The Butterfly, Country Life, The English Illustrated Magazine, The Graphic, The Humorist, London Opinion, The Longbow, The New Budget, The Pall Mall Magazine, Pick-Me-Up, Printer's Pie, Punch, The Sketch, The Sporting and Dramatic News, The Tatler, Toc H Annual, The Unicorn, The Windsor Magazine

References: Bénézit; Houfe; Johnson & Greutzner; Mallalieu; Mallett; Price; Thieme & Becker; Thorpe; Wa (1934); Waters; WW (1906); C. Wood; J.C. Wood; *Country Life* (April 20 1978); *Pearson's Magazine* no 22 (1906); *The Studio* special (1911); *The Windsor Magazine* 7 (1898); James L. Caw *Scottish Painting Past and Present* (T.C. & E.C. Jack 1908)

Charles Robert Ashbee (1863-1942)

Worked as C.R. Ashbee. Born at Isleworth in Middlesex. Educated at Wellington School and King's College, Cambridge. Articled to the Gothic Revival architect G.F. Bodley, then set up his own architectural practice. Like William Morris, he sought to develop art and handicraft as an instrument of social reform, and to this end he set up the School and Guild of Handicraft in the Mile End Road, East London in 1888, moving with it to the Cotswold village of Chipping Camden in 1902. He founded the Guild's Essex House Press in 1898 and superintended its work until 1906, when he passed it on to A.K. Coomeraswamy. He also designed jewellery and silverwork, and wrote a number of books on art, education and society. During World War I he served in the Middle East, and was appointed civic adviser to the City of Jerusalem (1916-22) to make recommendations on the preservation of buildings and the revival of Arab crafts. As a book illustrator, decorator and designer, Ashbee was involved exclusively with the Essex House Press. He designed for it two new typefaces—'Endeavour' and 'Prayer Book'—as well as illuminated capitals, head and tail pieces, vignettes and frontispieces. Some of these were engraved on wood by Ashbee himself, others by the Essex House craftsmen who included W.E. Hooper (formerly of the Kelmscott Press) and Bernard Sleigh*. Ashbee was an outstanding decorator and typographic designer,

but his pictorial illustrations are stilted in comparison with those of other Essex House artists who included Walter Crane*, F.L.M. Griggs*, Laurence Housman, T. Sturge-Moore*, E.H. New*, Reginald Savage* and Paul Woodroffe*. Member of the Art Workers' Guild (1897), elected Master of the Guild (1927).

Books illustrated include:
C.R. Ashbee Echoes from the City of the Sun (1905)
Cicero De Amicitia or the Book of Friendship (1904)
John Fischer A Mornynge Remembrance (frontispiece 1906)
Oliver Goldsmith The Deserted Village (frontispiece 1904)
Thomas à Kempis The Imitation of Christ (1904)
W. Shakespeare Poems (1900)
Percy B. Shelley Adonais (1900), Prometheus Unbound (frontis 1904)
Walt Whitman Hymn on the Death of President Lincoln (1901)
The Book of Common Prayer (1903)
The Prayer Book of King Edward VII (1903)
The Psalter or Psalms of David (1902)
The Rubaiyat of Omar Khayyam (1905)

References: DNB (1941-50); Johnson & Greutzner; Taylor; Thieme & Becker; Vollmer supp; *Art Journal* 1898, 1904; C.R. Ashbee *A Palestine Notebook 1918-23* (Heinemann 1923), *The Private Press: a study in idealism* (Essex House Press 1909); Colin Franklin *The Private Presses* (Studio Vista 1969); H.J.L.J. Massé *Art Workers' Guild 1884-1934* (Shakespeare Head Press 1935)

Leslie Atkinson (active 1946-67)

Illustrator, mainly of children's books, in pen and ink and occasionally half-tone washes. His style was sketchy and animated and, in the *Badger* books, influenced at times by the work of E.H. Shepard*. His most distinguished illustrations were for *This Unknown Island*, a descriptive work for adults, for which he produced evocative landscape drawings with considerable atmosphere.

Books illustrated include:
Ruth Ainsworth Roly the Railway Mouse (1967)
Louisa M. Alcott Little Men (1948)
Cecilia Knowles Hua Ma (1947)
Stuart Mais This Unknown Island (1946)
Geoffrey Trease Seven Kings to England (1955), A Ship to Rome (1972)
Elleston Trevor Badger's Beech (1948), The Wizard of the Wood (1948), Mole's Castle (1951), Sweethallow Valley (1951), Badger's Wood (1958)

Mabel Lucie Attwell (1879-1964)

Born Mile End, London, the ninth of ten children of a butcher. Studied at Regent School of Art and at Heatherley's School of Art, but, disliking the formal training, completed neither course. Married Harold Earnshaw* (1908). From 1911 until the end of her life she designed postcards for Valentines of Dundee. Following the success of a card depicting two children peering over the end of a bed at a mouse (entitled 'What's the good of a perfect day if you can't spend a perfect night') she developed a line in pictures of chubby children in situations with adult overtones and (possibly unconscious) suggestions of *double entendre*. A

Mabel Lucie Attwell. From *The Water Babies* by Charles Kingsley (Raphael Tuck, nd)

rapid and prolific worker, she also designed advertisements, posters, calendars, figurines and wall plaques (e.g. 'Please remember, don't forget, never leave the bathroom wet') and contributed to annuals and gift books. Some of her earlier books such as *Peter Pan* and *The Water Babies* were delicate and appealing but as she became a household name her drawing became increasingly stereotyped. She worked mainly in pen and ink and watercolour. Member SWA. She died at Fowey in Cornwall, where she had lived for many years.

Books illustrated include:
Mabel Lucie Attwell The Boo-Boos Series (1921-22), Baby's Book (1922), Fairy Book (1932), Happy-Day Tales (1932), Quiet Time Tales (1932), Great Big Midget Books (1934-35), Playtime Pictures (1935), Story Books (1943-45), Jolly Book (1953), Nursery Rhymes Pop-up Book (1958), Book of Verse (1960), Book of Rhymes (1962)
J.M. Barrie Peter Pan and Wendy (1921)
Lewis Carroll Alice in Wonderland (1910)
Charles Kingsley The Water Babies (nd)
Archibald Marshall Wooden (1920)
Mrs Molesworth The February Boys (1909)
Queen Mary, consort of King Ferdinand of Roumania Peeping Pansy (1919)
Grimm's Fairy Tales (nd)
Rainy-Day Tales (various authors, 1931)
Rock-Away Tales (various authors, 1931)

Periodicals: Cassell's Children's Annual, Father Tuck's Annual, Little Folks, Lucie Attwell's Annual, Pearson's Magazine

References: Doyle CL; Fisher p.350; Houfe; Johnson & Greutzner; Waters; *The Times* (12th December 1979)

Stephen André Augarde (b. 1950)

Works as Stephen Augarde. Born in Birmingham.

Studied at Somerset College of Art. Worked for the National Trust as a gardener for a year before taking a teacher training course in Devon. Author and illustrator of children's books, and a sign writer. His first four books were illustrated using gouache and pen and ink on dual-proven card (with a china-clay surface that can be scraped). For subsequent books he used rapidograph, watercolour and watercolour crayons.

Books illustrated include:
Stephen Augarde A Lazy Day (1974), The River That Disappeared (1974), The Willow Tree (1974), Pig (1976), Barnaby Shrew Goes to Sea (1978), Barnaby Shrew, Black Dan and the Mighty Wedgwood (1979), Mr Mick (1980), January Jo and Friends (1981)
Bill Gilham Septimus Fry FRS (1980)

Reference: ICB 4

Norman Ault (1880-1950)

Attended King Edward VI Grammar School in Birmingham, studied art and architecture at the West Bromwich School of Art (1895-1900) and later settled in Oxford. He contributed drawings to the *Strand Magazine* and to various children's annuals. Some of his early children's books were produced in collaboration with his wife (also an artist), and he became a close friend of H.R. Millar*. He made a special study of poetry, publishing several anthologies, and was made an Honorary MA (Oxon) for his work on Alexander Pope (1941). Among his other interests were experimental shadow-shows, and life in prehistoric times. His work shows a strong feeling for black and white, and his well-arranged compositions are informed with a sense of history and considerable imagination.

Books illustrated include:
Norman Ault Sammy the Snarleywink (1904), The Rhyme Book (1906), The Podgy Book (1907), Dreamland Shores (1920), Life in Ancient Britain (1920), The Poet's Life of Christ (1922)
Lewis Carroll Alice's Adventures in Wonderland (nd)
J. Connolly The Story of an Old Fashioned Doll (1905)
F.J. Harvey Darton The Seven Champions of Christendom (1913)
Lady Guest The Mabinogion (1902)
Wilhelm Hauff Caravan Tales (1912)
Thomas Babington Macaulay Lays of Ancient Rome (1911)
W.E. Sparkes New Tales of Old Times (1914)
Alfred, Lord Tennyson Poems (1913)
Grace I. Whitham Shepherd of the Green (1914)
M.B. Williams England's Story for Children (1908)
Chamber's Dramatic History Readers (1914-15)

Periodical: The Strand Magazine

References: Houfe; ICB 1; Vollmer supp; *Who Was Who* (1941-50)

John Austen (1886-1948)

Born in Kent. Trained as a carpenter. In 1906 he moved to London where he became what Dorothy Richardson described as a 'long-haired studio exquisite', attended life classes and participated enthusiastically in amateur dramatics. In 1925 he exhibited illustrations at the St George's Gallery with Harry Clarke* and Alan Odle*, (whom he regarded as one of the outstanding draughtsmen of the age and whose precarious career he from then on attempted to assist). In the late 1920s, illness forced a return to the country and he settled at Jesson in Kent, turning to rural pursuits such as gardening. He also held a teaching post at Thanet School of Art. His early illustrations, generally in pen and ink with cross hatching or flat colours owed much to his acknowledged enthusiasm for Aubrey Beardsley, modified by the then current Art Deco idiom. *The Studio* during this period praised his 'astonishing fertility in design combined with a power of imaginative penetration of no common order.' After the 1920s, his work began to lose its stylish effervescence as his images increasingly consisted of mannered, though still elegant, full-length figures in close-up, set in a very shallow picture space.' The majority of his wood engravings and pencil/wash drawings date from this time. He often took an active part in designing many of the books he illustrated.

Books illustrated include:
Aristophanes The Frogs (1937)
Jane Austen Persuasion (1946)
John Austen (ed) Rogues in Porcelain (1924)
Arnold Bennett The Old Wives' Tale (1941)
Francis Bickley The Adventures of Harlequin (1923)
Lord Byron Don Juan (1926)
J.V.P. David The Guardsman and Cupid's Daughter (1930)
Daniel Defoe Moll Flanders (1929)
Charles Dickens The Posthumous Papers of the Pickwick Club (1933)
Benjamin Disraeli Ixion in Heaven (1925), The Infernal Marriage (1929)
J.M. de Eca de Queiroz Perfection (1923)
Gustave Flaubert Madame Bovary (1928)
Anatole France The Gods are Athirst (1926)
Hugh L'Anson Fausset The Condemned (1922)
R.H. Keen The Little Ape and Other Stories (1921)
E.C. Lefroy Echoes from Theocritus (1922)
Alain-René le Sage The Adventures of Gil Blas (1937)
Charles Perrault Tales from Passed Times (1922)
E.J. Pratt The Witches Brew (1925), Daphnis and Chloe (1925)
L'Abbé Prévost Manon Lescaut (1928)
D.U. Radcliffe The Gypsy Dorelia (1932)
William Shakespeare Hamlet (1922), As You Like It (1930), The Comedy of Errors (1939)
T.G. Smollett The Adventures of Peregrine Pickle (1936)
Edmund Spenser The Faerie Queene (with A.M. Parker*—prepared 1939)
Laurence Sterne The Life and Opinions of Tristram Shandy (1928)
William Makepeace Thackeray Vanity Fair (1931)
Everyman and Other Plays (1925)

Periodical: The Golden Hind

References: ICB 1; Johnson & Greutzner; Vollmer; Wa (1934); *Drawing and Design* 12 (April 1921); *The Studio* 88 (1924), 89 (1925), special (1923-24, Winter 1931); John Austen *The ABC of Pen and Ink Rendering* (Pitman 1937); G. Montague Ellwood *The Art of Pen Drawing* (Batsford 1927); Dorothy M. Richardson *John Austen and the Inseparables* (William Jackson 1930)

Winifred Marie Louise Austen (1876-1964)

Later worked as Mrs Oliver Frick. Born Ramsgate, Kent. Studied under Mrs Jopling and C.E.

Swan and in the Zoological Gardens. Painter and etcher (with drypoint and aquatint) mainly of bird and animal subjects. In later years she lived in Orford, Suffolk. Elected SWA (1905), ARE (1907), RE (1922), RI (1933).

Books illustrated include:
Patrick Chalmers Birds Ashore and Aforeshore (1935)
Arthur Cooke At the Zoo (1920)
Kenneth Dawson Marsh and Mud Flat (1931), Just An Ordinary Shoot (1935)
E. Nesbit A Book of Dogs (1898)
Eric Parker Field, River and Hill (1927)

References: Bénézit; Guichard; Johnson & Greutzner; Thieme & Becker; Vollmer; Wa (1964); Waters; *The Studio* 61 (1941)

Robert Sargent Austin (1895-1973)

Worked as Robert Austin. Born in Leicester, brother of the painter and etcher F.G. Austin. Studied part-time at Leicester School of Art from the age of seven, and full time from the age of thirteen (1909-11). Worked as an apprentice printer and lithographer (1911-13). Attended the Royal College of Art on a scholarship (1914-16 and 1919-22) studying engraving under Frank Short. Served in the Royal Artillery (1916-19). Studied engraving on a scholarship at the British School in Rome (1922-23); elected to the Faculty (1926). Travelled in Germany, then returned to England (1925). Teacher of engraving at the Royal College of Art (1927-44) and Professor of Graphic Design (1948-55). He became known during the 1920s for his etchings and etching/engravings of Italian figure subjects, which were drawn with great precision, somewhat in the manner of Dürer. A sensitive topographer, he produced pencil landscape illustrations for travel books on which he collaborated with his wife Ada Harrison. His illustrative work also included humorous figures

Robert Austin. 'Oh dear! I do believe it will be wet' from *Northanger Abbey* by Jane Austen (Avalon Press, 1948).

sketches for children's books and small but very striking black and white line drawings for G.K. Chesterton's* *The Ballad of the White Horse.*

Books illustrated include:
Jane Austen Northanger Abbey (1948)
Robert S. Austin Surrey. A Sketch Book (1922), Warwick, Leamington and Kenilworth. A Sketch-Book (1920)
G.K. Chesterton The Ballad of the White Horse (1928), There and Back (1932)
Ada Harrison The Doubling Rod (1957)
Ada Harrison and Robert S. Austin Some Umbrian Cities (1925), A Majorca Holiday (1927), The Adventures of Polly Peppermint (1943), Lucy's Village (1945)

References: Bénézit; Chamot; Farr & Butlin; Guichard; Johnson & Greutzner; Vollmer; Wa (1934); Waters; *The OWS Club Volume* 33; *The Print Collector's Quarterly* 16; *The Studio* special (Spring 1929); Campbell Dodgson *A Catalogue of Etchings and Engravings by Robert Austin RE 1913-19* (Catalogue 2 Gallery 1930); M.C. Salaman *Robert Austin RE: Modern Masters of Etchings 25* (Studio series 1925-32)

Michael Ayrton (1921-75)

Born London, son of Gerald Gould, novelist, poet and literary critic, and Barbara Ayrton, Labour politician; he adopted his mother's name in order to appear among the As in alphabetically listed mixed exhibitions. Studied briefly at Heatherley's School of Art (1935). Travelled extensively in Europe, visiting Barcelona (during the Spanish Civil War), Vienna and Paris (where he shared a studio with John Minton*). In collaboration with Minton, he designed and supervised sets and costumes for John Gielgud's production of *Macbeth* (1940-42). Taught life drawing and theatre design at Camberwell School of Art (1942-44); succeeded John Piper* as art critic on *The Spectator* (1944-46) and also became known as a broadcaster on art and regular participant in the BBC radio's *Round Britain Quiz*. In 1951, he moved to Essex and, with technical advice from Henry Moore, began working as a sculptor. He travelled in Italy and Greece and became deeply interested in the myths of Icarus and Daedalus which provided the inspiration for many later works.

Throughout his career, Ayrton explored and dramatised situations containing strong elements of human tension: unidentified threats, doomed aspirations, suppressed violence. His early paintings, usually based on specific locations or individuals, were often literary and illustrative in approach, but his later exploration of sculptural form (and subsequent adoption of mythological subjects) enabled him to attempt more generalised and universally applicable images of powerful feeling. His forms, however, tended to be stylised rather than inventive. His book illustrations developed from his work as a painter, stage designer and sculptor, and usually reflected his current ideas in these fields. Most successful, perhaps, were his small line drawings (e.g. in *The Duchess*

of Malfi), which are spontaneous, graceful and unpretentious in contrast to the over-emphatic qualities of many of his more ambitious illustrations in half-tone or lithography. His work was admired by Wyndham Lewis*, who entrusted to him the illustrations for his novel *The Human Age*; though these drawings were not finished until after Lewis had become blind, he continued to supervise their execution closely (through descriptions).

Books illustrated include:
Lucius Apuleius (trans Robert Graves) The Golden Ass (1960)
John Arlott and Michael Ayrton Clausentum (1946)
Michael Ayrton Tittivulus or the Verbiage Collector (1953), The Testament of Daedalus (1962), Berlioz. A Singular Obsession (1969), The Minotaur (1970)
Giambattista Basile (trans R. Burton) The Pentameron (1952)
Henry Bett English Myths and Legends (1952)
Douglas G. Bridson The Quest of Gilgamesh (1972)
Richard Church North of Rome (1960)
J. Wentworth Day Ghosts and Witches (1954)
George Foa The Blood Rushed to my Pockets (1957)
Kay Fuller Forfeit (1954)
Cecil Gray Gilles de Rais (1945), The Bed (1946)
Dr E.J. Holmyard (ed) Ancestors of an Industry (1950)
John Keats Poems (1957)
P. Wyndham Lewis The Human Age (1956)

Michael Ayrton. From *The Bed* by Cecil and Margery Gray (Nicholson & Watson, 1946).

Louis MacNeice The Other Wing (1954)
Gavin Maxwell Ring of Bright Water (1960)
Thomas Nashe Summer's Last Will and Testament (1946), The Unfortunate Traveller (1948)
Plato The Trial and Execution of Socrates (1972)
Edgar Allen Poe Tales of Mystery and Imagination (1957)
Phoebe Pool Poems of Death (1945)
George Rylands (ed) A Distraction of Wits (1958)
William Shakespeare The Tragedy of Macbeth (1951)
David Cleghorn Thompson The Hidden Path (1943)
Paul Verlaine Fêtes Galantes (1941, unpublished), Femmes, Hombres (1971)
John Webster The Duchess of Malfi (1945)
Oscar Wilde The Picture of Dorian Gray (1948)

Periodical: Radio Times

References: Bénézit; Chamot, Farr & Butlin; Contemporary Artists; Contemporary Authors; Driver; Jacques; Phaidon; Thieme & Becker; Vollmer; Wa (1977); Waters 1, 2; *Motif* 7 (1951); *The Studio* 150 (1955), 156 (1958); *The Studio International* (August 1967); *Ayrton at Bruton* (Bruton Gallery 1971); *Word and Image* II (National Book League 1971); Michael Ayrton *Drawings and Sculpture* (Cory, Adams & Mackay 1962); James Laver *Paintings by Michael Ayrton* (Grey Walls Press 1947)

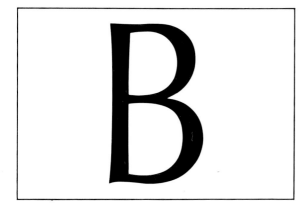

John Henry Frederick Bacon (c. 1866-1914)

Authorities disagree as to the year of his birth. He studied at the Royal Academy Schools and worked as a painter of domestic scenes, figures and occasionally portraits. As an illustrator, he worked in pen and ink and halftone, and, as he became better known, in full colour. His early illustrations were typical of their period, but as time went on, he tended to depict figures in increasingly exaggerated poses. In the full colour plates of later books, such as *Celtic Myth and Legend*, he was evidently aiming at something more elevated than mere illustration. Elected ARA (1903).

Books illustrated include:
H. Clarke The Ravensworth Scholarship (1895)
Mrs Craik John Halifax, Gentleman (1899)
Charles Dickens Dombey and Son (1902), Little Dorrit (1902)
Evelyn Everett-Green Priscilla (1900), Esther's Charge (1912)
W.H. Fitchett (intro) The King's Empire (1906)
Beatrice Harraden Things Will Take a Turn (with A.A. Dixon, 1894)
Nathaniel Hawthorne The Scarlet Letter and the House with the Seven Gables (1904)
Thomas Hughes Tom Brown's Schooldays (1906)
Charles Lamb Tales from Shakespeare (nd)
E. Nesbit and Doris Ashley Children's Stories from English History (with Howard Davie*, 1914)
C. Squire Celtic Myth and Legend (with others, 1912)

Periodicals: Black and White, Cassell's Family Magazine, The Girl's Own Paper, The Ludgate Monthly, The Quiver, The Windsor Magazine

References: Bénézit; Houfe; Mallalieu; Thieme & Becker; Thorpe; Vollmer; Waters; C. Wood; *Connoisseur* 38 p.202 (1914); *Magazine of Art* p.193 (1902)

Stanley Roy Badmin (b. 1906)

Born in Sydenham, London. Studied at Camberwell School of Art and at the Royal College of Art under Randolph Schwabe*. Subsequently a lecturer at the Central School of Arts and Crafts. His principal concern, as an artist, was with the countryside, and his work can be seen as part of the English pastoral landscape revival of the 1920s and 1930s. As an illustrator, he was particularly known for his knowledgeable depiction of trees, which he drew, often in pen and ink, with tautness and delicacy. He also worked in watercolour, and made etchings and lithographs. Elected ARE (1931), ARWS (1932), RE (1935), RWS (1939).

Books illustrated include:
S.R. Badmin Trees in Britain (1946), Village and Town (1949)
R.St B. Baker Famous Trees (1952)
P. Nicholson Country Bequest (nd)
Sir G. Stapleston Farm Crops in Britain (1955)
Ralph Wightman The Seasons (nd)

Periodicals: Fortune, Radio Times, The Tatler

References: Driver; Guichard; ICB 2; Jacques; Johnson & Greutzner; Wa (1980); Waters; *The OWS Club Volume* 37; *The Studio* 105 (1933), special (Spring 1929)

Bruce Bairnsfather (1888-1959)

Born Murree, India, the son of an army officer. Served in the Royal Warwickshire Regiment. On leaving the army, he studied at John Hassall's New Art School, then worked as an apprentice to a firm of electrical engineers. Army volunteer during World War I (wounded at Ypres); sent comic drawings from the front to *The Bystander*. These brash and simplified pen, pencil or halftone drawings extracted humour from the appalling conditions of trench warfare in a way that had immediate popular appeal, particularly among the troops themselves who recognised their authenticity. Bairnsfather was appointed as Officer Cartoonist in the Intelligence Department; his central character, 'Old Bill', became a household name, and afterwards sustained his creator in a postwar career as comic draughtsman, writer, lecturer and music-hall performer in England and America. During World War II, Bairnsfather was Official War Artist to the American Army in Europe.

Books illustrated include:
Captain B. Bairnsfather Bullets and Billets (1916), Fragments from France (c.1916), From Mud to Mufti (1919), More Fragments from France (c.1917)
Captain B. Bairnsfather and W.A. Muleh The Bairnsfather Case (1920)

Bruce Bairnsfather. 'What's that hat doin' floatin' round there, sergeant?'/ 'I think that's Private Murphy sittin' down, sir' from *Fragments from all the Fronts. Number Six* (The Bystander).

Captain A.J. Dawson For France (1916), Some Battle Stories (1916), Back to Blighty (1917)

Periodicals: The Bystander, Judge, Life, The New Yorker, Passing Show, The Tatler

References: DNB (1951-60); Houfe; Vollmer; Wa (1956); Waters; *The Strand Magazine* 51 (1916); Bruce Bairnsfather *Bairnsfather, a Few Fragments from his Life* (Hodder & Stoughton 1916), *The Bairnsfather Case* (Putnams 1920), *Wide Canvas* (John Lang 1939); Percy Bradshaw *They Make Us Smile* (Chapman & Hall 1942); T. and V. Holt *The Best Fragments from France* (Phin 1978)

Alan Baker (b. 1951)

Born in London, son of a welder. Studied at Croydon Technical College (1969-71), Hull University (1971-72), Croydon College of Art (1972-73) and Brighton College of Art (1973-76). An illustrator and author of children's books, he particularly favours fantasy and animal subjects. He works in a very detailed style in pen and ink, often with colour washes. His sister, Jeannie Baker (who lives in Australia), is also an illustrator and writer of children's books.

Books illustrated include:
Alan Baker Benjamin and the Box (1977), Benjamin Bounces Back (1978), Benjamin's Dreadful Dream (1980)
Eleanor Bourne Heritage of Flowers (1980)

Alan Baker. 'I think I'll just try to forget it and go to sleep' from *Benjamin's Dreadful Dream* (André Deutsch, 1980).

Deirdre Headon Mythical Beasts (1981)
Philippa Pearce The Battle of Bubble and Squeak (1978)

Reference: Contemporary Authors

Mary Baker (b. 1897)

Born Runcorn, Cheshire. Took a correspondence course in illustration at the Press Art School and attended Chester School of Art. Illustrated children's books written by her sister, Margaret, of which the first, *The Black Cats and the Tinker's Wife*, was turned down by several publishers, but eventually ran to many editions. In many of her illustrations she made effective use of silhouette, a technique then enjoying a considerable vogue. She was also a painter in watercolour and an amateur naturalist.

Books illustrated include:
Margaret Baker The Black Cats and the Tinker's Wife (1923), Pedlar's Ware (1925), The Little Girl who Curtsied (1925), The Dog, the Brownie and the Bramble Patch (1926), Pixies and the Silver Crown (1927), The Lost Merbaby (1927), Tomson's Hallowe'en (1929), The Best of Health (1930), Patsy and the Leprechaun (1932), Tell Them Again Tales (1933), Cats' Cradles for his Majesty (1933), Mrs

Mary Baker. From *Tell Them Again Tales* by Margaret Baker (University of London Press, 1933).

Bobbity's Crust (1937), Margaret and Mary Baker Story Book (1939), Lady Arabella's Birthday Party (1940), The Nightingale (1944), The Book of Happy Tales (1948), Seven Times Once Upon a Time (1948)

References: Eyre; ICB 1,2; Johnson & Greutzner; Vollmer; Wa (1934)

Ronald Edmund Balfour (1896-1941)

A generation after Aubrey Beardsley's death in 1898, his decorative style continued to exert an influence on graphic artists. In Balfour's black and white illustrations for *Omar Khaiyam* (published by Constable), there were distinct echoes of Beardsley, while the colour plates recalled the Danish/American illustrator Kay Nielsen. Nothing seems to have been recorded about Balfour's life or career.

Books illustrated include:
Constance Bridges Thin Air (1930)
E. Fitzgerald (trans) The Rubaiyat of Omar Khaiyam (1920)

References: Houfe; B. Reade and F. Dickinson *Aubrey Beardsley* (Victoria & Albert Museum catalogue 1966)

Frederick E. Banbery (active from 1938)

Works as Fred Banbery. Born in London. Studied at the Central School of Arts and Crafts. Staff artist with *The Times of India*, Bombay (1938-40). Royal Air Force pilot (1940-46). Since then he has worked as a freelance book and newspaper illustrator, and portrait painter. He succeeded Peggy Fortnum* as illustrator of the *Paddington*

Fred Banbery. From Paddington at the Tower by Michael Bond (Collins, 1975).

Bear picture books. His other book illustrations have been mainly for New York publishers including Simon & Schuster, Random House, Harper & Row and Viking. He works mainly in pen and ink and watercolour. Winner of the New York Art Director's Club Medal (1951) and the Philadelphia Art Director's Club Medal (1952). [Q]

Books illustrated include:
Michael Bond Paddington Bear (1972), Paddington's Garden (1972), Paddington at the Circus (1973), Paddington Goes Shopping (1973), Paddington at the Tower (1975), Paddington at the Seaside (1975), Paddington's Picture Book (1978)

Periodicals: Atlantic, Colliers, The Economist, Homes and Gardens, Ladies' Home Journal, The New Yorker, Saturday Evening Post, The Sunday Times, The Times of India, TV Times, The Wall Street Journal

Helen Brodie Cowan Watson Bannerman (1862-1946)

Worked as Helen Bannerman. Born Edinburgh. Much of childhood spent in Madeira (1864-74). Studied language and literature at St Andrew's University as an external student, and also in Germany and Italy. Married Will Bannerman (1889), a doctor in the Indian Medical Service, and spent almost thirty years in India. She wrote and illustrated *The Story of Little Black Sambo* during a two-day journey to Madras from the family's summer home in Kodai, where she had left her two daughters. It was taken to the London publisher Grant Richards by a friend who, without consulting the author, sold the copyright for five pounds. The book was an immediate success and has remained popular ever since. *The Story of Little Black Mingo* and those that followed (all set in India) were published by James Nisbet. Her illustrations, although obviously the

Helen Bannerman. From The Story of Little Black Quibba (James Nisbet, 1902).

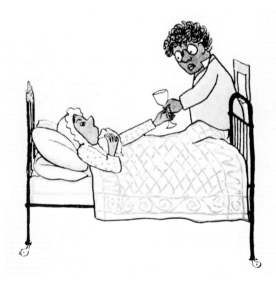

work of an amateur, were clear and straightforward, a fanciful view of the cruel side of animal life. Helen Bannerman returned to Edinburgh in 1918 and died there in 1946; *The Story of Little White Squibba* was completed by her daughter Day and published by Chatto and Windus in 1966.

Books illustrated include:
Helen Bannerman The Story of Little Black Sambo (1899), The Story of Little Black Mingo (1901), The Story of Little Black Quibba (1902), The Story of Little Degchie-head (1903), Pat and the Spider (1904), The Story of the Teasing Monkey (1906), The Story of Little Black Quasha (1908), The Story of Little Black Bobtail (1909), The Story of Sambo and the Twins (1937), The Story of Little White Squibba (1966)

References: Contemporary Authors; Doyle CL; Fisher p.174; ICB 1; Kirkpatrick; Elizabeth Hay *Sambo Sahib. The Story of Helen Bannerman* (Paul Harris 1981)

Anthony Raine Barker (1880-1963)

Born in Harrow. Worked as a painter, etcher, lithographer and wood engraver of landscapes and architectural subjects. In 1909, he won the Soane medal at the Institute of Architects. In 1912, he published a portfolio of Italian etchings. His children's books, which were written for his own amusement, were illustrated in a deliberately quaint chap-book style.

Books illustrated include:
A.R. Barker The Fairyland Express (1925), Hidden Gold (1926)

References: Bénézit; Guichard; Johnson & Greutzner; Vollmer; Wa (1934); Waters; *The Studio* special (1919)

Carol Mintum Barker (b. 1938)

Born in London. Studied at Bournemouth, Chelsea and the Central School of Arts and Crafts. Freelance illustrator since 1958. Her work, in pen and ink, watercolour, collage and wax, is decorative

Carol Barker. From *Storyteller's Choice* by Eileen Colwell (Bodley Head, 1963).

rather than spatial in character. H.E. Bates wrote *Achilles the Donkey* around her pictures.

Books illustrated include:
Carol Barker The Boy and the Lion (1968), Birds and Beasts (1972), An Oba of Benin (1976), A Prince of Islam (1976), Argun and his Village in India (1979), King Midas and the Golden Touch (nd)
H.E. Bates Achilles the Donkey (1962), Achilles and Diana (1963), Achilles and the Twins (1964)
Eileen Colwell Storyteller's Choice (1963)
Nicholas Fisk Emma Borrows a Cup of Sugar (1973)
Roger Lancelyn Green Ancient Greece (1962)
Janet McNeill It's Snowing Outside (1968)
Margaret Mahy Pillycock's Shop (1969), The Princess and the Clown (1971)
Richard Parker Lost in a Shop (1968)
Geraldine Symons Morning Glory (1966)
Norman Wymer Gilbert and Sullivan (1962)

References: ICB 3,4; Ryder

Cicely Mary Barker (1895-1973)

Born in Croydon, Surrey. Studied part-time at Croydon School of Art but was largely self-taught as an illustrator. Working mainly in watercolour but sometimes in black and white, she became one of the most accomplished children's illustrators of her period. Her works shows a Kate

Cicely Mary Barker. From her *Flower Fairies of the Spring* (Blackie, 1923).

Greenaway-like predilection for ravishingly pretty children in idealised village or rural settings; like Kate Greenaway, she was often her own versifier, and her books were thus largely of her own creation. She was best known for her flower fairies—appealing drawn children in picturesque botanic costumes, in marked contrast to the adult and essentially theatrical tradition earlier found in Walter Crane's* floral masques. Her books were mainly published by Blackie & Son. She also designed Christmas cards (published by the Girls' Friendly Society), and a stained glass window for St Andrew's Church, Croydon. One of her pictures was purchased by Queen Mary. She was a close friend of Margaret Tarrant*, and lived in Sussex for much of her life.

Books illustrated include:
C.M. Barker The Book of Flower Fairies (nd), Flower Fairies of the Spring (1923), Old Rhymes for all Times (1928), A Flower Fairy Alphabet (1934), A Little Book of Old Rhymes (1936), A Little Book of Rhymes New and Old (1937), The Lord of the Rushie River (1938), Flower Fairies of the Garden (1944), Groundsel and Necklaces (1946), Flower Fairies of the Wayside (1948), Fairies of the Flowers and Trees (1950), Flower Fairy Picture Book (1955), Lively Numbers (1957), Lively Words (1961), Beautiful Bible Pictures (1932), The Little Picture Hymn Book (1933), Rhymes Old & New (nd)

Periodical: Little Folks

References: Cope; Johnson & Greutzner; Vollmer; Wa (1977); Waters

Kathleen Frances Barker (from c.1933)

Worked as Kathleen Barker. Writer and illustrator of books about animals, especially dogs. She worked in pen and ink, or pencil, depicting dogs and other creatures with expertise and affection, keeping backgrounds and other subjects to a minimum. Mainly published by A. & C. Black, Harrap, Country Life and Heinemann.

K.F. Barker. 'K.D.O.H. and the Nidd Hounds crossing the river to take up the drag on the other bank' from *The Young Entry* by K.F. Barker (A. & C. Black, 1939).

Peter Barker-Mill. From *A Voyage Round the World* (Golden Cockerel Press, 1944).

Books illustrated include:
K.F. Barker Bellman, the Story of a Beagle (1933), Bellman Carries On (1933), Just Dogs (1933), Traveller's Joy (1934), Himself (1935), Champion. The Story of a Bull Terrier (1936), Just Pups (1937), Nothing But Horses (1938), Dog Days (1938), Rogues' Gallery (1939), The Young Entry (1939), The Mole Who Was Different (1955), The January Tortoise (1955), The Wood by the Water (1957), There are Tigers About (1958), Me and My Dog (1961)
M.E. Buckingham Phari (1933), Zong (nd)
Graham Grand The Silver Horn (nd)
Anna Sewell Black Beauty (1936)

Peter Barker-Mill (b. 1908)

Born Italy. Attended Sandhurst and served with Wiltshire Regiment (1930). Studied art under Iain MacNab* at Grosvenor School of Art (1934-36), then worked as a freelance artist (1937-39). Served in the Civil Defence Camouflage Unit (1940-44). Since 1945, he has worked for the Model and Graphics Department of the Ministry of Town and Country Planning and as a freelance artist and design consultant. Maker of animated films using paper puppets, also a mural and relief sculptor in a variety of media. Chairman of the Arnolfini Gallery, Bristol since 1961. In his book illustration, Barker-Mill uses black and white or two-colour wood engraving to achieve striking effects. Mainly published by the Golden Cockerel Press. [Q]

Books illustrated include:
Owen Rutter (ed) Bligh's Voyage in the Resource (1937), The First Fleet (1937)
Anders Sparrman A Voyage Round the World (1944)
Cecil Stewart Topiary (1949)

Periodical: The London Mercury

References: Balston EWE; Wa (1980); Waters; The Studio 139 (1950); Christopher Sandford Bibliography of the Golden Cockerel Press (Dawson 1975); Cock-a-Hoop (Private Libraries Association 1976)

Jill Barklem (b. 1951)

Maiden name: Gillian Gaze, under which she worked until 1980. Born Epping, Essex. Studied

Jill Barklem. 'They found him in the kitchen drinking mint-tea with Mrs Crustybread...' From her *Spring Story* (Collins, 1980).

at St Martin's School of Art. Freelance illustrator of children's books since 1974. Works in sepia ink and watercolour. In recent illustrations of small anthropomorphised mammals against a background of detailed and evocative habitats, she offers a bland but pleasant example in the Beatrix Potter* tradition. [Q]

Books illustrated include:
Jill Barklem The Brambly Hedge Books: Spring Story, Summer Story, Autumn Story, Winter Story (1980)
E. Margaret Clarkson Susie's Babies: a true story (1976)
Meryl Doney The Very Worried Sparrow (1978)
Gillian Gaze Everyday Graces (1975), Everyday Prayers (1975), Goodnight Prayers (1975), Sunday Prayers (1975), Prayers for Special Days (1978).
Janet and John Perkins Haffertee Finds a Place of His Own (1977), Haffertee Goes Exploring (1977), Haffertee Hamster Diamond (1977), Haffertee Hamster's New House (1977), Haffertee's First Christmas (1977)
Agnes Szudek Victoria Plumb (1978)
Ann Turnbull The Frightened Forest (1974)
The Lion Book of Children's Prayers (1977)

References: *Sunday Times* colour supplement (7th September 1980); *Woman's World* (November 1980)

Oswald Charles Barrett (1892-1945)

Worked as 'Batt'. Born in London. Studied at the Camden School of Art and, after army service in World War I, at Heatherley's School of Art and Goldsmith's School of Art. He contributed to the *Radio Times* from 1930 until his death, and was best known for his striking black and white portraits of musical composers in the *Radio Times* and in the *Oxford Companion to Music*. He also occasionally worked in halftone. At one time, he shared a studio with Eric Fraser*.

Books illustrated include:
Winifred Holtby The Astonishing Island (1933)
C.B. Purdom How Should We Rebuild London? (1945)
H.M. Raleigh The Chronicles of Slyme Court (1935)
Percy Scholes The Oxford Companion to Music (1938)

Periodicals: The Bystander, Current Literature, Radio Times

Reference: Driver

Henry Mayo Bateman (1887-1970)

Born to English parents in New South Wales, Australia, where his father owned an export and packing business. In 1889 the family returned to England and lived in various parts of London. With the encouragement of his parents, despite advice from the illustrator Phil May* to do nothing for the time being, he had decided by the age of 14 to be an artist. He studied initially at the Westminster School of Art and the Goldsmith's Insitute and then on the recommendation of John Hassall* he attended classes given by the Flemish artist Charles van Havermaet (1904-07). By this time, he was already contributing humorous drawings to *Scraps* and *The Royal Magazine* and, from 1904, he worked for *The Tatler*. He also took up amateur boxing, tap-dancing, golf and fishing—hobbies that were to prove valuable as sources for cartoon material. From 1912, he produced weekly drawings for the theatrical pages of the *Tatler* and designed a number of theatrical posters. During World War I he joined the London Regiment, but fell ill in 1915 and was discharged. The post-war years saw the beginning of his famous *The Man Who...* series of cartoons (Kenneth Bird* claimed to have originated the idea) and at the peak of his career in the 1930s he was earning between four and five thousand pounds from magazine cartoons, book illustrations and advertising. He drove the latest cars and built himself a house in Reigate, Surrey, where he lived for 14 years. He retired in 1939 and took up oil painting. In his last years he divided his time between his cottage on the edge of Dartmoor and Malta where he spent part of each winter; he died at Gozo. He was a member of the London Sketch Club and of the Chelsea Arts Club, and was a close friend of Fred

H.M. Bateman. 'The Renaissance—Leonardo da Vinci' From *Art ain't all Paint* by Jan Gordon (Feature Books, 1944).

Pegram*. Bateman was one of the first graphic artists to adopt a cinematic approach. The episodic format was by no means new, but Bateman brought to it techniques that were closely parallelled in the silent movie, such as the slow build-up to a climax or *dénouement*, and a new emphasis on gesture and facial expression: his practice of animating furniture props and even landscape for added emphasis recalled the work of early film cartoonists such as Pat Sullivan and Max Fleischer. Bateman's subject matter was drawn almost entirely from the social milieu of his immediate personal experience, but within this somewhat limited context he was often devastatingly effective, particularly when exploiting middle-class fears of exposure to ridicule for committing some unforgivable social gaffe.

Books illustrated include:
H.M. Bateman Burlesques (1916), A Book of Drawings (1921), More Drawings (1922), Suburbia (1922), Adventures at Golf (1923), A Mixture (1924), Colonels (1925), Rebound (1927), Bateman (1931), Brought Forward (1931), Considered Trifles (1934), The Art of Caricature (1936), On the Move in England (1940), The Man Who... and other drawings by H.M. Bateman (1975)
Sir Ernest Benn Mind Your Own Business (1946)
G. Brennard Walton's Delight (1953)
William Caine What a Scream (1927)
Lewis Carroll Further Nonsense Verse and Prose (1926)
Dudley Clark Bateman and I in Filmland (1926)
Desmond Coke Our Modern Youth (1924)
R.D. Cook Fly Fishing for Duffers (1934)
Geoffrey Dowd Whiffs from the Briny (1931)
James Ferguson The Table in a Roar (1933)
J. Gordon Art Ain't All Paint (1944)
A.P. Herbert Dolphin Square (1935)
William Koebel All Aboard (1923)
R.D. Peek Spinning for Duffers (1939)
Langford Reed The Complete Limerick Book (1924), Nonsense Verses (1925)
Robert K. Risk Songs of the Links (1919)
G. Robey After Dinner Stories (1920)
Henry Walbrook Gilbert and Sullivan Opera (1922)

Periodicals: The Bystander, The Captain, The Gaiety Magazine, The Grand Magazine, The Graphic, Holly Leaves, The Humorist, Hutchinson's Life, The London Magazine, London Opinion, Nash's Magazine, The Odd Volume, Pear's Annual, Pearson's Magazine, Printer's Pie, Punch, Radio Times, The Royal Magazine, Scraps, The Sketch, The Strand Magazine, The Tatler

References: Bénézit; Bradshaw; Cuppleditch; Doyle BWI; Houfe; ICB 1; Johnson & Greutzner; Low; Veth; Vollmer; Wa (1934); Waters; *Drawing and Design* (March 1923); *The Strand Magazine* (February 1916); *The Studio* special (Spring 1922, Autumn 1928); H.M. Bateman *By Himself* (Collins 1937); Michael Bateman (intro) *The Man Who Drew the Twentieth Century* (Macdonald 1969); Dudley Clark *Bateman and I in Filmland* (1926); John Jenson *The Man Who... and other drawings* (Eyre Methuen 1975)

John Yunge Bateman (active 1946-58)

An illustrator who was commissioned to work for the Golden Cockerel Press, during its period of decline, in a style similar but inferior to that of Buckland Wright*. Somewhat in the manner of Mark Severin*, he attempted to give a cultural veneer to 'page three' titillation. His best drawings are documentary close-ups of bees.

Books illustrated include:
J. Yunge Bateman How to Draw on Scraper Board (1947)

Charles N. Buzzard The Bumble Bee (1946), Shining Hours (1946)
Edward FitzGerald (trans) The Rubaiyat of Omar Khayyam (1958)
William Shakespeare The Rape of Lucrece (1948), Venus and Adonis (1948)
The Story of the Ant (1946)

Leo Bates (active from c.1920)

Portrait painter and illustrator of children's books. A dextrous, fluent, even slick draughtsman who turned his hand mainly to boys' adventure stories and girls' school stories. He worked mainly in pencil, occasionally adding white chalk highlights or grey washes for half-tone reproduction. Work published mainly by Blackie.

Books illustrated include:
Margaret Baker Nonsense Said the Tortoise (1949)
R.M. Ballantyne The Coral Island (1964)
Arthur Cooke Stephen Goes to Sea (1922), Planter Dick (1924), Ben's Adventure (1925)
Major J.T. Gorman The Lost Crown of Ghorpora (c.1930)
Rudyard Kipling Songs for Youth (c.1920)
Joanna Lloyd Catherine Goes to School (1945), Jane Runs Away From School (1946), Catherine, Head of the House (1947), Audrey, a New Girl (1948)
Percy Westerman A Shanghai Adventure (1928), At Grips with the Swastika (1940)

Reference: Johnson & Greutzner

Dora M. Batty (active 1924-44)

Illustrator in a decorative and stylised idiom. In her designs for *A Poet's Alphabet*, she combined emblems with calligraphy in a sprightly heraldic manner; by contrast, her illustrations for *The Giant Without a Heart* offered some broad effects of pattern and movement. Worked in pen and ink, scraperboard and gouache.

Books illustrated include:
D.M. Batty The Giant Without a Heart (1944)
W.H. Davies Secrets: Poems (1924), A Poet's Alphabet (1925), The Song of Love (1926), A Poet's Calendar (1927)

Batt.
See Oswald Charles Barrett.

Amelia Bäuerle (d. 1916)

Worked as Amelia Bowerley from around 1909. Born in London. Studied at the South Kensington Schools (under Frank Short), the Slade School of Fine Art, and later in Munich and Italy. Etcher, portrait painter and decorative illustator. Her illustrations show Art Nouveau influences. She worked generally in black and white with an easy flowing line, but she also, at times, used soft grounds and chiaroscuro. Elected ARE (1900).

Books illustrated include:
W.E. Cule Sir Constant (1899)
Frederick W. Farrar Allegories (1902)
J. Ingold Glimpses from Wonderland (1900)
Nathaniel Hawthorne A Wonder Book (nd)

Amelia Baüerle. 'Traversing the dark sea' from *Allegories* by Frederic W. Farrar (Longmans Green, 1902).

Nemo A Mere Pug (1897)
Alfred, Lord Tennyson The Day Dream (1901)
Ismay Thorn Happy-Go-Lucky (1894)

Periodicals: The English Illustrated Magazine, The Yellow Book

References: Baker; Guichard; Houfe; Johnson & Greutzner; Sketchley; Waters; C. Wood; *Art Journal* (1899); Walter Shaw Sparrow *Women Painters of the World* (Hodder & Stoughton 1905)

Lewis Christopher Edward Baumer (1870-1963)

Worked as Lewis Baumer. Born and brought up in St John's Wood, London. Encouraged by his parents to take up art, he attended St John's Wood Art School, the South Kensington Schools and the Royal Academy Schools. He painted flowers and portraits of women and children in watercolour, pastel and oil; worked in black and white and made etchings. From the 1920s he concentrated on drawing for *Punch* and other magazines. R.G.G. Price wrote of his *Punch* cartoons that 'he was in a way the leader and certainly the most popular of the social commentators, using "social" in the old rather than the new sense'. In his book illustrations, as in his other work, 'bright young things' predominated—charming, effervescent, weightless creatures, depicted with Baumer's characteristically light touch. Elected RI (1921).

Books illustrated include:
T.R. Arkell Winter Sportings (1929)
G. Barker The Harlequinade (1918)
Lewis Baumer Jumblies (1897), Did You Ever (1903), Bright Young Things (1928)
Ruth Berridge The Baby Philosopher (1898)
Enid Blyton Silver and Gold (1925)
J.B. Erntage Ski Fever (1936)
Harry Graham Departmental Ditties (1909), The Perfect Gentleman (1912), The Motley Muse (1913), The Complete Sportsman (1914), Canned Classics and other verses (nd)
Ian Hay The Lighter Side of School Life (1914), The Shallow End (1924)
Alfred Hyatt The Gift of Love (1911)
Washington Irving Old Christmas and Bracebridge Hall (1919)
L.T. Meade The Hill-Top Girl (1906)
Mrs Molesworth Hoodie (1897), The Boys and I (1898-1900), Hermy

(1898-1900), The Three Witches (1900), Miss Bouverie (1901), The Bolted Door and other stories (1906)
E. Nesbit The Story of the Treasure Seekers (with G. Browne* 1899)
William Makepeace Thackeray Vanity Fair (1913)
Fred Whishaw Elsie's Magician (1897)
Princess Mary's Gift Book (with others, nd)
The Queen's Gift Book (with others, nd)

Periodicals: The Bystander, The English Illustrated Magazine, The Graphic, The Harmsworth Magazine, Holly Leaves, The Idler, Illustrated Bits, The London Magazine, London Opinion, The Minster, The New Budget, The Pall Mall Budget, The Pall Mall Magazine, Pear's Annual, Pearson's Magazine, Pick-Me-Up, Printer's Pie, Punch, The Queen, The Royal Magazine, St James's Budget, The Sketch, The Strand Magazine, The Tatler, To-Day, The Unicorn

References: Baker; Bénézit; Guichard; Houfe; ICB 1; Johnson & Greutzner; Price; Sketchley; Thieme & Becker; Thorpe; Vollmer; Wa (1962); Waters; C. Wood; WW (1908); *The Girls' Realm Annual (1906); The Ludgate* (February 1897); *The Strand Magazine* (September 1916); *The Studio* 30, special (1911, Autumn 1933); G. Montague Ellwood *The Art of Pen Drawing* (Batsford 1927)

Edward Bawden (b. 1903)

Born Braintree, Essex. Studied at the Cambridge School of Art and the Royal College of Art (1922), where he worked under Paul Nash* and was a contemporary and close friend of Eric Ravilious* and Douglas Percy Bliss*. After gaining his Diploma in Book Illustration (1925), he continued to study engraving and book binding at the Central School of Arts and Crafts. Part time teacher of Graphic Design at the Royal College of Art (from 1930) and later at the Royal Academy Schools and Goldsmiths College School of Art. He worked regularly for the Curwen Press in the late 1920s and early 1930s.

Edward Bawden is a designer and illustrator of great originality with wide experience of different techniques and methods of reproduction. For illustration he draws in pen and ink with washes of clear colour on non-absorbent paper, but he has also worked with lithography, lino-cuts and occasionally stencils. An inspired and incisive draughtsman, he uses line with economy and a sharp wit. He has also produced delightful and accomplished water colours of Essex landscapes. As an official war artist, working with the British Army in France in 1940, he made a series of sensitive drawings, some of the best representing the battered harbour at Dunkirk; his later war work in the Middle East was even more descriptively powerful. Prize winner in the Francis Williams Book Illustration Award for 1977 and 1982. Elected RA (1956). [Q]

Books illustrated include:
Edward Bawden Hold Fast By Your Teeth (1963)
William Beckford Vathek (1958)
William Blake Tyger, Tyger (1974)
Christopher Bradby Well on the Road (1935)
Noel Carrington Life in an English Village (1949)
Joan Comay The World's Greatest Story (1978)
Gustave Flaubert Salammbô (1960)
Sir Alexander Gray (trans) Historical Ballade of Denmark (1958)
James Gray How Animals Move (1953)
Ambrose Heath Good Food (1932), More Good Food (1933), Good Savouries (1934), Good Soups (1935)

(Routledge & Kegan Paul 1954); Ruari McLean *Edward Bawden: A Book of Cuts* (Scolar Press 1978); J.M. Richards *Edward Bawden* (Penguin Modern Painters 1946)

Nicola Bayley (b. 1949)

Born in Singapore. Studied graphic design at St Martin's School of Art and illustration at the Royal College of Art. Soon after she left college, Jonathan Cape published her first illustrated children's book, *Nicola Bayley's Book of Nursery Rhymes*, which was outstandingly successful and was followed a year later by *Tyger Voyage*; both books were translated into seven languages. The fantasy world that she paints is secure and tranquil and full of carefully worked detail. Her jewel-like colours are sometimes applied with a distinctive stippling technique to produce a varied texture. She lives and works in Stockwell, South London.

Books illustrated include:
Richard Adams The Tyger Voyage (1976)
Nicola Bayley Book of Nursery Rhymes (1975), The Patchwork Cat (1981)
Christopher Logue Puss-in-Boots (1976)

Reference: ICB 4

Pauline Diana Baynes (b. 1922)

Married name: Pauline Diana Gasch. Born in Sussex. She spent her early childhood in India,

Edward Bawden. From *Life in an English Village*, with an introduction by Noel Carrington (Penguin Books, 1949).

Robert Herring Adam and Evelyn at Kew (1930)
Samuel Johnson Rasselas (1975)
Magda Joicey Cook-Book Note-Book (1946)
Andrew Lang Tales of Greece and Troy (1957)
Jack Lindsay (trans) Patchwork Quilt (c.1930)
D.M. Low London is London (1949)
Louis MacNeice The Sixpence That Rolled Away (1956)
Thomas More Utopia (1972)
Newman Neame Queen's Beasts (1953)
Robert Paltock The Life and Adventures of Peter Wilkins (1928)
Denis Saurat Death and the Dreamer (1946)
R.B. Serjeant The Arabs (1947)
William Shakespeare Henry IV Part II (1939)
Jonathan Swift Gulliver's Travels (1965), Gulliver's Travels: Lilliput and Brobdignag (1968)
Lloyd Thomas (ed) Traveller's Verse (1946)
Rex Warner The Gardener's Diary (1936), Greeks and Trojans (1951)
The Kynoch Press Diary and Note Book (1936)
The Oxford Illustrated Old Testament (1968)

Periodicals: Curwen Press Newsletter, House & Garden, The Listener, Vogue

References: Bénézit; Bland; Chamot, Farr & Butlin; Gilmour; Guichard; ICB 2; Jacques; Johnson & Greutzner; Lewis; Phaidon; Shone; Vollmer; Wa (1934); WaG; Waters; *Alphabet & Image* 2 (September 1946); *Artwork* 15 (1928); *Graphis* 17 (1947), 89 (1960); *Signature* 3 (July 1936); Douglas Percy Bliss *Edward Bawden* (Pendomer Press 1979); Robert Harling *Edward Bawden* (Art and Technics 1950); John Lewis *A Handbook of Type and Illustration* (Faber 1956); John Lewis and John Brinkley *Graphic Design*

Nicola Bayley. From *The Patchwork Cat* by Nicola Bayley and William Mayne (Cape, 1981).

later studying at the Farnham School of Art and the Slade School of Fine Art. During the war she worked for Army Camouflage, and then for the Admiralty Hydrographic Department. After the war she returned to her work as a painter (tempera), designer and illustrator. In 1968, she won the Kate Greenaway Medal for her illustrations to *A Dictionary of Chivalry*, and she was runner-up for the prize in 1972. Her fluent pen and ink style is particularly appropriate to line block reproduction. Her work is often inspired by medieval manuscripts (e.g. *Farmer Giles of Ham*, 1946) or by Persian miniatures (e.g. *The Horse and His Boy*, 1954), and is extremely decorative. The imaginative flair and lively attention to detail in her illustrations make them well-suited to the spirit of such books as the 'Narnia' series by C.S. Lewis. Publishers include Blackie, Allen & Unwin, Kestrel and Rupert Hart Davies. [Q]

Books illustrated include:
Richard Barber Companion to World Mythology (1979)
R.D. Blackmore Lorna Doone (1970)
Enid Blyton The Land of Far Beyond (1973)
Leonard Clark All Along Down Along (1971)
Rumer Godden The Dragon of Og (1981)
Rosemary Harris The Enchanted Horse (1982)
C.S. Lewis Chronicles of Narnia: The Lion, the Witch and the
    Wardrobe (1950), Prince Caspian (1951), The Voyage of the Dawn

Pauline Baynes. From *Prince Caspian* by C.S. Lewis (Geoffrey Bles, 1951).

S.G. Hulme Beaman. 'Again they stopped to peer round' from *The Children's Golden Treasure Book for 1937* edited by John R. Crossland & J.M. Parrish (Odhams).

Treader (1952), The Silver Chair (1953), The Horse and his Boy
    (1954), The Last Battle (1956)
Naomi Mitchison Graeme and the Dragon (1954)
Mary Norton The Borrowers Avenged (1982)
Iona and Peter Opie The Puffin Book of Nursery Rhymes (1963)
Philippa Pearce (ed) Stories from Hans Andersen (1972)
Helen Piers Snail and Caterpillar (1972), Grasshopper and Butterfly
    (1975), Frog and Water Shrew (1981)
Geoffrey Squire The Observer's Book of European Costume (1975)
Katie Stewart The Times Cookery Book (1972)
John Symonds Harold (1973)
J.R.R. Tolkien The Adventures of Tom Bombadil (1946), Farmer
    Giles of Ham (1946), Smith of Wootton Major (1946), Poems and
    Stories (1980)
Grant Uden A Dictionary of Chivalry (1968)
Alison Uttley The Little Knife Who Did All the Work (1962), Recipes
    from an Old Farmhouse (1966)
Jennifer Westwood Medieval Tales (1967), The Isle of Gramarie
    (1970), Tales and Legends (1971)

Periodical: The Sphere

References: Contemporary Authors; Doyle CL; Fisher pp. 30, 105, 131, 279, 287, 295, 302, 377; ICB 2,3; Wa (1980); *Growing Point* vol 16 no 8 (March 1978); *Library Association Record* vol 71 no 6 (June 1969); *Signal* (May 1973); *Smithsonian* (August 1975); *The Times* (October 17 1973)

BB

See Denys James Watkins-Pitchford.

Sydney George Hulme Beaman
(1887-1932)

Worked as S.G. Hulme Beaman. Born Tottenham, London. Performed in music hall acts while studying at Heatherley's School of Art. After World War I he set up a workshop in Golders Green making model theatres and carved wooden toys, which were later to become the *dramatis personae* of his illustrated children's books. In 1928, *Tales of Toytown* was taken up by the BBC's Children's Hour and formed the basis of the spectacularly successful series. Beaman contributed twenty-eight episodes before he died but the programme continued after his death until 1963. The original *Toytown* figures are now in the Bethnal Green Museum.

Cecil Beaton. 'He scorned the world, and his way of showing it was to wear his fell hat over one eyebrow after the manner of the peerless d'Artagnan' from *A Young Man Comes to London* by Michael Arlen (1932).

Books illustrated include:
S.G. Hulme Beaman Aladdin Retold (1924), Jerry and Joe (1925), Trouble in Toyland (1925), The Road to Toytown (1925), The Wooden Knight (1925), The Seven Voyages of Sinbad the Sailor (1926), Out of the Ark Books (1927), Tales of Toytown (1928), John Trusty (1929), Wireless in Toytown (1930)
Mrs H.C. Cradock The Smith Family (nd)
John Crossland and J.M. Parrish (ed) The Children's Golden Treasure Book for 1937
R.L. Stevenson The Strange Case of Dr Jekyll and Mr Hyde (1930)

Periodicals: The Golders Green Gazette, Little Folks, Radio Times

References: Doyle CL; Driver; Kirkpatrick; *The Observer* magazine (24th February 1980); *The Studio* special (Winter 1931); S.G. Hulme Beaman *The Book of Toytown and Larry the Lamb* (including biographical sketch by Hendrik Baker, Harrap 1979)

Cecil Walter Hardy Beaton (1904-80)

Worked as Cecil Beaton. Brought up in Hampstead, North London. Educated at Harrow School and Cambridge University. Celebrated photographer and stage designer who illustrated several of his own books with pen and ink sketches alongside his photographs. Particularly successful are the wittily *insouciant* line drawings in *New York*. His later illustrations have less spontaneity and panache.

Books illustrated include:
Michael Arlen A Young Man Comes to Town (1932)
Cecil Beaton The Book of Beauty (1930), Cecil Beaton's New York (1938), The Glass of Fashion (1954), The Face of the World (1957)
Richard Brinsley Sheridan The School for Scandal (1949)

References: Contemporary Authors; Johnson & Greutzner; Vollmer; Wa (1977); Cecil Beaton *Photobiography* (Odhams 1951), *Scrapbook* (Batsford 1937), *The Wandering Years* Diaries 1922-39 (1961), *The Years Between* Diaries 1939-44 (1965); James Danziger *Beaton* (Secker & Warburg 1980)

Roy Beddington (b. 1910)

Born in London, son of a barrister. Studied at Corpus Christi College, Oxford, then at the Slade School of Fine Art and in Florence. During World War II, he served with the Territorial Army in intelligence, and in H.M. Fisheries. Landscape painter, illustrator, author, poet and journalist. His fondness for fishing, gardening and natural history is reflected in the subject matter of his paintings and graphic work. In his illustration work, he uses watercolour, gouache, pen and wash, black and white (using litho chalk) and scraper board; for *The Adventures of Thomas Trout* he used three colour offset-litho (blue, red and black) instead of the five colour process common at the time. Publishers have included Country Life Books, Methuen and Geoffrey Bles. [Q]

Books illustrated include:
Roy Beddington The Adventures of Thomas Trout (1939), To Be a Fisherman (1955), The Pigeon and the Boy (1957, with new illustrations 1959), A Countryman's Verse (1981)
Sinclair Carr Alexander and the Angling (1936)
Douglas Carruthers Beyond the Caspian (1943)
Anthony Crossley The Floating Line for Salmon and Sea Trout (1938)
Stephen Gwynn The Happy Fisherman (1936), River to River (1937), Two in a Valley (1937)
J.W. Walker Riverside Reflections (1947)

Periodicals: Country Life, The Field

References: Wa (1980); Waters

Roy Beddington. 'Fishing on a mere.' Sepia illustration dated 1963.

Francis D. Bedford. From *Through Merrie England* by F.L. Stevens (Warne, 1928).

Francis Donkin Bedford (1864-1954)

Born in London. Studied architecture at the South Kensington and Royal Academy Schools. Articled to the architect Sir Arthur Blomfield for four years before embarking, in the 1890s, on a long and successful career in book illustration. He worked in black and white and full colour, and was one of the first artists to take advantage of the then newly developed four colour process. The interior and exterior settings for his drawings clearly reflected his architectural training and often showed a marked liking for the then popular 'Bedford Park' style; his figures and animals were lively and expressive. Work published mainly by Methuen and Grant Richards. Member of the Art Workers' Guild.

Books illustrated include:
S. Baring Gould Old Country Life (1890), The Deserts of Southern France (1894), Old English Fairy Tales (1895)
Jane Barlow (trans) The Battle of the Frogs and the Mice (1894), A Book of Nursery Rhymes (1897)
F.D. Bedford A Night of Wonders (1906)
George Clinch Kent (1903), The Isle of Wight (1904)
Charles Dickens The Chimes (1899), The Magic Fishbone (1921), A Christmas Carol (1923), The Cricket on the Hearth (1927)
Louise Field Two are Company (1905)
Oliver Goldsmith The Vicar of Wakefield (1898)
E.V. Lucas The Book of Shops (1899), Four and Twenty Toilers (1900), A Book of Verses for Children (c.1900), The Visit to London (1902), Old Fashioned Tales (1905), Forgotten Tales of Long Ago (1906), Runaways and Castaways (1908)
George MacDonald At the Back of the North Wind (1924), The Princess and the Goblin (1926)
Frank Leonard Stevens Through Merrie England (1928)
Ann and Jane Taylor The Original Poems and Others (1903)
William Makepeace Thackeray The History of Henry Esmond (1898)
G.E. Troutbeck Westminster Abbey (1900)

References: Baker; Bénézit; Doyle CL; Houfe; ICB 1; Johnson & Greutzner; Mallalieu; Muir; Peppin; Sketchley; Vollmer; Wa (1929); Waters 2; C. Wood; William Feaver *When We Were Young* (Thames & Hudson 1977)

Henry Maximilian Beerbohm (1872-1956)

Worked as Max Beerbohm. Born in London, half brother of the actor Sir Herbert Beerbohm Tree.

Educated at Charterhouse and Merton College, Oxford. In 1893, he was introduced by the painter William Rothenstein into the Aubrey Beardsley/ Oscar Wilde circle of artists and writers, among whom he established his already considerable reputation as a caricaturist, man-about-town and wit. In 1910 he moved to Rapallo, Italy where he remained for the rest of his life, returning to England only for visits. In 1943, Beerbohm was appointed Rede lecturer at Cambridge. Wireless broadcaster during World War II. Beerbohm's graphic work consisted of pen and pencil drawings, often tinted in watercolour or wash. Brilliantly capitalising on his lack of conventional graphic skill, he adopted a simplified and apparently naive drawing style which gave him freedom to exaggerate and select. Under the influence of the caricatures of Carlo Pellegrini ('Ape' of *Vanity Fair*), his early work often consisted of single, isolated figures, but from here it was a short step to developing imaginary situations and conversations among his chosen subjects. *Rossetti and his Circle* (which Gordon Ray rightly considers to be the only work in which Beerbohm can really be called an illustrator) contained subtly ironic glimpses into Pre-Raphaelite private moments, and here his acute perception of character, sensitivity to nuances of speech and close observation of domestic minutiae were unforgettably combined. Member of the Chelsea Art Club and of the NEAC

Max Beerbohm. 'Blue China' (Whistler and Carlyle) from his *Rossetti and his Circle* (Heinemann, 1922).

(1909). Founder member of the National Portrait Society. Knighted in 1939.

Books illustrated include:
Max Beerbohm Caricatures of Five and Twenty Gentlemen (1896), The Poet's Corner (1904), Caricatures by Max (1904), A Book of Caricatures (1907), The Second Childhood of John Bull (1911), A Christmas Garland (1912), Fifty Caricatures (1913), Seven Men (1919), A Survey (1921), Rossetti and his Circle (1922), Things New and Old (1923), Observations (1925), Heroes and Heroines of Bitter Sweet (1951), Zuleika Dobson (nd)

Periodicals: The Academy, The Butterfly, The Bystander, Cassell's Magazine, Daily Mail, Eureka, The Idler, John Bull, The Page, The Pall Mall Budget, The Pall Mall Magazine, Parade, Pearson's Magazine, Pick-Me-Up, Reveille, The Savoy, The Sketch, The Spectator, The Strand Magazine, The Tatler, The Unicorn, Vanity Fair, The Yellow Book

References: Bénézit; Chamot, Farr & Butlin; DNB (1951-60); Hammerton; Houfe; Johnson & Greutzner; Low; Phaidon; Price; Ray; Thorpe; Vollmer and supp; Wa (1934); Waters; *The Studio* special (1911, 1923-24, Autumn 1928, Autumn 1930); Max Beerbohm *Letters to Reggie Turner* (Hart-Davis 1964); S.N. Behrman *Conversations with Max* (Hamish Hamilton 1960); David Cecil *Max* (Constable 1964); William Feaver *Masters of Caricature* (Weidenfeld & Nicolson 1981); A.E. Gallatin *Sir Max Beerbohm* (Harvard University Press 1944); R. Hart-Davis *A Catalogue of the Caricatures of Max Beerbohm* (Macmillan 1972); Osbert Lancaster *Max's 'Nineties* (Hart Davis 1958); B. Lynch *Max Beerbohm in Perspective* (Heinemann 1921); John Rothenstein *The Artists of the 1890s* (Routledge 1928); Lance Sieveking *The Eye of the Beholder* (Hulton Press 1957)

Peggy Beetles (active 1956-60)

Children's book illustrator of the late 1950s. She worked in pen and ink, sometimes using flat colour washes. Her subject matter is the everyday world rather than fantasy, and her freely drawn figures are clearly sketched from life. Much of her work has been published by Hamish Hamilton.

Books illustrated include:
Mabel Allan The Secret (1956), The Runaway (1957), The Happiest Day (1958), The Old Pony (1959), Hide and Seek (1959), The Hidden Key (1960)
Mary Cockett Jan the Market Boy (1957), Bouncing Ball (1958), Seven Days with Jan (1960)
Pamela Mansbridge The Larks and the Linnets (1958)
John Pudney The Grandfather Clock (1957)

Reference: Fisher p.153

Peggy Beetles. From *Seven Days with Jan* by Mary Cockett (Brockhampton, 1960).

George Belcher 'Mr O'Shaughnessy' from *The Lighter Side of English Life* by F. Frankfort Moore (T.N. Foulis, 1913).

George Frederick Arthur Belcher (active 1875-1947)

Worked as George Belcher. Born London. Studied at Gloucester School of Art. Exhibited at the Royal Academy from 1909. He contributed drawings regularly to *Punch* from 1911, also to *Vanity Fair* and *The Tatler*. He enjoyed hunting and fishing. A painter and etcher of portraits, caricatures, sporting subjects and still life, he was however chiefly known for his humorous and sympathetic studies of working class life in chalk and charcoal. R.G.G. Price wrote, 'he drew the poor as a kindly gentleman who paid them to come and be drawn by him, not, like Phil May*, as somebody sketching the neighbours. But he drew very well indeed'. F.L. Emmanuel* suggests (in his book *Charles Keene* published by the Print Collector's Club, 1935) that Belcher was considerably influenced by Keene's* work. Elected ARA (1931), RA (1946).

Books illustrated include:
George Belcher Characters (1922), By George Belcher (1925), Taken
  from Life (1929), Potted Charm and Other Delicacies (1933)
F. Frankfort Moore The Lighter Side of English Life (1913)

Periodicals: The Graphic, The Odd Volume, The Owl, Printer's Pie,
Punch, The Tatler, Vanity Fair

References: Bénézit; Chamot, Farr & Butlin; Guichard; Houfe;
Johnson & Greutzner; Price; Vollmer; Wa (1929); Waters; *Drawing
and Design* (April 1923); *The Studio* 52 (1911), 86 (1923), special (1911,
1917, Spring 1922, Spring 1929); Percy Bradshaw *They Make Us Smile*
(Chapman & Hall 1942)

Robert Anning Bell (1863-1933)

Born in London. Worked for an architect before
studying at the Westminster School of Art, the
Royal Academy Schools, in Paris and under Sir
George Frampton. From 1894 he taught at Liverpool University and was appointed Head of Design
at Glasgow School of Art (1911) and Professor of
Design at the Royal College of Art (1918-24). A
close friend of the architect C.F.A. Voysey, Bell's
interest in working with architectural space found
expression in relief sculpture, stained-glass designs
and mosaics (i.e. for Westminster Cathedral). His
work as an illustrator is firmly rooted in the Arts
and Crafts tradition, and, as a contemporary of
Walter Crane* and Charles Ricketts*, his work
shows the same awareness of full-design and use
of decorative borders. His illustrations for children's books have a lightness and grace somewhat
akin to the work of Charles Robinson*. Elected
NEAC (1892-1902), ARWS (1901), RWS (1904),
ARA (1914), RA (1922); Master of the Art Worker's Guild (1921).

Robert Anning Bell. 'To Emilia Viviani' from
Shelley with an introduction by Walter Raleigh
(Bell, 1902).

Books illustrated include:
John Bunyan The Pilgrim's Progress (1898)
John Dennis (ed) English Lyrics from Spenser to Milton (1898)
A.B. Jameson Shakespeare's Heroines (1901)
John Keats Poems (1897), Odes (1901), Isabella and the Eve of St
  Agnes (1902)
John Keble The Christian Year (1895)
Charles Lamb Tales from Shakespeare (1899)
Robert Mack The Golden Treasury of Art and Song (1890)
Sir Walter Raleigh The Riddle (1895), The Milan (1898)
Ernest Rhys (ed) English Fairy Tales (with Herbert Cole*, 1913)
William Shakespeare A Midsummer Night's Dream (1895), The
  Tempest (1901)
Percy B. Shelley Poems (1902)
An Altar Book (1896)
Dent Banbury Cross series: Cinderella, Dick Whittington and his Cat,
  Jack the Giant Killer, The Sleeping Beauty (1894)
Grimm's Household Tales (1901)
Palgrave's Golden Treasury (1907)
Rubaiyat of Omar Khayyam (1902)

Periodicals: The English Illustrated Magazine, The Pall Mall
Magazine, The Windsor Magazine, The Yellow Book

References: Baker; Bénézit; Chamot, Farr & Butlin; Crane; Houfe;
ICB 1; Johnson & Greutzner; Lewis; Mallalieu; Muir; Pennell MI, PD;
Peppin; Ray; Sketchley; Taylor; Thieme & Becker; Thorpe; Vollmer;
Wa (1929); Waters; C. Wood; *The OWS Club Annual* Volume 12; *The
Studio* special 1897-98, 1898-99, 1900-01, Autumn 1914, Spring 1922,
Winter 1923-24

Jill Crawford Bennett (b. 1934)

Born in Johannesburg, South Africa; her childhood was spent in Jamaica. Studied at Wimbledon
School of Art and the Slade School of Fine Art.
Illustrator of children's books in black and white
and full colour.

Books illustrated include:
Joan Aiken The Cat-Flap and the Apple Pie and Other Funny Stories
  (1979), Black Eyes (1979)
Angela Bull The Accidental Twins (1982)
Charles Causley Figgie Hobbin (1979)
Helen Cresswell The Bagthorpe Saga (1977)
Roald Dahl Fantastic Mr Fox (1970), Danny, the Champion of the
  World (1975)
Dorothy Edwards The Magician Who Kept a Pub (1975)
Griselda Gifford Earwig and Beetle (1981)
Rosemary Harris I Want to be a Fish (1977)
Catherine Sefton The Emma Dilemma (1982)

Reference: ICB 4

Nicolas Clerihew Bentley (1907-78)

Born Highgate, London. Son of E.C. Bentley,
the novelist, leader writer for the *The Daily
Telegraph* and inventor of the four-line verse
form known as the 'clerihew'. Studied at University College School, London and at Heatherley's
School of Art. Before and after World War I
(during which he was deputy director of the Home
Intelligence Unit and editor in the Publications
Division of the Ministry of Information), he worked
freelance as a journalist, author and humorous
illustrator. Director of André Deutsch (from
1950). Drew the daily pocket cartoon for *The
Daily Mail* (1958-62). An editor for Sunday Times
Publications Ltd (1962-63) and for Thomas Nelson
& Son (1963-67). Nicolas Bentley's illustrations

Nicholas Bentley. 'Mr. Noel Coward was disillusioned and soured/By the lukewarm reception of his comedy/Introducing a real dromedary.* [*named Ethel]' from *More Biography* by E. C. Bentley (Methuen, 1929).

for Belloc's *New Cautionary Tales* (as successor to B.T. Blackwood*) established his importance as an illustrator. His stylish, witty and economical drawings, often depicting figures without background or setting, owed much to his admiration for the work of the French draughtsman Caran D'Ache and the Swede Olaf Gulbransson. He had an extensive knowledge of the Victorian period which proved invaluable in his work as an illustrator. Elected FSIA (1946) and FRSA (1974).

Books illustrated include:
Kingsley Amis On Drink (1972)
Michael Barsley This England 1940-1946 (1946)
Hilaire Belloc New Cautionary Tales (1930), Ladies Gentlemen (1932), Cautionary Verses (1940)
E.T.R. Benson and B.E. Asquith Foreigners (1935), Muddling Through (1936), How To Be Famous (1937)
E.C. Bentley More Biography (1929), Baseless Biography (1939), Clerihews Complete (with others, 1951)
Nicolas C. Bentley All Fall Down (1932), The Beastly Birthday Book (1934), Ready Refusals (1935), Die? I Thought I'd Laugh (1936), The Time of my Life (1937), Gammon and Espionage (1938), The Week-End Wants a Guest (1938), The Week-End Worries a Hostess (1938), Le Sport (1939), The Tongue-Tied Canary (1948), Third Party Risk (1953), The Floating Dutchman (1954), How Can You Bear to Be Human? (1957), Book of Birds (1965), The Victorian Scene (1968), Golden Sovereigns (1970)
Lawrence Durrell Stiff Upper Lip (1958), Sauve Qui Peut (1969)
T.S. Eliot Old Possum's Book of Practical Cats (1941)
B. Evans Comfortable Words (1963)
Roy Fuller Poor Roy (1976)
Barbara Hastings Lobby Lobster (1943), Mustapha Monkey (1945)

Hugh Kingsmill The Worst of Love (1931)
Eric Linklater The Wind on the Moon (1944)
Dorothy Lovell Silvanus Goes to Sea (1943), In the Land of the Thinsies (1944)
George Mikes How to be an Alien (1946), How to Scrape Skies (1948), Milk and Honey (1950), Wisdom for Others (1950), East Is East (1958), How To Be Inimitable (1960), Tango (1961), Eureka! Rummaging in Greece (1965), How To Be Decadent (1965), Tsi-Tsa: Biography of a Cat (1978)
J.B. Morton The Beachcomber Omnibus (1931), By the Way (1931), 1933 and Still Going Wrong! (1932), Morton's Folly (1933), Here and Now (1947)
Damon Runyon More Than Somewhat (1937)
John R. Russell The Duke of Bedford's Book of Snobs (1965)
Leonard Russell Parody Party (1936), Press Gang (1937)
Jerrard Tickell Gentlewomen Aim to Please (1938)
Auberon Waugh The Diaries of Auberon Waugh (1976)

Periodicals: Daily Mail, Private Eye, Radio Times, Sunday Telegraph

References: Contemporary Authors; Driver; Hillier; ICB 1; Lewis; Price; Wa (1980); Nicolas Bentley *A Version of the Truth* (André Deutsch 1980); William Feaver *Masters of Caricature* (Weidenfeld & Nicolson 1981)

Bernardette

See Bernardette Watts

Alfred Edmeades Bestall (b. 1892)

Born Mandalay, Burma. Son of a Methodist minister. Studied art on a scholarship at the Birmingham School of Arts and Crafts, and afterwards at the Central School of Arts and Crafts, London. After serving in Flanders during World War I

Alfred E. Bestall. 'The Rainbow Flowers, Act II. Dragonfly bows before the Sun' from *The Play's the Thing* by Enid Blyton (Newnes, 1927).

(1915-19), he worked in Fleet Street, contributing humorous illustrations to *Punch, The Tatler, The Bystander, Passing Show* and various lesser magazines. He also illustrated nearly fifty books including about half the *Literary and Dramatic Reading* series (Schofield & Sims), which were widely used in London schools. At one time he designed costumes and sets for Enid Blyton's *Twelve Plays for Children.* In 1936 he took over the *Daily Express* series of *Rupert Bear* strips from Mary Tourtel* and by the time he retired from morning paper work in 1965, he had produced over 270 Rupert adventures. He continued to draw for the *Rupert* annuals until 1973, and still contributes the occasional page to the newspaper. Bestall considers his graphic work to have been 'heavily influenced...by Joseph Pennell's *Pen Drawing and Pen Draughtsmen* also by *Punch* as it was fifty to seventy years ago—a weekly gallery in all that was best in British line work'. He has also worked in watercolour, oil and lithography. An origami enthusiast, he has twice had original models exhibited in Japan, and at the age of 86 was elected President of the British Origami Society. [Q]

Books illustrated include:
Enid Blyton The Play's The Thing (1927), Plays for Older Children (1941), The Boy Next Door (1944)
John Crompton The Hive (nd)
Alexandre Dumas The Three Musketeers (1950)
Agnes Frome The Disappearing Trick (1933)
Dudley Glass The Spanish Goldfish (1934)
Mary Inchfawn Salute to the Village (1943)
E. Jones Folk Tales of Wales (1947)
Literary and Dramatic Readings (with others, from 1928)
Mother Goose (1932)
Myths and Legends of Many Lands (Nelson 1934)
Rupert Annuals (1936-73)

Periodicals: Blackie's Annual, The Bystander, Daily Express, Gaiety Magazine, Passing Show, Punch, Schoolgirls' Own Annual, The Tatler

References: Doyle BWI; Wa (1980); Waters; Margaret Blount *Animal Land* (Hutchinson 1974)

Bettina

See Bettina Bauer Ehrlich.

John R. Biggs (b. 1909)

Born Derby. Studied at Derby School of Art (1931), Central School of Arts and Crafts (1931-38) under Noel Rooke* and Bernard Meninsky, and then at London University. Lecturer on graphic arts and printing at Chelsea School of Art (1938-39), London School of Printing (1938-49), and Norwich City Art School (1949-53). Head of Graphic Design at Brighton Polytechnic (1953-74). Has also taught overseas. Art Editor for SCM Press (1943-49); production manager at Country Life Books. Since 1930, he has run the private

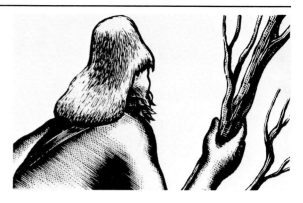

John R. Biggs. From *Robinson Crusoe* by Daniel Defoe (1938).

Hampden Press. Mainly a black and white illustrator, he uses pen and ink or wood engraving. His work is decorative and usually based on nature and he achieves effective tonal variety with strong contrasts and fine cross hatching. Lives in Brighton. Member of the Art Workers' Guild (1936), Master (1983); member SIAD; FRSA. [Q]

Books illustrated include:
John R. Biggs Sinfin Songs (1932), Three Sonnets (1932), Approach to Type (1949), Illustration and Reproduction (1950), The Use of Type (1954), Woodcuts (1958), The Craft of Lettering (1961), The Craft of the Pen (1961), The Craft of Woodcuts (1963), The Craft of the Script (1964), Basic Typography (1968), The Story of the Alphabet (1968), Lettercraft (1982)
Laurence Binyon Three Poems (1934)
Daniel Defoe Robinson Crusoe (2 vols 1938)
Wilfred Gibson A Leaping Flame (1935)
William J. Ibbett One Hundred Facets of Winter and Spring (1931)
Beverley Nichols Green Grows the City (c.1939)
Herbert Read A World Within a War (1943)
Edmund Spenser Epithalamion (1938)

References: Balston WEMEB; Garrett BWE, HBWE; Johnson & Greutzner; Wa (1980); Waters; John R. Biggs *Autobiographica* (Brighton Polytechnic 1974)

Percy J. Billinghurst (active 1898-1906)

Illustrator and book plate designer. Studied at Barnsbury School of Art and the Royal Academy Schools. He became a close friend of W. Heath Robinson*, and shared a studio with him. Langston Day describes Billinghurst as 'cautious and in delicate health' and records that 'having developed a technique for animal drawing he stuck to it and never tried anything else. Before many years his health grew worse and he died'. He drew animals with sympathy and humour, but his backgrounds were often naive or cursory, and he depicted humans with a measure of apparent distaste. He worked mainly in pen and ink, developing a fluent, well-modulated line.

Books illustrated include:
P.J. Billinghurst A Hundred Anecdotes of Animals (1901)
L. Dalkeith Beasts Shown to the Children (with others, 1906)
Jean de la Fontaine A Hundred Fables of La Fontaine (1900)
R. L'Estrange (trans) A Hundred Fables of Aesop (1899)

L.N. Parker Richard Wagner and the Ring of the Nibelungs (with C. Robinson*, nd)

References: Baker; Houfe; ICB 1; Sketchley; *The Studio* 14 (1898), special (1898-99, 1900-01); Langston Day *The Life and Art of William Heath Robinson* (Michael Joseph 1947)

Pearl Binder (b. 1904)

Married name: Lady Polly Elwyn Jones. Born in Fenton, Staffordshire, daughter of Maurice Binder, tailor. Brought up in Fenton and Manchester. Studied lithography at the Central School of Arts and Crafts, London. Freelance author and illustrator of books; lithographer and painter; writer and designer of picture programmes for BBC television since 1938. Worked in Government information press serice during World War II. She has also designed theatre costumes for her own plays and musicals (based on detailed research), small stained-glass window panels, and mugs and plates for Wedgwood; she occasionally lectures on specialist subjects (e.g. 'Symbols in Folk Art' and 'Pearly Kings and Queens'). Her favourite medium is lithography; she also works with wax crayons, gouache, collage and pastels. Some of her work makes a satirical comment on social life and its pretensions. She has been influenced by Daumier (in lithography), Picasso (in drawing) and primitive African, Indian and Polynesian art. [Q]

Books illustrated include:
Jane Austen Persuasion (1928)
Pearl Binder Odd Jobs (1935), Misha and Masha (1936), Russian Families (1942), Misha Learns English (1942), Muffs and Morals (1953), The Peacock's Tail (1958), Look at Clothes (1959), The English Inside Out (1961), Magic Symbols of the World (1972), Treacle Terrace (1974), The Pearlies (1975)
Pearl Binder and George Ordish Pigeons and People (1967), Ladies Only (1972)
Anthony Bland Treasure Islands (1977)
Thomas Burke The Real East End (1932)
Jack H. Driberg People of the Small Arrow (1930)
Josephine Gladstone Zadig (1976), Stories from Ladder Street (1979)
Philip Godfrey Back-Stage (1933)
Louis Golding The Dance Goes On (1937)
Coralie Hobson Bed and Breakfast (1926)
June Knox-Mawer South Sea Spell (1975)
Bert Lloyd The Golden City (nd)
Alan Lomax Harriet and her Harmonium (1955)
Bertha Malnick Everyday Life in Russia (1938)
Josephine Marquand Chi Ming and Tiger Kitten (1964), Chi Ming and the Lion Dance (1969), Chi Ming and the Jade Earring (1969)
Gérard de Nerval (trans Richard Aldington) Aurelia (1932)
Lancelot de G. Sieveking All Children Must be Paid for (1927)
John Skelton The Tunning of Elynour Rumming (1928)
Also educational books published by A. & C. Black

Periodicals: Daily Mail, Geographical Magazine, Harper's Bazaar, Housewife, The New Coterie, News Chronicle, The Observer, The Sketch, The Tatler, Vogue

References: ICB 1, 2; *The Studio* 95 (1928), special (Autumn 1928)

Helen Binyon (1904-79)

Born in Chelsea, London, daughter of Laurence Binyon, poet, writer and keeper of Prints and Drawings at the British Museum. Studied design and illustration at the Royal College of Art (1922-26) and in Paris (1927), and copper engraving at the Central School of Art, London (1928). She then worked as a part-time art teacher, also running a travelling marionette theatre with her twin sister Margaret. In 1940, she moved to Bath to draw charts for the Hydrographic Department of the Royal Navy, and later worked in the exhibitions section of the Ministry of Information, London (1942-45). Lecturer in design, watercolour, shadow puppetry at the Bath Academy of Art (1950-65). Her later work for the Arts Council and the Central School of Speech and Drama was concerned with puppetry. Her illustrative style was simple, usually pen and ink drawings for line block reproduction or reproduced in two colours as in the 'Binyon Books'. In her wood engraving, black tends to predominate with tones and textures achieved by dots, scratches and parallel lines. The illustrations, often of simple intimate scenes, have great charm and evoke a sense of period. Also a landscape painter in watercolour and lithographer. [Q]

Books illustrated include:
Jane Austen Pride and Prejudice (1938)
Helen Binyon The Children Next Door (1949), An Everyday Alphabet (1952), Puppetry To-day (1966)
Helen and Margaret Binyon The Binyon Books: The Birthday Party

Helen Binyon. 'Oh, I fell down! My poor knee! Is that blood?' from *Polly and Jane* by H. & M. Binyon (1940).

(1940), A Country Visit (1940), A Day at the Sea (1940), Polly and Jane (1940), Christmas Eve (1942), The Wet Afternoon (1942), The Picnic (1944), Polly Goes to School (1944), Polly and Jane's Houses (1949), The Railway Journey (1949)

Laurence Binyon Sophro the Wise (1926), Brief Candles (1938)
Maria Edgworth Angelina or L'Amie Inconnue (1933)
Vernon Knowles The Street of Queer Houses (1925)

References: Bénézit; Crouch; Garrett BWE, HBWE; Johnson & Greutzner; Vollmer; Wa (1980); *The Studio* special (Autumn 1938); *Shall We Join the Ladies?* (Studio One Gallery, Oxford 1979); A.C. Sewter *Modern British Woodcuts and Wood-Engravings in the Collection of the Whitworth Art Gallery* (Manchester 1962)

Cyril Kenneth Bird (1887-1965)

Worked as Fougasse. Born London, and son of England cricketer Arthur Bird. Educated at Cheltenham College. Studied engineering at King's College, London and attended art classes at the Regent Street Polytechnic and later at the School of Photo-engraving and Lithography in Bolt Court, Fleet Street, London. An officer in the Royal Engineers during World War I, he was blown up by a shell at Gallipoli (1915) and sustained injuries from which he was not expected to recover. No longer able to work as an engineer, and with a wife to support, he took a correspondence course in illustration from Percy Bradshaw's Press Art School. From 1916, his work was published in *Punch*. His pseudonym 'Fougasse' (a type of French mine noted for its unpredictable performance) was adopted to avoid confusion with the *Punch* contributor 'W. Bird' (Jack B. Yeats*). He became Art Editor (1937) and, with reluctance, Editor (1949-53) of *Punch* succeeding his friend E.V. Knox. During World War II, he designed posters for various government ministries, including his famous 'Careless Talk Costs Lives' series for the Ministry of Information. His style was notable for its increasingly pronounced linear simplicity. By the 1940s, all descriptive content was abandoned, and instead he favoured a highly characteristic graphic shorthand, with noses and feet often represented by a single line

Fougasse [Cyril Kenneth Bird]. 'Bear to the right' from his *You Have Been Warned* (Methuen, 1935).

and other parts of the body correspondingly reduced. With this apparently meagre formula he could encapsulate a surprisingly wide variety of situations, achieving an effect of effortlessness in the finished version with the help of numerous preparatory sketches. Like H.M. Bateman*, he often adopted an episodic format, and Bevis Hillier credits him with the original idea for Bateman's celebrated *The Man Who...* series.

Books illustrated include:
Eleanor Adlard Dear Turley (1942)
E.P.L. Bennett Southern Ways and Means (1931)
Arthur W. Bird Just a Few Lines (1943)
R.S.C. Brown Exploring the Avenues (1936)
Gerald Fleming Wall Pictures for Guided Composition (1957), Guided Composition for Students of English (1961)
Fougasse A Gallery of Games (1921), E and OE (1928), Fun Fair (1934), The Luck of the Draw (1936), Drawing the Line Somewhere (1937), Stop or Go. A Diary for 1939 (1938), Jotsam (1939), ...and the Gatepost (1940), The Changing Face of Britain (1940), Running Commentary (1941), Sorry—No Rubber (1942), Family Group (1944), The Neighbours (1954), The Good Tempered Pencil (1956)
Harry J.C. Graham The World's Workers (1928)
A.P. Herbert (intro) A School of Purposes (1946)
W.D.H. McCullough Aces Made Easy (1934) You Have Been Warned (1935)
Guy Reed The Little Lessi (1941)
Harry L. Wilson So This is Golf (1923)

Periodicals: The Bystander, The Graphic, London Opinion, Pear's Annual, Punch, The Sketch, The Tatler

References: Houfe; Johnson & Greutzner; Price; Wa (1968); *The Artist* 18 (1940); *The Strand Magazine* 61 (1921); Percy Bradshaw *They Make Us Smile* (Chapman & Hall 1942); Bevis Hillier (ed) *Fougasse* (Elm Tree Books 1977)

W. Bird

See Jack B. Yeats.

Balint Stephen Biro (b. 1921)

Works as Val Biro. Born Budapest, Hungary. Studied at Central School of Art. Served in National Fire Service during World War II. Worked for Sylvan Press (1945-48) and for John Lehmann (1948-53), and since then has worked freelance as an artist and writer. He has illustrated nearly 400 books, two thirds of which are for children and the rest for adults (gardening, cookery, travel, the countryside, memoirs and humour); uses pen and watercolour for children's books, and generally scraperboard and gouache for adult books, magazine work and book jackets. He is best known for his *Gumdrop* series of picture books published yearly since 1966 by Hodder and Stoughton. For children he writes largely from personal experience and in this series he relates the adventures of an Austin Clifton Heavy 12/4 1926 (his own) with a keen understanding of childish humour and sense of drama; the watercolour illustrations flow freely and relate directly to the texts. He is also a watercolour painter of architecture in landscape (this interest is evident in his illustration work) and a

Val Biro. From *Fire Engine by Mistake* by Leila Berg (Brockhampton, 1955).

designer for advertising and of commemorative medallions. Elected FSIA. [Q]

Books illustrated include:

Peter Allen Play the Best Courses (1973)
Stephen Andrews Cubs with a Difference (1973), Cubs Away (1974), Cubs on Saturday (1976)
Enid Bagnold Serena Blandish (1951)
Arnold Baines Discovering Chesham (1968)
Denys Baker Worlds Without End (1945)
Kate Barclay The Story of a Carrot (1944)
L. Frank Baum The Wonderful Wizard of Oz (1965), The Marvellous Land of Oz (1967)
Leila Berg Fire Engine by Mistake (1955), Andy's Pit Pony (1958), The Doctor (1972)
Val Biro Bumpy's Holiday (1943), Gumdrop: The Adventures of a Vintage Car (1966), Gumdrop and the Farmer's Friend (1967), Gumdrop on the Rally (1968), Gumdrop on the Move (1969) Gumdrop Goes to London (1971), The Honest Thief (1972), Gumdrop Finds a Friend (1973), Gumdrop in Double Trouble (1975), Gumdrop and the Steamroller (1976), Gumdrop Posts a Letter (1976), Gumdrop on the Brighton Run (1976), Gumdrop has a Birthday (1977), The Gumdrop Annual (1979), Gumdrop Gets His Wings (1979), Gumdrop Finds a Ghost (1980), Hungarian Folk Tales (1980), Gumdrop and the Secret Switches (1981), Gumdrop Makes a Start (1982), The Magic Doctor (1982), Fables from Aesop (1982), Little Gumdrop books (8 titles 1982-83), The Long Gumdrop (1983)
Donald Bisset Kangaroo Tennis (1968), Benjie and the Circus Dog (1969)
Enid Blyton Brer Rabbit Books (1975-76)
Edward Bohan The Writ of Green Wax (1970)
Dawn Bowker The Dinghy Stories (1973)
Norman J. Bull 100 Bible Stories (1980), 100 New Testament Stories (1981)
John Bunyan The Pilgrim's Progress (1951)
J. Corneille Journal of my Service in India (1966)
Fanny Craddock The Sherlock Holmes Cook Book (1976)
Thurlow Craig The Country Year (1964)
Norman Dale The Casket and the Sword (1956)
David Daniell Hideaway Johnny (1959)
Peter Dawlish The Seas of Britain (1963)
Joan Drake Sally the Seal (1968), James and Sally Again (1970), Mr Bubbus and the Railway Smugglers (1976)
Kenneth Grahame Tales from The Wind in the Willows (1983)
Elizabeth Goudge David and the Shepherd Boy (1954)
E.W. Hildick The Nose Knows (1974), Dolls in Danger (1974), The Case of the Condemned Cat (1975), The Menaced Midget (1975), The Case of the Nervous Newsboy (1976), A Cat Called Amnesia (1976), The Case of the Invisible Dog (1977)

Margaret Holden Kettleby's Zoo (1957)
Anthony Hope The Prisoner of Zenda (1961)
Ted Humphris Garden Glory (1969)
Nicholas Husk Zoo for the Zanies (1952)
Cyril Jackson No Bombs at all (1944), Airman's Song Book (1945)
Eric Leyland To Arms for the Queen (1956)
Jane MacMichael Tales of the Circus (1972)
Mary Moore Crusading Holiday (1946)
Geoffrey Morgan Soldier Bear (1970)
Beverley Nichols Down the Kitchen Sink (1974)
Richard Parker Escape from the Zoo (1945), A Camel From the Desert (1947), The Penguin Goes Home (1951)
J.B.H. Peel Country Talk (1972), More Country Talk (1973), New Country Talk (1975)
Jean Plaidy Victoria in the Wings (1972)
Michael Pollard The Reporter (1973)
Helen S. Rice Lovingly (1971), Prayerfully (1972), Thankfully (1975)
Daphne Rooke The Australian Twins (1954), The South African Twins (1953)
Kenneth Rudge Man Makes Towns (1963)
Eric Shipton That Untravelled World (1969)
Donald Sutherland Hear and Speak (1971)
Dora Thatcher Tommy the Tugboat series (from 1956), Henry the Helicopter series (from 1956)
H.E. Todd The Sick Cow (1974), George the Fire Engine (1976), The Roundabout Horse (1979), King of Beasts (1980), The Very Very Long Dog (1980), The Crawly Crawly Caterpillar (1980), The Big Sneeze (1981), Jungle Silver (1981), The Tiny Tiny Tadpole (1982), The Scruffy Scruffy Dog (1983)
Lord Tweedsmuir One Man's Happiness (1969)
Keith Waterhouse and Willis Hall Worzel Gummidge (1981), The St Michael Book of Worzel Gummidge Stories (1982)
Rosemary Weir What a Lark (1961), Soap-Box Derby (1962)
Fred Whitsey The Sunday Telegraph Gardening Book (1966)
William Wise The Terrible Trumpet (1969)

Periodical: Radio Times

References: Contemporary Authors; Driver; Fisher pp.93, 125, 132; ICB 2,3,4; Kirkpatrick; Usherwood; Wa (1980); *The Penrose Annual* 56 (1962)

Donald Bisset (b. 1910)

Born in London, son of a dress designer. Served in the Royal Artillery during World War II. Actor in the Royal Shakespeare Company, at the National Theatre and in films for television. Writer of more than forty children's books, many of which he has illustrated himself with humorous line drawings in

Douglas Bissett. From *Island Holiday* by Margaret McPherson in *Miscellany One* edited by Edward Blishen (Oxford University Press, 1964).

a naive style. He also designs childrens' posters. Work published principally by Methuen. [Q]

Books illustrated include:
Donald Bisset Anytime Stories (1954), Sometime Stories (1957), Next Time Stories (1959), This Time Stories (1961), Another Time Stories (1963), Talks with a Tiger (1967), Nothing (1969), Time and Again Stories (1970), Tiger Wants More (1971), Father Tingtang's Journey (1973), The Adventures of Mandy Duck (1974), 'Oh Dear' said the Tiger (1975), The Story of Smokey Horse (1977), The Adventures of Yak (1978), What Time Is It, when It Isn't (1980), Johnny Here and There (1981), The Tiger Who Rolled Uphill (1982), The Joyous Adventures of Smokey Boo (1982)
Edward Blishen (ed) Miscellany One (with others, 1964)

References: Contemporary Authors; Kirkpatrick

Basil Temple Blackwood (1870-1917)

Mainly worked as 'BTB' and sometimes as B.T. Blackwood. Third son of the 1st Marquess of Dufferin and Ava. Friend and contemporary of Hilaire Belloc at Oxford. Barrister at Law, 1900-14. In 1916 he became a Lieutenant in the Grenadier Guards and Private Secretary to the Lord Lieutenant of Ireland. Killed in action in 1917. Blackwood was untrained as an artist, and his crude but effective drawings sometimes recall the humorously childlike manner of Edward Lear. Gordon Ray comments 'Blackwood, who illustrated Belloc's first six children's books, knew how to give the poet's beasts a preternatural awareness that make them seem both shrewder and more congenial than their human associates.'

Books illustrated include:
Hilaire Belloc The Bad Child's Book of Beasts (1896), More Beasts (for Worse Children) (1897), The Modern Traveller (1898), A Moral Alphabet (1899), Cautionary Tales for Children (1907), More Peers (1911)

References: ICB 1; Ray; *The Studio* special (Autumn 1933); *After Alice* (Museum of Childhood catalogue 1977); R. Speaight *Hilaire Belloc* (Hollis & Carter 1957)

F.M.B. Blaikie (active 1906-14)

An artist about whose life nothing seems to be recorded. (S)he worked mostly in ink and pale wash somewhat in the style of F.D. Bedford*, but lacked Bedford's ability to create a whole scene, and depended on caricature rather than serious study for effect.

Books illustrated include:
Louey Chisholm Nursery Rhymes (1911)
Charles Dickens Nicholas Nickleby (c.1910)
Alice F. Jackson (retold by) The Childrens' Dickens (with others, 1906)
Foster Meadow Stories from the Arabian Nights (1906), The Farm (1908)
Jonathan Swift Gulliver's Travels (nd)
Theodore Wood The 'Dwellers' Series (1908)

Quentin Blake (b. 1932)

Born Sidcup, Kent. Son of a civil servant. Educated at Chislehurst, Sidcup Grammar School and

Quentin Blake. 'He fooled around with mud, and stomped and squelched and slithered through it.' From *How Tom Beat Captain Najork and his Hired Sportsmen* by Russell Hoban (Cape, 1974).

Cambridge University. Attended life classes at Chelsea College of Art. Tutor in illustration at the Royal College of Art (1965-78) and Head of the Illustration Department since 1978. He works in pen and ink and watercolour in a popular and unmistakable style, capturing essential character and movement with wit and gaiety in a few rapid strokes. *How Tom Beat Captain Najork and his Hired Sportsman* was joint winner of the Whitbread Award (1974) and *Mister Magnolia* was the winner of the Kate Greenaway Medal (1980). He has illustrated many editions of the BBC *Jackanory* television programme. Appointed RDI; elected FSIAD. [Q]

Books illustrated include:
Joan Aiken Arabel's Raven (1972), The Escaped Black Mamba (1973), The Bread Bin (1974), Tales of Arabel's Raven (1974), Mortimer's Tie (1976), Mortimer and the Sword Excalibur (1979), The Spiral Stair (1979), Arabel and Mortimer (1980), Mortimer's Portrait on Glass (1982)
Ted Allan Willie the Squowce (1977)
Aristophanes (trans Dudley Fitts) The Birds (1971)

Marjorie and Antony Bilbow Give a Dog a Good Name (1967)
Quentin Blake Patrick (1968), Jack and Nancy (1969), A Band of Angels (1969), Angelo (1970), Snuff (1973), Lester and the Unusual Pet (1975), Lester at the Seaside (1975), The Adventures of Lester (1977), Mr Magnolia (1980), Quentin Blake's Nursery Rhyme Book (1983)
Ellen Blance and Ann Cook Monster Books (24 titles 1976-78)
Elizabeth Bowen The Good Tiger (1970)
James Britton (ed) The Oxford Books of Stories for Juniors (3 vols 1964-66)
Geoffrey Broughton Listen and Read with Peter and Molly (1968), Success with English: The Penguin Course (1969), Peter and Molly (1972), Peter and Molly's Revision Book (1975)
Natalie Savage Carlson Pigeon of Paris (1972)
Patrick Campbell Come Here Till I Tell You (1960), Constantly in Pursuit (1962), How to Become a Scratch Golfer (1963), Brewing Up in the Basement (1963), Rough Husbandry (1965), The P-P-Penguin Patrick Campbell (1965), A Feast of True Fandangles (1979)
Lewis Carroll The Hunting of the Snark (1976)
Charles Connell Aphrodisiacs in Your Garden (1965)
Ruth Craft Play School Play Ideas (1971)
Rupert Croft-Cooke Tales of a Wicked Uncle (1963)
Bronnie Cunningham (ed) Funny Business (1978), The Puffin Joke Book (1974)
Roald Dahl The Enormous Crocodile (1978), The Twits (1980), George's Marvellous Medicine (1981), Revolting Rhymes (1982), The BFG (1982)
Gillian Edwards Hogmanay and Tiffany (1970)
Ezo My Son-in-Law the Hippopotamus (1962)
Sid Fleischman McBroom's Wonderful One-Acre Farm (1972), Here Comes McBroom! (1976), McBroom and the Great Race (1981)
Helen Jill Fletcher Put On Your Thinking Cap (1968)
Nils-Olof Franzen Agaton Sax and the Diamond Thieves (1965), Agaton Sax and the Scotland Yard Mystery (1969), Agaton Sax and the Max Brothers (1970), Agaton Sax and the Criminal Doubles (1971), Agaton Sax and the Colossus of Rhodes (1972), Agaton Sax and the London Computer Plot (1973), Agaton Sax and the League of Silent Exploders (1974), Agaton Sax and the Haunted House (1975), Agaton Sax and the Big Rig (1976), Agaton Sax and Lispington's Grandfather Clock (1968)
Gordon Fraser (ed) Your Animal Book (1969)
Clement Freud Grimble (1974)
Jonathan Gathorne-Hardy Cyril Bonhamy v. Madam Big (1981)
Stella Gibbons Cold Comfort Farm (1977)
J.B.S. Haldane My Friend Mr Leakey (1971)
Willis Hall The Incredible Kidnapping (1975), Kidnapped at Christmas (1975)
Bill Hartley (ed Roy McCarthy) Motoring and the Motorist (1965)
Thomas L. Hirsch Puzzles for Pleasure and Leisure (1966)
Russell Hoban How Tom Beat Captain Najork and his Hired Sportsmen (1974), A Near Thing for Captain Najork (1975), The Twenty Elephant Restaurant (1980), Ace Dragon Ltd (1980)
Evan Hunter The Wonderful Button (1961)
Norman Hunter Wizards are a Nuisance (1973)
F. Knowles and B. Thompson Eating (1973)
Edward Kovel Listen and I'll Tell You (1962)
Tony Lacey (ed) Up with Skool! (1981)
Fred Loads, Alan Gemmell and Bill Sowerbutts Gardeners' Question Time (1964, second series 1966)
D. Mackay, B. Thompson and P. Schaub Doctors and Nurses (1970), The Birthday Party (1970)
Margaret Mahy Non-stop Nonsense (1977), The Great Piratical Rumbustification (1978)
J.P. Martin Uncle (1964), Uncle Cleans Up (1965), Uncle and his Detective (1966), Uncle and the Treacle Trouble (1967), Uncle and Claudius the Camel (1969), Uncle and the Battle for Badgertown (1973)
John Moore (ed) The Boys' Country Book (1961)
John Moreton Punky: Mouse for a Day (1962)
Ogden Nash Custard and Company (1979)
Frances Gray Patton Good Morning, Miss Dove (1961)
Sylvia Plath The Bed Book (1976)
Ennis Rees Riddles, Riddles Everywhere (1964), Pun Fun (1965), Gillygaloos and Gollywhoppers (1969)
James Reeves Mr Horrox and the Gratch (1969)
Tim Rice and Andrew Lloyd Webber Joseph and the Amazing Technicolor Dreamcoat (1982)
H.P. Rickman Living with Technology (1969)
Michael Rosen Mind Your Own Business (1974), Wouldn't You Like To Know (1977), The Bakerloo Flea (1979), You Can't Catch Me (1981)

Barry Ruth Home Economics (1966)
Richard Schickel The Gentle Knight (1964)
R.C. Scriven The Thingummyjig (1973)
Joan Tate The Next-Doors (1964), Bits and Pieces (1967), Luke's Garden (1967)
H. Thomson The Witch's Cat (1971)
Robert Tibber Aristide (1966)
Jules Verne Around the World in Eighty Days (1966)
Carole Ward Play School Ideas 2 (1977)
Julia Watson The Armada Lion Book of Young Verse (1974)
Evelyn Waugh Black Mischief (1981), Scoop (1983)
Rosemary Weir Albert the Dragon (1961), Further Adventures of Albert the Dragon (1964), Albert the Dragon and the Centaur (1968)
John Yeoman The Boy Who Sprouted Antlers (1961), Alphabet Soup (1969), The Bear's Winter House (1969), The Bear's Water Picnic (1970), A Drink of Water (1970), Sixes and Sevens (1971), Mouse Trouble (1972), Beatrice and Vanessa (1974), The Puffin Book of Improbable Records (1975), The Young Performing Horse (1977), The Wild Washerwomen (1979), Rumbelow's Dance (1982)
Helen Young What Difference Does It Make, Danny? (1980)
A Band of Angels (Gordon Fraser 1969)
'Quote and Unquote' (Arcadia Press 1970)

Periodicals: Punch, The Spectator

References: Contemporary Authors; ICB 3,4; Jacques; Ryder; *Books for Keeps* 1 (March 1980); *Puffin Post* vol 17 no 8 (1973); *Punch* (15th December 1965); *Signal* (16th January 1975)

Zelma Blakeley (1927-78)

Born in London. Studied at Kingston School of Art (1939-42) under Wilfred Fairclough, and at the Slade School (1945-48) under Norman Janes* and John Buckland Wright*. Tutor at Heatherley's School of Art. Wood engraver. Lived near Ipswich, Suffolk. Elected ARE (1955), RE (1966).

Books illustrated include:
Ignacio Manuel Altamirano (trans Mary Allt) El Zarco the Bandit (1957)
Sheila Bishop Geordie's Mermaid (1961)
Helen Burke Kippers to Caviar (1965)
Rhoda Hoff Why They Wrote (1964)
Meta Mayne Reid With Angus in the Forest (1963)
André Simon English Fare and French Wines (1958)
John Varney Under the Sun (1964)
B.B.C. Book of the Countryside (Arthur Phillips 1963)
Bedside Book of Nature (Readers Digest 1959)
Treasure Trove (Longmans 1961)

References: Garrett BWE, HBWE; Wa (1980)

Edmund Blampied (1886-1966)

Born Jersey, Channel Islands, son of a farmer. Until he was fifteen, when he took art lessons in St Helier, he had never seen a town. In 1903, speaking little English, he began studying at Lambeth School of Art under Philip Connard*. He was soon employed to make topical pen and ink sketches for *The Daily Chronicle*. In 1905, he entered the London County Council School where he won a scholarship. He took up etching in 1913, and in 1925 he won a Gold Medal for lithography at the Paris International Exhibition. During World War II, he lived in St Aubin, Jersey and designed six Jersey occupation stamps and one of the Channel Island liberation stamps. He was a landscape and figure painter in oil and watercolour, etcher and lithographer, clay modeller and draughtsman. He was considered one of the leading British etchers of his day and was particularly acclaimed for his drypoints of farming and rural subjects. He also worked in black and white, pencil and watercolour, developing an easy, fluent and sometimes almost impressionist graphic style. Elected ARE (1920), RE (1921), RBA (1938).

Books illustrated include:
J.M. Barrie The Blampied Edition of Peter Pan (1939)
Edmund Blampied Bottled Trout and Polo (1936)
Ethel M. Dell The Way of an Eagle (1912)
Michael Fairless The Roadmender (1924)
John J. Farnol The Money Moon (1914), The Chronicle of the Imp (1915)
H.C. Hunt Hand-Picked Proverbs (1938), More Hand-Picked Proverbs (1940)
E. Nesbit Phoenix and the Carpet (1903), The House of Arden (1908)
Anna Sewell Black Beauty (c.1920)
R.L. Stevenson Travels with a Donkey (1931)
William R. Titterton Me as a Model (1914)

Periodicals: The Apple, The Bystander, The Daily Chronicle, The Graphic, Nash's Magazine, The Royal Magazine, The Sketch, The Strand Magazine, Sunday at Home, The Tatler

References: Bénézit; Guichard & appendix; Houfe; Johnson & Greutzner; Wa (1960); Waters; *Drawing and Design* (May 1923); *Fine Prints of the Year* (1923-37); *The Print Collector's Quarterly* vols 13, 19, 24; *The Studio* 83 (1922), 89 (1925), special (Spring 1922, Spring 1929, Winter 1931); Campbell Dodgson *A Complete Catalogue of the Etchings and Dry-Points of Edmund Blampied* (Halton & Truscott Smith 1926); M.C. Salaman *Modern Masters of Etching* vol 10 (Studio series 1925-32)

Douglas Percy Bliss (b. 1900)

Born in Karachi, India. Son of a chemist. Studied at Edinburgh University (M.A. Hons) and then painting at the Royal College of Art (1922-25). Painter, illustrator, pictorial satirist and writer on art: works include *A History of British Wood Engraving* (Dent 1928) and a monograph on Edward Bawden* (Pendomer Press 1979). Exhibited watercolours with his friends Bawden and Eric Ravilious* at St George's Gallery, 1927. Served with the Royal Air Force during World War II. Part-time tutor at Hornsey School of Art (1932-40), Blackheath School of Art (1934-40) and Harrow School of Art (1945-46). Director of Glasgow School of Art (1947-65). Bliss's early book illustrations consisted of wood engravings; influenced by Ethelbert White*, they were characterised by vigorous cutting with complex tonal and textural variations. Later he became impatient with the inherent limitations of the medium and in particular with the difficulty of achieving a satisfactory visual relationship between the 'dropped in' engravings and the surrounding text, and turned to pen and ink, sometimes with stencilled partial colour. His black and white illustrations for *Palace for Pleasure* (1929) demonstrate his fine penmanship and visual wit; he was an admirer of the French illustrator Edy Legrand (b. 1901) and his own work sometimes achieved a comparable panache. His pictorial satires (some reproduced in *The*

Edmund Blampied. 'A caterpillar has three pairs of proper legs and five pairs of improper ones.' From *More Hand-picked Howlers* by Cecil Hunt (Methuen, 1938).

Sketch during the 1930s), in watercolour and body-colour, showed the influence of Max Beerbohm*. His work has been published by Dent, Oxford University Press and the Folio Society. Elected member of SWE (1934) and RBA (1939).

Books illustrated include:
J.R. Allan The Farmer's Boy (1935)
E.P. Leigh Bennett Ghosts Grave and Gay (1930)
D.P. Bliss (ed) Border Ballads (1925), *(intro)* The Devil in Scotland (1934)
Cervantes The Spanish Lady (1928)
W.H. Gardner Salamander in Spring (1933)
Thomas Jefferson Hogg Memoirs of Prince Alexy Haimatoff (1952)
Samuel Johnson Rasselas (1926)

Douglas Percy Bliss. From *Rasselas* (1926).

Diana Bloomfield. From *Come Hither* collected by Walter de la Mare (Constable, 1960).

W. Painter Palace of Pleasure (1929)
Edgar Allan Poe Some Tales of Mystery and Imagination (1938)

Periodicals: The London Mercury, The Sketch, The Woodcut

References: Balston EWE, WEMEB; Garrett BWE, HBWE; Johnson & Greutzner; Lewis; Vollmer; Wa (1972); Waters; *Drawing and Design* (July 1926); *Fine Prints of the Year* (1935); *Graven Images* (Scottish Arts Council 1979); *The Studio* 98 (1929), special (Spring 1927, Spring 1930, Winter 1931, Winter 1936); Iain MacNab *A Student's Book of Wood-Engraving* (Pitman 1938)

Diana Bloomfield (b. 1916)

Maiden name: Diana Wallace. Born in Harrow, Middlesex. Studied at Harrow School of Art (1933-35). Fabric designer, calligrapher and wood engraver. Taught wood engraving at the City Literary Institute, London (1966-69) and more recently at the University of Sussex. She lives in Sussex and teaches wood engraving at the Gardner Centre for the Arts, University of Sussex, and painting in Seaford and Eastbourne. As a wood engraver, she has been influenced by the work of Thomas Bewick and particularly by that of Reynolds Stone*, whom she considers 'the great master of engraved bookplates and engraved lettering not just for this century but for all time' (quoted in *The Private Library*, 1974). Like Stone, she has engraved numerous bookplates; she has also illustrated a number of books with wood engravings, many for American publishers. As a quill pen letterer, she works in the tradition of Edward Johnstone. An adventurous traveller, she went on a Himalayan trek up the Annapurna range in 1978. [Q]

Books illustrated include:
Evelyn Ansell Twenty Five Poems (1963)
Walter de la Mare Come Hither (1960)
Eleanor Graham (ed) A Puffin Quartet of Poets
Sacheverell Sitwell (intro) Great Palaces (1964)
Colin Willock (ed) The Man's Book (1958)
Also numerous books first published in the United States

References: Garrett BWE, HBWE; *The Private Library* (Spring 1974); *Year Book of the American Society of Bookplate Collectors and*

Designers (1969-70); Brian North Lee *British Bookplates* (David & Charles 1979); Mark Severin and Anthony Reid *Engraved Bookplates* (Private Libraries Association 1972)

Muirhead Bone (1876-1953)

Born in a Glasgow suburb, one of eight children of a journalist. While studying to be an architect (1890-94), he attended evening classes at Glasgow School of Art. In 1901 he moved to London. He married Gertrude Dodd, a writer, and later illustrated several of her books. Bone was the first artist to receive government recognition as an Official War Artist (1916). From 1939 to 1946, he was Official War Artist to the Admiralty. He and his wife travelled extensively in France, Holland and Sweden and lived for several years in Italy and Spain. Died in Oxford and is commemorated with a memorial tablet in the crypt of St Paul's Cathedral, London. A painter, draughtsman and self-taught etcher, he was known for panoramic architectural and landscape views sometimes with tiny figures enhancing the illusion of scale; however, some of his book illustrations were more intimate in feeling. In 1937, he was knighted.

Books illustrated include:
Gertrude Bone Children's Children (1908), Old Spain (2 vols 1936), Days in Old Spain (1938), Came to Oxford (1952)

Muirhead Bone. Ship Building - 'A Shaft Bracket' from *The Western Front* (Part X, October 1917).

James Bone London Etching (1919), London Perambulator (1925),
   London Echoing (1948)
Sir Muirhead Bone Merchantmen-at-Arms (1949), Merchantmen
   Rearmed (1949)
Stephen Bone The English and their Country (1951)
C. Montague The Front Line (1916), The Western Front (1917)
J. Hamilton Muir Glasgow in 1901 (1901)

Periodical: The Yellow Book

References: Bénézit; Chamot, Farr & Butlin; DNB (1951-60);
Guichard; Houfe; Johnson & Greutzner; Pennell PD; Thieme &
Becker; Vollmer and supp; Wa (1952); Waters; WW (1908); *Fine
Prints of the Year* (1936, 1937); *The OWS Club Volume* 33; *The Print
Collector's Quarterly* 9; *The Studio* 147 (1954), special (1911, 1917,
Spring 1922, Winter 1931); James L. Carr *Scottish Painting Past and
Present (T.C. & E.C. Jack 1908); Campbell Dodgson Etchings and
Drypoints by Muirhead Bone* (Obach 1909); Sir Frederick Wedmore
Some of the Moderns (Virtue 1909)

Stephen Bone (1904-1958)

Born in Chiswick, London, son of Sir Muirhead
Bone*. Educated at Bedales School. Studied art
with his father and under Henry Tonks at the
Slade School of Fine Art (1922-24). He won a
gold medal at the Paris Exhibition (1924). In
1928, he executed a mural decoration for Piccadilly
underground station. He married Mary Adshead*
in 1929. Served as a war artist with the Navy (1942-
45). From 1948, he was art critic for *The Manchester
Guardian*, and a frequent guest on the BBC radio
show *The Critics*. Worked as a landscape and
portrait painter, lithographer, muralist and illustrator of books, book jackets and magazines. He
illustrated several books written by his mother
Gertrude Bone with woodcuts that combined
boldness with sensitivity. Elected NEAC (1932)
[Q].

Books illustrated include:
Gertrude Bone The Furrowed Earth (1921), Oasis (1924), Of the
   Western Isles (1925), The Hidden Orchis (1929), The Cope (1930)
Stephen Bone and Mary Adshead The Silly Snail (1942), The Little
   Boy and his House (1950), The Little Boys and their Boats (1953)
George Bourne A Farmer's Life (1922)
Julian Brooke The Military Orchid (1948)
W.H. Davies Selected Poems (1923)

Periodicals: The Illustrated London News, The Manchester Guardian,
New Statesman

Stephen Bone. 'I will make mention of the loving
kindness of the Lord' from *Oasis* by Gertrude
Bone (1924).

References: Bénézit; Chamot, Farr & Butlin; Crouch; DNB (1951-60);
ICB 2; Johnson & Greutzner; Vollmer; Wa (1958); Waters; *The Artist*
(March 1938); *The Studio* special (Spring 1927)

Peter Boston (b. 1918)

Born in Looe, Cornwall. Studied at King's College, Cambridge (1937-40), and at Liverpool
University School of Architecture (1946-49).
Army service in the Royal Engineers in North
Africa and Italy (1940-46). He has practised as an
architect since 1950, winning eight architectural
and Civic Trust awards. He has illustrated many
of the books written by his mother, Lucy Boston,
published in England (principally by Faber &
Faber and the Bodley Head) and abroad. Working
in pen and ink on scraper board, or with felt pen
on Whatman paper, he succeeds in creating a
highly imaginative atmosphere. He has also made
colour designs for the BBC *Jackanory* programme. [Q]

Books illustrated include:
Lucy M. Boston The Children of Green Knowe (1954), The Chimneys
   of Green Knowe (1958), Treasure at Green Knowe (1958), The
   River at Green Knowe (1959), A Stranger at Green Knowe (1961),
   An Enemy at Green Knowe (1964), The Sea Egg (1967), Nothing

Peter Boston. Frontispiece from *The Chimneys of
Green Knowe* by L.M. Boston (Faber, 1958).

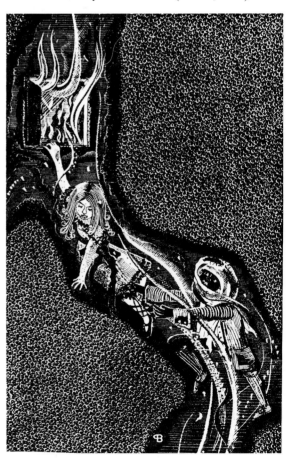

Said (1971), The Guardians of the House (1974), The Fossil Snake (1975), The Stones of Green Knowe (1976)

Reference: Fisher p.355

Hilda Boswell (1903-76)

Born London, daughter of an architect. Studied at Hornsey Art School and the Regent Street Polytechnic. Lived in North London from the age of eleven until her death. From the 1930s, she worked as a book illustrator. Her interests included reading, gardening and the countryside. She particularly admired the work of Beatrix Potter*, Kate Greenaway, Arthur Rackham* and Edmund Dulac*. Her preferred medium was watercolour. [Q]

Books illustrated include:
Hilda Boswell Jenny's Fairy Year (1945), The Little Birthday Horse (1950), Treasury of Nursery Rhymes (1959), Jingle Time (1960), Treasury of Fairy Tales (1962), Little Boy Blue Nursery Rhymes (1964), Little Crazy Car (1965), Treasury of Poetry (1968), Treasury of Children's Stories (1971), Omnibus (1972)
R.L. Stevenson A Child's Garden of Verses (1963)
My Book of Elves and Fairies (with others, nd)

James Boswell (1906-71)

Born New Zealand. Studied at the Elam School of Art, Auckland, and at the Royal College of Art, London (1925-29). Served in the army during World War II. He later became an art director of Shell (until 1947) and art editor of *Lilliput* (1947-50), commissioning work from (among others) Walter Trier*, Paul Hogarth* and Ronald Searle*. From 1951, he worked freelance as a painter, graphic artist and journalist. Executed a fifty-foot mural in the 'Sea and Ships' Pavilion for the Festival of Britain (1951). His graphic work was mainly in pen and ink or brush, sometimes with half-tone washes or spatter. His imagery was loosely based on that of the German artist, George Grosz, but seldom expressed the same bitter despair. Paul Hogarth considered that 'his illustrations have the quality of suggesting the emotional undertones of a situation without literally describing a particular incident' possessing 'some mysterious conjunction of aesthetic and purely human emotion which is the function of all illustrative art.' During the 1930s, he concentrated on satirical drawings of social subjects, but during and after the war, he often turned to a more realistic style of reportage. William Feaver considers him 'one of the finest graphic artists of this century'.

Books illustrated include:
Lawrnce Benedict The Paper Chase (1954)
F. De Roberte The Viceroys (1962)
Marcus Hayman The Adventures of the Little White Girl in her Search for Knowledge (1934)
Betty Holt All This and the Family Too (1960)
A.S. Jasper A Hoxton Childhood (1969)
Compton Mackenzie Little Cat Lost (1965)
David Malcolm The Winning Art (1958)

James Boswell. 'Note how the Stoat/Exemplifies bad habits:/Endowed by Nature with a turn of coat/And by upbringing with a lust for rabbits.' From *Low Life*, verses by John Pudney (Bodley Head, 1947).

Wolf Mankovitz A Kid for Two Farthings (1953)
John Pudney Low Life (1947)
Margaret Reynolds Prisoner at the Bar (1958)
Maurice Richardson The Exploits of Engelbrecht (1950)
L.C.T. Rolt Railway Adventure (1953)
Randall Swingler The Years of Anger (1946)
John Symonds The Dapplegray (1962), Conversations with Gerald (1974)

Periodicals: Daily Worker, Left Review, Lilliput, Punch, Radio Times

References: Bénézit; ICB 3; Jacques; Price; Usherwood; Vollmer supp; Waters 1, 2; *Design* (July 1971); James Boswell *The Artist's Dilemma* (Bodley Head 1947); William Feaver *Boswell's London* (Wildwood House 1978); Paul Hogarth *The Artist as Reporter* (Studio Vista 1967)

Beryl Antonia Botterill (1912-70)

Worked as 'Anton'. Married name: Antonia Yeoman. Born Brisbane, Australia, daughter of an English stockbroker; settled in England (1915). Having lost two of the fingers on her right hand in her early teens, she learned to write and draw with her left hand. Studied at the Royal Academy Schools (1928-30) and for a year under Steven Spurrier*. From 1932 to 1937, she freelanced as a fashion and commercial artist under the name of 'Botterill'. From 1937 to 1945, in partnership with her brother Harold Underwood Thompson, she produced humorous cartoons under the name 'Anton'. On the outbreak of war, he joined the

Anton (Beryl Botterill). From *How to Live like a Lord without really Trying* by Shepherd Mead (Macdonald, 1964).

Navy, and although he continued to contribute ideas, she took over the entire execution of the drawings, placing greater emphasis on linear elegance but retaining the characteristic style of shading (though in later years she sometimes used wash). She continued to contribute to numerous magazines and also undertook commercial work, book illustration and book jackets, portrait-drawing and occasional broadcasts. Elected FRSA and FSIA; the first (and so far only) female member of the *Punch* Toby Club. Served for several years, until her death, on the Council of the Artists' General Benevolent Institution.

Books illustrated include:
Desmond Briggs Entertaining Single Handed (1968)
E. Cleugh Without Let or Hindrance (1961)
P. de Polnay Travelling Light (1959)
C. Fullerton The Man Who Spoke Dog (1959)
V. Graham Here's How (1951)
A. Hilton This England (1952)
Margharita Laski Apologies (1955)
S. Mead How to Live Like a Lord without Really Trying (1964)
Victor Mollo Streamlined Bridge (1947)
E. Parr Grafters All (1964)
D. Parsons Can It Be True? (1953), Many a True Word (1958)
A.D. Wintle The Club (1961)

Periodicals: The Daily Telegraph, Evening Standard, Lilliput, London Opinion, Men Only, Night and Day, Pan, Punch, The Sketch, The Tatler

References: Price; Vollmer supp; Wa (1962); *Country Life* (December 1971); *Modern Living* (Winter 1953); *Readers Digest* (April 1977); *The Tatler* (January 1941); *Woman's Mirror* (9th October, 1965); *Way of the World* (Daily Telegraph album 1957-58); A. Andriola and M.

Casson *Ever Since Adam and Eve* (McGraw Hill 1955); Nicolas Bentley (ed) *The Shell Book of Motoring Humour* (Michael Joseph 1976); A. Havinden *Line Drawing for Reproduction: How to do it series no 4* (Studio 1941); D.B. Wyndham Lewis (ed) *I Couldn't Help Laughing* (Lindsay Drummond 1941); I. Scott (ed) *British Cartoonists Album no. 2* (Panther 1963)

Amelia Bowerley.
See Amelia Bauerle.

Alexander Stuart Boyd (1854-1930)

Sometimes worked as 'Twym'. Born in Glasgow, son of a muslin manufacturer. On leaving school he worked for six years in a bank, then in 1880 studied art for several months at Heatherley's School of Art. He subsequently contributed to numerous magazines including the Glasgow illustrated paper *Quiz* (1881-1901), and was on the staff of *The Graphic* and *The Daily Graphic*. In his early years he often worked under the pseudonym 'Twym', an arbitrary combination of letters. In 1891 he moved to London and from 1894 contributed intermittently to *Punch*. He emigrated in 1912 to New Zealand where he later became President of the Auckland Society of Artists. His wife, Mary, was a writer and they collaborated on several travel books. In common with other *Graphic* artists of the period such as Reginald Cleaver*, Boyd developed an essentially journalistic black and white technique, concentrating on the essential elements of a scene and depicting them in a simple, easily reproduced style. His drawings lacked the smoothness and polish of Cleaver's, and were much less even in quality, but they often retained a feeling of spontaneity and revealed a talent for expressive portrait caricature.

Books illustrated include:
Charles Blatherwick Peter Stonnor (with James Guthrie*, 1884)
A.S. Boyd Sweet Briar... (1886), The Gailes of '89 (1889), When We Were Laddies at the Scüle (1902), Glasgow Men and Women (1905)
Mary Stuart Boyd Our Stolen Summer (1900), A Versailles Christmas-Tide (1901), The Fortunate Isles (1911)
Robert Burns The Cotter's Saturday Night (1905)
Joan Dane Prince Madog (1909)
Hugh Haliburton Horace in Homespun (1900)
Bret Harte The Bell Ringer of Angel's (with others, 1894), A Protegée of Jack Hamlin's (with others, 1894)
Jerome K. Jerome Novel Notes (with others, 1893), John Ingerfield (with J. Gulich, 1894)
Ian Maclaren Martha Spreuill (1887), The Days of Auld Lang Syne (1898), Rabbi Sanderson (1898)
Frank Matthew At the Rising of the Moon (with F. Pegram 1893)
Charles Murray Hamewith... (1917)
Will Roberts The Birthday Book of Solomon Grundy (1884)
R.L. Stevenson A Lowland Sabbath Morn (1898)
George E. Todd The Sketch-Book of the North (1896)
Israel Zangwill Ghetto Tragedies (1894)

Periodicals: The Baillie, Black and White, The Daily Graphic, Good Words, The Graphic, The Idler, The London Magazine, The Odd Volume, The Pall Mall Magazine, Punch, Quiz, The Strand Magazine

References: Baker; Bénézit; Johnson & Greutzner; Hammerton; Houfe; Mallalieu; J.G. Reid; Sketchley; Thorpe; Vollmer supp; Wa (1929); Waters; C. Wood; *Alphabet & Image* 2 (September 1946); *The Ludgate* (January 1897)

Dorothea Braby. Wood engraving for tailpiece from *91st Psalm* (Golden Cockerel Press, 1943).

Dorothea Paul Braby (b. 1909)

Born in London. Studied at the Central School of Arts and Crafts under John Farleigh* (1926), in Florence (1927), at Heatherley's School of Art (1928-30) and in Paris (1930). Subsequently worked freelance (1930-60). As a mainly black and white illustrator, she makes wood engravings or works in pen and ink. Most of her illustrative work has been for private presses, especially the Golden Cockerel Press. Influences on her style include the work of Eric Fraser* and C.W. Bacon. She is also active as a jacket designer, portrait painter and in advertising. [Q]

Books illustrated include:
Dorothea Braby (ed) The Commandments (1946)
V.G. Calderon The Lottery Ticket (1945)
Ida Clyde Clarke Men Who Wouldn't Stay Dead (1936)
Emily Eden The Semi-Attached Couple (1955)
Gwyn Jones (trans) Sir Gawain and the Green Knight (1952), The Saga of Llywarch the Old (1955)
Gwyn Jones and Thomas Jones (trans) The Mabinogion (1948)
John Keats Poems (1950)
John Amos Komensky (trans Count Lutzow) The Labyrinth of the World and the Paradise of the Heart (1950)
Christopher Whitfield Mr Chambers and Persephone (1937), The Ninety-First Psalm (1943)
Oscar Wilde Lord Arthur Savile's Crime (1954)

Periodicals: Courier, The Observer, Radio Times

References: Garrett BWE, HBWE; Wa (1980); Waters; *The Studio* 133 (1947); *Shall We Join the Ladies?* (Studio One Gallery, Oxford 1979); Dorothea Braby *The Way of Wood Engraving* (Studio 1953)

R.A Brandt (b. 1906)

Born in Hamburg, Germany, a British subject by birth; he settled in England in 1933. He studied art briefly at Amédée Ozenfant's school in London, and in Paris. He taught at the London College of Printing during the 1950s, 1960s and 1970s, and at the Byam Shaw School of Art. He lives in London. For book illustration, he has worked in various media including pencil or bodycolour or with frottage (as in *The Earth-Owl and other Moon People*). His work is notable for its compelling imagery in which there are often overtones of the sinister or macabre.

Books illustrated include:
Honoré de Balzac The Devil's Heir (1945)
Ted Hughes The Earth Owl and Other Moon People (1963)
Stephen MacFarlane The Story of a Tree (1946)
Rabelais Gargantua and Pantaginel (1945)
The Fisherman's Son (1944)
'Come not Lucifer!' (1945)

Frank William Brangwyn (1867-1956)

Born in Bruges, Belgium, son of a Welsh architect who, at that time, was manager of a carpet factory. In 1877, the family returned to London. From 1882 to 1884, he worked in William Morris's Oxford Street workshop enlarging tapestry cartoons. Worked as a sailor from 1887 to 1894, visiting many parts of the world. More or less a self-taught artist, he became known internationally for his easel paintings and large-scale murals. Also a printmaker and designer of furniture, carpets, textiles, ceramics, stained glass, metalwork and jewellery, and schemes for interior and street decorations and pageants. His book illustrations were executed in crayon, ink, watercolour

R.A. Brandt. 'The three clerks of St Nicholas' from *The Devil's Heir and other tales from 'Les Contes Drolatiques'* by Honoré de Balzac (John Westhouse, 1945).

and gouache in various combinations and also included some etchings, lithographs and wood-engravings. Like all his work, they were executed with speed and energy, and had much in common with his large-scale pictures which were admired for their vitality, technical bravura and dramatic tonal contrasts. Despite the popular acclaim there remained a few critics, one of whom, Douglas Percy Bliss*, penetratingly observed that all Brangwyn's work suffered from 'slipshod construction, obscured but not concealed by the noisy rhetoric of his style'. His reputation as a painter and printmaker declined after his death. Elected RBA (1890), ROI (1893), ARA (1904), RE (1907), PRBA (1913), HRSA (1914), RSW (1917), HRMS (1918), RA (1919), ARWS (1921). He was knighted in 1941. There is a Brangwyn Museum at Bruges in Belgium, and the William Morris Gallery at Walthamstow has a room devoted to his work.

Books illustrated include:
Christian Bourman The Bridge (1926)
Frank Brangwyn and H. Preston Windmills (1923)
Frank Brangwyn and W. Shaw Sparrow A Book of Bridges (1915)
Cervantes Don Quixote (1898)
G.K. Chesterton The Way of the Cross (1935)
S.R. Crockett Tales of Our Coast (1896)
George Cupples A Spliced Yarn (1899)
George Emslie The Last of the Wooden Walls of England (1944)
E. Hutton The Pageant of Venice (1922)
C.J. Hyne The Captured Cruiser (1893), The Rubaiyat of Omar Khayyam (1919)
A.W. Kinglake Eothen (1913)
R. Leighton The Wreck of the Golden Fleece (1893)
Eden Philpotts The Girl and the Faun (1917)
Sir Walter Raleigh The Last Flight of the Revenge (1908)
William C. Russell Collingwood (1891)
Frank Rutter The British Empire Panels designed for the House of Lords (1933)
Michael Scott Cruise of the Midge (2 vols, 1894), Tom Cringle's Log (2 vols, 1898)
Thomas Shelton (trans) The History of Don Quixote (4 vols 1898)
Robert Southey The Life of Nelson (1911)
Hugh Stokes Belgium (1916)

Periodicals: The Acorn, The Apple, Form, The Graphic, The Idler, The Neolith, The Pall Mall Budget, The Pall Mall Magazine, Reveille, The Venture

References: Baker; Bénézit; Chamot, Farr & Butlin; Guichard; Houfe; Johnson; Johnson & Greutzner; Lewis; Mallalieu; Phaidon; Shone; Sketchley; Thieme & Becker; Thorpe; Vollmer & supp; Wa (1934); Waters; C. Wood; *Artwork* 1 (1924); *Drawing and Design* (May 1925); *Magazine of Art* 2 (1904); *The Studio* 12 (1898), 40 (1907), 52 (1911), 59 (1913), 72 (1918), 83 (1922), 121 (1941), 145 (1953) special (Summer 1902, Winter 1913, Autumn 1914, 1917, 1919, Spring 1922, Spring 1927, Spring 1929, Autumn 1930); Cyril G.E. Bunt *Sir Frank Brangwyn* (F. Lewis 1949); William de Bellaroche *Brangwyn's Pilgrimage* (Chapman & Hall 1948); Herbert Furst *The Decorative Art of Frank Brangwyn* (John Lane 1924), *Frank Brangwyn: Modern Woodcutters* no 2 (Morland Press 1920); W. Gaunt *The Etchings of Frank Brangwyn: A Catalogue Raisonné* (The Studio 1925-32); G.F. Sandilands *Frank Brangwyn: Famous Watercolour Painters* (The Studio 1928); Walter Shaw Sparrow (ed) *Frank Brangwyn and his Work* (Kegan Paul 1910)

John Bratby (b. 1928)

Born in Wimbledon, Surrey. Studied at Kingston School of Art (1948-50) and at the Royal College of Art (1950-54). Winner of the *Daily Express* Young Artists' Competition (1955) and the Guggenheim Award for Great Britain (1956 and 1958). Taught at Carlisle College of Art (1955-56) and the Royal College of Art (1957-58). During the 1950s he emerged as a prominent painter of 'kitchen sink' subjects, developing a highly individual linear impasto style. His graphic work is equally recognisable, but more concentrated in effect; here he uses pen line in combination with broader strokes of solid black to create powerful imagery with strikingly animated surface qualities. Elected ARA (1959), RA (1971). Member of the London Group. [Q].

Books illustrated include:
John Bratby Breakdown (1960), Breakfast and Elevenses (1961), Brake Pedal Down (1962), Break 50 Kill (1963)
Joyce Cary The Horse's Mouth (1969)
Ronald Duncan Tale of Tales (1974)
Oxford University Press Bible (3 of 6 vols 1968-69)

References: Bénézit; Contemporary Artists; Parry-Crooke; Phaidon; Vollmer supp; Wa (1980); Waters; *The Studio* 155 (1958)

Horace Walter Bray (1887-1963)

Born West Ham, London. Apprenticed to a scene painter; attended Westminster School of Art before 1914. In 1924, Bray accepted an invitation from his friend R.A. Maynard* to work at the Gregynog Press. In 1930, they both left to start the Raven Press at Harrow Weald; in 1934, the press was dissolved and Bray returned to scene painting. he retired to live at Finchingfield, Essex in 1958. He was an accomplished wood engraver, but his chief strength as an illustrator and decorator lay in an intelligent eclecticism, and an ability to make sensitive adaptations from past styles and motifs to harmonise with his texts.

Books illustrated include:
Lord D. Cecil Sir Walter Scott (1933)
Charles Lamb The Essays of Elia (nd)
Thomas Love Peacock The Misfortunes of Elphin (1928)
Ernest Rhys The Life of St David (with R.A. Maynard*, 1927)
William Shakespeare Venus and Adonis (1931)
Philip E. Thomas Chosen Essays (1926)
Henry Vaughan Poems (with R.A. Maynard*, 1924)
Helen Waddell The Abbé Prévost (1933)
The Autobiography of Edward, Lord Herbert of Cherbury (1928)
The Book of Tobit (1931)
The Plays of Euripides (with R.A. Maynard*, 1927)

References: Balston WEMEB; *The Private Library* (Winter 1973, Autumn 1974)

Gretchen E. Breary (active 1943-63)

Writer and illustrator of books for young children in black and white and full colour, published mainly by George Newnes during the post-war years.

Books illustrated include:
G.E. Breary The Bear Nobody Wanted (1944), Polly, Wolly and Doodle (1944), The Bunnies' Boarding School (1945), Hanky, Panky and the Hedgepig (1945), Polly, Wolly and the Beggar's Baby

John Bratby. From his own *Breakfast and Elevenses* (Hutchinson, 1961).

(1946), The Further Adventures of the Woodle Bear (1946), Those Boarding School Bunnies Again (1946), Hanky on Tom Tiddler's Grounds (1946), The Toy Cupboard ABC (1950), Talking of Many Things (1963)
Charles Kingsley The Water Babies (1948)
Malcolm Saville Mystery at Witchend (1943)

Nicholas Stephen Brennan (b. 1948)

Born in Coventry. Studied at Coventry College of Art and, while still a student, wrote and illustrated *Jasper and the Giant*. He works in a humorous vein in detailed outline and wash, often using white flashes to suggest shiny surfaces.

Books illustrated include:
Nicholas Brennan Jasper and the Giant (1970), The Blundle's Bad Day (1974), The Magic Jacket (1976)
Ruth Jennings In the Bin (1979)
Kaye Webb and Treld Bicknell (ed) Puffin's Pleasure (with others, 1976)

Reference: ICB 4

Bernard Brett (b. 1925)

Born in Birmingham. Educated at Hove County Grammar School, Sussex, and Todmorden Grammar School. Studied at Brighton College of Art.

During World War II, he served in the Royal Navy (1943-46). Lecturer at Wolverhampton College of Art (1951-55) and Head of Department (1955-57). Director of a design consultancy (1959-67). Vice-Principal at East Surrey College of Art (1967-75). Editor and designer of a house journal (from 1979). Writer and editor, designer, typographer and printmaker. For illustration, he uses a variety of media—pen, pen and wash, pencil, crayon, gouache, watercolour and combinations of these, often superimposed, using resist techniques. He also works with various printing methods, including 'mock woodcuts'. His work is often visually rich, with considerable tonal and textural variety and evocative colour harmonies. [Q]

Books illustrated include:
Bernard Brett Captain Cook (1970), Bernard Brett's Book of Explorers (1973), Monsters (1976), Ships (1979), A Young Person's Guide to Ghosts (1981), A Young Person's Guide to Witchcraft (1981)
Arthur Catherall Keepers of the Castle (1970)
Julia Clark Crab Village (1954)
Eilis Dillon The Hamish Hamilton Book of Wise Animals (1975)
Kathleen Fidler Pirate and Admiral (1974)
Nicholas Ingman Story of Music (1972), What Instrument Shall I Play? (1975), Gifted Children of Music (1978)
Eve Sutton Moa Hunter (1978)
Ada Williams Between the Lights (1952)
S.F. Wooley The Romans (1972)

Periodical: The American Traveller

Reference: ICB 4

Molly Mary Elizabeth Brett
(active since 1934)

Works as Molly Brett. Born in Croydon, Surrey, daughter of animal painter Mary Gould Brett. Studied illustration on a correspondence course at the Press Art School. Since 1934, she has worked as a freelance writer and illustrator of children's books, nursery pictures, and designer of greetings cards and wrapping paper. She works in line and watercolour, preferring animal, bird and other subjects from nature. Much of her work has been published by the Medici Society. [Q]

Books illustrated include:
Molly Brett The Little Garden (1936), The Story of a Toy Car (1938), Drummer Boy Duckling (1945), Mr Turkey Runs Away (1947), Follow Me Round the Farm (1947), Puppy School-Days (1948), Master Bunny the Baker's Boy (1950), Robin Finds Christmas (1961), Tom Tit Moves House (1962), A Surprise for Dumpy (1965), The Untidy Little Hedgehog (1966), The Forgotten Bear (1968), Two in a Tent (1969), Flip Flop's Secret (1970), Paddy Gets Into Mischief (1972), Jiggy's Treasure Hunt (1973), The Hare in a Hurry (1975), Midget and the Pet Shop (1975), The Party That Grew (1976), The Jumble Bears (1977), The Molly Brett Picture Book (1979), An Alphabet Book (1980), The Runaway Fairy (1981-82), Goodnight Time Tales (1981-82)
Mrs Maitland Nimmo The Bed That Learnt How to Fly (1963), Through the Magic Mirror (1963)
Also a number of educational books for Collins.

Periodicals: Puck, Tiny Tots

References: Contemporary Authors; Cope; Wa (1980)

Eleanor Fortescue Brickdale. 'With everything that pretty bin/My lady sweet, arise! Arise, arise! From *The Book of Old English Songs and Ballads* (Hodder & Stoughton, c.1918).

Eleanor Fortescue Brickdale (1871-1945)

Daughter of a barrister. Studied at the Crystal Palace School of Art and the Royal Academy Schools, where she was a prize-winning student. Painter of figure compositions in oil and water-colour, graphic artist and stained glass designer. She was a friend of Byam Shaw*, several of whose pictures she owned, and by whom she was clearly influenced. Her early illustrations were inexpensively produced in black and white, but as her reputation increased, she was given the chance to work in colour. She was acclaimed, somewhat over-enthusiastically, by *The Studio* as 'a lady of real genius'. She had a penchant for garden idylls with medieval maidens among roses, hollyhocks and half-timbered cottages and depicted detail with Pre-Raphaelite expertise. Her illustrations were published principally by Hodder & Stoughton and Chatto & Windus. Elected ARWS (1902), RWS (1919).

Books illustrated include:
Eleanor Fortescue Brickdale Golden Book of Famous Women (1919), Carols (1925), Golden Book of Songs and Ballads (nd)

Robert Browning Pippa Passes (1908), Men and Women (1908), Dramatis Personae (1909), Dramatic Romances and Lyrics (1909)
Dion Clayton Calthrop A Diary of an 18th Century Garden (1926), The Gentle Art (1927)
William M. Canton The Story of St Elizabeth of Hungary (1913)
Michael Fairless The Gathering of Brother Hilarious (1913)
Mary MacGregor The Story of St Christopher (c.1921)
Francis Palgrave The Golden Treasury (1925)
Alfred, Lord Tennyson Poems (1905), Idylls of the King (1911)

References: Bénézit; Houfe; ICB 1; Johnson & Greutzner; Mallalieu; Ray; Sketchley; Thieme & Becker; Vollmer; Wa (1934); Waters; C. Wood; *Art Journal* (1907); *The Studio* 13 (1898), 23 (1901), special (1898-99, 1900-01, Spring 1905, Autumn 1914, 1923-24); Walter Shaw Sparrow *Women Painters of the World* (Hodder & Stoughton 1905)

Raymond Redvers Briggs (b. 1934)

Works as Raymond Briggs. Born in London, son of a milkman. Studied at Wimbledon School of Art (1949-53) and, after National Service, at the Slade School of Fine Art (1955-57). Since 1957, he has been a full-time illustrator and author, mainly of children's books; since 1961, he has been a part-time lecturer in illustration at Brighton Polytechnic. He won the Kate Greenaway medal for *The Mother Goose Treasury* (1966) and *Father Christmas* (1973), the first book for which he adopted the distinctive strip-cartoon format that he has since used frequently. *The Snowman* had no words, and was adapted by him for television (December 1982); *When the Wind Blows*, a powerful condemnation of nuclear defence (for adults), was adapted for radio (February 1983) and the theatre (April 1983). An accomplished draughtsman, he works in line and watercolour, gouache, pencil and crayons.

Books illustrated include:
Raymond Briggs The Strange House (1961), Midnight Adventure (1961), Ring-a-Ring-O'Roses (1962), Sledges to the Rescue (1963), The White Land (1963), Fee Fi Fo Fum (1964), The Mother Goose Treasury (1966), Jim and the Beanstalk (1970), Father Christmas (1973), Father Christmas Goes on Holiday (1975), Fungus the Bogeyman (1977), The Snowman (1978), Gentleman Jim (1980), When the Wind Blows (1982)
Virginia Haviland The Fairy Tale Treasury (1972)
Ruth Manning-Sanders (ed) A Book of Magical Beasts (1970)
Ian Serraillier The Tale of Three Landlubbers (1970)
Elfrida Vipont The Elephant and the Bad Baby (1969)

References: Doyle CL; Eyre; ICB 3, 4; Ryder; *The Sunday Times* 20th January 1980; *After Alice* (Museum of Childhood catalogue 1977)

Raymond Briggs. From his own *Father Christmas* (Hamish Hamilton, 1973)

Leonard Robert Brightwell (b. 1889)

Born in London. Spent childhood in Clapham and Chiswick, London. He drew animals from the age of six, and professionally from the age of sixteen, when he began contributing to *Punch* (1905-29). He studied at Lambeth School of Art. Contributed to many comic magazines including *Punch* (1905-29). He served in the army during World War I and as an air-raid warden in World War II. As a member of the Marine Biological Association (1922), he joined many scientific and commercial deep-sea trawling expeditions. He worked in pen and ink, ink and wash, and sometimes in full colour. While his educational and scientific drawings are usually clear and informative, his humorous and descriptive work is more sketchy in execution. He was an admirer of the work of fellow animal draughtsmen J. Cecil Aldin*, A. Shepherd* and Harry Rountree*. Fellow of the Zoological Society of London (1906).

Books illustrated:
Edward H. Barker A British Dog in France (1913)
Edward G. Boulenger A Naturalist at the Zoo (1926)
O. Bowen Taddy Tadpole (1946)
L.R. Brightwell A Cartoonist Among Animals (1921), The Tiger in Town (1930), On the Seashore (1934), Zoo Calendar (1934), A Seashore Calendar (1935), The Zoo You Knew (1936), Neptune's Garden (1937), The Dawn of Life (1938), The Garden Naturalist (1941), Rabbit Rearing (1944), Sea-Shore Life in Britain (1947), The Pond People (1949), The Story Book of Fish, Fishermen and the Home (1951), The Story Book of Pets and how to keep them (1951), The Story Book of Animals and the Home (1952), The Story Book of Jungle to Home (1952), The Zoo Story (1952), Down to the Sea (1954), Trimmer. The Tale of a Trawler Tyke (1956)

L.R. Brightwell. 'The show-off' from *Zoo Calendar* (Hutchinson, 1934).

Joyce L. Brisley. 'The Little Girl Who Couldn't Play' from *The Holiday Book* (nd).

Francis Buckland Buckland's Curiosities of Natural History (1948)
Hugh Chesterman The Odd Spot (1928)
Ellen Davies Our Friends at the Farm (1920)
Charles Evans Reynard the Fox (1921)
Leslie Mainland Zoo Saints and Sinners (1925)
Sister Margaret Zoo Guy'd (1935)
Mildred Swannell Animal Geography (1930)

Periodicals: The Boy's Own Annual, The Boy's Own Paper, The Bystander, The Captain, Cassell's Children's Annual, The Daily Mail, The Gaiety Magazine, The Humorist, The Sporting and Dramatic News, London Opinion, Puck, Punch, The Quiver

References: Cuppleditch; Doyle BWI; Houfe; ICB 1; Johnson & Greutzner;

Joyce Lankester Brisley (1896-1978)

With her sister Nina, she wrote and illustrated stories from early childhood. Many of these appeared in a magazine they produced called *The Wanderer*. Having seen this magazine, Lord Northcliffe interviewed them in 1911 and they were soon contributing to *Home Chat*. When their parents separated, they moved to London with their mother; they studied at Lambeth School of Art for two years and, with their sister Ethel, a miniature painter, exhibited together at the Royal Academy. Joyce became well known for her *Milly-Molly-Mandy* stories which originally appeared in instalments in *The Christian Science Monitor* and were first published in book form by Harrap in

1928. Milly-Molly-Mandy was followed by other characters such as the wooden peg dolls Purl and Plain. Her illustrations consisted of clear, easily reproduced outline drawings. Though her range was narrow, she depicted her chosen subjects with assurance and consistency. The modest vignettes, often single figures or motifs, with which she enlivened pages of text, were arguably the best work she produced.

Books illustrated include:
Joyce Lankester Brisley Milly-Molly-Mandy Stories (1928), More of Milly-Molly-Mandy (1929), Lamb's Tales and Suchlike (1930), Further Doings of Milly-Molly-Mandy (1932), The Dawn Shops and other stories (1933), Marigold in Grandmother's House (1934), My Bible Book (1940), Adventures of Purl and Plain (1941), Milly-Molly-Mandy Again (1948), Another Bunchy Book (1951), Milly-Molly-Mandy and Co (1955), Children of Bible Days (1970)
Mrs H.C. Cradock Adventures of a Teddy Bear (1934), More Adventures of a Teddy Bear (1935), In Teddy Bear's House (1936), Teddy Bear's Shop (1939), Teddy Bear's Farm (1941)
'Mrs Herbert Strang' (ed) The Golden Book for Girls (c.1936), Apple Blossom (with others, nd)
Elizabeth Wetherell The Wide Wide World (1950)
Ursula Moray Williams Adventures of a Little Wooden Horse (1938), Pretenders' Island (1940)
The Holiday Book (nd)

Periodicals: The Christian Science Monitor, Home Chat, Watkin's Annual

References: Contemporary Authors; Johnson & Greutzner; Kirkpatrick; Wa (1934); *After Alice* (Museum of Childhood catalogue 1977); Frank Waters *The Joyce Lankester Brisley Book* (Harrap 1981)

Nina Kennard Brisley (d. 1978)

Sister of Joyce Lankester Brisley*, she also studied at the Lambeth School of Art and exhibited at the Royal Academy. Her simple line-block illustrations, which resemble her sister's work, have considerable appeal. She is also known to have designed some posters.

Books illustrated include:
Elinor M. Brent-Dyer A Head Girl's Difficulties (1923), The Maids of La Rochelle (1924), The School at the Chalet (1925), Jo of the Chalet School (1926), The Princess of the Chalet School (1927), The Head Girl of the Chalet School (1928), The Rivals of the Chalet School (1929), The Chalet School and Jo (1931), The Exploits of the Chalet Girls (1933), Jo Returns to the Chalet School (1936), The New Chalet School (1938)
Elizabeth Clark More Stories and How to Tell Them (1928), The Tale that had no Ending (1929), Twenty Tales for Telling (1933), Standard Bearers (1934), Tales for Jack and Jane (1936), Story Books (1936), Tell Me a Tale (with Tony Brisley, 1938), A Little Book of Bible Stories (1938), Twilight and Fireside (1942), Sunshine Tales for Rainy Days (1948)
M.M. Hayes The Book of Games (with M. Tarrant*, 1920)
Dr Norman The Secret of the Beeches (1950)
Elsie Oxenham The School without a Name (1924), Ven at Gregory's (1925), Deb at School (1929), Dorothy's Dilemma (1930), Deb of Sea House (1931)
SPCK Giant Picture Books (with E.A. Wood*, 1950)

Periodicals: Wilfred's Annual, Wonder Books

References: Johnson & Greutzner; Wa (1929); Frank Waters *The Joyce Lankester Brisley Book* (Harrap 1981)

Charles Edmund Brock (1870-1938)

Often worked as C.E. Brock. Born Holloway, London. His father became Reader in Oriental

C.E. Brock. 'A shabby-genteel personage…with a dry suspicious look' from *The Holly Tree and the Seven Poor Travellers* by Charles Dickens (Dent, 1900).

Languages at Cambridge University and soon after Charles's birth the family moved to Cambridge. Here Brock studied under the sculptor Henry Wiles, and by the age of 21 was an established book and magazine illustrator, in a style initially somewhat influenced by Hugh Thomson*. He shared a studio with his younger brother, H.M. Brock*, and together they assembled a collection of antique furniture and costumes for use as 'props' in period illustrations. The brothers' illustrations show undeniable similarities but, in general, Charles's work was more tranquil both in subject and treatment, and more delicate in style. He was also a portrait and genre painter in oil and watercolour. Elected RI (1908).

Books illustrated include:
Canon Atkinson Scenes in Fairyland (1892)
Jane Austen Pride and Prejudice (1896), Northanger Abbey (1907), Mansfield Park (1908), Sense and Sensibility (1908), Emma (1909), Persuasion (1909)
James Barr The Humour of America (1893)
R.D. Blackmore Lorna Doone (1910)
Emily Brontë Wuthering Heights (1933)
Francis Hodgson Burnett Little Lord Fauntleroy (1925)
Hans Casenov The Humour of Germany (1893)
James Fennimore Cooper The Pathfinder (1900), The Prairie (1900)
Ethel Corkey The Magic Circle (1924)
William Cowper John Gilpin (1898)
Daniel Defoe Robinson Crusoe (1898)
E.M. Delafield The Unlucky Family (1914)
Charles Dickens The Holly Tree and the Seven Poor Travellers (1900), The Chimes (1905), A Christmas Carol (1905), The Cricket on the Hearth (1905), The Haunted Man (1907), Dr Marigold (1908), Martin Chuzzlewit (1923), Posthumous Papers of the Pickwick Club (1930), Nicholas Nickelby (1931)

George Eliot Silas Marner (1905)
Juliana Horatia Ewing Mrs Overtheway's Remembrances (1911)
Eleanor Farjeon Martin Pippin in the Apple Orchard (1921)
Jeffery Farnol The Broad Highway (1912), The Honorable Mr
   Tawnish (1913)
A.G. Gardiner Pebbles on the Shore (1917)
Mrs Gaskell Cranford (1904)
W.S. Gilbert The Mikado (with W.R. Flint*, 1928), The Yeoman of
   the Guard (with W.R. Flint*, 1928)
Oliver Goldsmith The Vicar of Wakefield (1898)
Washington Irving Christmas at Bracebridge Hall (1906)
J.R. Johnson The Parachute and other Bad Shots (1891), The Knight
   of Grazinbrook (1893)
Annie Keary Heroes of Asgard (1930)
Charles Kingsley Westward Ho! (1896)
Rudyard Kipling All the Puck Stories (with H.R. Millar*, 1935),
   Rewards and Fairies (1910)
Charles Lamb Essays of Elia (1900), The Works of... (12 vols 1903)
Charles and Mary Lamb Mrs Leicester's School (1904)
Anne Manning The Household of Sir Thomas More (1906)
Mrs Mitford Our Village (1904)
Mrs Molesworth The Cuckoo Clock (1931)
Sir Walter Scott Ivanhoe (1897), The Lady of the Lake (1898)
R.L. Stevenson Catriona (1928)
F. Stockton Rudder Grange (1914)
Herbert Strang Bright Ideas (1920), Winning His Name (1922), True as
   Steel (1923)
Theodora Wilson Through the Bible (with H.M. Brock*, 1936)
The Works of John Galt (10 vols 1936)

Periodicals: Blackie's Children's Annual, The Captain, Cassell's
Family Magazine, Chums, The Girls' Budget, The Girls' Realm, Good
Words, The Graphic, Herbert Strang's Annual, The Jolly Book, Little
Folks, The Odd Volume, The Pall Mall Magazine, Pearson's
Magazine, The Quiver, The Sunday Magazine, Tuck's Annual, The
Windsor Magazine.

References: Baker; Bénézit; Bradshaw; Doyle BWI, CL; Hammerton;
Houfe; ICB 1; Johnson & Greutzner; Mallalieu; Muir; Sketchley;
Thorpe; Vollmer; Wa (1934); Waters; C. Wood; *The Book Lover's
Magazine* 6 (1905); *The Ludgate* (April 1897); *The Junior Bookshelf*
vol 22 no 4 (1958); *The Studio* 68 (1916), special (1900-01, 1911,
Autumn 1914, 1923-24); Clifford M. Kelly *The Brocks* (Charles Skilton
1975)

Henry Matthew Brock (1875-1960)

Born in Cambridge, younger brother of Charles
Edmund Brock*. Studied at Cambridge School of
Art. Lived and worked in Cambridge in close
contact with his brother. By the mid-1890s he was
a popular and prolific illustrator, and continued
working until his eyesight began to fail in 1950.
Unlike C.E. Brock, he worked almost entirely in
pen and ink so that even his coloured illustrations
were basically tinted line drawings. His early work
resembled his brother's, but he was a more rapid
worker and soon developed an individual graphic
style marked by a fluent and vigorous line and
smoothly applied hatching used for glossy surface
effects. His flair for drama and action helped him
to achieve considerable popularity as an illustrator of boys' stories. A Gilbert and Sullivan
devotee, he designed a number of posters for the
D'Oyly Carte during the 1920s. He was a friend of
Harry Rountree* and an admirer of (among others)
Arthur Rackham*, Edmund Dulac*, Russell Flint*
and H.M. Bateman*. In an appendix to C.M.
Kelly's *The Brocks*, the illustrator A.E. Bestall*
makes the following observations: 'C.E. was
probably the last of the era of perfectionists that

Apouyon calleth
down to the ground
the Christian

H.M. Brock. From *The Pilgrim's Progress* by
John Bunyan (Seeley, Service, c.1900).

produced Railton and Thomson, and so far as I
know he never descended from his high standard.
H.M. must have been a man of greater power and
all-round knowledge, infallible in portraying anatomy and action, so sure in the accuracy of his
drawing that he was almost independent of his
media, and over the years he found short-cuts
that increased his output. This retained all his
powerful effects but was a disappointment to those
who knew his potential.' Elected RI (1906).

Books illustrated include:
Louisa M. Alcott Little Women (1904)
Hans Andersen Fairy Tales and Stories (1905)
H.M. Brock The Book of Fairy Tales (1914)
John Bunyan The Pilgrim's Progress (1900)
Louey Chisholm The Golden Staircase (with C.E. Brock*, 1928)
James Fennimore Cooper The Deerslayer (1900), The Last of the
   Mohicans (1900)
Norman James Davidson A Knight Errant and his Doughty Deeds
   (1911)
Charles Dickens The Old Curiosity Shop (1932), Christmas Tales
   (1932)
John Drinkwater All About Me (1928), More About Me (1929)
Juliana Horatia Ewing Jackanapes and Other Tales (1913)
Mrs Gaskell Cranford (black and white 1898, colour 1912)

Charles Kingsley Westward Ho! (1903), The Heroes (1928)
Compton Mackenzie (intro) A Book of Nursery Tales (1934)
Captain Marryat Jacob Faithful (1895)
Beverley Nichols A Book of Old Ballads (1934)
Sir Walter Scott Waverley (1899)
William Shakespeare King Richard II (1899)
R.L. Stevenson Treasure Island (1928), The Black Arrow (1928), The
     Master of Ballantrae (1928), Kidnapped (1928)
William Makepeace Thackeray Ballads and Songs (1896), Henry
     Esmond (1902)
Lewis Wallace Ben Hur (1902)
G.J. Whyte-Melville Black but Comely (1899), Digby Grand (1900),
     Cerise (1901), Kate Coventry (1901)
Theodora Wilson Through the Bible (with C.E. Brock*, 1938)

Periodicals: Blackie's Children's Annual, The Boy's Own Paper, The
Captain, Cassell's Children's Annual, Cassell's Family magazine,
Chums, Fry's Magazine, Fun, The Girls' Realm, Good Words, The
Grand Magazine, The Graphic, The Harmsworth Magazine, Herbert
Strang's Annual, Holly Leaves, The Humorist, Little Folks, The
London Magazine, The Odd Volume, The Oxford Annual for Boys,
Pear's Annual, Pearson's Magazine, The Penny Magazine, Printer's
Pie, Punch, The Quiver, The Royal Magazine, The Sketch, The
Sphere, The Strand Magazine, The Tatler, The Windsor Magazine.

References: Baker; Bénézit; Doyle BWI, CL; Houfe; ICB 1; Johnson
& Greutzner; Mallalieu; Muir; Price; Sketchley; Thorpe; Vollmer; Wa
(1934); Waters; *The Booklover's Magazine* 6 (1905); *The Studio* special
(1911, Autumn 1914); Clifford M. Kelly *The Brocks* (Charles Skilton
1975)

Winifred Bromhall (active 1923-45)

Born Walsall, Birmingham, where she spent her
childhood. Studied at Queen Mary's College and
Walsall Art School. Emigrated to America in
1924. Illustrator of children's books in a linear
style and whimsical mood, typical of the period.

Books illustrated include:
Winifred Bromhall Belinda's New Shoes (1945)
Elizabeth Martineau des Chesnez Lady Green Satin and her Maid
     Rosette (1923)

Leslie Brooke. 'Till the Hippopotami/Said: 'Ask
no further "What am I?" ' from his *Johnny
Crow's Garden* (Warne, 1903).

Walter de la Mare A Child's Day (1923)
Catherine Perry The Island of Enchantment (1926)

References: ICB 1,2

Iris Brooke (b. 1908)

Married name: Mrs Giffard. Studied at the Royal
College of Art (1926-29). *English Children's
Costume* (1930) made an immediate impact with
its attractive economical line drawings, and subsequent works consolidated her reputation as a
writer and illustrator of books on historical costume.
Her occasional departures from this field (e.g.
Arpies and Sirens, 1942) have been in a humorous
vein.

Books illustrated include:
Iris Brooke English Children's Costume since 1775 (1930), English
     Costume in the Age of Elizabeth (1933), English Costume of the
     Seventeenth Century (1934), English Costume of the Late Middle
     Ages (1935), A History of English Costume (1937), English Costume
     1900-50 (1951), Four Walls Adorned (1952), Pleasures of the Past
     (1955), Dress and Undress (1958), Costume in Greek Classic Drama
     (1962), Medieval Theatre Costume (1967);
Susan Knowles Arpies and Sirens (1942)
James Laver English Costume of the Nineteenth Century (1929),
     English Costume of the Eighteenth Century (1931)
C.M. Matthews and C.E. Carrington A Pageant of Kings and Queens
     (1937)

References: Wa (1964); *The Studio* special (Winter 1931)

Leonard Leslie Brooke (1862-1940)

Born in Birkenhead, Cheshire, son of a rope and
sail manufacturer. A three-month visit to Italy
with an aunt in 1880 confirmed his determination
to become an artist. He studied at Birkenhead
Art School (1880-82), St John's Wood Art School
(1882-84) and the Royal Academy Schools (1884-
88). He worked as a portrait and occasional landscape painter and illustrator. He worked initially
for publishers Blackie and Cassell, then Fisher
Unwin and Dent and, in 1891, succeeded Walter
Crane as illustrator of Mr Molesworth's annual
books for children, published by Macmillan. He
illustrated his first book for Warne (*The Nursery
Rhyme Book*) in 1897, and from then on Warne
was his principal publisher. The first book that he
wrote, *Johnny Crow's Garden,* was based on a
rhyming game that he played as a child with his
father and elder brothers. His most successful
drawings were of animals, which he characteristically depicted clothed and standing upright,
with unmistakable twinkling eyes and an appearance of sly humour. His work in this vein was
widely imitated and he was, with his contemporaries, Beatrix Potter* and J.A. Shepherd*,
one of the leading animal illustrators of his generation. He drew with a sensitive but firm line in
pen and ink, sometimes adding watercolour washes.

Books illustrated include:
Annie Armstrong Marian (1892)

Christopher Brooker. 'Merlissa Benck's expression had become hard and eager; she was like a hound picking up an interesting scent...' From *Auntie Robbo* by Ann Scott-Moncrieff (Constable, 1959).

L. Leslie Brooke Johnny Crow's Garden (1903), The History of Tom Thumb (1904), The Story of the Three Little Pigs (1904), The Story of the Three Bears (1905), The Golden Goose (1905), Johnny Crow's Party (1907), The Tailor and the Crow (1911), Oranges and Lemons (1913), The Man in the Moon (1913), This Little Pig Went to Market (1922), Little Bo-Peep (1922), Ring o' Roses (1922), Johnny Crow's New Garden (1935)
Robert Browning Pippa Passes (1898)
Robert H. Charles A Roundabout Turn (1930)
Evelyn Everett-Green Miriam's Ambition (1889), The Secret of the Old House (1890)
Brothers Grimm The House in the Wood and some other old fairy stories (1909)
Eleanor H. Hayden Travels Round our Village (1901)
Sir George F. Hill The Truth about Old King Cole (1910)
Eva Knatchbull Hugessen A Hit and a Miss (1893)
Lawrence P. Jacks Mad Shepherds... (1923)
Andrew Lang The Nursery Rhyme Book (1897)
Emily Lawless The Book of Gilly (1908)
Edward Lear The Jumblies and other nonsense verses (1900), Nonsense Songs (1900), The Pelican Chorus and other nonsense verses (1900)
George Macdonald The Light Princess (1890)
Mrs Molesworth Nurse Heatherdale's Story (1891), The Girls and I (1892), Mary (1893), My New Home (1894), Sheila's Mystery (1895), The Carved Lions (1895), The Oriel Window (1896), Miss Mouse and her Boys (1897)
Thomas Nash A Spring Song (1898)

Mary Rowsell Thorndike Manor (1890)
E.H. Strain School in Fairyland (1896)
Ismay Thorn Bab (1892)
Anthony Trollope Barchester Towers (1924)
Amy Walton Penelope and Others (1896)
Roma White Brownies and Rose Leaves (1892), Moonbeams and Brownies (1894)

Periodicals: The English Illustrated Magazine, The Odd Volume, The Parade, Pearson's Magazine

References: Baker; Bénézit; Crouch; Eyre; Fisher pp.117, 161; Houfe; ICB 1; Johnson; Johnson & Greutzner; Kirkpatrick; Mallalieu; Muir; Sketchley; Thieme & Becker; Vollmer supp; Waters; C. Wood; *The Junior Bookshelf* vol 16 no 2 (1952); *The Studio* special (1897-98, 1900-01); Henry Brooke *Leslie Brooke And Johnny Crow* (Warne 1982); William Feaver *When We Were Young* (Thames & Hudson 1977)

Christopher Brooker (active from 1955)

Pen and ink illustrator. He worked with a fine line in a distinctive scribbly style to achieve evocative effects.

Books illustrated include:
Eilis Dillon Aunt Bedelia's Cats (1958)
Patricia Lynch Brogeen and the Princess of Sheen (1955), Cobbler's Luck (1957), Brogeen and the Black Enchanter (1958), The Stone House at Kilgobbin (1959), The Lost Fisherman of Carrigmor (1960)
William Mayne The Rolling Season (1960), The Fishing Party (1960)
Philip Rush Apprentice at Arms (1960)
A.C. Stewart The Boat with Reeds (1960)
A. Stephen Tring Pictures for Sale (1958)

Robert Broomfield (b. 1930)

Born in Old Portslade Village, Sussex. Studied at Brighton College of Arts and Crafts. Visualiser in the creative art department of the S.H. Benson Advertising Agency in London (1955-57). Has worked freelance since 1957 as a designer of greetings cards and posters, cartoonist and illustrator of children's books and educational books (for German and English publishers). He works in pen and watercolour wash or coloured inks and occasionally wood engraving, and considers himself to have been broadly influenced by Thomas Rowlandson and his contemporaries. [Q]

Books illustrated include:
Anon (with additional verses by John Ruskin) Dame Wiggins of Lee and her Seven Wonderful Cats (1963)
Robert Broomfield The Baby Animal ABC (1964), The Toy ABC (1964), Animal Babies (1973), Toys (1974)
Dorothy Clewes The Purple Mountain (1962)
Anita Hewett Mrs Mopple's Washing Line (1966), Mr Faksimily and the Tiger (1967)
Denys Parsons What's Where in London (1961)

References: ICB 3,4; *Good Housekeeping* February 1978

Gordon Frederick Browne (1858-1932)

Worked as Gordon Browne. Born in Surrey. Younger son of illustrator Hablôt Knight Browne*. He studied at Heatherley's School of Art and at the South Kensington Schools where he insisted —contrary to accepted practice—on drawing only from life. He began accepting commissions as an illustrator while still a student (his father had been partly incapacitated by illness in 1867 and money was in short supply), and during his long and prolific career he contributed thousands of drawings to family and children's magazines, and illustrated several hundred books (often for Blackie). For narrative illustration he drew freely in ink with hatched shading of varying intensity accented at points to emphasise composition or action. Although he had originally trained to draw on wood, his style adapted well to reproduction by photomechanical means, and he also worked effectively in halftone. Unlike many minor illustrators, he took great care over the interpretation of his texts, reading every manuscript twice, first to comprehend the plot and again to explore the pictorial possibilities. Painstaking in historical research and detail, he assembled a large reference collection of mainly mid 17th-century arms and weapons. He also sketched constantly from life and, like his contemporary Harry Furniss*, had a remarkable flair for capturing movement, particularly of humans and horses. However, he seemed to underestimate the impact of facial expression in narrative illustration; though he worked hard at 'character' physiognomies, there was a curious uniformity in the rather 'aesthetic' features of his heroes, heroines and children. His humorous drawings sometimes appeared as illustrations for his own comic books written under the pseudonym 'A. Nobody'—here his style was considerably simplified and sometimes contained distinct echoes of the work of Phil May*. Despite his undeniable talent, Browne has never received the critical acclaim accorded to his contemporaries Hugh Thomson* and the Brocks*; this is probably due partly to the fact that he never developed a long-term association with an author of note (as did his father with Charles Dickens), and partly because much of his vast output was published in very cheap editions. Nevertheless on the grounds of energy, competence, reliability, and sheer volume he must be rated among the important illustrators of his time. He lived for many years at Richmond, Surrey. Elected RBA (1891) and RI (1896).

Books illustrated include:

Grant Allen An African Millionaire (1897), Miss Cayley's Adventures (1899), Hilda Wade (1900)

Hans Andersen Fairy Tales (1902)

Sir Edwin Arnold The Book of Good Counsels (1909)

Helen Atteridge Bunty and the Boys (1888), Butterfly Ballads (with others, 1898)

Comtesse d'Aulnoy Fairy Tales (1888)

Alice Banks Chirp and Chatter (1888)

R.D. Blackmore Lorna Doone (1911)

Gordon Browne Hop o' my Thumb (1886), Beauty and the Beast (1887), Nonsense for Somebody (1895), Some More Nonsense (1896), A Nobody's Scrapbook (1900)

Cervantes History of Don Quixote (1921)

Alice Corkran Down the Snow Stairs (1887)

Samuel Rutherford Crockett Surprising Adventures of Sir Toady Lion (1897)

F.J.H. Darton The Merry Tales of the Wise Men of Gotham (1907)

Gordon Browne. 'How now! A rat? Dead, for a ducat, dead!' from *The Shakespeare Story Book* by Mary MacLeod (Wells Gardner, 1902).

Daniel Defoe Robinson Crusoe (1885)

F.H.K. de la Motte Fouqué Sintram and his Companions, and Undine (1896)

Evelyn Everett-Green Dick and Dorrie (1906), Dick and Dorrie at School (1911)

Juliana Horatia Ewing Old Fashioned Fairy Tales (with A.W. Bayes, 1882), The Story of a Short Life (1885), Mary's Meadow (1886), Melchior's Dream (1886), Dandelion Clocks (1887), The Peace Egg and a Christmas Mumming Play (1887), Snapdragons (1888)

B.L. Farjeon Christmas Angel (1885)

William Frederick Farrar Eric or Little by Little (1899), St Winifred's (1900)

G. Manville Fenn Devon Boys (1887), Syd Belton (1891)

Jean Froissart Stories from Froissart (1899)

Thomas Guthrie Paleface and Redskin (1898)

George Halse The Legend of Sir Juvenis (1886)

G.A. Henty Facing Death (1882), True to the Old Flag (1883), By Sheer Pluck (1884), With Clive in India (1884), St George for England (1885), In Freedom's Cause (1885), For Name and Fame (1886), Under Drake's Flag (1887), With Wolfe in Canada (1887), Bonny Prince Charlie (1888), Orange and Green (1888), The Lion of St Mark (1889), With Lee in Virginia (1890), Held Fast for England (1892)

Hitopadesa The Book of Good Counsels (1893)

Silas Hocking One in Charity (1893)

Edwin Hodder Thrown to the World (1885)

Ascott R. Hope The Day after the Holidays (1875), Stories of Old Renown (1883), The Hermit's Apprentice (1886), The Seven Wise Scholars (1887)

Frank Hudson The Origins of Plum Pudding (1889)

Washington Irving Rip van Winkle (1887)

Harry Jones Prince Boohoo and Little Smuts (1896)

William Lancaster The Log of the Flying Fish (1887), The Doctor of the Juliet (1892)

Andrew Lang Prince Prigio (1889), Prince Ricardo of Pantouflia (1893)

Amy Le Feuvre The Buried Ring (1905), Christina and the Boys (1906), Robin's Heritage (1907), Oliver and the Twins (1922)

Mary MacLeod The Shakespeare Story Book (1902)

John Masefield A Book of Discoveries (1910)

Mrs Molesworth Five Minutes' Stories (with others, 1888), Great Uncle Hoot-Toot (with others, 1889), The Red Grange (1891), Stories for Children in Illustration of the Lord's Prayer (1897)

Alice T. Morris Our Wonderful World (nd)

E. Nesbit The Story of the Treasure Seekers (with Lewis Baumer*,

1899), The New Treasure Seekers (with Lewis Baumer*, 1904)
Barry Pain Graeme and Cyril (1893)
Charles Reade The Cloister and the Hearth (with others, 1912)
Talbot Baines Reed My Friend Smith (1889)
W. Clarke Russell Master Rockafeller's Voyage (1891)
George Edmund B. Saintsbury National Rhymes of the Nursery (1897)
Walter Scott Ivanhoe (1893), Guy Mannering (1893), Count Robert of
    Paris (1893)
William Shakespeare Works (8 vols with others, 1888), Macbeth (1899)
R. L Stevenson The Pavilion on the Links (1913)
Jonathan Swift Gulliver's Travels (1886)
Georgina M. Synge Great Grandmama (1891)
William Makepeace Thackeray The Rose and the Ring (1909)
Ethel Turner The Wonder-Child (1901)
Percy Westerman The Young Cavalier (1911)
A Apple Pie (1890)
Dr Jollyboy's ABC (1898)
Fairy Tales from Grimm (1895)

Periodicals: Andy, Atlanta, Aunt Judy's Magazine, Black and White, The Boy's Own Paper, The Captain, Chums, The Girls' Realm, Good Words, The Graphic, Herbert Strang's Annual, The Illustrated London News, The Leisure Hour, Little Folks, The Penny Magazine, Puck, The Quiver, The Strand Magazine.

References: Baker; Bénézit; Doyle BWI, CL; Eyre; Fisher p.172; Harper; Houfe; ICB 1; Johnson & Greutzner; Lewis; Mallalieu; Muir; Sketchley; Thieme & Becker; Thorpe; Vollmer; Wa (1929); Waters; *The Boy's Own Annual* 42 (1919/20); *The Leisure Hour* (1901-02); *The Studio* special (1897-98, 1900-01, 1911).

Thomas Arthur Browne (1872-1910)

Sometimes worked as Tom Browne. Born in Nottingham. Left school at eleven to help support his family. Worked in the Nottingham lace market. Apprenticed to a firm of lithographers (c.1886). Began contributing to *Scraps* around 1889. Moved to London around 1893 and embarked on a full-time career as a comic illustrator, achieving huge success with his strip cartoon tramp *Weary Willie and Tired Tim* in *Chips* (from 1896). From then on he was in great demand as a strip cartoon artist, but also found time for humorous sketches and caricatures, designing cards and advertisements, figure painting, easel painting and establishing a lithographic firm of his own in Nottingham. Browne drew with exceptional facility and panache. He has often been compared to Phil May*—by whom he was almost certainly influenced—but his work was coarser, more mannered and basically more conventional; there are also stylistic echoes of John Hassall*. Working almost entirely for magazines, he was among the most widely known and popular humorous artists of his generation. Elected RBA (1898), RMS (1900), RI (1901). Member of London Sketch Club (President 1907-08).

Books illustrated include:
A. E. Jackson The Simpsons of Coe (frontispiece 1900)
Barry Pain The One Before (1902)
Tom Browne's Clyde Sketchbook (1897)
Tom Browne's Annuals (1904-05)

Periodicals: The Big Budget, The Boy's Own Paper, The Captain, Cassell's Children's Annual, The Chicago Tribune, Chips, Chums, Comic Cuts, Dan Leno's Comic Journal, The Funny Wonder, The Graphic, The Halfpenny Comic, The New York Herald, The New York Times, The Penny Magazine, Pick-me-up, Printer's Pie, Punch, Scraps, The Sketch, The Windsor Magazine.

References: Bénézit; Cuppleditch; Doyle Cl, BWI; Hammerton; Houfe; Johnson & Greutzner; Mallaliu; Vollmer; Waters; C. Wood; Alan Aldridge *The Penguin Book of Comics* (Penguin 1967); A.E. Johnson *Tom Browne RI* (A. & C. Black 1909)

Violet E. Brunton (1878-1951)

Born in Brighouse, Yorkshire. Daughter of Arthur and Annie Brunton, both painters. Studied at Southport School of Art, Liverpool School of Art and the Royal College of Art. Lived in Streatham, London, and later in Chorleywood, Hertfordshire. She specialised in miniature painting, but was also interested in sculpture, wood-carving and numerology. Her illustrations, described by C. Lewis Hind in his introduction to *Ecclesiasticus* as 'decoratively modern', are extremely stylised with varied surface textures and little spatial depth. Elected RMS (1925).

Books illustrated include:
C. Lewis Hind (intro) Ecclesiasticus or The Wisdom of Jesus the Son of Sirach (1927)
Romer Wilson Green Magic (1928), Silver Magic (1929)

References: Bénézit; Johnson & Greutzner; Wa (1929); Waters

Lillian L. Buchanan (active from c.1954)

Illustrator of children's books and gift books; principal illustrator of H.E. Todd's *Bobby Brewster* series.

Books illustrated include:
Enid Blyton The Mystery of the Missing Man (1956), The Mystery of the Strange Messages (1957), The Mystery of Banshee Towers (1966)
Malcolm Saville Four and Twenty Blackbirds (1959)
H.E. Todd Bobby Brewster series (1954)
My Book of Elves and Fairies (with others, nd)
Popular Book for Girls (with others, nd)
The Schoolgirl's Story Book (with others, nd)
Warne's Happy Book for Girls (with others, nd)

Reference: Fisher p.49

Alec Buckels (active 1923-45)

Painter, wood engraver and etcher; illustrator and writer of children's books. Malcolm C. Salaman wrote in *The Studio* of his wood engravings, 'he uses his graver with exquisite sensitiveness to build up an elaborate pictorial statement that shall seem very simple.' However, his children's illustrations in black and white and full colour, though often superficially attractive, were surprisingly erratic in drawing and penmanship. Elected ARE (1924).

Books illustrated include:
Alec Buckels Adventures of Bunny Buffin (1933), Billy Bobtail (1933), Plays for Little Players (1935), Stories of Bunny Buffin (1945)
Walter de la Mare Miss Jemima (1925), Come Hither (1928)
Laurence Housman Turn Again Tales (1930)
Alison Uttley The Adventures of No Ordinary Rabbit (1937), Tales of the Four Pigs and Brock the Badger (1939), Six Tales of the Four Pigs (1941)

Periodical: Joy Street

Alec Buckels. From *Number One Joy Street* (Blackwell, 1923).

References: ICB 1; Johnson & Greutzner; Wa (1929); Waters; *Graven Images* (Scottish Arts Council 1979); *The Studio* special (Spring 1927, Spring 1930)

George Buday (b. 1907)

Born in Kolozsvar, Transylvania (then part of Hungary). Educated at the Presbyterian College, Kolozsvar and the University of Szeged (Hungary); studied art under the watercolourist I. Deak, and as an apprentice in the studios of G. Daday and L. Meczner in the Transylvanian Museum. He exhibited in Hungary from 1924, and also abroad. After becoming acquainted with the work of the University Settlements in the East End of London, he was one of the organisers of the Agrarian Settlement Movement in Hungary and of its later development, the College of Arts, of which he was President until 1938. Appointed lecturer in Graphic Arts at Franz Joseph University (1934). Rome scholar (1936-37). Won travelling scholarship to London (1937) and settled in England. Broadcaster in BBC European service (1941); worked for the Political Warfare Department of the British Foreign Office (1942-45), and was Director of the Hungarian Cultural Institute, London (1948-49).

He began wood engraving in 1928 after his first visit to England and has worked freelance as an illustrator (mainly wood engravings), first in Hungary, from 1931, and subsequently in Britain; he is also a writer on graphic art (e.g. *The History of the Christmas Card*, 1954). In 1953, he acquired a Victorian Albion printing press on which he hand-sets and prints bibliophile booklets and

George Buday. 'The Muses, still with freedom found,/Shall to thy happy coast repair' from *Britannia* (Times Literary Supplement, April 1941).

broadsheets. Having developed an interest in the use of portraiture on book-covers, title pages and frontispieces, he received commissions from Penguin Classics and the Oxford Standard Authors series. He is profoundly interested in folk art and traditional culture, his research into these fields has often formed the basis of his own work. Albert Garrett observes that 'the British school of wood engraving which initially attracted Buday to live in this country, can now justly claim him as one of its masters' (*A History of British Wood Engraving* 1978). Elected ARE (1938), RE (1953), SWE (1954). Member Art Workers Guild (1941). [Q]

Books illustrated include:
George Buday Little Book: Hungarian Folktales (1943), 2nd Little Book (1944), 3rd Little Book: A Christmas Keepsake (1945), 4th Little Book: The Hearth (1947), 5th Little Book: Hungarian Folktales (1948), 6th Little Book: The 'Sentiment'... (1949), 7th Little Book: Old Charms and Spells... (1950), 8th Little Book: The Language of Flowers (1951), 9th Little Book: Graven Adages or Proverbs Illustrated (1952), 10th Little Book: Cries of London, Ancient and Modern (1953), 11th Little Book: The Rules of Etiquette for Ladies and Gentlemen (1954), 12th Little Book: Proverbial Cats and Kittens (1955), Multiple Portraiture (1980)
J.C. Fennessy The Siege of Elsinor (1948)
Edward FitzGerald (trans) The Rubaiyat of Omar Khayyam (1947)
Lewis Gielgud (ed and trans) The Vigil of Venus (1952)
F. Kabraji The Cold Flame (1956)
Arthur Koestler Darkness at Noon (1980)
François Mauriac The Life of Jesus (1937)
Elizabeth Moberly Marian Trilogy (1977)
Joseph Moxon (ed H. Davis and Harry Carter) Mechanick Exercises (1962)
Bill Naughton Pony Boy (1946)
Ovid (trans Godfrey Turton) The Art of Cosmetics (1974)
Alexander Pope Poetical Works (1967)
Alexander Pushkin (trans R. Edmonds) The Queen of Spades and other stories (1962)
Amina Shah (trans) Arabian Fairy Tales (1969)

Periodicals: John O' London's Weekly, Lilliput, London Mercury,
The Times Literary Supplement

References: Garrett BWE, HBWE; Johnson & Greutzner; Vollmer;
Wa (1980); Waters; Curt Visel *Illustration* 63 8 Jahrgang, Heft 1 (April
1971) pp.2-7; G. Ortutay *George Buday's Wood Engravings* (Magyar
Helikon, Budapest 1970)

Percy Bulcock (1877-1914)

Studied at the Liverpool School of Art. Worked
as a black and white artist and lithographer. He
died in Liverpool. In style, his book illustrations
broadly resembled those of his exact contemporary Henry Ospovat*, but his draughtsmanship
was exceptionally weak, and his line inert and
scratchy. His facial types were based on those of
Dante Gabriel Rossetti.

Books illustrated include:
D.G. Rossetti The Blessed Damozel (1900)
Alfred, Lord Tennyson A Dream of Fair Women (1902)

Periodical: The Dome

References: Baker; Houfe; Johnson & Greutzner; Sketchley

René Bull (c.1870-1942)

Born in Dublin. Studied engineering in Paris

René Bull. 'Noureddin enters the Forbidden
Room' from *The Arabian Nights* retold by Gladys
Davidson (Blackie, 1912).

where he met the outstanding humorous draughtsman Caran d'Ache and decided to take up art.
Moved to London to study and soon began contributing to illustrated magazines (1892). As 'special
artist' (from 1896) on *Black and White*, he reported from Armenia, India, the Greco-Turkish
War, Kitchener's Sudan campaign, and the Boer
War (during which he escaped from Ladysmith on
the last train before the seige), augmenting his
on-the-spot sketches with photographs and written descriptions. During World War I, he served
in the RNVR and the Royal Air Force, working
for the Air Ministry after the war. He was a
sleight-of-hand aficionado, and model railway enthusiast with a track circuiting the dining room of
his flat in Baron's Court, London. A capable and
assured draughtsman with a distinct comic talent,
he used his first-hand knowledge of Eastern costume and custom to achieve striking effects in the
richly coloured illustrations for *The Arabian
Nights* and *The Rubaiyat of Omar Khayyam*.
Founder member of the London Sketch Club.

Books illustrated include:
Hans Andersen Fairy Tales (nd)
Jean de la Fontaine Fables (with C. Moore Park*, 1905)
Rose Fyleman A Garland of Roses (1928)
Joel C. Harris Uncle Remus (1906)
A.E. Johnson The Russian Ballet (1913)
P. Mérimée Carmen (1916)
Jonathan Swift Gulliver's Travels (1928)
The Arabian Nights (1912)
Rubaiyat of Omar Khayyam (1913)

Periodicals: Black and White, The Bystander, Cassell's Family
Magazine, Chums, The English Illustrated Magazine, Freeman's
Weekly, Gaiety Magazine, The Graphic, Illustrated Bits, The
Illustrated London News, The Lady's Realm, The London Magazine,
London Opinion, The Ludgate Monthly, Pall Mall Budget, Pearson's
Magazine, Pick-Me-Up, Printer's Pie, The Royal Magazine, St Paul's,
The Sketch, The Strand Magazine, The Tatler, To-Day

References: Cuppleditch; Houfe; Johnson & Greutzner; Peppin;
Thorpe; Waters 2; *The Ludgate* (January 1897); *The Studio* special
(Autumn 1914); Cecil Aldin *Time I Was Dead* (Eyre & Spottiswoode
1934); David Cuppleditch *The John Hassall Lifestyle* (Dilke Press
1980); Pat Hodgson *The War Illustrators* (Osprey 1977); Peter Johnson
Front Line Artists (Cassell 1978)

Anne Bullen (b. 1914)

Animal painter and illustrator. Studied at the
Académie Julian in Paris and at the Chelsea School
of Art. Lived in Dorset. Her book illustrations, in
crayon and pen and ink, were exclusively of horse
subjects.

Books illustrated include:
Anne Bullen Ponycraft (1956), Showing Ponies (1964), Horseman's
    Week End Book (nd), Young Horsebreakers (nd)
Joanna Cannan A Pony for Jean (1936)
Monica Edwards A Wish for a Pony (1947), No Mistaking Corker
    (1947),
The Summer of the Great Secret (1948), The Midnight Horse (1949)
Rosamund Oldfield and Anne Bullen Darkie, the Life Story of a Pony
    (1950)
Ruth Manning-Sanders Mystery at Penmarth (1940)
Diana Pullein Thompson I Wanted a Pony (1946)

References: Wa (1962); *After Alice* (Museum of Childhood catalogue
1977)

Anne Bullen. 'He looked like a dream' from *I Wanted a Pony* by Diana Pullein Thompson (Collins, 1946).

Averil Mary Burleigh (d. 1949)

Studied at Brighton School of Art. Painter of landscapes and figure subjects in watercolour, oil and tempera. Married flower and landscape painter Charles H.H. Burleigh. Elected ASWA (1922), RI (1936), ARWS (1939).

Books illustrated include:
Leolyn L. Everett Thistledown (1927)
John Keats The Poems of John Keats (1911)
William Shakespeare Macbeth (nd), The Merchant of Venice (nd)

References: Bénézit; Johnson & Greutzner; Vollmer; Wa (1948); Waters 1, 2

Philip Burne-Jones (1861-1926)

Son of the celebrated painter and designer Sir Edward Burne-Jones. Educated at Marlborough College and at Oxford. Painter of portraits, fanciful subjects and landscapes; in his later years he gave up painting in favour of drawing and caricature. His book illustrations, which were mostly in pen and ink, sometimes in full colour, were often uneasy juxtapositions of naturalistic reportage and humorous simplification. He lived in London and Rottingdean, Sussex, and eventually committed suicide.

Books illustrated include:
L.C.A. Chamisso de Boncourt Peter Schlemil (1899)

Sir Philip Burne-Jones Dollars and Democracy (1904), With Amy in Brittany (1905)
Maurice Hewlett The Little Iliad (1915)
W. Meinhold The Amber Witch (1895)
Fables by Fal (1898)

References: Bénézit; Houfe; Johnson & Greutzner; Waters; C. Wood

John Mackintosh Burningham (b. 1936)

Works as John Burningham. Born Farnham, Surrey. Studied at the Central School of Arts and Crafts (1956-59). Writer and illustrator of children's books and occasionally designed posters (e.g. for London Transport). Winner of Kate Greenaway Medals for *Borka* (1963) and *Mr Gumpy's Outing* (1970). He works in a wide range of media, sometimes within a single work, as in *Come Away from the Water, Shirley* (1977), where 'reality', shown in line with pale crayon tints, is contrasted with the vivid colour washes of the 'daydream' pages. His imagery is simplified and he sometimes successfully adopts a child-like drawing style to increase the sense of participation of young readers.

Books illustrated include:
John Burningham Borka (1963), Trubloff (1964), Humbert (1965), Harquin (1965), Cannonball Simp (1966), Seasons (1969), Mr Gumpy's Outing (1970), Around the World in Eighty Days (1972), Mr Gumpy's Motor Car (1973), Come Away from the Water, Shirley (1977), The Shopping Basket (1980), Avocado Baby (1982)
Ian Fleming Chitty-Chitty-Bang-Bang (1964)
Letta Shatz The Extraordinary Tug-of-War (1968)

References: Contemporary Authors; Doyle CL; Eyre; Hürlimann; ICB 3, 4; Kirkpatrick; Lewis; *The Junior Bookshelf* vol 28 no 3 (1964)

Edward John Burra (1905-76)

Worked as Edward Burra. Born in London, son of a solicitor. Spent childhood and much of his life in Rye, Sussex. Studied at Chelsea School of Art (1921-23) and at the Royal College of Art (1923-24). In spite of delicate health, he made frequent visits to Paris and the South of France

John Burningham. From his *Harquin. The Fox Who Went Down to the Valley* (Cape, 1967).

Edward Burra. From *The Voyage of Magellan* by
Laurie Lee (John Lehmann, 1948).

(with Paul Nash* in 1930) and in 1934 to Mexico
and America. Member of Unit One, organised by
Nash and including Edward Wadsworth* among
its members (1933). Contributor to the *International Surrealist Exhibition* in London (1936)
and, in the same year, to *Fantastic Art, Dada
Surrealism* in New York. Designer of sets and
costumes for ballet and opera. Burra was an
important English Surrealist in whose work 'the
grotesque and fantastic tradition in Northern
Europe flowered magnificently' (Richard Shone).
He generally worked in a mixture of watercolour
and gouache but also did some wood engravings
and pen and ink drawings. William Feaver writes
of him, 'As a painter, Burra's speciality is sinister
characters and shady transactions in fancy locales.
Huckleberry Finn, one of the few books he has
illustrated, suited his devices.' Elected ARA
(1963); awarded CBE (1971). OBE (1971).

Books illustrated include:
Laurie Lee The Voyage of Magellan (1948)
Mark Twain Huckleberry Finn (1947)
Humbert Wolfe ABC of the Theatre (1934)

References: Bénézit; Chamot, Farr & Butlin; Contemporary Artists;
Johnson & Greutzner; Lewis; Phaidon; Rothenstein; Shone; Vollmer;
Waters; William Feaver *When We Were Young* (Thames & Hudson
1977); Anthony Powell *To Keep the Ball Rolling vol III Messengers of
Day* (Heinemann 1978); John Rothenstein *Edward Burra* (Penguin
1945)

Dorothy Mary L. Burroughes (d. 1963)

Worked as Dorothy Burroughes. Born in London. Studied at the Slade School of Fine Art, at
Heatherley's School of Art and in Germany.
Worked as a painter and poster and lino-cut artist
as well as an illustrator of children's books. Elected RBA (1925).

Books illustrated include:
Dorothy Burroughes Amazing Adventures of Little Brown Bear

(1930), Jack Rabbit (1931), Harris the Hare and his own True Love
(1933), The Home the Moles Built (1939), Niggs, the Little Black
Rabbit (1940), The Pigs Who Sailed Away (1944), The Magic Herb
(1944), The Conceited Frog (1949), Hans Britterman and the Silver
Skates (nd), The Heart of the Ancient Wood (nd), How Nature
Helps You (nd), A Story of the Penguins (nd), The Robin and the
Wren (nd), The Little Gentleman in Black Velvet (nd)
Rose Fyleman Fifty-one New Nursery Rhymes (1931)

References: Johnson & Greutzner; Vollmer; Wa (1929); Waters

Doris Burton (active c.1926-31)

Book illustrator in black and white and full colour
about whom nothing seems to have been recorded.

Books illustrated include:
Sir Harold E. Boulton The Huntress Hag of the Blackwater (1926)
Mrs H.C. Cradock Elizabeth (1930), Barbara and Peter (1931)
Brian Rhys A Book of Ballads (1929)

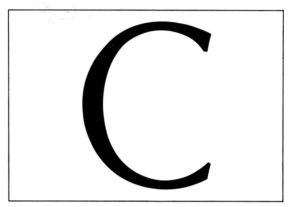

Lindsay Cable. ' "I like reading too," she smiled'
from *Blackie's Children's Annual*, 37th year.

Dion Clayton Calthrop. 'The Satyr' from *Psyche* (Alston Rivers, nd).

W. Lindsay Cable (active 1927-51)

Illustrator, mainly of girls' school stories, in pen and ink, brush and ink, and pencil. Initially, her work was rather reminiscent of fashion plates, but by the 1940s it had become more independent in style, employing a good range of textures and shading.

Books illustrated include:
Enid Blyton The Second Form at St Clare's (1944), Fifth Formers at St
  Clare's (1945), The Naughtiest Girl in the School (1951)
Angela Brazil The School on the Loch (1946), Monitress Merle (1947)
Geoffrey Trease Running Deer (1941)

Periodicals: The Girls' Budget, Little Folks

Edmund G. Caldwell (1852-1930)

Born in Canterbury, Kent. Landscape and animal painter. Lived in London (1881 and 1898), Swanley in Kent (1887), Guildford in Surrey (1890), and Hampstead, London (1902-25).

Books illustrated include:
Maud Brindley Lives of the Fur Folk (1910)
Henry A. Bryden Animals of Africa (1900)
James Percy Fitzpatrick Jock of the Bushveld (1907)
V. Hesketh Pritchard Hunting Camps in Wood and Wilderness
  (1910)

Periodical: The Sporting and Dramatic News

References: Bénézit; Fisher p.158; Houfe; ICB 1; Johnson & Greutzner; Thieme & Becker; Waters; C. Wood

Dion Clayton Calthrop (1875-1937)

Born at Regent's Park, London, into a theatrical family. Educated at St Paul's School. Studied art at St John's Wood School, London and in Paris at Julian's and Colarossi's. During the 1890s, worked freelance as a painter, graphic artist and magazine illustrator. Co-editor of *The Idler* with Sidney Sime*. Later worked as studio assistant to Byam Shaw*. From about 1906, he concentrated on writing and soon made his name as an essayist, novelist and playwright. He also worked as a stage designer. He settled in Dorchester, Dorset, during the late 1920s. As a graphic artist, he never really developed a style of his own; his figures, in particular, tended to be strongly reminiscent of Byam Shaw's. Thorpe considered that he had 'a pleasant sense of fantasy in delicate line': this is best seen in *A Guide to Fairyland* (1905).

Books illustrated include:
Dion Clayton Calthrop A Guide to Fairyland (1905), English Costume
  (4 vols, 1906), Psyche (nd)

Periodicals: The Butterfly, The Dome, The Idler, The Pall Mall
Magazine, Pick-me-up, The Quartier Latin

References: Bénézit; Houfe; Johnson & Greutzner; Thieme & Becker;
Thorpe; Vollmer; Waters 2; WW (1911); *The Studio* special (Autumn
1914); Dion Clayton Calthrop *My Own Trumpet, Being the Story of My
Life* (Hutchinson 1935)

David Young Cameron (1865-1945)

Son of a Scottish minister and brother of Katherine Cameron*. Initially studied art in evening classes at Glasgow School of Art while embarking on a career in commerce, then entered the Royal Institution in Edinburgh (1885), where he took up etching. Appointed Official War Artist to the Canadian Government (1917) and knighted (1924). Appointed King's Painter and Limner in Scotland (1933). He made his name with landscape etchings, paintings and drawings, most often depicting his native Scottish countryside. His style was free and evocative, and remained remarkably consistent throughout his long and successful career. His book illustrations are in a vein very similar to his other work. Elected RE (1895), ROI (1902), RSW (1906), RWS (1915), RSA (1918), RA (1920) and HRSW (1934).

Books illustrated include:
John Buchan The Scholar Gypsies (1896)
R.B. Cunningham-Graham District of Montieth (1930)
E.P. Eardley-Wilmot and F.C. Streatfield Charterhouse, Old and New
  (1895)
Seton P. Gordon Highways and Byways in the Central Highlands
  (1948)
Sir Herbert Maxwell The Story of the Tweed (1905)
Robert Renwick The Barony of Gorbals (1900)

R.L.Stevenson Le Roman du Prince Othon (1896)
Isaak Walton The Compleat Angler (1902)
Sir William Watson The Tomb of Burns (1904)
Gilbert White The Natural History of Selborne (1902)

Periodicals: The Artist, Black and White, Good Words, The Ludgate Quarterly, The Quarto, The Yellow Book

References: Bénézit; Chamot, Farr & Butlin; DNB (1941-50); Guichard; Houfe; Johnson & Greutzner; Vollmer and supp; Wa (1927); Waters; C. Wood; *The OWS Club Volume* 27; *The Studio* 5 (1895), 36 (1905), 44 (1908), 55 (1912), specials (1898-99, 1900-01, Summer 1902, Spring 1905, 1911, Winter 1913, Autumn 1914, 1917, Autumn 1930); *The Etching and Drypoints of Sir D.Y. Cameron* (Print Collectors Club 1947); Arthur M. Hind *The Etchings of D.Y. Cameron* (Halton & Truscott Smith 1924); David Martin *The Glasgow School of Painting* (G. Bell 1897); Frank Rinder *D.Y. Cameron* Jackson Wylie 1932; M.C. Salaman *Modern Masters of Etching* vols 7, 33 (The Studio Series 1925-32)

Katharine Cameron (1874-1965)

Married name: Mrs Arthur Kay. Born Glasgow, sister of Sir D.Y. Cameron*. Studied at Glasgow School of Art and at Colarossi's in Paris. Lived in Stirling and Edinburgh. According to John Russell Taylor, 'her first and real love was landscape and flower painting. She drifted into book illustration because she was asked to, went on illustrating as long as people went on asking her and then returned happily to landscape and flower painting

Katharine Cameron. From *The Water-Babies* by Charles Kingsley (T.C. & E.C. Jack, nd).

with never a second thought, only keeping some of her books, which she never took seriously, on the insistence of her husband.' This lack of enthusiasm for illustration is often apparent in her figure and animal subjects, in which she only occasionally freed herself from schoolgirl whimsy to produce a striking image. Her flower illustration, on the other hand, is crisp, vital and sensitive, and shows the influence of the Glasgow School and the Japanese print. Elected RSW (1897), ARE (1920).

Books illustrated include:
James Aitken In A City Garden (1913)
Katharine Cameron Iain, the Happy Puppy (1934)
Louey Chisholm In Fairyland (1904), The Enchanted Land (1906), Celtic Tales (1910)
Flora Grierson Haunting Edinburgh (1929)
Charles Kingsley The Water-Babies (nd)
Mary Macgregor Stories of King Arthur's Knights (1905)
Amy Steedman Legends and Stories of Italy for Children (1909)
Philip Thomas The Flowers I Love (1916)
Iolo Williams Where the Bee Sucks (1929)
Aucassin and Nicolette (1908)

Periodical: The Yellow Book

References: Bénézit; Chamot, Farr & Butlin; Guichard; Houfe; ICB 1; Johnson & Greutzner; Taylor; Thieme & Becker; Wa (1964); Waters; *The Studio* 17 (1899), 30 (1903-04), 36 (1906), 37 (1906) 60 (1913-14); Walter Shaw Sparrow *Women Painters* (Hodder & Stoughton 1905); H. Wright 'The Etchings of Katharine Cameron' in *International Studio* 75

John F. Campbell (active 1909-c.1930)

Illustrator of boys' adventure stories. He specialised in action-packed scenes painted in watercolour and reproduced in halftone or full colour. He is sometimes confused with John P. Campbell* who was working during the same period. He signed his work 'John F. Campbell'.

Books illustrated include:
Edward Gilliatt Heroes of Modern Crusades (with others, 1909), Heroes of the Elizabethan Age (with others, 1911), Heroes of Modern Africa (with others, 1911), Daring Deeds of the Indian Mutiny (1918)
R.L. Stevenson The Black Arrow (1915)
Percy Westerman Under King Henry's Banner (1914)
The Golden Picture Book of Red Indians (nd)

John Patrick Campbell (active 1900-19)

Occasionally worked as Seaghan MacCathmhaoil. Illustrator and poster designer who lived in Belfast and had no formal art training. He was best known for his decorative illustrations of Celtic songs and legends: these were characterised by heavy outlines enclosing areas of varied, closely drawn texture, and strong contrasts of black and white. He also provided illustrations for some of the Irish text publications of the Gaelic League. In a very different vein, he illustrated a number of school stories by Angela Brazil, which were published by Blackie. For these halftone plates he worked in bodycolour, densely applied to create broad effects of light and shade.

John P. Campbell. 'Saba appears to Finn' from
Celtic Romances (1910).

Books illustrated include:
Angela Brazil The Fortunes of Philippa (1907), The School by the Sea
   (1907), The New Girl at St Chad's (1912), A Harum Scarum
   Schoolgirl (1919)
C. Milligan Fox Four Irish Songs (nd)
Mary A. Hutton The Tain (1907)
Celtic Romances (1910)
The Shanachie (frontis 1903)

Periodical: Uladh

References: Bénézit; Houfe; Thieme & Becker; Waters 2; *The Studio*
48 (1910), special (1911, Autumn 1914)

Estella Louis Michaela Canziani
(1887-1964)

Worked as Estella Canziani. Born in London,
daughter of an Italian civil engineer and portrait
painter Louisa Starr. Studied at Erskine Nichols's
school in South Kensington and at the Royal
Academy Schools (c.1904). Painter, muralist,
writer and illustrator. Collected, painted and
wrote on peasant costumes and crafts. Worked as
a medical illustrator and cast-maker during World
War I. Her book illustrations were in pen and ink,
and watercolour. Elected ARBA (1919), RBA
(1930). Fellow of the Royal Geographical Society
and member of the Tempera Society.

Books illustrated include:
Estella Canziani Costumes, Traditions and Songs of Savoy (1911),
   Through the Appenines and the Lands of the Abruzzi (1928), Round
   about Three Palace Green (1939), Oxford in Pen and Brush (nd)
Walter de la Mare Songs of Childhood (1923)
Eleanor S. Rouhde Oxford's College Gardens (1932)
Eleanor S. Rouhde and Estella Canziani Piedmont (1913)
Elfrida Vipont Good Adventure (1931)

References: Bénézit; Houfe; ICB 1; Johnson & Greutzner; Vollmer;
Wa (1914); Waters; Estella Canziani *Round about Three Palace Green*
(Methuen 1939)

Edward Carrick.
See Edward Anthony Craig

John P. Campbell. ' "Could you do me a
kindness, Miss?" she asked' from *A Harum-
Scarum Schoolgirl* by Angela Brazil (Blackie,
1919).

Anne Gillmore Carter (active 1929-30)

Very little has been recorded about the life of this
artist, who seems to have had an exceptionally
short working career. Her book illustrations consist mainly of wood engravings in a simplified,
somewhat archaic style: an example of the widespread influence of Eric Gill* on illustrators of
the period.

Books illustrated include:
Shaw Desmond Tales of the Little Sisters of Saint Francis (1929)
Laurence Housman Turn Again Tales (with others, 1930)
The Book of Tobit: Bible (1929)

Reference: Johnson & Greutzner

Frederick Carter (1883-1967)

Born in Bradford, Yorkshire; son of a shipping
merchant. Studied civil engineering and sur-
veying, then art in London, Paris and Antwerp
(Académie Royale des Beaux-Arts), and etching
under Frank Short. Winner of three successive
gold medals for book illustration in the National

Competition, South Kensington. Painter, draughtsman, etcher, engraver, and writer on the arts and mysticism. Contributed book reviews to *The Nation*. A friend of fellow symbolist A.O. Spare*, with whom he experimented in automatic drawing during the 1920s. His own drawing style was inspired by Albrecht Dürer and Daniel Vierge and by the poster art of Cheret and Willette; it is characterised by broken, overlapping curved outlines and by high-minded 'significant' imagery in a style that sometimes descends into banality. He lived in Liverpool and later in St John's Wood, London. Elected ARE (1910-16, re-elected 1922).

Books illustrated include:
Thomas Burke 'Will Someone Lead Me to a Pub?' (1936)
Lord Byron Manfred (1929)
Frederick Carter London at Night. A Sketchbook (1914), The Dragon of the Alchemists (1926), Gold Like Glass (1932)
John Gawsworth The Flesh of Cypris (1936)
H. Heine Florentine Nights (1933)
W.J. Tarling Café Royal Cocktail Book (1937)
The Works of Cyril Tourneur (1930)

References: Guichard; Houfe; Johnson & Greutzner; Vollmer; Wa (1962); Waters; Victor Arwas *Alastair* (Thames & Hudson 1979); John Gawsworth *Ten Contemporaries* (Joiner & Steele 1933); *British Print Makers of the 1920s and 1930s* (Michael Parkin Fine Art catalogue, October/November 1974); *The Print Collector's Quarterly* 20

Christopher Chamberlain

See Diana Copley

Charles Henry Chapman (b. 1879)

Born in Thetford, Norfolk. He made humorous drawings in his spare time while apprenticed to an architect; contributed to numerous boys' magazines from 1900. In 1911, he joined the staff of *The Magnet* and succeeded Arthur Clarke* as illustrator of the *Billy Bunter* stories, continuing until *The Magnet* ceased pubication in 1940. He took over as illustrator of the Billy Bunter books after the death of R.J. Macdonald* in 1955. Brian Doyle writes, 'Chapman's graphic pictures of Bunter and the rest of the Greyfriars characters were—and are—superb, and caught the magical atmosphere of Hamilton's writing perfectly'. (*The Who's Who of Children's Literature*).

Books illustrated include:
Frank Richards Backing up Billy Bunter (1955), The Banishing of Billy Bunter (1956), Billy Bunter Afloat (1957), Billy Bunter's Bolt (1957), Billy Bunter the Hiker (1958), Billy Bunter's Bargain (1958), Bunter Comes for Christmas (1959), Bunter Out of Bounds (1959), Bunter Keeps it Dark (1960), Billy Bunter at Butlins (1961), Billy Bunter's Treasure-Hunt (1961), Bunter the Ventriloquist (1961), Billy Bunter's Bodyguard (1962), Bunter the Caravanner (1962), Just Like Bunter (1963), Big Chief Bunter (1963), Bunter the Stowaway (1964), Thanks to Bunter (1964), Bunter the Sportsman (1965), Bunter's Last Fling (1965)

Periodicals: The Big Budget, The Boy's Friend, The Boys' Herald, The Boys' Leader, The Boy's Own Paper, The Captain, Chips, Chums, Comic Cuts, The Daily Graphic, The Dreadnought, The Jester, The Magnet, Marvel, The Penny Pictorial Magazine, Pluck, Scraps, The Scout

References: Doyle BWI, CL; Houfe

Gaynor Chapman (b. 1935)

Born in London. Studied at Epsom School of Art (1951-52), Kingston School of Art (1952-55) and the Royal College of Art (1955-58). Illustrator for the publisher Thames & Hudson (1958-60). Lecturer at Brighton College of Art (1958-63) and visiting lecturer at Kingston Polytechnic, Brighton Polytechnic, Ealing Technical College and Richmond-upon-Thames College. Freelance illustrator, graphic designer and printmaker since 1960. Much of her work has been in graphic design with commissions from London Transport, Air France, BP, Shell, the Central Office of Information, British Travel and Holidays Association, American Express, etc. She was also responsible for a 20 ft mural in the SS *Dover* and for wallpaper designs for ICI. As an illustrator, she often works in colour, using designer's gouache, poster colour, waterproof ink or candle wax and turpentine. *The Luck Child* (1968) was runner-up for the Kate Greenaway Medal. She lives in Surrey. Elected FSIA in 1979.

Books illustrated include:
Hans Andersen The Jumping Match (1973)
Edward Bacon (ed) Vanished Civilizations (1963)
Edward Blishen (ed) Miscellany Two (1965)
Alexis Brown Treasure in Devil's Bay (1962)
M. Burton and W. Shepherd The Wonder Book of Our Earth (c.1960)
Eilis Dillon The Wise Man on the Mountain (1969)
Brothers Grimm The Luck Child (1968)
Mimoko Ishii The Dolls' Day for Yoshiko (1965)
Stuart Piggot (ed) The Dawn of Civilization (with others, 1961)

C.H. Chapman. ' "I won't come!" howled Bunter' from *Big Chief Bunter* by Frank Richards (Cassell, 1963).

Kurt Rowland (ed) Wealth from the Ground (1962), Our Living World
(1964)
Mervyn Skipper The Fooling of King Alexander (1967)
Donald Swann Around the Piano with Donald Swann (1979)
Elfrida Vipont The Story of Christianity in Britain (1960)
Aesop's Fables (1971)

Periodicals: Aerial, The Director, Esso Magazine, Family Magazine,
Homes and Gardens, Living, Radio Times

Michael Alan Charlton (b. 1923)

Works as Michael Charlton. Born in Poole,
Dorset. Studied at Poole School of Art and Edinburgh College of Art. Illustrator of children's
books in black and white and full colour. He
draws fluently using either a pen or a brush and
often creates appropriate surface textures with a
variety of media and techniques. He lives in Dorset.

Books illustrated include:
M.E. Almedingen Land of Muscovy (1971)
Freddy Bloom The Boy Who Couldn't Hear (1977)
Elizabeth Fanshawe Rachel (1975)
Kathleen Fidler The Desperate Journey (1964)
Molly Holden The Unfinished Feud (1970)
Marie Hynds Frog Paper (1977), The House of the Future (1977), The
Mint Market (1977), Oliver's Photo (1977)
Susan Lapsley I Am Adopted (1974)
H.W. Longfellow The Song of Hiawatha (1975)
Desmond Skirrow The Case of the Silver Egg (1966)
Rosemary Sutcliff The High Deeds of Finn MacCool (1967)
Guido Waldman I Went to School One Morning (1978)
Jennifer Westwood Gilgamesh and other Babylonian Tales (1968)

Reference: ICB 4

Michael Charlton. From *The Case of the Silver
Egg* by Desmond Skirrow (Bodley Head, 1966).

G.K. Chesterton. 'The Art of Biography/Is
different from Geography./Geography is about
Maps,/But Biography is about Chaps.' from
Biography for Beginners by E.C. Bentley
(Werner Laurie, 1905).

Gilbert Keith Chesterton (1874-1936)

Worked as G.K. Chesterton. Born Campden
Hill, London, son of an estate agent. Studied art
briefly at St John's Wood and at the Slade School
of Fine Art (1892-95). Attended lectures on English literature at University College, London.
Worked as a publisher's assistant and began writing
for magazines. From 1925, he edited his own
paper, *G.K.'s Weekly,* to which Eric Gill* was the
chief contributor of designs. Chesterton illustrated several of his own books in a bold cartoon-
like style. An anthology of his work covering 30
years, *The Coloured Lands* (1938), contains good
examples of his humorous, slightly slapdash style.
(Copies of this book are now extremely rare, since
most of the stock was destroyed in the blitz.) He
also illustrated eleven books by his close friend
Hilaire Belloc.

Books illustrated include:
Hilaire Belloc The Great Inquiry (1903), Emmanuel Burden (1904),
The Green Overcoat (1912), Mr Petrie (1925), The Haunted House

(1926), The Emerald (1926), But Soft, We Are Observed! (1928), The Missing Masterpiece (1929), The Man Who Made Gold (1930), The Postmaster-General (1932), The Hedge and the Hose (1936)
G.K. Chesterton Greybeards at Play (1900), The Club of Queer Trades (1905), The Coloured Lands (1938)
E.C. Bentley Biography for Beginners (1905)
Clerihews Complete (with others, 1951)
Nicolas C. Bentley All Fall Down (1932), The Beastly Birthday Book (1934), Ready Refusals (1935), Die? I Thought I'd Laugh (1936), The Time of my Life (1937), Gammon and Espionage (1938), The Week-End Wants a Guest (1938), The Week-End Worries a Hostess (1938), Le Sport (1939), The Tongue-Tied Canary (1948), Third Party Risk (1953), The Floating Dutchman (1954), How Can You Bear to Be Human? (1957), Book of Birds (1965), The Victorian Scene (1968), Golden Sovereigns (1970)
Lawrence Durrell Stiff Upper Lip (1958), Sauve Qui Peut (1969)
T.S. Eliot Old Possum's Book of Practical Cats (1941)
B. Evans Comfortable Words (1963)
Roy Fuller Poor Roy (1976)
Barbara Hastings Lobby Lobster (1943), Mustapha Monkey (1945)

Born in Kiu-Kiang, China. Studied chemistry at Nanking University, then became local district governor in the provinces of Anhui and Kiangsi. Moved to England (1933). Lecturer in Chinese language and literature at London University. Became full-time painter and writer (1940). Designed costumes and sets for the Sadler's Wells ballet, *The Birds*. Eventually settled in New York. Much of Chiang Yee's creative work had its roots in his fascination with the differences between oriental and western cultures. This was particularly evident in his *Silent Traveller* series, in which he brought Chinese iconography and traditions of draughtsmanship and iconography to European and American environments, often with delightful results. His children's books seem to be mainly Chinese in inspiration and idiom.

Chiang Yee. 'An Imaginary Scot' from his *The Silent Traveller in Edinburgh* (Methuen, 1948).

Books illustrated include:
Chiang Yee Chin-pao and the Giant Pandas (1939), Chin-pao at the Zoo (1941), Lo Cheng. The Boy Who Wouldn't Keep Still (1941), The Men of the Burma Road (1942), Dabbitse (1944), The Story of Ming (1944), Yebbin—A Guest from the Wild (1947), The Silent Traveller in Lakeland (1937), The Silent Traveller in London (1938), The Silent Traveller in War Time (1940), The Silent Traveller in the Yorkshire Dales (1942), The Silent Traveller in Oxford (1944), The Silent Traveller in Edinburgh (1948), The Silent Traveller in New York (1950), The Silent Traveller in Dublin (1953), The Silent Traveller in Paris (1956), The Silent Traveller in Boston (1960), The Silent Traveller in San Francisco (1964)

References: ICB 1,2; Wa (1977); *The Studio* 113 (1937); Chiang Yee *A Chinese Childhood* (Methuen 1940)

Richard Chopping (active 1939-45)

Illustrator of natural history subjects and children's books. Among the former, *Butterflies in Britain*, in the Picture Puffin series, (drawn direct on the litho plate) is handled with assurance and a fine decorative sense. Chopping also contributed nature subjects and other illustrations to the Bantam Picture Book series —these are lively and humorous but sometimes slightly grotesque. *Mr Postlethwaite's Reindeer*, a hardback, is illustrated in line. He designed the dust jackets for Jonathan Cape's editions of the James Bond novels in a detailed surrealist style.

Books illustrated include:
Richard Chopping Butterflies in Britain (1943), A Book of Birds (1944), The Old Woman and the Pedlar (1944), The Tailor and the Mouse (1944), Wild Flowers (1944), Mr Postlethwaite's Reindeer (1945)

Reference: Johnson & Greutzner

Ralph Nicholas Chubb (1892-1960)

Worked as Ralph Chubb. Born in Harpenden, Herts. Educated at St Albans Grammar School. Won a classics scholarship to Cambridge, and, after serving in France during World War I, at the Slade School of Fine Art (1919-22). Landscape

Ralph Chubb. From *A Fable of Love and War* (1925).

and figure painter, poet and mystic. Taught art part-time at Bradfield College (1924-27) and life drawing at St Martin's School of Art (1930-33). He was a close friend of Leon Underwood*, with whom he shared a deep interest in gipsy life and culture, spending much time in gipsy camps. In 1922, Chubb set up a private press and from then on published his own work, mostly in very small hand-bound editions, using wood engraving and later lithography for the illustrations and often also for the text. Many of his designs were striking and romantic, but with unquestionably pederastic overtones. He was a great admirer of William Blake, and his handwritten 'illuminated prophecies' were inspired by him.

Books illustrated include:
Ralph Chubb Manhood (1924), A Fable of Love and War (1925), The Sacrifice of Youth (1925), The Cloud and the Voice (1927), The Book of God's Madness (1928), Songs of Mankind (1930), The Sun Spirit (1931), The Heavenly Cupid (1934), Songs Pastoral and Paradisal (1935), Water-Cherubs (1936), The Secret Country (1939), The Child of Dawn (1948), Flames of Sunrise (1953), Treasure Trove (1957)

Periodical: The Island

References: Bénézit; Garrett BWE, HBWE; Johnson & Greutzner; Vollmer; Wa (1960); Waters; *Book Design and Production* vol 3 no 2 (1960); *The Private Library* vol 3 no 3, vol 3 no 4 (1970); *The Studio* 92 (1926); Ralph Chubb *Woodcuts* (Andrew Block 1928)

James Clark (1858-1943)

Studied at the South Kensington Schools and in Paris. Art examiner for Cambridge Examinations Board and the Government Board of Education. Painter (oil and watercolour), pastel draughtsman, fresco painter, stained glass designer. As an illustrator, Clark concentrated on biblical and religious subjects, for which he drew on his experiences as a traveller in the Holy Land. His work was conventional in treatment and very competently executed; he was one of the relatively small number of illustrators of his generation who completely mastered working for the four-colour process. Elected member NEAC (1886), ROI (1891), RI (1903).

Books illustrated include:
John Bunyan The Pilgrim's Progress (1911)
James Neil Everyday Life in the Holy Land (1913)
The Life of Our Lord (1920)
The Palestine Pictorial Bible (1906)
The Pictorial New Testament (1902)

References: Bénézit; Johnson & Greutzner; Mallalieu; Waters; C. Wood

Henry Patrick Clarke (1889-1931)

Worked as Harry Clarke. Born in Dublin, son of a church decorator and stained glass artist. After working for a Dublin architect (1904-05), he studied briefly in London (1906) and then on a scholarship at the Dublin Metropolitan School of Art

(1910-13) where he specialised in stained glass and won three gold medals for the subject in national competitions. Further scholarships enabled him to study the medieval cathedral windows of France. After returning to Dublin, he worked independently on stained glass commissions from his father's studio, and took over the business on his father's death in 1921. He worked as an occasional book illustrator (mainly for the publisher, Harrap) from 1916, and taught illustration at evening classes at the Metropolitan School of Art (1918-23). He also worked as a mural painter, textile designer and decorator. He died in Switzerland of tuberculosis.

The embellished linear style of his illustrations was clearly inspired by Aubrey Beardsley (whose work he saw at the Irish International Exhibition of 1907). Throughout his illustrative work, decorative elegance was combined with an atmosphere of dark intensity, often enhanced by closely textured surface patterns and dominant areas of black. Like Beardsley, his imagery often contained ingenious sexual allusions, but these were often combined with images drawn from ecclesiatical iconography. Another important influence was *fin-de-siècle* symbolism, and his biographer, Nicola Gordon Bowe, considered him 'the leading symbolist artist of Ireland'. She also drew attention to the 'peculiarly medieval' quality of his mind.

Books illustrated include:
Hans Andersen Fairy Tales (1916)
J.W. von Goethe Faust (1925)
Edgar Allen Poe Tales of Mystery and Imagination (1919)
A.C. Swinburne Selected Poems (1928)
Lettice d'O. Walters The Year's at the Spring (1920)
The Fairy Tales of Charles Perrault (1922)

Periodical: The Golden Hind

References: Bénézit; Houfe; Johnson; Johnson & Greutzner; Peppin; Vollmer; Wa (1934); Waters; *Drawing and Design* (July 1925); *The Studio* 78 (1920), 89 (1925), 90 (1925), special (Autumn 1914, Spring 1922, 1923-24); Nicola Gordon Bowe *Harry Clarke* (Douglas Hyde Gallery catalogue, Dublin 1979)

Harry Clarke. Headpiece from *Faust* by J.W. von Goethe (Harrap, 1925).

Ralph Cleaver (1893-1932)

Brother of Reginald Cleaver*, and like him, worked for *The Graphic* and the *Daily Graphic* in the clean hard linear style favoured by those publications. Thorpe considered him superficially clever but thought that he lacked his brother's fine draughtsmanship.

Books illustrated include:
James Bank The Mating of Clopinda (1909)
Reginald Summerlays Here's Horse Sense (1932)

Periodicals: The Daily Graphic, The Graphic, The Illustrated London News, Judy, Punch, The Spectator

References: Bénézit; Houfe; Thieme & Becker; Thorpe; *The Studio* special (1900-01)

Reginald Thomas Cleaver (d. 1954)

Worked as Reginald Cleaver. Black-and-white illustrator on the staff of *The Graphic* and *The Daily Graphic*. He developed a very distinctive style, replacing cross-hatching with immaculate, almost mechanical shading using parallel lines, which gave an appearance of hardness and polish to the surfaces. His work reproduced perfectly by line block, even on inexpensive paper. Thorpe considered him 'an accurate draughtsman with great mastery of the pen, a clean, sure, open line, a great gift of portraiture and a sense of humour... His early drawings were characterised by less certainty but greater freedom than his later work, from which he eliminated cross-hatching and produced his tones by an almost mechanical shading with parallel lines... His drawings printed perfectly and must have rejoiced the hearts of the printer and the editor.' His few book illustrations were in the same highly accomplished manner as his magazine illustrations.

Books illustrated include:
Reginald Cleaver A Winter Sport Book (1911), Included in the Trip (1921)
Humorous Tales from Rudyard Kipling (1931)

Periodicals: The Daily Graphic, The Graphic, Punch

References: Houfe, Pennell MI, PD; Price; Thorpe; Waters 2

Rene Cloke (active from 1943)

Born Plymouth, Devon. Works as a postcard and greetings card designer, and as an author and illustrator of stories for very young children. Her work has been published principally by the Medici Society, Dixons, Wheaton, Blackie, Collins, Dean, Ward Lock and Warne. Works in black and white line or full colour, mainly depicting nursery animals and pixies. Lives in South London. [Q]

Books illustrated include:
Enid Blyton Mister Meddle's Muddles (1950)
Lewis Carroll Alice in Wonderland (1944), Alice through the Looking-Glass (1950)

Rene Cloke. 'When Brer Fox went down, his weight pulled Brer Rabbit up!' from *Uncle Remus* by Joel Chandler Harris (P.R. Gawthorn, nd).

Rene Cloke Mr Podge of Oaktree Lodge (1943), Chickweed (1946), The Little Roundabout Horse (1955), Tippety Is Snowed Up (1955), Barnaby's Cuckoo Clock (1958), Dumpling Wants a House (1958), The Flying Frog (1958), Merry's New Hat (1958), Tufty Paints his Door (1958), Patrick's Caravan (1958), Paul Piglet Keeps Shop (1959), Popkyn the Pedlar (1959), Snowy for Sale (1961), Adventure in Acorn Wood (1962), The Dragonfly series (8 books, 1965), No Dogs, Please! (1967), Rene Cloke's Bedtime Book (1977)
Joel Chandler Harris Uncle Remus (nd)
Ben Royle Red Riding Hood Goes to the Teddy-Bear's Picnic (1943)
Modwena Sedgwick A Tale for Pebblings Village (1960), A Play for Pebblings Village (1961)
Hans Andersen Fairy Tales (1947)
Beauty and the Beast (1947)
Little Folk's First Book (1964)
Little Folk's Second Book (1966)
My Best Book of Enid Blyton Stories (1980)
Nursery Rhymes (1962)
Nursery Tales (1963)
The Sleeping Beauty (1947)
Truth in a Tale series (1949)

Reference: Cope

Ruth Cobb (active 1902-53)

An illustrator and writer whose books were produced in two distinct phases (1902-11 and 1929-53), separated by a period of nearly 20 years during which she apparently published nothing. In her earlier phase, she gradually emerged from youthful uncertainty and occasional clumsiness, while

Ruth Cobb. 'He seemed to travel with the speed of lightning over the ground' from her *A Wishing Cap* (nd).

her later work, consisting of both children's illustrations and topographical pencil drawings for adults, was, within certain limits, capable and self-assured. Some of her pen and ink children's illustrations resemble those of Joyce Lankester Brisley* in their effective use of outline. Many of her later drawings reveal an interest in historical and vernacular styles, particularly of buildings.

Books illustrated include:
Ruth Cobb Baby Ballads (1911), This Way to London (1936), The Golden Thread (1937), This Way to the Castle (1937), Brown, Jones and Robinson (1937), Adventure at Dial House (1938), Village Story (1945), Country Town Story (1946), A Sussex Highway (1946), Travellers to the Town (1953)
Charles S. Goodsman This Happy Home (1944)
Richard Hunter Dollies (1902), More Dollies (1903), Irene's Christmas Party (1904), Somewhere Street (1933)
Edward Shirley Sea and Sand (1904), The Wander-Voyage (1906), Sinbad the Sailor (1908), Tommy's Adventures in Fairyland (1908), A Trip to Fairyland (1908)
'Mrs Herbert Strang' (ed) The Golden Book for Girls (with others, c.1936)
L.G. Strong Patricia Comes Home (1929), The Old Argo (1931)

Periodicals: The Chatterbox, Playtime Annual, The Prize, Puck, Punch, The Wonderland Annual.

Anthony Colbert (b. 1934)

Born on the Isle of Wight. Studied at West Sussex College of Arts and Crafts, Worthing, on a scholarship. After studio and agency work, he joined the editorial staff of *The Observer,* where he learned about print, layout and design. Freelance illustrator and teacher from 1968. He often uses gouache resist or similar techniques, or makes offset drawings (a form of monoprint)—processes that introduce the possibility of a 'controlled accident' and thus introduce an element of surprise into his work. Publishers include Kestrel, Macmillan and Heron. [Q]

Books illustrated include:
Anne Brontë The Tenant of Wildfell Hall (1969)
Anthony Colbert Amanda Has a Surprise (1971), Amanda Goes Dancing (1972)
Eileen Colwell Round About and Long Ago: Tales from the English Countries (1972), Tales from the Islands (1972)
George Eliot Adam Bede (1969)
Robert Furneaux Volcanoes (1974), Buried and Sunken Treasure (1974)
Maxim Gorky The Spy (1969)
Neil Grant Stagecoaches (1977)
Edward Hyams The Changing Face of England (1973)
D.H. Lawrence The Lost Girl (1969)
Vadim Netchayev Petya and his Dog (1975)
Tony Parker Five Women (1965), People of the Streets (1968)
Jim Riordan Tartar Tales (1977)
H.G. Wells The Research Magnificent (1969)
My England (anthology, 1973)

Anthony Colbert. From *The Research Magnificent* by H.G. Wells (Heron Books, 1969).

Periodicals: Drum, The Guardian, New Society, Nova, The Observer, Radio Times, The Spectator, The Times, The Times Educational Supplement

References: Contemporary Authors; Jacques

Herbert Cole (1867-1930)

Illustrator in black and white and in colour, heraldic expert, bookplate designer, engraver and painter, based in London. Around 1910, he was teaching at Camberwell School of Art with A.S. Hartrick* as a colleague. A capable draughtsman, he was well able to take advantage of photomechanical reproduction. He worked with invention, charm and skill, though not without any outstanding degree of imagination. Sketchley, writing in 1903, regarded Cole as one of a group of graphic artists whose style derived (in intention at least) from the 1860s, while Houfe suggests influences as diverse as Charles Keene (on his early humorous work) and Walter Crane (on his page designs). Echoes of the influential linear style of Cole's contemporary, E.J. Sullivan*, can also be found.

Books illustrated include:
B.H.A. The Village of Eynsford (with Frederick Adcock, 1908)
Richard Barham The Ingoldsby Legends (1903)
William Canton A Child's Book of Warriors (1912)
Herbert Cole Heraldry and Floral Forms Used in Decoration (1922)
Samuel Taylor Coleridge The Rime of the Ancient Mariner (1900)
Edward FitzGerald The Rubaiyat of Omar Khaiyam (1905)
Jean Froissart Chronicles of England, France and Spain (1908)
Christopher Hare The Story of Bayard (1911)
Winifred Hutchinson The Sunset of Heroes (1911)
Walter Raymond The Book of Simple Delights (nd)
Walter Rhys (ed) Fairy-Gold (1906), English Fairy Tales (with R.A. Bell*, 1913)
Sir John Suckling Ballade (1901)
Jonathan Swift Gulliver's Travels (1900)
Queen Mab's Fairy Realm (1901)

Periodicals: Form Fun, The Pall Mall Magazine

References: Bénézit; Houfe; Johnson & Greutzner; Sketchley; Thieme & Becker; Thorpe; A.S. Hartrick A Painter's Pilgrimage through Fifty Years (Cambridge University Press 1939)

Derek Collard (b. 1936)

Born in London. Studied at South East Essex School of Art. Illustrator of children's and educational books, printmaker, painter and lecturer. In his illustrations, he works in pen and ink, sometimes with colour washes. His style is characterised by heavy outlines, often contrasting with fine-lined internal detail.

Books illustrated include:
John Bailey Gods and Men (with others, 1981)
Elisabeth Beresford The Wombles Gift Book (with Margaret Gordon, 1975)
Derek Collard At the Zoo (1977), In the Jungle (1977), In the Park (1977), On the Beach (1977), Opposites (1981)
L.A. Hill Contextualised Vocabulary Tests (1975)
Ann Jungman The Dragon Becomes a Pet (1978), The Dragon in Love (1978), The Dragon Joins the Army (1978), The Dragon of Yong-Wong (1978)
Felicia Law Topics (1975)
Jo Manton The Flying Horses (1977)
Sheila McCullough The Island of Solomon Dee (1980), The Journey

through the Strange Land (1980), The Mystery of the 'Blue Whale' (1980), The Silver Ship (1980)
Walt Morey The Bear of Friday Creek (1971)
Robert Nye Poor Pumpkin (1971)
Philippa Pearce The Squirrel Wife (1971)
Helen Sergeant Danny on the Motorway (1975)

Reference: ICB 4

George Edward Collins (1880-1968)

Son of Charles Collins, painter. Studied at Epsom School of Art, Surrey, and at Lambeth School of Art, London. Taught art at King Edward VI School, Guildford (1911-47). Painter in watercolour and etcher of natural subjects. His black and white illustrations, drawn with a meticulous line, were careful and restrained; his colour work naturalistic and low key. Elected RBA (1905), ARCamA (1915), RCamA (1941).

Books illustrated include:
Patrick Chalmers Green Fields and Fantasy (1934)
John R. Jefferies Wild Life in a Southern County (1937)
Gilbert White The Natural History and Antiquities of Selborne (1911)

References: Bénézit; Johnson & Greutzner; Mallalieu; Vollmer; Waters

Philip Connard (1875-1958)

Born in Southport, Lancashire. While working as a house painter, he attended evening art classes, and won a National Scholarship in textiles to the Royal College of Art. In 1898, he won the British Institution prize and went to Paris to study under Laurens and Constant. After 1901, he taught at Lambeth School of Art. He was a close friend of the landscape painter Wilson Steer. During World War I, he served in the Royal Field Artillery as a captain before becoming official war artist to the Royal Navy (1916-18). Executed murals for the Queen's Dolls' House at Windsor (1924) and for the liner Queen Mary (1935). Keeper of the Royal Academy (1945-49). He did very few book illustrations, and his drawings are described by Thorpe as 'very mannered and very like Reginald Savage*'. Commander of the Royal Victorian Order (1950). Elected NEAC (1909), ARA (1918), RA (1925), RI (1927), ARWS (1933), RWS (1934).

Books illustrated include:
Robert Browning The Statue and the Bust (1900)
Stephen Phillips Marpessa (1901)

Periodicals: The Dome, The Idler, The Quartier Latin

References: Bénézit; Chamot, Farr & Butlin; DNB 1951-60; Houfe; Johnson & Greutzner; Sketchley; Thieme & Becker; Thorpe; Vollmer; Waters; Art Journal (1909); The Studio 85 (1923), special (1923-24); F. Wedmore Some of the Moderns (Virtue 1909)

Diana Heather Copley (b. 1920)

Works as Heather Copley. Born and brought up in Staffordshire. Studied at Clapham School of

Art, London, and at the Royal College of Art. Married Christopher Chamberlain (b.1918, Worthing, Sussex). Served in the Civil Defence during World War II. Part-time lecturer at St Martin's School of Art, London, painter and illustrator. She sometimes collaborated on books with her husband, and their respective contributions (unsigned) are virtually indistinguishable. Adept at pastiche, they adapt their style to fit their subject; thus, the drawings for *Heroes of Greece and Troy* are in the manner of Greek vase paintings, and those for *Tales of Ancient Egypt* recall tomb paintings of that epoch.

Books illustrated include:
Leonard Clark (ed) Drums and Trumpets (1962)
Roger Lancelyn Green Heroes of Greece and Troy (with C. Chamberlain, 1960), Tales of Ancient Egypt (1967)
Eric de Maré London's River (with C. Chamberlain, 1964)

References: ICB 3; Ryder

Harold Copping (1863-1932)

Studied at the Royal Academy Schools and in Paris on a Landseer Scholarship. He was an accomplished illustrator working mainly in colour in a conventional style typical of his period. In Thorpe's opinion: 'Harold Copping's work, capable and honest as it was, does not inspire any great enthusiasm; there are so many artists doing illustrations equally satisfactory in literal translation and equally lacking in strong personal individuality.' To achieve authenticity for his illustrations for the Bible, he travelled in Palestine; the resulting edition of 1910 (known as 'the Copping Bible') was a best-seller and led to many more Bible and Bible story commissions. He also published watercolour sketches made during a trip to Canada. He lived for many years at Sevenoaks, Kent.

Books illustrated include:
Ellinor Adams A Queen among Girls (1900)
Louisa M. Alcott Little Women (1912), Good Wives (1913)
Doris Ashley Children's Stories from Longfellow (with others, nd)
H. Barrow-North Jerry Dodds, Millionaire (c.1898)
John Bunyan The Pilgrim's Progress (1903), Grace Abounding (1905)
Nora Chesson Children's Stories from Tennyson (with others, nd)
Arthur Copping A Journalist in the Holy Land (1911), The Golden Land (1911)
Mary Angela Dickens Children's Stories from Dickens (c.1911)
Charles Dickens A Christmas Carol (1920), Character Sketches from Boz (1924)
John Finnemore Three School Chums (1907)
Eleanor Helme The Perfect Friend (1929)
S. K. Hocking Rex Raynor (nd), Where Duty Lies (nd)
Charles Kingsley Westward Ho! (1903)
S. Kupford Hammond's Hard Lines (1894)
Amy Le Feure Joy Cometh in the Morning (1917)
A. Stronach A Newnham Friendship (nd)
Ethel Thurner Miss Bobbie (1897), The Cub (1915), John of Gaunt (1916), Captain Cub (1917), St Tom and the Dragon (1918), Brigid and the Cub (1919), Laughing Water (1920), King Anne (1921), Jennifer, J. (1922), Nicola Silver (1924), Judy and Punch (1928)
The Bible Story Book (1923)
The Copping Bible (1910)
The Little Child (1914)
My Bible Book (1931)
A Picture ABC Book of Jesus (1956)

LITTLE NELL

Harold Copping. 'Little Nell' from *Children's Stories from Dickens* by Mary Angela Dickens (Raphael Tuck, c.1911).

Periodicals: Black and White, The English Illustrated Boys' Magazine, The Girl's Own Paper, The Girls' Realm, The Harmsworth Magazine, The Leisure Hour, Little Folks, Pearson's Magazine, The Quiver, The Royal Magazine, The Temple Magazine, The Windsor Magazine

References: Bénézit; Doyle BWI; Houfe; ICB 1; Johnson & Greutzner; Thorpe; Vollmer supp; Waters; C. Wood; *The Leisure Hour* photo (1901-02)

Jennie Corbett (active from 1960s)

Author and decorative illustrator, mainly of nature subjects, in pen and ink.

Books illustrated include:
Leonard Clark Four Seasons (1975)
Jennie Corbett How-do-you-do Cookery (1965), How-do-you-do Dogs and Cats (1966), How-do-you-do Gardening (1966), How-do-you-do Indoor Plants (1966), How-do-you-do Sewing (1966), How-do-you-do Garden Birds (1967)
Anita Hewett The Pebble Nest (1965)
David Ross Blackbird (1968)
Alison Uttley The Mouse, the Rabbit and the Little White Hen (1966), Enchantment (1966), The Little Red Fox and the Big Big Tree (1968)

Reference: Fisher p.48

Hilda Cowham (1873-1964)

Married name, Mrs Edgar Lander. Born in Westminster. Studied at Wimbledon School of Art and then at Lambeth School of Art on a scholarship. She won a prize in a competition in *The Studio*. This led to magazine commissions, and her work soon became well known. She was one of the first women artists to work for *Punch*. She often drew with a brush, and her style, almost calligraphic in its simplicity, seemed to reflect the influences of the Japanese woodcut and of Art Nouveau. Many of her halftone illustrations were printed from originals painted in flat colours. Hammerton, writing in 1904, ranked her as a female humorous artist with Edith Farmiloe*, Rosamond Praeger*, Florence Upton* and Alice B. Woodward. She was also a painter of domestic scenes and landscapes, and an etcher, and married watercolour painter and etcher Edgar Lander.

Books illustrated include:
Hilda Cowham Fiddlesticks (1900), Blacklegs (1911), Curly Heads and Long Legs (1914)
A. Golsworthy Ping Pong People (c.1905)
Raymond Jacberns The Record Term (c.1910)
John Lea Willie Wimple's Adventures (1908)
Phyllis Morris The Adventures of Willy and Nilly (1921)
Elsie Player 'Our Generals' (1903)
Our Darling's Own Book (with others, 1912)

Periodicals: Father Tuck's Annual, The Girls' Realm, The Graphic, Little Folks, Moonshine, Pearson's Magazine, Pick-me-up, Playbox Annual, Playtime Annual, Puck, Punch, The Queen, The Royal Magazine, The Sketch, The Sphere, Sunday at Home, Tiny Tots

References: Bénézit; Guichard; Hammerton; Johnson & Greutzner; Mallalieu; Vollmer; Wa (1960); Waters

Hookway Cowles (active 1948-65)

Black and white illustrator of mainly classic adventure stories during the 1950s and 1960s. He worked competently in the sketchy style typical of the period, using vigorous shading to create dramatic tonal contrasts. He illustrated many of the Rider Haggard stories in an edition published by Macdonald.

Books illustrated include:
Alexandre Dumas The Three Musketeers (1950)
H. Rider Haggard Allan Quartermain (1949), The Brethren (1952), Heart of the World (1954), King Solomon's Mines (1956), Ayesha (1956), Cleopatra (1958), Marie (1959), Finished (1962), Maiwa's Revenge (1965), Benita (1965)
G.A. Henty The Cornet of Horse (1953)
Charles Kingsley Westward Ho! (1948)
Walter Scott Kenilworth (1953)
Henry Treece Wickham and the Armada (1959)

Reference: ICB 2

Elijah Albert Cox (1876-1955)

Born in Islington, London. Studied at the People's Palace Technical School in London. Worked as designer for a manufacturing chemist, then as assistant to Frank Brangwyn*. He designed posters for shipping and railway companies, as well as a number of mural panels and painted landscapes. His work as an illustrator clearly shows Brangwyn's influence. Elected RBA (1915), RI (1921), ROI (c.1924).

Books illustrated include:
Charles Kingsley Westward Ho! (1923)

Thomas Babington Macaulay Lays of Ancient Rome (1926)
Percy Westerman A Mystery of the Broads (1930)
Rubaiyat of Omar Khayyam (1944)
Selfridge's Schoolboys' Story Book (with others, nd)

Periodical: The Golden Hind

References: ICB 1; Johnson & Greutzner; Vollmer; Wa (1950); Waters

Edward Anthony Craig (b. 1905)

Worked as Edward Carrick. Born in London, son of Edward Gordon Craig. Lived with his father in Italy 1908-27, with an interval of three years in England during World War I, during which he acted with his grandmother, Ellen Terry, in numerous charity matinées. Returned to England in 1927 and worked in London as a painter, wood engraver, graphic artist, and theatre and film designer. From 1939 he concentrated on film work, becoming a leading art director during the 1940s and 1950s. His pleasant and sometimes striking book illustrations, consisting of wood engravings and pen and ink drawings, dated from the earliest years of his career and showed the influence of his father's ideas.

Books illustrated include:
Edmund Blunden In Summer (1931)
William Davies In Winter (1931)
G.W. Jones The Georgics (1931)
André Maurois A Voyage to the Islands of the Articoles (1928)
Herbert E. Palmer In Autumn (1931)
Edward Selsey So Far So Glad (c.1930)
Edith Sitwell In Spring (1931)

References: Bénézit; Contemporary Authors; Johnson & Greutzner; Vollmer; Waters 2; Wa (1934); *The Studio* special (Spring 1930)

Edward Henry Gordon Craig (1872-1966)

Worked as Edward Gordon Craig. Son of actress Ellen Terry and architect E.W. Godwin, father of Edward Anthony Craig*. After eight years as an actor, he became interested in wood engraving and came under the influence of William Nicholson* and of James Pryde* from whom he learned how to simplify his designs. He travelled in Germany and Italy from 1903 and published a portfolio of etchings in 1908. Thereafter, he combined theatre design and production with writing and engraved illustration. He was an original member of the SWE (1920). Craig was obsessed with the idea of the book as a complete work of art. Paper, printing, page design and binding were of equal importance to him, and he experimented endlessly. He was deeply influenced by Italian Renaissance woodcuts, and in his own work used a variety of techniques, including speckled dot work, white lines combed against flat black area, and the lowering of the black to obtain lighter effects, as in his masterpiece, the illustrations to the Cranach Press edition of *Hamlet*. Above all, his dramatic inheritance and training enabled him to dispose

Edward Gordon Craig. 'Hamlet Greeting the Actors' from *Hamlet* (Cranach Press, 1927).

his forms effectively in space, and the extremely simple sets he designed for his stage productions were paralleled in his illustrations.

Books illustrated include:
Edward Gordon Craig Book of Penny Toys (nd), The Art of the
  Theatre (1905), Books and Theatres (1925)
Chambers MacFall Sir Henry Irving (with others, 1930)
Haldane MacFall The Splendid Wayfaring (with others, 1913)
T.E. Pemberton Ellen Terry and her Sisters (1902)
William Shakespeare The Tragedie of Hamlet (1927)
Hugo von Hofmannsthal The White Fan (1905)
W.B. Yeats Plays for an Irish Theatre (1913)

Periodicals: The Dome, The Marionette, The Mask, The Page

References: Balston EWE, WEMEB; Bliss; Bénézit; Bryan; Garrett BWE; Guichard; Hofer; Houfe; Johnson & Greutzner; Phaidon; Ray; Taylor; Thieme & Becker; Vollmer; Wa (1934); Waters; *The Print Collector's Quarterly* 9; *The Studio* 23 (1901), special (1898-99, Spring 1927, 1927, Spring 1930, Winter 1931); Denis Balet *Edward Gordon Craig* (Heinemann 1966); Edward Gordon Craig *Gordon Craig* (Gollancz 1968), *Index to the Story of My Days* (Hulton Press 1957, new edition with introduction by Peter Holland, Cambridge University Press 1981), *Nothing or the Bookplate* (Chatto & Windus 1924), *Woodcuts and some Words* (Dent 1924); Fletcher & Rood *Edward Gordon Craig* (Society for Theatre Research 1967); Basil Gray *The English Print* (A. & C. Black 1937); Holbrook Jackson *The Printing of Books* (Cassell 1938); Janet Leeper *Edward Gordon Craig* (Penguin 1948); George Nash *Edward Gordon Craig* (HMSO 1967); Enid Rose *Gordon Craig and the Theatre* (Samson Low 1931); Catherine Valogne *Gordon Craig* (Paris 1953)

Dorothy Craigie (b. 1908)

Writer and illustrator of children's books. For her decorative, animated designs, she often uses flat, bright colour.

Books illustrated include:
Ruth Ainsworth Rufty Tufty the Golliwog (1952), Rufty Tufty at the
  Seaside (1954), Rufty Tufty Goes Camping (1956), Rufty Tufty Runs
  Away (1957)
M.E. Atkinson Chimney Cottage (1947)
Dorothy Craigie Summersalts Circus (1947), The Little Balloon
  (1953), Akoo and the Crocodile who Cried (1954), Akoo and the Sad
  Small Elephant (1954), The Little Parrot who Thought He Was a

Pirate (1954), The Saucy Cockle (1955), Tim Hooley's Hero (1957),
  Captain Flint series (1957-60), Tim Hooley's Haunting (1958),
  Nicky and Nigger and the Pirate (1960), Nicky and Nigger Join the
  Circus (1960)
Graham Greene The Little Train (1946), The Little Fire Engine
  (1950), The Little Horse Bus (1952), The Little Steamroller (1953)
Catherine Storr Clever Polly and other stories (1952)

Periodicals: The Sphere, The Tatler

References: Fisher pp. 182-183; ICB 2

Walter Crane (1845-1915)

Born in Liverpool, son of portrait miniaturist Thomas Crane. He was apprenticed (1859-62) to the wood engraver W.J. Linton and was taught to draw on wood by Linton's partner Orrin Smith. He also studied at the Zoological Gardens and attended drawing classes at Heatherley's School of Art. He worked for the engraver and printer Edmund Evans during the 1860s and 1870s, first designing covers for 'yellowbacks' and soon afterwards illustrating the inexpensive children's 'toy' books that established his reputation. They represented the first successful attempt to mass-produce well drawn, designed and printed books in colour for young children. Crane approached their educational function very seriously, using images and detail from a wide range of sources to create imaginative and decorative designs. In use of colour and outline, the books were to some extent influenced by Japanese woodblock prints. He also worked in black and white, illustrating books by Mrs Molesworth in a relatively naturalistic manner, as well as books of poetry with hand-drawn lettering surrounded by drawn images in a manner inspired by William Blake. His creative approach to page design was evident throughout his work, and he was one of the first illustrators to acknowledge the visual unity of the double page spread. Though trained as a draughtsman for wood engraving, he transferred very successfully to working for photomechanical reproduction when this was introduced at the beginning of the 1890s. He continued as a prolific and influential illustrator to the end of his life, further developing his individual vein of fantasy in coloured picture books such as *A Masque of Days* (1901) and *Flowers from Shakespeare*. *The Walter Crane Readers* by Nellie Dale remained in widespread use for many years and must have exercised a formative influence on many artists among the generation that started work in the 1920s and 1930s.

Crane's involvement in the arts encompassed textiles, wallpaper, cards and calendars, tiles, costumes for masques, at least one trades union banner, and easel paintings (mainly of allegorical subjects). He was at the forefront of the Arts and Crafts movement (and his own work had played a significant part in the development of the Aesthetic style of the late 1870s and 1880s). He was first President of the Art Workers' Guild (1884) and President of the Arts and Crafts Exhibition Society (1889). He joined William Morris's Socialist League (1883) and the Fabians (1885). He was part-time Director of Design at Manchester School of Art (1893-97) and Principal of the Royal College of Art (1898-99). Elected RI (1882, resigned 1886), ROI (1893), ARWS (1888), RWS (1899).

Books illustrated include:
H.C. Beeching (ed) A Book of Christmas Verse (1895)
Lucy Crane The Baby's Opera (1877), The Baby's Bouquet (1878), Art and the Formation of Taste (with T. Crane, 1882), Household Stories from the Brothers Grimm (1882), The Baby's Own Aesop (1887)
Walter Crane Toybooks (1865-76), The Quiver of Love (with Kate Greenaway, 1876), New Series of Picture Books (1885-86), The Sirens Three (1886), Legends for Lionel (1887), Flora's Feast (1889), Queen Summer (1892), A Floral Fantasy in an Old English Garden (1898), A Flower Wedding, Described by Two Wallflowers (1905), Flowers from Shakespeare's Garden (1906)
Nellie Dale The Walter Crane Readers (1898-99)
Agnes de Havilland Stories from Memel (1864)
Margaret Deland The Old Garden and other verses (1893)
Mary A. de Morgan The Necklace of Princess Florimunde (1880)
F.S. Ellis The History of Reynard the Fox (1894)
Ennis Graham The Cuckoo Clock (1877)

Walter Crane. From Household Stories from the Brothers Grimm (Macmillan, 1882).

THE ·ALMOND·TREE·

"KYWITT, KYWITT, KYWITT, I CRY,
OH WHAT A BEAUTIFUL BIRD AM I!"

Henry Gilbert King Arthur's Knights (1911), Robin Hood and the Men of the Greenwood (1912), The Knights of the Round Table (1915), Robin Hood and his Merry Men (1915)
E.J. Gould The Children's Plutarch (1906)
Mrs Burton Harrison Folk and Fairy Tales (1885)
Elizabeth Harrison The Vision of Dante (1894)
Nathaniel Hawthorne Transformation (1865), A Wonderbook for Boys and Girls (1892)
Arthur Kelly The Rosebud and other tales (1909)
Charles Lamb A Masque of Days (1901)
Mark Lemon Wait for the End (1866)
Mary MacGregor The Story of Greece (1913)
Theodore Marzials Pan Pipes (1883)
Brothers Mayhew The Magic of Kindness (1869)
J.M.D. Meiklejohn The Golden Primer (2 vols, 1884-85)
Mrs Molesworth Tell Me a Story (1875), Carrots (1876), Grandmother Dear (1878), The Tapestry Room (1879), A Christmas Child (1880), The Adventure of Herr Baby (1881), Rosy (1882), Two Little Waifs (1883), Christmas-Tree Land (1884), Us. An Old Fashioned Story (1885), Four Winds Farm (1886), Little Miss Peggy (1887), A Christmas Posy (1888), The Rectory Children (1889), The Children of the Castle (1890)
William Morris The Story of the Glittering Plain (1894)
Judge Parry (retold by) Don Quixote of La Mancha (1900)
R.E.J. Reid The Book of Wedding Days (1889)
William Shakespeare The Tempest (1893), The Merry Wives of Windsor (1893), Two Gentlemen of Verona (1894)
Edmund Spenser The Faerie Queen (1895), The Shephearde's Calendar (1898)
George Warr (intro) Echoes of Hellas (1887)
Oscar Wilde The Happy Prince and other tales (with P. Jacomb-Hood*, 1888)
J.R. Wise The New Forest (1863), The First of May (1881)
The Turtle Dove's Nest and other nursery rhymes (with others, 1890)

Periodicals: The Argosy, Atalanta, The Churchman's Shilling Magazine, The Clarion, The Commonwealth, The English Illustrated Magazine, Entertaining Things, Every Boy's Magazine, Fun, Good Words, The Graphic, Justice, Little Folks, London Society, Once a Week, The People's Magazine, Punch, The Strand Magazine, Time, Tinsley's Magazine, Woman's World, The Yellow Book

References: Baker; Bénézit; Bland; Crane; DNB (1912-21); Doyle CL; Garrett HBWE; Hardie; Harper; Houfe; ICB 1; Johnson; Johnson & Greutzner; McLean; Mallalieu; Muir; Pennell MI, PD; Peppin; Ray; F. Reid; Taylor; Thieme & Becker; Waters; White; C. Wood; *Art Annual* (Easter 1898); *Artwork* 22 (1930); *The Studio* special (1894, 1897-98, 1899-1900, 1900-01, Autumn 1914, 1917, 1923-24, Autumn 1933); Walter Crane *An Artist's Reminiscences* (Methuen 1907), *The Bases of Design* (G. Bell 1898), *Cartoons for a Cause* (reprinted Journeyman Press 1976), *The Claims of Decorative Art* (Lawrence & Bullen 1892), *Ideals in Art* (G. Bell 1905), *Line and Form* (G. Bell 1900), *Moot Points* (B.T. Batsford 1903); Rodney K. Engen *Walter Crane as a Book Illustrator* Academy 1975; P.G. Konody *The Art of Walter Crane* (G. Bell 1902); Gertrude Massé *A Bibliography of First Editions of Books Illustrated by Walter Crane* (Chelsea Publishing Co 1923); Isobel Spencer *Walter Crane* (Studio Vista 1975)

Charles E. Crombie (active 1904-32)

Caricaturist, also a magazine, postcard and book illustrator, and poster designer. He worked mainly in watercolour.

Books illustrated include:
Allan The Canny Scot (1932)
Charles Crombie Laws of Cricket (1906), Motoritis (1906), Simple Simon and his Friends (1906)
J.H.L. Sherratt The Goblin Gobblers (1910)
W.M. Thackeray Vanity Fair (1924)

Periodicals: The Bystander, The Graphic, The Illustrated London News, Printer's Pie

Reference: Houfe

Cyrus Cincinnato Cuneo (1879-1916)

Born in San Francisco, into an Italian family.

Flyweight boxing champion of San Francisco at the age of 19; used his prize money to travel to Paris. He enrolled at Colarossi's studio and became one of Whistler's trusted students; he also helped to set up an afternoon drawing class with Edith Oenone Somerville* (1899) and partly supported himself by giving boxing lessons. On his marriage to Nell Tenison* in 1903 he settled in London, and there achieved immediate success as an illustrator. He worked regularly for *The Illustrated London News*, contributing drawings of Canada (which he visited to carry out a commission for the Canadian Pacific Railway), a series of 'unconventional portraits' of celebrities, scenes from London's underworld, and a record of four double-page drawings on the occasion of King Edward VII's funeral. He worked with considerable panache in crayon or in black and white oil on board painted without preliminary pencil drafts. During World War I, he painted war subjects in London (and the proceeds from the sale by auction of one of these canvasses paid for two motor ambulances for the front). Elected ROI (1908); member of the Langham Sketch Club.

Books illustrated include:
J.F. Fraser Life's Contrasts (with others, 1908)
C. Gilson The Lost Column (1908)
H. Rider Haggard Nada the Lily (1906), The People of the Mist (1906)
Bessie Marchant A Countess from Canada (1911)
C.G.D. Roberts The Backwoodsman (with others, c.1910)
Herbert Strang A Gentleman at Arms (with T.H. Robinson, 1914)
Robert Vernède The Fair Dominion (1911)
Marriott-Watson The Privateer's (1907)
Claude White and H. Harper Heroes of the Air (1912)
Selfridges Schoolboys' Story Book (with others, nd)

Periodicals: The Girls' Realm, Herbert Strang's Annual, The Illustrated London News, The Pall Mall Magazine, Pearson's Magazine, The Quiver, The Royal Magazine, The Strand Magazine, The Wide World Magazine, The Windsor Magazine.

References: Bénézit; Bradshaw; Cuppleditch, Doyle BWI; Houfe; Johnson & Greutzner; Thieme & Becker; Thorpe; Vollmer; Waters; Terence Cuneo *The Mouse and his Master* (New Cavendish Books 1977)

Terence Tenison Cuneo (b. 1907)

Born in Shepherd's Bush, London, son of illustrators Cyrus Cuneo* and Nell Tenison*. As a child, he was taught painting by his mother, but was later more influenced by his father's work. He studied at the Chelsea School of Art. He was most active as an illustrator during the 1930s when he contributed extensively to a number of magazines and annuals, especially *The Illustrated London News*. During and after World War II he became a successful commercial and popular painter specialising in industrial subjects and machinery (particularly railways), portraits of eminent sitters (including the Queen, Field Marshal Montgomery, and Edward Heath) and fantasy

genre (often featuring anthropomorphised mice). He lives in East Moseley, Surrey.

Books illustrated include:
Terence Cuneo Sheer Nerve (1939), Tanks and How to Draw Them (1943)
Mary England (ed) Warne's Happy Book for Girls (with others, c.1938)
G.G. Jackson Travel Ways (nd)
Scott The Treasure Trail (1931)
Percy Westerman Tales of the Sea (1934), Alan Carr in Command (1943), Engage the Enemy Closely (1944), Secret Country (1944), By Luck and Pluck (1946), Squadron Leader (1946)
The Blue Book for Boys (Hodder & Stoughton, with others nd)
Sea Stories and other stories (Raphael Tuck, with others nd)

Periodicals: Autocar, Blackie's Annual, The Boy's Own Paper, The Champion Annual, Christian Herald, Chums, Good Housekeeping, The Illustrated London News, Little Folks, The London Magazine, The Magnet, Motor, Nash's Magazine, The Oxford Annual, Picture Post, The Strand Magazine, Tuck's Annual, The Wide World Magazine, The Windsor Magazine

References: Doyle BWI; Johnson & Greutzner; Vollmer supp; Wa (1980); Waters; *The Studio* 132 (1946), 148 (1954); Terence Cuneo *The Mouse and his Master* (New Cavendish Books 1977)

Dora Curtis (active 1899-1914)

Figure painter, based in London, about whom little is known. Illustrator of books and magazines for older children. Her work was well drawn and composed, somewhat in the manner of Howard Pyle, but using little imagination.

Books illustrated include:
Stories of King Arthur and the Round Table (1905)
Tales from the Arabian Nights (with T.H. Robinson, 1914)

References: Fisher p.240; Houfe; Johnson & Greutzner

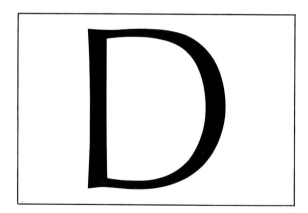

Frank Dadd (1851-1929)

Born in London, cousin of Kate Greenaway. Studied at the South Kensington School of Art and at the Royal Academy Schools. On the staff of *The Illustrated London News* (1878-84) and of *The Graphic* (from 1884). Lived in London, Surrey, and Devon. Painter in oil and watercolour, as well as an illustrator of romantic, biblical and genre subjects and boys' adventure stories in black and white and full colour. He made particularly effective use of body colour. Some of the best examples of his work were the highly finished watercolours published in *Pear's Annual*, *The Graphic* Christmas numbers, and *Holly Leaves*, in which the scenes were often set in the early 19th century.

Books illustrated include:
C.E.M. The Mill in the Valley (1885)
G. Manville Fenn Dick o' the Fens (1888), Quicksilver (1889)
Mrs Molesworth The Abbey by the Sea (1887)
J.H. Newman Lead, Kindly Light (1887)
Max Pemberton Beatrice of Venice (1904)
G.R. Simms Nat Harlowe, Mountebank (1902)

Periodicals: The Boy's Own Paper, The Cornhill Magazine, The Graphic, Holly Leaves, The Illustrated London News, The Leisure Hour, Pear's Annual, The Quiver, The Windsor Magazine

References: Bénézit; Chamot, Farr & Butlin; Houfe; Johnson & Greutzner; Mallalieu; Thieme & Becker; Thorpe; Vollmer supp; Wa (1927); Waters; *Who Was Who* (1924-40); C. Wood; *The Leisure Hour* (photo 1901-02); *The Studio* special (1906)

Eric Fitch Daglish (1894-1966)

Born in London. Studied at Hereford County College and at London and Bonn Universities. Naturalist and illustrator of books on natural history published mainly by Dent (1926-48). He learned wood engraving from his friend Paul Nash* (c.1919) and three of his engravings were exhibited at the opening event of the Society of Wood Engravers in 1920. As a wood engraver, he worked with a very fine white line, depicting animals, birds and plants with a naturalist's sympathy and eye for detail. Fellow engraver Douglas Percy Bliss* praised his careful designs and 'creatures beautifully patterned with thin white lines' but observed that 'in his preoccupation with pattern and colour he neglects form' (*A History of Wood Engraving*). Daglish lived near Paul Nash at Dymchurch in Kent during the 1920s and later near Aylesbury, Buckinghamshire. Elected ARE (1931) but resigned in the same year; member SWE (1922).

Books illustrated include:
Eric Fitch Daglish Marvels in Plant Life (1924), Woodcuts of British Birds (1925), The Book of Garden Animals (1928), Life Story of Birds (1930), Life Story of Beasts (1931), A Nature Calendar (1932), Children's Nature Series (1932-34), Open Air Library (1932-38), The Dog Owner's Guide (1933), Animals in Black and White (1936), The Junior Bird Watcher (1936), The Book of the Dachsund (1937), Birds of the British Isles (1948), The Dog Breeder's Annual (1951), Enjoying the Country (1952), The Pet-Keeper's Manual (1958), The Beagle (1961), Dog Breeding and Management (1962), The Basset Hound (1964)
J.H.C. Fabre Animal Life in Field and Garden (1926)
Edward Grey Fly Fishing (1930)
H.T. Massingham Birds of the Sea-Shore (1931)
E.M. Nicholson Birds in England (1926)
P.E. Thomas The South Country (1932)
Henry David Thoreau Walden (1927)
Izaak Walton The Compleat Angler (1927)
Gilbert White The Natural History of Selborne (1929)

Periodicals: Form, The Woodcut

References: Balston EWE, WEMEB; Bliss; ICB 1, 2; Johnson &

C. Reginald Dalby. From *Tank Engine Thomas Again* by Revd W. Awdry (Kaye & Ward, 1949).

Greutzner; Vollmer; Wa (1970); Waters; *The Print Collector's Quarterly* vol 17; *The Studio* special (Spring 1927, Spring 1931); *Graven Images* (Scottish Arts Council 1979)

C. Reginald Dalby (b. 1904)

Born in Leicester. Studied at Leicester College of Art (1917-21). He worked as a commercial designer for Victor Ward (1921-26) before becoming a freelance commercial artist (1926-40). During World War II, he served in the Royal Air Force and in intelligence. In 1946, he returned to commercial and fine art work. He was the illustrator of the first ten of the popular 'Engine Books' written by Reverend W. Awdry and published by Edmund Ward, and his clear, descriptive, full-colour plates made a significant contribution to the early success of the series. He is currently writing an autobiographical fantasy. [Q]

Books illustrated include:
Revd W. Awdry The Three Railway Engines (1945), Thomas the Tank Engine (1946), James the Red Engine (1948), Tank Engine Thomas Again (1949), Troublesome Engines (1950), Henry the Green Engine (1951), Toby the Tram Engine (1952), Gordon the Big Engine (1953), Edward the Blue Engine (1954), Four Little Engines (1955), Percy the Small Engine (1956)
C. Reginald Dalby Tales of Flitterwick Harbour (1955)
R.P. Littlewood Quentos Illustrados (1974)

Reference: Fisher p.344

Anne Dalton (b. 1948)

Born in London. Studied at Camberwell School of Art and Hornsey College of Art, and later taught part-time at a South London school. She works in a fine pen line or in full colour in considerable detail, often adapting her imagery from medieval manuscripts or paintings.

Books illustrated include:
Penelope Lively Boy Without a Name (1975)
James Reeves The Shadow of the Hawk (1975)
Hilary Seton The Stonemason's Boy (1975)
Richard Barber Tournaments (1978)

Reference: ICB 4

Biddy Darlow (b. 1910)

Married name: Mrs Richard Haslam. Born in Maidenhead, Berkshire. Studied at the Royal College of Art, Académie Ranson in Paris, Chelsea School of Art, and the City and Guilds School of Art. Taught at the Ruskin School of Drawing, Oxford (1934-35), Dartington Hall Senior School (1936-39) and Bath Academy (1945-48). Chairman of Oxford Art Society. Printmaker, painter in oil and watercolour, and book illustrator. Her work displays a well-developed decorative sense and a firm touch reflecting the disciplines of etching and wood-engraving. In *Fifteen Old Nursery Rhymes* she made effective use of lino prints. [Q]

Books illustrated include:
Biddy Darlow Fifteen Nursery Rhymes with New Linocuts by Biddy Darlow (1935), Shakespeare's Lady of the Sonnets (1974)
Elizabeth Hamilton The Year Returns (1952)

Reference: *The Studio* special (Autumn 1938)

Howard Davie (active 1914-35)

Nothing appears to have been recorded about the life or career of this illustrator. He seems to have worked only for the publisher Raphael Tuck. His illustrations consist mainly of watercolours executed with great neatness and precision, which are consequently well suited to being reproduced. His black and white drawings have controlled, regular

Howard Davie. 'The Eldest of the Nymphs went down, and into a dark cavern' from *The Heroes of Greek Fairy Tales* by Charles Kingsley (Raphael Tuck, 1941).

shading, rather in the manner of Linley Sambourne.

Books illustrated include:
Charles Kingsley The Heroes of Greek Fairy Tales (1924)
Alfred Miles Brave Deeds by Brave Men (with others, 1935)
E. Nesbit and Doris Ashley Children's Stories from English History (with others, 1914)
Lilia Romano Children's Stories from Italian Fairy Tales and Legends (1921)
Rose Yeatman Woolf The Seven Champions of Christendom (nd)

Muriel Dawson (active 1920-62)

Studied at the Royal College of Art. Watercolour painter as well as a book illustrator in pen and ink, watercolour and gouache. Her pleasant, freely drawn sketches of children in *Wonderful Days* (1929) were typical of their period.

Books illustrated include:
Muriel Dawson My Book of Nursery Rhymes (1944), Another Lovely Book of Nursery Rhymes (1945), Happy Days (1945)
Muriel Dawson and Clare Dawson The Childhood of Jesus (1962)
Charles Kingsley The Water Babies (1920)
Austin Latham Wonderful Days (1929)
The Rose Fyleman Birthday Book (with Margaret Tarrant*, 1932)

Reference: Waters

Jessie Mabel Dearmer (1872-1915)

Worked as Mabel Dearmer. Maiden name: Jessica Mabel White. Born London. Studied portrait painting under Professor Herkomer at Bushey. Married Reverend Percy Dearmer, also a writer. Dramatist and designer of book plates and posters, as well as author and illustrator of popular children's books. She was an early friend of Laurence Housman* who considered that 'in her beginnings [she] was one of the most amusing people I have ever met... She had social ambitions and liked to be surrounded by an admiring crowd; probably even then she did not know that the charm of her work lay not in it cleverness but in its exuberant spirits and simplicity... She became 'good' and it did not improve her for it diminished her sense of humour and still more the unconscious comedy of her behaviour.' (*The Unexpected Years*, 1937). Her illustrations in black and white and full colour have a pleasant liveliness and period quality. She died of enteric fever while attached to the Stobart Hospital Mission in Serbia during World War I.

Books illustrated include:
Mabel Dearmer Roundabout Rhymes (1898), The Book of Penny Toys (1899), The Noah's Ark Geography (1900), The Noisy Years (1902), The Orangery. A Comedy of Tears (1904), The Difficult Way (1905), A Child's Life of Christ (1906), Gervase (1909), Non Pilgrim: a Play... (1909), The Playmate: a Christmas Mystery (1910), The Soul of the World (1911), The Dreamer: a Poetic Drama (1912), The Cockyolly Bird. The book of the play (1914), Brer Rabbit and Mr Fox (1914), Letters from a Field Hospital (1915), Don Quixote. A Romantic Dream (nd)
Laurence Housman The Seven Young Goslings (1899)
Evelyn Sharp Wymps (1897), All the Way to Fairyland (1898)

Periodical: The Yellow Book

Jean de Bosschère. 'She meant to keep her there until she had grown bigger and fatter.' From his *Beasts and Men, folk tales collected in Flanders* (Heinemann, 1918).

References: Bénézit; Houfe; Thieme & Becker; WW (1914); *The Poster* vol 2 no 7 (1899); *The Studio* special (1897-98); Laurence Housman *The Unexpected Years* (Jonathan Cape 1937)

Jean de Bosschère (1878-1953)

Born in Uccle, Belgium, son of a botanist. Studied at the Beaux Arts d'Anvers. A man of wide talents and culture, he was a poet, novelist and critic, painter, etcher, book illustrator and binder, a collector of fine books and had a particular interest in archaeology and history. Until 1915, he worked as a writer and artist in Paris and Brussels, where his friends included the writers Max Elskamp, Andres Suarez, Paul Claudel and Paul Valéry. In 1915, he arrived almost penniless in Britain and taught French and Latin at a school in Greenwich. He was soon moving in *avant-garde* circles, with T.S. Eliot and Ezra Pound among his friends. He lived in Hampstead in North London and Cranley in Surrey, before returning to the continent probably in 1920. For the next five years (1920-25), he lived mainly in Italy, then moved to Paris (1926) and in 1929 settled on a substantial estate at Vulaines, near Fontainebleau, where he built himself a villa and surrounded himself with paintings and rare books, pheasants and peacocks. He became a French citizen in 1951.

De Bosschère had a particularly lively sense of the relationship between verbal and visual images, and his own poems were almost always accompanied by paintings, etchings or drawings inspired by the same theme. The first book that he both wrote and illustrated, *Béâle-Gyne*, was published in 1909 and he began illustrating the works of others only in 1917 during his period in England. Between 1916 and 1942, a substantial amount of his work was published by British publishers, particularly by Heinemann, John Lane and the Fortune Press. His graphic work was remarkably individual, although it has been compared with the work of Aubrey Beardsley (in the case of his children's books) or even with paintings by 14th and 15th century Flemish artists. His illustrations for his own poems were often abstract and informal, reflecting something of the widespread interest in the subconscious that was playing an important part in Dadaism and the Surrealist movement at the same time; there were also echoes of Cubism and of Symbolism. De Bosschère once commented that he preferred line drawings to be integrated with the text so that the general homogeneity of the book remained undisturbed, *(The Bookman, 1920)*. His own illustrations were reproduced by a variety of means, including etchings and full colour plates, while in *Job Le Pauvre* (1923), the line block illustrations were printed on brightly coloured pages distributed through the text.

Books illustrated include:
E. & J. Anthony The Fairies Up-to-Date (1925)
Marcel Ayme The Green Mare (1938)
Boccaccio The Decameron (1930)
Cervantes The History of Don Quixote de la Mancha (1922)
Honoré de Balzac Ten Droll Tales (1926)
Jean de Bosschère 12 Occupations (1916), The Closed Door *(translated by F.S. Flint 1917)*, Beasts and Men (ed, 1918), The City Curious (1920), Weird Islands (1921), Job Le Pauvre (1923), The House of Forsaken Hope (1942)
Gustave Flaubert The First Temptation of St Anthony (1924)
P. Louÿs The Songs of Bilitis (1933)
W. Bashyr Pickard The Adventures of Alcassini (1936)
Plato The Symposium (1932)
May Sinclair Uncanny Stories (1923)
Straton Strato's Boyish Muse (1932)
Jonathan Swift Gulliver's Travels into Lilliput and Brobdingnag (1920)
Christmas Tales of Flanders (1917)
The Golden Asse of Lucius Apuleius (1923)
The Love Books of Ovid (1925)

Periodicals: The Little Review, The Monthly Chapbook, The New Coterie, Reveille

References: Bénézit; ICB 1; Johnson; Peppin; Waters 2; Vollmer; *The Bookman* (Christmas 1920); *The Private Library* vol 4 no 3 (1971); *The Studio* 78 (1920); *The Times Literary Supplement* (13th September 1917); S. Putnam *The World of Jean de Bosschère* (Fortune Press 1932); M. Sinclair (intro) *The Closed Door* by Jean de Bosschère (Bodley Head 1917)

Stephen Baghot De La Bere (1877-1927)

Born Leicestershire. Educated at Ilkley College, Yorkshire. Studied in Leicester and at the Westminster School of Art. Lived in Kensington, London. Watercolour painter and illustrator. The heavy black outlines and flat washes of his coloured book illustrations were clearly influenced by the work of fellow London Sketch Club member,

John Hassall*. He was a close friend of Edmund Dulac* who considered that De La Bere's work work 'foreshadowed that of Klee'. In his black and white work, he experimented with different techniques in hatching, with curious and rather obtrusive effects. Elected RI (1908).

Books illustrated include:
Cervantes Adventures of Don Quixote (1905), The Life of Lazarillo de Tomes (1908)
A.R. Hope Moncrieff The Adventures of Punch (1905)
Jonathan Swift Gulliver's Travels (1904)

Periodical: The Illustrated London News

References: Houfe; Johnson; Johnson & Greutzner; Vollmer; Waters; *The Studio* 30 (1904); Colin White *Edmund Dulac* (Studio Vista 1976)

Thomas C. Derrick (1885-1954)

Born Bristol. Studied at the Royal College of Art, London, where he later taught decorative painting. During World War I, he commissioned a series of lithographic prints by prominent artists for *British Work* and *British Ideals*. A regular contributor to *Punch* and illustrated books and ephemera for the St Dominic's Press. His illustrations were characterised by a taut, energetic line; he was adept at transposing medieval imagery into a modern decorative idiom, and his treatment of contemporary themes was stylish and witty.

Books illustrated include:
Cyril Argentine Alington Cautionary Catches (1931)
Hilaire Belloc Nine Nines (1931)
Ambrose Bierce Babble Sketches (1930)
Boccaccio The Decameron (1920)
G.K. Chesterton The Turkey and the Turk (1930)
Richard Dark Shakespeare (1931), The Hilarious Universe (1932), Jobs for Jane (1934)
Jean de La Fontaine Les Fables (1910)
Richard Haklyut The Principal Navigations...of the English Nation (1927)
C.E.M. Joad The Untutored Townsman's Invasion of the Country (1946)
Vincent McNabb God's Book (1935)
Stephen L. Robertson The Shropshire Racket (1937)
Frederick S. Thacker Kennet Country (1932)
Arthur Tooth Here Begynneth ye Storie of ye Palmerman (1914)
Everyman (Dent 1927)
The Muses (1933)
The Prodigal Son and other Parables (1931)

Periodicals: The London Mercury, Punch, Time and Tide

References: Balston WEMEB; Houfe; ICB 1; Johnson & Greutzner; Price; Vollmer; Wa (1954); Waters 1, 2; *The Studio* special (Winter 1931, Autumn 1938)

Charles Maurice (1883-1908) and Edward Julius Detmold (1883-1957)

Worked as Maurice and Julius Detmold. Twins born in Putney and privately educated by an uncle. They studied animal life in the Zoological Gardens and worked in close association, painting, drawing and etching bird and animal subjects. They

E.J. Detmold. 'The Spider and the Wasp' from *Rainbow Houses for Boys and Girls* built by Arthur Vine Hall (Cape, 1923).

collaborated on several books before Charles Maurice ended his life by inhaling chloroform in 1908. Edward Julius went on to become one of the most interesting of the gift book illustrators, specialising in animals and plants, which were drawn with exactitude and sympathy, and often placed in fantastic architectural or landscape settings. In its delicacy of outline and subtle colour harmonies, his work shows the influence of oriental miniature painting. In the early 1920s, he retired to Montgomeryshire, and eventually committed suicide himself. Both brothers were elected ARE (1905), but resigned a few months after.

Books illustrated by Edward Julius Detmold include:
Edward Julius Detmold The Fables of Aesop (1909)
Florence E. Dugdale (Mrs Thomas Hardy) The Book of Baby Beasts (with others, 1911), The Book of Baby Birds (with others, 1912), The Book of Baby Pets (with others, 1915)
Joan H.C. Fabre Fabre's Book of Insects (1921)
Arthur V. Hall Rainbow Houses for Boys and Girls (1923)
William H. Hudson Birds in Town and Village (1923)
Charles J. Kaberry The Book of Baby Dogs (1915), Our Little Neighbours (1921)
Rudyard Kipling The Jungle Book (with Charles Maurice Detmold, 1908)
Camille Lemonnier Birds and Beasts (1911)
M.P.M.B. Maeterlinck The Life of the Bee (1911), Hours of Gladness (1912)
Pictures from Birdland (with Charles Maurice Detmold, 1899)
Princess Mary's Gift Book (with others, nd)
Tales from the Thousand and One Nights (1924)

Periodical: The Illustrated London News

References: Bénézit; Guichard; Houfe; ICB 1; Johnson; Johnson &

Greutzner; Mallalieu; Peppin; Thieme & Becker; Vollmer; Wa (1934); Waters 1, 2; C. Wood; *The Print Collector's Quarterly* 9; *The Studio* 51 (1911); E.J. Detmold *Life* (Dent 1921); David Larkin *The Fantastic Creatures of Edward Julius Detmold* (Pan 1976), *The Fantastic Kingdom* (Ballantine 1974)

Carolyn Dinan (active from 1969)

Illustrator of children's books principally for Faber & Faber.

Books illustrated include:
Joy Allen Boots for Charlie (1975)
Helen Cresswell At the Stroke of Midnight (1973), A Kingdom of Riches (1981)
Joyce Gard Handysides Shall Not Fall (1975)
Geraldine Kaye Tim and the Red Indian Headdress (1973)
Gene Kemp Tamworth Pig Saves the Trees (1973), Tamworth Pig and the Litter (1975), Ducks and Dragons (1980), Dog Days and Cat Naps (1980) The Clock Tower Ghost (1981)
Janet McNeill Umbrella Thursday (1969)
Pamela Oldfield Melanie Brown Climbs a Tree   (1972)
Annie Schmidt Bob and Jilly (1977)
Robin Stemp Guy and the Flowering Plum (1980)
Catherine Storr Puss and Cat (1969)
Joan Tate Jock and the Rock Cakes (1973)
Rosemary Weir Uncle Barny and the Sleep-Destroyer (1974), Uncle Barny and the Sleep-Drink (1977)

Mary Dinsdale (active from 1963)

Born in Guildford, Surrey. Studied at Guildford School of Art (1936-39). Began drawing for magazines in 1945 and has illustrated numerous children's and educational books.

Books illustrated include:
Mary Cockett Strange Valley (1967), Frankie's Country Day (1968),

Mary Dinsdale. 'Mrs Willy's Dog' from *The Lost Money* by Mary Cockett (Macmillan, 1968).

The Lost Money (1968), The Wedding Tea (1970), The Marvellous Stick (1972), Monster on the River (1979)
Lettice Cooper Bob-a-Job (1963)
Marjorie Darke Kipper's Turn (1976)
Meindert de Jong The Easter Cat (1972)
James Elliot Living in Hospital (1975)
Kathleen Fidler Turk the Border Collie (1975)
Geraldine Kaye Joanna All Alone (1974)
Anne Knowles Flag (1976)
Elinor Lyon Echo Valley (1966)
Sheila McCullagh Princess Ugly-Face (1976)
Margaret Mahy The Pirate Uncle (1977)
William Mayne Robin's Real Engine (1972)
Joan Phipson Hide Till Daytime (1977)
Pamela Rogers Sometimes Stumps (1975)
Noel Streatfeild Ballet Shoes for Anna (1972)
Joan Tate Ben and Annie (1963), The Ball and the Tree House (1969)
Jill Paton Walsh The Dawnstone (1973)
Ursula Moray Williams Man on a Steeple (1971)

Periodicals: Argosy, Economist, Good Housekeeping, Lilliput, Radio Times, The Strand Magazine

References: ICB 4; Usherwood

Arthur A. Dixon (active 1893-1920)

Figure painter and illustrator who lived in London, Sussex and Hertfordshire. His book illustrations,

A.A. Dixon. 'The Beginning of Friendship' from *The Red Knight* by G.I. Witham (Blackie, 1911).

mainly in full colour or half tone, were conventional and prosaic with sentimental overtones, but generally competent.

Books illustrated include:
Doris Ashley Children's Stories from Longfellow (nd), Tales of King Arthur and the Knights of the Round Table (nd)
Angela Brazil The Nicest Girl in the School (nd)
Frances Browne Granny's Wonderful Chair (nd)
Nora Chesson Children's Stories from Tennyson (nd)
Mrs Craik A Noble Life (1912)
Charles Dickens The Holly Tree (1899), Child Characters from Dickens (1905), American Notes (1912)
Evelyn Everett-Green The King's Butterfly (1900), A Princess's Token (1902), In a Land of Beasts (1906)
Mrs Gaskell Cranford (1906), North and South (1910)
Wilhelm Hauff Fairy Tales (1910)
Washington Irving Christmas at Bracebridge Hall (1905), Tales of the Alhambra (with H.M. Brock*, 1923)
C.M.D. Jones The Candle of the North (1924)
John Keats Poetical Works (nd)
Charles Kingsley The Water Babies (1903)
E.F.L. Laboulaye Fairy Tales (1909)
Andrew Lang Tales of a Fairy Court (1907)
Henry Longfellow The Courtship of Miles Standish (1906), Evangeline (nd)
Emma Marshall Cross Purposes (1900)
Mrs Molesworth The Mystery of the Pinewood (1903)
Dorothea Moore Terry the Girl Guide (1912)
Elsie Oxenham Schoolgirls and Scouts (1914), The Abbey Girls (1920)
Seraphima Pulman Children's Stories from Russian Fairy Tales and Legends (1917)
Alfred, Lord Tennyson Complete Works (with others, nd), Poems (with others, nd)
William Makepeace Thackeray The History of Henry Esmond (1903)
T.W. Wilson The New Testament Story (nd), Stories from the Bible (1914)
G.I. Witham The Red Knight (1911)
May Wynne When Auntie Lil Took Charge (nd)

Periodicals: Collins Children's Annual, Pearson's Magazine, Tuck's Annual

References: ICB 1; Johnson & Greutzner; Thieme & Becker; Waters; C. Wood

Andrew Dodds (b. 1927)

Born Gullane, Scotland, and grew up in Essex. Studied at North East Technical College and School of Art, and at the Central School of Arts and Crafts (1947-50). Lecturer at St Martin's School of Art (1950-70), and subsequently Principal Lecturer in the Department of Art and Design, Suffolk College. Like a number of graphic artists of the post-war generation, he used the constructional devices of the Euston Road School of Artists (measuring points, direction lines, etc.) mainly for their decorative effect. His illustrations are based on fact rather than fantasy, and are marked by a feeling for well-ordered design. Publishers include Nelson, Dent, Longmans and Michael Joseph. [Q]

Books illustrated include:
Eric Allen Smitty and the Plural of Cactus (1963), Smitty and the Egyptian Cat (1966)
Richard Armstrong Island Odyssey (1963), The Big Sea (1964)
Charles Edwin Benham Essex Ballads (1960)
Christopher Hibbert London (1969)
Charles Loewenthal London: Biography of a city (1969)
Joan Morgan The Casebook of Capability Morgan (1965)
Bill Naughton A Roof Over Your Head (1967)
Eva Nendick Silver Bells and Cockle Shells (1971)
'Miss Read' Country Bunch (1963), Hob and the Horse Bat (1965)

Andrew Dodds. From *Essex Ballads* by Charles Benham (Benham & Co, 1960).

Philip Reder Epitaphs (1969)
L.E. Snellgrove From Kitty Hawk to Outer Space (1960)
Wynford Vaughan-Thomas Madly in all Directions (1967)
Voldemar Veedam and Carl V. Wall Sailing to Freedom (1961)
Marjorie Ward The Blessed Trade (1971)
Heat (Allied Ironfounders 1952)

Periodicals: Homes and Gardens, Radio Times

References: Driver; Ryder; Usherwood; Wa (1980)

James H. Dowd (1884-1956)

Draughtsman, etcher and painter, particularly known for his depictions of children. *Important People* and *People of Importance*, collections of fluent, stylish pencil drawings of children and babies, were widely admired and had considerable influence during the 1930s. He began contributing to *Punch* in 1906 and later became the magazine's first film cartoonist, until he was succeeded by R.S. Sherriffs* in 1948. He lived in London.

Books illustrated include:
James H. Dowd The Doings of Donovan in and out of Hospital (1918)
John Drinkwater Robinson of England (1937)
Brenda E. Spender Important People (1930), People of Importance (1934), Serious Business (1937)

Periodicals: The Graphic, Punch

References: Houfe; Johnson & Greutzner; Price; Wa (1934); Waters;

Apollo 10 (1929); William Feaver *Masters of Caricature* (Weidenfeld & Nicolson 1981)

Barry Driscoll (active 1960s)

A capable illustrator of animals who works with a brush outline and wash reproduced in halftone, sometimes with partial colour and spattered texture.

Books illustrated include:
Joseph Chipperfield Lone Stands the Glen (1966)
René Guillot Mokokambo, the Lost Land (1961), King of the Cats (1962), Mountain with a Secret (1963)
Desmond Morris Apes and Monkeys (1964), The Big Cats (1965)
William Swinton Digging for Dinosaurs (1962)
Henry Williamson Tarka the Otter (1964)

References: Fisher p.341; ICB 3

Violet Hilda Drummond (b. 1911)

Works as Violet Drummond. Married name: Mrs Anthony Swetenham. Born London. Studied at St Martin's School of Art (1939-42). Painter and lithographer, author and illustrator of children's books in ink-and-wash and colour, and illustrator

J.H. Dowd. 'The Menace of the Talkies' from *Review of Revues* edited by C.B.C. (Cape, 1930).

A COMFORTABLE SEAT IS PRO-VIDED, WITH AN UNINTERRUPTED VIEW —

OR YOU CAN BE IN THE FRONT ROW FOR LESS MONEY, WITH AN EVEN BETTER VIEW —

THINK OF ME, LITTLE PAL!

J·H·DOWD

AND SEE AND HEAR —

THE REAL STUFF.

V.H. Drummond. From her *The Flying Postman* (1948).

of humorous adult books. Has drawn, written and produced eighteen cartoon films for the BBC, based on the *Little Laura* books. Winner of the Kate Greenaway Award for illustrations to *Mrs Easter and the Storks* (1957). In her children's illustrations, Violet Drummond cheerfully abandons spatial and anatomical conventions in a spontaneous style which is both expressive and witty.[Q]

Books illustrated include:
Geoffrey Bles The Title's My Own (1952)
Helen Cresswell The Piemakers (1967)
Eilis Dillon Wild Little Horse (1955)
V.H. Drummond Phewtus the Squirrel (1939), Mrs Easter's Parasol (1944), Miss Anna Truly (1945), Lady Talavera (1946), The Charming Taxicab (1947), The Mountain That Laughed (1947), Tidgie's Innings (1947), The Flying Postman (1948), Little Laura on the River (1960), Little Laura and her Best Friend (1963), Little Laura and the Thief (1963), Miss Anna Truly and the Christmas Lights (1968), Mrs Easter and the Golden Bounder (1970), Mrs Easter's Christmas Flight (1972), I'll Never Be Asked Again (1979)
Lawrence Durrell Esprit de Corps (1957)
Barbara Ireson Liza and the Helicopter (1958)
Angela Jean The Kingdom of the Winds (1957)
Alastair Miller The Quest of the Catnip Mouse (1967)
Eric Partridge The Shaggy Dog Story (1953)
Thomas A. Powell Here and There a Lusty Trout (1947)
Arnold Silcock Verse and Worse (1952)
Barbara Sleigh Carbonel King of the Cats (1955)
J.K. Stanford The Twelfth (1944)

References: Contemporary Authors; Crouch; Eyre; Fisher pp.123, 248; Hürlimann; ICB 2,3,4; Kirkpatrick; Wa (1980); Waters 2; *The Junior Bookshelf* vol 13 no 3 (1949)

Ella Du Cane (active 1890-1930)

Lived in London. Watercolour painter of landscapes, flowers, figures and buildings. Her book illustrations consist of topographical landscapes in watercolour, executed with assurance and invariably reproduced in colour.

Books illustrated include:
P. Bagot The Italian Lakes (1905)

Ella Du Cane The Nile Water-colours (1931)
Florence Du Cane The Flowers and Gardens of Japan (1908), The
    Flowers and Gardens of Madeira (1909), The Canary Islands (1911)
J. Finnemore Japan... (1907, 1930)
John A. Todd The Banks of the Nile (1913)

References: Johnson & Greutzner; Waters 2; C. Wood

Janet Duchesne (b. 1930)

Married name: Mrs Lonsdale. Born in London.
Studied at Bromley College of Art and the Royal
Academy Schools. Since 1956, she has worked
freelance, mainly as an illustrator of children's
books for Hamish Hamilton's 'Antelope' and
'Gazelle' series. She uses pen and ink, sometimes
with watercolour washes. Her early drawing is in
the sketchy 'multiple outline' style characteristic
of much work in the 1950s and 1960s; in her more
recent illustration there is greater emphasis on
texture and shading. She also paints landscapes,
makes small sculptures in bronze, and writes
children's stories.

Books illustrated include:
Joy Allen Stitches for Charlie (1980)
Kenneth Allen The Story of London Town (1967)
Bernard Ashley Dinner Ladies Don't Count (1981), Linda's Lie (1982)
Evelyn Davies Cam (1980)
Richard Dennant The Video Affair (1981)
Janet Duchesne Two to Five Books (1963), Richard Goes Sailing
    (1966), Peach Pudding (1978)
Jacynth Hope-Simpson Danger on the Line (1962), The Ninepenny
    (1964), The Witches' Cave (1964)
Delia Huddy Creaky Knees (1978)
Jean MacGibbon Peter's Private Army (1960), Red Sail, White Sail
    (1961), The Red Sledge (1962), The View-Finder (1963), Sandy in
    Hollow Tree House (1967), The Tall Ship (1967), The Great-Great
    Rescuers (1967)
William Mayne The Glass Ball (1961), Plot Night (1963), The Big
    Wheel and the Little Wheel (1965)
Maureen O'Donnell The Lorry Thieves (1961)
Pamela Oldfield Children of the Plague (1979)
Joan Phipson The Crew of the 'Merlin' (1966)
Mary Ray The Eastern Beacon (1965), Standing Lions (1968), Spring
    Tide (1969)
Pamela Rogers All Change (1974)
Margaretha Shemin The Little Riders (1964)

Janet Duchesne. From *The Lorry Thieves* by
Maureen O'Donnell (Hamish Hamilton, 1961).

Joan Smith November and the Truffle Pig (1977)
Dinah Starkey Monsters, Dragons and Sea-Serpents (1979)
Judith Stinton Tom's Tale (1983)
Elfrida Vipont The Offcomers (1965)
Simon Watson Venus Pool (1975)

References: ICB 3,4; Ryder

Ambrose Dudley (active 1890-1922)

Landscape and portrait painter who lived in London
and exhibited at the Royal Academy from time to
time. His book illustrations (black and white and
full colour) were conventional in both imagery
and technique.

Books illustrated include:
Robert Browning The Pied Piper of Hamelin (1912)
Geoffrey Chaucer The Prologue to the Canterbury Tales (1907)
Daniel Defoe Robinson Crusoe (1922)
Ambrose Dudley The Dudley Portfolio of the Pilgrim's Progress (1908)
Mrs D.V. Greet The Story of the Golden Owl (1893)
E. Nesbit The Revolt of the Toys (1902)
M. von Pochhammer Six Stories (1900)
Catherine Shaw Suffer Little Children (1910), Long Ago in Bible
    Lands (1911)
Viator Overland to Persia (1906)
L.L. Weedon Old Testament Stories (nd)
Stories from the Book of Books (1914)
Everyman—A Morality Play (1906)

References: Houfe; Johnson & Greutzner

Emma S. Duffin (active 1927-36)

A children's illustrator about whom nothing seems
to have been recorded; probably an amateur.

Books illustrated include:
E.S. Duffin The Magic Watch (1927), The Tale of Li-Po and Su-Su
    (1927)

Edmund Dulac (1882-1953)

Born Toulouse, France, son of a textile salesman.
Studied law at Toulouse University. Attended the
art school in Toulouse for three years and won a
scholarship to the Académie Julian in Paris, but,
disliking it, remained there for only three weeks.
Already an anglophile and an admirer of British
book illustration, he became a regular contributor
to *The Pall Mall Magazine* (1904), settled in London (1905) and became a British subject (1912).
His annual exhibitions at the Leicester Galleries
(1907-15) were sponsored by Hodder and Stoughton, publishers of his Gift Books during these
years. He also drew and painted portraits and
caricatures, and designed costumes and scenery
for the theatre (including plays by his close friend
W.B. Yeats). After World War I (when the market for expensive illustrated books subsided), he
turned his talents to caricature, interior and furniture design, medals, book-plates, playing cards,
bank notes and stamps (he regarded his World
War II designs for the stamps and banknotes of

Edmund Dulac. 'The City in the Sea' from *The Bells and other poems* by Edgar Allan Poe (Hodder & Stoughton, 1912).

Free France as one of his most important achievements). Also a skilled musical performer and composer, in an oriental mode.

As an imaginative book illustrator, Dulac ranks with Arthur Rackham*, although his work was very different; while Rackham relied mainly on his wiry, fluent line, Dulac, more painterly in approach, explored his subject through studied compositions and, by exploiting new printing developments, through an expressive use of colour then unprecedented in book illustration. During the years 1907 to 1912, identified by Colin White as his 'blue period', Dulac produced many of his most evocative and atmospheric plates. Thereafter his knowledge of art styles (and in particular his passionate interest in Persian miniatures) led to greater eclecticism, and in this later period he often abandoned western 'photographic' perspective, in favour of the multiple viewpoint of oriental and medieval art. He used pastiche, particularly in his caricatures, with outstanding subtlety and wit. A meticulous draughtsman, he devised a method of working on tracing paper to refine figure poses and compositions.

Books illustrated include:
Helen V. Beauclerk The Green Lacquer Pavilion (1926), The Love of the Foolish Angel (1929)
Edmund Dulac Lyrics Pathetic and Humorous from A-Z (1908), Fairy Book (1915), Picture Book for the French Red Cross (1915)
Nathaniel Hawthorne Tanglewood Tales (1918)
Laurence Housman (retold by) Princess Badoura, a tale from the Arabian Nights (1913)
Edgar Allan Poe The Bells and other poems (1912)
Alexander Pushkin The Golden Cockerel (1950)
Queen Marie of Roumania The Dreamer of Dreams (1915), The Stealers of Light (1916)
Leonard Rosenthal The Kingdom of the Pearl (1920)
William Shakespeare The Tempest (1908)
M.M. Stawell Fairies I Have Met (1910), My Days with the Fairies (1913)
R.L. Stevenson Treasure Island (1927)

Periodicals: American Weekly, Good Housekeeping, The Graphic, The Illustrated London News, The Outlook, The Pall Mall Magazine, The Strand Magazine.

References: Bénézit; Crouch; Cuppleditch; DNB (1951-60); Doyle CL; Houfe; ICB 1, 2; Johnson; Johnson & Greutzner; Lewis; Low; Peppin; Ray; Thieme & Becker; Vollmer; Wa (1952); Waters; *Nash's Magazine* 77 (1926); *The Strand Magazine* 61 (1921); *The Studio* 45 (1909), special (Autumn 1914, Spring 1922, 1923-24, 1927, Autumn 1928, Winter 1931); William Feaver *Masters of Caricature* (Weidenfeld & Nicolson 1981); David Larkin *Dulac* (Coronet Books 1975); Colin White *Edmund Dulac* (Studio Vista 1976).

Gilbert Dunlop (active 1949-66)

A prolific children's book illustrator during the postwar period. He worked in pen or brush and ink or full colour, producing cheerful uncomplicated illustrations. Work published mainly by Nelson and Collins.

Books illustrated include:
Enid Blyton The Rockingdown Mystery (1949), The Rubadub Mystery (1952), The Mystery That Never Was (1961), The Rilloby Fair Mystery (1965), Ring O'Bells Mystery (1965), The Ragamuffin Mystery (1966)
Gilbert Dunlop The Baby Elephant (1948)
Mary Gervaise Golden Path Pets (1957)
Pamela Mansbridge Family Adventure (1953), Riverside Adventure (1954), The Children in the Square (1955), A House for Five (1956), Holiday in London (1960), The Creek Street Jumble (1961), Battle Tunes at Bindleton (1964)

John Dyke (b. 1935)

Born in Alcester, Warwickshire. Served in the Royal Navy (1952-59), then studied at Birmingham College of Art (1959-62). Lecturer at Folkestone School of Art (1967-71) and at Amersham College of Further Education. Freelance illustrator

John Dyke. From *Pigwig and the Pirates* by John Dyke (Methuen, 1979).

Will Dyson. 'Spread of terror/Shade of Bismarck:/Ah, my dear Moltke, he is succeeding in spreading terror—in the wrong direction!' from *Kultur Cartoons* (Stanley Paul, 1915).

since 1962. His early illustrations were mainly for educational books including Macmillan's 'Nipper' and 'Little Nipper' series, and Longman's 'Breakthrough Books'. More recently he has illustrated a number of children's books of his own, notably the lively 'Pigwig' titles for Methuen. He works in pen and ink with watercolour, or occasionally gouache, in a very individual style characterised by broken outlines and dappled colours. Also a painter, puppet-maker and designer of animated films.[Q]

Books illustrated include:
Gwen Clemens Shapes and Words (1980)
John Dyke Peter and the Pier (1968), Magic Colour (1974), Columbus Mouse (1975), Pigwig (1978), Pigwig and the Pirates (1979), Pigwig and the Crusty Diamonds (1982)
Dorothy Edwards Dad's New Car (1976)
Marion Green The Magician Who Lived in the Mountain (1977)
Fran Hunia The Elves and the Shoemaker (1978), The Sly Fox and Red Hen
Rose Impey The Ladybird Book of Fairy Tales (with others, 1980)
Ives McGee Oliver the Famous Birdman (1976)
Vernon Mills Tom Thumb (1979)
Sheila Parker and Alan Ward Sciencewise (1978)
Edward Ramsbottom and Joan Redmayne Secret Island (1975), In the Air (1977)
Ann Thwaite Rose in the River (1975)
Nicholas Tucker In the Picture (1976)
Anne-Cath Vestly The Eight Children Series (1973-79)

Periodicals: Child Education, Junior Education

References: Contemporary Authors

William Henry Dyson (c.1880-1938)

Worked as Will Dyson. Born Ballarat, Australia. Contributed to the *Sydney Bulletin* and the *Melbourne Herald*. Moved to London in 1909 and became the chief cartoonist on the *Daily Herald* (1913-25 and 1931-38). He was official war artist to the Australian armed forces during World War I and revisited Australia, 1925-30. He befriended David Low* on his arrival in London in 1919. Low, who admired his work, later observed that Dyson's early cartoons contained 'a sardonic disrespect for orthodox standards that was an emetic for the complaisant.' Dyson's best work, mostly dating from before 1920, had an iconographic freedom and ideological fervour that distinguished it from the output of other cartoonists of the period. Although he was principally a political cartoonist, he is included here for his wittily caricatured illustrations for Gerald Gould's *Lady Adela* (1920). He was married to children's illustrator Ruby Lind.

Books illustrated include:
W.H. Dyson War Cartoons (1916), Australia at War (1918), Artist among the Bankers (1933)
Gerald Gould Lady Adela (1920)
E. Patand and E. Pouget Syndicalism and the Co-operative Commonwealth (1913)
H.G. Wells (intro) Kultur Cartoons (1915)
The Martyrs of Tolpuddle (1934)

Periodicals: The Daily Herald, The London Mercury, The Melbourne Herald, The Odd Volume, Pearson's Magazine, Reveille, The Sydney Bulletin

References: Hillier; Houfe; Johnson & Greutzner; Low; Vollmer supp; Waters 2; *The Studio* special (Autumn 1928); C.R. Ashbee *Caricature* (Chapman & Hall 1928); William Feaver *Masters of Caricature* (Weidenfeld and Nicolson 1981); John Geipel *The Cartoon* (David & Charles 1972)

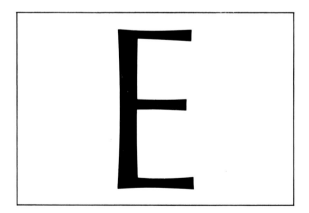

Harold C. Earnshaw (d. 1937)

Studied art in London. Lost his right arm in World War I, but taught himself to draw left-handed. His work appeared regularly in children's annuals and anthologies, where his drawings and colour plates can be seen to echo the work of John Hassall* in their humour and bold conception. He married

Mabel Lucie Attwell*, and is thought to have been responsible for some of the more naturalistic parts of her drawings, such as the animals. Worked extensively for the publisher Blackie and designed many colour covers. Member of the London Sketch Club and the Chelsea Arts Club, and a golfing companion of Harry Rountree*. Died as a result of his war injuries.

Books illustrated include:
Cynthia Asquith (ed) The Flying Carpet (with others, 1926)
Charles Greig The Rebel Cadets (1908)
Elsie Oxenham At School with the Roundheads (1915), The School of Ups and Downs (1918), A Go-Ahead Schoolgirl (1919)
T.B. Reed The Willoughby Captains (1910)
Walter Scott Ivanhoe (c.1930)
The Golden Budget of Nursery Stories (nd)
The King Who Was Never in Time (Playbox Annual 1910)
Princess Mary's Gift Book (with others, nd)

Periodicals: The Boy's Own Annual, The Captain, Cassell's Children's Annual, Chums, The Graphic, The Jolly Book, Little Folks, Playbox Annual, Punch

References: Cuppleditch; Doyle BWI; Houfe; Johnson & Greutzner; *The Times* (12th December 1979)

Janina Ede (b. 1937)

Married name: Mrs Zbinden. Born in Southampton. Studied at Winchester School of Art (1953-57). Has since worked as a freelance illustrator and book jacket designer, with commissions from publishers including Heinemann, Macmillan Educational, Faber & Faber and Heron Books. She has worked in pen and ink, gouache and pencil, and in 1977 adopted scraperboard for *Einar and the Seal.* Her work is decorative, with textures created by various techniques including spatter and off-printing from leaves, fabrics, etc. She draws animals with sympathy and a feeling for movement. She lives in rural Hampshire. [Q]

Books illustrated include:
Anton Chekhov Stories (1974)
Colette My Apprenticeships (1972), Music Hall Sidelights (1972)
Freda Collins The Pack Mascot (1962), The Patchwork Pack (1967)
Colquhoun and Guergady Sur les Routes de France (1960), Les Duttons en Route (1966)
Helen Cresswell A Gift from Winklesea (1969)
Patrick Duggan The Travelling People (1964), The Travelling Boy (1965)
Harry Fleming White Witch's Secret (1966)
Leon Garfield Adventures of the Boy and the Monkey (1976)
Marjorie Gayler It's the New Sound (1964), Operation Hotel (1968)
David George Einar and the Seal (1977)
Jane Holiday Biddy's Talking Pineapple (1980)
Clare Maxwell-Hudson The Natural Beauty Book (1976)
'Margett' It's Sunny Outside (1974), Hard and Soft (1974)
Somerset Maugham Theatre (1975)
Margaret J. Miller Mousetails (1967), Willow and Albert (1968), Willow and Albert Are Stowaways (1970), The Big Brown Teapot (1979), The Mad Muddle (1982)
Yvonne Mitchell Cathy Away (1964), Cathy At Home (1964)
Gwynedd Rae Mostly Mary (1968), All Mary (1968), Mary Plain on Holiday (1969), Mary Plain and the Twins (1970), Mary Plain's Big Adventure (1970), Mary Plain V.I.P. (1970), Mary Plain Goes to America (1971), Mary Plain in Trouble (1972), Mary Plain's Whodunnit (1973)
Bohumil Riha Johnny's Journey (1971)
Modwena Sedgwick Matilda's Special Plate (1969)
Septima and 'Margett' Child's Play (1969), More Child's Play (1970)

Nevil Shute The Rainbow and the Rose (1975)
R.L. Stevenson Travels with a Donkey (1972), An Amateur Emigrant (1974)
Margaret Storey The Mollyday Holiday (1971), The Sleeping Witch (1971), A War of Wizards (1976)
Morna Stuart Marassa and Midnight (1966)
Pamela Sykes Air Day for the Brownies (1968), The Brownies at the Zoo (1969), The Brownies at the Fire (1970), The Brownies on Television (1972), The Brownies in Hospital (1974), The Brownies Throw a Party (1976)
W.M. Thackeray The History of Henry Esmond (1976)
Alison Uttley Lavender Shoes, Eight Tales of Enchantment (1970)
Alison Winn Helter Skelter (1966)

Periodicals: Homes and Gardens, Vogue

Reference: Ryder

Gunvor Edwards (active from 1958)

Maiden name: Gunvor Övden. Born in Uppsala, Sweden. Studied at Gun Zetterdahls School of Painting, Sweden, and at the Regent Street Polytechnic, where she took a course in illustration under Stuart Tresilian*. Illustrator of children's and educational books. She is married to Peter Edwards*. In her independent work, her lively outline drawings, often with flat colour washes, retain a distinctive Scandinavian flavour. [Q]

Books illustrated include:
Louisa M. Alcott Little Women (1975)
Margaret Stuart Barry Maggie Gumption (1979), Maggie Gumption Flies High (1981)
Gerard Bell The Smallest King in the World (1968)
Mary Hayley Bell Whistle Down the Wind (1958)
Elisabeth Beresford Snuffle to the Rescue (1975)
Eileen Colwell Tell Me Another Story (1964)
Gunvor Edwards Cat Samson (1978), Grandmother's Donkey (1982)
Frederick Grice Tales and Beliefs (1974)
Jennie Hawthorne The Mystery of the Blue Tomatoes (1958)
M.C. Ibbetson Daniel's Shed (1974)
J. Clement Jones James and Susan in the Country (1959)
Felicia Law Something to Make (1971), Bad Boys (1972), Going to School (1980)
Francis Lindsay Mr Bits and Pieces (1976)
Kathleen Mackenzie Garden Railway (1966)
E.M. Matterson Play with a Purpose for Under Sevens (1975)
Johanna Bugge Olsen Stray Dog (1966)
Barbara Sleigh Ninety-Nine Dragons (1974)
Barbara Softly Magic People (1966), More Magic People (1969)

Gunvor Edwards. 'The first fish laughed and said, "No, you would drown without us." ' from *Danny Fox Meets a Stranger* by David Thomson (Penguin, 1968).

Helen Thomas A Book of Children's Parties (1976)
David Thomson Danny Fox (1966), Danny Fox at the Palace (1968), Danny Fox Meets a Stranger (1968)
Anne-Cath Vestly Aurora and the Little Blue Car (1974), Aurora and Socrates (1975), Aurora in Holland (1976)
Stig Weimar Norway Is Like This (1979)
Ursula Moray Williams Cruise of the 'Happy-Go-Gay' (1967), Tiger-Nanny (1973)
Robina Beckles Willson Musical Merry-go-round (1977)
Also educational titles published principally by Nelson.

Periodicals: The Egg, Puffin Post

Reference: ICB 4

Lionel Dalhousie Robertson Edwards (1878-1966)

Usually worked as Lionel Edwards. Born in Oxfordshire, son of a doctor. Studied under A.S. Cope and Frank Calderon at the School of Animal Painting, Kensington, London. Reporter of the Lisbon revolution of 1910 for *The Graphic*. Served in the Army Remount Service during World War I. Worked regularly for *Punch* during the 1920s and became a popular contributor of hunting scenes to sporting and society magazines, and a well-known sporting painter. Settled in Salisbury, Wiltshire. Edwards was widely regarded as a sporting artist of the first rank. Guy Paget considered that 'he can paint a Hunt scurry as good and life-like as Ferneley, on a background worthy of Birket Foster...no man softens his outlines with mist as he does, and at the same time retains their truth and weight.' As an illustrator, he worked in watercolour and body colour, pen and ink, wash, pencil, crayon and charcoal. Member of the London Sketch Club. Elected RCamA (1926), RI (1927).

Books illustrated include:
E.A.H. Alderson Pink and Scarlet (1913)
Richard Ball Hounds Will Meet (1931)
Muriel Bowen Irish Hunting (1955)
Patrick R. Chalmers The Horn (1937)
Moyra Charlton Tally Ho (1930), Echoing Horn (1939)

Lionel Edwards. 'An error of judgement' from *The Wiles of the Fox* by Lionel Edwards (The Medici Society & Sporting Gallery, 1932).

Crascredo Sense and Sensibility (1926), Country Sense and Common Sense (1928)
Lionel Dawson Sport in War (1936)
G.A.B. Dewar The Pageant of the English Landscape (1924)
Lionel Edwards Hunting and Stalking the Deer (1927), Hunting Sketch Book (1928), Huntsmen Past and Present (1929), My Scottish Sketch Book (1929), The Wiles of the Fox (1932), A Leicestershire Sketch Book (1935), Sketches in Stable and Kennel (1936), Seen from the Saddle (1937), My Irish Sketch Book (1938), Famous Foxhunters (1938), The Lighter Side of Sport (1940), Getting to Know Your Pony (1948), The Fox (1949), Beasts of the Chase (1950), The Servant the Horse (1952), Sportsman's Sketchbook (1953)
William Fawcett Thoroughbred and Hunter (1934)
Mark Flint Grig the Greyhound (1938)
Golden Gorse Moorland Mousie (1929), Older Mousie (1932)
S.G. Goldschmidt Bridle Wise (1927)
Adam L. Gordon Sporting Verse (1927)
Eleanor E. Helme Mayfly (1935), Shank's Pony (1946)
A.H. Higginson Letters from an Old Sportsman to a Young One (1929)
Beatrice Holden They're Away (1945)
N. Kalashnikov Jumper (1948)
Rudyard Kipling The Fox Meditates (1933)
R.C. Lyle Brown Jack (1934), The Aga Khan's Horses (1938), Royal Newmarket (1945)
Edward MacDermot The Devon and Somerset Staghounds (1936)
M.F. MacTaggart Mount and Man (1925)
G.J.W. Melville Songs and Verses (1924)
Pamela M. Morris Topper (1947)
Will H. Ogilvie Galloping Shoes (1922), Scattered Scarlet (1923), Over the Grass (1925), A Handful of Leather (1928), Collected Sporting Verse (1932)
K.M. Peyton Sabre, the Horse from the Sea (1948), Mandrake (1949)
Frances Pitt Betty (1943)
Rancher Forrad-on! (1930), Tally-Ho Back! (1931)
Eric Roberts Somewhere in England (1929)
Sabretache Shires and Provinces (1926)
Anna Sewell Black Beauty (1946)
R.L. Stevenson The Black Arrow (1957)
A.G. Street Moonraking (1936)
Anthony Trollope Hunting Sketches (1952)
Richard G. Verney Hunting the Fox (1925)
Joyce M. Vivian Riding with Reka (1937)
Harold F. Wallace A Stuart Sketchbook (1934)
R.E.E. Warburton Hunting Songs (1925)

Periodicals: The Bystander, Country Life, The Graphic, Herbert Strang's Annual, Holly Leaves, Pearson's Magazine, Printer's Pie, Punch, The Strand Magazine, The Tatler

References: Bénézit; Cuppleditch; Houfe; ICB 1,2; Johnson & Greutzner; Vollmer; Wa (1934); Waters; J.C. Wood; Lionel Edwards *Reminiscences of a Sporting Artist* (Putnam 1947); Guy Paget *Sporting Pictures of England* (Collins 1942)

Peter William Edwards (b. 1934)

Born in London, son of a bus driver and fireman. Educated at Quintin School; studied at Regent Street Polytechnic (1950-54). Army service (1955-56). Since then, he has worked independently in Sweden (1956-58) and in London (from 1958) as a muralist, children's book writer and illustrator, writer of educational books, and painter (portraits and landscapes). For illustration, he initially used gouache and acrylics applied thickly, but later worked towards thin, transparent colour washes with pen and ink. He varies his style according to the demands of the subject, sometimes adopting a humorous cartoon-like idiom for the figures. In 1957, he married the Swedish artist Gunvor Övden (Gunvor Edwards*); they live in Greenwich with their six children.

Books illustrated include:
Revd W. Awdry Railway series (last nine titles 1963-72)
E. Berridge That Surprising Summer (1971)
S. Buckland English on Line (1980-82)
John O.E. Clark Chemistry (1971)
Dorothy Clewes Wilberforce and the Slaves (1961), Skyraker and the Iron Imp (1962)
M. Coles and B. Lord Access to English (4 titles, 1975-80)
Wilkie Collins The Moonstone (1961)
H.L. Davies Honey in the Horn (1961)
John Denton The Colour Factory (1976)
M. Dickens The Great Escape (1971)
Dorothy Edwards A Look, See and Touch Book (1976), A Walk Your Fingers Story
Peter Edwards Simply Salt (1978), Simply Sell (1978), Simply Size (1978), Simply Song (1978), Simply Soup (1978), Simply Stones (1978)
Michael Holt Puma Puzzles (1980)
Michael Holt and Ronald Ridout The First Big Book of Puzzles (1972), The Second Big Book of Puzzles (1973), The Third Big Book of Puzzles (1979)
C. Mackenzie The Dining Room Battle (1972)
Sybil Marshall Nicholas and Finnegan (1977)
Carl Memling Seals for Sale (1964)
Laurence Meynell Tony Trotter and the Kitten (1971)
H. Mills Prudence and the Pill (1965)
E. Ramsbottom Ideas 2 (1970), Young Ideas Books 3,4,6 (1971)
Kenneth Rudge Man Builds Houses (1963)
D.R. Sherman Old Mali and the Boy (1966)
Elfrida Vipont Search for a Song (1962)
John Wyndham The Chrysalids/Trouble with Lichen (1960)

Reference: ICB 4

Beresford Egan (b. c.1906)

Born in England and educated in South Africa. Worked in a bank before becoming sports cartoonist for the *Rand Daily Mail* in Johannesburg. Returned to England in 1926. Satirical draughtsman, painter, novelist and playwright. Influenced by Aubrey Beardsley, many of his illustrations were in a fantastic/erotic vein.

Books illustrated include:
N. Balehin Income and Outcome (1936)
Charles Baudelaire Les Fleurs du Mal (1929)
Beresford Egan The Sink of Solitude (1928), Pollen. A Novel in Black and White (1933), But the Sinners Triumph (1934), Epitaph. A Double-bedside Book for Singular People (1943), Epilogue (1946)
Beresford Egan and B. de Shane De Sade (1929)
Pierre Loüys The Adventures of King Pausole (1929), Aphrodite (1929)
Lucian (of Samosata) Cyprian Masques (1929)
P.R. Stevensen Policeman of the Lord (1929)

Periodicals: London Opinion, Pearsons Magazine, Rand Daily Mail, The Royal Magazine

References: Taylor; *Arts and Crafts* vol 2 no 2 (1928); Paul Allen *Beresford Egan* (Scorpion Press 1966); Beresford Egan *Epitaph* (Fortune Press 1943)

Bettina Ehrlich (b. 1903)

Maiden name: Bettina Bauer. Works as a writer and illustrator under the name 'Bettina'. Born in Vienna and studied at the Academy of Applied Arts there. Later settled in London. Painter and textile designer. Her first English book, *Poo-Tsee the Water-Tortoise* (1943), is fancifully and decoratively illustrated with colour and black and white lithographs. More recently, she has worked

Bettina Ehrlich. '…Poo-Tsee made himself look like a stone as his mother had taught him. So the cook threw him out of the window' from her *Poo-Tsee the Water Tortoise* (Chatto & Windus, 1943).

in watercolour for reproduction by offset lithography. She always designs the layout and jackets for her books and works for publishers in Britain, the United States, Germany and Japan. [Q]

Books illustrated include:
Bettina Poo-Tsee the water tortoise (1943), Show Me Yours (1944), Cocolo (1945), Trovato (1959), Paolo and Panetto (1960), For the Leg of a Chicken (1962), Francesco and Francesca (1962), Dolls (1963), Of Uncles and Aunts (1963), The Goat Boy (1967), Sardines and the Angel (1967), Neretto (1970), A Day in Venice (1973)
Giles Saint Cèrère Poiuwayu and the Rainbow (1958)
John Hosier The Sorcerer's Apprentice (1960)

References: Contemporary Authors; Crouch; Hürlimann; ICB 2, 3, 4

Susan Einzig (b. 1922)

Born in Berlin, daughter of a businessman. Studied at the Central School of Arts and Crafts (1939-42); worked in industry until the end of World War II. Part-time lecturer at Camberwell School of Art, London (1946-50), St Martin's School of Art (1948-51), Beckenham School of Art (1959-60), and Chelsea School of Art (1959-65), where she became senior lecturer in drawing and illustration in 1965. She made her name as an illustrator with her pen and ink drawings for *Tom's Midnight Garden* (1958), which received widespread acclaim. Among contemporary painter/illustrators, the main influence on her work has been Carel Weight*. [Q]

Books illustrated include:
Gillian Avery (ed) In the Window Seat (1960)
Charlotte Brontë Jane Eyre (1961)
Hester Burton (ed) Her First Ball (1959)
Noel Carrington Mary Belinda and the Ten Aunts (1946)

Susan Einzig. From *The Vengeance of the Gods* by Rex Warner (MacGibbon & Kee, 1954).

Alphonse Daudet Sappho (1954)
Margaret Love An Explorer for an Aunt (1960)
Eduard Mörike Mozart on the Way to Prague (1946)
E. Nesbit The Bastables (1965)
Philippa Pearce Tom's Midnight Garden (1958)
Elizabeth Poston The Children's Song Book (1961)
Barbara Sleigh The Seven Days (1958)
Eleanor Spence Lillypilly Hill (1960)
Rex Warner The Vengeance of the Gods (1954)

Periodicals: The Compleat Imbiber, Contact, Good Housekeeping, Homes and Gardens, House and Garden, Lilliput, News Chronicle, Radio Times, Reader's Digest, The Saturday Book, The Strand Magazine, The Tatler, Vogue, The Young Elizabethan, and the house magazines of ICI, BP, Yardleys, Watneys and Whitbreads

References: Crouch; Driver; Eyre; Fisher p.27; ICB 3; Jacques; Ryder; Usherwood

John Shenton Eland (1872-1933)

Born Market Harborough, Northamptonshire. Studied at the Royal Academy Schools and in Paris. Worked in London (1895-1913), Paris and New York as an aquatinter, sculptor, lithographer, portrait painter (mostly of the English aristocracy), watercolourist and illustrator of children's books. Died in New York. As book illustrations, his sketches have an *insouciant*, if slightly offhand, charm. In *Flower Legends*, he makes good use of

colour lithography to create particularly pretty effects. Member of the Senefelder Club.

Books illustrated include:
The Duchess of Buckingham and Chandos The Story of Willy Wind and Jock the Cheese (1905)
Hilda Murray Flower Legends for Children (1901)

References: Bénézit; Johnson & Greutzner; Thieme & Becker; Vollmer; Waters

Mildred E. Eldridge (b. 1909)

Born Wimbledon, South London. Studied at Wimbledon School of Art, the Royal College of Art and the British School in Rome. Painter, often of botanical and biological subjects; contributor to the Culpeper Society's 'Herbals'.

Books illustrated include:
Walter de la Mare The Three Royal Monkeys (1946), The Three Mulla Mulgars (1970)
Mildred Eldridge Gwenno the Goat (1957)
Hilda W.W. Leyel Compassionate Herbs (1946)
Henry Williamson The Star-Born (1948)

References: Fisher p.345; ICB 2; Johnson & Greutzner; Wa (1980); Waters; *The OWS Club Volume* 34

Lionel Ellis (b. 1903)

Born Plymouth, Devon, son of a dockyard mechanic. Studied on scholarships at Plymouth School of Art (1918-22) and at the Royal College of Art (1922-24). Travelling scholarship to Florence and Rome (1926). Lecturer in painting at Wimbledon School of Art (1937-68). In 1953, he bought a small estate, where he has lived as a recluse since his retirement, growing much of his own food. Painter in oil and tempera of portraits, flowers, landscapes, figures and horses, stone carver, modeller in clay and wax, and wood engraver. As a book illustrator, he worked only for the Fanfrolico Press. F.J. Harvey Darton wrote in *The Studio* special (Winter 1931) of his monochrome illustrations for *Delighted Earth* that 'if Rubens had had the chance to illustrate Herrick he might conceivably have produced something like this.' His impressive wood engravings for *Theocritus*, on the other hand, owe more in conception and anatomical treatment to Michaelangelo, whom Ellis considers 'the greatest of all artists'. Elected ARCA (1924), FRSA (1951). [Q]

Books illustrated include:
Robert Herrick Delighted Earth (1927)
Jack Lindsay (trans) Theocritus (1929)
The Complete Poetry of Gaius Catullus (1929)

Periodical: The London Aphrodite

References: Johnson & Greutzner; Vollmer; Wa (1980); Waters; *The Studio* special (Winter 1931); Harry Chaplin *The Fanfrolico Press* (Wentworth Press 1976); Jack Lindsay *Fanfrolico and After* (Bodley Head 1962)

Beatrice Elvery. 'I am the candleholder of the king' from *Heroes of the Dawn* by Violet Russell (Maunsel, 1913).

Beatrice Elvery (1883-1970)

Born in Dublin. Studied at the Dublin School of Art and at the Slade School of Fine Art (winning the Taylor scholarship three times and bronze and silver medals). Taught at the Dublin Metropolitan School of Art. In 1912, she married the second Baron Glenavy. Salaman described her graphic work as 'imaginatively expressive and decorative.' She worked principally as a painter (which is evident in her manner of handling colour plates) and as a modeller. Some of her black and white drawings clearly reveal the imprint of the stained glass designs for which she was also known. Elected ARHA (1932), RHA (1934).

Books illustrated include:
K.F. Purdon Candle and Crib (1920)
Violet Russell Heroes of the Dawn (1913)

References: Houfe; Johnson & Greutzner; *The Studio* special (Autumn 1914)

Alfred Thomas Elwes (active 1867-1911)

During the 1870s, Elwes worked as the chief natural history draughtsman for *The Illustrated*

London News. His oeuvre consisted almost entirely of mammal and bird subjects, which he could draw convincingly in both humorous and naturalistic veins; his backgrounds and occasional ancillary humans were not generally treated with as much authority.

Books illustrated include:
John Bailey The Story of Papa's Wise Dogs (1867)
A.T. Elwes Neptune (1869), A Pleasant History of Reynard the Fox (1873), Picture Lessons in Natural History (1878), Animal Drawings (1882), How to Draw Animals, Birds and Dogs (1882), The Zoo Past and Present (1905)
Lilian Gask Bird Wonders of the Zoo (1911)
J.C. Harris Uncle Remus (1883)
R.B. Sharpe Wonders of the Bird World (1898)
Uncle Charlie The Favourite Picture Book (with others, 1879)

Periodicals: The Cornhill Magazine, The Girl's Own Annual, The Graphic, The Illustrated London News, Little Folks

Reference: Houfe

Rowland Emett (b.1906)

Born in London, the son of an amateur inventor. Studied at Birmingham School of Arts and Crafts. Worked in a commercial art studio in Birmingham until 1939, when he made his first contribution to *Punch*. During World War II, he was employed as a draughtsman in the development of jet engines. Designed the Far Wittering and Oyster Creek Railway for the Festival of Britain Battersea Pleasure Gardens (1951). He subsequently designed murals and advertisements (for Shell, Guinness, etc.), painted, made lithographs, and invented such items as a Hush-A-Bye Hot Air Rocking Chair, a Forget-Me-Not Computer, and the Exploratory Moon-Probe Lunacycle. As a delineator of fantastic machines, he has inevitably been compared with W. Heath Robinson*, but his fragile, elegant contrivances in their Gothic settings are far removed from the do-it-yourself ingenuity of the earlier artist's contraptions. He lives and works in Sussex.

Books illustrated include:
Walter de la Mare Peacock Pie (1941), Bells and Grass (1941)
R. Emett Engines, Aunties and Others (1943), Anthony and Antimacassar (1943), Sidings and Suchlike (1946), Home Rails Preferred (1947), Saturday Slow (1948), Buffer's End (1949), Far Twittering (1949), High Tea, Infused by Emett (1950), The Forgotten Tramcar (1952), Nellie Come Home (1952), New World for Nellie (1952), The Early Morning Milk Train (1976), Alarms and Excursions (1977)
A. Guinness Hobby Horses (1958)

Periodicals: Cosmopolitan, Harper's Bazaar, Holiday, Life, Mademoiselle, Punch, This Week

References: *Contemporary Authors*; Fisher p.27; Hillier; ICB 2; Vollmer supp; Price; Wa (1980); WaG; John Geipel *The Cartoon* (David & Charles 1972)

Cicely Englefield (b. 1893)

Born in London, but spent her childhood in rural Kent. She studied at St Martin's School of Art and the Central School of Arts and Crafts. She illustrated her numerous children's books with wood engravings (her preferred medium), pen and ink drawings, watercolours and lithographs. In her wood engravings, she uses simplified animal forms and strong black on white contrasts to create cheerful vigorous effects that successfully combine a nursery idiom with a quite sophisticated use of the medium. She achieves some interesting page designs in her drawn and lithographed books, most of which were published by John Murray.

Books illustrated include:
Cicely Englefield George and Angela (1932), Katie the Caterpillar (1933), Billy Winks (1934), The Tale of a Guinea Pig (1935), A House for a Mouse (1936), Squishy Apples (1937), Bennie Black Lamb (1938), Connie the Cow (1939), Jeremy Jack, the Lazy Lamb (1940), Bert the Sparrow (1941), Monty the Frog (1941), Feather the Foal (1942), The Tale of a Tadpole (1945)

Reference: ICB 1

Jacob Epstein (1880-1959)

Born in New York. Studied at the Art Students' League (c.1896) and in Paris (1902). Settled in London (1905) and became a British subject (1907). Worked in Paris (1909-13). Founder member of the London Group (1913) and closely associated with the Vorticists (1914-15), who included Wyndham Lewis* and Edward Wadsworth*. In later life, he was known for his expressively modelled portrait busts, which formed a striking contrast to his simplified, angular carved pieces. His powerful, uninhibited book illustrations, mainly drawn in chalk, show a sculptor's preoccupation with the human form. Honorary doctorate, Oxford University (1953); knighted (1954).

Books illustrated include:
Charles Baudelaire Les Fleurs du Mal (1940)
Jacob Epstein Seventy Five Drawings (1929)
H. Hapgood The Spirit of the Ghetto (1902)
M. Oyred The Book of Affinity (1933)
The Old Testament (1929-31)

References: Bénézit; Chamot, Farr & Butlin; Contemporary Artists; DNB (1951-60); Phaidon; Thieme & Becker; Vollmer and supp; Wa (1934); Waters; *The Studio* 79 (1920), 103 (1932), special (Autumn 1930); Richard Buckle (intro) *Jacob Epstein: Let There Be Sculpture: An Autobiography* (Michael Joseph 1940, Hulton Press 1955), *Jacob Epstein: Sculptor* (Faber & Faber 1963); Jacob Epstein and A. Haskell *The Sculptor Speaks* (Heinemann 1931); Lady Epstein and Richard Buckle *Epstein Drawings* (Faber & Faber 1962); L.B. Powell *Jacob Epstein* (Chapman & Hall 1932); B. Van Dieren *Epstein* (John Lane 1920); H[ubert] W[ellington] *Jacob Epstein* (Ernest Benn 1925)

Nellie Erichsen (active 1882-1917)

Lived in Tooting, South London, and worked as a painter and illustrator, and as a translator and editor of contemporary drama. She edited the Duckworth Modern Plays series (1895-1901) with R. Brimley Johnson and was the first translator into English of August Strindberg's *The Father* (1899). As an illustrator, she found her true field

in architectural and landscape subjects, which she depicted with accuracy, clarity and a concern for graphic technique. However, the feeling of detachment sometimes present in her work suggests the use of photographs for reference or as source material.

Books illustrated include:
J.B. Firth Highways and Byways in Derbyshire (1905)
Edmund Gardner The Story of Florence (with others, 1898)
Lina Duff Gordon The Story of Assisi (1900)
Edward Hutton Highways and Byways in Somerset (1912), Highways and Byways in Wiltshire (1917)
A.J. Lawley The Story of Verona (1902)
F. Luetzow The Story of Prague (1902)
T. Okey The Story of Venice (1905)
Henrik Pontoppidan Emanuel (1896), The Promised Land (1896)
Janet A. Ross Florentine Villas (1901), The Story of Pisa (1909), The Story of Lucca (1912)
Norwood Young The Story of Rome (1901)
The Novels of Susan E. Ferrier (6 vols 1894)

Periodical: The English Illustrated Magazine

References: Baker; Bénézit; Houfe; Johnson & Greutzner; C. Wood

Treyer Meredith Evans (b. 1889)

Born in Chichester, son of a dentist. Advertising

Treyer Evans. 'It's exactly right as it is' from *Loyal to the School* by Angela Brazil (Blackie, nd).

and press illustrator employed by C. Arthur Pearson (1909) and Edward Hulton (1910). He was a bright, stylish illustrator who worked in pen and ink or pencil, often with broad expanses of shading. However his style varied according to his subject—for example, in *Will You Come As Well* (Milne-like verses about children), he adopted a technique similar to that of E.H. Shepard*. He lived at Gerrard's Cross, Buckinghamshire.

Books illustrated include:
Anthony Armstrong England Our England (1948)
Enid Blyton The Christmas Book (1944), The Mystery of the Vanished Prince (1951), The Mystery of the Strange Bundle (1952), The Mystery of Holly Lane (1953), The Mystery of Tally-Ho Cottage (1954)
Angel Brazil Loyal to the School (nd), A Fortunate Term (1921)
Fay Inchfawn Will You Come As Well? (1931), The Verse Book of a Garden (1932)
M. Proctor Three Wise Men (1958)
Geoffrey Trease The Hills of Varna (1948)

Periodicals: The Girls' Realm, The Humorist, Little Folks, London Magazine, Punch, Scout, The Sketch, The Strand Magazine, The Tatler

References: Fisher p.23; Vollmer; Wa (1934)

Ethel Fanny Everett (active 1900-39)

Born London and educated at Mary Datchelor School before entering the Royal Academy Schools. Portrait painter of children and illustrator of children's books. Lived in London.

Books illustrated include:
Enid Blyton Silver and Gold (1927)
M. Dowson Elizabeth Ann's Delight (1922)
L.G. Eady Elizabeth's Book (1928)
Rose Fyleman Old-Fashioned Girls (1928)
Charles Kingsley The Water Babies (1910)
Old Fairy Tales (1927)
Old Nursery Rhymes (1927)

Periodicals: Aunt Judy's Magazine, The Jolly Book

References: Houfe; Johnson & Greutzner; Vollmer; Wa (1934); Waters

Fred R. Exell (active from 1954)

Lecturer at St Martin's School of Art. Illustrator in pen and ink, particularly of historical subjects. His early work is distinguished by very carefully modulated hatched shading, while his later illustration is freer and more linear in approach.

Books illustrated include:
Joseph Chipperfield A Dog Against Darkness (1963)
J. Meade Faulkner Moonfleet (1962)
Kathleen Fidler Flodden Field September 9 1513 (1971), The '45 and Culloden (1973)
R.L. Stevenson Kidnapped (1964)
Donald Suddaby Village Fanfare (1954)
Geraldine Symons The Rose Window (1964), The Quarantine Child (1966)

Periodical: Radio Times

Reference: Usherwood

D.C. Eyles (d. 1975)

An illustrator who worked for boys' story books, annuals and magazines. His work, which was typical in its field, was drawn in a bold, simplified style that derived ultimately from the 'classic' early illustrators of the century such as H.E. Brock*, though the images were adapted and coarsened so that they could be reproduced on cheap paper.

Books illustrated include:
John R. Crossland & J.M. Parrish (ed) The Children's Wonder Book (with others, 1933)
'Mrs Herbert Strang' (ed) The Golden Wonder Book (with others, nd)
Percy Westerman The Mystery of Nix Hall (1950)
The Big Christmas Wonder Book (with others, 1935)
Selfridge's Schoolboys' Story Book (with others, nd)
Thrilling Air Stories (with others, nd)

Periodicals: The Big Budget, Champion Annual, Chums, Holiday Annual, Little Folks, The Scout

John Eyre (d. 1927)

Born in Staffordshire. Studied at the South Kensington School of Art. Worked as a genre painter in watercolours (mainly of religious themes), enameller and pottery designer. A good deal of Eyre's not very distinguished black and white work suffered from cheap 'process' reproduction. His colour illustrations, which fared rather better,

F.R. Exell. Frontispiece for *Moonfleet* by J. Meade Faulkner (Penguin, 1962).

revealed more painterly qualities. A number of his *Evangeline* drawings bore a distinct resemblance to Frank Dicksee's earlier illustrations of the same poem. Lived in London and at Petworth, Sussex. Elected RBA (1896), RI (1917).

Books illustrated include:
Washington Irving Rip Van Winkle (nd)
Henry Longfellow Voices of the Night (1899), Evangeline (1902)
M.B. Manwell Carol Adair (1899)
Alfred, Lord Tennyson In Memoriam (1902)
Old Ballads (1906)
Old Time Ballads (1902)

References: Houfe; Johnson & Greutzner; Thieme & Becker; Vollmer supp; Waters; C. Wood

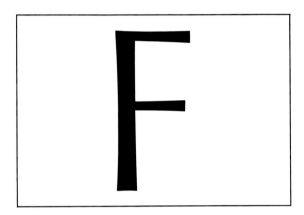

Pearl Falconer (active from 1960s)

Born in Dundee. Studied at St Martin's School of Art and under Bernard Meninsky at the Central School of Arts and Crafts. Painter of portraits and murals, magazine and children's book illustrator, and costume designer for films. In her illustrations, she works with a spontaneous, economical pen line, sometimes emphasised with areas of solid black. Elected FSIA.

Books illustrated include:
Natalie Savage Carson The Happy Orpheline (1960), The Orphelines in the Enchanted Castle (1963), A Pet for the Orphelines (1963)
Penelope Farmer The China People (1960)
Mary Treadgold The Winter Princess (1962)

Periodicals: Harper's Bazaar, The Listener, The New York Herald Tribune, The New York Times, Radio Times

References: ICB 3; Jacques; Ryder; Usherwood; *The Junior Bookshelf* vol 27 no 1 (1963)

Joan Jefferson Farjeon (b. 1913)

Born in London, daughter of novelist and playwright Joseph Jefferson Farjeon and niece of children's writer Eleanor Farjeon. Studied at Westminster School of Art. A professional stage designer and scene painter for over 50 years, she was responsible for the sets and costumes of the plays by her close friend Nicholas Stuart Gray between 1949 and 1970; she also illustrated many

of his books and plays for children. She worked mainly in pen and ink (apart from cover designs which were mostly two or three colour). Her illustrations are finely shaded and decorative, with elements of the whimsical and picturesque. [Q]

Books illustrated include:
Nicholas Stuart Gray Beauty and the Beast (1951), The Tinder-Box (1951), The Princess and the Swineherd (1952), The Hunters and the Henwife (1954), The Marvellous Story of Puss in Boots (1955), The Imperial Nightingale (1957), New Clothes for the Emperor (1957), The Other Cinderella (1958), The Seventh Swan (1962), The Stone Cage (1963), New Lamps for Old (1968)

Reference: ICB 2

John Frederick William Charles Farleigh (1900-65)

Worked as John Farleigh. Born in London. Left school at the age of fourteen to take up a five year apprenticeship to the Artists' Illustrators (a commercial graphics firm). For 10 years, he attended evening classes in life drawing at the Bolt Court School, Fleet Street, London. After army service (1918-19), studied under Noel Rooke* (and Bernard Meninsky) at the Central School of Arts and Crafts (1919-22). Art teacher at Rugby School (1922-24). From 1925, he taught antique and still-life drawing at the Central School. Worked for

Pearl Falconer. From *The Happy Orpheline* by Natalie Savage Carlson (Blackie, 1960).

John Farleigh. 'In an eveningtide David arose from his bed, and walked upon the roof, he saw a woman washing herself...' From *The Story of David* (A. & C. Black, 1934).

the Golden Cockerel and Shakespeare Head Presses to which he was introduced by Rooke. During the 1940s, he was director of the Sylvan Press. President of the Arts and Crafts Exhibition Society (1940-46). Head of the book illustration department at the Central School (1947-48). Honorary Chairman of the Crafts Centre of Great Britain (1950-64). Painter, wood engraver, lithographer, black and white artist, broadcaster and writer.

Farleigh was an outstanding book illustrator, using wood engraving (his favourite medium) and pen and ink with equal success. He was one of the first engravers to work extensively for general publishers rather than for private presses, making his name with the widely acclaimed illustrations for Bernard Shaw's *The Adventures of the Black Girl in her Search for God* (Constable 1932), which sold out within a few days of publication. Writing four years later, Clare Leighton* detected an alteration in Farleigh's style, considering that 'he has lately veered towards the Blair Hughes-Stanton* school, so that his work is distinctly different from what it was in the days when he first became well known.' (*The Studio* special, Winter 1936). During the 1930s, his work was occasionally marred by an unsettled relationship between naturalistically treated figures or faces and formal, linear elements of design, a problem brilliantly resolved in his pen and ink drawings of ghosts in *Haunted England* (1951). Elected LG (1927), RE (1948); awarded CBE (1949).

Books illustrated include:
Ethel Armitage A Country Garden (1936)
W.J. Brown The Gods had Wings (1936)
John Bunyan The Pilgrim's Progress (nd)
Samuel Butler The Way of all Flesh (1934)
Walter de la Mare Stories from the Bible (1933)
Lovat Dickson Hortensius, Friend of Nero (1936)
John Farleigh Graven Image (1940), It Never Dies (1946)
Cicely Hamilton Little Arthur's History of the 20th Century (1933)
Christina Hole Haunted England (1951)
Claude Houghton Three Fantastic Tales (1934)
D.H. Lawrence The Man Who Died (1935)
Jack Lindsay Storm at Sea (1935)
Cunliffe Owen The Precursors (1934)
George Bernard Shaw The Adventures of the Black Girl in her Search for God (1932), Short Stories, Scraps and Shavings (1933), Prefaces (1934), Back to Methuselah (1938)
Sacheverell Sitwell Old Fashioned Flowers (1939)
Jonathan Swift Selected Essays (1925)
Dr Tucker The Disappointed Lion (1937)
R. Turner Spotted Dog: A Book of English Inn Signs (1948)
Complete Homer (1929-32)
Odes of Pindar (1928-29)
Plutarch's Lives (1937)
The Story of David (1934)

References: Balston EWE, WEMEB; Bénézit; Garrett BWE, HBWE; Gilmour; Johnson & Greutzner; Lewis; Vollmer; Wa (1972); Waters; *The Studio* 108 (1934), 123 (1942), special (Spring 1927, Winter 1936, Autumn 1938); *A Guide to the Practice of Illustration* (SIA Lectures 1937); Dorothea Braby *The Way of Wood Engraving* (Studio 1953); John Farleigh *Graven Image, Typography and Illustration* (Royal Society of Art, Cantor Lecture 1938) (Macmillan 1940); Christopher Sandford *Bibliography of the Golden Cockerel Press* (Dawson 1975), *Cock-a-Hoop* (Private Libraries Association 1976); A.C. Sewter *Modern British Woodcuts and Wood Engravings in the Collection of the Whitworth Art Gallery* (Manchester 1962)

Edith Farmiloe (active 1893-1908)

Maiden name: Edith Parnell. Second cousin of the Irish patriot Charles Parnell. The slum children of her clergyman husband's parish in Soho (London) formed the subject of many of her illustrated books. Her work has affinities with that of Phil May* and Tom Browne*, but is less naturalistic and more stylised than either of theirs. She drew in bold outline, without shading and often without backgrounds, depicting her ragamuffin subjects with humour and considerable sympathy. Elected ASWA (1905), SWA (1907).

Books illustrated include:
Edith Farmiloe 'Chousers' and other stories (1898), Chapel Street Children (1900), Piccalilli (1900), Little Citizens (1901), Young George (1901), Mr and Mrs Tiddiwinks (1902), One Day (1903), Mr Biddle and the Dragon (1904), Elizabeth-over-the-way (1905)
V. Lucas All the World Over (1898)
W. Parnell Rag, Tag and Bobtail (1899)

Periodicals: The Child's Pictorial, Little Folks, Pearson's Magazine

References: Bénézit; Houfe; Johnson & Greutzner; Thieme & Becker; *The Studio* 18 (1900), special (1900-01)

Herbert Granville Fell (1872-1951)

Born in London. Educated at Kings College School. Studied art at Heatherley's School of Art and in France, Belgium and Germany. First exhibited at the Royal Academy at the age of 19, and at about the same time began drawing for magazines. He illustrated and decorated books from around 1895 with many of his early commissions coming from the publisher Dent. In about 1900, he was appointed Director of Drawing, Painting and Design at the Royal Albert Memorial College at Exeter; he was also art advisor for some twenty years to the decorative bookbinder Cedric Chivers of Bath, designed stained glass and metalwork, and was an active member of the Art Workers' League. From 1907, he was Art Editor of George Newnes's book department, and of various magazines including *The Ladies' Field* (1907-19), *The Strand Magazine* (1910-12) and *The Woman at Home*. He was later Editor of *The Connoisseur* and his extensive writing on art included monographs on Vermeer and Cézanne. Fell's book illustrations and decorations, in black and white and full colour, were well within the traditions of Art Nouveau, often emphasising the Celtic elements in the style. Thorpe's appraisal of him as 'another artist of the academic school deriving much of his inspiration from the work of William Morris and Walter Crane' is accurate but unnecessarily dismissive. He was an outstandingly professional linear draughtsman, able to organise his ideas into coherent, satisfying and often evocative designs.

Books illustrated include:
Nathaniel Hawthorne A Wonder Book and Tanglewood Tales (1910)
Constance Maud Wagner's Heroes (1895)
E. Nesbit The Book of Dragons (1900)
Ali Baba and the Forty Thieves (1895)
The Book of Job (1896)
Cinderella and Jack and the Beanstalk (1895)
The Fairy Gifts and Tom Hickathrift (1895)
Our Lady's Tumbler (1894)
The Serious Poems of Thomas Hood (1901)
Song of Solomon (1897)
Wonder Stories from Herodotus (1900)

Periodicals: The English Illustrated Magazine, The Ladies' Field, The Ludgate Monthly, The Pall Mall Magazine, The Windmill

References: Baker; Bénézit; Houfe; Johnson & Greutzner; Sketchley; Thieme & Becker; Thorpe; Vollmer; Wa (1950); Waters; C. Wood; *Apollo* 54 (1951); *The Connoisseur* 128 (1952); *The Studio* 2 (1894), 142 (1951), special (1897-98, 1898-99, 1899-1900, 1900-01, Spring 1914); H.G. Fell *The Future of the Illustrator* (Press Art School supplement 1912); Holbrook Jackson *The 1890s* (Grant Richards 1913)

Ronald George Ferns (b. 1925)

Works as Ronald Ferns. Studied at St Martin's School of Art from the age of fourteen. Worked in the art department of a publishing firm, and as a scene painter, before becoming a freelance magazine and advertising illustrator. Illustrated a children's feature in *Good Housekeeping* from 1946 for about twenty years. Designed a mural for the Festival of Britain, sets and costumes for the Ballet Rambert's *Fate's Revenge*, and carpets for the Time-Life Building in London. His early book illustrations were in gouache; subsequently, he has used pen and ink line with neatly hatched shading in controlled, stylish designs.

Books illustrated include:
Lewis Carroll Alice Versary (1959)
Lettice Cooper Garibaldi (1964)
Arthur Guiness, Son & Co Untopical Songs (1953)
Gladys Williams Semolina Silkpaws Comes to Town (1962), Fireworks for Semolina Silkpaws (1964), Semolina Silkpaws' Motor-Car (1968)

Periodicals: Country Fair, Good Housekeeping, Harper's Bazaar, Housewife, Lilliput, Scope, Vogue

References: ICB 3; Wa (1966)

Joseph Finnemore (1860-1939)

Born in Birmingham. Studied at Birmingham School of Art and in Antwerp under Verlat. Travelled around Europe, visiting France, Germany, Greece, Malta, Turkey and Russia. After returning to England (1881) he was employed as a 'special' artist by *The Graphic* and later *The Sphere* (for which he covered the Boer War). His first illustrations of fiction appeared in *The Boy's Own Paper* (1884) and he was soon much in demand as an illustrator of adventure stories. He was a regular contributor to *Black and White*, specialising in military uniforms and fencing. Finnemore also made a reputation as a painter of adventure scenes, and as a portrait painter, medallist and etcher. His illustrations, in pen and ink, halftone, and, less often, in full colour, are reasonably competent and in many ways typify the 'action pictures' of the late Victorian and Edwardian eras. Elected RBA (1893), RI (1898), RBSA (1901).

Books illustrated include:
G. Allen The White Man's Boot (1888)
Daniel Defoe Robinson Crusoe (nd)
J. Finnemore The Animals' Circus (1915)
Henry Gilbert The Book of Pirates (1916)
James Glass Chats Over a Pipe (1922)
G.A. Henty When London Burned (1895)
Charles Kingsley Westward Ho! (1925)
Mrs Molesworth Philippa (1896)

J. Finnemore. 'I resolved to watch' from *Robinson Crusoe* by Daniel Defoe (Children's Press, nd).

William Shakespeare The Merry Wives of Windsor (1897)
W.G. Stables Kidnapped by Cannibals (1900)
J. Wyss Swiss Family Robinson (1897)

Periodicals: Black and White, The Boy's Own Paper, Cassell's Family Magazine, Cassell's Saturday Journal, Chums, The English Illustrated Magazine, The Girl's Own Paper, The Graphic, The Quiver, The Sphere, The Strand Magazine, The Windsor Magazine, The Wide World Magazine

References: Bénézit; Doyle BWI; Houfe; Johnson & Greutzner; Mallalieu; Thieme & Becker; Thorpe; Vollmer supp; Wa (1934); Waters; C. Wood

Charlotte Firmin (b. 1954)

Born London, daughter of Peter Firmin*. Studied at Hornsey College of Art (1972-73) and Brighton Polytechnic (1973-76). Freelance writer and illustrator of children's books since 1975. Works in pen and ink and watercolour. Publishers of her work include A. & C. Black and André Deutsch.

Books illustrated include:
Birthe Alton The Magic of Ah (1980)
Terry Deary The Custard Kid (1978), Calamity Kate (1980), The Lambton Worm (1981)
Mary Dickinson Alex's Bed (1980), Alex and Roy (1981), Alex and the Baby (1982)
Annabel Farjeon The Cock of Round Hill (1977)
Charlotte Firmin Hannah's Great Decision (1978), Claire's Secret Ambition (1979), Eggbert's Balloon (1979), The Eggham Pot of Gold (1979), Egglantine's Party (1979), The Giant Egg Plant (1979)
Hugo Rice The Remarkable Feat of King Caboodle (1978)

Periodical: The Egg

Peter Firmin (b. 1928)

Born Harwich, Essex. Studied illustration at Colchester School of Art (1944-47) and, after National Service in the Royal Navy, graphic design and book production at the Central School (1949-52), where he studied lino and wood cutting under Gertrude Hermes*. He began working freelance as a magazine illustrator while employed as a glass cutter and painter in a stained glass studio (1953-55) and as a general artist in an advertising studio (1955-57), contributing some of the first illustrations to the *New Scientist*. He has collaborated with writer Oliver Postgate since 1958, initially on 'cutprice cardboard cartoons' and then on animated puppet and cartoon films for television; among their creations have been *The Clangers, Alexander the Mouse, Noggin the Nog, Bagpuss* and *Ivor the Engine*, all of which have later reappeared in books. Firmin also made the puppet 'Basil Brush' for television, and wrote the subsequent series of *Basil Brush* stories (published by Kaye & Ward). He has recently invented a new character, Bramwell the rat, for a series of books in the form of the rat's diaries, the first of which is *The Winter*

Peter Firmin. From *Noggin and the Whale* by Oliver Postgate (Edmund Ward, 1965).

Diary. For book illustration, he usually works in pen and ink, often with colour washes, using realistic detail to give conviction to unlikely or fantastic situations. As a collector of 19th-century illustrated books, he feels that he has been influenced (in particular) by the works of the Cruikshanks, Jean Grandville and James Gillray. Among 20th-century illustrators, he admires the work of W. Heath Robinson* and James Boswell*. He lives near Canterbury, Kent, in the same village as Oliver Postgate. His two eldest daughters (of six) are both illustrators, Charlotte and Hannah Firmin. [Q]

Books illustrated include:
Peter Firmin Basil Brush Goes Boating (1969), Basil Brush Goes Flying (1969), Basil Brush in the Jungle (1970), Basil Brush at the Seaside (1970), Basil Brush and the Dragon (1971), Basil Brush Finds Treasure (1971), Basil Brush Builds a House (1973), Basil Brush Gets a Medal (1973), Basil Brush and the Windmills (1979), Basil Brush on the Trail (1979), Three Tales of Basil Brush (1979), Chicken Stew (1981), The Winter Diary of a Country Rat (1981)
Peter Meteyard Stanley: the Tale of the Lizard (1979)
E. Nesbit The last of the Dragons (1980), Mélisande (1981)
Oliver Postgate Noggin the King (1965), Noggin and the Whale (1965), Ice Dragon (1968), The Firecake (1969), The Island (1969), The Omruds (1969), The Flowers (1971), The Pie (1971), The Game (1972), The Monster (1972), Nogbad the Elephant (1972), Nogbad Comes Back (1972), Noggin and the Dragon (1972), Noggin and the Moon Mouse (1972), Noggin and the Storks (1973), Bagpuss in the Sun (1974), Bagpuss on a Rainy Day (1974), King of the Nogs (1974), The Blackwash (1975), The Icebergs (1975), Nogmania (1977), Ivor the Engine: First Story (1977), Snowdrifts (1978), Dragon (1978), The Elephant (1978), Tricks and Tales (1982)

Periodicals: Country Fair, Good Eating, New Scientist, Radio Times, Scope TV Times

References: Fisher p.144; *Books for Keeps* (School Bookshop Association July 1980)

Anne Harriet Fish (d. 1964)

Worked as 'Fish'. Married name: Mrs Sefton. Born Bristol. Studied under John Hassall* and at

Fish (Anne Harriet Fish). 'Shoemakers had to invent something' from *Gin and Ginger* by Lady Kitty Vincent (John Lane, The Bodley Head, 1927).

the London School of Art and in Paris. She lived in London, at East Grinstead, Sussex and at St Ives, Cornwall. She was a mainstay of *The Tatler* during the 1920s and 1930s, contributing drawings and caricatures in a mannered Art Deco idiom somewhat resembling the work of Aubrey Hammond*, but deriving ultimately from Aubrey Beardsley's work. Cornelis Veth regarded her as one of the most important social satirists of the day. He wrote that she depicted modern society with modern boldness, using its own weapons to attack it with cynical understanding—'the mock naîveté of her drawings makes the shamelessness of the subjects acceptable... It is a world where the girls, emancipated in the wrong way, are masters of a piteous situation' He saw her drawings as 'morally speaking...cruel, almost perverse, without however being wholly vicious.' Today her economical and polished designs come across as amusingly sharp, satirical commentaries on the

flapper lifestyle. In graphic style and often in subject, her book illustrations resemble her magazine drawings.

Books illustrated include:
Anne Harriet Fish Awful Weekends and Guests (1938)
Fowl The New Eve (1917), The Third Eve Book (1919)
Gilbert Frankau One of Us (1917)
Harry Graham The World We Laugh In (1924)
Ruth Holmes The Clock and the Cockatoo (1922)
Sydney Tremayne Tatlings (1922)
Lady Kitty Vincent Lipstick (1925), Sugar and Spice (1926), Gin and Ginger (1927)
The Rubaiyat of Omar Khayyam (1922)

Periodicals: Cosmopolitan, Eve, Harper's Bazaar, London Calling, Nash's Magazine, Printer's Pie, Punch, The Tatler, Vanity Fair, Vogue

References: Guichard; Houfe; Johnson & Greutzner; Veth; Wa (1964); Waters; *The Studio* special (Autumn 1928); G. Montague Ellwood *The Art of Pen Drawing* (Batsford 1927).

Thomas Henry Fisher (1879-1962)

Worked as Thomas Henry. Born Eastwood, Nottinghamshire. Studied at Nottingham School of Art. He worked as a lithographer (his first job was the 'sailor' trade-mark for Player's cigarettes) and poster designer before becoming a regular contributor of cartoons and humorous illustrations to newspapers and magazines. His forte was the funny side of school life and he illustrated the first 34 of Richmal Crompton's 'William' books in pen and ink in a cheerful, effective and remarkably

Thomas Henry (Fisher). ' "I've jus' remembered," said William, "that I saw someone at the fête in a coat exactly like that one what you've got on." ' From *William the Outlaw* by Richmal Crompton (Newnes, 1927).

consistent style. Although the first of these books was published in 1922, Fisher did not meet Richmal Crompton until 1954.

Books illustrated include:
Richmal Crompton Just William (1922), More William (1923), William Again (1923), William the Fourth (1924), Still William (1925), William the Conqueror (1926), William the Outlaw (1927), William in Trouble (1927), William the Good (1928), William (1929), William the Bad (1930), William's Happy Days (1930), William's Crowded Hours (1931), William the Pirate (1932), William the Rebel (1933), William the Gangster (1934), William the Detective (1935), Sweet William (1936), William the Snowman (1937), William the Dictator (1938), William the A.R.P. (1939), William and the Evacuees (1940), William Does His Bit (1941), William Carries On (1942), William and the Brains Trust (1945), Just William's Luck (1948), William the Bold (1950), William and the Tramp (1952), William and the Moon Rocket (1954), William and the Space Animal (1956), William's Television Show (1958), William the Explorer (1960), William's Treasure Trove (1962), William and the Witch (with Henry Ford, 1964)

Periodicals: The Boy's Own Paper, The Captain, Chums, Crusoe, Happy Magazine, Home Magazine, The Humorist, Nottingham Guardian, Passing Show, Punch, The Windsor Magazine

References: Doyle BWI, CL

Nicholas Fisk (b. 1923)

Born London. Served in the Royal Air Force during World War II. Head of Creative Department of Percy Lund, Humphries & Co. Author and illustrator of children's books published principally by Hamish Hamilton. Since the early 1970s, he has concentrated on unillustrated science fiction writing.

Books illustrated include:
Lettice Cooper The Bear Who Was Too Big (1963)
Eric Fenby Menuhin's House of Music (1969)
Nicholas Fisk Look at Cars (1959), The Bouncers (1964)
William Mayne Skiffy (1972)
Geoffrey Morgan Tea with Mr Timothy (1966)

References: Contemporary Authors; Kirkpatrick

Dennis Flanders (b. 1915)

Educated at Merchant Taylors' School, London. Studied at the Regent Street Polytechnic, the Central School of Art and St Martin's School of Art. Served in the army during World War II. Topographical and architectural draughtsman in pencil and watercolour; 'special' artist on *The Illustrated London News* (1956-64). He has been working for several years on a series of 224 drawings in colour and in black and white for a book called *Dennis Flanders' Britain*. He lives in London. Elected RBA (1970), ARWS (1970), RWS (1976); member of the Art Workers' Guild (Master 1975). [Q]

Books illustrated include:
Michael Brander Soho for East Anglia (1963)
Alastair M. Dunnett Land of Scotch (with others, 1953)
Richard Edmonds Chelsea: From the Five Fields to the World's End (1956)
Dennis Flanders The Twelve Great Livery Companies (1974)

C.V. Hancock East and West of Severn (with J. Porteous Wood, 1956)
John Raynor A Westminster Childhood (1973)
Gwen Wade Yorkshire Sketchbook (with others, 1947)
J.R. Walbran A Visit to Bolton Priory (1948)

Periodicals: The Birmingham Post, The Builder, The Daily Telegraph, The Field, Radio Times, The Sphere, The Sunday Times, Yorkshire Post

W. Claude Flight (1881-1955)

Son of Walter Flight FRS. Trained as an engineer and worked as a librarian and beekeeper before entering Heatherley's School of Art (1913); returned to Heatherley's after World War I and concentrated on lino-cuts. Taught at Iain Macnab's* Grosvenor School of Modern Art (where pupils included Eileen Mayo*), and at a number of summer schools; became an early proponent of the psychotherapeutic possibilities of art. Lived in London and Wiltshire and (from 1926) in a cave (inhabited by humans since prehistoric times) near Guyon, France. In 1920, he met former Slade student Edith Lawrence (1890-1973), a painter and textile printer; they soon became inseparable, collaborating on exhibitions, setting up an interior design business (from 1927), and writing and illustrating books. They pioneered the use of lino prints in books, using the medium to create powerful, rhythmical images that seemed to be held on the page surfaces only by their formal qualities of design. S.C. Kaines-Smith considered that Flight succeeded in imposing order on the kaleidoscopic movement of Futurist art, especially that of Gino Severini, and that his work 'carried the aesthetic aspects of Futurism beyond any point reached by its originators'. Flight organised exhibitions of British linocuts at the Redfern Gallery (1929-37). Also a teacher and writer. Elected ARBA (1923), RBA (1925).

Books illustrated include:
Claude Flight Tinker Tailor (1929), Animal, Vegetable or Mineral (1931)
Claude Flight and Edith Lawrence Christmas and other Feasts and Festivals (1936), A Little About Art (1938), A Little About Art (1938), A Little About History (1938)

References: Bénézit; Johnson & Greutzner; Vollmer; Wa (1954); Waters; *Apollo* 14 (1931); *The Studio* special (Spring 1927); *British Print Makers of the 1920s and 1930s* (Michael Parkin catalogue 1974); *Claude Flight and his Circle* (Michael Parkin catalogue 1975); Claude Flight *The Art and Craft of Lino Cutting and Printing* (B.T. Batsford 1934), *Linocuts* (John Lane 1927); S.C. Kaines-Smith *Painters of England* (Medici Society 1934)

William Russell Flint (1880-1969)

Worked as Russell Flint. Born Edinburgh, son of artist F.W. Flint. For six years from the age of fourteen, he was apprenticed to a firm of lithographers and attended art classes in Edinburgh. Moved to London (1900), where he first found work as a medical illustrator. Joined the staff of

The Illustrated London News and enrolled at Heatherley's School of Art. Visited Italy (1912-13) and on his return studied etching at Hammersmith School of Art (1914). Served in the Royal Naval Volunteer Reserve and the Royal Air Force during World War I. He made his name as a technically brilliant watercolourist, specialising in scenes with sunlit, semi-nude nymphets, which, reproduced as prints, found a ready market. He had comparable success with his highly polished colour illustrations for lavishly produced gift books, mainly published by the Medici Society. These virtuoso set-pieces, rather in the manner of Byam Shaw*, were usually greeted with great praise by public and critics alike. A more balanced appraisal came from F.J. Harvey Darton in *Modern Book Illustration in Great Britain and America (The Studio* special Winter 1931); writing about Flint's illustrations for the Medici *Chaucer*, he praised their 'lucid and harmonious' colour and design, but criticised them as mere costume pieces, lacking curiosity and insight into character. He concluded 'there is nothing stimulating or provocative in such pictures. The "reader" is not brought into vivid contact with a fresh mind, or illuminated anew as to the author's personality.' This evaluation did nothing to hinder Flint's triumphant progress in the upper echelons of the Establishment. Elected RI (1912), RSW (1913), RWS (1917), ARA (1924) and RA (1933), RE (1931) and PRWS (1936-56). He was knighted in 1947.

Books illustrated include:
Matthew Arnold The Scholar Gipsy and Thyrsis (1910)
Robert Burns Songs and Lyrics (1911)
Geoffrey Chaucer The Canterbury Tales (1913)
Sir W.R. Flint Models of Propriety (1951), Minxes Admonished or
   Beauty Reproved (1955), Shadows in Arcady (1965), Breakfast in
   Périgord (1968)
W.S. Gilbert The Mikado (with C.E. Brock*, 1928), The Yeomen of
   the Guard (with C.E. Brock*, 1929)
H. Rider Haggard King Solomon's Mines (1905)
Robert Herrick One Hundred and Eleven Poems (1955)
Homer The Odyssey (1924)
Dr Montague James (intro) The Book of Tobit and History of Susanna
   (1929)
Thomas à Kempis (intro Wilfrid Raynal) The Imitation of Christ (1908)
Charles Kingsley The Heroes (1912)
Andrew Lang (trans) The Idylls of Theocritus, Bion and Moschus
   (1922)
Sir Thomas Malory Le Morte D'Arthur (4 vols 1910-11)
M.F. Pidansat de Mairobert Memoirs of Madame du Barry (1956)
The Thoughts of the Emperor Marcus Aurelius Antonius (1910)
Judith (1928)
The Song of Songs (1909)

Periodicals: Black and White, Cassell's Magazine, The English
Illustrated Magazine, The Graphic, The Illustrated London News, The
Pall Mall Magazine, Pearson's Magazine, The Sketch, The Tatler

References: Bénézit; Bradshaw; Guichard; Houfe; ICB 1; Johnson &
Greutzner; Mallalieu; Thieme & Becker; Vollmer; Wa (1960); Waters;
The Studio 60 (1914), special (Autumn 1914, 1923-24, Winter 1931);
William Russell Flint *Drawings* (Collins 1950), *An Autobiography: In
Pursuit* (Medici Society 1970); Arnold Palmer *More Than Shadows*
(The Studio 1943); Malcolm Salaman *Modern Masters of Etching* no 27

W. *Russell Flint.* From *The Imitation of Christ* by Thomas à Kempis with an introducton by Wilfrid Raynal (Chatto & Windus, 1908).

(The Studio 1925-32); G.F. Sandilands *William Russell Flint: Famous
Watercolour Painters* (*The Studio* 1928)

Gareth Floyd (b. 1940)

Born in Whiston, Lancashire. Spent his childhood in Halesworth, Suffolk, and studied at Lowestoft School of Art, Guildford School of Art and Brighton College of Art. Secondary school teacher at Orpington (1963-64); lecturer in illustration at Leicester College of Art (1964-67). Since 1967, he has combined freelance illustration with an active political life as a County Councillor (Guildford Borough Council and Surrey County Council) and parliamentary candidate (Aldershot 1974). His book illustrations are in pen and ink, sometimes with watercolour washes, and are lively, naturalistic and informal in treatment. He was a regular contributor to *Cricket* magazine before its demise, and now contributes regularly to the BBC's *Jackanory* programme and also to other television programmes. [Q]

Books illustrated include:
Richard Armstrong The Mutineers (1968)
Margaret Baker The Sand Bird (1973), Lock Stock and Barrel (1974)
Martin Ballard Bristol (1966), The Emir's Son (1967), Rome and

Empire (1970), The Cross and the Sword (1970), Faith and Violence (1970), Sails and Guns (1970), Europe Reaches Round the World (1970), Kings and Courtiers (1970), Revolutions and Steam Engines (1971), The Age of Progress (1971), The World at War (1971)

Roy Brown The Thunder Pool (1971)

Hester Burton Otmoor for Ever (1968), Through the Fire (1969)

Betsy Byars The Midnight Fox (1970)

Joseph Chipperfield Storm Island (1970)

Mary Cockett Boat Girl (1972), Backyard Hospital (1976)

Helen Cresswell The Signposters (1968), The Night-Watchmen (1969), The Game of Catch (1969), The Wilkses (1970), Up the Pier (1971)

Gillian Cross Save Our School (1981)

Joan de Hamel Take the Long Path (1978)

Lavinia Derwent The Boy in the Bible (1973)

Charles Dickens Great Expectations (1970)

Peter Dickinson The Gift (1973)

Eilis Dillon The Five Hundred (1972)

R.P.A. Edwards The Tower Block (1969), The By-Pass (1969), The New Town (1970), The Branch Line (1970)

R.M. Fisher Stories about the Sparks Family (1976)

John L. Foster My Friend Cheryl (1975)

Joyce Gard The Hagwaste Donkeys (1976)

Gwen Grant Private—Keep Out (1979), Knock and Wait (1981)

Margaret Greaves The Snake Whistle (1980)

Angela Grunsell Jackdaw, Jackdaw (1980)

Rob Grunsell Stan the Stammer (1980)

Michael Hardcastle Holiday House (1977), Crash Car (1977), Fire on the Sea (1977), Strong Arm (1977)

Cynthia Harnett The Writing on the Hearth (1971)

Clifford B. Hicks Alvin Fernald, Mayor for a Day (1975)

Mollie Hunter The Bodach (1970), The Wolf King (1975)

Alan C. Jenkins The Man Who Rode a Tiger (1975)

Geraldine Kaye The Raffle Pony (1966), Tawno Gypsy Boy (1968), Nowhere to Stop (1972), Billy-Boy (1975), Children of the Turnpike (1976)

Betty Lee The City-on-the-Water (1976)

Penelope Lively The Whispering Knights (1971)

Cecil Maiden Castle Dangerous (1975)

Laurence Meynell The Great Cup Tie (1974)

Peggy Miller Life in Elizabethan London (1976)

Eileen Molony Giant, Spriggan and Buccaboo (1980)

Bill Naughton The Goalkeeper's Revenge and other stories (1976)

Richard Parker Second-Hand Family (1965), He is Your Brother (1974)

P.D. Pemberton Richard's M-Class Cows (1975)

Madeleine Polland Prince of the Double Axe (1976)

Ray Pope The Model Railway Men (series from 1970)

Sheena Porter The Knockers (1965)

Christine Pullein-Thompson Book of Pony Stories (1975), Strange Riders of Black Pony Inn (1976)

'Miss Read' Animal Boy (1975)

James Reeves Two Greedy Bears (1974)

Meta Mayne Reid The Plotters of Pollnashee (1973)

Mary Schroeder By Winding Water (1976)

Ian Serraillier Havelock the Warrior (1968)

Leonard Smith The New House (1975)

Eleanor Spence The Year of the Currawong (1965)

Catherine Storr Kate and the Island (1972), February Yowler (1982)

Ann Turnbull The Wolf King (1975)

Ronald Welch The Hawk (1967)

Barbara Willard The Grove of Green Holly (1967), Hurrah for Rosie (1968), Royal Rosie (1968), The Lark and the Laurel (1970), The Miller's Boy (1976)

Periodicals: Car, Cricket, Ford Times, The Sunday Telegraph

References: Eyre; Fisher p.342; ICB 4

Charles James Folkard (1878-1963)

Worked as Charles Folkard. Born Lewisham, London, son of a printer. Became an expert conjurer, and, while designing his own programmes, discovered his preference for drawing. Studied at

Charles Folkard. 'The great teeth of the animal closed upon a mouthful of the sacred vestments…' from *The Princess and Curdie* by George Macdonald (Dent, 1949).

Gareth Floyd. From *The Grove of Green Holly* by Barbara Willard (Constable, 1967).

various schools of art including the St John's Wood School of Art and Goldsmith's College School of Art. He illustrated nursery literature and children's classics in black and white and full colour with professionalism, often combining naturalistic detail with a strong element of caricature. He was the creator of the *Daily Mail* children's strip cartoon *Teddy Tail* (1915) which continued until 1960, and the author of a number of children's plays and pantomimes. He lived in London, Kent and Sussex.

Books illustrated include:
Richard Barham The Jackdaw of Rheims (1913)
Dorothy Black The Magic Egg (1922)
Arthur Brook Witch's Hollow (1920)
Lewis Carroll Alice's Adventures in Wonderland (1929)
Alice Daglish and Ernest Rhys The Land of Nursery Rhyme (1932)
Lucy Mary Jane Garnett Ottoman Wonder Tales (1915)
William Glover British Fairy and Folk Tales (1920)
Roger Lancelyn Green The Book of Nonsense (1956)
Alice Hoffman The Children's Shakespeare (1911)
S.Z. Kossak Troubles of a Gnome (1928)
Charles and Mary Lamb Tales from Shakespeare (1926)
Lorenzini Pinocchio (1914)
George Macdonald The Princess and Curdie (1949), The Princess and the Goblin (1949)
H.A. Nybloe Jolly Calls (nd)
Eden Philpotts The Flint Heart (1910)
J.R. Wyss Swiss Family Robinson (1910)
Aesop's Fables (1912)
The Arabian Nights (1913)
Grimm's Fairy Tales (1911)
Mother Goose's Nursery Rhymes (1919)
Mother Goose's Nursery Tales (1923)
Ottoman Wonder Tales (1915)

Periodicals: Daily Mail, Little Folks, Printer's Pie, Tatler, Teddy Tail Annual, Watkin's Annual

References: Cope; Doyle BWI, CL; Houfe; ICB 1; Wa (1962); Waters

Henry Justice Ford (1860-1941)

Usually worked as H.J. Ford. Born in London, into a cricketing family. Studied at Clare College, Cambridge (first class, Classical tripos, 1882), at the Slade School of Fine Art, and at Sir Hubert Von Herkomer's Bushey School of Art. Served as a private in the Artists' Rifles during World War I. He was a prolific illustrator, especially of anthologies of children's fairy and folk tales and poetry. His best known illustrations were for the coloured Fairy Books, edited by Andrew Lang (to whom he was introduced by Percy Jacomb-Hood*). The eleven books in this series, published by Longman, Green & Co. between 1889 and 1913, each had a cloth binding in the colour of the title, gold-printed in a design by Ford, and were profusely illustrated with full page and smaller pen and ink drawings, and (in the later books) some colour plates. The slightly diffident pen work in the earliest one, *The Blue Fairy Book* (1889), soon developed into the strong confident line of his mature work. His images were widely imaginative, and often romantic in feeling, and were given conviction by his detailed draughtsmanship and instinct for

H.J. Ford. 'Old Eric catches Hans' from *Hans, the Mermaid's Son* in *The Pink Fairy Book* edited by Andrew Lang (Longmans Green, 1901).

clear, dramatic design. He was a friend of Sir Edward Burne-Jones, whose influence can be seen in Ford's 'aesthetic' female types as well as in the air of dreamlike fantasy in much of his work. Houfe notes the influence of some of the earlier Pre-Raphaelites in the brilliant colour and detail in the plates of some of his later books, and that of Walter Crane* on his black and white drawings. Ford was also a painter and pastellist, exhibiting portraits, landscapes and mythological subjects. He lived in London and Dorset.

Books illustrated include:
E.F. Benson David Blaize and the Blue Door (1918)
F.W. Bourdillon A Lost God (1891)
Arthur Brookfield (ed) Aesop's Fables (1888)
John Bunyan The Pilgrim's Progress (1921)
Revd W. Lowther Clarke The Parables (1921), St Peter and St Paul (1922)
Harry P. Greene Pilot and other stories (1916)
M.R. James Old Testament Legends (1913)
Andrew Lang (ed) The Blue Fairy Book (with G.P.J. Hood*, 1889), The Red Fairy Book (with L. Speed*, 1890), The Green Fairy Book (1892), The True Story (with others, 1893), The Yellow Fairy Book (1894), The Blue True Story Book (with others, 1896), The Animal Story Book (1896), The Pink Fairy Book (1897), The Red True Story Book (1897), The Arabian Nights Entertainment (1898), The Red Book of Animal Stories (1899), The Grey Fairy Book (1900), The Violet Fairy Book (1901), The Book of Romance (1902), The Disentanglers (1902), The Crimson Fairy Book (1903), The Brown Fairy Book (1904), The Red Romance Book (1905), The Orange Fairy Book (1906), The Olive Fairy Book (1907), Tales of Greece and Troy, The Marvellous Musicians and other stories (1909), The Lilac Fairy Book (1910)

References: Baker; Bénézit; Houfe; ICB 1; Johnson; Johnson & Greutzner; Pennell MI, PD; Peppin; Sketchley; Thieme & Becker; Vollmer supp; Wa (1929); Waters; C. Wood; *The Studio* special (1897-98)

Michael Foreman (b. 1938)

Born in Pakefield, Suffolk. Studied at Lowestoft School of Art and at the Royal College of Art. Lecturer at St Martin's School of Art (1963-65), the London College of Printing (1967-68), the Royal College of Art (1968-70) and the Central School of Arts and Crafts (1972). Art Director of *Playboy Magazine*, Chicago (1965) and *King Magazine*, London (1966). Painter, etcher, illustrator and writer of children's books. His illustrative work is distinctive: he often works in colour or halftone, creating luminous effects with veils of thinly diluted pigment over delicate pencil outlines; in his etched illustrations, he uses soft ground techniques to achieve subtle tonal gradations. His imagery, ostensibly decorative, humorous or with a sometimes child-like appearance, often has menacing or bizarre overtones. He is widely travelled and derives inspiration from many sources. He was winner of first prize in the Francis Williams Book Illustrations Award (1972 and 1977) and the Silver Eagle Prize at the Festival International du Livre, Nice, France (1972), the Graphics Prize at Bologna (1982) and the Kurt Maschler Award (1982). He lives in South Kensington, London. [Q]

Books illustrated include:
Barbara Adachi Living Treasures of Japan (1973)
C.H.O'D. Alexander Fisher v. Spassky (1972)

Michael Foreman. From his *The Perfect Present* by Michael Foreman (Hamish Hamilton, 1967).

Hans Andersen Classic Fairy Tales (1977)
Allen Andrews Plantaganet Pig (1980)
Sheila Burnford Noah and the Second Flood (1973)
Angela Carter French Fairy Tales (1981)
Janet Charters The General (1961)
Derek Cooper The Bad Food Guide (1966)
Donald Davie Essex Poems (1969)
Charles Dickens A Christmas Carol (1983)
Peter Dickinson Tales from the Old Testament (1980)
Janice Elliott The Birthday Unicorn (1970)
William Fagg Living Arts of Nigeria (1972)
Michael Foreman The Two Giants (1966), The Perfect Present (1967), The Great Sleigh Robbery (1968), Horatio (1969), Moose (1971), Dinosaurs and all that Rubbish (1972), War and Peas (1974), All the King's Horses (1976), Panda and his Voyage of Discovery (1977), Panda's Puzzle (1977), Panda and the Odd Lion (1979), Trick a Tracker (1980), Panda and the Odd Lion (1981), Land of Dreams (1982)
Alan Garner The Stone Book (1976), Tom Fobble's Day (1976), Granny Reardun (1977), The Aimer Gate (1978), The Girl of the Golden Gate (1979), The Golden Brothers (1979), The Princess and the Golden Mane (1979), The Three Golden Heads of the Well (1979)
Peter Harris The Monkey and the Three Wizards (1976)
Cledwyn Hughes The King Who Lived on Jelly (1963)
Aldous Huxley After Many a Summer (1980)
Terry Jones Fairy Tales (1981), Erik the Viking (1983)
Leonore Klein Huit Enfants et un Bébé (1966)
Robert McCrum The Magic Mouse and the Millionaire (1982)
Georgess McHargue Private Zoo (1975)
Nanette Newman Cat and Mouse (1983)
Eric Partridge Comic Alphabets (1964)
Anthony Paul The Tiger Who Lost His Stripes (1980)
Helen Piers Longneck and Thunderfoot (1982)
Mabel Watts I'm for You—You're for Me (1967)
Oscar Wilde The Selfish Giant (1978), The Nightingale and the Rose (1980)
Jane Yolen Rainbow Rider (1975)

Periodical: Ambit

References: ICB 4; Kirkpatrick; *Graphis* 187; *Idea* 150; *Isis* (1967)

Amédée Forestier (1854-1930)

Of French origin according to Harper, and Belgian according to Houfe. Joined the staff of *The Illustrated London News* as a 'special' artist (1882-99), covering mainly ceremonial and state functions in Britain, Europe and North Africa. In later life, he settled in Dulwich, South London, and pursued an interest in archaeology. His pen and ink line was described by Harper as 'singularly scratchy', but he was skilled at working in wash, using well articulated tonal gradations with accented highlights and shadows, that reproduced well. He also worked in watercolour, mainly for topographical works, achieving convincing atmospheric effects. Elected RA, ROI.

Books illustrated include:
B.G. Ambler Alfred, Lord Tennyson (1911)
S.L. Bensusan William Shakespeare—His Homes and Haunts (1910), William Wordsworth—His Homes and Haunts (nd)
Walter Besant The World Went Very Well Then (1897)
Wilkie Collins Blind Love (1890)
Amédée Forestier The Roman Soldier (1928)
G. Garcia The Actor's Art (1882)
S. Baring Gould Pablo the Priest (1899)
Frances E. Greville William Morris (1912)
Bret Harte Barker's Luck (1896)
F.F. Moore The Jessamy Bride (1897)
D.C. Murray and Henry Herman Paul Jones's Alias (1890)
G.W.T. Ormonde West Flanders (1906), Brabant and East Flanders

Amedée Forestier. 'Elleray, Windermere—House of Professor Wilson' from *William Wordsworth—His Homes and Haunts* by S.L. Bensusan (T.C. & E.C. Jack, nd).

(1907), Liège and the Ardennes (1908), Belgium (1909)
B.E.O. Pain The Romantic History of Robin Hood (1898)

Periodicals: The Girl's Own Paper, The English Illustrated Magazine, The Illustrated London News

References: Harper; Houfe; Johnson & Greutzner; Thorpe; Vollmer supp; C. Wood

Archibald Stevenson Forrest (1869-1963)

Usually worked as A.S. Forrest. Born in Greenwich, London. Educated at the Roan School, Greenwich; studied at Westminster School of Art, the City and Guilds' College, and at Edinburgh School of Art. He travelled widely, recording his impressions in bold, confident studies in crayon pencil and wash, charcoal, pen and ink, watercolour, bodycolour and oil. Among his children's books, his illustrations for the startlingly xenophobic *Pictures for Little Englanders* (1900) show the influence of John Hassall* and Tom Browne* in their simplification and resemblance to caricature. He concentrated on landscape painting during the latter part of his life. Lived in Essex, Blackheath (South London) and later in Sussex.

Books illustrated include:
S.L. Bensusan Morocco (1904), Picturesque Normandy (1905)
F.T. Bullen Back to Sunny Seas (1905)
Arthur Cooke Blackbeard's Boy (1928)
George Eliot Adam Bede (1933)
John Finnemore Morocco (c.1908)
Archibald S. Forrest A Tour through Old Provence (1911)
Archibald S. Forrest and Henry Bagge Switzerland (1915)
F.G. Green Pictures for Little Englanders (1900)
John Henderson A Tour through the West Indies (1905), A Tour through Jamaica (1906)
M.A.S. Hume A Tour through Portugal (1907)
Charles Kingsley Westward Ho! (1934)
W.H. Koebel South America (1912)
H.E. Marshall Stories of Robin Hood (1905), Our Island Story (1909)
M. Merrythought Martin Merrythought's Child's Guide to London (1922)
Percy Westerman Trapped in the Jungle (1947)

Periodicals: Black and White, The Idler, Illustrated Bits, Judy, Moonshine

References: Houfe; Johnson & Greutzner; Thorpe; Water; C. Wood; James L. Caw *Scottish Painting Past and Present* (T.C. & E.C. Jack, 1908)

Margaret Emily Noel Fortnum (b. 1919)

Usually works as Peggy Fortnum. Born Harrow-on-the-Hill, Middlesex. Educated at St Margaret's School, Harrow. Joined the Auxiliary Territorial Service (1942-43); discharged, after injury, with a

A.S. Forrest 'He stood there holding the magic sword in his hand' from *The Coming of Arthur* in *Our Island Story* by H.E. Marshall (T.C. & E.C. Jack, 1909).

Peggy Fortnum. 'Rebecca Ann, Rebecca Ann, what have you done with the watering-can?' from *Adventures with Benghazi* by Rose Fyleman (Eyre & Spottiswoode, 1946).

pension and war grant on which she studied at the Central School of Arts and Crafts. An introduction by John Farleigh* (then Art Director at the Sylvan Press) led to publishers' commissions, and she continued as a book illustrator (of some 70 titles, mainly for children) until 1975. Her light-hearted pen and ink sketches did much to enliven the first eleven book in Michael Bond's *Paddington Bear* series (1958-74). She also paints, in oil and watercolour, and has exhibited in England and America; she has also designed textiles (1947-51). [Q]

Books illustrated include:
Elisabeth Beresford Two Gold Dolphins (1961)
Leila Berg Trust Chunky (1954), Little Pete Stories (1959)
Michael Bond A Bear Called Paddington (1958), More About
   Paddington (1959), Paddington Helps Out (1960), Paddington
   Abroad (1961), Paddington at Large (1963), Paddington Marches
   On (1964), Adventures of Paddington (1965), Paddington at Work
   (1966), Paddington Goes to Town (1968), Paddington Takes the Air
   (1970), Paddington on Top (1974), Paddington on Stage (1974)
Helen Cresswell Where the Wind Blows (1966)
Eleanor Farjeon Grannie Gray (1956), The Children's Bells (1957)
Peggy Fortnum Running Wild (1975)
Rose Fyleman Adventures with Benghazi (1946)
Jane Gardam A Few Fair Days (1971)
Kenneth Grahame The Reluctant Dragon (1959)
Muriel Hooper The Goose Girl (1960)
Ursula Hourihane Pedlar Pete's Enchanted Toys (1948)
Margaret Jowett Candidate for Fame (1955)
Patricia Lynch Brogeen Follows the Magic Tune (1952), Brogeen and
   the Green Shoes (1953), The Bookshop on the Quay (1956), The Old
   Black Sea Chest (1958), Jinny the Changeling (1959)
Margaret Mackay Dolphin Boy (1963)
Beverley Nichols The Mountain of Magic (1950)
Josephine Poole A Dream in the House (1961)
James Reeves (ed) The Rhyming River (Book IV): An Anthology of
   Verse (1959)
Meta Mayne Reid The Tinkers' Summer (1965)
Joan G. Robinson When Marnie was There (1967)
Diana Ross The Enormous Apple Pie (1951)
C. Fox Smith Seldom Seen (1954)
Catherine Storr Rufus (1969)

Noel Streatfeild Thursday's Child (1970)
Oscar Wilde The Happy Prince and other stories (1968)
Ursula Moray Williams The Adventures of a Little Wooden Horse
   (1959)

References: Crouch; Fisher pp. 186, 199, 267-68; ICB 2,3,4; Ryder; Wa (1980); Peggy Fortnum *Running Wild* (Chatto & Windus 1975)

Marcia Lane Foster (b. 1897)

Married name: Mrs Dudley Jarrett. Born at Seaton, Devon. Studied at the St. John's Wood School of Art, then at the Royal Academy Schools and, at the same time, at the Central School of Arts and Crafts under Noel Rooke*. Wood engraving became, and remained, her favourite medium. She worked in advertising, as a book illustrator, and as an occasional painter of portraits. She was employed for about 20 years by William Hollins and Co. designing children's wear advertisements for Viyella and Clydella, and publicity material for Kodak, Cadbury, Nestlé, TCP, Bovril and Clark's Shoes. The publication of *Let's Do It* (1938), a collection of charcoal sketches of children at play in a similar vein to J.H. Dowd's* *People of Importance* (1934), established her reputation as

Marcia Lane Foster. 'He marched on along the white, respectable road' from *The Golden Journey of Mr Paradyne* by William J. Locke (John Lane, 1924).

an artist who could capture the lively movement of children, and this (slightly to her regret) determined to a large extent the subsequent character of her commissions. Her earlier book illustrations included a number of wood engravings, and these shared with her drawings the qualities of clarity and animation. Elected ARE (1959).

Books illustrated include:
Margaret Baker Lions in the Potting Shed (1954), Acorns and Aerials (1956)
Kitty Barne Dusty's Windmill (1949), Barbie (1952), Rosina and Son (1956)
Viola Bayley Paris Adventure (1954), Lebanon Adventure (1955), Kashmir Adventure (1956), Turkish Adventure (1957), The Shadow on the Wall (1958), Corsican Adventure (1958), Swedish Adventure (1959), Mission on the Moor (1960), London Adventure (1962), Italian Adventure (1964), Scottish Adventure (1965), Welsh Adventure (1966), Austrian Adventure (1968)
M.C. Carey Nicky Goes Ashore (1957)
Marcia Lane Foster Let's Do It (nd)
Anatole France The Merrie Tales of Jacques Tournebroche (1923), Little Sea Dogs (1925)
Kenneth Grahame The Headswoman (1921)
Lorna Hill The Vicarage Children (1961)
James Kinross Blackfoot Lagoon (1950)
William J. Locke The Golden Journey of Mr Paradyne (1924)
Cyrus Macmillan Canadian Fairy Tales (1922)
William Mayne Underground Alley (1958)
G. Plummer My Bible Stories (1963)
Malcolm Saville The Ambermere Treasure (1953)
Eleanor Spence The Summer in Between (1959)
Noel Streatfeild The Children in Primrose Lane (1941)
Netta Syrett Tinkelly Winkle (1923)
Pamela Whitlock (ed) The Opera Book (1956)

References: Balston WEMEB; Bénézit; Houfe; ICB 1, 2; Johnson & Greutzner; Vollmer; Wa (1980); Waters; The Studio special (Spring 1927, Spring 1930); Campbell Dodgson Contemporary English Woodcuts (Duckworth 1922)

William Foster (1853-1924)

Second son of the Victorian watercolourist and illustrator Myles Birket Foster. Studied at Heatherley's School of Art. Worked in watercolour as an ornithological draughtsman, and as a humorous illustrator of children's books in black and white and colour, specialising in animals. He lived in Surrey.

Books illustrated include:
May Clarissa Byron The Bird Book (1915)
William Foster Follies, Foibles and Fancies of Fish, Flesh and Fowl (1889), A Frog He Would A Wooing Go (1890), Keeper Jocks (1904)
Charles Johns British Birds in their Haunts (1909)
Edward Lear Nonsense Drolleries (1889)

References: Bénézit; Houfe; Johnson & Greutzner

George Algernon Fothergill (1868-1945)

Born at Leamington, Warwickshire. Studied medicine at Edinburgh University. He practised as a doctor in Darlington, Co Durham before becoming a professional artist. Settled in West Lothian, Scotland (1913). Landscape and portrait painter, lithographer, pottery decorator, bookplate designer; experimenter in collotype and tri-colour printing. His book illustrations and decorations were mainly in pen and ink.

Books illustrated include:
G.A. Fothergill A Riding Retrospect (1895), An Old Ruby Hunt Club Album (1899), A North Country Album (1901), Notes from the Diary of a Doctor, Artist and Sportsman (1901), Sketch Books (from 1903), Stories and Curiosities of Edinburgh and Neighbourhood (1910), British Fire-Marks from 1680 (1911), The National Stud—Gift to the State (1916), An Artist's Thoughts in Verse and Design (1919)

References: Houfe; Johnson & Greutzner; Mallalieu; Vollmer supp; Wa (1934); Waters 1, 2; C. Wood

Fougasse

See Cyril Kenneth Bird.

Claud Lovat Fraser (1890-1921)

Born in London, son of a solicitor. Educated at Charterhouse. Articled to his father (1908), then entered Westminster School of Art, where he studied under W.R. Sickert. By 1912, he was producing decorative pen and ink drawings for book plates and greetings cards; in 1913, he began publishing chapbooks and ballad-sheets. After being invalided out of the Army (1916), he achieved rapid success as a theatre designer with *As You Like it* and *The Beggars' Opera* (Lyric, Hammersmith, London 1920). Through joining the Design and Industries Association in 1917, he met Harold Curwen who commissioned from him pattern papers, borders, vignettes and illustrations for the Curwen Press. Towards the end of his life, he became a close friend of Paul Nash*. He died suddenly from heart failure after an operation. In her account of the Curwen Press, Pat Gilmour describes Fraser as an artist 'in conscious revolt against pomposity and academism and charmed by the simplicity of such things as the woodcuts of Joseph Crawhall...' He made a number of woodcuts, but worked mainly in pen and ink, using a broad reed nib and often adding flashes of brilliantly coloured ink. John Russell Taylor describes him as an 'exponent of quaintness' but sees his work as a late manifestation of the branch of Art Nouveau that produced the Beggarstaff brothers and Edward Gordon Craig* (*The Art Nouveau Book in Britain* 1966). His drawings were often tiny, his subjects frequently gathered from the past, especially the 18th and 19th centuries, and his style had a compelling effervescence particularly appreciated during wartime and in the period of post-war austerity.

Books illustrated include:
Walter de la Mare Peacock Pie (1924)
John Gay The Beggar's Opera (1921)
Carlo Goldoni The Liar (1922)
John Hilton and Joseph Thorp Change, the Beginning of a Chapter (with others, 1919)
R. Hodgson and L. Fraser Flying Fame (1913)
Haldane Macfall The Splendid Wayfaring (with others, 1913)
Walter de la Mare Peacock Pie (1924)
J.E.C. Nodier The Luck of the Bean-Rows. A Fairytale for Lucky Children (1921), The Woodcutter's Dog (1921)

Claud Lovat Fraser. From *The Splendid Wayfaring* by Haldane Macfall (1913).

Hayter Preston The House of Vanities (1922)
Joseph Thorp Apropos the Unicorn (with others, 1920)
Sir Herbert Beerbohm Tree Thoughts and Afterthoughts (1913)
Poems from the Works of Charles Cotton (1922)
Curwen Press: Book of Types and Ornaments (1928), A Specimen
   Book of Pattern Papers (1928)
Heleion Hill (1921)
The Lute of Love. An Anthology (1920)
Nurse Lovechild's Legacy (1916)
Nursery Rhymes (1919)
Pirates (1921)
The Windmill (with others, 1923)

Periodicals: The Apple, The Art Chronicle, The Beacon, The
Chapbook, Drama, Form, Hearth and Home, The Imprint, The
Onlooker, Pan

References: Bénézit; Crouch; DNB (1912-21); Gilmour; Houfe; ICB
1; Johnson & Greutzner; Lewis; Mallalieu; Taylor; Vollmer; Waters;
Alphabet and Image 7 (1948); *The Bookman* (August 1921); *The
Fleuron* 1 (1923); *Form* no 3 vol 1 (January 1922); *The Studio* 77 (1919),
special (1927); *Catalogue of Exhibition* (Hull University, 1968); *Warrack
and Perkins Catalogue* 24 (c.1978); John Drinkwater and Albert
Rutherston *Claud Lovat Fraser* (Heinemann 1923); G. Lovat Fraser
(intro) *Claude Lovat Fraser* (Victoria & Albert 1968); Pat Gilmore
Artists at Curwen (1977); *63 Unpublished Designs by Claude Lovat
Fraser* (1924); Haldane Macfall *The Book of Lovat* (Dent 1923);
Christopher Millard *The Printed Work of Claude Lovat Fraser*
(Danielson 1923); Herbert Simon *Song and Words* (Allen & Unwin
1973)

Eric George Fraser (b. 1902)

Works as Eric Fraser. Born Westminster, London,
son of a solicitor's clerk and a headmistress. Educated at Westminster City School; while still a
pupil there, he attended W.R. Sickert's evening
classes at Westminster School of Art. Studied at
Goldsmith's College School of Art on a scholarship (1919). Taught lithography at Goldsmith's
(1923-24), fashion and figure composition at the
Reimann School, Westminster (1938-39), and
graphic design at Camberwell School of Art (1928-
40). He has been active in many fields including
black and white illustration, etching, lithography,
mural and easel painting, and stained glass design.
Perhaps best known as a graphic artist, he has
illustrated books for many publishers (including
the Golden Cockerel Press and the Folio Society),
and made drawings for magazines (including the
Radio Times since 1926) and advertisements (for
British Rail, the General Post Office, Shell and
the Ministry of Information, among others). He
works mainly in black ink, with white overlaid to
give something of the quality and definition of a
wood engraving. His book and advertising illustrations exemplify his capable draughtsmanship
and ability to create striking and memorable
images. [Q]

Books illustrated include:
Richard Cavendish (ed) Legends of the World (1983)
Alessandro Manzoni (trans Archibald Colquhoun) The Betrothed
   (1969)
Mardrus and Mathers (trans) The Book of the Thousand Nights and
   One Night (vols I & III, 1958)
Ippolito Nievo (trans Lovett F. Edwards) The Castle of Fratta (1954)
Ovid The Art of Love (1971)
Barbara Léonie Picard Tales of the British People (1961)
Maria de Zayas y Sotomayer (trans John Sturrock) A Shameful
   Revenge and other stories (1963)
Tacitus (trans G.G. Ramsay) The Reign of Nero (1952)
J.R.R. Tolkien Lord of the Rings (with Queen of Denmark, 1977).

Eric Fraser. 'Devil Leaping' from *English Legends* (Batsford, 1950).

The Hobbit (1979)
Paul Turner (trans) The Ephesian Story (1957)
Richard Wagner The Ring (1976)
Complete Works of Shakespeare
English Legends (1950)
Folklore, Myths and Legends of Britain (1973)
The Golden Fleece (1965)
Joan of Arc (1974)
A Life of Christ (1977)
Myths of the Sudan and Egypt (1977)
Pioneers Against Germs (1962)
Pioneers in Astronomy (1964)
Sir William and the Wolf (1959)
The Voyage of Odysseus (1973)

Periodicals: Britannia & Eve, The Bystander, Harper's Bazaar, The Leader, Lilliput, The Listener, Nash's Magazine, Punch, Radio Times, Vogue

References: Bland; ICB 2; Jacques; Johnson & Greutzner; Usherwood; Vollmer supp; Wa (1980); Waters; *Graphis* 7 (1951), 13 (1957); *Illustrators* 27 (1980); *The Studio* special (Autumn 1928); John Austen *An ABC of Pen and Ink Rendering* (Pitman 1937); Alec Davis *The Graphic Work of Eric Fraser* (Uffculme Press 1974); Ashley Havinden *Line Drawing for Reproduction* (Studio 1941)

Peter Fraser (b. 1888)

Born in the Shetland Islands. Worked in the City (1907-10). Served in France during World War I. Studied at the Central School of Arts and Crafts. As an illustrator, he specialised in routinely cheerful animal drawings in a cartoon style for magazines and children's books.

Books illustrated include:
Edith and Peter Fraser Jack and Jock's Great Discovery (1944), Camping Out (1945)
Peter Fraser Funny Animals (1921), Tufty Tales (1932), Moving Day (1945)
Wilfrid H. Harrison Humour in the East End (1933)
Susan Rye The Blackberry Picnic (1946), Bevis and the Giant (1948)

Periodicals: Punch, The Sketch, Tatler

References: Vollmer; Wa (1934); Waters 2

Barnett Freedman (1901-58)

Born in the East End of London, son of Russian Jewish immigrants. A sickly child, he had little formal education, but taught himself to draw and play the violin during four years in hospital. Worked as an office boy, stone-mason's assistant and architect's assistant. Attended evening classes at St Martin's School of Art for five years, then studied at the Royal College of Art on a scholarship (1922-25). After two years of near starvation, he began receiving book illustration commissions (1927), and from then on worked extensively for the Curwen and Baynard Presses, designing advertisements, posters (including work for London Transport and Shell), calendars, cards and a large number of book jackets (mainly for Faber). Taught at the Royal College of Art and the Ruskin School of Drawing, Oxford. He married Claudia Guercio*, with whom he had studied at the Royal College, and lived in Kensington, London. Official

Barnett Freedman. 'Love thwarted and unrequited' from *Love* by Walter de la Mare (Art & Technics, 1948).

war artist for the Royal Air Force (1940), and for the Admiralty (1941-46). Though he was also an easel painter, Freedman is now mainly remembered as a lithographer and illustrator. He found, in autolithography, a responsive medium that gave full scope to his fluent graphic abilities, and he soon acquired an outstanding command of the technique. Encouraged by Harold Curwen, he developed a method of simulating lithography by drawing in chalk for line block reproduction, first using this process for the small 'dropped in' images in *Lavengro* (1932). His *magnum opus* was the American edition of *War and Peace* (1938), illustrated with colour lithographs. He was an inspired book artist who could combine firm design with sympathetically drawn figures, and a feeling of spatial breadth for which he often adopted an elevated viewpoint. Created CBE (1946). Elected Royal Designer for Industry (1949).

Books illustrated include:
Laurence Binyon The Wonder Night: Ariel Poem (1927)
George Borrow Lavengro (1936)
Charlotte Brontë Jane Eyre (1942)
Emily Brontë Wuthering Heights (1940)
Roy Campbell Choosing a Mast (1931)
Walter de la Mare News: Ariel Poem (1930), Love (1943), Ghost Stories (1956)
Charles Dickens The Adventures of Oliver Twist (1939)

Barnett Freedman The Technique of Colour Printing by Lithography (1940), Colour Printing (1945)
Siegfried Sassoon Memoirs of an Infantry Officer (1931)
William Shakespeare Henry IV Part I (1939)
Edith Sitwell Victoria of England (1935)
Leo Tolstoy War and Peace (1938), Anna Karenina (1950)
Emlyn Williams Readings from Dickens (1953)

Periodical: Curwen Press Newsletter

References: Bénézit; Bland; Chamot, Farr & Butlin; DNB (1951-60); Gilmour; ICB 1,2; Johnson & Greutzner; Lewis; Vollmer and supp; Wa (1956); Waters; *Motif* 1 (1958); *Penrose Annual* (1950); *Signature* 2 (1936), 5 (1937); *The Studio* 109 (1935), 156 (1958), special (Autumn 1938); *Catalogue of Arts Council Memorial Exhibition* (1958); Edward Ardizzone *Baggage to the Enemy* (John Murray 1941); John Lewis and John Brinkley *Graphic Design* (Routledge & Kegan Paul 1954); Jonathan Mayne *Barnett Freedman* (Art & Technics 1948); Herbert Simon *Song and Words* (Allen & Unwin 1973)

Claudia Freedman

See Claudia Guercio.

Barbara Constance Freeman (b. 1906)

Born in Ealing, Middlesex, daughter of William Freeman, writer. Studied at Kingston School of Art. She worked in London in a West End wall-paper studio, then as a painter (1926-27) and as a freelance illustrator (from 1928). She began writing in 1956, and illustrates her own books. Since early childhood she has lived near London in a mid-Victorian house with a large garden, which has influenced her stories and provided material for her drawings. She works in pen and ink, and sometimes with watercolour washes. [Q]

Books illustrated include:
Enid Blyton The Treasure Hunters (1950)
Frances Browne Granny's Wonderful Chair (nd)
Barbara C. Freeman Timi (1961), Two-Thumb Thomas (1961), A Book by Georgina (1962), Broom-Adelaide (1963), The Name on the Glass (1964), Lucinda (1965), The Forgotten Theatre (1967), Tobias (1967), The Other Face (1975), A Haunting Air (1976), A Pocket of Silence (1977), The Summer Travellers (1978), Snow in the Maze (1979), Clemency in the Moonlight (1981)
Charles Perrault The Sleeping Beauty and Other Tales (1954)
Antonia Ridge Jan and his Clogs (1951), Jan Klaassen Cures the King (1952), Puppet Plays for Children (1953), Never Run from the Lion and Another Story (1958)
Stories from Hans Andersen (1949)
Stories from Grimm (1949)

References: Contemporary Authors; Kirkpatrick

Terence Reginald Freeman (b. 1909)

Born and grew up in London; later lived in Tunbridge Wells. Studied at Clapham School of Art and at the Royal College of Art, studying Florentine Renaissance draughtsmanship with a view to painting murals. He taught in various preparatory and public schools and Art schools, and worked briefly in an advertising agency and for films. He was a prolific illustrator of children's books, producing unpretentious, reliable pen and ink drawings with a firm line and varied shading and texture.

Books illustrated include:
Mabel Allan Chiltern Adventure (1950), The Vine-Clad Hill (1956), The Conch Shell (1958), Pendron Under the Water (1961)
Margaret Joyce Baker Treasure Trove (1952), The Young Magicians (1954), The Bright High Flyer (1957), Tip and Run (1958), Homer Goes on Stratford (1958), Homer in Orbit (1961), Into the Castle (1962), Homer Goes West (1965)
Margaret Curry London (1958)
Kathleen Fidler The Brydons Look for Trouble (1950), The Brydons in a Pickle (1950), Surprises for the Brydons (1950), The Brydons Get Things Going (1951), St Jonathan's in the Country (1951), More Adventures of the Brydons (1952), The Brydons Catch Queer Fish (1952), The Brydons Stick at Nothing (1952), The Brydons at Smugglers' Creek (1952), The Brydons Abroad (1953), The Brydons on the Broads (1955), Challenge to the Brydons (1956), The Brydons at Blackpool (1960), The Brydons Go Canoeing (1963)
Pamela Mansbridge The Larchwood Mystery (1960)
Malcolm Saville Treasure at Amorys (1964)
A. Stephen Tring (pseud) Penny Dreadful (1949), The Cave By The Sea (1950), Penny Triumphant (1953), Penny Penitent (1953), Penny Puzzled (1955), Penny Dramatic (1956), Penny in Italy (1957)
Elfrida Vipont The Lark in the Morn (1948), The Lark on the Wing (1950), The Family at Dowbiggins (1955), The Spring of the Year (1957), More About Dowbiggins (1958), Changes at Dowbiggins (1960)
Ronald Welch The Gauntlet (1951)

Reference: ICB 2

Fiona French (b. 1944)

Born in Bath, Somerset. Studied painting and printmaking at Croydon College of Art (1961-66). Illustrator of children's books since 1967, working exclusively for the Oxford University Press until 1978. Part-time lecturer at Wimbledon School of Art (1970-71), Leicester Polytechnic (1973) and Brighton College of Art (1974). Assistant to the painter Bridget Riley for a short period. She works in colour in various media including ink, gouache, watercolour and crayon, adapting her style to the subject of each book; thus the illustrations for *The Blue Bird* are based on Chinese 'willow pattern' designs, and those for *City of Gold* on medieval stained glass. [Q]

Books illustrated include:
R. Blythe Clowns and Clowning (1978), Fabulous Beasts (1978)
Fiona French Jack of Hearts (1970), Huni (1971), The Blue Bird (1972), King Tree (1973), City of Gold (1974), Aio the Rainmaker (1975), Matteo (1976), Hunt the Thimble (1978), The Princess and the Magician (1981), John Barleycorn (1982)
Margaret Mayo The Book of Magical Birds (1977)
Oscar Wilde (adapted by Jennifer Westwood) Star Child (1979)

References: Contemporary Authors; ICB 4; Kirkpatrick

Rowel Boyd Friers (b. 1920)

Works as Rowel Friers. Born in Belfast, Northern Ireland. Studied part-time at Belfast College of Art (1935-43) while working as a poster designer and commercial lithographer. Advertising, television and stage designer, cartoonist, portrait painter and muralist. Contributor of weekly topical cartoons to the *Belfast Telegraph* and *The Irish Times*. His illustrations are humorous and exact, drawn in a cartoon-like linear style. Elected member RUA (1940) and Ulster Watercolour Society (1977).

Books illustrated include:
Ted Bonner Don't Shoot I'm Not Well (1974)
Cyril Cusack The Humour is on Me (1980)
Rowel Boyd Friers Wholly Friers (1948), Mainly Spanish (1951), Riotous Living (1971), Pig in the Parlour (1972), The Book of Friers (1973), The Revolting Irish (1974), On the Borderline (1982)
Robert Harbinson Tattoo Lily (1961)
Florence Mary McDowell Other Days Around Me (1966), Roses and Rainbows (1972)
Janet McNeill My Friend Specs McCann (1955), A Pinch of Salt (1956), A Light Dozen (1957), Specs Fortissimo (1958), Special Occasions (1958), This Happy Morning (1959), Various Specs (1961), Try These for Size (1963), Best Specs (1970)
Palmer and Lloyd A Brew of Witchcraft (1966), Moonshine and Magic (1967); The Obstinate Ghost (1968), Starlight and Spells (1969)
Wendy White The Beedy Book (1965)

Periodicals: Belfast Telegraph, Daily Express, Dublin Opinion, Irish Times, London Opinion, Punch, Radio Times, Sunday Independent

References: Fisher p.327; ICB 2; Wa (1980); Waters

Charles Front (b. 1930)

Born in London. Studied at Northampton School of Art, South East Essex School of Art, and at the Slade School of Fine Art, where he was taught by Edward Ardizzone* and Lynton Lamb*. He worked for various advertising agencies before becoming a full-time children's illustrator. He works in pen and ink, sometimes with water-colour washes.

Books illustrated include:
Pamela Binns Flavio and the Cats of Rome (1976)
Nancy Chambers Stickleback, Stickleback (1977)
Marjorie Darke The Big Brass Band (1976)
Sheila Front Raffan and Jeremy (1969), The Three Sillies (1974), The Golden Goose (1977)
Margaret MacPherson The Boy on the Roof (1974)
F.E. & F.J. Schonell Essential Read-Spell (vol 3 1979)
Shirley Steen (ed) A Child's Bible (1969)

Reference: ICB 4

Brian Froud (b. 1948)

Born in Winchester. Studied at Maidenhead College of Art, and then joined Artist Partners, an agency for graphic artists. He worked from their London studio for three years and then moved to Chagford in Devon. As an illustrator, he works in pen or pencil, with films of muted colour some-times applied with an air brush. His work depicts an imaginary world peopled with strange atavistic non-human creatures, faeries, primeval plants and mysterious machines. Stylistically and occas-ionally in his imagery, Froud's work has echoes of Arthur Rackham*. The visual elements in the film *The Dark Crystal* (1982) were based on his designs.

Books illustrated include:
Brian Froud and Alan Lee Faeries (1978)
J.J. Llewellyn The Dark Crystal (1982)
Margaret Mahy The Man Whose Mother Was a Pirate (1972), The Railway Engine and the Hairy Brigands (1973), The Ultra-Violet Catastrophe (1975), The Wind Between the Stars (1975)

Mary Norton Are All the Giants Dead? (1975)

References: ICB 4; David Larkin (ed) *The Land of Froud* (Pan 1977)

Rosalie Kingsmill Fry (b. 1911)

Usually works as Rosalie K. Fry. Born on Van-couver Island, Canada, but has lived in England since the age of four. Studied at Central School of Arts and Crafts (1929-34). Served in Women's Royal Naval Service during World War II. Author and illustrator of children's books. She works in pen and ink and watercolour. Published in Britain by Dent and Hutchinson. [Q]

Books illustrated include:
Rosalie K. Fry Baby's Progress Book (1944), Lost in the Dew (1944), Adventure Downstream (1946), In a Rock Pool (1947), Cherrywinkle (1951), The Little Gipsy (1951), Pipkin the Woodmouse (1953), Two Little Pigs (1953), Deep in the Forest (1955), The Wind Call (1955), Deep in the Forest (1956), Lucinda and the Painted Bell (1956), Child of the Western Isles (1957), Secret of the Forest (1958), Lucinda and the Sailor Kitten (1959), Fly Home Colombina (1960), The Mountain Door (1960), Princess in the Forest (1961), The Echo Song (1962), The Riddle of the Figurehead (1963), Secrets (1973)
Charles Kingsley The Water Babies (1957)
Marjorie Knight The Land of Lost Handkerchiefs (1954)
Modwena Sidgwick Jan Perry Stories (1955), More Jan Perry Stories (1957), New Jan Perry Stories (1959)
A large number of other titles published in America.

Periodicals: Collins' Children's Annual, Country Life, The Countryman, The Lady, Nursery World, Parents

References: Contemporary Authors, ICB 2,3,4; Kirkpatrick

Harry Furniss (1854-1925)

Born Wexford, Ireland, son of an English civil engineer. Educated at the Wesleyan College, Dublin. Studied art at the Royal Hibernian Academy Schools. Moved to London (1873) and soon established himself as a graphic artist working for magazines; joined the staff of *The Illustrated London News* (1876), and visited the Chicago World Fair as special artist. Contributed regularly to *Punch* from 1880 and joined its staff (1884) working mainly as a parliamentary caricaturist; some of his inventions became classics, most notably his aggrandisement of Mr Gladstone's collars—his treatment of Gladstone was undoubt-edly sharpened by his own opposition to Irish Home Rule. He left *Punch* precipitately (1894) after a disagreement over fees; his departure de-prived him of a highly appreciative public and (worse) of a reporter's ticket to the House of Commons. Resourcefully, he founded *Lika Joko* which merged after a year with the *Pall Mall Budget* to form *The New Budget*. He was continually in demand as a lecturer, and travelled extensively abroad. He turned to cinematography in later life and worked in New York (1912-14) as a writer, producer and actor. Furniss was an exceptionally prolific and facile draughtsman, adept at cap-turing movement and facial likenesses, and had a flair for topicality. These qualities, combined with an instinct for visual analogy and transposition, made him an outstanding commentator and cartoonist. His rapid throw-away style was less well suited to book illustration, with its opportunities for a more considered approach, and the challenge of depicting imaginary characters and situations failed to inspire his best work. Of his children's illustrations (which included Lewis Carroll's two *Sylvie and Bruno* books), Gleeson White observed: 'there is an irrepressible sense of movement and of exuberant vitality in his figures, but, all the same, they are more like Fred Walker's idyllic youngsters having romps than like real everyday children'. ('Children's Books and their Illustrators' in *The Studio* special 1897-98). His daughter Dorothy contributed drawings to a few of her father's books.

Books illustrated include:
Arthur A'Beckett The Comic Blackstone (1886)
Elinor Adams Miss Secretary Ethel (1898)
F.M. Allen Brayhard (1890)
Walter Besant All in a Garden Fair (1884)
Maggie Browne Wanted—a King (1890)
F.C. Burnand The Incompleat Angler (1887)
Lewis Carroll The Stay of Sylvie and Bruno (1889),
    Sylvie and Bruno Concluded (1893)
Norley Chester Olga's Dream (1892)
E.B.V. Christian Cricket Sketches (1896)
L.T. Courtenay (pseud) Travels in the Interior (1887)
H. de F. Cox Yarns Without Yawns (1923)
John Davidson Perfervid (1890)
Charles Dickens Complete Edition (1910)
B.L. Farjeon Shadows on the Snow (1904)
G.E. Farrow The Wallypug of Why (with Dorothy Furniss, 1895), The
    Missing Prince (with Dorothy Furniss, 1896)
Harry Furniss A River Holiday (1883), Parliamentary News (1885),
    How he did it (1887), Pictures at Play (1888), MPs in Session (1889),
    Royal Academy Antics (1890), Flying Visits (1892), The Grand Old
    Mystery Unravelled (1894), Australian Sketches (1899), Harry
    Furniss at Home (1903), How to Draw in Pen and Ink (1905),
    Friends without Faces (1905), Poverty Bay: a nondescript novel
    (1905), Deceit (1917), My Bohemian Days (1919), Some Victorian
    Women (1923), Some Victorian Men (1924), The Two Pins Club
    (1925)
H.E.A. Gingold Financial Philosophy (1902)
Edwin Hamilton The Moderate Man (1888)
G.A. Henty Seaside Maiden (1880)
Horace Leonard Romps at the Seaside and Romps in Town (1885)
Henry W. Lucy A Diary of the Salisbury Parliament (1892)
R. Marshall The Haunted Major (1902)

Harry Furniss. 'He's swallowed it!' from *Gamble Gold* by Edward Abbot Parry (Heinemann, 1907).

E.T. Milliken More Romps (1886)
C.M. Norris Hugh's Sacrifice (1886)
Edward A. Parry Gamble Gold (1907)
James Payn The Talk of the Town (1884)
Mabel H. Spielmann Littledom Castle and other tales (1903)
Laurence Sterne Tristram Shandy (1883)
William Makepeace Thackeray Complete Edition (1911)
Frederick Wicks My Undiscovered Crimes (1909)

Periodicals: Black and White, Cassell's Family Magazine, The Daily News, The English Illustrated Magazine, Good Words, The Graphic, The Illustrated London News, The Sporting and Dramatic News, Lika Joko, London Society, The New Budget, The Pall Mall Budget, Pearson's Magazine, Printer's Pie, Punch, The St James's Budget, The Sketch, The Strand Magazine, The Windsor Magazine, Zozimus

References: Baker; Bénézit; DNB (1922-30); Doyle CL; Fisher p.371; Hammerton; Harper; Houfe; ICB 1; Johnson & Greutzner; Low; Pennell MI, PD; Price; Sketchley; Spielmann; Thieme & Becker; Thorpe; Vollmer supp; Waters; C. Wood; WW (1914); *The English Illustrated Magazine* 26 (1902); *The Magazine of Art* 14; *The Strand Magazine* 38 (1909); *The Studio* 89 (1925), special (1897-98, 1923-24, Autumn 1928); *English Influences on Vincent Van Gogh* (University of Nottingham/AC catalogue 1974-75); William Feaver *Masters of Caricature* (Weidenfeld & Nicolson 1981); Harry Furniss *Confessions of a Caricaturist* (T. Fisher Unwin 2 vols 1901-02)

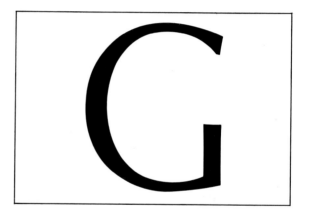

Ethel Leontine Gabain (1883-1950)

Worked as Ethel Gabain. Born in Le Havre, France. Studied at the Slade School of Fine Art, the Central School of Arts and Crafts (1906), at Chelsea and in Paris (1908). Contributed to the Senefelder Club's first exhibition (1910). Married artist John Copley (1913); they settled at Lingfield, Kent and were among the first artists to attempt to earn a living from their lithographs. She was also a painter and etcher. In 1933 she was awarded the De Lazlo silver medal for a portrait of Flora Robson (which was later purchased by Manchester Art Gallery). Official war artist (1940). Her book illustrations consist of lithographs (*Jane Eyre*) and crayon drawings (*The Warden*); they are theatrical in treatment and emotionally highly charged. Elected RBA (1932), ROI (1933), SWA (1934).

Books illustrated include:
Charlotte Brontë Jane Eyre (1923)
Anthony Trollope The Warden (1926)

References: Guichard; Johnson & Greutzner; Vollmer; Wa (1934); Waters; *Drawing and Design* 18 (October 1921); *The Print Collector's*

Quarterly vol 10; *The Studio* 135 (1948), special (1917, 1919, 1923-24); Harold J.L. Wright *The Lithographs of John Copley and Ethel Gabain* (Albert Roullier Art Galleries, Chicago 1924)

Gay John Galsworthy (b. 1932)

Born near Lisbon, Portugal. Studied at Hammersmith School of Art and at the South West Essex Technical College and School of Art. After doing National Service (1955-57), he taught at a Hertfordshire secondary modern school (1958-59) and worked for a firm of commercial illustrators and designers, Kempster & Evans (1959-60). Since 1960, he has illustrated a wide range of books including African school books, handbooks, and titles on natural history and folklore, for many publishers. He also works as a sculptor and mural painter, and lives in Essex. [Q]

Books illustrated include:
Victor Canning The Runaways (1977)
V.B. Chhiba Dangerous Thieves (1976)
Roy Day All about House Repair and Maintenance (1976)
Tony Deane & Tony Shaw The Folklore of Cornwall (1975)
Cyprian Erwenski The Rainbow-tinted Scarf (1975)
Christina Hole English Traditional Customs (1975)
Geraldine Kay Kassim and the Sea Monkey (1967), The Sea Monkey (1968)
Mapie, Contesse de Toulouse Lautrec Good French Cooking (1966)
Stan Learoyd The Conservation and Restoration of Antique Furniture (1982)
Ernest W. Marwick The Folklore of Orkney and Shetland (1975)
John Milne The Long Tunnel (1980)
Kingsley Palmer The Folklore of Somerset (1976)
Roy Palmer The Folklore of Warwickshire (1976)
Barbara Léonie Picard Hero-Tales from the British Isles (1963), Celtic Tales (1964)
Enid Porter The Folklore of East Anglia (1974)
R. Rumharack Singh Caribbean Primary Agriculture (9 titles, 1981)
Jacqueline Simpson The Folklore of Sussex (1973), The Folklore of the Welsh Border (1976)
John Steinbeck (retold by Martin Winks) Of Mice and Men (1975), *(retold by M.J. Paine)* The Red Pony (1976)
Joan Tate Crow and the Brown Boy (1976), Polly and the Barrow Boy (1976)
Joseph O. Tolutri Physical Education in Primary Schools (1976)
Katie Thear Part Time Farming (1982)
Johann Wyss Swiss Family Robinson (1970)

Periodical: Housewife

Reference: Fisher p.309

Reginald William Gammon (b. 1894)

Born in Petersfield, Hampshire. Studied art under Frank Patterson (1910-14). Painter in oil and watercolour and commercial illustrator. His book illustrations consist mainly of sketches in pencil or pen and ink, and are factual rather than imaginative in approach, and drawn in a rapid style typical of the 1930s.

Books illustrated include:
Stanley R. Baron Westward Ho! From Cambria to Cornwall (1934)
G. Bramwell Evans Romany, Muriel and Doris (1939), Out with Romany by the Sea (1941)
H. Rand A Book of Petersfield (1927)

Periodicals: Cyclist's Touring Club Gazette, News Chronicle, Scout

References: Houfe; Johnson & Greutzner; Vollmer; Wa (1980); Waters

Alfred Clive Gardiner (1891-1960)

Born in Blackburn, Lancashire, son of A.G. Gardiner, an editor of *The Daily News*. Educated at University College School, London. Attended the Slade School of Fine Art (1909-12) and the Royal Academy Schools (1913-14). After World War I, he taught art at Goldsmith's College School of Art, becoming Headmaster in 1929 and Principal in 1952. He designed posters for London Transport and Shell, painted murals, portraits and landscapes, and illustrated books (mainly in line). He was most important for his influence as a teacher; Graham Sutherland*, one of his pupils, wrote: 'I, for one, certainly owe him a debt which I can never repay.'

Books illustrated include:
'Alpha of the Plough' [A.G. Gardiner] Leaves in the Wind (1921), Many Furrows (1924)
James L. Campbell Miracle of Peille (1930)
William L. Courtney Pillars of Empire (1918)
Alfred G. Gardiner The War Lords (1915)

References: Bénézit; Johnson & Greutzner; Vollmer; Waters 2; *Clive Gardiner* (Arts Council Exhibition catalogue 1963)

Mary Gardiner (active 1935-63)

Illustrator in pen and ink of books written by Grace James and published by Frederick Müller. She worked in outline, sometimes with decorative looped shading on the contours, and her style remained consistent throughout her career.

Books illustrated include:
Grace James John and Mary (1935), More About John and Mary (1936), John and Mary Abroad (1937), John and Mary, Detectives (1938), John and Mary's Secret Society (1939), The Blakes and the Blacketts (1939), John and Mary's Visitors (1940), New Friends for John and Mary (1941), John and Mary and Miss Rose Brown (1942), John and Mary at School (1943), John and Mary's Youth Club (1945), John and Mary at Riverton (1946), The Adventures of John and Mary (1947), John and Mary's Aunt (1950), Nibs (1951), Nibs of the New World (1953), John and Mary in Rome (1954), John and Murray's Fairy Tales (1955), John and Mary By Land and Sea (1956), John and Mary's Japanese Fairy Tales (1957), John and Mary and Lisetta (1958), John and Mary's Treasures (1960), John and Mary Revisit Rome (1963)

Reference: *The Junior Bookshelf* vol 12 no 1 (1948)

Reginald Gammon. From *Out with Romany by the Sea* by G. Bramwell Evans (University of London Press, 1941).

James Gardner (b. 1907)

An internationally-known designer. After leaving school he spent six years designing for Cartier. He then turned to graphic work, mainly for advertising, and also illustrated the first titles in Noel Carrington's celebrated 'Picture Puffin' series of lithographed children's books. Immediately after World War II he designed the *Britain Can Make It* exhibition for the Council of Industrial Design (Victoria & Albert Museum 1946). He was a member of the design team for the Festival of Britain (1951) with overall responsibility for the Battersea Pleasure Gardens for which he created the Tree Walk, the Largest Tent in the World, the Showboat, and numerous fountains, illuminations and cane furnishings. A further achievement was the British Government Pavilion at the Brussels Exhibition (1958); he was subsequently responsible for the design of the Pilkington Glass Museum at St. Helen's in Lancashire, the interior of the New Commonwealth Institute in Kensington, London, and the remarkable Evoluon Museum at Eindhoven, Holland. Awarded OBE.

Books illustrated include:
James Gardner Drawing for Advertising (1938), How they Fly (1939), On the Farm (1940), War in the Air (1940)

References: Mary Banham & Bevis Hillier (ed) *A Tonic to the Nation* (Thames & Hudson 1976); *The House and Garden Dictionary of Design and Decoration* (Collins 1973)

Phyllis Gardner (b. 1890)

Born Cambridge, England. Educated at St Felix's School, Southwold. Studied at the Slade School of Fine Art, the British Museum, and at the Frank Calderon School of Animal Painting. Partner in the Asphodel Press with her sister Delphis Gardner (b. 1900) who had also studied at the Slade. They collaborated on the illustration of several books, making small-scale wood engravings sometimes in a chapbook style: their work is generally indistinguishable. They lived at Maidenhead, Berkshire, working as printers and woodcarvers as well as wood engravers. Phyllis also painted in watercolour and tempera.

Books illustrated include:
May W. Cannan The House of Hope (1923)
S. Casson Rupert Brooke and Skyros (1921)
Antonio Cippico Carme Umanistico (1923)
Delphis Gardner The Latin Writings of Saint Patrick (1932), The Tale of Troy (with Delphis Gardner, 1924-25)
Mary Gardner Plain Themes (1913), Songs of the Broads (1924)
Walter Scott Alice Brand (with Delphis Gardner, 1932), The Irish Wolfhound (with Delphis Gardner, 1931), Lyke-Wake Dirge (1926)

References: Balston WEMEB; Johnson & Greutzner; Vollmer; Wa (1934); Waters

William Biscombe Gardner (c.1847-1919)

Lived in London, Surrey, and Tunbridge Wells, Kent. He worked as an etcher and engraver, contributing in this capacity to *The Illustrated London News* and *The Graphic*. Also a landscape painter in oil and watercolour. His book illustrations consist of meticulously detailed topographical landscapes in watercolour.

Books illustrated include:
A.R.H. Moncrieff The Peak Country (1907), Derbyshire (1907)
W.T. Shore Canterbury (1907), Kent (1907)

Periodicals: The English Illustrated Magazine, The Graphic, The Illustrated London News, The Pall Mall Magazine

References: Bénézit; Houfe; Johnson & Greutzner; Pennell MI; Thieme & Becker; Waters; C. Wood

Eve C.R. Garnett (active from 1927)

Born in Worcestershire. Studied at Chelsea Polytechnic School of Art and the Royal Academy Schools, to which she was awarded a five-year scholarship at the School of Painting, and the Creswick prize and silver medal. Since then, she has worked as a painter in oil and watercolour (including large-scale mural works on canvas), and as a writer and illustrator of children's books. Her extensive travels have taken her to Kashmir, New Zealand, and eight times across the Arctic circle. While still a student, she collected material for *The London Child* (1927), and was appalled by the poverty and squalor of much working class

Eve Garnett. 'Blocking the pavement outside the Home and Continental Stores with their respective prams' from *The Family from One End Street* (Frederick Muller, 1937).

life; the direction of her work was then influenced by her determination to improve conditions of the poor through publicity and propaganda. Among the engaging wispy-haired, knock-kneed urchins of *The London Child* can be found the prototypes of Lily-Rose Ruggles and the other children in *The Family from One End Street* (which won the Carnegie Gold Medal in 1937) and its sequels. Eve Garnett's simple linear style of illustration altered very little during her career.

Books illustrated include:
Eve Garnett The Family from One End Street (1937), *(foreword by Walter de la Mare)*, 'Is it well with the Child?' (1938), In & Out & Roundabout (1948), A Book of the Seasons (1952), Further Adventures of the Family from One End Street (1956), Holiday at the Dew Drop Inn (1962), *(foreword by Professor Bloch-Hoell)* To Greenland's Icy Mountains (1968), Lost and Found: Four Stories (1974)
Norman Hunter The Bad Barons of Crashbania (1932)
James Reeves (ed) A Golden Land (with others, 1958)
Evelyn Sharp The London Child (1927)
R.L. Stevenson A Child's Garden of Verses (1948)

References: Contemporary Authors; Crouch; Doyle Cl; Eyre; ICB 2; Johnson & Greutzner; Kirkpatrick; Vollmer; Wa (1980); *The Junior Bookshelf* vol 2 no 4 (1938); Alec Ellis *Chosen for Children* (Library Association 1977)

Rachel Alice Garnett (d. 1940)

Maiden name: Rachel Alice Marshall. Daughter of an architect, and first wife of Bloomsbury writer David Garnett, several of whose books she illustrated. She used straight-forward wood cutting and engraving techniques to create images that have considerable charm and individuality.

Books illustrated include:
David Garnett Lady into Fox (1922), A Man in the Zoo (1924) The Grasshoppers Come (1931)
R.A. Garnett A Ride on a Rocking-Horse (1917)
T.F. Powys Black Bryony (1930), The Key of the Field (1930)

References: Balston WEMEB

Gillian Gaze

See Jill Barklem.

Kathleen Gell (b. 1913)

Maiden name: Kathleen Reid. Daughter of a clergyman. She studied art privately in Newton Abbot and in Manchester. She provided pen and ink and watercolour illustrations for many small junior educational books published by Basil Blackwell, and illustrated other stories for children. [Q]

Books illustrated include:
Enid Blyton The Children at Happy House (1946), The Happy House Children Again (1947), A 2nd Book of Naughty Children (1947), The Red-Spotted Handkerchief (1948), Jinky's Joke, and other stories (1949), The Yellow Story Book (1950), Benjy and the Others (1955)
Olive Denn Come In (1946)
Kathleen Gell An Alphabet (1956)

R.A. Garnett. From *A Man in the Zoo* by David Garnett (Chatto & Windus, 1924).

J.G. Hughes A King in the Oak Tree (1965)
A. Stephen Tring Penny and the Pageant (1959), Penny Says Good-Bye (1961)

David Gentleman (b. 1930)

Born in London. Studied at St Albans School of Art (1947-48) and the Royal College of Art, London (1950-53), where he later taught (1953-55). Since then, he has worked freelance from his studio in Camden Town, London, making drawings, watercolours and lithographs of landscapes and buildings, and designing murals, posters, bookjackets, postage stamps, and a wide variety of other design and illustration commissions. His book illustrations have included limited editions of a number of classic works as well as books by several contemporary writers, some of them for children. He has written and illustrated several children's books and one on design, as well as a book of watercolour drawings of contemporary Britain. Many of his illustrations have been engraved on wood and some lithographed; more often, however, he draws in pen and ink with watercolour. As an illustrator, he uses pen and ink, wood engraving, and water-colour. His work is always immaculately presented; his wood engravings reveal a master of pastiche, convincingly and often humorously adopting the style and iconography of his subject's period. Elected RDI (1970); member AGI.

Books illustrated include:
John Russell Brown Shakespeare and his Theatre (1981)
John Clare The Shepherd's Calendar (1964)
Peter Ede Bridges on the Backs (1961)
George Ewart Evans Pattern Under the Plough (1966), Where Beards
    Wag All (1970), The Strength of the Hills (1983)
David Gentleman Design in Miniature (1972), Fenella in Greece
    (1967), Fenella in Ireland (1967), Fenella in the South of France
    (1967), Fenella in Spain (1967), A Cross for Queen Eleanor (1979),
    David Gentleman's Britain (1982)
Patience Gray and Primrose Boyd Plat du Jour (1957)
H. Rider Haggard King Solomon's Mines (1970)
Russell Hoban The Dancing Tigers (1978)
Rudyard Kipling The Jungle Book (1968)
John Langstaff The Golden Vanity (1972), St George and the Dragon
    (1973)
John Stallworthy A Familiar Tree (1978)
Flora Annie Steel Tales of the Punjab (1973)
J.R. Wyss Swiss Family Robinson (1963)
The Ballads of Robin Hood (1977)
The Poems of John Keats (1966)

References: Contemporary Authors: Fisher pp.226, 291; Garrett BWE, HBWE; ICB 4; Jacques; Lewis; Ryder; WaG; John Lewis *A Handbook of Type and Illustration* (Faber 1956)

Charles March Gere (1869-1957)

Born in Gloucester. Studied at the Birmingham School of Art and afterwards taught there, contributing (with A.J. Gaskin) to its success as a centre for illustration and book-design during the 1890s. Profoundly influenced by the ideas of William Morris, the Birmingham artists sought inspiration from medieval printed books and from the woodcuts of Dürer and Holbein. They believed that illustration and typography should complement each other as elements in a book's overall design, and emphasised graphic and decorative qualities rather than illusion, modelling or depth. Avoiding the pitfall of over-elaboration and prettiness inherent in this approach, Gere's drawings are restrained and workmanlike in manner and display an impressive command of draughtsmanship and design. He worked with Morris at the Kelmscott Press, and later at the Ashendene Press. Pen and ink draughtsman, wood engraver, painter and designer of embroidery and stained glass. In 1902, he settled in Gloucestershire and devoted his efforts increasingly to landscape painting. Elected RBSA (1906), NEAC (1911), ARWS (1921), RWS (1927), ARA (1933), RA (1939).

Books illustrated include:
Thomas A Kempis The Imitation of Christ (1894)
R. Nisbet Bain Russian Fairy Tales (1893)
A.J. Gaskin A Book of Pictured Carols (1893)
Thomas Malory Le Morte D'Arthur (1913)
William Morris News from Nowhere (1893)
Alice Sargant The Fairy Fowk's Rade (1896)

Ruth Gervis. From *Ballet Shoes* by Noel Streatfeild (1936).

Periodicals: The English Illustrated Magazine, The Quest, The Yellow Book

References: Baker; Bénézit; Crane; Houfe; ICB 1; Johnson & Greutzner; Mallalieu; Pennell M1; Sketchley; Thieme & Becker; Thorpe; Vollmer; Wa (1927); Waters; C. Wood; *The Studio* 59 (1913), 80 (1920), special (Christmas 1894).

Ruth S. Gervis (b. 1894)

Maiden name: Ruth Streatfeild. Born Frant, Sussex, daughter of the Revd William Streatfeild (later Bishop of Lewes) and sister of the children's novelist, Noel Streatfeild. A delicate child, she was often away from school because of illness and had plenty of time to draw. She studied art at various private studios and art schools and has since worked as an illustrator, landscape painter and occasional sculptor. She taught art at Sherborne School (1941-52) and at Lord Digby's School, Sherborne, and has worked in a local museum. [Q]

Books illustrated include:
Kitty Barne Young Adventurers (1936), She Shall Have Music (1938),
    Family Footlights (1939), Visitors from London (1941), In the Same
    Boat (1945), Musical Honours (1947)
Enid Blyton The Saucy Jane Family (1947), The Seaside Family
    (1950), The Pole Star Family (1950), The Buttercup Farm Family
    (1951), The Very Big Secret (1952), The Caravan Family (1953)
Noel Streatfeild Ballet Shoes (1936)
Mary Treadgold No Ponies (1946)

References: ICB 1; Johnson & Greutzner; Wa (1954)

David L. Ghilchick (b. 1892)

Born in Romania. Studied art at Manchester and at the Slade School of Fine Art, London, and later worked as a painter of landscapes and figure subjects. As a contributor to *Punch* (1920-39), he specialised in social and domestic subjects in the tradition of Lewis Baumer, and his book illustrations are often in a similar vein. Typically his work is lively—sometimes almost slapdash in appearance—with frequent use of hatching.

D.L. Ghilchik 'The "Happy Medium" is our Spirits quest' from *The Rubaiyat of a Golfer* by J.A. Hammerton (Country Life, 1946).

Member of the London Sketch Club; founder member SWE (1920); elected ROI.

Books illustrated include:
D. Ghilchick Children (1961)
J.A. Hammerton The Rubaiyat of a Golfer (1946)

Periodical: Punch

References: Cuppleditch; Johnson & Greutzner; Price; Wa (1960); Waters

Robert John Gibbings (1889-1958)

Usually worked as Robert Gibbings. Born Cork, Ireland, son of clergyman. He briefly attended medical school, then studied at the Slade School of Fine Art and at the Central School of Arts and Crafts under Noel Rooke*. Wounded at Gallipoli during army service in World War I. After the war, he supported himself as a freelance artist/engraver. He founded the Society of Wood Engravers in 1919, and bought the Golden Cockerel Press in 1924. As a printer of fine editions, he often worked in collaboration with Eric Gill*, and commissioned wood-engraved illustrations from John Nash*, David Jones*, Eric Ravilious*,

Blair Hughes-Stanton*, John Farleigh*, and Agnes Miller Parker*. A visit to Tahiti in 1929 inspired *Ioriana* (1932), the first of many books that he both wrote and illustrated over the next 25 years. Financial problems led to the sale of the Press (1933). Gibbings later settled in Berkshire and lectured in book production at Reading University (1939-42). His experience in publishing and printing made Gibbings exceptionally sensitive to the relationship between illustration and the printed page. He regarded wood engravings primarily as ornaments that should harmonise with the refinement and finish of the typeface used in the book. His own engravings were characterised by exceptional economy and precision. In his early work (coinciding with his period at the Golden Cockerel Press), outlines were often replaced by articulated areas of black and white (showing Rooke's influence); his later work became more descriptive, with white line details worked into the areas of black, reflecting his acute powers of observation. Founder member of the SWE (1920).

Books illustrated include:
Samuel Butler Erewhon (1923)

Robert Gibbings. 'St Brendan and the Sea Monsters' from *Beasts and Saints* translated by Helen Waddell (Constable, 1934).

Henry Carey Songs and Poems (1924)
A.E. Coppard Pelagea and other poems (1926), Count Stephan (1928), The Man from Kilsheelan (1930), The Hundredth Story (1931), Crotty Shinkwin and the Beauty Spot (1932), Rummy (1932)
Charles Darwin The Voyage of HMS Beagle (1956)
Pierre de Bourdeille The Lives of Gallant Ladies (1924)
Eleanor Doorly The Insect Man (1936), The Microbe Man (1938), The Radium Woman (1939)
J.H. Driberg Initiation (1932)
Lord Dunsany Lord Adrian (1933)
J.H. Fabre Marvels of the Insect World (1938)
Gustave Flaubert Salammbô (1931)
Esther Forbes A Mirror for Witches (1928)
Robert Gibbings The Seventh Man (1930), Ioriana! A Tahitian Journal (1932), A True Tale of Love in Tonga (1935), The Wreck of the Whale-ship Essex (1935), Coconut Island (1936), John Graham, Convict 1924 (1937), Blue Angels and Whales (1938), Sweet Thames Run Softly (1940), Coming Down the Wye (1942), Lovely is the Lee (1945), Kiwis in Captivity (1947), Over the Reefs (1948), Sweet Cork of Thee (1951), Coming Down the Seine (1953), The Discovery of Tahiti (1955), Trumpets from the Montparnasse (1955), Till I End My Song (1957)
Viscount Grey Falloden Papers (1926), The Charm of the Birds (1927)
Godfrey P. Harrison A Bird Diary (1936)
Francis Hickes (trans) The True Historie of Lucian the Samosatenian (1927)
John Keats Lamia and other poems (1928)
Francis Macnamara (ed) Miscellaneous Writings of Henry VIII (1924)
Thomas Mallory Le Morte D'Arthur (3 vols 1936)
E. Powys Mathers Red Wise (1926), The Circle of the Seasons (1929)
Herman Melville Typee (1938)
H.E. Palmer The Roving Angler (1933)
Llewellyn Powys Glory of Life (1934), The Twelve Months (1937)
Alexander Pushkin The Tale of the Golden Cockerel (1936)
Owen Rutter (ed) The Journal of James Morrison (1935), Mr Glasspoole and the Chinese Pirates (1935), The Voyage of the Bounty's Launch (1934)
George Scott-Moncrieff A Book of Uncommon Prayer (1937)
William Shakespeare Othello (1939)
Jonathan Swift Miscellaneous Poems (1928)
Henry Thoreau Where I Lived and What I Lived For (1924)
Helen Waddell Beasts and Saints (1934)
Chester Mystery Plays: Samson and Delilah (1925), The Deluge (1927)

Periodicals: The Golden Hind, The Woodcut

References: Balston EWE, WEMEB; Crouch; DNB (1951-60); Eyre; Garrett BWE, HBWE; Guichard; ICB 1,2; Johnson & Greutzner; Lewis; Vollmer; Wa (1956); Waters; *Alphabet and Image* 8 (Winter 1948); *The Junior Bookshelf* vol 4 no 4 (1940); *The Studio* 76 (1919), 110 (1935), special (1919, Spring 1927, Spring 1930, Winter 1936, Autumn 1938); *Graven Images* (Scottish Arts Council 1979); Thomas Balston *The Wood Engravings of Robert Gibbings* (Art & Technics 1949); Patience Empson *The Wood Engravings of Robert Gibbings* (Dent 1959); A. Mary Kirkus *Robert Gibbings: A Bibliography* (Dent 1960); Christopher Sandford *Bibliography of the Golden Cockerel Press* (Dawson 1975), *Cock-a-Hoop* (Private Libraries Association 1976); A.C. Sewter *Modern British Woodcuts and Wood Engravings in the Collection of the Whitworth Art Gallery* (Manchester 1962)

Iris Giffard

See Iris Brooke.

Phillida Gili (b. 1944)

Maiden name: Phillida Stone. Born in Newbury, Berkshire, daughter of Reynolds Stone*. Studied at the Ruskin School of Drawing, Oxford (1961-64), the Central School of Arts and Crafts in London (1964-65), and illustration and graphics at St. Martin's School of Art (1965-68). Co-owner,

with her husband Jonathan Gili, of a small publishing company, Warren Editions, specialising in illustrated books. She works freelance as an illustrator (mostly of children's books) in pen and ink, watercolour, coloured pencils, and occasionally wood-engravings. [Q]

Books illustrated include:
Ken Ansden Up the Crossing (1981)
Margaret Baker Juby (1970)
Hilaire Belloc A Remaining Christmas (1976)
John Betjeman Archie and the Strict Baptists (1977)
Alexander Dumas (trans Douglas Munro) The Nutcracker (1976)
Eileen Dunlop A Flute in Mayferry Street (1976)
Elizabeth Gili Apple Recipes from A-Z (1975)
Phillida Gili The Lost Ears (1970), Dottie (1973), ABC (1974), Demon Daisy's Dreadful Week (1980), The Lost Ears (1981), Fanny and Charles (1983)
H.S. Vere Hodge Five Overs and Two Wides (1975)
Christopher Matthew Loosely Engaged (1980)
Harriet Mott The Year of the Fire (1974)
Alicia Pearson Memories of my Childhood (1976)
Ray Pope One's Pool (1969)
Mary Schroeder My Horse Says (as Phillida Stone 1963, redrawn 1967)
Barbara Willard Spell Me a Witch (1979)
The Woman's Hour Yearbook (1981)

Arthur Eric Rowton Gill (1882-1940)

Worked as Eric Gill. Born in Brighton, son of a Nonconformist (later Church of England) clergyman. Studied for two years at Chichester Technical and Art School, then served a three-year apprenticeship with the London architect Douglas Caroë while attending evening classes in masonry at Westminster Technical Institute, and in lettering at the Central School of Arts and Crafts under Edward Johnstone* (with whom he shared lodgings 1902-04). He was employed mainly as a letter-cutter until 1909 when, encouraged by the art critic Roger Fry, he turned to figure carving in wood and stone. He became a Roman Catholic (1913) and carved a series of reliefs for Westminster Cathedral (1913-18). After World War I, he received many commissions for carved and lettered war memorials. In 1918, he formed a religious order of artist-craftsmen called the Guild of St Joseph and St Dominic, which was

Eric Gill. From *The Song of Songs* (1925).

based at Ditchling, Sussex (where he had lived since 1907); among its associates were Philip Hagreen* and David Jones*. He moved with his extended family to Capel-y-ffinn in the Black Mountains of Wales in 1924, and finally settled at Piggots, near High Wycombe, Buckinghamshire, in 1928, where he established workshops and a printing press. As his reputation as a sculptor grew, he received many important public commissions including carvings for Broadcasting House, London (1929), relief panels for the Palestine Museum, Jerusalem (1935) and for the League of Nations Hall at Geneva (1936).

Between 1915 and 1939, Gill illustrated 138 books, mainly with wood engravings. He met Noel Rooke* in Edward Johnstone's classes and was initially drawn towards wood engraving for its lettering possibilities, first attempting pictorial engraving in around 1906. His early book illustrations were engraved in white line, but, as he became more concerned with book design, he felt that the predominantly black images produced by this method were too heavy in the context of the printed page, and he turned to black-line for illustration in the mid-1920s. During this period, he also experimented with intaglio printing from wood blocks, before taking up copper engraving (c.1924). In his wood engravings of the 1930s, he often introduced hatched or stippled shading, creating effects of relief modelling that echoed his sculptural work. 15 of his books were commissioned and published by the Golden Cockerel Press under the directorship of Robert Gibbings*. Of these, The Four Gospels (1931), with images inspired by early Christian manuscripts, has been widely considered his masterpiece. His early illustration was mainly for the St Dominic Press and he also worked for a number of other private presses including the Cranach Press, as well as for commercial publishers such as Faber & Faber, Dent (the New Temple Shakespeare edition) and Jonathan Cape. His involvement with typeface design was a natural corollary of letter-cutting and wood engraving. In all, he designed ten typefaces: two of the most successful, Perpetua (1927) and Sans Serif (now generally called Gill Sans, 1928), were designed for the Monotype Corporation and still remain in use.

Many of Gill's ideas derived from those of the late 19th century Arts and Crafts movement—in particular his opposition to mechanisation and his commitment to the Guild of Handicraft ideal. On the other hand, his imagery owed much to 20th century modernism—especially in its discovery and re-evaluation of 'primitive' forms of art. Another essentially post-Victorian aspect of his work was his celebration—in drawing, engraving, sculpture and writing—of the sensual and erotic qualities of nudity. His importance as a book illustrator, however, rests above all on the outstanding aesthetic and technical qualities of his engraving and on his ability to form every visual component of the printed page—illustration, type and design—into a coherent and inspired whole. On a different level, his role as a pioneer in the wood engraving revival and his use of the medium for illustration did much to attract attention towards the private press movement—the major outlet and source of support for many wood engravers during the 1920s. Founder member SWE (1920); Hon. ARIBA (1935), RDI (1936), ARA (1937) and honorary associate of the Royal Society of British Sculptors.

Books illustrated include:
Theodore Besterman (ed) The Travels and Sufferings of Father Jean de Brébent (1938)
Geoffrey Chaucer Troilus and Criseyde (1927), Canterbury Tales (1929-31)
G.K. Chesterton Gloria in Profundis (1927)
Enid Clay Sonnets and Verses (1925), The Constant Mistress (1934)
Frances Coinford Autumn Midnight (1923)
John Donne Holy Sonnets (1938)
Eric Gill Wood Engravings (1924), Verses (1926), Engravings (1929), Clothes (1931), Clothing without Cloth (1931), Sculpture and the Living Model (1932), Engravings 1928-1933 (1934), Quia Amore Langueo (1937), Twenty-Five Nudes (1938), In a Strange Land (1944), First Nudes (1954), Nudes (nd)
J. Maritain The Philosophy of Art (1923)
E.P. Mathers Procreant Hymn (1926)
Patrick Miller The Green Ship (1936)
Thomas More Utopia (1929)
D. Pepler The Devil's Devices (1915), The Way of the Cross (1917), Nisi Dominus (1919)
Plato The Phaedo (1930)
T.F. Powys Uncle Dottery (1930)
St John of the Cross The Song of the Soul (1927)
William Shakespeare Hamlet (1933), Henry VIII (1939)
W.H. Shewring (trans) The Passion of Perpetua and Felicity (1929)
Canticum Canticorum (1931)
The Four Gospels of the Lord Jesus Christ (1931)
The Lord's Song (1934)
The Passion of the Lord Jesus Christ from the Gospel according to St Matthew (1926)
The Song of Songs (1925)
Songs to our Lady of Silence (1920)

Periodicals: Change, The Fleuron, The Game, G.K.'s Weekly, The Newsleader Book, The Woodcut

References: Balston EWE, WEMEB; Bénézit; Bland; Bliss; Chamot, Farr & Butlin; Garrett BWE, HBWE; Hofer; Lewis; Phaidon; Thieme & Becker; Vollmer; Wa (1929); Waters; Who Was Who (1929-40); *Alphabet and Image* 3 (December 1946); *The Fleuron* 7 (1930); *The Print Collector's Quarterly* vol 15; *The Studio* 99 (1930), 121 (1941), special (Spring 1927, Autumn 1930, Winter 1931, Winter 1936, Autumn 1938); *The Engraved Work of Eric Gill* (Victoria & Albert Museum catalogue 1963); Douglas Cleverdon Engravings by Eric Gill (Fanfare Press 1929, Faber 1934); Eric Gill *Autobiography* (Cape 1940); Evan R. Gill *Bibliography of Eric Gill* (Cassell 1953), *The Inscriptional Work of Eric Gill* (Cassell 1964); Sister Elizabeth Marie Eric Gill, 20th Century Book Designer (Scarecrow Press, New York 1962); J.F. Physick *The Engraved Work of Eric Gill* (H.M. Stationery Office 1963); J.K.M.R[Rothenstein] *Eric Gill* (Benn 1927); W. Shewring (ed) *Letters of Eric Gill* (Cape 1947); Robert Speaight *The Life of Eric Gill* (Methuen 1966); J. Thorp *Eric Gill* (Jonathan Cape, 1929); Malcolm Yorke *Man of Flesh and Spirit* (Constable 1981)

Margery Jean Gill (b. 1925)

Usually works as Margery Gill. Born in Scotland. Studied at Harrow School of Art, then took etching

Margery Gill. From *Let the Balloon Go* by Ivan Southall (Methuen, 1968).

and engraving courses at the Royal College of Art. She has illustrated children's books since 1954, working mainly in black and white in a sketchy linear style. [Q]

Books illustrated include:
Ruth Arthur Dragon Summer (1962), A Candle in Her Room (1966), Requiem for a Princess (1967), Portrait of Margarita (1968), The Whistling Boy (1969), The Saracen Lamp (1970), The Little Dark Thorn (1971), The Autumn People (1973), After Candlemass (1974), On the Wasteland (1975), An Old Magic (1977)
Anne Barrett Midway (1967)
Elisabeth Beresford The Hidden Mill (1965), Peter Climbs a Tree (1966), Looking for a Friend (1967)
Barbara Bingley The Story of a Tit-Be and His Friend (1962)
Lucy Boston The Castle of Yew (1965)
Frances Hodgson Burnett A Little Princess (1961)
Mary Cockett Twelve Gold Chairs (1967), The Wild Place (1968)
Susan Coolidge What Katy Did (1968)
Susan Cooper Over Sea, Under Stone (1965)
Jean Craig What Did You Dream? (1964)
Helen Cresswell The Weather Cat (1971), Jane's Policeman (1972) The Long Day (1972), The Bower Birds (1973), Butterfly Chase (1975)
Walter de la Mare Tom Tiddler's Ground (1961), Poems (1962)
Rosalie K. Fry The Castle Family (1965), September Island (1965)
Eleanor Graham (ed) A Thread of Gold (1964)
Roger Lancelyn Green Mystery at Mycenae (1957), The Luck of Troy (1961)
René Guillot The Blue Day (1958)
E. Hamilton The Heavenly Carthorse (1958)
Anita Hewett Honey Mouse and other stories (1957), A Hat for Rhinoceros and other stories (1959), The Tale of the Turnip (1961), The Elworthy Children (1963), Animal Story Book (with Charlotte Hough, 1972)
E.W. Hildick Lemon Kelly Digs Deep (1964)
Charles Kingsley The Water Babies (1960)

Margaret Kornitzer Mr Fairweather and his Family (1960)
Andrew Lang (ed) Fifty Favourite Fairy Tales (1963), More Favourite Fairy Tales (1967)
Margaret Mahy The Bus Under the Leaves (1975)
William Mayne The Last Bus (1962), A Parcel of Trees (1963), Sand (1964), A Day Without Wind (1964), The Old Zion (1966)
Norah Montgomerie (ed) This Little Pig Went to Market (1966)
Michael Morpurgo The Nine Lives of Montezuma (1980)
Christina Rossetti Doves and Pomegranates (1971)
José Sanchez-Silva The Boy and the Whale (1963)
David Severn Three at Sea (1959)
Ivan Southall Let the Balloon Go (1968)
Noel Streatfeild Bertram (1959), Apple Bough (1962), When the Sea Wailed (1974)
R.L. Stevenson A Child's Garden of Verses (1946)
Edward Thomas Four and Twenty Blackbirds (1965)

References: Eyre; Fisher p.219; ICB 3,4; Ryder; *The Junior Bookshelf* vol 30 no 5 (1966); *Penrose Annual* 56 (1962)

J.L. Gilmour

See Lillian Amy Govey.

Louise M. Glazier (active 1899-1912)

Illustrator, writer and bookplate designer, who is known to have worked in Belgium and Surrey, England. She was an early autographic wood engraver (or possibly cutter), using the medium to create simplified white line images, often of children. Her topographical pen and ink drawings were more conventional.

Books illustrated include:
G.F. Edwards Old Time Paris (1908)
Louise M. Glazier A Book of Thirty Woodcuts (1903), Animal's Tags and Tails (1910), A Book of Babes (1911), The Field-Flower's Lore (1912)
Helumac Australian Wonderland (1899)

Periodicals: The Dome, The Venture

References: Houfe; Johnson & Greutzner; Taylor

Paul Goble (b. 1933)

Born in Surrey. Studied at the Central School of Art and Design. Freelance industrial designer (1960-68); senior lecturer in three-dimensional design at Ravensbourne College of Art (1968-77). Fascinated since childhood by the life and culture of American Indians, he first visited Red Indian country in 1959 and has returned regularly since 1972; he has been adopted into the Sioux and Yakima tribes. He works mainly in full colour and his style of illustration is closely based on Indian art. Won the Caldecott medal with *The Girl who Loved Wild Horses.* Many of his books were written in collaboration with his first wife Dorothy.

Books illustrated include:
Paul Erdoes (ed) The Sound of Flutes and other Indian Legends (1976)
Dorothy and Paul Goble Red Hawk's Account of Custer's Last Battle (1969), A Hundred in the Hands: Brave Eagle's Account of the Fetterman Fight (1972), Lone Bull's Horse Raid (1973), The Friendly Wolf (1974)
Paul Goble The Girl who Loved Wild Horses (1978)

References: Contemporary Authors; ICB 4

Warwick Goble. 'The strange story of the golden comb' from *Green Willow and other Japanese Fairy Tales* by Grace James (Macmillan, 1910).

Warwick Goble (d. 1943)

Born and educated in London. After leaving school, he spent several years with a printing firm where he learned chromolithography and commercial design; he also studied at Westminster School of Art, before joining the staff of *The Pall Mall Gazette* and later *The Westminster Gazette*. He lived in London and Surrey and travelled extensively in Europe and the Orient. He was best known for his watercolour illustrations for gift books such as *Green Willow, and other Japanese Fairy Tales* (1910). From his printer's training, he gained an understanding of colour reproduction, and from his interest in Chinese and Japanese art, a feeling for surface design and composition. He was a reliable and accomplished illustrator, but the spark of originality was strangely absent, and he took few risks, so his work remained atmospheric and polished, but bland.

Books illustrated include:
J. Barlow Irish Ways (1909)

G.B. Basile Stories from the Pentamerone (1911)
D.M.M. Craik The Fairy Book (1913), John Halifax, Gentleman (1914)
S.R. Crockett Lad's Love (1897)
Revd Lal B. Day Folk Tales of Bengal (1912)
J.S. Fletcher The Cistercians in Yorkshire (1919)
F.A. Gasquet The Greater Abbeys of England (1908)
Grace James Green Willow, and other Japanese fairy tales (1910)
Charles Kingsley The Water Babies (1909)
D.A. Mackenzie Indian Myth and Legend (1913)
A. van Millingen Constantinople (1906)
Mrs Molesworth The Grim House (1899)
Dora Owen The Book of Fairy Poetry (1920)
C. Sourabji Indian Tales of the Great Ones (1916)
R.L. Stevenson Kidnapped (1925), Treasure Island (1923)
H.G. Wells The War of the Worlds (1898)
Elinor Whitney Tod of the Fens (1928)
The Modern Reader's Chaucer (1912)

Periodicals: The Boy's Own Paper, The Captain, The Illustrated London News, Little Folks, The Minister, The Pall Mall Budget, The Pall Mall Gazette, Pearson's Magazine, The Strand Magazine, The Westminster Gazette, The Wide World Magazine, The Windsor Magazine.

References: Bénézit; Fisher p.356; Houfe; ICB 1; Johnson; Johnson & Greutzner; Thieme & Becker; Thorpe; Vollmer; Wa (1927); Waters; C. Wood

John Strickland Goodall (b. 1908)

Works as John S. Goodall or J.S. Goodall. Born Heacham, Norfolk, son of a heart specialist. After leaving Harrow School, he worked in the studios of Sir Arthur Cope RA and E. Watson Nicol under whom he 'was taught with loving care to be a mid-Victorian art student' (*The Connoisseur,* July 1968). He also studied under Harold Speed and at the Royal Academy Schools (c.1930). Served in the Royal Norfolk Regiment (1939-46). He concentrated on line drawing in the 1930s, and began to paint in watercolour while stationed in India at the end of World War II. Since then, his extensive travels (e.g. twice round the world on a cargo boat) have provided him with many landscape subjects; he also paints conversation pieces and late 19th-century pastiches in watercolour and gouache. As an illustrator, he works in black and white (sometimes in silhouette), and full colour, turning his 'Victorian' early training to good account in evocative period tableaux. In his wordless picture books he evolved an effective method of telling stories by means of half pages placed between each double-page spread. Elected RBA, RI. [Q]

Books illustrated include:
Reginald Arkell Trumpets over Merriford (1955)
Sydney Blow Through the Stage Door (1958)
C.W. Cooper Town and Country (1937)
Mary Dale Mrs. Dale's Friendship Book (1961)
Simon Dewes Suffolk Childhood (1959)
J.S. Goodall Dr Owl's Party (1954), Field-Mouse House (1954), The Adventures of Paddy Pork (1968), Shrewbettina's Birthday (1970), Jacko (1971), Paddy's Evening Out (1973), Creepy Castle (1975), An Edwardian Summer (1976), Paddy Pork's Holiday (1976), The Surprise Picnic (1977), An Edwardian Christmas (1977), An Edwardian Diary for 1979 (1978), The Story of an English Village (1978), An Edwardian Holiday (1978), An Edwardian Season (1979), Paddy's New Hat (1980), Escapade (1980), Lavinia's

London, and Hertfordshire. After some experiments with wood engraving, lithography and etching, he turned to copper engraving in 1923, and from then on worked entirely in this medium, basing his technique, and to a considerable extent his iconography, on 17th-century examples. He engraved cards and bookplates, including a series (from 1937) for the Royal Library at Windsor, and was responsible for reintroducing copper engraving as a book illustration technique. He was encouraged in this by the Nonesuch Press, with which he was closely associated (1923-29), and for whom he produced full-page illustrations, vignettes, and some of his earliest examples of title pages, embellished with architectural motifs in a Renaissance manner. Describing Gooden's work, Campbell Dodgson wrote, 'Craftsmanship, scholarship, taste, wit, and the careful nicety with which this true artist engraves an ornament, puts pen to paper, or affixes a seal, commend his work to the admiration of amateurs who can appreciate, if they cannot themselves actually possess, engravings consistently maintained at so high a level of achievement'. Elected RMS (1925), ARE (1931), RE (1933), ARA (1937), RA (1946); he was awarded a CBE (1942) and was a member of the Faculty of Engraving at the British School in Rome.

S.F. Gooden. From *Ulick and Soracha* by George Moore (Nonesuch Press, 1926).

J.S. Goodall. 'Who are you' from *Trumpets over Merriford* by Reginald Arkell (Michael Joseph, 1955).

Cottage (1981), Before the War (1981), Shrewbettina Goes to Work (1981), Paddy Finds a Job (1981)
Roger Lancelyn Green The Land of the Lord High Tiger (1958)
Kathleen Jarvis Diary of a Parson's Wife (1958)
Frank Knight The Golden Monkey (1953)
Laurence Meynell Bridge Under the Water (1954)
E. Nesbit Five Children and It (1948), The Phoenix and the Carpet (1948), The Story of the Amulet (1949)
'Miss Read' Village School (1955), Thrush Green (1975), Battle at Thrush Green (1975), No Holy for Miss Quinn (1976)
Ian Serraillier Fight for Freedom (1965)
Frank Swinnerton Reflections from a Village (1969)

Periodical: Radio Times

References: Contemporary Authors; Driver; ICB 2, 4; Wa (1980); Waters; *The Connoisseur* vol 168 no 677 (July 1968)

Stephen Frederick Gooden (1892-1955)

Often worked as S.F. Gooden. Son of a picture dealer and a descendant of the wood engraver Henry Linton (1815-99). Educated at Rugby School and studied art at the Slade School of Fine Art (1909-13). Served in France during World War I (1914-17); subsequently lived in Middlesex,

Books illustrated include:
Abraham Cowley (trans) Anacreon (1923)
Mona Gooden The Poet's Cat (1946)
G.R. Hamilton The Latin Portrait (1923)
O. Henry The Gift of the Magi (1939)
Edward Marsh (trans) The Fables of Jean de la Fontaine (1931)
George Moore The Brook Kerith (1929), Peronnik the Fool (1933), Ulick and Soracha (1926)
Siegfried Sassoon Vigils (1934)
C. Singer The Earliest Chemical Industry (1948)
Aesop's Fables (1936)
The Apocrypha (1929)
The Nonesuch Bible (1924-27)
The Pythian Odes of Pindar (1928)
Rubaiyat of Omar Khayyam (1940)
Songs of the Gardas (1925)

References: Bland; DNB (1951-60); Guichard; Johnson & Greutzner; Lewis; Vollmer; Wa (1929); Waters; *Fine Prints of the Year* (1925, 1932-37); *The Print Collectors Quarterly* vols 19, 28; *The Studio* 130 (1945), special (1923-24, Spring 1927, Autumn 1938); Campbell Dodgson *An Iconography of the Engravings of Stephen Gooden* (Elkin Mathews 1944)

Cora Josephine Gordon (d. 1950)

Studied at the Slade School of Fine Art, and in Brussels. Painter, wood engraver and etcher. Contributed articles to *The Studio* during the 1940s. Co-author and illustrator of travel books with her husband Godfrey Jervis Gordon*. Elected ARBA (1939), RBA (1940), SWA.

Books illustrated: *See* Godfrey Jervis Gordon

Periodical: Coterie

References: Johnson & Greutzner; Vollmer; Wa (1934); Waters

Godfrey Jervis Gordon (1882-1944)

Worked as Jan Gordon. Born Finchampstead, Berkshire. Educated at Marlborough College and Truro School of Mines, and worked as a mining engineer until 1909. Art critic on *The New Witness* (1916-19), *The Athenaeum* (1919), *Land and Water* (1920) and *The Observer*. Painter, etcher, lithographer and writer. Co-author and illustrator with his wife Cora Gordon* of travel books. Initially his illustrations were more professional and assured than those of his wife, but in their later books (in which the drawings were generally unsigned), their work was practically indistinguishable. It was always boldly executed, usually in chalk or pen and ink. Elected RBA (1935).

Books illustrated include:
G.J. Gordon A Balkan Freebooter (1916), On a Paris Roundabout (1927)
G.J. & C. Gordon Misadventures with a Donkey in Spain (1922), Poor Folk in Spain (1922), Two Vagabonds in the Balkans (1925), Two Vagabonds in Languedoc (1925), Two Vagabonds in Sweden and Lapland (1926), Two Vagabonds in Albania (1927), On Wandering Wheels (1929), Star-Dust in Holywood (1930), Three Lands on Three Wheels (1932), The London Roundabout (1933), Portuguese Somersault (1934)
Herbert Strang (ed) The Big Book for Boys (with others nd)

References: Houfe; Johnson & Greutzner; Vollmer; Wa (1934); Waters; *The Artist* vol 4 nos 1-4 (1932)

Jan Gordon

See Godfrey Jervis Gordon.

Margaret Anna Gordon (b. 1939)

Born in London, daughter of two performing musicians. She studied at St Martin's School of Art, Camberwell School of Arts and Crafts, and the Central School of Arts and Crafts. After leaving college, she taught art part-time for five years and married a publisher whom she met while seeking freelance work as an illustrator. In her black and white drawings she tends to combine quite detailed treatment of background and setting with cartoon-like simplification of the principal figures. In her colour work, she sometimes employs the technique of drawing in ink or gouache over candle-wax.

Books illustrated include:
Elisabeth Beresford The Wombles (1968), The Wombles at Work (1973), The Wombles Gift Book (1975), The Snow Wombles (1975), Tomsk and the Tired Tree (1975), Wellington and the Blue Balloon (1975), Orinoco Runs Away (1975), The Wombles to the Rescue (1975), The MacWombles's Pipe Band (1976), Madame Cholet's Picnic Party (1976), Bungo Knows Best (1976), Tobermory's Big Surprise (1976), The Wombles Go Round the World (1976)
Helen Cresswell A House for Jones (1969)
Kevin Crossley-Holland The Green Children (1966), The Callow Pit Coffer (1968), The Pedlar of Swaffham (1971)
Alison Jezard Albert in Scotland (1969), Albert's Christmas (1970)
George Macbeth Noah's Journey (1966)
Emma Smith Emily's Voyage (1962)

References: Fisher p.385; ICB 3,4; *After Alice* (Museum of Childhood Catalogue 1977)

Philip Gough (b. 1908)

Born Warrington, Lancashire. Studied stage design at Liverpool School of Art. Spent two years in a commercial studio and designed sets and costumes for about twenty-five productions for London theatres. Since World War II, he has concentrated on the decorative illustration of

Philip Gough. From A Bunch of Blue Ribbons by M.M. Johnson (Skeffington, 1951).

books and covers in a style that sometimes recalls Rex Whistler*. His interest in the architecture, furniture and decoration of the late 18th and early 19th centuries is reflected in his work. He lives in Chelsea, London.

Books illustrated include:
Cynthia Asquith The Children's Ship (1950)
Jane Austen Emma (1948), Pride and Prejudice (1951)
Lewis Carroll Alice and Wonderland and Through the Looking Glass (nd)
M. Clive Christmas with the Savages (1955)
Gordon Cooper An Hour in the Morning (1971)
Eleanor Farjeon The New Book of Days (1941), The Old Nurse's Shopping Basket (1949)
Rosalie K. Fry Gypsy Princess (1969)
Roger Lancelyn Green Ten Tales of Adventure (1972)
Lord Holden Purgatory Revisited (nd)
M.M. Johnson A Bunch of Blue Ribbons (1951)
Barbara Léonie Picard The Mermaid and the Simpleton (1949), Three Ancient Kings (1972)
Philip Rush Frost Fair (1965)
Ian Serraillier The Franklin's Tale, (retold 1972)
Barbara Sleigh Jessamy (1967)
Sir W. Beach Thomas A Year in the Country (1950)
John Rowe Townsend A Wish for Wings (1972)
Philip Turner Colonel Sheperton's Clock (1964)
Hans Andersen's Fairy Tales (1946)

References: ICB 2,4

Alexander Carruthers Gould (1870-1948)

Often worked as Alec Carruthers Gould. Born Woodford, Essex, son of Sir F.C. Gould*. He lived in London and Somerset, becoming a well-known landscape painter. Writing about his early black and white illustrations, Thorpe described him as 'a weak solution of his father'.

Books illustrated include:
Grant Allen Michael's Crag (with F.C. Gould, 1893)
E.W. Hendy Wild Exmoor through the Year (1930)
Cyril Hurst Scrap-Ironies (1905)

Periodical: The Windsor Magazine

References: Bénézit; Johnson & Greutzner; Thieme & Becker; Thorpe; Wa (1929); Waters; C. Wood

Francis Carruthers Gould (1844-1925)

Born Barnstable, Yorkshire, son of an architect. He drew political caricatures from the age of 11. At the age of 16, he entered a bank, and at 20 joined a London stockbroker's office and for the next 20 years he worked on the stock exchange. He then embarked on a career as a cartoonist, and became art editor and caricaturist of *The Pall Mall Budget* (1887-93) and of *The Westminster Gazette* (1893-1914). In 1894, he founded his own paper, *Picture Politics*, which ran until 1914. An ardent Liberal, his most outstanding success as a caricaturist was his depiction of the Conservative politician Joseph Chamberlain. He received a knighthood after the Liberal election victory of 1906. Gould had no formal training as a draughtsman and was under no illusions about his artistic

stature. However, he was an extremely sharp observer of face and gesture and of the political scene, and drew well enough to communicate his ideas clearly and directly. He was one of the first political cartoonists to attempt to capture changes in his sitters' appearance rather than remaining content with a static formula. A keen amateur naturalist, he often used his knowledge of bird and animal life in his interpretations of human character and situation.

Books illustrated include:
H.M. Batson A Book of the Country and the Garden (1903)
H. Begbie Great Men (1901), The Political Struwwelpeter (1899), The Struwwelpeter Alphabet (1900)
C.M. Brentano Fairy Tales from Brentano (1885), New Fairy Tales from Brentano (1888)
C. Geake and F.C. Gould John Bull's Adventures... (1904)
F.C. Gould Ah Chin Chin (1880), Explorations in the Sit-tee Desert (1880), The 'Unted Artist; or, the 'Orrible Dream (1880), Froissart's Modern Chronicles (1902-08), Wild Nature in Pictures, Rhymes and Reasons (1903), Political Caricatures (1904), The Gould-en Treasury (1906)
Sir Wilfred Lawson Cartoons in Rhyme and Line (1905)
H.W. Lucy Peeps at Parliament (1903), Later Peeps at Parliament (1904)
A. Matheson Snowflakes and Snowdrops (1900)
H.H. Munro The Westminster Alice (1902)
P.V. Ramaswami Raju (ed) Indian Fables (1901)
E.H. Spender The Story of the Home Rule Session (1893)
R.E. Welsh The Capture of the Schools (1903)

Periodicals: Cassell's Family Magazine, Fun, The Leisure Hour, The Pall Mall Budget, The Pall Mall Gazette, The Strand Magazine, The Westminster Gazette

References: Bénézit; DNB (1937); Hammerton; Houfe; Johnson & Greutzner; Low; Thieme & Becker; Thorpe; Waters; C. Wood; *The Leisure Hour* photo (1901-02); *Magazine of Art* New Series 1 1903; *The Studio* special (1900-01); William Feaver *Masters of Caricature* (Weidenfeld & Nicolson 1981)

Lilian Amy Govey (1886-1974)

Sometimes worked under the pseudonym J.L. Gilmour. Lived at Stoke Newington as a child

Lilian A. Govey 'He thought he had never seen any one look so old!' from *The Old Fairy Tales* (Nelson, c.1936).

and in Clissold Park, North London; during World War I, she settled in Sussex. Writer and illustrator of children's stories for publishers Dean and Son, Harrap, Wells, Gardner & Darton, and Humphrey Milford, for whom she also designed postcards. Her work was somewhat similar in style to that of Anne Anderson* (another contributor to 'Mrs. Strang's' annuals for children), but her style was less consistent and her line less sure.

Books illustrated include:
Agnes Grozier Herbertson The Book of Happy Gnomes (1924), Dean's Happy Common Series (1920)
Constance Heward Grandpa and the Tiger (1924)
'Mrs Herbert Strang' Nursery Rhymes from Animal Land (1934), The Rose Fairy Book (1912), The Violet Book for Children (with others, nd)
The Old Fairy Tales (c. 1936)

Periodicals: Cassell's Children's Annual, Little Folks, Mrs Strang's Annual for Children

Reference: Cope

Rigby Graham (b. 1931)

Born Stretford, Lancashire. Studied at Leicester College of Art. Taught at Ellis Boys' School, Leicester (1954-56). From 1956, he lectured in printing and graphic design at Leicester College of Art and is now principal lecturer in Art at Centre for Postgraduate Studies, Leicester Polytechnic. Represented Britain at Leipzig International Book Illustration Exhibitions (1971, 1977, 1982). Landscape painter, printmaker (lithographs, wood and lino cuts, monotypes), pen and ink draughtsman; influenced by the 'romantic' artists of the 1940s, especially Graham Sutherland* and John Minton*. He has illustrated over 200 books and pamphlets, many for private presses, including his own. [Q]

Books illustrated include:
John Best Poems and Drawings in Mud Time (1960), Nine Gnats (1964)
Salvador Jacinto de Medina El Icaro (1965)
Lord de Tabley The Churchyard in the Sands (1964)
Jill Gascoigne & Derrick Goodwin The Living Theatre (1962)
Rigby Graham Slieve Bingian (1968), An Alderney Afternoon (1969), The Casquets...the most dangerous Channel Islands (1972), Edmund Spenser's Kilcolman (1975), James Joyce's Tower, Sandycove (1975), Patterned Papers (1978)
Penelope Holt A Sicilian Memory (1963)
Penelope Holt and Edmund Thorpe Gold and Books (1969)
Peter Hoy Silence at Midnight (1967)
Frederico Garcia Lorca Llanto por Ignacio Sanchez Mejias (1962)
Douglas Martin Kirby Hall (1960)
Spike Milligan Values (1968)
R.H. Mottram Twelve Poems (1968)
Israel Perkins In Favour of Bundling (1963)
Rainer Maria Rilke Die Sonnette an Orpheus (1959)
Thea Scott Fingal's Cave (1962)
P.B. Shelley Lines Written among the Euganean Hills (1961)
David Tew The Oakham Canal (1968)
Oscar Wilde The Nightingale and the Rose (1961)

References: *The American Book Collector* vol 16, no 5 (1966); *The Bulletin* Malta (29 June 1979, 28 December 1979); *The Daily News* Malta (29 May 1979, 10 July 1979); *Quarterly Newsletter of Book Club*

Rigby Graham. From *The Living Theatre* by Jill Gascoigne and Derrick Goodwin (Pandora Press, 1962).

of California vol XL, no 4 (1975); *Saghtar* (Oct. 1979); *The Times* Malta (14 April 1979); Brian Allison *Rigby Graham* (Bosworth Gallery, Desford 1981); Patrick Bridgwater *Rigby Graham* (Brewhouse Press 1969); John Cotton *Rigby Graham* (Hemel Hempstead Art Trust 1977); John Cotton and Victor Bennet *Rigby Graham* (Victoria Gallery, Harrogate 1977); Hans van Eijk, *Rigby Graham* (Cog Press, Leicester 1979); Michael Felmingham *Graham's Leicestershire* Gadsby Gallery, Leicester 1976; Colleen Foord *Rigby Graham* (Leicester Polytechnic 1981); Patricia Graham *Rigby Graham* (Wymondham Art Gallery, Leicestershire 1979); Anne Greer *Rigby Graham* (Brian Mills 1981; A.A.C. Hedges *Rigby Graham, Paintings* (Yarmouth 1964); Harry Johnson *Rigby Graham* Littack, Ember Press vol 4 no 1 (November/December 1975); Mary Lynn *Rigby Graham* (Rawlins Art Centre, Quorn 1978); Julie Mellors *Rigby Graham and the Private Press in Leicestershire* (Loughborough 1979); Toni Savage and Hugh Collinson *Rigby Graham* (Gadsby Gallery 1963); Alan Tucker *Rigby Graham* (Gadsby Gallery 1974); Alan Tucker and Michael Freestone *Rigby Graham* (Brewhouse Press 1971); Maurice Willoughby *Rigby Graham* (Crescent Theatre, Birmingham 1967)

Janet and Anne Grahame-Johnstone (active from 1958)

Children's book illustrators specialising in large, brightly coloured gift books (mainly published by Dean), in which the full-page illustrations normally surround the passages of text. Their work represents a recent manifestation of the nursery

tradition mass-marketed by Mabel Lucie Attwell*
and updated by Hilda Boswell*, characterised by
unfailing sentimentality and a palpable determination to please.

Books illustrated include:
Enid Blyton Tales of Ancient Greece (nd)
Lewis Carroll Alice in Wonderland (1968)
Paul Gallico Miracle in the Wilderness (1975)
J. and A. Grahame-Johnstone A Child's Book of Prayers (1968), An
 Enchanting Book of Nursery Rhymes (c.1972), Gift Book of Prayers
 or Children (1975), Dean's Gift Book of Hans Christian Andersen
 Fairy Tales (1975), Little Jesus Pop-up-Book (1976), Dean's Gold
 Star Book of Cowboys (1976), Dean's Gold Star Book of Indians
 (1977), Bible Stories and Prayers for Children (1978), A Book of
 Children's Rhymes (1978), Dean's Gift Book of Nursery Rhymes
 Old and New (1978), Ten Little Dogs (1979), The Wonderful Story
 of Cinderella (1979), The Wonderful Story of Puss in Boots (1979),
 The Wonderful Story of Snow White and the Seven Dwarfs (1979),
 Santa Claus is Coming to Town (c.1980), Santa's Toy Shop (c.1980)
Anne Graham Johnstone Santa's Toy Shop (1979), Santa Claus is
 Coming to Town (1979)
Roger Lancelyn Green Tales of the Greeks and Trojans (1964),
 Myths from Many Lands (1965), Folk Tales of the World (1966),
 Sir Lancelot of the Lake (1966), Jason and the Golden Fleece (1968)
Heinrich Hoffman Struwwelpeter (1950)
John Pudney Crossing the Road (1958)
Virginia Salmon Supreme Book of Bible Stories (1977)
Dodie Smith The Hundred and One Dalmatians (1956)

Reference: Fisher p.196

Elisabeth Grant (active from 1960)

Children's book illustrator who worked mainly in
pen and ink in a sketchy style typical of the 1960s,
with varied hatched and off-printed texture and
shading. She also designed covers in full colour
for Puffin paperbacks.

Books illustrated include:
Mollie Hunter The Spanish Letters (1964), A Pistol in Greenyards
 (1965)
Patricia Lynch Sally from Cork (1960), Ryan's Fort (1961)
Rosemary Weir No Sleep for Angus (1969)

Reference: Fisher p.149

Millicent Ethelreda Gray (b. 1873)

Born in London. Studied at the Cope and Nicol
School and at the Royal Academy Schools. As an
illustrator she worked in watercolour for rather
expensively produced books with tipped-in colour
plates. Her illustrations were in a closely-worked
style, with furnishings and settings carefully depicted, but her treatment of figures was often
uncertain. She was also a painter.

Books illustrated include:
Louisa M. Alcott Little Women (1922)
Mabel and Lilian Quiller-Couch (ed) A Book of Children's Verse
 (1920)
Princess Mary's Gift Book (with others, c.1915)
The Queen's Gift Book (with others, c.1915)

Reference: Houfe

John Frederic Greenwood (1885-c.1954)

Born at Rochdale, Lancashire. Studied at Shipley

Janet & Anne Grahame-Johnstone. From *The
Hundred and One Dalmatians* by Dodie Smith
(Heinemann, 1956).

Art School (1904-07), Bradford College of Art
(1907-08) and at the Royal College of Art (1908-
11). Etcher and wood engraver. Taught at Battersea Polytechnic and Bradford College of Art, and
was Head of the Design School at Leeds College
of Art until 1948. His book illustrations consisted
of well-executed wood engravings of landscapes.
Elected RBA (1940), ARE (1922), RE (1939).

Books illustrated include:
Serid Evans A Short History of Ely Cathedral (1927)
J.F. Greenwood The Dales are Mine... (1952), Scarborough and
 Whitby (1920), Twenty-four Woodcuts of Cambridge (1926)
Reginald L. Hine A Short History of St Mary's, Hitchin (1930)

References: Balston WEMEB; Garrett BWE, HBWE; Johnson &
Greutzner; Vollmer; Wa (1924); Waters; *The Studio* special (Spring
1927, Spring 1930, Winter 1936); Campbell Dodgson *Contemporary
English Woodcuts* (Duckworth 1922)

Barbara Greg (b. 1900)

Born at Styal, Cheshire. Studied at the Slade
School of Fine Art (1919-23), the Central School
of Art (1921-23) and Westminster School of Art
(1926-27). Married Norman Janes* (1925). Some
of her earliest designs were for book endpapers
printed from wood and lino blocks. From 1926 to
1930, she and her husband produced a number of
wood engravings on musical subjects for pianola
rolls. Except in her early endpaper designs, she
used the white line technique of wood engraving,
reflecting her admiration for the work of Thomas
Bewick. All her book illustrations depict scenes
from nature and the countryside. Later in her
career, she worked in watercolour and made coloured linocuts. Member of Manchester Academy
of Fine Art (1925); elected ARE (1940), FRE
(1946), SWE (1952).[Q]

Books illustrated include:
G.L. Ashley-Dodd A Fisherman's Log (1929)

Ian Niall The Poacher's Handbook (1950), Fresh Woods (1951), Pastures New (1952)

E.L. Grant Watson Enigmas of Natural History (1936), More Enigmas of Natural History (1937), Wonders of Natural History (reprint of above two books 1947)

Periodicals: Country Fair, Countrygoer, Country Life

References: Garrett BWE, HBWE; Johnson & Greutzner; Vollmer; Wa (1980); Waters; *Fine Prints of the Year* (1937); *The Studio* special (Spring 1927, Spring 1930); Wilfred Gregson *A Student's Guide to Wood Engraving* (Batsford 1953)

Peter Ronald Gregory (b. 1947)

Born in Ilford, Essex. Studied at Walthamstow School of Art. Illustrator of mainly non-fiction children's books in pen and ink, sometimes with transparent washes and bodycolour. In his early work (influenced by the American artist Ken Dallisson) successive redefinitions of his subjects were retained, with no attempt to erase discarded lines, but in recent years—in response to publishers' demands—he has removed traces of his earlier ideas from finished drawings.

Books illustrated include:
Frank Bell Shen Stories/The Lioness (1979), Shen Stories/Trapped (1979)
John Denton On the Railway (1976), On the Road (1977)
John Dyson Know Your Car (1975)
Harry Hossent The Beaver Book of Trees (1980)
Edward Hyams Working for Man (1975)
Jack London The Call of the Wild (1976)
Josephine Ross Lord Mountbatten (1981), Thomas Edison (1982)
Ruth Thomson Henry Ford (1973)
Grant Uden High Horses (1976)

Reference: ICB 4

Maurice William Greiffenhagen (1862-1931)

Born in London. Studied at the Royal Academy Schools, where he won the Armitage Medal, the Cartoon Medal and various other prizes. He became well known as a magazine and book illustrator (often of 'society' subjects) during the 1890s, working mainly in black and white. Houfe detects the infuence of Phil May* in his freedom and economy of line; certainly he enjoyed and exploited the new opportunities offered by the development of line block reproduction, and developed a dashing pen and ink style. For his later illustrative work (mainly for books), he often worked for halftone reproduction, handling wash and bodycolour with panache. For full colour illustration he used deep rich hues. His work tended to be peopled with healthy square-jawed outdoor types (prototypes of the typical boys' adventure heroes of the inter-war period), and he was a noted illustrator of the works of H. Rider Haggard. After 1900, Greiffenhagen concentrated increasingly on portrait painting and became much less prolific as an illustrator; he also worked as a

decorative artist and poster designer. He was head of the Life Department at Glasgow School of Art (1906-29). One of the earliest members of the NEAC (1886); elected ARA (1916) and RA (1922).

Books illustrated include:
S.R. Crockett Strong Mac (1904)
W.L. Crowdy 'Dorothy' Sketches (1887)
J.M. Forman Bianca's Daughter (1910)
Edward Fitzgerald (trans) Rubaiyat of Omar Khayyam (1909)
A.H. Gilkes Kallistratus (1897)
Rider Haggard She (1887), Allan's Wife (1889), Cleopatra (1889), Montezuma's Daughter (1894), Swallow (1899), Ayesha (1905)
W.W. Jacobs The Lady of the Barge (1902), Many Cargoes (1912)
A.C. Kennedy Pictures in Rhyme (1891)
A.H. Norway Naples Past and Present (1905)
C.F. Parsons Some Thoughts at Eventide (1910)
M. Pemberton The Gold Wolf (1903), White Walls (1910)
H.M. Vaughan The Naples Riviera (1907)
R.H.E. Wallace Lieutenant Bones (1918)

Periodicals: Black and White, The Butterfly, The Daily Chronicle, The Illustrated London News, Judy, The Lady's Pictorial, The Pall Mall Budget, The Pall Mall Magazine, Pick-Me-Up, The Sketch, The Sphere, The Unicorn, The Windsor Magazine

References: Bénézit; Chamot, Farr & Butlin; DNB (1931-40); Harper; Houfe; ICB 1; Johnson & Greutzner; Pennell MI, PD; Sketchley; Thieme & Becker; Thorpe; Vollmer; Waters; C. Wood; *The Studio* 9 (1896-97), 88 (1924); *The Windsor Magazine* (December 1897); Bevis Hillier *Posters* (Weidenfeld & Nicolson 1969)

Vivien Gribble (d. 1932)

Married name: Mrs Douglas Doyle Jones. Studied in Munich, at the Slade School of Fine Art, and under Noel Rooke* at the Central School of Arts and Crafts. She exhibited with the Society of Wood Engravers from 1921, and illustrated several books for Duckworth, including *Six Idillia of Theocritus* (1922), one of the first books in the new style of wood engraving developed in the 'twenties. Her wood-engraved illustrations were frequently in the form of vignettes, and head or tail pieces. Her work was formal and simplified, with heavy black outlines and sometimes patterned backgrounds; her style was described by D.P. Bliss* as having ' "gentlemanly" restraint and severity'. She sometimes introduced white-line engraving into her later work.

Books illustrated include:
Lucius Apuleius Cupid and Psyche (1935)
Thomas Hardy Tess of the D'Urbervilles (1926)
J. Hilton and J. Thorp Change, the beginning of a Chapter (with others, 1919)
John Keats Odes (1923)
Alfred, Lord Tennyson Three Psalms, lxi, cxxi, cxlii (1912), Songs from 'The Princess' (1924), Six Idillia of Theocritus (1922)

Periodicals: Change, Country Life, The Golden Hind, London Mercury

References: Balston EWE, WEMEB; Johnson & Greutzner; Vollmer; Wa (1929); Waters; *The Studio* special (1919, Spring 1927, Winter 1931); Campbell Dodgson *Contemporary English Woodcuts* (Duckworth 1922); Herbert Furst *The Modern Woodcut* (Bodley Head 1924); A.C. Sewter *Modern British Woodcuts and Wood-Engravings in the Collection of the Whitworth Art Gallery* (Manchester 1962); Bernard Sleigh *Wood Engraving Since 1890* (Pitman 1932)

Frederick Landseer Maur Griggs
(1876-1938)

Often worked as F.L. Griggs. Born Hitchin, Hertfordshire, son of a baker. At the age of 20, he began an architectural training, but after two years, with the encouragement of Joseph Pennell*, turned instead to drawing and illustration. From 1900, he worked on Macmillan's 'Highways and Byways' series, illustrating thirteen volumes in pen and ink or pencil and acquiring, in the process, an intimate knowledge of vernacular and ecclesiastical building styles. In 1904, he joined the Guild of Handicraft at Chipping Campden, Gloucestershire, and during the following years was associated with the furniture maker Ernest Gimson. He made his first experiments in etching in 1896, and later became well known for his work in the medium. He also designed lettering, typefaces and book covers, and painted in watercolour. As an architect, he designed cottages and extensions to old buildings and was responsible for a number of war memorials after World War I. The slump of 1929 led to a decreasing number of commissions, and he died in relative poverty.

Griggs's work was inspired by a profound love of old buildings, particularly of the medieval period. His early illustrations had affinities with those of E.H. New*, but he soon developed a freer and more responsive personal style of

Frederick L. Griggs. 'The Castle Moat, Burwell' from *Highways and Byways in Cambridge and Ely* by Edward Conybeare (Macmillan, 1910).

drawing; some of his etchings showed the influence of Samuel Palmer in the taut intensity of their line. Elected ARE (1916), RE (1918), ARA (1922), Hon. ARIBA (1926), RA (1931), and member of the Council of the Society for the Protection of Ancient Buildings.

Books illustrated include:
A.C. Bradley Highways and Byways in South Wales (1903)
Edward Conybeare Highways and Byways in Cambridge and Ely (1910)
E.C. Cook Highways and Byways in London (1902)
H.A. Evans Highways and Byways in Northamptonshire and Rutland (1918), Highways and Byways in Oxford and the Cotswolds (1905)
J.B. Firth Highways and Byways in Leicestershire (1926) Highways and Byways in Nottinghamshire (1916)
Reginald L. Hine Charles Lamb and his Hertfordshire (1949)
W. Huyshe Royal Manor of Hitchin and its Lords, Harold and The Balliols (1906)
E.V. Lucas Highways and Byways in Sussex (1904)
M.P. Milne-Home Stray Leaves from a Border Garden (1901)
W.F. Rawnsley Highways and Byways in Lincolnshire (1914)
Harry Roberts The Chronicle of a Cornish Garden (1901)
Percy Bysshe Shelley The Sensitive Plant (1902)
C.K. Shorter Highways and Byways in Buckinghamshire (1910)
H.W. Tomkins Highways and Byways in Hertfordshire (1902)
J.E. Vincent Highways and Byways in Berkshire (1906)

Periodicals: The London Mercury, The Oxford Almanack

References: Bénézit; Guichard; Houfe; Johnson & Greutzner; Mallalieu; Pennell PD; Sketchley; Thieme & Becker; Vollmer; Wa (1927); Waters; *Fine Prints of the Year* 1923-25, 1928-37; *The Print Collector's Quarterly* vols 11, 20, 26, 40; *The Studio* 82 (1921), 116 (1938), special (1900-01, 1911, Autumn 1914, Spring 1922, Spring 1929, Autumn 1938); F.A. Comstock *A Gothic Vision: F.L. Griggs and his Work* (Boston Public Library 1966); G. Montague Ellwood *The Art of Pen Drawing* (Batsford 1927); M.C. Salaman *Modern Masters of Etching* vol 12 (The Studio series 1925-32)

Rosemary Ann Grimble (b. 1932)

Works as Rosemary Grimble. Born in Kiribati, Central Pacific. Daughter of the Colonial administrator and writer Sir Arthur Grimble. She was educated in France and has subsequently travelled widely. Painter (oil and watercolour) and photographer; freelance designer and illustrator of books, magazines and newspapers. For illustration, she works with a fine pen and ink line, in a style that gradually gained assurance. She is also a writer and broadcaster on travel subjects. [Q]

Books illustrated include:
Paula Fox How Many Miles to Babylon? (1972)
Sir Arthur Grimble Return to the Island (1957)
Ian Grimble Scottish Clans and Tartans (endpapers 1973)
Rosemary Grimble Jonothon and Large (1965), Migrations, Myth and Magic from the Gilbert Islands (1970), The Thief Catcher and other stories from Ethiopia (1972)
Jocasta Innes The Pauper's Homemaking Book (1976)
Naomi Mitchison Alexander the Great (1964)
Prince Modupe I Was a Savage (1958)
L.E. Snellgrove From Coracles to Cunarders (1962)
R.L. Stevenson Treasure Island (1959)
House and Garden Books: Book of Interiors (1962), The Modern Interior (1964), Guide to Interior Decoration (1967)
Songs of Greece (Sunday Times 1968)
Longman's Then and There Series: Ancient Greece (1965)

Periodicals: Cyprus Magazine, The Field, Go, The Guardian, Harper's Bazaar, House and Garden, The Observer, The Sunday Times, The Times, Vogue

Mary E. Groom (active 1920s and 1930s)

At Leon Underwood's* Art School (when she had started in 1921), she was introduced to wood engraving by a fellow student who had previously studied under Robert Gibbings*; others at the school who took up engraving included Blair Hughes-Stanton*, Gertrude Hermes*, Agnes Miller Parker* and soon afterwards Underwood himself. A distinct group within the broader wood-engraving movement, these artists formed the nucleus of the English Wood Engraving Society, which broke away from the Society of Wood-Engravers in 1925 and was re-united with it in 1932. Mary Groom's engravings have the delicate line characteristic of this group and she sometimes used a multiple graver, which she had helped to re-introduce from France. Her work is generally in white line, with little tonal contrast or textural variety, and there is frequently an element of primitivism in her drawing.

Books illustrated include:
John Milton Paradise Lost (1937)
W.O.E. Oesterley (intro) Roses of Sharon (1937)

Periodical: The Island

References: Balston EWE, WEMEB; Johnson & Greutzner; *The Penrose Annual* vol 41 (1939); *The Studio* special (Spring 1930, Winter 1936, Autumn 1938); Christopher Sandford, *Bibliography of the Golden Cockerel Press* (Dawson 1975)

William Henry Charles Groome (active 1881-1914)

Landscape painter; illustrator of adventure stories in black and white, halftone and full colour. Lived in Ealing, West London. Elected RBA (1901).

Books illustrated include:
R.M. Ballantyne The Gorilla Hunters (nd)
G. Manville Fenn Fix Bay'nets (1899)
John Finnemore A Boy Scout in the Balkans (1913), Brother Scouts (1911), Foray and Fight (1906), His First Term (1909)
G.A. Henty Dash and Daring (1898), Hazard and Heroism (1904), Steady and Strong (1905)
W.H.G. Kingston Afar in the Forest (1912), Old Jack (nd)
Amy le Feuvre Brownie (1900), Thoughtless Seven (1900), Us, and Our Donkey (1909), A Little Listener (1910), Us, and Our Empire (1911), Laddie's Choice (1922), His Little Daughter (c.1930)
A. Weber When I'm a Man (1888)
The Silver Flagon (1896)

Periodicals: Chums, The Illustrated London News, Little Folks, The Sunday Magazine, Young England

References: Bénézit; Houfe; Johnson & Greutzner; Thieme & Becker; Thorpe; Waters 2; C. Wood

Imre Anthony Sander Gross (b. 1905)

Works as Anthony Gross. Born in Dulwich, London, son of a geographer father and a playwright mother. Studied in London at the Slade School of Fine Art and the Central School of Arts and Crafts under Robbins, in Paris at the Académie Julian and the Ecole des Beaux Arts, and

Anthony Gross. From *Sixe Idyllia of Theocritus* (Clover Hill Editions, New York, 1971).

in Madrid; settled in Paris (1926). In partnership with Hector Courtland Hoppin, he made three animated films: *La Joie de Vivre* (1932), *Fox Hunt* (produced by Alexander Korda, (1937) and *Round the World in Eighty Days* (held up during World War II and edited by the British Film Institute in 1955). His first book illustrations — some 70 line drawings and eight etchings for Jean Cocteau's *Les Enfants Terribles* —were published in a limited edition in Paris in 1937. He served as an official war artist in Africa, India, Burma and Europe (1940-45). Taught at the Central School of Arts and Crafts (1948-55); and was head of the Etching and Engraving Department at the Slade School of Fine Art (1955-71). He spends half the year in Greenwich, London, and half in France.

Gross's graphic work is characterised by its versatile and vigorous quality of line; indeed, Jonathan Mayhew considers that 'If there is one quality rather than another which is admirable, it is, I think, the artist's power to give full rein to the nervous brio of his line while never letting it get out of hand' (*Image* 4). Of *The Forsyte Saga*, John Lewis writes 'It will stand as an example of what can be done when a graphically minded painter turns his hand to illustration'. Member of London Group (1948-71); elected ARA (1979), RA (1980), Hon RE (1979); awarded CBE (1982). [Q]

Books illustrated include:
Emily Brontë Wuthering Heights (1947)
John Galsworthy The Forsyte Saga (1950)
E. and J. de Goncourt Germinie Lacerteau (1955)
Anthony Gross (preface David Garnett) The Very Rich Hours of Le
    Boulvé (1980)
Henry James English Hours (1960)
Theocritus (ed Douglas Cleverdon) Six Idyllia (1971)

Periodicals: Radio Times, The Strand Magazine

References: Bénézit; Bland; Chamot, Farr & Butlin; Driver;
Guichard; Jacques; Johnson & Greutzner; Lewis; Parry-Crooke;
Underwood; Vollmer; Wa (1980); WaG; Waters; *Image 4* (1950); *The
Studio* 153 (1957); Diana Klemin *The Illustrated Book* (Bramhall
House, New York 1970); John Lewis *A Handbook of Type and
Illustration* (Faber 1956); Graham Reynolds *The Etchings of Anthony
Gross* (Victoria and Albert Museum 1968)

Ralph Gore Antony Groves-Raines (b. 1928)

Works as Antony Groves-Raines. Born in Ireland;
his artist mother had studied under J.A. McNeill
Whistler. Studied at Cambridge and in France
and Germany with a view to a career in the dip-
lomatic service, but instead, decided to take up
painting as a profession. He settled in Ireland.
His book illustrations in black and white, often
with added colour or halftone, have a taut fastidious line, and he adapts his style to the demands
of his text with intelligence and wit. He also designs
book jackets.

Books illustrated include:
H.A. The Golden String (1947)
A. Groves-Raines The Tidy Hen (1961),
John Langstaff Alice, a Forethought (1938), Prodigies and Prodigals
    (1947), A Guinness Sportfolio (c.1950), Alice, Where Art Thou?
    (1952), What Will They Think of Next? (1954), Can This Be Beeton?
    (1956), On Christmas Day in the Morning (1959), My Goodness! My
    Gilbert and Sullivan! (1961)
Lays of Courtly Love (nd)

References: ICB 3; Vollmer supp; Wa (1977); Diana Klemin *The
Illustrated Book* (Bramhall House, New York 1970)

Beatrice Claudia Guercio (b. 1904)

Worked as Claudia Guercio and, under her married
name, as Claudia Freedman. Born in Formby,
Liverpool, into a Sicilian family. Studied at Liverpool School of Art and at the Royal College of
Art. Married Barnett Freedman* (1930). Painter,

Claudia Guercio. From *Review of Revues* edited
by C.B.C. (Cape, 1930).

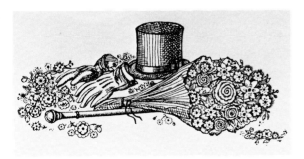

pen and ink illustrator, designer (e.g. an alphabet
of initials for the Baynard Press and book covers).

Books illustrated include:
C.B.C. (ed) Review of Revues (1930)
Walter de la Mare A Snowdrop (1929)
Claudia Freedman My Toy Cupboard (nd)
Eleanor Graham (ed) The Puffin Book of Verse (1953)
The Curwen Press Miscellany (with others, 1931)
German Tales and Legends (1925)

References: Johnson & Greutzner; Wa (1972); Waters; Herbert Simon
Song and Words (Allen & Unwin 1973)

James Joshua Guthrie (1874-1952)

Often worked as James Guthrie. Born Glasgow,
son of a metal merchant. Studied in the evenings
at Heatherley's School of Art and with the British
Museum Students' Group while working in the
family firm in London. He was a painter, illustrator, book and bookplate designer, etcher and
wood-engraver, printer, writer and poet; a significant figure in the early development of the
private presses, and in the parallel revival of
wood-engraving as an art form. In 1895, he founded
The Elf, a magazine for which he produced text
and illustrations; hand printed at the Old Bourne
Press, it appeared intermittently until 1902. From
1897 to 1899, he worked full time as Reginald
Hallward's* assistant. In 1899, he founded the
Pear Tree Press at Gravesend, Kent (moving to
South Harting in 1901 and Flansham in 1906). He
undertook the whole production process, illustrating, engraving and designing its publications
(of which he was often also the author), and exper-
imenting with intaglio plates and hand colouring
techniques. He developed a characteristic graphic
style, described by John Russell Taylor as 'a sort
of folk-weave art nouveau'. His imagery is often
reminiscent of the black and white drawings of
D.G. Rossetti or Samuel Palmer in atmosphere
and dramatic intensity. He wrote extensively on
book and book-plate design.

Books illustrated include:
J.D.B. Echoes of Poetry (1908)
H. Beardsell Pillow Fancies (1901), Garden Fancies (1904)
William Blake Songs of Innocence (1939)
Charles Blatherwick Peter Stonnor (with A.S. Boyd*, 1884)
Gordon Bottomley The End of Frescoes from Buried Temples (1928),
    Midsummer Eve (1905), The Riding to Lithend (1909), The Viking's
    Barrow at Littleholme (1930)
William Collins Ode to Evening (1937)
Mrs Davidson The Garden of Time (1896)
A.F.S. and E. de Passemere Wedding Bells (1895)
Vivian Ellis Epode (1915)
James J. Guthrie An Album of Drawings (1900), My House in the
    World (1919)
Frances H. Low Little Men in Scarlet (1896)
John Milton Hymn on the Morning of Christ's Nativity (1904)
H. Monro Trees (1916)
Edgar Allan Poe Some Poems (1901-1908)
Dante Gabriel Rossetti The Blessed Damozel and Hand and Soul
    (1903)
P.E. Thomas A Friend of the Blackbird (1938)
Mrs Williams The Floweret (1902)
The Beatitudes from the Sermon on the Mount (1905)

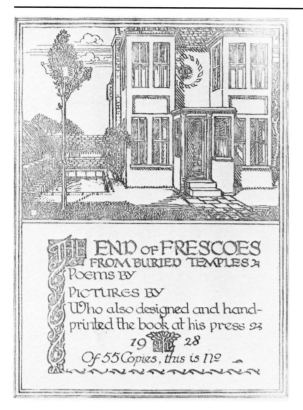

James Guthrie. From *The End of Frescoes from Buried Temples* by Gordon Bottomley (1928).

Periodicals: The Dome, The Idler, The Page, The Pall Mall Gazette, The Quartier Latin, The Page, Root and Branch, The Windmill, The Yellow Book

References: Baker; Bénézit; Houfe; Johnson & Greutzner; Pennell PD; Sketchley; Taylor; Thieme & Becker; Vollmer; Wa (1927); Waters; C. Wood; *The Studio* special (1898-99); Gordon Bottomley (intro) *James Guthrie: His Book of Book-Plates* (Otto Schulze 1907); James L. Carr *Scottish Painting Past and Present* (T.C. & E.C. Jack 1908); James J. Guthrie *An Account of the Aims and Intentions of his Press, with a list of Books* (Pear Tree Press 1905), *On the Art of the Book* (Lexington 1952); Robin Craig Guthrie *James Guthrie: Biographical Notes* (Lexington 1953)

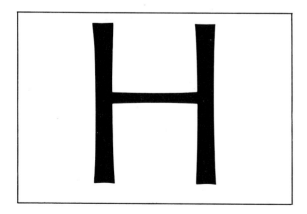

Philip Hagreen (1890-1965)

Poet and illustrator. One of the original members of the Society of Wood Engravers, which was founded in his studio (1920). Became a member of Eric Gill's* religious guild of artists at Ditchling, Sussex (1921), and joined Gill (taking his family with him) at Capel-y-ffin, Abergavenny (1924-25). Left through ill-health and lived mostly in France until 1932; returned to Ditchling and worked as a guild member until 1955. He published several books of his own poetry. Although Hagreen was principally concerned with wood engraving and lettering, his book illustrations consist mainly of line drawings in pen and ink. His simplified two-dimensional style shows the influence of Gill.

Books illustrated include:
Lucius Apuleius The Golden Ass (1924)
John Hilton and Joseph Thorp Change, the Beginning of a Chapter (with others, 1919)
A.R. Le Sage The Devil on Two Sticks (1927)
Thomas Moult (ed) The Best Poems of 1922, 1923 and 1924
Rhyme Sheets The White Window (1920)
Jane M. Strachey Nursery Lyrics (1922)

References: Balston EWE; Johnson & Greutzner; Waters 2; *The Studio* special (Spring 1927); Campbell Dodgson *Contemporary English Woodcuts* (Duckworth 1922); Herbert Furst *The Modern Woodcut* (Bodley Head 1924); A.C. Sewter *Modern British Woodcuts and Wood-Engravings in the Collection of the Whitworth Art Gallery* (Manchester 1962)

Kathleen Hale (b. 1898)

Married name: Mrs McClean. Born in Broughton, Scotland. Studied at Manchester School of Art, Reading University College of Art (1916-18), the Central School of Arts and Crafts (1928-30) and the East Anglian School of Painting and Drawing under Cedric Morris (1938). Painter in oil and watercolour, and printmaker (lithographs and lino-cuts). She worked in a variety of jobs after first leaving college, before establishing herself as a book illustrator and designer of book jackets and posters. Her most famous character, Orlando the Marmalade Cat, was originally created for her two sons. The first Orlando book appeared in 1938 and, with its large format and brilliantly coloured, freely drawn lithographed illustrations, was a landmark in children's publishing. It was followed by another 18 Orlando titles, all illustrated in Kathleen Hale's characteristic manner. The imagery is lively and humorous, with naturalistically treated cats contrasting with bizarre caricatures of humans. Kathleen Hale has travelled widely—in Europe, Scandinavia, Morocco, the Lebanon and Peru—and lives in Oxford. Elected FSIA and awarded the OBE (1976). [Q]

Books illustrated include:
Kathleen Hale Orlando the Marmalade Cat: Camping Holiday (1938), Orlando the Marmalade Cat: A Trip Abroad (1939), Orlando's Evening Out (1941), Orlando's Home Life (1942), Orlando the Marmalade Cat Buys a Farm (1942), Henrietta the Faithful Hen (1943), Orlando the Marmalade Cat: His Silver Wedding (1944), Orlando the Marmalade Cat Becomes a Doctor (1944), Orlando's Invisible Pyjamas (1947), Orlando the Marmalade Cat Keeps a Dog

(1949), Orlando the Judge (1950), Orlando's Country Life Peep Show Book (1950), Puss-in-Boots: A Peep Show Book (1951), Orlando the Marmalade Cat: A Seaside Holiday (1952), Manda (1952), Orlando's Zoo (1954), Orlando the Marmalade Cat: The Frisky Housewife (1956), Orlando's Magic Carpet (1958), Orlando the Marmalade Cat Buys a Cottage (1963), Orlando and the Three Graces (1965), Orlando the Marmalade Cat Goes to the Moon (1969), Orlando the Marmalade Cat and the Water Cats (1972), Henrietta's Magic Egg (1973)
Mary R. Harrower I Don't Mix Much with the Fairies (1928), Plain Jane (1929)
Evelyn Waugh Basil Seal Rides Again (1963)

Periodicals: The Christian Science Monitor, Homes and Gardens, Vogue

References: Contemporary Authors; Crouch; Doyle CL; Fisher pp.138, 251, 265; Hürlimann; ICB 2,3,4; Johnson & Greutzner; Kirkpatrick; Lewis; Vollmer supp; Wa (1962); Waters; WW (1980); *The Junior Bookshelf* vol 11 no 1 (1947); William Feaver *When We Were Young* (Thames & Hudson 1977)

Robert Hales (active from 1967)

Children's book illustrator. He worked mainly in black and white in a style typical of the 1960s.

Books illustrated include:
Joseph Chipperfield Rex of Larkbarrow (1969), Banner (1972), Lobo (1974)
Dorothy Clewes A Bit of Magic (1967), Peter and the Jumble (1969), Library Lady (1970)
Mary Cockett Something Big (1968)
Peter Dickinson Heartsease (1969), The Devil's Children (1970)
Leon Garfield Baker's Dozen (1973)
Tim Hopkins Nobody Pushes Me Around (1980)
Elyne Mitchell Moon Filly (1968)
Reginald Ottley Rain Comes to Yamboorah (1967)
Rosemary Weir The Foxwood Flyer (1968)
Ursula Moray Williams Traffic Jam (1971)

Arthur Henderson Hall (1906-83)

Born in Sedgefield, County Durham, son of an estate bailiff. He was an apprentice joiner carpenter from the age of thirteen for four years. He studied at Accrington and Coventry Schools of Art, then at the Royal College of Art, London, under William Rothenstein; won the Prix de Rome for engraving (1931) and attended the British School in Rome for two years. Part-time teacher at Kingston and Central School of Art (1939-40). Served in the army and the Royal Air Force during World War II. Part-time teacher of drawing at the Central School of Arts and Crafts (1946-52), and Head of the School of Graphic Design at Kingston School of Art (1952-74). Painter in watercolour and oil, etcher, glass designer and illustrator of children's and gardening books. Hall's crisp black and white illustrations for the horticultural books of E.R. Janes published by Penguin demonstrate that diagrammatic clarity can be achieved without the sacrifice of stylistic independence. Member RE, RWS, SIA and London Group.[Q]

Books illustrated include:
Ruth Ainsworth Bedtime Book (1974)
Mark Dallow Heir of Charlecote (1955)
Roger Lancelyn Green Robin Hood (1956)

E.R. Janes The Flower Garden (1952), The Vegetable Garden (1954), Growing Vegetables for Show (1956), Flower-Growing for Shows (1959)
Sheila McCullagh Jacca and the Talking Dog (1978)
Betty Sherman George Moves House (1978)
Mark Twain The Adventures of Tom Sawyer (1950), The Adventures of Huckleberry Finn (1953)
The Children's Guide to Knowledge (Odhams Press 1949)
History of England (Odhams Press, nd)
Library of the Garden (Reader's Digest 1963)

References: Johnson & Greutzner; Vollmer; Wa (1980); Waters

Douglas Hall (b. 1931)

Born in Doncaster, Yorkshire. Studied at Doncaster School of Art (1947-48), Leeds College of Art (1948-50) and, after National Service, at the Royal College of Art, London (1953-56). Freelance illustrator and book jacket designer since 1956, working mainly for Hutchinson. He describes his illustrative work as 'loosely academic with a pinch of humour'. Part-time teacher of portrait painting and drawing since 1976; works in Tunbridge Wells, Kent. [Q]

Books illustrated include:
Lillian Beckwith Hills is Lonely (1959), Sea for Breakfast (1961), Loud Halo (1964), Rope in Case (1968), About My Father's Business

Douglas Hall. 'The flat was in a mews and all the mews round about looked exactly the same' from *The Battle of Wednesday Week* by Barbara Willard (Constable, 1963).

(1971), Lightly Poached (1973), Beautiful Just! (1975), Hebridean Cook Book (1976), Bruach Blend (1978)
Lewis Carroll Alice in Wonderland (1960)
Douglas Hall Douglas Hall's Animal Nursery Rhymes (1979)
Roger Lancelyn Green The Land Beyond the North (1958)
George MacBeth The Rectory Mice (1982)
Margaret Macpherson The Rough Road (1966)
Janet McNeill Just Turn the Key (1976)
Evelyn Prentis A Nurse in Time (1977), A Nurse in Action (1978), A Nurse in Parts (1980), A Nurse Near By (1981), A Turn for the Nurse (1982)
Doris Rybot My Kingdom for a Donkey (1963)
Sally Sheringham Splodge Pig (1983)
John Rowe Townsend Pirate's Island (1968)
Maurice Wiggin A Cottage Idyll (1969)
Barbara Willard The Battle of Wednesday Week (1963), Three and One to Carry (1964), Charity at Home (1965)
James Dillon White The Fursedown Comet (1970)
More Stories from Listen with Mother (1983)

References: ICB 3,4

Adelaide Hallward
See Reginald F. Hallward.

Reginald F. Hallward (1858-1948)
Studied at the Slade School of Fine Art and the Royal College of Art. Painter, designer of stained glass and embroidery, lithographer and writer. He ran the Woodland Press at Gravesend, Kent and published a number of his own books and those of his wife Adelaide (written under her maiden name: Bloxham). These attractive volumes, printed lithographically and sometimes hand-coloured, often have handwritten passages in the manner of William Blake's *Songs*; the landscape treatment of many of the plates shows some affinity with the work of Hallward's one-time assistant James Guthrie*. Gleeson White considered that 'Mr and Mrs Reginald Hallward eschew the pretty-pretty and are bent on producing really decorative pages' ('Children's Books and Their Illustrators' in *The Studio* special, 1897-98).

Books illustrated include:
E.L. Farrar Stories from the Bible (1896)
Reginald Hallward Flowers of Paradise (1889), Vox Humana (1900), The Religion of Art (1917)

References: Houfe; Johnson & Greutzner; Pennell MI; Vollmer supp; Waters; C. Wood; *The Studio* special (1897-98)

Aubrey Hammond (1894-1940)
Born Folkestone, Kent. Studied at the London and Byam Shaw Schools of Art and at the Académie Julian, Paris. Teacher of commercial and theatrical design at the Westminster School of Art. A pen and ink draughtsman, stage and poster designer and caricaturist, his illustrations are clearly drawn and amusing, in an unmistakably 1920s style.

Books illustrated include:
Dora Greville (ed) The Diary of Mr Niggs (1932)

Lewis Melville The London Scene (1926)
Peter Traill Under the Cherry Tree (1926)

Periodical: Nash's Magazine

References: Cuppleditch; Johnson & Greutzner; Vollmer supp; Wa (1934); *The Studio* special (1927, Autumn 1928); Bohun Lynch A History of Caricature (Faber & Gwyer 1927)

Gertrude E. Demain Hammond (1862-c.1952)
Born in Brixton, London, sister of illustrator Chris Hammond (1861-1900). Studied at Lambeth School of Art (1879) and the Royal Academy Schools (1885). Painter, and illustrator in full colour, halftone and black and white. Thorpe rightly considered that, although less popular, she was a better draughtsman than her sister. Elected RI (1896).

Books illustrated include:
E.D. Adams A Girl of To-day (1898)
F.C. Armstrong A Fair Claimant (1900)
Dorita F. Bruce Dimsie Moves Up Again (1922), Dimsie Among the Prefects (1923)
John Bunyan The Pilgrim's Progress (1916)
Thomas Carter Shakespeare's Stories of the English Kings (1912)
Audrey Curtis The Artist of Crooked Alley (1896), Little Miss Curlylocks (1896), Old Moneybags' Grandson (1897)
J.H.K. Denny The Clever Miss Follett (1893)
Charles Dickens The Personal History of David Copperfield (1915)
Mrs Molesworth Jasper (1906), The Little Guest (1907), Fairies—of Sorts (1908), The Story of a Year (1910), Fairies Afield (1911)
Rose Mulholland Cynthia's Bonnet Shop (1900)
Mrs E.R. Pitman Life's Daily Ministry (c.1900)
E.F. Pollard The King's Signet (1900)
M. Corbet Seymour Nicola (1893)
Edmund Spenser Stories from the Faerie Queene (1909)
Douglas Stedman The Story of Hereward (1909)
Katharine Tynan The Handsome Brandons (1898)
Charles Young Harald, First of the Vikings (1911)
The Works of William Shakespeare (1922)

Periodicals: Black and White, The Idler, The Lady's Pictorial, The Ludgate Monthly, Madame, The Minster, Pick-Me-Up, The Queen, The Quiver, St Paul's Magazine, The Yellow Book

References: Bénézit; Houfe; ICB 1; Johnson & Greutzner; Mallalieu; Thieme & Becker; Thorpe; Waters 1, 2; C. Wood; Walter Shaw Sparrow *Women Painters of the World* Hodder & Stoughton 1905

Nina Hamnett (1890-1956)
Born in Tenby, South Wales, daughter of an army officer. She studied at the Pelham School of Art and at the London School of Art under Frank Brangwyn*, Joseph Simpson* and William Nicholson*. A painter, she was a friend of Modigliani and of Henri Gaudier-Brzeska, and worked at Roger Fry's Omega Workshops. She uninhibitedly recalled her bohemian life in Paris and London in her two books of autobiographical anecdotes. Her book illustrations (pen and ink line drawings without hatching) are refreshingly spontaneous and direct.

Books illustrated include:
Nina Hamnett Laughing Torso (1932)
Seymour Leslie The Silent Queen (1927)
Osbert Sitwell The People's Album of London Statues (1928)

W. Lee Hankey. From *The Deserted Village* by Oliver Goldsmith (Constable, 1909).

Periodicals: The Gypsy, The New Coterie

References: Houfe; Johnson & Greutzner; Vollmer supp; Wa (1934); Waters; *Artwork* 2 (1924); Nina Hamnett *Laughing Torso* (Constable 1932), *Is She a Lady? A Problem in Autobiography* (Alan Wingate 1955); Jack Lindsay *Fanfrolico and After* (Bodley Head 1962)

Frank Hampson (b. 1918)

Born in Audenshaw, near Manchester. Worked as a messenger (1932-34) and clerk (1934-38) for the Post Office. Served in the army during World War II. He was the creator of the celebrated full colour cartoon strip *Dan Dare* on the front page of the *Eagle* comic (1950-60), successfully modifying the American *Marvel* comic style to appeal to more delicate British sensibilities. His illustrations for various Ladybird titles have on the whole been less distinguished. He works in ink, pen and wash, acrylics and oils and acknowledges the influence of, among others, Charles Keene* and Phil May*. He has travelled extensively in Russia, Asia and Europe. [Q]

Books illustrated include:
Frank Hampson Man from Nowhere (1979), Rogue Planet (1980), Road of Courage (1981)
Ladybird titles: Nursery Rhymes, Kings and Queens of England, Through the Ages Food, Marie Curie, Through the Ages Transport

Periodicals: Anvil, Eagle, Meccano Magazine, The Post (U.P.W. magazine)

William Lee Hankey (1869-1952)

Born Chester. Attended evening classes at Chester School of Art while working as a designer of furniture and textiles. Awarded a scholarship to the Royal College of Art (1894), but disliked the system there and left to continue his studies in Paris. Taught etching at Goldsmith's College, London (1907-12). Served as a reconnaissance instructor in the Artists' Rifles during World War I. Lived in London, but had a studio in Pulborough, Sussex, which he often lent to friends, including Frank Reynolds* and James Thorpe (later the author of *English Illustration—The Nineties*). He was a landscape and portrait painter in oil and watercolour and a noted etcher who experimented with different types of ground. His book illustrations consist of sensitive watercolours and gouaches, and simple but effective pen and ink drawings. Founder member of the London Sketch Club (president, 1904). Elected RBA (1896, resigned 1900), RI (1896-1906, 1918-24), RMS (1896), ROI (1901), ARE (1909), RE (1911), ARWS (1925), RWS (1936).

Books illustrated include:
Oliver Goldsmith The Deserted Village (1909)
Maurice Maeterlinck It's the Child's Turn Now (nd)
Izaak Walton The Compleat Angler (1913)

Periodical: The Flag

References: Bénézit; Cuppleditch; Guichard; Houfe; ICB 1; Johnson & Greutzner; Mallalieu; Thieme & Becker; Vollmer and supp; Wa (1934); Waters; C. Wood; *The Studio* 36 (1906), 54 (1912), 74 (1918), special (Spring 1906, Winter 1913, Autumn 1914, 1917); Martin Hardie *The Etched Work of William Lee Hankey* (Lefèvre 1921)

Dudley Hardy (1867-1922)

Born in Sheffield, son of the marine painter T.B. Hardy. Studied in Düsseldorf (where he found himself at odds with the academic training of Crola and Löwenstein, and was expelled in 1884), in Antwerp under Verlat, and in Paris at Colarossi's. After returning to London, he worked freelance as a painter (exhibiting at the Royal Academy of Art from 1885), as a magazine and as a book illustrator, and poster designer. He was a very rapid worker in a wide range of media and, perhaps inevitably, his work was uneven in quality. A.E. Johnson considered that the essence of his style was its spontaneity and observed that he had 'the power to set down, without effort, the passing impressions of his mind.' These mental impressions were, at best, popular rather than profound, and he turned out large numbers of pot-boilers; these often consist of the Oriental and Breton peasant and oriental scenes then in vogue and (for magazines) 'countless sketches in black and white of attractive little milliners and beauteous "corypées" of the stage, whose gay and frisky "insouciance" has endeared them to the amorous heart of the public' (A.E. Johnson). In a similar vein, Hardy contributed a successful series of opera sketches to *Punch*. He was probably most widely known for his strikingly animated poster designs, which had an enormous impact and did much to set off the 'poster boom' at the beginning of the century. He designed the celebrated 'Yellow Girl' poster (inspired, perhaps, by the American R.F. Outcault's 'Yellow Kid') which advertised Jerome K. Jerome's new weekly newspaper *To-Day*, the 'Gaiety Girl' (influenced by the French poster designer Jules Cheret), and a highly successful series for the Savoy Theatre. He lived in the West London artists' suburb, Bedford Park. Member of the Langham Sketch Club and London Sketch Club. Elected RBA (1889), RI (1897), ROI (1898), RMS.

Books illustrated include:
E.H. Cooper Wyemarke and the Sea-Fairies (1899), The Stock
    Exchange in the Year 1900 (1900)
Bret Harte The Bell Ringer of Angels (1897)
R. Strong Sensations of Paris (1912)
J. Tresahar Temptation (1901)
F.E. Weatherly 'Lays for the Little Ones' (1898)
Alice Werner The Humour of Holland (1894)

Periodicals: Ariel, Black and White, The English Illustrated
Magazine, Eureka, The Flag, The Gentlewoman, The Idler, Illustrated
Bits, The Illustrated London News, The Lady's Pictorial, Little Folks,
The London Magazine, The Longbow, The Ludgate Monthly, The
Minster, The Pall Mall Budget, Pearson's Magazine, Pick-Me-Up,
Printer's Pie, Punch, St Paul's Magazine, The Sketch, The Windsor
Magazine

References: Bénézit; Bradshaw; Cuppleditch; Harper; Houfe; Johnson
& Greutzner; Thieme & Becker; Thorpe; Waters; C. Wood; *Art
Journal* 1897; *The Studio* 8 (1896), special (Spring 1906); Cecil Aldin
Time I Was Dead (Eyre & Spottiswoode 1934); David Cuppleditch
The John Hassall Lifestyle (Dilke Press 1980); A.E. Johnson *Dudley
Hardy RI, RMS* (A. & C. Black 1909)

Evelyn Stuart Hardy (b. 1870)

Sister of Paul Hardy*. Writer and illustrator of children's books, in black and white and full colour and illustrator in black and white of military subjects. The captions to *Friends of Jesus* (Shaw's Hardy Picture no. 114) indicate a series of no fewer than 977 Bible pictures for Shaw; the style of these competent but unremarkable watercolours suggests that they might have been painted in the early 1920s.

Books illustrated include:
Hans Christian Andersen Fairy Tales (1904)
Romesh Dutt (ed) Maha Bharata (1899)
Brothers Grimm Fairy Tales (with others, 1898)
E. Stuart Hardy Happy Times (1900), Laugh and Play (1900), Merry
    Folk (1900)
Valmiki Ramayana (1900)
Lucy Weedon Nursery Tales (1903)
Friends of Jesus (1949)
Old Mother Goose Nursery Rhymes (nd)
Stories from the Book of Books (1914)

Periodicals Cassell's Children's Annual, Chums, The Gentlewoman,
Little Folks, Our Jabberwock, The Penny Magazine, St James's
Budget, The Sporting and Dramatic News

References: ICB 1; *Pearson's Magazine* vol 2, pp. 109-110

John Hargrave. 'The merchant and his oil-skin' from *Black Tales for White Children* (Constable, 1914).

Paul Hardy (b. 1862)

Born near Bath, Somerset, son of artist David Hardy and brother of Evelyn Stuart Hardy*. Lived at Bexley Heath, Kent, and Chobham, Surrey. Illustrator, watercolour painter and metal worker. A prolific illustrator of adventure stories, especially in magazines, and a contributor to *Chums* for over forty years (1896-1940). Brian Doyle, who considers his work 'distinctive and accomplished', comments that his forte was figures in action. Hardy was attentive to historical detail, particularly the rigging of ships and period costume (of which he formed a collection to be worn by the models from whom he generally drew). Most of his book illustrations were in halftone. He also achieved recognition for his metal models of antique ships.

Books illustrated include:
Mrs S.D.S. Barker Our Pets (1887)
Cervantes The Adventures of Don Quixote (1911)
Mary H. Debenham The Whispering Winds (c.1900)
C.G. Harper The Smugglers (1909)
Bret Harte Barker's Luck (with others, 1896)
G.A. Henty A Jacobite Exile (1894)
Thomas Hughes Tom Brown's Schooldays (1914)
Thomas Babbington Macaulay The Lays of Ancient Rome (1907)
L. Malet Little Peter (1888)
Mrs E.R. Pitman Florence Godfrey's Faith (c.1900), Garnered
    Sheaves (c.1900)
J.H. Spettigue A Pair of Them (1900)

Amelia Stirling The Reign of Princess Naska (1899)
Sarah Tyler A Loyal Little Maid (1900)

Periodicals: Black and White, The Boy's Own Paper, The Captain,
Cassell's Family Magazine, Cassell's Saturday Journal, The
Chatterbox, Chums, The English Illustrated Magazine, The
Gentlewoman, The Girl's Own Paper, The Girl's Realm, Good Words,
The Ludgate Monthly, Our Jabberwock, The Pall Mall Magazine,
Pearson's Magazine, The Penny Magazine, The Prize, The Quiver, The
St James's Budget, St Paul's Magazine, Scout, The Sporting and
Dramatic News, The Strand Magazine, The Windsor Magazine, Young
Britain

References: Doyle BWI; Houfe; ICB 1; Johnson & Greutzner;
Thorpe; C. Wood

John Gordon Hargrave (b. 1894)

Son of landscape painter Gordon Hargave. Writer
and, at 17, chief cartoonist on the London *Evening
News*. As a black and white illustrator, he worked
with a heavy, disjointed line, sometimes with
passages of mechanical tone.

Books illustrated include:
John Hargrave The Totem Talks (1918)
C.H. Stigland Black Tales for White Children (1914)
Jonathan Swift Gulliver's Travels (1909)
William Makepeace Thackeray The Rose and the Ring (1909)

Periodicals: Evening News, The Illustrated London News

References: Houfe; Waters 2; *The Studio* special (Autumn 1914)

Cynthia Mary Harnett (1893-1981)

Usually worked as Cynthia Harnett. Born in Kensington, London. Studied at Chelsea School of
Arts and Crafts, and then under her cousin, the
artist and writer G. Vernon Stokes, with whom
she collaborated on several children's books from
the 1930s. Her delicate pen and ink drawings are
quietly informative, with a great deal of well-
researched period detail. The second book she
wrote, *The Wool-Pack* (1951), won the Carnegie
Medal. Work mainly published by Collins.

Books illustrated include:
Cynthia Harnett The Great House (1949), The Wool-Pack (1951),
    Ring Out, Bow Bells! (1953), The Green Popinjay (1955), Stars of
    Fortune (1956), The Load of Unicorn (1959), A Fifteenth Century
    Wool Merchant (1962)
Cynthia Harnett and G. Vernon Stokes The Pennymakers (1937),
    David's New World (1937), Junk, the Puppy (1937), Banjo, the
    Puppy (1938), To Be a Farmer's Boy (1940), Mudlarks (1940),
    Mountaineers (1941), Ducks and Drakes (1942), Bob-Tale Pup
    (1944), Sand Hoppers (1946) Two and a Bit (1948), Follow My
    Leader (1949), Pets Limited (1950)

References: *Contemporary Authors*; Doyle CL; Eyre; Fisher pp. 63,
257; ICB 2; Kirkpatrick

Derrick Harris (1919-60)

Born Chislehurst, Kent. Studied at the Central
School of Arts and Crafts, under Noel Rooke*
and John Farleigh*. Wood engraver and illustrator. His illustrations for the Folio Society are
bold, humorous and decorative in a deliberately
archaic style.

Cynthia Harnett. 'She held the light for Ned'
from *The Great House* by Cynthia Harnett
(Methuen, 1949).

Books illustrated include:
John Barclay Euphormio's Satyricon (1954)
Henry Fielding Joseph Andrews (1953), The History of Tom Jones
    (1959)
Tobias Smollett Humphrey Clinker (1955)

Periodical: The Radio Times

References: Jacques; Usherwood; Vollmer supp; Wa (1956)

Charles Harrison (d. 1943)

Worked as an actor before becoming an illustrator and cartoonist. His early 'Toy' books were
weak pastiches of Walter Crane* and Randolph
Caldecott, but he soon developed an individual
style of humorous drawing and became a regular
contributor to *Punch* (1896-1914). He was also,
for some time, cartoonist on the *Daily Express*.
He lived in London and was a member of the
London Sketch Club. In an obituary notice in *The
Times*, he was remembered as 'first and foremost
a black and white artist with a very distinct style
of his own, working with a strong black line that
was decorative rather than expressive, and well
suited to reproduction on any surface of paper.
Harrison was essentially a "fun maker" with a
rather schoolboyish sense of humour that presented no difficulties to the simplest mind, and a
large public will hear of his death with regret.'

Books illustrated include:
R. Andom Troddles and Us and Others (1901)
S.H. Hamer Master Charlie (1899)
Charles Harrison Charles Harrison's Shilling Toy Books: The Prince and the Penny, Grandma's Nursery Rhymes, Rhymes and Jingles, with novel pictures, The Prince and the Penny (1883), A Humorous History of England (1920)
C. Harrison & W.K. Haselden Accidents Will Happen (1907)
Frederick F. McCabe A Living Machine (1921)
H. Rowan London Japanned (1910)

Periodicals: Boy's Champion, Cassell's Saturday Journal, Chums, Daily Express, Daily Mail, Evening News, Funny Folks, The Humorist, Jester, Little Folks, The Pall Mall Budget, The Pall Mall Gazette, The Penny Magazine, Printer's Pie, Puck, Punch, St James's Budget, Scraps, The Strand Magazine

References: Doyle BWI; Hammerton; Houfe; Thorpe; Waters 2; *The Times* (obit 21st December 1943)

Emma Florence Harrison
(active 1877-1925)

Worked as Florence Harrison. Children's illustrator and verse writer. Her early work combines the influence of Art Nouveau with characterisation similar to that of Randolph Caldecott. Later, when she was working for Dent, her drawings became more commonplace, ending as a pastiche of contemporary styles.

Books illustrated include:
Florence Harrison Rhymes and Reasons (1905), The Rhyme of a

Florence Harrison. 'They Were Quarrelling Over a Ball' in *The Princess Seeks a Shadow* from *My Fairy Tale Book* (Blackie, c.1919).

Charles Harrison. From *The Swoop, or How Clarence Saved England* by P.G. Wodehouse (Alston Rivers, 1909)

Faun, and other verse (1907), In the Fairy Ring (1908), Elfin Song (1912), Tales in Rhyme and Colour (1916), The Pixy Book (1918)
Agnes G. Herbertson Tinkler Johnny (1916)
William Morris Early Poems (1914)
Christina Rossetti (intro Alice Meynell) Poems (1910)
Netta Syrett Godmother's Garden (1918)
Alfred, Lord Tennyson Guinevere and other poems (1911)
My Fairy Tale Book (c.1919)

Periodical: The Girls' Budget

References: Houfe; C. Wood

Dick Hart (b. 1920)

Born on the Isle of Sheppey, Kent. Studied at Rochester School of Art, the Royal Academy Schools, the Royal College of Art and the Ecole des Beaux Arts in Paris. Lecturer in graphic design at the Regent Street Polytechnic. As an illustrator, he has worked mainly in black and white, using a dry brush to achieve roughly textured, almost lithographic effects; his figures are often drawn in close-up. Elected MSIA.

Books illustrated include:
Joan Aiken The Kingdom and the Cave (1960)
Gillian Avery The Warden's Niece (1957), Trespassers at Charlcote (1958)
Leila Berg My Dog Sunday (1968)
Richard Blythe Danger Ahead (1951)
Anita Hewett Piccolo (1960), Piccolo and Maria (1962)
Reginald Maddock The Widgeon Gang (1964)
James Reeves The Pillar-Box Thieves (1965)
Catherine Storr Lucy (1961), Lucy Runs Away (1962)
Noel Streatfeild Day Before Yesterday (1956)
Elizabeth Stucley Magnolia Buildings (1960)
John Rowe Townsend Gumble's Yard (1961)
Jules Verne (trans Joyce Gard) Journey to the Centre of the Earth (1961)

References: Eyre; Fisher pp.166, 200; ICB 2; Ryder

Frank Hart (1878-1959)

Born Brighton, Sussex. Studied at Heatherley's School of Art under John Crompton. Painter, black and white illustrator, writer and lecturer. Contributed regularly to *Punch*. Lived in Sussex at Lewes (1921) and Eastbourne (1933).

Books illustrated include:
Frank Hart Dolly's Society Book (1902), The Best Nursery Rhymes (1910), The Animals Do Their Bit in the Great War (1918), Andrew, Bogie and Jack: Three Dogs (1919), One Long Holiday! (1921), Everyhorse (1935)

Periodicals: Country Life, The Field, The Graphic, Punch, The Temple Magazine.

References: Houfe; Johnson & Greutzner; Vollmer; Wa (1958); Waters

Archibald Standish Hartrick (1864-1950)

Often worked as A.S. Hartrick. Born in Bangalore, India, son of a soldier. Educated at Fettes College and Edinburgh University; then studied art at the Slade School of Fine Art, London (1884-85), and in Paris at the Académie Julian (1885-86). In France, he became a friend of Gauguin, Van Gogh, and later Toulouse-Lautrec. Back in London, he joined the staff of *The Graphic* (1890-93) and *The Pall Mall Budget* and worked for various other magazines. He shared a studio with E.J. Sullivan* and was a close friend of Phil May*, J.J. Guthrie* and Joseph Pennell*. During the 1890s, he was a founder and committee member of the Chelsea Arts Club and later vice-president of the Senefelder Club (for lithographers). He lived in Gloucestershire during the early 1900s. From 1908, taught at the Camberwell School of Art, London, where his pupils included David Jones*, and from 1914 at the Central School of Arts and Crafts. Hartrick was a discerning observer of the art world and was highly esteemed by his fellow artists. He was well known for his black and white

A.S. Hartrick. 'Chiswick House, from the Lake' from *Recording Britain* Vol I (Cambridge University Press, 1946).

magazine work during the 1890s and later for his drawings and prints of rural subjects. His work is unpretentious and drawn with sensitivity and atmosphere, although it is sometimes weak in basic construction. Elected NEAC (1893), ARWS (1910), RWS (1920); awarded OBE (1948).

Books illustrated include:
George Borrow Wild Wales (nd)
Frances Marion Crawford The Little City of Hope (1908)
Maurice Hewlett The Forest Lovers (1909)
Rudyard Kipling Soldiers' Tales (1896)
Arnold Palmer Recording Britain (4 vols, 1946-49)
E.R. Pennell Tantallon Castle (1895)
Nancy Price Vagabond's Way (1914)
R.L. Stevenson The Body Snatcher (nd)

Periodicals: Black and White, The Butterfly, Cassell's Family Magazine, Daily Chronicle, Daily Graphic, The Graphic, Harmsworth's Magazine, The Ludgate Monthly, The Neolith, The New Budget, The Pall Mall Budget, The Pall Mall Magazine, Pearson's Magazine, Pick-Me-Up, The Quiver, The Sketch, The Strand Magazine, The Yellow Book

References: Bénézit; Chamot, Farr & Butlin; Guichard; Houfe; Johnson & Greutzner; Mallalieu; Pennell PD; J.G. Reid; Sketchley; Thieme & Becker; Thorpe; Vollmer; Waters; C. Wood; *Drawing and Design* 3 (1923); *The OWS Club Volume* 30; James L. Caw *Scottish Painting Past and Present* (T.C. & E.C. Jack, 1908); A.S. Hartrick *A Painter's Pilgrimage Through Fifty Years* (Cambridge University Press 1939)

John Hammond Harwood (1904-1980)

Born Darwen, Lancashire. Educated at Ripon School, Yorkshire. Studied at Harrogate School of Art (1921-24) and at the Royal College of Art (1924-28). Principal of Gloucester School of Art (1939-45) and of Sheffield School of Art (1945-64). Honorary Fellow of Sheffield Polytechnic (1969), Freeman of the Worshipful Company of Goldsmiths. Painter in oil and watercolour, writer and illustrator of children's books.

Books illustrated include:
John Harwood The Old Woman and Her Pig (1945), Puffin Rhymes (1945), The Yuletide Cottage (1945), A Christmas Manger (1954)
Richard Parker A Moor of Spain (1953)
Barbara Euphan Todd Worzel Gummidge and Saucy Nancy (1947)
Hope C. White and John Harwood Bible Picture Books (from 1945)

References: Johnson & Greutzner; Vollmer; Wa (1980); Waters

Joan Hassall (b. 1906)

Born in Kensington, London, daughter of John Hassall*. Educated in London and Surrey. She studied at Roehampton Froebel Training College (1922-25), London School of Art (1925-27), Royal Academy Schools (1928-33) and at evening classes at the LCC School of Photo-Engraving in Bolt Court, Fleet Street (1931-34). Taught book production at Edinburgh College of Art (1940-46). Her first illustrative commission was for a wood engraved title page for *Devil's Dyke* (Heinemann 1936), a book of poems by her brother, Christopher Hassall. Since then, she has worked as a wood engraver (and occasionally on scraperboard) in a meticulous style influenced by Thomas Bewick, often on small blocks for inclusion in pages of text. Also a painter in oils and designer of book plates and of pamphlets for British Rail, British Waterways, British Transport Hotels and the National Book League. She designed the invitation for the coronation of Queen Elizabeth II. She gave up engraving in 1974 because of failing sight. Interested in early music, and a performer on many early instruments. Elected ARE (1938), SWE (1947), RE (1948); member of the Art Workers' Guild (Master 1972). [Q]

Books illustrated include:

Jane Austen Pride and Prejudice (1957), Sense and Sensibility (1958), Mansfield Park (1959), Northanger Abbey (1960), Persuasion (1961), Emma (1962), Shorter Works (1963)
Richard Church Small Moments (1957)
Mrs Gaskell Cranford (1940)
Bernard Gooch The Strange World of Nature (1950)
Christopher Hassall Devil's Dyke (title page, 1936), Penthesperon (title page, 1938)
Margaret Lane The Brontë Story (1953), The Drug-Like Brontë Dream (1980)
Eric Linklater Sealskin Trousers (1947)
Thomas Malory Lancelot and Elaine (1947)
Miss Mitford Our Village (1946)
Iona and Peter Opie The Oxford Book of Nursery Rhymes (1955)
R.L. Stevenson A Child's Garden of Verses (1946)
Anthony Trollope The Parson's Daughter (1949), Mary Gresley (1951)
Pamela Whitlock (ed) All Day Long (1954)
Andrew Young Collected Poems (1950)
F. Brett Young Portrait of a Village (1937)
Collected Poems of Robert Burns (1964)
51 Poems by Mary Webb (1950)
The Roman Missal (1949)
The Saltire Chapbooks 1 (1943), 2 (1944), 3-5 (1945), 6 (1946), 8 (1947), 9 (1948), 10 (1950), 12 (1951)

Periodical: The Saturday Book (1955)

References: Balston EWE; Barrett BWE, HBWE; Bénézit; ICB 2; Jacques; Johnson & Greutzner; Vollmer supp; Wa (1980); WaG; Waters; *Image* 5 (1950); *Motif* 2 (1959); *The Private Library* vol 7 no 4 (1974); *Signature* 1 (July 1946); *Graven Images* (Scottish Arts Council 1979); David Cuppleditch *The John Hassall Lifestyle* (Dilke Press 1980); Ruari McLean *The Wood Engravings of Joan Hassall* (Oxford University Press 1960)

John Hassall (1868-1948)

Born Walmer, Kent, son of a naval officer. Educated in Devon and Heidelberg, Germany. During a brief period of farming in Canada, he began contributing to *The Graphic*. He studied art in Antwerp under Professor van Havermaet and his son Charles (1891-94) and in Paris at the Académie Julian, where he became familiar with Art Nouveau and the work of Alphonse Mucha. Back in England, he soon made his name as a cartoonist and advertising artist, designing some of the most effective posters of his day, including the unforgettable 'Skegness Is So Bracing' (1908). He began illustrating children's books in the late 1890s in a cheerfully jaunty style, using the bold outlines and flat colour washes that often characterised his posters. Houfe notes a resemblance to the Japanese print in the decorative, two-dimensional qualities of his work, though it is not clear whether

Joan Hassall. From *Sealskin Trousers and other stories* by Eric Linklater (Hart-Davis, 1947).

he used these as a direct source. He was one of the first members of the London Sketch Club, becoming President (1903), and was a close friend of fellow members Cecil Aldin*, René Bull*, Dudley Hardy* and Phil May*. With Charles van Havermaet, he founded the New Art School (later the Hassall Art School of Art) and ran it for over 20 years. Among its pupils were 'Fish'*, Harry Rountree*, Bert Thomas* and H.M. Bateman*, who later wrote, '…his energy and output at the time was really amazing. He worked in pretty well every known and unknown medium and like as not he would be discovered engaged on several pictures at once. It was all done as if it was a great joke, and he never appeared to take his work seriously, but there was no doubt about the results being effective.' His daughter is the wood engraver Joan Hassall*. Elected RI (1901) and RMS (1901).

Books illustrated include:

Thomas Arkell A Children's Painting Book (1914)
C.H. Avery Through the Wood (1907)
G.C. Bingham Six and Twenty Boys and Girls (1902)
R. Carse The Pantomime ABC (1902)
Cumberland Clark The Humours of Bridge (1902)
Walter Emanuel People (1903), Paris—Not to Mention Monte Carlo (1906), One Hundred Years Hence (1911), Tommy Lobb (1912), Keep Smilin' (1914)
G.E. Farrow An ABC of Everyday People (1902), Absurd Ditties (1903), Round the World ABC (1904)
G.E. Farrow and May C. Gillington Ruff and Ready (1905)
May C. Gillington Friday and Saturday (1910)
B. Girvin Good Queen Bess 1533-1603 (1907)
S.H. Hamer The Princess and the Dragon (1908)
John Hassall and Cecil Aldin Two Well-Worn Shoe Stories (1899)
Keble Howard Potted Brains (1909), Love and a Cottage (1913)
H.N. Hutchinson Primeval Scenes (1899)
Walter C. Jerrold Mother Goose's Nursery Rhymes (1909)
A.L. Liberty A Day in Tangier (1913)
R.H. Lindo With Love from Daddy (1918)
P. Montrose Oh! My Darling Clementine (1900)
Charles Perrault The Sleeping Beauty and other tales (1912)
E. Shirley The Twins (1927)
A.A. Spurr A Cockney in Arcadia (1899)
Blackie's Popular Fairy Tales (1921)
Blackie's Popular Nursery Rhymes (1921)
Blackie's Popular Nursery Stories (1931)
Grimm's Fairy Tales (1902)

Gulliver's Travels (c.1910)
Mother Goose's Nursery Rhymes (c.1914)
The Old Nursery Stories and Rhymes (1904)
Robinson Crusoe (nd)
The Swiss Family Robinson (nd)

Periodicals: The Boy's Own Paper, The Captain, Cassell's Magazine, The Daily Graphic, Eureka, The Flag, The Graphic, The Happy Annual, Holly Leaves, The Idler, Illustrated Bits, The Illustrated London News, Judy, Little Folks, London Opinion, Moonshine, The New Budget, The Odd Volume, The Pall Mall Magazine, Pear's Annual, Pearson's Magazine, Pick-Me-Up, The Poster, Printer's Pie, Punch, St Paul's Magazine, The Sketch, The Strand Magazine, The Tatler

References: Bénézit; Cuppleditch; DNB (1941-50); Doyle BWI; Hammerton; Houfe; Johnson & Greutzner; Mallalieu; Thieme & Becker; Thorpe; Vollmer supp; Wa (1934) Waters; C. Wood; *Art Journal* (1900) *Cassell's Magazine* (1905, 1908); *The Studio* 36 (1906), special (1900-01, Spring 1906, 1911); H.M. Bateman *By Himself* (Collins 1937); David Cuppleditch *The John Hassall Lifestyle* (Dilke Press 1980); A.E. Johnson *John Hassall RI* (A. & C. Black 1907).

John Hassall. From Ye Berlyn Tapestrie: Wilhelm's Invasion of Flanders *(Studio, nd).*

William Hatherell (1855-1928)

Studied at the Royal Academy Schools after working in the City of London for a time. Painter of historical and literary subjects and later a popular magazine illustrator in both Britain and America, on the staff of *The Graphic* from the early 1890s. Initially he received most of his book commissions from Cassell's (including one for over 300 drawings in *Picturesque Australasia*). Bradshaw describes his work on 'pictorial duets' (double page spreads shared, for speed, between two artists) with fellow *Graphic* illustrators, among them Frank Dadd*, H.M. Paget* and Balliol Salmon*. Whenever possible, he worked from life, handling his media (pencil and wash, pen and ink, watercolour, body colour and oil) with a high degree of professional assurance. Elected RI (1888), ROI (1898), RWA (1903).

Books illustrated include:
J.M. Barrie Sentimental Journey (1897)
E.J. Bradley Annals of Westminster Abbey (with H.M. Paget and F.S. Walker, 1895)
Mrs Molesworth The Next-Door House (1892)
E.R. Pennell Tantallon Castle (with others, 1895)
R.L. Stevenson Island Nights' Entertainment (1893)
Mark Twain The Prince and the Pauper (1923)
Picturesque Australasia (nd)
Shakespeare's Tragedy of Romeo and Juliet (1912)

Periodicals: Black and White, Cassell's Family Magazine, Cassell's Saturday Journal, Chums, The English Illustrated Magazine, The Graphic, Harper's Magazine, Nash's Magazine, The Pall Mall Budget, Pear's Annual, Pearson's Magazine, The Quiver, The Strand Magazine, The Windsor Magazine, Young England

References: Bénézit; Bradshaw; Chamot, Farr & Butlin; Houfe; ICB 1; Johnson & Greutzner; Mallalieu; Thieme & Becker; Thorpe; Waters; C. Wood

Irene Beatrice Hawkins (b. 1906)

Born in Yorkshire. Studied at York School of Art (initially at evening classes) and at the Royal College of Art (1929-33). Worked for a year at the Curwen Press learning about printing methods,

type layout and lithography, and later for *Country Life* as a layout artist. Subsequently she worked freelance as a painter, lithographer and illustrator of children's books, as well as teaching painting and drawing at York School of Art. As an illustrator, she worked in pen and ink or lithography, specialising in whimsical or semi-fantastic stories to which she brought considerable charm and a feeling for atmosphere. During the 1950s she contributed a weekly full-page drawing to *Robin*, Hulton Press's Magazine for very young children, and illustrated the first *Andy Pandy* book (subsequent titles based on this television character were illustrated by Matvyn Wright*). She settled at Lewes, Sussex in 1951.

Books illustrated include:
Dorothy Clewes The Cottage in the Wild Wood (1945), The Stream in the Wild Wood (1946), The Treasure in the Wild Wood (1947), The Fair in the Wild Wood (1949)
Walter de la Mare The Old Lion and Other Stories (1942), The Magic Jacket and Other Stories (1943), The Scarecrow and Other Stories (1945), The Dutch Cheese and Other Stories (1946), Collected Stories for Children (1947)
John Gilmour Wild Flowers of the Chalk (1947)
Freda Lingstrom and Maria Bird Andy Pandy, the Baby Clown (1953)
Dorothy Ann Lovell Lolly Popkin (1944)
R.J. Macgregor Chi-Lo the Admiral (1940)
Elizabeth Ramal Timothy (1943)
Diana Ross The Tooter and Other Nursery Tales (1951), Ebenezer the Big Balloon (1952)
Alison Uttley Nine Starlight Tales (1942), Cuckoo Cherry-Tree (Faber 1943), The Spice Woman's Basket and Other Tales (1944), The Cobbler's Shop and Other Tales (Faber 1950)
Stories from the Bible (1947)

References: ICB 2; Johnson & Greutzner

Sheila Hawkins (b. 1905)

Born in the goldfields of Kalgoorlie, Western Australia; spent much of her childhood in bush country and had a large collection of animals and insects. She was educated at Toorak College,

Melbourne, and studied briefly at the Art School of the Australian National Gallery before leaving to become a commercial artist. She moved to London in 1931 and has lived there ever since. While looking for a job, she illustrated her first children's book, *Black Tuppeny* (1932). After the first of Geraldine Elliot's stories about African animals (1939), she became known for her humorous animal illustrations (mainly in pen and ink, charcoal or lithography) and since then has worked for various publishers including Faber & Faber, Penguin, Heinemann and Methuen. She was one of the first artists to contribute to the Puffin Picture Books. During the 1930s, she worked in the studio of Shell Mex Advertising (the first woman to be employed there), and, during World War II, as an artist for the Royal Australian Air Force.

Books illustrated include:
Peggy Barnard Wish and the Magic Hut (c.1953)
Maurice Burton More Animals (1966)
Geraldine Elliott The Long Grass of Whispers (1939), Where the Leopard Passes (1949), The Hunter's Cave (1951)
Sheila Hawkins Black Tuppeny (1932), Ena-Meena-Mina Mo (1935), Appleby John, the Miller's Lad (1938), The Panda and the Piccaninny (1939), A Book of Fables adapted from Aesop (1940), The Bear Brothers' Shop (1942), The Bear Brothers' Holiday (1942), Animals and Birds of Australia (1947), Australian Animals and Birds (1962)
Geraldine Kaye Kofi and the Eagle (1963)
Aaron Judah Tommy with the Hole in his Shoe (1957), Tales of Teddy Bear (1958), Henrietta Hen (1958), Miss Hare and Mr Tortoise

Sheila Hawkins. From *Henrietta in Love* by Aaron Judah (Faber, 1961).

(1959), Basil Chimpy Isn't Bright (1959), Henrietta in the Snow (1960), Basil Chimpy's Comic Light (1960), Henrietta in Love (1961), The Elf's New House (1962), The Careless Cuckoos (1963), On the Feast of Stephen (1965)
Douglas Lord Kiwi Jane (1962)
Patricia Lynch Long Ears (1954)
Robert Nye March Has Horse's Ears (1966), Taliesen (1966)
Ruth Park Air Life for Grandee (1964)
Mervyn Skipper The Meeting Pool (1953)
James Stagg Bran of the Moors (1961)
Chetham Strode Three Men and a Girl (1958), Top of the Milk (1959)
Ailsa Wills Boy of the Mohawks (1963)

Periodicals: Farmer's Weekly, The Nursery World, N.S.W. School Magazine

References: ICB 1; Johnson & Greutzner

Raymond Humphrey Millis Hawthorn (b. 1917)

Works as Raymond Hawthorn. Born in Poole, Dorset, son of a teacher/painter. Studied at Coventry School of Art (1935-39) and then at Hornsey College of Art, London (1939-40), under Norman Janes*. After army service in World War II, he lectured at various colleges of art before joining the staff of the Laird School of Art (subsequently Wirral College of Art, Design and Adult Studies), in Birkenhead (1947-78). In his wood engravings, he combines symbolic and realistic content with abstract treatment. The example of Blair Hughes-Stanton* and Gertrude Hermes* can be seen in his concern for textural variety and technical experiment. Elected ARE (1960), RE (1975). [Q]

Books illustrated include:
Flavius Arrianus (trans Aubrey de Selincourt) The Life of Alexander the Great (1970)
Kenneth Fenwick (ed) The Third Crusade (1958)
Herodotus (trans Kenneth Cavander) The Struggle for Greece (1959)
Pierre Choderlos de Laclos (trans Richard Aldington) Les Liaisons Dangereuses (1962)
Plutarch (trans Ian Scott-Kilvert) The Rise and Fall of Athens (1967)
Betty Radice (trans) Abelard and Heloise: The Story of his Misfortunes and Personal Letters (1977)
Gaius Suetonius Tranquillus (trans Robert Graves) The Twelve Caesars (1964)

References: Garrett BWE, HBWE; Vollmer supp; Wa (1956); Waters

Margaret Lynette Hemmant (b. 1938)

Works as Lynette Hemmant. Born in London, daughter of a mining engineer. Childhood spent in South Wales, Australia and in the Home Counties. Studied illustration at St Martin's School of Art (1952-58). Freelance illustrator since 1958, working sometimes in black and white, but mostly sometimes in colour (acrylic, coloured inks and crayons). She also paints portraits, landscapes, flowers and animals, makes etchings, and has designed a set of Christmas stamps for the island of Guernsey (1982). She lives in London. [Q]

Books illustrated include:
Jane Austen Pride and Prejudice (1980)
R.H. Barham The Jackdaw of Rheims (1976)
Irene Byers Tiptoes Wins Through (1976)
Mary Cockett Acrobat Hamster (1965), Sunflower Giant (1966)
Helen Cresswell The Barge Children (1968)

Lynette Hemmant. From *Elegant Patty* by Mary Treadgold (Hamish Hamilton, 1967).

Charles Dickens A Christmas Carol (1978)
Dorothy Edwards The Read-to-me Story Book (1974)
Rachel Field Poems for Children (1978)
Edward FitzGerald (trans) The Rubaiyat of Omar Khayyam (1979)
Jacynth Hope-Simpson The High Toby (1966)
Marie Hynds The Wishing Bottle (1975)
G.F. Lamb More Good Stories (1975)
Rosemary Manning Boney Was a Warrior (1966), The Rocking Horse (1970)
Ruth Manning-Sanders The Crow's Nest (1965)
Joan Phipson A Lamb in the Family (1966)
Jenny Seed Small House, Big Garden (1965), Timothy and Tinker (1967), Canvas City (1968)
Jenny Taylor and Terry Ingleby Messy Malcolm's Birthday (1978), Messy Malcolm's Dream (1981)
Barbara Euphan Todd The Box in the Attic (1970), The Ward from France (1972)
Mary Treadgold Elegant Patty (1967), Poor Patty (1968)
Geoffrey Trease The Dutch Are Coming (1965)
Rosemary Weir Summer of the Silent Hands (1969)
Barbara Willard The Suddenly Gang (1963), The Pet Club (1967)

Keith Henderson (b. 1883)

Born in Scotland, son of painter Joseph Henderson Educated at Marlborough School. Studied at the Slade School of Fine Art and in Paris, where he met Edmund Dulac* and shared a studio with Maxwell Armfield* and Norman Wilkinson of Four Oaks*. His early work consisted mainly of portraits. During World War I, he served with the Cavalry on the Western Front. After the war, he settled in Scotland, but also painted in France, Cyprus, Egypt, South America and Central Africa. He was an official war artist attached to the Royal Air Force during World War II. He moved to London in 1971. He was a painter and muralist, pastel draughtsman and illustrator in pen and ink, pencil and watercolour, and scraperboard. As a black and white draughtsman he was outstanding, combining formal strength with striking decorative effects. He used scraperboard with great boldness in white-line drawings and in passages of tonal counterpoint, and was one of the few artists

to avoid the pitfall of scratchy over-elaboration inherent in the medium. He was elected RP (1912), ARSW (1930), ARWS (1930) and RWS 1937, ROI (1934), and awarded the OBE.

Books illustrated include:
Janet Beith No Second Spring (1933), Sand Castle (1936)
Geoffrey Chaucer The Romaunt of the Rose (with Norman Wilkinson*, 1908)
Neil M. Gunn Highland Pack (1949)
Thomas Hardy Under the Greenwood Tree (1913)
Keith Henderson Letters to Helen (1917), Palm-Groves and Humming Birds (1924), Prehistoric Man (1927)
W.H. Hudson Green Mansions (1926), The Purple Land (1929)
Stuart Piggott Scotland Before History (1956)
William H. Prescott The Conquest of Mexico (2 vols 1922)
G. Whitworth and Keith Henderson A Book of Whimsies (1909)
Burns—By Himself (1938)

Periodical: The Tatler

References: Houfe; ICB 1; Johnson & Greutzner; Vollmer; Wa (1934); Waters; *Antiquarian Book Monthly Review* 2 (1975); *The Studio* 90 (1925), special (Autumn 1914, 1923-24); Keith Henderson *Pastels* Studio 1952

Thomas Barclay Hennell (1903-45)

Born in Ash, Kent, son of a clergyman. Educated at Bradfield College, Berkshire. Studied art at

Keith Henderson. 'Porter, sir?' from *Sand Castle* by Janet Beith (Hodder & Stoughton, 1936).

Regent Street Polytechnic (1921-28) and received encouragement from A.S. Hartrick*. In the early 1930s, he taught art at schools—in Bath and Bruton. From then on, he concentrated on writing and art, putting his profound knowledge of the country-side into quiet drawings and watercolours of great individuality. From 1931, he was a close friend of Edward Bawden*, Paul Nash* and Eric Ravilious*. He suffered a mental breakdown (1932-35), which he described with great vividness in *The Witnesses* (1938). In 1943, he became an official war artist replacing his friend Eric Ravilious (d.1942) in Iceland. He was then sent to the Far East attached to the Royal Air Force; he died on active service in Jakarta. Elected ARWS (1938), RWS (1942), NEAC (1943).

Books illustrated include:
Thomas Hennell Change in the Farm (1934), The Witnesses (1938), The Countryman at Work (1947)
H.J. Massingham A Countryman's Journal (1939), Country Relics (1939), Chiltern Country (1940), The Natural Order (1945)
Dr C.S. Orwin Farm and Fields (1944)
Clarence Henry Warren The Land Is Yours (1943), Miles from Anywhere (1944)

References: Chamot, Farr & Butlin; Johnson & Greutzner; Vollmer; Wa (1934); Waters; *Alphabet & Image* 4 (April 1947); *The Countryman* 54 (1957); *The OWS Club Volume* 21, 28; T.B. Hennell *The Witnesses* (Peter Davies 1938), *intro* H.J. Massingham, *The Countryman at Work* (Architectural Press 1947), *Lady Filmy Fern* (Hamish Hamilton 1980)

Thomas Henry

See Thomas Henry Fisher.

Robert Norman Hepple (b. 1908)

Worked as Norman Hepple. Born in London. Studied at Goldsmith's College and the Royal Academy Schools. He served in the National Fire Service, and was its official war artist (1941-44). Since then he has become an established portrait and subject painter, sculptor and engraver. His stylish and convincing book illustrations (gen-erally brush and poster black) date from the early years of his career, and were influenced by Muir-head Bone*, E.J. Sullivan* and F.L.M. Griggs*. He lives in Richmond, Surrey. Elected NEAC (1947), RP (1948), ARA (1954), RA (1960); Pres-ident RP (1979). [Q]

Books illustrated include:
John Buchan (intro Hilaire Belloc) English Literature (1934)
Peter Dawlish Peg-Leg and the Fur Pirates (1939)
Arthur Milton Huntingdon The Ladies of Vallbona (1934)
Elfrida Vipont Blow the Man Down (1939)
Mary Webb The Golden Arrow (1930), Gone to Earth (1931), The House in Dormer Forest (with others, 1931), The Spring of Joy (1937)

Periodicals: Britannia, Nash's Magazine

References: Johnson & Greutzner; Vollmer; Wa (1980); Waters; *The Artist* (April 1980); *Drawing and Design* (1927); *The Illustrated London News* 222 (1953) p.687; *The Studio* special (Winter 1931)

Philip Hepworth (active 1947-50)

Illustrator in pen and ink mainly for Faber & Faber. He worked with a crisp, deliberate line, and often created attractive (though not always consistent) effects of chiaroscuro with decor-atively hatched shading.

Books illustrated include:
R.J. MacGregor Chi-Lo the General (1947)
Meriol Trevor The Forest and the Kingdom (1949), Hunt the King, Hide the Fox (1950)
Alison Uttley John Barleycorn (1948)

Gertrude Hermes (1901-83)

Born in Bromley, Kent, of Anglo-German parent-age. Studied at Beckenham School of Art, Kent (1919-20) and the Leon Underwood* School (1921-25). Prix de Rome (1925). She was married to Blair Hughes-Stanton* from 1926 to 1932 and collaborated with him on engravings for the Cresset Press edition of *Pilgrim's Progress* (1928). Also worked for the Gregynog Press from 1931. In 1939, she joined the Westminster Schools of Art, teaching life drawing, and from 1945, she was at

Norman Hepple. From The Spring of Joy by Mary Webb with introductions by Walter de la Mare and Martin Armstrong (Cape, 1937).

Camberwell and St Martin's School of Art, teaching wood engraving. During World War II, she worked in Canada as a tracing and precision draughtsman for aircraft factories and shipbuilders. She resumed teaching in London (1945), and later became a staff member at the Central School of Arts and Crafts and (from 1966) the Royal Academy Schools. At various times she worked as a sculptor, wood engraver, lino and wood cutter, mosaic designer and metal worker. One of the most versatile and accomplished of the 20th-century white-line wood engravers, Hermes worked with a pliant, responsive line of varying weight, using her tools (including the multiple graver) with imagination to achieve varied effects of light, texture and 'colour'. Her feeling for design is particularly evident in her flower illustrations, in which she often adopted the device of removing the woodblock corners to emphasise shape and outline. Lived in London. Member of the London Group (1935); included in the National Register of Industrial Designers (1938). Elected SWE (1935), RE (1951), ARA (1963), RA (1971). [Q]

Books illustrated include:
John Bunyan The Pilgrim's Progress (with Blair Hughes-Stanton, 1928)
T.S. Eliot Animula (1929)
Irene Gosse A Florilege Chosen from the Old Herbals (1931)
Richard Jeffries The Story of My Heart (1939)
Naomi Mitchison The Alban Goes Out (1939)
R.H. Mottram Strawberry Time (1934)
Christopher Sandford (trans) The Garden of Caresses (1934)
P.L. Travers I Go by Sea, I Go by Land (1941)
Izaak Walton The Compleat Angler (1939)
The Apocrypha (1929)

Periodical: The Woodcut

References: Balston EWE, WEMEB; Chamot, Farr & Butlin; Garrett BWE, HBWE; Vollmer; Wa (1980); Waters; *The Print Collector's Quarterly* 16; *The Studio* 123 (1942), special (Spring 1927, Winter 1936); *Shall We Join the Ladies?* (Studio One Gallery, Oxford 1979); Basil Gray *The English Print* (A. & C. Black 1937); Clare Leighton *Wood Engravings and Woodcuts* (Studio 1932); A.C. Sewter *Modern British Woodcuts and Wood Engavings in the Collection of the Whitworth Art Gallery* (Manchester 1962)

P.B. Hickling (active 1908-c.1960)

Illustrator in black and white, halftone and full colour. His early illustrations, mainly in pen and ink, were typical of their period. Much later he illustrated Noel Barr's animal stories for Ladybird Books in bright, luminous, slightly hazy colour.

Books illustrated include:
Noel Barr The Inquisitive Harvest Mouse (1949), Tiptoes the Mischievous Hen (1949), The Wise Robin (1950), Beaky, the Greedy Duck (1951), The Conceited Lamb (1951), The Discontented Pony (1951), Mick the Disobedient Puppy (1952), Ned the Lonely Donkey (1952), Cocky the Lazy Rooster (1953), The Sleepy Water Vole (1955)
J.F. Fraser Life's Contrasts (with others, 1908)
Charles F. Parsons 'All Change Here!' (with Mary Stevens, 1916)

Periodicals: The Boy's Own Paper, The Girl's Own Paper, The Girls' Realm, Little Folks, The Penny Magazine, Punch, The Quiver, Young England

Don Higgins (b. 1928)

Born in Ilford, Essex, son of a salesman. Studied at Wimbledon School of Art (1942-47) and the Royal College of Art (1952-55). Graphic designer for the BBC (1955-60); freelance illustrator (1955-64), working mainly in black and white, using pen and ink, pen and wash, and various techniques on acetate. Since 1963, he has concentrated on writing and directing films. [Q]

Books illustrated include:
Michel-Aimé Bandony Bruno, King of the Wild (1960)
E.R. Braithwaite Paid Servant (1962)
John Buchan The Thirty-Nine Steps (1959)
Cervantes Don Quixote (1962)
C.S. Forester Brown on Resolution (1959), Death to the French (1959), The Gun (1959), Payment Deferred (1959)
René Guillot Elephant Road (1959)
Oakly Hall Warlock (1959)
René Hardy Lost Sentinel (1960)
Jean Laborde Falcon and the Dove (1961)
John Ryder Six on the Black Art (with others, 1961)
David Stephen Rory the Roebuck (1961)
Hildegard Swift Railroad to Freedom (1960)

Periodical: Radio Times

References: Jacques; Ryder; Usherwood

Rowland Hilder (b. 1905)

Born Long Island, USA; his family returned to England in 1915 and settled in New Cross, London. Studied at Goldsmith's College of Art with a view to becoming a marine painter. Studied etching and illustration under E.J. Sullivan* (1924-27). Landscape and marine painter in oil and watercolour, and researcher into printing techniques. He taught at Goldsmith's College (1929-41) and also lectured at the Slade School of Fine Art, the Central School of Arts and Crafts, the Royal College of Art and Farnham School of Art. During World War II, he served in the camouflage section of the Royal Engineers (1942). Director of the Heron Press and Royle Publications. He has worked extensively for advertising and has achieved wide popularity as a printmaker and artist, with evocative views of the English countryside, often featuring winter scenes, and published as greetings cards. His book illustrations were considerably more varied and animated in subject and style. He has also made etchings and lithographs, and in 1924 produced the first silk-screen print made in Britain. A friend of C. Walter Hodges* (who also studied under Sullivan), Laurence Irving*, Dr Richard Southern and D.P. Bliss*. Elected RI (1938). [Q]

Books illustrated include:
Harold Avery No Surrender (1933)
J.M. Fisher Birds and Beasts (with Maurice Wilson, 1956)
C. Fox-Smith True Tales of the Sea (1932)
Rowland Hilder Horse Play (1946)
Geoffrey Grigson The Shell Guide to Flowers of the Countryside (1955)
John Lesterman The Adventures of a Trafalgar Lad (1926), A Sailor of

Napoleon (1927), A Pair of Rovers (1928), The Second Mate of the
   Myradale (1929)
John Masefield The Midnight Folk (1927)
Herman Melville Moby Dick (1926)
Monica Redlich Five Farthings (1939)
R.L. Stevenson Treasure Island (1929), Kidnapped (1930)
L.G. Strong They Went to the Island (1940)
Mary Webb Precious Bane (1929)
Percy Westerman The Riddle of the Air (1925), East in the 'Golden
   Grain' (1925), The Luck of the 'Golden Dawn' (1926), The Junior
   Cadet (1927), Chums of the 'Golden Vanity' (1927), The Senior
   Cadet (1931), All Hands to the Boats (1932), The Black Hawk
   (1934), The Red Pirate (1935)

Periodicals: Good Housekeeping, Nash's Magazine, Radio Times, The
Sphere

References: Crouch; Doyle CL; Johnson & Greutzner; Vollmer; Wa
(1980); Waters; *The Artist* 10 (1936); *Reader's Digest* (February 1983);
The Studio 91 (1926), 119 (1940), 138 (1949); Rowland Hilder *Starting
with Watercolours* (Studio Vista 1966), *Painting Landscapes in
Watercolour* (Collins, 1983); John Lewis *Rowland Hilder, Painter and
Illustrator* (Barrie & Jenkins 1978)

Francis E. Hiley (active c.1910-37)

An illustrator who often contributed to cheap,
anthology story books were typical of the genre.
A mediocre draughtsman who worked in pen and
ink, halftone and full colour.

Books illustrated include:
Angela Brazil The School at the Turrets (1935), An Exciting Term
   (1936), Jill's Jolliest School (1937)
Cardinal Newman The Dream of Gerontius (1911)
Walter Scott Kenilworth (1932)
'Mrs Herbert Strang' (ed) The Golden Book for Girls (with others, nd)

Periodical: The Big Budget

Ellen G. Hill (active 1863-1912)

Studied under J. Cross in London and J.B.J.
Trayer in Paris. A portrait and figure painter, she
worked in London and exhibited at the Royal
Academy from 1873. She was the daughter of
penal reformer Frederick Hill, and niece of the
postage stamp inventor Rowland Hill and sister
of Constance Hill whose books she illustrated.
Ellen Hill's book illustrations consist of very well-
researched interiors and landscapes, carefully and
delicately drawn in pen and ink.

Books illustrated include:
Constance Hill Jane Austen, Her Homes and Her Friends (1902),
   Juniper Hall (1904), The House in St Martin's Street (1907), Maria
   Edgeworth and Her Circle in the Days of Buonaparte and Bourbon
   (1909), Fanny Burney at the Court of Queen Charlotte (1912)
Frederick Hill (ed Constance Hill) Autobiography (1894)
A London Garden (1895)

References: Bénézit; Clayton; Johnson & Greutzner; Thieme &
Becker; C. Wood

Vernon Hill (b. 1887)

Born in Halifax, Yorkshire. He was apprenticed
to a trade lithographer at 13, by the age of 18, he
was a student teacher at night school to classes of
mill hands. At 21, he was working under the illustrator and poster designer John Hassall*. He

Vernon Hill. From Canto vii of *The New Inferno*
by Stephen Phillips (John Lane, 1911).

became a sculptor in wood, ivory and bronze; a
draughtsman, lithographer, etcher and engraver.
His remarkable illustrations for *The New Inferno*
and *Ballads Weird and Wonderful* in pencil and
pen, combine a sculptor's understanding of the
human form with a strong feeling for Art Nouveau
design.

Books illustrated include:
E. Cammaerts Belgian Poems (1915)
Richard Chope Ballads Weird and Wonderful (1912)
Stephen Graham Tramping with a Poet in the Rockies (1922)
Stephen Phillips Jr The New Inferno (1911)
The Arcadian Calendar for 1910 (1909)

References: Guichard; Houfe; Johnson; Johnson & Greutzner;
Peppin; Vollmer; Wa (1934); Waters; *The Studio* special (1911,
Autumn 1914, Spring 1922, 1923-24, Spring 1929)

George Him (b. 1900)

Born in Lodz, Poland, son of Jacob Himmelfarb,
a manufacturer. Educated in Warsaw; studied at
the State University, Moscow (1917-18), Berlin
and Bonn Universities (1920-24), and at the State
Academy for Graphic Arts, Leipzig (1925-28). In

1933, he formed a design partnership with Jan Lewitt*, and the two artists worked together as Lewitt-Him until c.1954, illustrating books and designing advertisements and exhibitions. They moved to London in 1937. Throughout the partnership, they collaborated as closely as possible at every stage of their work, and it remained virtually impossible to distinguish the individual hand of either artist in any of their combined undertakings. After 1954, Him continued to illustrate children's books, and his independent work retained the crispness, vitality and humour that had characterised the productions of the partnership. Also working independently, he designed toys and animated films, and painted topographical landscapes. He was a senior lecturer at Leicester Polytechnic (1969-77). Prizewinner in the Francis Williams Book Illustration Awards of 1977; appointed RDI (1978). [Q]

Books illustrated include:
Leila Berg (ed) Folk Tales (1966), Little Nippers (1975)
Cervantes Don Quixote (1980)
Frank Herrmann The Giant Alexander (1964), The Giant Alexander and the Circus (1966)
George Him The Football's Revolt (with Jan Lewitt, 1939), Polish Panorama (with Jan Lewitt, 1941), Israel, the Story of a Nation (1958), 25 Years of the Youth Aliyah, Facts about Israel (1961)
Alina Lewitt Blue Peter (with Jan Lewitt, 1943), Five Silly Cats (with Jan Lewitt, 1944)
Stephen Potter Squawky (1964)
Lynn Reid-Banks Adventures of King Midas (1976)
Jim Rogerson King Wilbur the Third (1976), King Wilbur the Third and the Bath (1976), King Wilbur the Third and the Bicycle (1976), King Wilbur the Third Rebuilds his Palace (1976), King Wilbur the Third's Birthday Present (1976)
Diana Ross The Little Red Engine Gets a Name (with Jan Lewitt, 1942)
Ann Thwaite The Day with the Duke (1969)
Julian Turvim Locomotive (with Jan Lewitt, 1939)

Periodical: The New Middle East (covers)

References: Crouch; Hürlimann; ICB 1,2,3; Lewis; Vollmer supp; WaG; *Graphis* 74 (1927), 94 (1961); William Feaver *When We Were Young* (Thames & Hudson 1977)

David Hockney (b. 1937)

Born in Bradford, son of a clerk. Educated at Bradford Grammar School; studied at Bradford College of Art (1953-57) and the Royal College of Art (1959-62), where he won several awards. Internationally known painter, draughtsman, stage designer and etcher. Taught etching at Maidstone College of Art (1962-63); visiting lecturer at the University of Iowa (1964), University of Colorado (1965) and University of California (1966-67). He has travelled widely and has lived in London, Paris and Los Angeles. His book illustrations consisted of etchings which were published as individual prints in limited editions as well as in book form. Most widely known were his 39 plates for *Six Tales from the Brothers Grimm* (1969-70)—mass produced in an inexpensive small format in addition to the full-size limited edition.

His choice of stories in this anthology was determined by his view of their illustrative possibilities, and the resulting images are particularly rich in visual jokes and allusions. Instead of aquatinting, he experimented with superimposed layers of fine cross-hatching to create tone. *The Blue Guitar* (1977) originated as a group of hardground, softground and aquatint etchings, each printed from two copper plates in a selection of five colours; these were then reproduced in book format, accompanied by the Wallace Stevens poem that had inspired them. [Q]

Books illustrated include:
C.P. Cavafy 14 Poems (1967)
David Hockney (with Stephen Spender) China Diary (1982)
Wallace Stevens The Blue Guitar (1977)
The Oxford Illustrated Bible: Book of Nehemiah (1968)
Six Tales from the Brothers Grimm (1970)

References: Chamot, Farr & Butlin; *Contemporary Artists*; Parry-Crooke; Phaidon; Rothenstein 3; Mark Glazebrook (ed) *David Hockney: Paintings, Prints and Drawings 1960-70* (Whitechapel Gallery catalogue 1970); David Hockney *Seventy-Two Drawings* (Cape 1971), *Travels with Pen, Pencil and Ink* (Petersburg Press 1978); Stephen Spender (intro) *Catalogue of Hockney Exhibition at Musée des Arts Décoratifs, Paris* (1974); Nikos Stangos (ed) *David Hockney* (Thames & Hudson 1976)

Cyril Walter Hodges (b. 1909)

Works as C. Walter Hodges. Born Beckenham, Kent, son of an advertising manager. Educated at Dulwich College (1922-25); studied at Goldsmith's College of Art under E.J. Sullivan* (1925-28). Since 1928, he has designed stage sets for various theatres (including the Mermaid and St George's Theatres, London), and since 1931, he worked as an illustrator of books and magazines and for advertisements. He has also painted murals at the Chartered Insurance Institute (1934) and the UK Provident Institute (1957) and has designed exhibitions and educational filmstrips. He served in the Army during World War II. Lecturer at Brighton Polytechnic School of Art and Design (1959-69). His detailed and authoritative book, *Shakespeare's Theatre* (1964), was awarded the Kate Greenaway Medal for its illustrations. He has also written novels and short stories for children. Hodges has illustrated more than 90 books, mainly in pen and ink or watercolour. While the influence of E.J. Sullivan* is visible in the fluent quality of his line, he developed very early a distinctive graphic 'handwriting' that has remained consistent throughout his career despite stylistic modifications. Fidelity to his texts and convincing characterisations have ensured his continued appreciation by adult as well as child readers. [Q]

Books illustrated include:
Margaret Baker Hannibal and the Bears (1965)
Robert Browning The Pied Piper of Hamelin (1971)
Gerald Bullett The Happy Mariners (1935)
Samuel Taylor Coleridge The Rime of the Ancient Mariner (1971)
Elizabeth Goudge Sister of the Angels (1939), Smoky-House (1940), The Little White Horse (1946), Make-Believe (1949)

C. Walter Hodges. '...walked in single file like Indians' from *The New Treasure Seekers* by E. Nesbit (Ernest Benn, 1947).

Robert Graves The Siege and Fall of Troy (1962)
G. B. Harrison New Tales from Shakespeare (1938), New Tales from Malory (1939), New Tales from Troy (1940)
C. Walter Hodges Columbus Sails (1939), The Flying House (1947), Shakespeare and the Players (1948), The Namesake (1964), Shakespeare's Theatre (1964), The Marsh King (1967), The Overland Launch (1970), Playhouse Tales (1974), The Emperor's Elephant (1975), Plain Lane Christmas (1978)
Charles Kingsley Westward Ho! (1949)
Ruth Manning-Sanders Red Indian Folk and Fairy Tales (1960)
William Mayne A Swarm in May (1955), Chorister's Cake (1956), Cathedral Wednesday (1960)
E. Nesbit The Story of the Treasure Seekers (1947), The New Treasure Seekers (1947), The Would-Be-Goods (1947)
Barbara Léonie Picard Ransom for a Knight (1956)
Rhoda Power Redcap Runs Away (1952)
Ian Serraillier They Raced for Treasure (1946), Flight to Adventure (1947), There's No Escape (1950), The Silver Sword (1956)
C. Fox Smith The Ship Aground (1940), Painted Ports (1948)
L. G. Strong King Richard's Land (1933), Mr Sheridan's Umbrella (1935)
Rosemary Sutcliff The Chronicles of Robin Hood (1950), The Armourer's House (1951), The Queen Elizabeth Story (1951), Brother Dusty-Feet (1952), The Eagle of the Ninth (1954), The Shield Ring (1956)
Lowell Swortzell Here Come the Clowns (1978)
Geoffrey Trease Crown of Violet (1952)
Henry Treece Castles and Kings (1959)
Barbara Willard The Richleighs of Tantamount (1966)

Periodical: Radio Times

References: Crouch; Doyle CL; Driver; Fisher pp. 12, 82, 149; ICB 1,2,3,4; Jacques; Kirkpatrick; Usherwood; Vollmer supp; Wa (1980); *The Junior Bookshelf* vol 5 no 2 (1941), vol 15 no 3 (1951); Marcus Crouch *The Nesbit Tradition* (Benn 1972)

Edward S. Hodgson (active 1908-36)

Landscape painter who exhibited at the Royal Academy and lived at Bushey, Hertfordshire. Illustrator of boys' adventure stories in pen and ink, halftone and full colour.

Books illustrated include:
Percy Westerman A Lad of Grit (1908), The Sea Monarch (1912), Rounding Up the Raider (1916), Winning His Wings (1919), The Salving of the 'Fusi Yama' (1920), The Third Officer (1921), Clipped Wings (1923), Unconquered Wings (1924), Fosdyke's Gold (1932), Captain Frick (1936)

Periodicals: The Captain, Chums, The Girls' Realm, Herbert Strang's Annual, The Quiver

References: Houfe; Johnson & Greutzner

Robert Hodgson (active 1950s and 1960s)

A pen and ink illustrator who worked in the free, sketchy style typical of the period.

Books illustrated include:
Elisabeth Kyle Caroline House (1955), Queen of Scots (1957), Maid of Orleans (1957)
Reginald Maddock Corrigan and the White Cobra (10 vols 1956-63), Rocky and the Lion (1957), The Time Maze (1960), The Tall Man from the Sea (1962), Rocky and the Elephant (1962)
Geoffrey Trease Change at Maythorn (1962)
Mark Twain The Prince and the Pauper (1968)
Barbara Willard The Horse with Roots (1959)

Gerard Hoffnung (1925-59)

Born Berlin; moved to London (1938). Studied at Hornsey and Harrow Schools of Art. Taught art at Stamford School (1944) and Harrow School (1945). Cartoonist, illustrator and painter, broadcaster, impresario and amateur musician. He contributed to *Lilliput* from the age of 15 and to numerous magazines internationally; staff artist on the London *Evening News* and *Flair* magazine (New York). He also originated and organised the Hoffnung Festival Concerts, made broadcasts on BBC radio and television, and spoke regularly at the Oxford and Cambridge Unions. As a black and white artist, he was particularly known for his wittily inventive musical cartoons, in which orchestral performers and their instruments were affectionately depicted in a vein of comic fantasy reminiscent of Edward Lear.

Books illustrated include:
James Broughton The Right Playmate
Colette (trans Christopher Fry) The Boy and the Magic (1964)
Percy Cudlipp Bouverie Ballads (1955)
Gerard Hoffnung The Maestro (1953), The Hoffnung Symphony Orchestra (1954), The Hoffnung Music Festival (1956), The Hoffnung Companion to Music (1957), Hoffnung's Musical Chairs (1958), Hoffnung's Acoustics (1959), Ho Ho Hoffnung (1959), Birds, Bees and Storks (1960), Hoffnung's Little Ones (1961), Hoffnung's Constant Readers (1962), Hoffnung's Encore (1968), Hoffnung's Harlequinade (1979)
Elizabeth Pakenham Points for Parents (1954)
John Symonds The Isle of Cats (1955)

Periodicals: Evening News, Flair, Housewife, Lilliput, Punch, Radio Times, The Strand Magazine, The Tatler

References: Jacques; Vollmer supp; Wa (1958); WaG; Waters; *O Rare Hoffnung* (Putnam 1960); William Feaver *Masters of Caricature* (Weidenfeld & Nicolson 1981)

Arthur Paul Hogarth (b. 1917)

Works as Paul Hogarth. Born Kendal, Cumbria,

son of a master butcher and farmer. Studied at Manchester College of Art (1933-36) and at St Martin's School of Art, London (1938-40). Worked as assistant to James Boswell* (1946-48). Lecturer at the Central School of Arts and Crafts (1950-54), senior lecturer at Cambridge School of Art (1959-61), tutor at the Royal College of Art (1964-71) and visiting lecturer there (1971-82).

Since 1954, when he visited China, he has worked as an artist-reporter and social commentator, as well as illustrating Victorian classics and contemporary works of fiction. A specialist in architectural history, he has worked for the US National Trust, the National Geographic Society Book Service and the Smithsonian Publishing Task Force, and has written and illustrated a series of guidebooks on American cities. During the 1950s and 1960s, he worked mainly in charcoal or very soft pencil on high quality paper, but more recently much of his work has been in colour, and he has made lithographic prints. Hogarth considers that his work lies 'within the peculiarly English tradition of topographical drawing or watercolour blended with caricature,' and feels that travel has played a decisive part in the formation of his style and methods. He acknowledges the influence (at various times) of the Victorian illustrator Arthur Boyd Houghton (on whom he published a monograph in 1982), James Boswell* and Ronald Searle*, a close friend with whom he travelled widely in post-war Europe. Doctor of the Royal College of Art; elected ARA (1973), FSIA, RDI (1979). Prize winner in the Francis Williams Book Illustration Award for 1982.

Books illustrated include:
Louisa M. Alcott Little Men (1963)
Brendan Behan Brendan Behan's Island (1962), Brendan Behan's

Paul Hogarth. From Brendan Behan's Island: an Irish Sketchbook by Brendan Behan (Hutchinson, 1962).

New York (1964)
Nigel Buxton America (1979)
Arthur Catherau Jungle Trap (1958)
Arthur Conan Doyle The Adventures of Sherlock Holmes (1958)
Robert Graves Majorca Observed (1965), Poems (1980)
O. Henry Short Stories (1960)
Paul Hogarth Defiant People: Drawings of Greece Today (1953), Looking at China; with the journal of an artist (1955), People Like Us; Drawings of South Africa and Rhodesia (1958), Irish Sketchbook (1962), Creative Pencil Drawing (1964), Creative Ink Drawing (1968), American Album (1973), Drawing Architecture (1979)
Alaric Jacob A Russian Journey (1969)
Doris Lessing Going Home (1957)
Malcolm Muggeridge London à la Mode (1966)
Richard Parker Lion at Large (1959)
Elisabeth Sheppard-Jones Scottish Legendary Tales (1962)
Siegfried Sassoon Memoirs of a Fox-Hunting Man (1977), Memoirs of an Infantry Officer (1981)
Stephen Spender America Observed (1979)
Hugh Johnson's Wine Companion (1983)

Periodicals: Chance, The Daily Telegraph, Fortune, The Illustrated London News, Lilliput, Sports Illustrated

References: Contemporary Authors; Jacques; Vollmer; Wa (1980); WaG; *Architectural Review* (August 1955, March 1969); *Arts Review* 22 (14th March 1970); *The Association of Illustrators' Newsletter* (1977); *Designer* (November 1979); *Graphis* 79, 103, 148; *Illustrators* vol 27 (1982); Donald Drew Egbert *Social Radicalism and the Arts* (Knopf, New York 1970); Paul Hogarth *American Album* (Lion & Unicorn Press 1973), *Artist as Reporter* (Studio Vista 1967), *Creative Ink Drawing* (Pitman 1968), *Creative Pencil Drawing* (Studio Vista 1964, Pitman 1981), *Drawing Architecture* (Pitman 1973), *Drawing People* (Watson Guptill, New York 1970), *Drawings of Poland* (Wydawnictwo Artystczno-Graficzne, Warsaw 1954); Diana Klemin *The Illustrated Book* (Bramhall House, New York 1970)

Edith Blackwell Holden (1871-1920)

Married name: Mrs Smith. Born in Moseley, near Birmingham, daughter of Arthur Holden, proprietor of a paint and varnish firm. Studied at Birmingham School of Art and under Joseph Denoval Adam at his school at Craigmill, Stirling. She taught at a private art school (1906-09), married sculptor Ernest Smith (1911) and died by drowning in the River Thames. Painter in oil and watercolour of animals and plants; illustrator of several children's books. She contributed about 40 illustrations to *The Animals' Friend*, the magazine of the National Council for Animal Welfare. However, she remained more or less unknown until the discovery and publication of her 'Nature Notes' for 1906 under the title of *The Country Diary of an Edwardian Lady* (1977).

Two of her sisters, Evelyn and Violet, also studied at the Birmingham School of Art. Evelyn contributed one illustration to *The Yellow Book* (vol 9) and Violet contributed one to A.J. Gaskin's *A Book of Pictured Carols* (1893); together they illustrated *The Real Princess* by Blanche Atkinson (1894) and *The House That Jack Built* (1895).

Books illustrated include:
Helen van Cleve Blankmeyer Three Goats Gruff (nd)
Margaret Gatty Daily Bread (1910)
Edith Holden The Country Diary of an Edwardian Lady (1977)
Martin Merrythought Animals Around Us (1912)
Margaret Rankin Woodland Whisperings (1911)

Rowena Stott The Hedgehog Feast (1978)

Periodicals: The Animals' Friend, Mrs Strang's Annual for Children

References: Johnson & Greutzner; Edith Holden *The Country Diary of an Edwardian Lady* (Michael Joseph/Webb & Bower 1977); Ina Taylor *The Edwardian Lady* (Webb & Bower 1980)

Everard Hopkins (1860-1928)

Born in Hampstead, London, brother of illustrator Arthur Hopkins and of the poet Gerard Manley Hopkins. Educated at Charterhouse School; studied at the Slade School of Fine Art. Watercolourist, and book and magazine illustrator in black and white and occasionally in full colour. Sketchley considered that 'Mr Arthur Hopkins and his brother Mr Everard Hopkins are careful draughtsmen of some distinction without much spontaneity or charm of manner...'

Books illustrated include:
Maxwell Gray A Costly Freak (1894)
Laurence Sterne A Sentimental Journey (1910)
Alfred, Lord Tennyson The Princess (1911)

Periodicals: Atalanta, Black and White, The Graphic, The Illustrated London News, Punch, The Quiver

References: Bénézit; Houfe; Johnson & Greutzner; Sketchley; Spielmann; Thieme & Becker; Thorpe; Waters; C. Wood

William Thomas Horton (1864-1919)

Born in Brussels. Educated at Brighton Grammar School. Articled to a Brighton architect, then studied at the Royal Academy Architectural Schools (1887). He developed a dislike for architecture and abandoned it in 1893 in favour of painting and drawing. In the same year, he published a novel, *The Mystic Will*, and brought out the four issues of *Whispers, A Magazine for Surrey Folk*. He became involved in spiritualism and led an increasingly solitary life in Brighton and London although he did visit Russia, America and South Africa. In his graphic work, he was influenced by the French artist Théophile-Alexandre Steinlen (1859-1923) and inspired by the work of Aubrey Beardsley (another former pupil of Brighton Grammar School). Ingpen records that 'he would sometimes speak of the beauty of Beardsley's line almost in despair.' However, Horton's drawing had qualities of directness and clarity, even if it lacked Beardsley's sophistication and complexity; his imagery was often powerful and original—he believed it to be inspired by some occult influence. His friend W.B. Yeats observed in his introduction to Horton's *A Book of Images* (1898): 'his images are few, though they are becoming more plentiful, and will probably always be but few... there must always be a certain monotony in the work of the symbolist, who can only make symbols out of the things that he loves.'

Books illustrated include:
H. Rider Haggard The Mahatma and the Hare (with H.M. Brock*, 1911)
William T. Horton A Book of Images (1898), The Grig's Book (1900), The Way of the Soul, A Legend in Line and Verse (1910)
Edgar Allan Poe The Raven, The Pit and the Pendulum (1899)

Periodicals: The Academy, The Dome, The Green Sheaf, Pick-Me-Up, The Savoy, Whispers

References: Houfe; Johnson & Greutzner; Peppin; Ray; Taylor; Waters 2; *The Studio* special (1899-1900, 1911, Autumn 1914); Roger Ingpen *William Thomas Horton: a selection of his Work and a Biographical Sketch* (Ingpen & Grant 1927)

Helen Charlotte Hough (b. 1924)

Works as Charlotte Hough. Born Brockenhurst, Hampshire, daughter of a doctor father and musician mother. Received no formal art training. Illustrator, writer of children's books and adult detective stories, and occasional etcher. She has travelled widely in South America, the Galapagos Islands, Australia and elsewhere, and contributed a series of humorous travel articles to *The Spectator*. For illustration, she works in colour and in

Charlotte Hough. From her *The Homemakers* (Hamish Hamilton, 1957).

pen and ink (her favourite medium). Her drawings, while slight, are effective and lively. She is one of the many artists whose black and white style contains echoes of E.H. Shepard*, although she disclaims any conscious influence from that quarter. [Q]

Books illustrated include:
M.E. Atkinson The House on the Moor (1948), The Thirteenth Adventure (1949), Steeple Folly (1950), Castaway Camps (1951), Hunter's Moon (1953), The Barnstormers (1953)
Marcel Aymé The Wonderful Farm (1952)
Bruce Carter Peril on the Iron Road (1953), Gunpowder Tunnel (1955)
Ethelind Fearon The Sheepdog Adventure (1953)
Anita Hewett Elephant Big and Elephant Little (1955), The Little Yellow Jungle Frogs (1956), Animal Story Book (1972)
Charlotte Hough Jim Tiger (1956), Morton's Pony (1957), The Home-Makers (1957), The Story of Mr Pinks (1958), The Hampshire Pig (1958), The Animal Game (1959), The Trackers (1960), Algernon (1961), Three Little Funny Ones (1962), Anna and Minnie (1962), The Owl in the Barn (1964), More Funny Ones (1965), Red Biddy (1966), Sir Frog (1968), Educating Flora (1968), A Bad Child's Book of Moral Verse (1970), Queer Customer (1972), Wonky Donkey (1975), Bad Cat (1975), Pink Pig (1975), Charlotte Hough's Holiday Book (1975), The Mixture as Before (1976), Verse and Various (1979), The Bassington Murder (1980)
Richard Hough Galapagos (1975)
April Jaffé The Enchanted Horse (1953)
Lorna Lewis Mystery at Winton's Park (1952), Hotel Doorway (1953)
Laurence Meynell Smokey Joe Books (1952-56)
Marjorie Oliver Land of Ponies (1951)
Anna Sewell Black Beauty (1954)
Ann Stafford Five Proud Riders (1953)
Barbara Euphan Todd The Boy with the Green Thumb (1956)
A. Stephen Tring Barry books (1951-54)

Periodicals: The New Yorker, Puffin Post

References: ICB 2; Kirkpatrick

Alan Howard (b. 1922)

Born in Nottingham, son of a teacher. Educated at Nottingham High School. Read classics and history at Caius College, Cambridge, then studied at Nottingham College of Art and Crafts. Since 1952, he has worked as a layout and graphic artist, exhibition and book-jacket designer and a book illustrator, as well as designing various book jackets and contributing to illustrated miscellanies. In illustration, his aim is 'to interpret both the letter and the spirit of the story in visual terms, and at the same time produce something that is attractive enough to make people want to buy it.' He is particularly successful at capturing the element of magic in folk or fairy tales, and his work combines humour with a strong decorative sense. [Q]

Books illustrated include:
Robert Browning The Pied Piper of Hamelin (1967)
Arswyd Y Byd Gwasg Gomer (1976)
Chwyrlibwm Gwasg y Sir (1974)
Richard Coe (trans) Crocodile (1964)
Kevin Crossley-Holland The Faber Book of Northern Legends (1977), The Faber Book of Northern Folk-Tales (1980)
Mary Daunt The Roundabout Horse (1960)
Walter de la Mare Tales Told Again (1959)
Eilis Dillon The Voyage of Maelduin (1969)
Erik Hutchinson Roof-Top World (1956), Night of the Michaelmas Moon (1961), Limping Ginger of London Town (1962)

Alan Howard. From *The Day Grandfather Tickled a Tiger* by Ruskin Bond in *Allsorts 5* edited by Ann Thwaite (Macmillan, 1972).

Rhiannon Davies Jones Hwiangerddi Gwreiddiol (1973)
T. Llew Jones Helicopter! Help! (1974), Tân ar y Comin (1975)
Kathleen Lines (ed) The Faber Story Book (1961), Tales of Magic and Enchantment (1966)
Mitchell and Blyton The Faber Book of Nursery Songs (1968)
Carol Odell Johnny's Hunger Strike (1960)
Elfyn Pritchard Y Gath a Gollod ei Grwndi (1975)
Sergei Prokofiev Peter and the Wolf (1951)
Catherine Storr The Painter and the Fish (1975)
Jill Tomlinson The Bus that Went to Church (1965), Patti Finds an Orchestra (1966)
David Walker The Fat Cat Pimpernel (1958), Pimpernel and the Poodle (1959)
Anwn P. Williams Antur Elin a Gwenno (1976)
Megan Williams Pecyn Deg (1977)
Dick Whittington and his Cat (1967)
David and Goliath (1970)

References: Contemporary Authors; Eyre; Hürlimann; ICB 2, 3

Gwynedd M. Hudson (active 1910-1935)

Studied at the Municipal School of Art, Brighton, Sussex; lived nearby in Hove. Painter, poster designer, decorative illustrator in black and white with one or two colours, and in full colour.

Books illustrated include:
J.M. Barrie Peter Pan and Wendy (1931)
Lewis Carroll Alice's Adventures in Wonderland (1922)

References: Houfe; Johnson & Greutzner; Waters 2; *The Bookman Christmas Number* (1922)

Arthur Hughes (1832-1915)

Born in London. Studied under Alfred Stevens at the Government School of Design at Somerset House (1846), and at the Royal Academy Schools (from 1847). There he met the young artists of the Pre-Raphaelite Brotherhood (formed 1848): John Everett Millais, William Holman Hunt and Dante Gabriel Rossetti. Though never formally a member of their group, he was deeply and permanently influenced by their ideas, painting techniques and approach to black and white illustration. Hughes shared with Millais and Rossetti the illustrations for *The Music Master* (1855), but his most notable period as an illustrator was that of his association with the writer George MacDonald. Many of MacDonald's books, including *At the Back of the North Wind,* for which he made over 70 drawings, and *The Princess and the Goblin,* appeared initially in serial form in *Good Words for the Young* between 1868 and 1873; they elicited from Hughes images of outstanding imaginative and emotional intensity. He was essentially a Victorian illustrator, but comes within the scope of this volume for his 1905 illustrations to George MacDonald's posthumously published *Phantastes,* and for his son Greville MacDonald's stories, published 1911-13. These late illustrations were directly reproduced by line block, revealing the full extent of the artist's linear sensitivity and delicacy and making it a matter for considerable regret that his earlier illustrations had to be reproduced as wood engravings. Hughes lived quietly at Kew Green, London from 1860. He was awarded a Civil List pension in 1912.

Books illustrated include:
William Allingham The Music Master (with D.G. Rossetti and J.E. Millais, 1855)
Thomas Gordon Hake Parables and Tales (1872)
Thomas Hughes Tom Brown's Schooldays (1869)
Henry Kingsley The Boy in Grey (1871)
George MacDonald Dealings with the Fairies (1867), England's Antiphon (originally 3 parts, 1868), At the Back of the North Wind (1871), Ronald Bannerman's Boyhood (1871), the Princess and the Goblin (1872), The History of Gutta-Percha Willie (1873), (ed Greville MacDonald) Phantastes (1905)
Mrs George MacDonald Chamber Dramas (1870)
Greville MacDonald Jack and Jill (1870), The Magic Crook (1911), Trystie's Quest (1912)
Francis Turner Palgrave Five Days' Entertainments at Wentworth Grange (1868)
Christina Rossetti Sing Song (1872), Speaking Likenesses (1874)
Alfred, Lord Tennyson Enoch Arden (1866)
R.A. Willmott (ed) Poets of the Nineteenth Century (with others, 1857)
Thomas Woolner My Beautiful Lady (1866)
Babies' Classics (1904)
Christmas Carols (with others, 1874)
Mother Goose (with others, 1870)
National Nursery Rhymes (with others, 1870-71)
Sinbad the Sailor (1873)

Periodicals: The Cornhill Magazine, Good Cheer, Good Words, Good Words for the Young, The Graphic, The London Home Monthly, London Society, The Queen, The Sunday Magazine

References: Bénézit; Bland; Crane; DNB (1912-21); Doyle CL; Houfe; ICB 1; Johnson & Greutzner; Mallalieu; Muir; Pennell MI; Peppin; Ray; Thieme & Becker; Thorpe; Vollmer supp; Waters; C. Wood; *Art Journal* (1904); *Burlington Magazine* 28 (1915-16); *The Studio* special (1897-98, Spring 1922, 1923-24, Autumn 1933); William E. Fredeman *Pre-Raphaelitism. A Bibliocritical Study* (Harvard University Press, Cambridge Massachusetts 1965); Forrest Reid *Illustrators of the Sixties* (Faber & Gwyer 1928); Gleeson White *English Illustration 'The Sixties' 1855-70* (Constable 1897)

Shirley Hughes (b. 1927)

Married name: Mrs John Vulliamy. Born in Hoylake, near Liverpool, daughter of a department store owner. Educated at West Kirby High School.

Shirley Hughes. From *Mary Ann Goes to Hospital* by Mary Cockett (1961).

Studied drawing and costume design at Liverpool School of Art, and drawing and lithography at the Ruskin School of Drawing, Oxford. Since then, working freelance, she has illustrated more than 200 books for British, American and Dutch publishers. As an 'intimate chronicler of familiar childhood experience', she has developed a distinctive, easily recognisable way of drawing children, winning the Kate Greenaway Medal (1977) with *Dogger.* For black and white work, she uses pen and ink, sometimes with brushed-in areas of solid black; for colour, she works up from a fine sepia brush drawing, adding chalk, watercolour, gouache, and finally black ink. Experiments with the comic strip format (i.e. *Up and Up,* 1978) were inspired by the work of the American graphic artists Winsor McCay and George MacManus. She is a visiting lecturer at the Ruskin School and occasional lecturer elsewhere on the art of picture book making. [Q]

Books illustrated include:
Alison Abel (ed) Make Hay while the Sun Shines (1977)
Louisa M. Alcott Little Women (1960)
Ruth Ainsworth The Phantom Fisherboy (1974), The Phantom Roundabout (1977), The Pirate Ship and other stories (1980)
Mabel Esther Allan The Wood Street Secret (1968), The Wood Street Group (1970), The Wood Street Rivals (1971), The Wood Street Helpers (1973), Away from Wood Street (1975)
Hans Andersen Fairy Tales (1961), More Fairy Tales (1970)
Anne Barrett The Journey of Johnny Rew (1954)
Nina Bawden The Witch's Daughter (1966), Squib (1971)
Donald Bisset Little Bear's Pony (1966), Hazy Mountain (1975)

Angela Bull Wayland's Keep (1966)
Dorothy Butler Babies Need Books (1980)
Nan Chauncy World's End Was Home (1952)
Leonard Clark (ed) Flutes and Cymbals (1968)
Dorothy Clewes Adventure on Rainbow Island (1957), The Lost
     Tower Treasure (1960), Operation Smuggler (1964), The Jade Green
     Cadillac (1958)
Mary Cockett Rolling On (1960), Mary Ann Goes to Hospital (1961),
     The Cottage by the Lock (1962)
Sara Corrin (ed) Stories for 9-5 Year-Olds (5 vols), Stories for Under
     Fives (1974)
Dorothy Edwards All About My Naughty Little Sister, When My
     Naughty Little Sister Was Good (1968), My Naughty Little Sister
     Goes Fishing (1976), My Naughty Little Sister and Bad Harry's
     Rabbit (1977), My Naughty Little Sister at the Fair (1980)
Alison Farthing The Gauntlet Fair (1974)
Elizabeth Goudge The Lost Angel (1971)
Helen Griffiths Moshie Cat (1969), Frederico (1971)
Roger Lancelyn Green Tales the Mouse Told (1965)
Eric Houghton Summer Silver (1963)
Shirley Hughes Lucy and Tom's Day (1960), The Trouble with Jack
     (1970), Lucy and Tom Go to School (1973), Sally's Secret (1973),
     Helpers (1975), It's too Frightening for Me! (1976), Lucy and Tom at
     the Seaside (1976), Dogger (1977), Up and Up (1978), Here Comes
     Charlie Moon (1980), Lucy and Tom's Christmas (1981), Alfie Gets
     in First (1981), Alfies's Feet (1982), Charlie Moon and the Big
     Bonanza Bust-Up (1982)
Barbara Ireson (ed) The Faber Book of Nursery Stories (1966)
Josephine Kamm Where Do We Go from Here? (1972)
Geraldine Kaye Eight Days to Christmas (1970)
Margaret McPherson The Shinty Boys (1963), The New Tenants
     (1968)
Margaret Mahy The First Margaret Mahy Story Book (1972), The
     Second Margaret Mahy Story Book (1973), The Third Margaret
     Mahy Story Book (1975)
William Mayne Follow the Footprints (1953), The World Upside
     Down (1954), The Toffee Join (1968)
Helen Morgan Meet Mary Kate (1963), A Dream of Dragons (1965),
     Mary Kate and the Jumble Bear (1967), Mrs Pinny and the Blowing
     Day (1968), Satchkin Patchkin (1970), Mary Kate and the School
     Bus (1970), Mother Farthing's Luck (1971), Mrs Pinny and the Salty
     Sea Day (1972)
Jenny Overton The Thirteen Days of Chrsitmas (1972)
Charles Perrault Cinderella (1970)
Sheila Porter The Bronze Chrysanthemum (1961)
Joan Robinson The House in the Square (1972)
Diana Ross William and the Lorry (1956), The Merry-Go-Round
     (1963)
Ruth Sawyer Roller Skates (1964)
'Septima' Something to Do (1966)
Ian Serrailler Guns in the Wild (1956), Katy at Home (1957), Katy at
     School (1959)
Barbara Sleigh The Smell of Privet (1971)
Barbara Softly Plain Jane (1961), Place Mill (1962), A Stone in a Pool
     (1964)
Mary Stewart The Little Broomstick (1971)
Margaret Storey The Smallest Doll (1956), Kate and the Family Tree
     (1965), The Smallest Bridesmaid (1966)
Noel Streatfeild The Bell Family (1954), New Town (1960)
Ann Thwaite Home and Away (1967)
Ruth Tomalin The Snake Crook (1976)
Alison Uttley Tim Rabbit's Dozen (1964)
Elfrida Vipont Flowering Spring (1960)
Mary Welfare Witchdust (1980)
Ursula Moray Williams A Crown for a Queen (1968), The Toymaker's
     Daughter (1968), The Three Toymakers (1970), Malkin's Mountain
     (1971), Bogwoppit (1978)
Helen Young A Throne for Sesame (1977)

Periodical: Cricket

References: *Contemporary Authors*; Eyre; Fisher pp.206, 232; ICB
3, 4; Kirkpatrick; *Word and Image* (1977)

Blair Rowlands Hughes-Stanton
(1902-81)

Worked as Blair Hughes-Stanton. Born in London
son of landscape painter Sir Herbert Hughes-

Stanton. Studied at the Byam Shaw School (1919-
22), Royal Academy Schools (1922-23), and wood
engraving at the Leon Underwood* School (1923-
25). During his marriage to Gertrude Hermes*
(1926-32), he collaborated with her on twelve
engraved plates for the Cresset Press edition of
The Pilgrim's Progress (1928). He succeeded
Robert Maynard* as director of the Gregynog
Press (1931), and later, with his second wife, Ida
Graves, set up the Gemini Press. He taught drawing
at Westminster School of Art (1934-39) and wood
engraving at Colchester School of Art (1945-47),
St Martin's School of Art (1947-48) and the Central
School of Arts and Crafts (1948-80).

Hughes-Stanton worked mainly for the private
presses and involved himself with most of the
processes of book production including design,
typesetting, printing, binding, and designing and
cutting typefaces. He was technically one of the
most skilled of 20th-century wood engravers, a
pioneer in the revival of white-line engraving and
also in the use of the multiple graver to create
vibrant half-tone effects, which he offset with

Blair Hughes-Stanton. Frontispiece for *Mother
and Child* by Ida Graves (Fortune Press, c. 1942).

areas of white and solid black. His exceptionally fine line has made much of his work impossible to reproduce by photomechanical processes. During the 1920s and early 1930s, his imagery tended to be anthropomorphic and influenced by paleolithic cave paintings; but it later became abstract. Badly wounded during World War II, he was unable to return to wood engraving, but continued to paint, draw, produce multicoloured linocuts and teach part-time. Winner of the International Prize for engraving at the Venice Biennale (1938). Member SWE and London Group; founder member of the International Society of Wood Engravers (1953).

Books illustrated include:
John Bunyan The Pilgrim's Progress (with Gertrude Hermes*, 1928)
Samuel Butler Erewhon (1932)
Arthur Calder-Marshall A Crime against Cania (1934)
John Collier The Devil and All (1934)
Walter de la Mare Alone (1927), Self to Self (1928)
Thomas de Quincey Confessions of an English Opium Eater (1948)
Simon Gantillon Maya (1930)
Ida Graves Epithalamion (1934)
W.J. Gruffyd Caniadau (1932)
T.O. Brian Hubbard Tomorrow Is a New Day (1934)
D.H. Lawrence Birds, Beasts and Flowers (1930), The Ship of Death and other poems (1933)
T.E. Lawrence Seven Pillars of Wisdom (1926)
Christopher Marlowe The Tragicall History of Doctor Faustus (1933)
John Mavrogordata Elegies and Sons (1934)
John Milton Comus (1931), Four Poems (1933)
Velona Pilcher The Searcher (1929)
Christopher Sandford Primeval Gods (1934)
The Apocalypse (1929)
The Apocrypha (1929)
Ecclesiastes (1934)
The Lamentations of Jeremiah (1934)
The Revelation of St John the Divine (1932)
Also works published by Allen Press, California

Periodical: The Woodcut

References: Balston EWE, WEMEB; Bland; Garrett BWE, HBWE; Johnson & Greutzner; Lewis; Vollmer; Wa (1934); Waters; *Image* 6 (1951); *The Print Collector's Quarterly* vols 16 and 21; *The Studio* special (Spring 1927, Winter 1936, Autumn 1938); *The Times* obituary (10th June 1981); Dorothea Braby *The Way of Wood Engraving* (Studio 1953); Basil Gray *The English Print* (A. & C. Black 1937); Christopher Sandford *Bibliography of the Golden Cockerel Press* Dawson 1975; A.C. Sewter *Modern British Woodcuts and Wood-Engravings in the Collection of the Whitworth Art Gallery* (Manchester 1962)

Graham Humphreys (b. 1945)

Born in Solihull, Warwickshire. Studied at Sutton Coldfield School of Art and Leicester School of Art until 1967. Lecturer at Birmingham Polytechnic. Freelance book illustrator in black and white, and colour; primarily interested in historical subjects, especially sailing ships.

Books illustrated include:
Richard Armstrong The Albatross (1970)
Michael Brown Sailing Ships (1975)
J.H. Crockatt The Battle of Marston Moor (1976)
Neil Grant Smugglers (1978)
Alan C. Jenkins The Winter-Sleeper (1977)
Benjamin Lee The Frog Report (1974)
Reginald Maddock Northmen's Fury (1970)
Kenneth Ridge The Mud Scene (1975)

Pamela Rogers Big Stick and Little Who (1976)
Jenny Seed The Sly Green Lizard (1973)
John Rowe Townsend The Intruder (1969)
Philip Turner Wig-Wig and Homer (1969)
Barbara Willard Chichester and Lewes (1970)

Reference: ICB 4

James Hunt (b. 1908)

Book illustrator in black and white, and colour.

Books illustrated include:
John Beaton A Day at the Sea (1978), A Day on the Farm (1978)
Elisabeth Beresford The Secret Railway (1973)
Roy Brown A Saturday in Pudney (1966), The Battle against Fire (1966), The Viaduct (1967), The Day of the Pigeons (1968), The Wapping Warrior (1969), The River (1970), The Battle of Saint Street (1971), The Big Test (1976)
Roger Clare Islands (with others, 1971)
Alwyn Cox Two in a Boat (1971)
James Hunt Let's Be Friends (1975), Let's Be Joyful (1975), Let's Look at Jesus (1975), Let's Start Again (1975)
Samuel Johnson The Fountains (1978)
Patricia Lynch The Kerry Caravan (1967)
Hilary Spiers Freddy Is a Monster (1976), What Size Am I? (1976)

Pat Hutchins (b. 1942)

Maiden name: Pat Goundry. Born at Scorton, Yorkshire. Studied at Darlington Art School and

James Hunt. ' "There it goes!" said the bearded man, pointing with his stick.' from *The Day of the Pigeons* by Roy Brown (Abelard-Schumann, 1968).

at Leeds College of Art. Moved to London and became an assistant art editor at the advertising agency J. Walter Thompson for two years. She accompanied her husband to New York and, while living there for 18 months, produced *Rosie's Walk*, a picture story with very few words that has remained one of her better-known works. All her books have been published on both sides of the Atlantic, by Macmillan and Greenwillow in the New York and by The Bodley Head in London. She works in pen and ink with gouache and watercolour in a decorative style that has affinities with folk art. She won the Kate Greenaway Medal with *The Wind Blew* in 1974. She lives in North London and visits New York regularly. [Q]

Books illustrated include:
Pat Hutchins Rosie's Walk (1968), Tom and Sam (1969), The Surprise Party (1970), Clocks and More Clocks (1970), Changes, Changes (1971), Titch (1972), Goodnight, Owl! (1973), The Silver Christmas Tree (1974), The Wind Blew (1974), Don't Forget the Bacon (1976), Follow That Bus (1977), Happy Birthday Sam (1978), One-eyed Jake (1979), The Best Train Set Ever (1979), The Tale of Thomas Mead (1980), I Hunter (1982), You'll Soon Grow into them Titch (1983)

References: ICB 4; *Books for Keeps* no 5 (November 1980); *Graphis* vol 27 (1971-72); *The Writer's Directory* (1976-78)

Clarke Hutton (b. 1898)

Born in London. From 1916 to 1925, worked as assistant to 'Carl Wilhelm' (real name William Pitcher), a stage designer, mainly of ballets, at the Empire Theatre, Leicester Square, London. In 1926, Hutton visited Italy for six months and while there resolved to become a painter. On his return, he joined A.S. Hartrick's* lithographic class at the Central School of Arts and Crafts (1927) and on Hartrick's retirement took over the class as teacher until 1968. He turned to book illustration in the 1930s, finding that it provided a more reliable source of income than painting, and has since illustrated about 50 books for British and American publishers including the Oxford University Press, Cassells, the Folio Society, Chatto and Windus, and (in America) the Limited Editions Club of New York, Scribners and Houghton Mifflin. His illustrations consist mainly of lithographs, which have become increasingly bold and striking in treatment during his career. Through strong contrasts of tone and colour, animated compositions and often figures seen in close-up, his compositions project themselves forward from the page surface (an illusion further increased in several of his more recent books) by the device of dispensing with borders and extending the full-page illustrations to the paper's edge. He lives in London, where he now adds painting to his other activities. [Q]

Books illustrated include:
Michael Blakeway A Roundhead Soldier (1965)

Clarke Hutton. From *Pilgrim's Progress* by John Bunyan (SCM, 1947).

Charlotte Brontë Villette (1967)
John Bunyan The Pilgrim's Progress (1947)
Douglas Byng Byng Ballads (1935)
Noel Carrington Popular Art in Britain (1945)
Richard Church Cave (1950)
Henry Commager A Picture History of the United States (1958)
Joseph Conrad Almayer's Folly (1962)
Raymond M. Crawford A Picture History of Australia (1962)
Mabel E. George A Picture History of Great Discoveries (1954)
Thomas Gray Elegy Written in a Country Churchyard (1928)
John Hampden A Picture History of India (1965)
Clarke Hutton The Hare and the Tortoise (1939), A Country ABC (1940), Fifteen Nursery Rhymes (1941), Punch and Judy (1942), A Picture History of France (1951)
Thomas L. Jarman A Picture History of Italy (1961)
John Millican Rivers in the Desert (1982)
E. Nesbit The House of Arden (1967)
Alexander Pushkin (trans Gillon Aitken) The Queen of Spades: The Captain's Daughter (1970)
Walter Scott Kenilworth (nd)
R.L. Stevenson The Beach of Palesa (1959)
Noel Streatfeild Harlequinade (1943), The Circus is Coming (1948)
W.M. Thackeray The History of Henry Esmond (1950)
Tim Towle The Seven Deadly Sins (1980)
William Toye and Ivon Owen A Picture History of Canada (1956)
M.E. von Almedingen A Picture History of Russia (1964)
Eleven Chinese Proverbs (1975)
The Seven Deadly Sins (1980)
The Tale of Noah and the Flood (1946)

References: ICB 1,2,3,4; Johnson & Greutzner; Wa (1980); Waters; William Feaver *When We Were Young* (Thames & Hudson, 1977)

William Henry Hyde (1858-c.1925)

Born in New York. He studied in Paris under Boulanger and also trained as an engraver. He worked as an illustrator and landscape painter, exhibiting at the Royal Academy from 1889 and at the Paris Exposition in 1900. He settled in London and (c.1896) married Kate Rogers, a flower painter of pottery for Doulton's and former student at Lambeth School of Art. They later moved to Surrey. Hyde's English book illustrations consist of watercolours, wash drawings, pen and ink drawings, and etchings, and were almost invariably of landscape subjects. He used tone with subtlety—Sketchley observed that he could 'graduate from black to white with remarkable minuteness and ease'—and colour with richness and bravura. He went in for dramatic Turner-like skies, often painting directly into the sun, and could create striking effects of atmosphere.

Books illustrated include:
Hilaire Belloc The Old Road (1904), The Stane Street (1913)
Edward Garnett The Imaged World (1894)
Maurice Hewlett The Spanish Jade (1908)
A.E. Housman A Shropshire Lad (1908)
Ford Madox Hueffer The Cinque Ports (1900)
George Meredith The Nature Poems of George Meredith (1898)
Alice Meynell London Impression (1898)
John Milton L'Allegro and Il Penseroso (1896), Poetical Works (1904)
Eric Parker A West Surrey Sketch Book (1913)
Percy Bysshe Shelley Nature Poems (1911)
The Victoria History of the Counties of England: Hampshire, Norfolk (1901)

Periodicals: Harper's Magazine (New York), The Pall Mall Magazine, The Yellow Book

References: Baker; Bénézit; Houfe; Johnson & Greutzner; Sketchley; Thieme & Becker; Thorpe; Vollmer; Waters 2; C. Wood; *The Artist* (January 1898); *The Studio* 38 (1906)

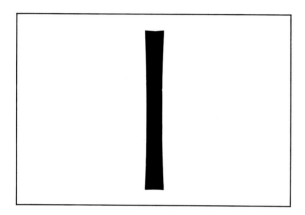

Nancy Innes (active 1942-47)

Illustrator in pen and ink who worked for Faber and Faber during the 1940s. Her rather scratchy line and inexpert draughtsmanship suggest that she had no formal art education. However, her drawings appeared attractive enough in the context of the excellent design of Faber books of the period.

Books illustrated include:
Alexie Gordon and T. Bliss Come into the Kitchen (1947)
Nancy Innes Ring-a-Ring of Roses, an ABC (1942)
Diana Ross Nursery Tales (1944)
Alison Uttley The Weather Cock and other Stories (1945)

Ionicus

See Joshua Charles Armitage.

Beryl Irving (active 1926-59)

Occasional book illustrator. She worked in pen and ink, sometimes with colour. Her illustrations for *The Dawn Child*, an early book, recall the work of Jessie M. King* in style, though not in

subject. Her later work consists of mainly small drawings, executed rather in the manner of A.K. MacDonald*.

Books illustrated include:
Beryl Irving The Dawnchild (1926)
Eric Parker (ed) The Shooting Man's Week End Book (1943), The Countryman's Week End Book (1946), The Cat Lover's Week End Book (1959)

Laurence Henry Forster Irving (b. 1897)

Works as Laurence Irving. Born London. Son of the celebrated actor-manager Henry Irving. Studied at the Byam Shaw School and at the Royal Academy schools. During World War I, he served as a captain in the Royal Air Force (1915-19). He became a stage designer and worked as Art Director of the Douglas Fairbanks films *The Iron Mask* and *The Taming of the Shrew* (1928-29). He was also a painter of landscapes and marine subjects. His book illustrations are vigorously drawn in brush or pen and ink, often with bold tonal contrasts. He was a friend of Rowland Hilder*. Member of the Society of Marine Artists.

Books illustrated include:
W. Bligh Bligh and the Bounty (1936)
G.W. Bullett The Spanish Caravel (1927)

Laurence Irving. From *Philip the King* by John Masefield (Heinemann, 1927).

Richard Church Dog Toby (1953)
Joseph Conrad The Mirror of the Sea (1935)
A.J.B.M.R. de Saint-Exupéry Flight to Arras (1955)
R. Hakluyt A Selection of the Principal Voyages…of the English Nation (1926)
L.H.F. Irving Windmills and Waterways (1927), Henry Irving. The Actor and his World (1951), Hakluyt's Voyages (nd)
John Masefield Philip the King (1927)
F.V. Morley River Thames (1926)
H. Reckitt The Adventure of Ann and the White Seals (1930)
M.F.E. Stewart The Wind Off The Small Isles (1968)
Emily Wooldridge The Wreck of the Maid of Athens (1952)

References: Johnson & Greutzner; Vollmer; Wa (1972); Waters; *The Studio* special (1927)

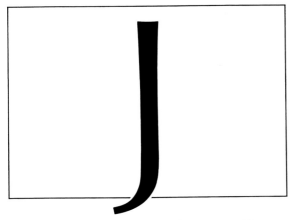

Albert Edward Jackson (1873-1952)

Often worked as A.E. Jackson. Born in London. Studied at Camden School of Art. Worked as an illustrator for the Amalgamated Press (1893-1947). Painter in oil and watercolour and children's book illustrator. His draughtsmanship was uneven, and, lacking a definite style of his own, he tended to absorb the styles and mannerisms of others—for example, some of his black and white work is reminiscent of H.R. Millar* and his full colour work at times resembles that of Arthur

A.E. Jackson. ' "You are making fun of me!" Molly said to the Moon boys' from *Molly and the Moon Boys* in *The Playbox Annual (1921).*

"You are making fun of me!" Molly said to the Moon boys

Rackham*, Anne Anderson* or Charles Robinson*. Nevertheless his earlier designs have a degree of modest charm. Member of the East Sussex Arts Club.

Books illustrated include:
Lewis Carroll Alice's Adventures in Wonderland (1915)
Daniel Defoe Robinson Crusoe (nd)
Charles Kingsley The Water Babies (1920)
Charles Lamb Tales from Shakespeare (1918)
Frederick Marryat Children of the New Forest (1934)
B.S. Woolf The Twins in Ceylon (1913)
Tales from the Arabian Nights (Ward Lock 1920)

Periodicals: Cassell's Children's Annual, The Girl's Realm, Little Folks, The London Magazine, Playbox Annual, Pearson's Magazine, The Quiver, The Royal Magazine, The Strand Magazine

References: Wa (1952); Waters; C. Wood

Michael Jackson (active from 1972)

Book illustrator in pencil and pen, sometimes with watercolour washes.

Books illustrated include:
Gillian Avery Book of the Strange and Odd (1975)
Tilla Brading Pirates (1976)
Marjorie Darke Ride the Iron Horse (1973), The Star Trap (1974)
Andrew Green The Ghostly Army (1980)
Anita Harper Ella Climbs a Mountain (1977)
Robert Leeson Maroon Boy (1974)
Richard Parker One Green Bottle (1973)
Ursula Moray Williams The Kidnapping of my Grandmother (1972)

Helen Mary Jacobs (1888-1970)

Worked as Helen Jacobs. Born in Ilford and brought up in Stoke Newington, North London, sister of the humorous writer W.W. Jacobs. Studied at West Ham School of Art. As an illustrator in watercolour and pen and ink, she worked for many publishers including Hodder & Stoughton, Ward Lock, Thomas Nelson and the S.P.C.K. Her later illustrative work consisted mainly of drawings for schoolbooks and primers published by Nisbet. She lived in Winchmore Hill, North London, and during her later years taught art at a primary school in Stoke Newington.

Books illustrated include:
Mabel Allan The Exciting River (1951)
Maud M. Higham Let's Paint Pictures of China (1947)
Helen Mary Jacobs The Open Road (1936)
Ethel L. MacPherson Native Fairy Tales of South Africa (1919)
Netta Syrett Magic London (1922)
Tales for Two (Dean nd)

Periodicals: Cassell's Children's Annual, Little Folks, Playbox Annual, Rainbow Annual, Wonder Annual

References: Cope; Johnson & Greutzner; Vollmer; Wa (1934); Waters

George Percy Jacomb-Hood (1857-1929)

Born in Redhill, Surrey. Studied at the Slade School of Fine Art (where he won a travelling scholarship and the Poynter Prize) and under J.P. Laurent in Paris. He was an etcher, a prolific

Robin Jacques. From *Vanity Fair* by W.M. Thackeray (Folio Society, 1963).

portrait painter and magazine illustrator. As correspondent for *The Graphic*, he attended the first Olympic Games in Athens (1896) and visited India in 1902, 1905 and 1911. When invited by Andrew Lang to illustrate *The Blue Fairy Book* (1889), he introduced H.J. Ford* as his collaborator, and it was Ford who continued as illustrator of the rest of the series. As a graphic artist, Jacomb-Hood was at his best with straightforward reportage and description. Evidently a convivial character, he wrote an autobiography *With Brush and Pencil* (1925), which was rich in good-natured anecdotes about his fellow-artists. Elected RE (1881) and served on the council, RBA (1884), founder-member NEAC (1886), RP (1891), ROI (1902). Vice president of the Royal British Colonial Society of Artists.

Books illustrated include:
E.F. Benson The Vintage (1898)
L.H. Grindon Lancashire (with others, 1882)
H. Rider Haggard Lysbeth (1901)
E.E. Hale In His Name (1884)
Andrew Lang The Blue Fairy Book (with H.J. Ford*, 1889)
Lewis Morris Odatis (1892)
W.C. Perry The Boy's Iliad (1902)
M. Seeley Stories from the Best Book (1881)
Oscar Wilde The Happy Prince and other tales (1888)

Periodicals: Black and White, The Graphic, The Illustrated London News, Punch, The Quarto, The Sunday Magazine

References: Bénézit; Houfe; Johnson & Greutzner; Sketchley; Thieme & Becker; Thorpe; Vollmer; Wa (1929); Waters; C. Wood; *The Burlington Magazine* 47 (1925); G.P. Jacomb-Hood *With Brush and Pencil* (John Murray, 1925)

Robin Jacques (b. 1920)

Born Chelsea, London, son of a professional soldier. Hattie Jacques, the well-known actress, was his sister. Educated at the Royal Masonic Schools, Bushey, Hertfordshire. Worked in an advertising agency before serving in the army during World War II. Art editor of *The Strand Magazine* (1948-51). Lecturer at Brighton (1947-48) and Harrow (1977-79) Schools of Art, and visiting lecturer at Canterbury College of Art (1979). He lived in France (1964-72), and has visited Mexico, South Africa, and the U.S.A. He has contributed drawings to the *Radio Times* since 1939 and worked as a freelance illustrator and designer of books, book jackets and magazines since 1945. His work is meticulously executed with a fine pen line, sometimes with added watercolour or coloured ink washes. For historical illustrations he undertakes detailed research into period costumes, furniture and architecture. He particularly enjoys illustrating 19th-century French and English romantic literature. Author of *Illustrators at Work* (Studio, 1963) and the pen and ink section of *Illustration and Graphic Design* (Phaidon, 1980). [Q]

Books illustrated include:
Lynne Reid Banks The Indian in the Cupboard (1980)
Henry Bell Youth (1947)
Gordon Cooper A Time in a City (1972), A Second Springtime (1973), Hester's Summer (1974), A Certain Courage (1975)
Helen Cresswell The White Sea Horse (1964), A Tide for the Captain (1967), The Sea Pipe (1968)
John K. Cross The Angry Planet (1945)
Patrick de Heriz Fairy Tales with a Twist (1946)
Charles Dickens Doctor Marigold (1945)
George Eliot Middlemarch (1972)
Eleanor Farjeon Kings and Queens (1983)
Washington Irving Alhambra Tales (1946)
James Joyce Dubliners (1954), Portrait of the Artist as a Young Man (1956)
Ruth Manning-Sanders A Book of Giants (1962), A Book of Dragons (1964), A Book of Dwarves (1964), A Book of Witches (1965), A Book of Wizards (1966), A Book of Ghosts and Goblins (1968), A Book of Sorcerers and Spells (1973), A Book of Monsters (1975)
Beverley Nichols The Wickedest Witch in the World (1971)
André Norton Steel Magic (1965)
E.O. Parnott Limericks (1983)
Sheena Porter The Hospital (1973)
W.M. Thackeray Vanity Fair (1963)
Ann Thwaite The House in Turner Square (1960)
Ruth Tomalin A Stranger Thing (1975)

Periodicals: Daily Express, Housewife, Leader, Lilliput, The Listener, Nova, Observer, Punch, Radio Times, The Saturday Book, The Sphere, The Strand Magazine, Sunday Times, Vogue

References: Doyle CL; Driver; Eyre; ICB 2, 3, 4; Ryder; Usherwood;

Vollmer supp; Wa (1980); *Alphabet & Image* 7 (1948); *Illustrators* 33 (1980); Diana Klemin *The Illustrated Book* (Bramhall House, New York 1970)

Gilbert James (active 1886-1926)

Born in Liverpool; while living there became a friend of Sidney Sime*. He moved to London in about 1892. His first important commission was from *The Sketch* (May 1894) and for the next decade he was much in demand as a magazine illustrator. He had a preference for symbolic and oriental subjects which he depicted in a restrained hieratic style. Arthur Lawrence (in an interview in *The Idler*, 1900) observed that 'No artist... has been made the subject of such extremes of valuation as Mr Gilbert James', and indeed his work, which could be assured and atmospheric, seemed just as often to be unconvincing and banal. His halftone illustrations, especially those published by Dent, were particularly hesitant. However, he was appreciated by Thorpe who referred to his 'excellent drawings' and by Holbrook Jackson who considered him among the distinctive artists of the 1890s. He was also a watercolour painter.

Books illustrated included:
Lucius Apuleius Cupid and Psyche (1906)
Matthew Arnold Poems (1905)
Edward Fitzgerald (trans) The Rubaiyat of Omar Khaiyam (1904)
J.W. von Goethe Faust (1904)
Edith Holland The Story of the Buddha (1916)
Montague R. James The Five Jars (1922)
V.M. Petrovic Hero Tales and Legends of the Serbians (with others, 1914)
William J. Sanderson Mind your own Buzziness (1912)
James Spence The Myths of Mexico and Peru (with others, 1913)
Alfred Lord Tennyson Poems (1907)
Ralph W. Trine In Tune with the Infinite (1926)
Aucassin and Nicolette (1905)
The Book of Ruth and Esther (1905)
Christmas Carols (1906)
The Song of Songs (1906)
The Story of Patient Griselda (1906)
Tristan and Iseulte (1911)

Periodicals: The Butterfly, The English Illustrated Magazine, The Idler, The Ludgate Monthly, Pick-me-up, The Quartier Latin, The Sketch

References: Houfe; ICB 1; Johnson & Greutzner; Mallett supp; Thorpe; Waters 2; *The Idler* 16 (1900); *The Sketch* (March 1897); Holbrook Jackson *The 1890s* (Grant Richards 1913)

Norman Thomas Janes (1892-1980)

Worked as Norman Janes. Born Egham, Surrey. Studied at the Regent Street Polytechnic (1909-14) and during the same period worked freelance as a designer of advertising for colour printers. After army service he studied at the Slade School of Fine Art (1919-22)—drawing and painting under Henry Tonks and Walter Russell, wood engraving under W. Thomas Smith; he attended evening classes in etching at the Central School of Arts and Crafts under W.P. Robins and studied under Sir Frank Short at the Royal College of Art

(1923-24). His teaching career began in 1922 with a part-time post at Queen Alexandra Hospital Home for Discharged Soldiers, Roehampton; he later lectured in etching and wood engraving at Hornsey School of Art (1928-60) and the Slade (1936-50). Principally a landscape artist in watercolour, etching (usually drypoint or aquatint), wood engraving, and sometimes in oils. In addition to his illustrated books, from 1926 to 1930, he was assisted by his wife Barbara Greg* (they married in 1925), and produced a number of wood engravings depicting scenes from the lives of composers to decorate pianola rolls published by the Aeolian Company. During the 1920s and 1930s, he designed music covers and other small illustrations for the Oxford University Press music department and book jackets for various publishers. He made some striking wood engravings as illustrations for *Heroes and Kings* in which his style is bold but formal, rather in the manner of Vivien Gribble*. Elected ARE (1921), FRE (1938), SWE (1952), ARWS (1957), RWS (1960). [Q]

Books illustrated include:
Leonard Merrick Four Stories (1925)
Wilfred Partington Smoke Rings and Roundelays (1924)
Charles Williams Heroes and Kings (1930)

References: Garrett BWE, HBWE; Guichard; Johnson & Greutzner; Vollmer; Wa (1980); Waters; *Amateur Artist* (September/October 1967); *The Artist* (February 1961); *The OWS Club* vol 49, 55 obit; *The Studio* special (Spring 1927, Spring 1930, Winter 1936); Herbert Furst *The Modern Woodcut* (John Lane 1924)

Faith Jaques (b. 1923)

Born in Leicester. Studied at Leicester School of Art and the Central School of Arts and Crafts. Visiting lecturer at Guildford and Hornsey School of Art. She has worked as a freelance illustrator since 1949, and during the 1960s and 1970s became

Norman Janes. From *Heroes and Kings* by Charles Williams (1930).

popular as an illustrator of children's stories and novels, working for publishers Heinemann, The Bodley Head, Chatto & Windus and André Deutsch, and others. She works mainly in pen and ink, and her drawings are easily recognised by their closely worked linear style and characteristic treatment of facial detail. She has also designed three British commemorative stamps (1960-61).

Books illustrated include:
Gillian Avery A Likely lad (1971)
Helen Cresswell Lizzie Dripping by the Sea (1974), Lizzie Dripping and the Little Angel (1974), Lizzie Dripping Again (1974), More Lizzie Dripping (1974)
Roald Dahl Charlie and the Chocolate Factory (1967), Charlie and the Great Glass Elephant (1973)
Leon Garfield The Cloak (1976), Moss and Blister (1976), Apprentices (1977), The Valentine (1977), Labour in Vain (1977)
Faith Jaques Tilly's House (1979)
Josephine Kamm The Story of Mrs Pankhurst (1961), Joseph Paxton and the Crystal Palace (1967)
M.M. Kaye The Ordinary Princess (1980)
Andrew Lang The Red Fairy Book (1973)
E. Nesbit The Old Nursery Stories (1975)
Philippa Pearce What the Neighbours Did and Other Stories (1972)
Jean Rhys The Wide Sargasso Sea (1968), Voyage in the Dark (1969)
Margery Sharp The Magical Cockatoo (1974), Bernard the Brave (1976)
Margaret Stavride (commentary) The Hugh Evelyn History of Costume (1966)
Mary Treadgold The Humbugs (1968)
Henry Treece The Windswept City (1967)
Ivan Turgenev (trans David Magarshack) The Torrents of Spring (1967)
Barbara Willard (ed) Field and Forest (1975)
Ursula Moray Williams Mog (1969), Johnnie Golightly and his Crocodile (1970), A Picnic with the Aunts (1972), Grandpapa's Folly and the Woodworm-Bookworm (1974)

Periodical: Radio Times

References: Contemporary Authors; Fisher pp.62, 68; Driver; ICB 4; Jacques; Usherwood; Wa (1972)

Daphne B. Jerrold (active 1927-32)

Lived in Hampstead, London. Flower painter; book illustrator in black and white line, in a somewhat immature style.

Books illustrated include:
Lady Cynthia Asquith (ed) Sails of Gold (with others, 1927), The Children's Cargo (with others, 1930)
Rose H. Heaton Mr Manners (with others, 1932), The Perfect Christmas (1932)

Reference: Johnson & Greutzner

Patrick A. Jobson (b. 1919)

Works as Pat Jobson. Born in Ilford, Essex, son of artist Frank Mears Jobson. Studied with Alfred Hayes (1931-37) and at North Tottenham Polytechnic. Served in Royal Navy (1940-46). Sign painter, landscape and marine artist, and black and white illustrator. In his illustrations, Jobson showed aptitude for depicting ships, landscapes and animals; he works in an open style with prominent hatching that owes something to the influence of Frank Brangwyn*. Founder Member of RSMA

Faith Jaques. ' "How much easier life in the doll's house would have been without all that ironing," thought Tilly wistfully' from her *Tilly's House* (Heinemann, 1979).

(resigned), PS (c.1958, resigned), SGA (1949-58, 1982); founder member of Wapping Group of Artists and Langham Sketch Club. [Q]

Books illustrated include:
Janet Carruthers The Forest Is My Kingdom (c.1951)
Peter Dawlish Dauntless Finds Her Crew (1947), The First Tripper (1947), Dauntless Sails Again (1948), Dauntless and the Mary Baines (1949), Peg-Leg and the Fur Pirates (1949), North Sea Adventure (1949), Captain Peg-Leg's War (1949), Dauntless Takes Recruits (1950), Aztec Gold (1951), Dauntless Sails In (1952), The Bagoda Episode (1953), Dauntless in Danger (1954), He Went with Drake (1955), Dauntless Goes Home (1960)
Leighton Houghton Haunted Creek (1953)
Frank Knight Voyage to Bengal (1954), Clippers to China (1955), Mudlarks and Mysteries (1955), The Bluenose Pirate (1956), Please Keep off the Mud (1957), The Patrick Steamboat (1958), He Sailed with Blackbeard (1958), Shadows on the Mud (1960), The Slaver's Apprentice (1961), The Golden Monkey (nd)
Jack Lindsay The Dons Sight Devon (1951)
J. Strang Morrison Wind Force Seven (nd)
Philip Rush He Went with Dampier (1957)
Marjorie Sankey Unwilling Stowaway (1959)
Percy Westerman A Midshipman of the Fleet (1954), Daventry's Quest (1955)

References: ICB 2; Wa (1980); Waters; Denys Brook-Hart *Twentieth Century British Marine Painting* (Antique Collectors' Club 1981)

Pat Jobson. From *Dauntless in Danger* by Peter Dawlish (1954).

A. Garth Jones 'Such notes, as, warbled to the string/Drew iron tears down Pluto's cheek' from *Il Penseroso* in *The Minor Poems of John Milton* (Bell, 1898).

Alfred Garth Jones (1872–c.1930)

Born and educated in Manchester. Studied in London at the Westminster School of Art and the Slade School of Fine Art, in Paris at the Académie Julian, and finally at the South Kensington Schools, where he founded, edited and contributed to an illustrated magazine *The Beam*. Settled in Chelsea and became visiting Master of Design at Lambeth and Manchester Schools of Art. His range included landscape painting, illustration, poster design, mosaic work (e.g. for Hull School of Art) and stained glass (e.g. for Cardiff City Hall). As a graphic artist he first became known in Paris, where he contributed to *La Revue Illustrée*. His drawings show the influence of the Arts and Crafts Movement and like many of his generation he held Japanese woodcuts and the prints and drawings of Dürer in particular regard. Thorpe considered that 'his work differs from that of many of the contemporary decorative artists

mainly by reason of his strong masculine method. His drawing is generally sure and sound, his sense of decoration simple and original, and he shows too, a fine feeling for colour and the judicious use of black'. In addition to illustrations, he designed a number of endpapers and title pages for the publisher George Newnes. His later drawings reflect his admiration for the work of E.J. Sullivan*.

Books illustrated include:
A.J. Boyer d'Agen Le Livre d'Heures d'un Cadet de Gascoigne (1902)
Jérôme Doucet Contes de Haute-Lisse (1899), Contes de la Fileuse (1900)
Charles Lamb The Essays of Elia (1902)
Charles H. Smith Fairy Tales from Classic Myths (1894)
Jonathan Swift The Journal to Stella (1904)
Alfred, Lord Tennyson In Memoriam (1901)
The Minor Poems of John Milton (Endymion series 1898)
Miscellaneous Works of Oliver Goldsmith (1905)
Queen Mab's Fairy Realm (with others, 1901)

Periodicals: The Beam Century Magazine, Form, The Golden Hind, The Graphic, The London Magazine, The Quartier Latin, The Quarto, Revue Illustrée, Scribner's Magazine

References: Baker; Bénézit; Crane; Houfe; Peppin; Sketchley; Thieme & Becker; Thorpe; Vollmer; Wa (1929); C. Wood *The Studio* special (1900-01, Autumn 1914)

Barbara Jones (d. 1978)

Born in Croydon, Surrey. Studied at the Royal College of Art. Writer and illustrator of books on design history and style; landscape painter, muralist and mosaic designer, also exhibition designer. For the Festival of Britain (1951), she designed the seaside section of *The Coastline of Britain*, a mural for the Television Pavilion, lion and unicorn figures for the Lion and Unicorn Pavilion,

Barbara Jones. 'Blaise Hamlet, Gloucestershire' from *On Trust for the Nation* by Clough Williams Ellis (Paul Elek, 1947).

and organised the Exhibition of British Popular and Traditional Art at the Whitechapel Gallery. Her work depicted the style and detail of buildings and man-made objects from the past. She had a remarkable sensitivity to qualities of atmosphere and the individual characteristics of places and things, evinced in spirited, appreciative pen and ink drawings. Fellow of the Royal Anthropological Institute and FSIA.

Books illustrated include:
Bertram C.W. Ellis On Trust for the Nation (1947)
Wyndham Gooden This or That? (1947)
Barbara Jones The Isle of Wight (1950), The Unsophisticated Arts (1951), Follies and Grottoes (1953), English Furniture at a Glance (1954), Design for Death (1963)
Recording Britain (1946)

References: Jacques; Wa (1980); Waters 2; The Times (obituary 7th September 1978); Mary Banham & Bevis Hillier (ed) A Tonic to the Nation (Thames & Hudson 1976)

David Michael Jones (1895-1974)

Worked as David Jones. Born Brockley, Kent, son of a printer's manager from Wales. Studied at Camberwell School of Art (1909-15) under A.S. Hartrick*, Herbert Cole* and Reginald Savage*. Served in the Royal Welsh Fusiliers (1915-18), then attended Westminster School of Art (1919-21). Became a Roman Catholic (1921) and went to work with Eric Gill* at Ditchling, Sussex (1922). There he studied woodwork and wood engraving, and made some illustrations for the St Dominic's

David Jones. 'Noah' from *The Chester Play of the Deluge* edited by J. Isaacs (Golden Cockerel Press, 1927).

Press. Admitted as a Tertiary of the Order of St Dominic (1923) and moved with Gill to Capel-y-ffin, Wales in 1924. In 1925, he illustrated the first of a number of books for the Golden Cockerel Press. Like the rest of his work, his book illustrations were imbued with his intensely personal vision. With delicate outlines and partial shading or colour, sensitively modulated, he created images of great visual and symbolic complexity, often placing them protectively within a shallow or up-tilted picture space. In his wood engravings, he sometimes used white-line to describe relatively simplified forms. He was also a pencil draughtsman and painter in watercolour. As a writer, he was best known for *In Parenthesis* (Faber & Faber 1937), a poetic account of his experience in World War I.

Books illustrated include:
Roy Campbell The Gum Trees (1930)
S.T. Coleridge The Rime of the Ancient Mariner (1929)
Sir Francis Coventry The History of Pompey the Little (1926)
T.S. Eliot The Cultivation of Christmas Trees (1954)
Eleanor Farjeon The Town Child's Alphabet (1924)
J. Isaacs (ed) The Chester Play of the Deluge (1927)
David Jones The Anathemata (1952)
Harold Munro The Winter Solstice (1928)
Hilary Pepler A Rosary Calendar (1930)
W.H. Shewring Hermia and Some Other Poems (1930)
Jonathan Swift Gulliver's Travels (2 vols 1925)
Alfred, Lord Tennyson The Morte d'Arthur (1940)
The Book of Jonah (1926)
Libellus Lapidum (1924)
Llyfr y Pregeth-wr: Ecclesiastes (1927)
Oxford Book of English Verse (1939)
Seven Fables of Aesop (1928)

Periodical: The Woodcut

References: Balston EWE, WEMEB; Bénézit; Chamot, Farr & Butlin; Contemporary Authors; Garrett BWE, HBWE; Guichard; Hofer; Johnson & Greutzner; Phaidon; Rothenstein 2; Vollmer; Wa (1934); Waters; Artwork 23 (1930); Motif 7 (1961); Signature 8 (1949); The Studio 149 (1955), special (Spring 1930); The Twentieth Century (July 1960); Word and Image 4 (National Book League 1972); David Jones (Arts Council catalogue 1954); Dr D. Blamires David Jones Artist and Writer (Manchester University Press 1971); Paul Hills (intro) David Jones (Anthony d'Offay Gallery 1979); Robin Ironside David Jones (Penguin 1949); David Jones Epoch and Artist (Faber 1959); Kathleen Raine David Jones and the Actually Loved and Known (Golgonooza Press 1978), David Jones, Solitary Perfectionist (Golgonooza Press 1975); Christopher Sandford Bibliography of the Golden Cockerel Press (Dawson 1975), Cock-a-Hoop (Private Libraries Association 1976)

Harold Jones (b. 1904)

Born in Romford, Essex. Initially destined for a career as a farmer, he went to work on a farm but after twelve months' trial decided against it. He studied art at Goldsmith's College (1921) under E.J. Sullivan*, then took a job and attended evening classes at Camberwell School of Arts and Crafts. He was awarded a Royal Exhibition to the Royal College of Art (1924-28), where he studied drawing, design and engraving; he was profoundly influenced by the disciplined, academic draughtsmanship of William Rothenstein. He taught at Bermondsey Central School for Boys (1930-34),

Harold Jones. From *Lavender's Blue* compiled by Kathleen Lines (Oxford University Press, 1954).

and was visiting lecturer at the Ruskin School of Drawing, Oxford (1937-40), where Albert Rutherston* was Master, and at the Working Mens' College in North London. After war service in a map reproduction section of the Royal Engineers, he lectured part-time at Chelsea College of Art (1945-58). He has been active as a book illustrator since 1937, working in pen and ink, sometimes with colour washes, in a style distinguished by a firm but sensitive pen line and controlled cross-hatching. His drawings are both decorative and spatially well-ordered, and at their best have an undemonstrative tonality reminiscent of Italian *quattrocento* painting. In most of his illustrated books he was also responsible for the design. He has been widely recognised as one of the most interesting professional illustrators of the 20th century. *Lavender's Blue* (1954) was included in the honours list for the Hans Christian Award (1956) and received the ALA Award in America. He has also designed book jackets for Chatto & Windus and The Bodley Head, and is a painter (oil and watercolour) and printmaker (etchings, wood engravings and lithographs). He has lived in Putney, South London, for many years. [Q]

Books illustrated include:
M.E. Atkinson August Adventure (1936), Mystery Manor (1937), The Compass Point North (1938), Smuggler's Gap (1939), Crusoe Island (1941)
William Blake Songs of Innocence (1958)
Colin Brooks The First Hundred Years (1947)
Robert Browning The Pied Piper of Hamelin (1962)
Lewis Carroll The Hunting of the Snark (1975)

Paul Ries Collin Calling Bridge (1976)
Walter de la Mare This Year: Next Year (1937)
Henry Fagen Ninya (1956)
M. Fisher Open the Door (1965)
T.E. Gregory The Westminster Bank (1936)
Cecil A. Joll Diseases of the Thyroid Gland (1932)
Harold Jones The Visit to the Farm (1939), The Enchanted Night (1947), The Childhood of Jesus (1964), There and Back Again (1977), Silver Bells and Cockle-shells (1979), Tales from Aesop (1981)
Charles Kingsley The Water Babies (1961)
Naomi Lewis The Silent Playmate (1979)
Kathleen Lines Four to Fourteen (1950), Lavender's Blue (1954), Once in Royal David's City (1956), A Ring of Tales (1958), Jack and the Beanstalk (1960), Noah and the Ark (1961)
Penelope Lively Voyage of the QV66 (1978)
Ruth Manning-Sanders The Town Mouse and the Country Mouse (1977)
John Pudney Selected Poems (1947)
Donald Suddaby Prisoners of Saturn (1957)
Elfrida Vipont (ed) Bless this Day (1958)
The Complete Greek Stories of Nathaniel Hawthorne (1964)
The Fairy Stories of Oscar Wilde (1976)
Songs from Shakespeare (1961)

References: Chamot, Farr & Butlin; Crouch; Hürlimann; ICB 1,2,3; Johnson & Greutzner; Vollmer supp; Wa (1980); Waters; *The Junior Bookshelf* vol 5, no 2 (1941), vol 12, no 4 (1948); William Feaver *When We Were Young* (Thames & Hudson 1977)

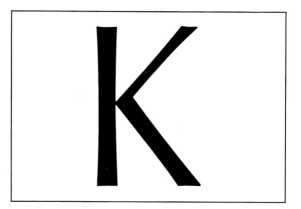

Edmond Xavier Kapp (1890-1978)

Born in London. Educated at Owen's School and Christ's College, Cambridge. Studied art in London, Paris and Rome. Caricaturist and portrait painter. As a caricaturist, he was influenced early on by Max Beerbohm*; stylistically his work reflected his interest in Japanese art and in contemporary modern movements such as Cubism. His drawings were most often in chalk, but he occasionally worked in a fine pen line, sometimes with wash, or in pencil, adapting his style and method to his response to the personality of the subject. He did very little book illustration in the accepted sense, but published a number of collections of caricatures, sometimes (as in *Pastiche*, 1926) with passages of text. J.B. Manson in *The Studio* described him as a '*distillateur*' of the perfume of personality' (1919). After the 1920s he concentrated on painting and serious portraiture. He served in the British Expeditionary Force during World War I. During World War II, he was an

Official war artist (1940-41) and later Official Artist to UNESCO (1946-47).

Books illustrated include:
Lawrence Binyon and W.H. Davies (intro) Reflections, a Second Series of Drawings (1922)
Yvonne Cloud and Edmond Kapp Pastiche, a Music Room Book (1926)
Laurence Housman Trimblerigg, a Book of Revelation (1924)
Edmond Kapp Personalities (1919), Minims (1925), Ten Great Lawyers (1925)

Periodicals: The Apple, The Listener, The Manchester Guardian, The New Statesman, The Observer, The Sunday Times, Time and Tide

References: Houfe; Johnson & Greutzner; Vollmer; Wa (1980); Waters; *Drawing and Design* 3 (1923); *The Studio* 77 (1919), 161 (1961), special (Autumn 1928); *Typography* 4 (1937); *British Print Makers of the 1920s and 1930s* (Michael Parkin catalogue October/November 1974); William Feaver *Masters of Caricature* (Weidenfeld & Nicolson 1981); Bohun Lynch *A History of Caricature* (Faber & Gwyer 1927)

Helen Kapp (b. 1901)

Born in London. Studied at the Slade School of Fine Art, Central School of Arts and Crafts, and in Paris. Director of Wakefield City Art Gallery (1951-61) and Abbot Hall Art Gallery, Kendal (1961-67). Painter in oil and watercolour, wood engraver; author of *Enjoying Pictures* (Routledge and Kegan Paul 1975). Her pen and ink drawings are spontaneous and humorous in appearance. Her illustrations were published at various times by Dent, Gollancz, Routledge & Kegan Paul, Robert Hale and the Medici Society.

Books illustrated include:
Gerald Bullett (ed) Seed of Israel: Tales from the English Bible (1927)
Basil Collier and Helen Kapp Take Forty Eggs (1938)
James Laver (intro) Toying with a Fancy (1948)
Harold Morland Fables and Satires (1945)

References: Johnson & Greutzner; Vollmer; Wa (1980); Waters

Edward McKnight Kauffer (1890-1954)

Born in Montana, U.S.A. and grew up in Indiana. Became assistant scene painter at Evansville Grand Opera House (c.1903). Studied art in San Francisco, Chicago (where he saw the controversial Armory Show of modern European art), Munich and Paris. Moved to London (1914) where, on the recommendation of John Hassall*, he approached Frank Pick, then commercial manager of the Underground Electric Railways company. For the next 25 years he was the main designer of London Underground posters under Pick's patronage, and also designed posters for numerous other companies, including Shell Petroleum. He worked as an easel painter until 1920, but from 1921 concentrated on commercial work: poster, theatre and exhibition design, interior and mural decoration, book illustration and designs for costumes, carpets and textiles. Founder member of the London Film Society (1925), for which he

E. McKnight Kauffer. From *Elsie and the Child* by Arnold Bennett (Cassell, 1929).

designed posters. An American citizen, he moved to New York after the outbreak of World War II (1940), but there his career declined. In 1950, he married designer Marian Dorn (illustrator of William Beckford's *Vathek* (1929), who had been his companion since 1923. Kauffer's illustrations for English publishers date from the period 1926-31. Though commissioned by several publishers (the Nonesuch Press, Faber and Faber, Etchells and Macdonald and Cassell), his books were mainly printed at the Curwen Press where the *pôchoir* (hand-stencilled) colouring method was being developed. This technique enabled exact colour harmonies to be reproduced, and captured a feeling of spontaneity often lost in mechanical reproduction. Kauffer's illustrations exploited this technique in ways that were both inventive and subtle. His graphic style in posters and illustrations reflected contemporary movements; ideas drawn from cubo-vorticist sources during the 1920s were followed by surrealist-inspired free association during the 1930s. However, these sources were always entirely assimilated into his own very individual visual language. F.J. Harvey Darton observed that 'work like E. McKnight Kauffer's is often, as in his *Don Quixote* (Nonesuch Press) not "illustration" in any usual sense at

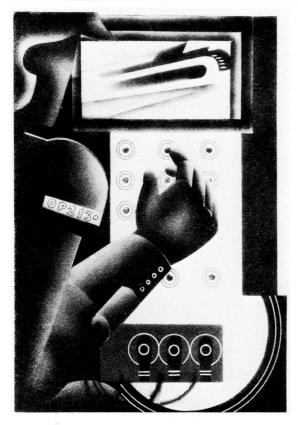

E. McKnight Kauffer. 'War in 2030' from *The World in 2030 AD* by the Earl of Birkenhead (Hodder & Stoughton, c.1930).

all but an imaginative projection from the artist's mind...' (*The Studio* special Winter 1931). Paul Nash*, writing in *Signature* (1935), considered Kauffer 'responsible, above anyone else, for the change in attitude towards commercial art in this country...his influence as an applied draughtsman has been immensely important.'

Books illustrated include:
Arnold Bennett Elsie and the Child (1929), Venus Rising from the Sea (1931)
Lord Birkenhead The World in 2030 (c. 1930)
Richard Burton The Anatomy of Melancholy (1925)
Cervantes Don Quixote (1930)
Daniel Defoe Robinson Crusoe (1929)
T.S. Eliot Journey of the Magi (1927), A Song for Simeon (1928), Marina (1931), Triumphal March (1931)
W.H. Hudson Green Mansions (1944)
Christopher Isherwood Lions and Shadows (1938)
Hermann Melville Benito Cereno (1926)
Edgar Allan Poe Complete Poems and Stories (1946)
Carl Van Vechten Nigger Heaven (nd)

Periodicals: The Apple, Fanfare, Radio Times

References: Bland; Driver; Gilmour; Houfe; ICB 1; Johnson & Greutzner; Lewis; Vollmer; Wa (1934); Waters 2; *The Studio* 79 (1920), 97 (1929), special (1927, Autumn 1930, Winter 1931); *The Thirties* (Arts Council catalogue 1979); Roger Fry *Transformations* (Chatto & Windus 1926); Mark Haworth-Booth *E. McKnight Kauffer, a Designer and his Public* (Gordon Fraser 1979); Bevis Hillier *Posters* (Weidenfeld & Nicolson 1969); Nikolaus Pevsner *Studies in Art, Architecture and Design* vol II (Thames & Hudson 1968).

Cecil Keeling (b. 1912)

Born Teddington, Middlesex. Studied at Putney School of Art (1930-34) and Chelsea School of Art (1935-36) while working for a printing firm, then became a designer for the Public Relations division of the British Broadcasting Corporation. After wartime army service in Italy and the Middle East, he rejoined the BBC as a designer in the publicity department. Since then he has concentrated on producing work for reproduction as a typographer and illustrator in a variety of media including wood and lino engraving and, increasingly, scraperboard. His style, with its strong blacks and bold tonal contrasts, is geometric and stylised, with varying tool marks used to emphasise the page surface and give overall textural consistency. Member RE, SWE, Art Workers' Guild (1945) and FSIA.

Books illustrated include:
Oliver Goldsmith The Citizen of the World (1969)
Cecil Keeling A Modicum of Leaves (1943), Pictures from Persia (1947), Hermstrong, or Man as he is not (1960)
Percy B. Shelley Zastrozzi (1955)

Periodicals: The Listener, Radio Times

References: Garrett BWE, HBWE; Jacques; Usherwood; Vollmer supp; WaG; *Graphis* 62; Christopher Sandford *Cock-a-Hoop* (Private Libraries Association 1976)

Henry Weston Keen (1899-1935)

Line draughtsman, engraver and lithographer

Cecil Keeling. 'Baghdad' from his *Pictures from Persia* (Robert Hale, 1947).

strongly influenced by Aubrey Beardsley*. He illustrated several books for the Bodley Head.

Books illustrated include:
Richard Garnett The Twilight of the Gods (1924)
Voltaire Zadig and other Romances (1926)
John Webster The Duchess of Malfi and the White Devil (1930)
Oscar Wilde The Picture of Dorian Gray (1925)

Periodical: The Golden Hind

Reference: Johnson

Charles William James Keeping (b. 1924)

Usually works as Charles Keeping. Born in Lambeth, London. Educated at the Frank Bryant School, Kennington, London. Served as a telegraphist in the Royal Navy (1943-46) before studying art at the Regent Street Polytechnic (1946-52), where he later became a visiting lecturer in lithography (1956-63). Also a visiting lecturer in drawing and lithography at Croydon College of Art (1962-78) and at Camberwell School of Art (from 1979). Illustrator, designer and writer of children's books and lithographer. Winner of the Kate Greenaway Medal with *Charlie, Charlotte and the Golden Canary* (1967) and *The Highwayman* (1981), and of the Bratislava Biennale Golden Apple Award (1975), and prize winner in the Francis Williams Book Illustration Award for 1972 and 1977. One of the best known illustrators of the 1960s and 1970s, Keeping combines an individual drawing style and a feeling for design and structure with the ability to evoke atmosphere and create a convincing world of the imagination. He works in black or coloured ink, mostly on a fine Whatman or Hodgkinson 'bank note' paper and sometimes on plastic (Cobex). *Joseph's Yard* and *Through the Window* have been made into television plays.

Books illustrated include:
Eric Allen The Latchkey Children (1974)
E.A. Almedingen The Knights of the Golden Table (1963), The Treasure of Siegfried (1964)
Bernard Ashley Terry on the Fence (1975), Break in the Sun (1980)
Nina Bawden The Robbers (1979)
Paul Berna Flood Warning (1962)
Edward Blishen Miscellany One (with others, 1964)
Emily Brontë Wuthering Heights (1964)
Marie Butts Champion of Charlemagne (1967)
Charles Causley The Sun, Dancing (1982)
Edna Walker Chandler With Book on her Head (1967)
Ruth Chandler Three Trumpets (1962)
Leonard Clark The Tale of Prince Igor (1979)
William Cole The Poet's Tales (1971)
Wilkie Collins The Moonstone (1963)
Clare Compton Harriet and the Cherry Pie (1963)
Joseph Conrad The Shadow-Line, and Within the Tides (1962)
Lee Cooper Five Fables from France (1970), The Strange Feathery Beast (1973)
Kenneth Crossley-Holland King Horn (1964), The Wildman (1976), Beowulf (1982)
Henry Daniel-Rops The Life of Our Lord (1965)
Mitchell Dawson The Queen of Trent (1961)
Charles Dickens Pickwick Papers and Great Expectations (1981), Our

Mutual Friend and Edwin Drood (1982), David Copperfield (1983)
Fyodor Dostoyevsky The Idiot (1971)
Kathleen Fidler Tales of Pirates and Castaways (1960), Tales of the West Country (1961)
Guthrie Foote Merrily on High (1959)
Leon Garfield and Edward Blishen The God Beneath the Sea (1970), The Golden Shadow (1973)
Alan Garner Elidor (1965)
Kenneth Grahame Dream Days (1962), The Golden Age (1962)
Nicholas Stuart Gray Grimbold's Other World (1963), Mainly in Moonlight (1965), The Apple-Stone (1969), Over the Hills to Babylon (1970)
Roger Lancelyn Green The Tale of Ancient Israel (1969)
Nigel Grimshaw The Angry Valley (1970)
Elizabeth Grove Whitsun Warpath (1964)
René Guillot Tipiti the Robin (1962)
H. Rider Haggard King Solomon's Mines (1961)
Helen Hoke Weirdies (1973), Monsters, Monsters, Monsters (1974), Spooks, Spirits and Spectres (1975)
James Holding The King's Contest (1964), The Sky-Eater (1966), Poko and the Golden Demon (1968)
Victor Hugo Les Misérables (1976)
Mollie Hunter Patrick Kentigern Keenan (1963), The Kelpie's Pearls (1964), Thomas and the Warlock (1967)
Aldous Huxley After Many a Summer (1969), Time Must Have a Stop (1969)
Lewis Jones The Birds and Other Stories (1973)
Ted Kavanagh Man Must Measure (1955)
Charles Keeping Black Dolly (1966), Shaun and the Cart-Horse (1966), Charley, Charlotte and the Golden Canary (1967), Alfie and the Ferry Boat (1968), (ed) Tinker Tailor: Folk Songs (1968), Joseph's Yard (1969), Through the Window (1970), The Garden Shed (1971), The Spider's Web (1972), Richard (1973), The Nanny Goat and the Fierce Dog (1974), The Railway Passage (1974), (ed) Cockney Ding Dong (1975), Wasteground Circus (1975), Inter-City (1976), River (1979), Willie's Fire Engine (1980), The Highwayman (1981)
Charles Kingsley The Heroes (1970)
Rudyard Kipling The Beginning of the Armadilloes (1982)
Frank Knight (ed) They Told Mr Hakluyt (1964)
David Kossoff The Little Book of Sylvanno (1975)
Erich Maria Lemarqué All Quiet on the Western Front (1966)
Marian Lines Tower Blocks (1975)
Walter Macken Island of the Great Yellow Ox (1966), The Flight of the Doves (1968)
W. Somerset Maugham The Mixture as Before (1968), Of Human Bondage (nd)
Margaret J. Miller Knights, Beasts and Wonders (1969)
John Reginald Milsome Damien the Leper's Friend (1965)
John Stewart Murphy Bridges (1958), Roads (1959), Canals (1961), Ships (1962), Railways (1964), Wells (1965), Dams (1966), Harbours and Docks (1968)
Ira Nesdale Riverbend Bricky (1960), Bricky and the Hobo (1964)
Robert Newman The Twelve Labors of Hercules (1972)
Barbara Leonie Picard Lost John (1962)
Richard Potts An Owl for his Birthday (1966), The Haunted Mine (1968), A Boy and his Bike (1976)
Eric and N.I.S. Protter Celtic Folk and Fairy Tales (1967)
James Reeves (ed) The Cold Flame (1967), An Anthology of Free Verse (1968)
R.E. Rogerson Enjoy Reading! (1971)
Philip Rush The Castle and the Harp (1963)
Ian Serraillier I'll Tell You a Tale (1973)
Mary Francis Shura The Valley of the Frost Giants (1971)
Nevil Shute On the Beach (1970), Ruined City (1970)
Jacoba Sporry The Story of Egypt (1964)
Roger Squire Wizards and Wampum (1972)
Forbes Stuart The Magic Horns (1974), The Mermaid's Revenge (1980)
Rosemary Sutcliff The Silver Branch (1957), Warrior Scarlet (1958), The Lantern Bearers (1959), Knight's Fee (1960), Beowulf (1961), Dawn Wind (1961), Heroes and History (1965), The Mark of the House Lord (1965), Dragon Slayer (1966), The Capricorn Bracelet (1973), Blood Feud (1977)
Ursula Synge Weland, Smith of the Gods (1972)
Joan Tate Jenny (1964), The Next-Doors (1964), Mrs Jenny (1966)
Denys Thompson and R.J. Harris Your English (1965)
P.L. Travers About Sleeping Beauty (1975)
Geoffrey Trease Bent is the Bow (1965), The Red Towers of Granada (1966)
Henry Treece The Horned Helmet (1963), The Children's Crusade

Charles Keeping. From *Flood Warning* by Paul Berna (Bodley Head, 1962).

(1964), The Last of the Vikings (1964), Splintered Sword (1965), The Dream-Time (1967), Swords from the North (1967), The Invaders (1972)
Horace Walpole The Castle of Otranto (1969)
John Watts Early Encounters (1970)
H.G. Wells Mr Britling Sees It Through (1969)
Frederic Westcott Bach (1967)

Periodical: Radio Times

References: *Contemporary Authors*; Crouch; Eyre; Fisher pp.10, 74, 96; Hürlimann; Jacques; Kirkpatrick; Ryder; Usherwood; Justin Wintle and Emma Fisher *The Pied Pipers* (Paddington Press 1974)

Felix Kelly (b. 1916)

Born in Auckland, New Zealand. Settled in London (1938) and served in the Royal Air Force during World War II. As a romantic painter in gouache and oil, he was influenced early on by Surrealism. He is also a graphic artist and has designed stage productions at the Old Vic and Sadlers Wells theatres, London. His colour illustrations for Herbert Read's *The Green Child* are (like his paintings) dreamlike and theatrical. In Elizabeth Burton's domestic histories, his evocative, finely textured pen and ink drawings endow household objects with mystery and romance.

Books illustrated include:
Elizabeth Burton The Elizabethans at Home (1958), The Georgians at Home (1967), The Jacobeans at Home (1967), The Early Victorians at Home (1972)
Herbert E. Read The Green Child (1945)

References: Contemporary Artists; Vollmer; Wa (1980); Waters; Herbert Read (intro) *Paintings by Felix Kelly* (Falcon Press 1946)

A.E. Kennedy (active 1924-1965)

A prolific and cheerful illustrator of mainly animal subjects who worked in black and white, and in full colour.

Books illustrated include:
Arthur Groom Farmyard Friends (1965)
A.E. Kennedy Gay Gambols (1925)
Lesley Kennedy For the Tinies (1930), For the Toddlers (1931), Holiday Friends (1932)
R.J. Macgregor The Adventures of Grump (1946)
Antonia Ridge The Handy Elephant (1946), Rom-Bom-Bom (1946), Endless and Co (1948), Galloping Fred (1950)
David Stephen Timothy's Book of Farming (1963)
Ethel Talbot Baby Animals (1928)
Alison Uttley Sam Pig Goes to Market (1941), Sam Pig and Sally (1942), Sam Pig at the Circus (1943), The Adventures of Tim Rabbit (1945), Sam Pig in Trouble (1948), Macduff (1950), Yours ever, Sam Pig (1951), Sam Pig and the Singing Gate (1955), Tim Rabbit and Company (1959), Sam Pig Goes to the Seaside (1960)
Constance Wickham Countryside Folk (1938)
Also a number of books for Blackie.

Reference: Fisher p.319

Richard Pitt Kennedy (b. 1910)

Works as Richard Kennedy. Born in Cambridge. Educated at Marlborough School, left at the age of 16 and entered the Hogarth Press as a publisher's apprentice under Leonard and Virginia Woolf. He subsequently worked for a silkscreen

A.E. Kennedy. 'Then Sam picked up a whistle' from *Sam Pig Goes to Market* by Alison Uttley (Faber, 1941).

printer in an advertising agency, and as an illustrator of jokes for *Strang's Weekly News*. He studied art briefly at the Central School for Arts and Crafts and the Regent Street Polytechnic in London (1932-33). He illustrated his first book while serving in the Royal Air Force during World War II. Since then he has become a prolific illustrator, mainly of children's books. His work has included 42 books for backward readers published by Benn, and a number of stills for the BBC *Jackanory* series. Recently he has worked for the Whittington Press. He draws mainly in pen and ink (often with wash) in a free sketchy style that reflects his admiration for the drawings of Henri Gaudier-Brzeska. He also works in full colour, and has published an edition of etchings *Lovers and Friends* (1977).[Q]

Books illustrated include:
H. Acker Lee Natoni: Young Navajo (1962)
Marigold Armitage A Long Way to Go (1973)
Iftikhar Azmi The Garden of the Night (1977)
Margaret Joyce Baker Castaway Christmas (1963), Cut Off from Crumpets (1964), Home from the Hill (1968)
J.M. Barrie Peter Pan (1967)
Paul Berna The Horse Without a Head (1958)
Paul Biegel The Twelve Robbers (1974)
Keith Bosley Tales from the Long Lakes (1966)
Agnes Campbell New Tales from Old (1956)
Joan E. Clapton Up, Down and Sideways (1946)
Pauline Clarke The White Elephant (1952)
Helen Cresswell Bluebirds over Pit Row (1972), Roof Fall! (1972)
A.J. Dawson Finn the Wolfhound (1964)
Walter de la Mare Poems and Stories (1952)
Eilis Dillon The Lost Island (1952), The San Sebastian (1953), The House on the Shore (1955), The Island of Horses (1956), The Singing Cave (1959), The Fort of Gold (1961), The Coriander (1963), A Family of Foxes (1964), The Sea Wall (1965), The Lion Cub (1966), The Road to Dunmore (1966), The Cruise of the Santa Maria (1967), The Key (1967), The Seals (1968), Under the Orange Grove (1968), A Herd of Deer (1969), The King's Room (1970), Living in Imperial Rome (1974)
Monica Edwards Under the Rose (1968)
Eleanor Farjeon Martin Pippin in the Apple Orchard (1952)
Elizabeth Goudge I Saw Three Ships (1969)

Richard Kennedy. From *A Long Way to Go* by Marigold Armitage (Faber & Faber, 1973).

René Guillot The Fantastic Brother (1961), Riders of the Wind (1961)
Aaron Judah God and the Sourpuss (1959)
Richard Kennedy A Boy at the Hogarth Press (1972), A Parcel of Time (1977)
Clive King 22 Letters (1966), Snakes and Snakes (1975)
Astrid Lindgren Pippi Goes Abroad (1957), Pippi in the South Seas (1957), Pippi Longstockings (1957)
Trevor Maine Blue Veil and Black and Gold (1961)
Manfred Michael Timpetill (1951)
Beverley Nichols The Stream that Stood Still (1948)
Baroness Orczy The Scarlet Pimpernel (1961)
Richard Parker A Valley Full of Pipers (1962), Perversity of Pipers (1964)
Stephanie Plowman Sixteen Sail in Aboukir Bay (1956)
James Reeves The Road to a Kingdom (1965)
Meta Mayne Reid Carrigmore Castle (1954), Tiffany and the Swallow Rhyme (1956), The Cuckoo at Coonean (1956), Strangers at Carrigmore (1958), Sandy and the Hollow Book (1961), The Tombermillin Oracle (1958)
David Severn Drumbeats (1953)
Noel Streatfeild Wintle's Wonders (1957)
Elizabeth Stucley The Secret Pony (1950)
Rosemary Sutcliff Simon (1953), Outcast (1955)
Joan Tate Wild Martin and the Crow (1967)
Geoffrey Trease No Boats on Bannermore (1949), Under Black Banner (1950), Black Banner Players
Henry Treece Desperate Journey (1954), Ask for King Billy (1955), Hunter Hunted (1957)

Periodical: Strang's Weekly News

References: Crouch; Eyre; Fisher pp.205, 275; ICB 2, 3, 4; Ryder; Wa (1980); Richard Kennedy *A Boy at the Hogarth Press* (Penguin 1972), *A Parcel of Time* (Whittington Press 1977)

Eric Henri Kennington (1888-1960)

Worked as Eric Kennington. Born in Chelsea, London, son of painter Thomas Benjamin Kennington. Studied at St Paul's Art School, Lambeth School of Art (1905-07) and the City and Guilds School. He had little success as a black and white illustrator and took up portraiture. Invalided out of the army (1915), he was appointed an Official War Artist. In 1922, he travelled for five months with T.E. Lawrence to Cairo, Jerusalem, Beirut and Damascus for five months making portrait studies of Arabs later used to illustrate *The Seven Pillars of Wisdom* (1926). On his return, he took up sculpture and executed a number of public commissions (e.g. war memorial in Battersea Park and sculptures at the Shakespeare Memorial Theatre, Stratford-on-Avon). He was again appointed an Official War Artist in World War II, by which time he was working mainly in pastel or crayon. Most of his book illustrations consisted of portrait drawings in these media, but for *The Powers of Light* (1932) he produced some remarkable line drawings printed over colour: expressionist in feeling and drawn with a free, varied line, they were very different in feeling from his straightforward portraits. Elected ARA (1951), RA (1959).

Books illustrated include:
B.L. Bowhay Caspar (frontis 1930)
John Brophy Britain's Home Guard (1945)
Eric Kennington Tanks and Tank Folk (1943)
T.E. Lawrence The Seven Pillars of Wisdom (1926), Revolt in the Desert (with others, 1927)

Eric Kennington. 'Coast defence searchlight: Lancashire Home Guard' from *Britain's Home Guard* by John Brophy (Harrap, 1945).

Naomi Mitchison The Powers of Light (1932)
The Legion Book (with others, 1925)

References: Bénézit; Chamot, Farr & Butlin; DNB (1951-60); Johnson & Greutzner; Phaidon; Thieme & Becker; Vollmer and supp; Waters; *Apollo* 3 (1926); *Drawing and Design* 9 (January 1921); *The Studio* 94 (1927), 112 (1936), 133 (1947); C. Dodgson and C.E. Montague (intro) *British Artists at the Front* (Country Life/George Newnes 1918)

Sarah Kensington (b. 1949)

Born in Pinner, Middlesex. Studied at a secretarial school in London and then at Harrow School of Art. Freelance illustrator in pencil, often with superimposed colour washes, in a style that frequently approaches photo-realism.

Books illustrated include:
H. Gautier and G. Braughton Let's Go (1975)
Penny Hughes Kelligant Pig and Other Stories (1979)
Richard Mabey Street Flowers (1976)
David McKay Helping (1973)
Mary Elwyn Patchett The Brumby (1974)
Geoffrey Smith Sure and Simple Gardening (1976)

Reference: ICB 4

James Macara Kenward (b. 1908)

Born in New Eltham, Kent, son of a Lloyds insurance broker. He worked at Lloyds (c.1925-28) and from then on freelance as writer, artist and illustrator. Studied at Brighton College of Art. Gunner in the Royal Artillery during World War II; now a pacifist. He has illustrated a number of his own books with delicate drawings in various combinations of pen, pencil, crayon and wash.

Books illustrated include:
James Kenward The Roof Tree (1938), Prince Foamytail or Professor Tovey's Invention (1946), The Poor Author (1959), The Market Train Mystery (1960), The Story of the Poor Author and Some of the Stories that he had told (1960)

Reference: Contemporary Authors

William Kermode (active 1930s)

Studied at the Grosvenor School of Modern Art under Iain Macnab*; then worked as a book and commercial illustrator. His best book illustrations consist of wood and lino cuts executed in a deliberately crude and archaic manner, which are possibly influenced by the woodcuts of the German *Die Brücke* group (1905-15). He used a broad, simplified line with striking black and white contrasts that are particularly effective in *The Specialist*

William Kermode. 'Gentlemen, you are face to face with the champion privy builder of Sangamon County' from *The Specialist* by Charles Sale (Putnam, New York, 1930).

—the hilarious vernacular monologue of a privy-builder—and in *The Patriot's Progress*, the experiences of a private soldier in World War I, of which F.J. Harvey Darton wrote 'the woodcuts convey strength, endurance, monotony, the grim and bloody soil of the trenches...' (*Modern Book Illustration in Great Britain and America*); however, David Bland described them as linocuts and considered that they were far too heavy for the page.

Books illustrated include:
F.B. Austin Tomorrow (1930)
H.F.G. Heard The Emergence of Man (1931)
M. Il'in Moscow Has a Plan (1931)
William Kermode Drawing on a Scraperboard for Beginners (1936)
Charles Sale The Specialist (1930)
S.T. Warner A Moral Ending and Other Stories (frontis 1931)
Henry Williamson The Patriot's Progress (1930)

Periodicals: The Artist, The London Mercury, Radio Times, The Woodcut

References: Bland; *The Artist* 13 (1937); *The Studio* special (Winter 1931); F.J. Harvey Darton *Modern Book Illustration in Great Britain and America*

Henry Wright Kerr (1857-1936)

Born in Edinburgh. Studied in Dundee and at the Royal Society of Arts School. Portrait painter, working in Scotland and Holland. His book illustrations consist of portrait and figure studies in watercolour. Elected ARSA (1893), RSA (1909), RSW (1899), RSA (1909).

Books illustrated include:
George Birmingham The Lighter Side of Irish Life (1911)
John Galt Annals of the Parish (1910), The Last of the Lairds (1926)
Edward B. Ramsay Reminiscences of Scottish Life and Character (1909)

References: Bénézit; Guichard; Houfe; Johnson & Greutzner; Mallalieu; Vollmer; Waters; C. Wood

Mary M. Kessell (b. 1914)

Born in London. Studied at Clapham School of Art (1935-37) and at the Central School of Arts and Crafts (1937-39) in London. Official War Artist, working in Germany (1945). Lecturer in drawing at the London School of Printing (from 1957). Muralist (e.g. at Old Westminster Hospital and Imperial Chemical House, Millbank), designer and illustrator in freely drawn outline, sometimes with wash.

Books illustrated include:
Mary Kessell A Visit to India for Oxfam (1969)
Thomas Moult (ed) Best Poems of 1937 (1938)
Osbert Sitwell Mrs Kimber (1937)
Ivan Turgenev A Sportsman's Notebook (1959)

References: Chamot, Farr & Butlin; Vollmer; Waters; Mary Kessell *Experiment in Embroidery Design* (Needlework Development Scheme 1950)

Joan Kiddell-Monroe (1908-72)

Born Clacton-on-Sea. Studied at Willesden and Chelsea Schools of Art. Worked initially in an

Joan Kiddell-Monroe. 'Raoul of Cambrai' from *French Legends, Tales & Fairy Stories* retold by Barbara Léonie Picard (Oxford University Press, 1955).

advertising studio and then turned freelance. In 1936, she married Webster Murray, illustrator for *The Tatler* and *The Sketch* and portrait painter. From 1944, she concentrated on book illustration. She travelled in Africa during the 1950s, and eventually settled in Mallorca. Joan Kiddell-Monroe was one of the outstanding professional illustrators of her generation, and her drawings combined a fluent, well-modulated line with a rhythmic and elegant decorative sense. She had a keen eye for detail, and this contributed to her ability to adapt her style in sympathy with the varied sources and subjects of her texts. Her versatility is clearly shown in the *Oxford Myths and Legends* series —folk tales collected from many parts of the world. She was particularly fond of drawing animals, and often included them in her designs. She worked mainly in black and white, sometimes with one added colour, and sometimes with the full colour range. [Q]

Books illustrated include:
Kathleen Arnott African Myths and Legends (1962)

Kitty Barne The Easter Holidays (1935)
Cyril Birch Chinese Myths and Fantasies (1961)
Pearl S. Buck The Water-Buffalo Children (1945), The Dragon Fish (1946)
Hester Burton The Great Gale (1960)
Nada Curcija-Prodanovic Yugoslav Folk-Tales (1957)
F. Fraser Darling Sandy the Red Deer (1950)
E. Dixon (ed) Fairy Tales from the Arabian Nights (1951)
Charles Downing Russian Tales and Legends (1956)
E. Fenton Sher, Lord of the Jungle (1962)
Reginald Forbes-Watson Ambari! (1952), Shifta! (1954)
Robert Graves Myths of Ancient Greece (1961)
J.E.B. Gray Indian Tales and Legends (1961)
Roger Lancelyn Green A Book of Myths (1965)
Frederick Grice The Moving Finger (1962)
Gwyn Jones Welsh Legends and Folk-Tales (1955), Scandinavian Legends and Folk-Tales (1956)
Joan Kiddell-Monroe In His Little Black Waistcoat (1939), In His Little Black Waistcoat to China (1940), Ingulabi (1943), Little Skunk (1943), Wau-Wau, the Ape (1947), In His Little Black Waistcoat to India (1948), In His Little Black Waistcoat in Tibet (1949)
Charles Kingsley The Heroes (1963)
Andrew Lang Adventures of Odysseus (1962)
Muriel Levy The Circus (1948)
Henry Longfellow Song of Hiawatha (1960)
Patricia Lynch Long Ears (1943), The Boy at the Swinging Lantern (1952), Delia Daly of Galloping Green (1953), Orla of Burren (1954), The Twisted Key (1964)
Helen and William McAlpine Japanese Tales and Legends (1958)
D. Martin Munya the Lion (1946)
Fritz Müller-Guggenbühl Swiss-Alpine Fairy-Tales (1958)
Ogden Nash Girls are Silly (1964)
Mary Norton The Magic Bed-Knob (1945)
Barbara Leonie Picard The Odyssey of Homer (1952), Tales of the Norse Gods and Heroes (1953), French Legends, Tales and Fairy Stories (1955), German Hero-Sagas and Folk-Tales (1958), The Iliad of Homer (1960)
James Reeves English Fables and Fairy Stories (1954)
Malcolm Saville All Summer Through (1951), Christmas at Nettleford (1953), Spring Comes to Nettleford (1954), The Secret of Buzzard Scar (1955)
David Severn Rick Afire! (1942), A Cabin for Crusoe (1943), Waggon for Five (1944), A Hermit in the Hills (1945), Forest Holiday (1946), Ponies and Poachers (1947), The Cruise of the 'Maiden Castle' (1948), Treasure for Three (1949), Crazy Castle (1951), Burglars and Bandicoots (1952)
Philip M. Sherlock West Indian Folk-Tales (1966)
N.B. Taylor The Aeneid of Virgil (1961)
Lorna Wood The People in the Garden (1954), Rescue by Broomstick (1954), The Hag Calls for Help (1959), Seven-League Ballet Shoes (1959), Hags on Holiday (1960), Hag in the Castle (1962), Hags by Starlight (1970)

References: Contemporary Authors; Crouch; Doyle CL; Eyre; Fisher p.95; ICB 2, 3

Jessie Marion King (c. 1875-1949)

Married name: Mrs E. A. Taylor. Usually worked as Jessie M. King. Studied at Glasgow School of Art where she was influenced by Charles Rennie Mackintosh and his circle. Visited France and Italy on a travelling scholarship and was particularly impressed by Botticelli's drawings in the Uffizi. In 1898, her work attracted the attention of *The Studio* and became widely known through its pages. She taught book decoration at the Glasgow School of Art (1902), and in the same year, won a gold medal for book design at the Turin International Exhibition of Modern Decorative Art. During the following years she worked as a muralist, designer of fabric, jewellery and costume, and as a book illustrator and book cover designer. She moved to Paris in 1911, and for the next two years ran the Shealing Atelier for Fine Art with her husband, artist Ernest Archibald Taylor. While in Paris, she was inspired by the Russian Ballet to experiment with colour; after her return to Scotland (1913), she took up pictorial batik, and gradually devoted less time to illustration. She eventually settled at Kircudbright. Her work, while bearing the imprint of the Glasgow school, was extremely individual. John Russell Taylor, who considered her work worthy of comparison with that of Aubrey Beardsley and Charles Ricketts*, wrote, 'the image she conjures up of pale ladies festooned in stars and attended by flights of birds, of wan haloed knights, lost in reverie and drifting through wispy landscapes of faint transfigured trees and insubstantial dream castles of the mind, is not quite like anything else in art, and once entered, never wholly escaped from.' She worked with a delicate line in pen and ink, sometimes with colour washes. Curiously, she never really overcame the problems of assimilating written titles into her pictorial designs, and her hand drawn lettering often strikes a discordant note. Elected ASWA (1925).

Jessie M. King. From *The Defence of Guenevere* by William Morris (John Lane, 1904).

HE·DID·NOT·HEAR·HER·COMING·AS·HE·LAY·

Books illustrated include:
E. Archambeau The Book of Bridges (1911)
George Buchanan Jephtha (1902)
Churton Cairns Shelley (1968)
L. Cross The Book of Old Sundials and Their Mottoes (1914)
Sebastian Evans (trans) The High History of the Holy Graal (1903)
James Hogg Kilmeny (1912), Songs of the Ettrick Shepherd (1912)
John Keats Isabella or the Pot of Basil (1914)
Jessie M. King Budding Life. A Book of Drawings (1906), Budding
   Life. A Book of Flowers (1908), Dwellings of an Old World Town
   (1909), The Grey City of the North (1910), The City of the West
   (1911), The Little White Town of Never-Weary (1917), How
   Cinderella Was Able to Go to the Ball (1924), Kircudbright, a Royal
   Borough (1934)
Charles Kingsley The Heroes of Greek Fairy Tales (1907)
Rudyard Kipling L'Habitation Forcée (1921), The Jungle Book (nd)
John Milton Comus (1906)
William Morris The Defence of Guenevere and other poems (1904)
Oscar Wilde A House of Pomegranates (1915)
W.B. Yeats Spenser (1908)
Good King Wenceslas. A Carol (1919)
Our Trees and How to Know Them (1908)

Periodical: The Studio

References: Bénézit; Houfe; Johnson; Johnson & Greutzner;
Mallalieu; Peppin; Ray; Taylor; Thieme & Becker; Vollmer; Waters;
C. Wood; *The Studio* 15 (1889) p.278, 26 (1902), 36 (1905-06) p.241, 60
(1914), special (1899-1900, 1900-01, 1911, Autumn 1914); James L.
Caw *Scottish Painting Past and Present* (T.C. & E.C. Jack 1908),
Cordelia Oliver *Jessie M. King* (Scottish Arts Council 1971); Walter
Shaw Sparrow *Women Painters of the World* (Hodder & Stoughton
1905)

Ronald Edward King (b. 1932)

Works as Ron King and Ronald King. Born in
Sao Paulo, Brazil, where he spent his childhood.

Ronald King. Serigraph from *Macbeth* by
William Shakespeare (Circle Press, 1970).

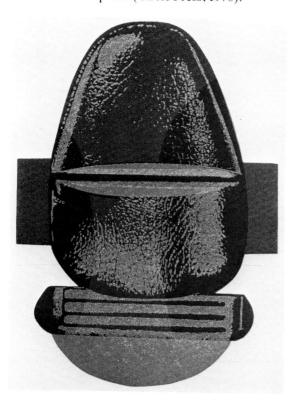

Educated at Ardingly College, Sussex (1946-51)
and studied at Chelsea School of Art (1951-55);
was awarded a Biddulph Painting Scholarship
(1954-55). Painter, printmaker (etching, silk
screen and lithography) and letterpress printer.
Art assistant and art editor for Maclean Hunter
publications, Canada (1956-60). Lecturer at
Farnham School of Art (1960-64). Founded and
runs the Circle Press, Guildford, Surrey (since
1967), publishing classic and contemporary texts
in limited editions, illustrated with autographic
prints (especially screen prints). All of his books
have been published in limited editions by the
Circle Press. [Q]

Books illustrated include:
Geoffrey Chaucer The Prologue
Anthony Conran Claim, Claim, Claim (1969)
Roy Fisher Neighbours we'll not Part Tonight (1957), Bluebeard's
   Castle (1972), Scenes from the Alphabet (1978)
Keith Please Chesil Bank South (1975)
William Shakespeare Macbeth (Arden version 1970), Antony and
   Cleopatra (nd)
The Song of Solomon (King James version 1969)

Reference: *Arts Review* (9th June 1978)

John Lockwood Kipling (1837-1911)

Studied art at the South Kensington Schools.
Teacher of architectural sculpture at the Bombay
School of Art. He later became Principal of the
Mayo School of Art in Lahore and Curator of the
Central Museum (1975-93). Author and illustrator in pen and ink of *Beast and Man in India*,
although he became more widely known as the
illustrator of his son Rudyard Kipling's* *Jungle
Books* in pen and ink and halftone, and of *Kim*
and *Valmiki* with modelled reliefs in clay, photo-
graphed and reproduced by the halftone process.

Books illustrated include:
John L. Kipling Beast and Man in India (1891)
Rudyard Kipling The Jungle Book (with W.H. Drake, 1894), The
   Second Jungle Book (with others, 1895), Kim (1901)
Valmiki The Iliad of the East (1908)

Periodical: Cassell's Magazine

References: Houfe; Mallalieu; Waters 2; *The Times* (obituary 30th
January 1911)

Joseph Rudyard Kipling (1865-1936)

Worked as Rudyard Kipling. Son of John Lock-
wood Kipling* and a celebrated writer. His highly
imaginative black and white illustrations for *The
Just So Stories for Little Children* are an indispen-
sable element in these now classic tales.

Book illustrated:
Rudyard Kipling Just So Stories for Little Children (1902)

References: Bénézit; DNB (1901-50); Doyle CL; Houfe; Kirkpatrick;
Peppin; *The Studio* special (Autumn 1933); Lord Birkenhead *Rudyard
Kipling* (Weidenfeld & Nicolson 1978); C.H. Brown *Rudyard Kipling*
(Hamish Hamilton 1945); C.E. Carrington *Rudyard Kipling*

Rudyard Kipling. 'The Animal that came out of the sea and ate up all the food that Suleiman-bin-Daoud had made ready for all the animals in all the world' from *Just So Stories* (Macmillan, 1902).

(Macmillan 1955); R. Lancelyn Green *Kipling and the Children* (Elek 1965); Holbrook Jackson *The 1890s* (Grant Richards 1913); J.C. Kernahan *Nothing Quite Like Kipling Had Happened Before!* (Epworth Press 1944); J.McG. Stewart *Rudyard Kipling: A Bibliographical Catalogue* (OUP 1960); Rosemary Sutcliff *Rudyard Kipling* (Bodley Head 1960)

Anne Knight (b. 1946)

Born in Sussex. Studied at Brighton College of Art and St Martin's School of Art. Illustrator of children's books in pen, pencil and sometimes full colour.

Books illustrated include:
Jane Counsel Mostly Timothy (1971)
Helen Cresswell The Beetle Hunt (1973)
Susan Dickinson Stories for Bedtime (1975)
E.C. Ellis Mr and Mrs Vinegar (1971)
Marie Hynds The Fire Bell (1975)
Felicia Law Red (1976)
Brian Lee Late Home (1976)

Reference: ICB 4

David Knight (1923-82)

Born Coulsdon, Surrey. Studied at Wimbledon School of Art under E.J. Sullivan. From 1948 he worked as a freelance illustrator of books, magazines, advertisements, and as an architectural draughtsman; his linear pen and ink drawings show a concern for spatial construction and depth. R.D. Usherwood commented: 'Knight has a gift for suggesting the atmosphere of architecture and in particular that charm of the irregularity of contrasting elements which in the 18th century they called 'sharawaggi' (*Drawing for the Radio Times* 1961). He also illustrated the BBC series of pamphlets 'French for Schools'. [Q]

Books illustrated include:
Giovanni Arpino The Novice (1950)
Anne Barrett Songberd's Grove (1957)
Sarah Churchill A Thread in the Tapestry (c.1960)
S. Cunningham-Brown Crowded Hour (1980)
P. Elek This Other London (1951)
Eleanor Farjeon Mrs Malone (1950)
Paul Gallico The Small Miracle (1951)
A.P. Herbert The Singing Swan (1970)
L. Lafitte Eau Trouble (1962)
Elizabeth Macdonald The Incredible Magic Plant (1975)
O.S. Manders Mrs Manders' Cookbook (1968)
William Mayne Earthfasts (1973)
Lawrence Meynell The Young Architect (1958)
Roger W. Pilkington Boats Overland (1962), Small Boat to Bavaria (1962)
John Pudney The Smallest Room (1955)
Jo Rice Mortimer Also (1970), The Day the Queen was Crowned (1979)
Cecil Roberts Wine is the Horizon (c.1960)
Philip Rush That Fool of a Priest (1970)

David Knight. 'It was as though they had managed to transfer themselves from one world into another, entirely, different; out of a slummy town and into the country' from *Songberd's Grove* by Anne Barrett (1957).

Reginald L. Knowles. 'Down came the Trolls' from *Norse Fairy Tales* by P.C. Asbjörnsen and J.I. Moe, selected and adapted by Sir George Dasent (S.T. Freemantle, 1910).

Roger Vailland The Law (1958)
Hugh Walpole Mr Perrin and Mr Traill (1964)
Also the Pepe books (Faber), Don Quixote (Faber), The Small Boat series (Macmillan)

Periodicals: Good Housekeeping, Harper's Bazaar, House and Garden, Radio Times

References: Jacques; Ryder; Usherwood; Wa (1972)

Horace J. Knowles (active 1908-48)

His style is very similar to that of his brother, Reginald Knowles* with whom he sometimes collaborated. He drew firmly, usually in pen and ink and had a strong feeling for the whole page design.

Books illustrated include:
P.C. Asbjörnsen and J.I. Moe Norse Fairy Tales (with R. Knowles*, 1910)
A.M. Buckton Eager Heart (1931)
B. Buxton My First Book of Prayers (1932)
A.G. Chant The Legend of Glastonbury (1948)
Lee Holme Legends from Fairy Land (with R. Knowles, 1908)
J.H.L. Hunt The Months (1936)
Horace Knowles Peeps into Fairyland (1924), Countryside Treasures (1046)

The Beacon Books (1932)

Periodical: Cassell's Children's Annual

Reference: Houfe

Reginald Lionel Knowles (active 1905-49)

Best known as the designer for Dent's Everyman Series from 1905, for which he used distinctive double facing title pages heavily bordered with twining patterns and incorporated lettering. A different design was commissioned for each of the thirteen groups of work published. He also designed the endpapers with the Everyman quotation (used for the whole series) as well as the spine designs and lettering. His work reflects the influence of William Morris, and the style of the Arts and Crafts Movement. His book illustrations have a sense of fantasy, and a very strong feeling for page design. Sometimes he collaborated with his brother Horace J. Knowles*.

Books illustrated include:
P.C. Asbjornsen and J.I. Moe Norse Fairy Tales (with H. Knowles, 1910)
W.G. Brown My River and Some Other Waters (1947), Angler's Almanac (1949)
Marie de France Old World Love Stories (1913)
Holme Lee Legends from Fairy Land (with H. Knowles, 1908)

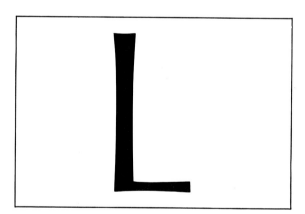

Lynton Harold Lamb (1907-77)

Worked as Lynton Lamb. Born in India; spent his childhood in London. Educated at Kingswood School, Bath. Worked in an office for two years before studying at the Central School of Arts and Crafts (1927-30) where he studied painting under Bernard Meninsky*, wood engraving and book illustration under Noel Rooke*, and lithography under A.S. Hartrick*. He then joined the publishing side of the Oxford University Press in London, with the job of redesigning Bible and prayer book bindings, returning to the Central School for a few hours each week to study bookbinding under Douglas Cockerell. He succeeded

Lynton Lamb. Frontispiece: 'There were a great many crossing lines at the station' from *The Railway Children* by E. Nesbit (Benn, 1957).

Cockerell as part-time lecturer in the early 1930s and continued until the outbreak of war in 1939. During World War II he served with the Royal Engineers, working in camouflage. Lecturer at the Slade School of Fine Art (1950-71) and visiting lecturer at the Royal College of Art (1956-70). He worked as a painter, lithographer and illustrator, and designed advertisements, bookplates, postage stamps and book bindings (notably the Bible used at the coronation of Elizabeth II). His early book illustrations consisted of wood engravings for the Shakespeare Head, Fulcrum and Golden Cockerel Presses, but after the war he used pen and ink or, less frequently, lithography for his illustrative work. In his pen and ink drawings, the line was often broken into a series of dots and strokes, suggesting the play of light and giving the images a painterly and sometimes impressionist appearance. In both pen drawings and lithographs, he often drew directly on to the paper or plate without preparatory sketches. At the same time, he was meticulous in his historical research and—particularly in his pen drawings—created evocations of

the past that were both atmospheric and convincing. He was appointed a Royal Designer for Industry (1974). He lived at Sanden in Essex. Member London Group (1935); SWE, FRSA (1953), RDI (1974).

Books illustrated include:
Lydia Avilov Chekhov in my Life (1950)
H.E. Bates A German Idyll (1932)
William Bligh Log of the 'Bounty' (1937)
Henri Bosco The Boy and the River (1956), The Fox and the Island (1958), Barboche (1959)
Charlotte Brontë Jane Eyre (1955)
Angela Bull Friend with a Secret (1965)
Ivor Brown Winter in London (1951)
Wilkie Collins The Woman in White (1956), The Moonstone (1963)
Charles Dickens Hard Times (1959)
George Eliot Silas Marner (1953)
C.S. Emden Gilbert White in his Village (1956), Poets in their Letters (1959)
Ida Gundy Staying with the Aunts (1963)
Philip Gosse An Apple a Day (1948)
Thomas Hardy Our Exploits at West Poley (1952)
James Hawker A Victorian Poacher (1961)
Robert Herrick The Music of the Feast (1968)
Thea Holme The Carlyles at Home (1965)
Henry James Washington Square (1963)
Lynton Lamb County Town Backs and Fronts in Kennelsford (1950), Cat's Tales (1959)
William Mayne The Member for the Marsh (1956), A Grass Rope (1957), The Twelve Dancers (1962), Words and Music (1963)
E. Nesbit The Railway Children (1957)
Arnold Palmer Moveable Feasts (1952)
D. Parry Jones Welsh Country Characters (1952)
Plato Lysis (1930)
James Reeves The Strange Light (1964)
William Sansom Lord Love Us (1954)
Siegfried Sassoon The Memoirs of a Fox-Hunting Man (1971), The Memoirs of an Infantry Officer (1974)
David Severn Foxy Boy (1959)
Christopher Smart A Song to David (1965)
B.A. Smith Dean Church (1958)
Stephen Spender Sirmione Peninsula (1954)
George W. Stonier Round London with the Unicorn (1951)
Flora Thompson Lark Rise to Candleford (1939), Still Guides the Stream (1948)
Anthony Trollope Can You Forgive Her? (1948), The Two Heroines of Plumpington (1953)
Thomas Walker Aristology, or the Art of Dining (1965)
Sir Hugh Walpole The Apple Trees (1932)
Isaak Walton The Compleat Angler (1949)
H.G. Wells Tono-bungay (1960)
The Kitchen Garden in Harvest, vol 2 (1968)
Queen Victoria at Windsor and Balmoral (1959)
The Quiet Spirit (1946)

Periodicals: Chambers Journal, The Field, Radio Times, Signature

References: Balston EWE; Bland; Driver; Garrett BWE, HBWE; Gilmour; ICB 2, 3; Jacques; Ryder; Usherwood; Wa (1977); WaG; Waters; *Alphabet & Image* 5 (1947); John Lewis and John Brinkley *Graphic Design* (Routledge 1954); George Mackie *Lynton Lamb, Illustrator* (Scolar Press 1979); Christopher Sandford *Bibliography of the Golden Cockerel Press* (Dawson 1975)

H.G.C. Marsh Lambert
(active c.1919-30)

Illustrator and writer of stories for young children, particularly in 'The Shakespeare series' published by Allday Ltd. She also worked for Blackie and Ward Lock. She worked in pen and ink outline, usually colour, in a characteristically 1920s style with echoes of Millicent Sowerby*, Agnes Richardson and Mabel Lucie Attwell*.

H.G.C. Marsh Lambert. From *Rob and Rab* in *The Playbox Annual* (1921).

Books illustrated include:

H.G.C. Marsh Lambert Red Riding Hood, Baby Bunch, Goldilocks and the Three Bears (all 1920); The 'Tiny Elf' series: The Holly Bush Elf, Bunny Boy, Robin Red, Ann and the Goblins, Cross Patch, Mistress May and Little Midget (Shakespeare series, 1921); The Jumble Book no 1, The Jumble Book no 2 (Shakespeare series, 1921); Baby Bunting's Big Book (1924), Baby Bunting's Big Play Book (1925), Baby Bunting's Book of Games (1925), Baby Bunting's Book of Toys (1925), Baby Bunting's Big Bedtime Book (1925), Bo-Peep's Big Nursery Story Book, Little Bo-Peep's Animal Story Book, Little Bo-Peep's Simple Story Book (all 1927); Jack and Jill's Bedtime Story Book, Jack and Jill's Fireside Story Book, Jack and Jill's Big Story Book (all with others, 1928); The Bonnie Big Story Book (with others, 1929), Ring O' Roses Story Book (with others, 1929), The Rock-a-Bye Story Book (with others, 1929), The Nuts an' May Story Book (with others, 1930), The Ding Dong Bell Story Book (with others, 1930), The Big Cosy Corner Story Book (with others, 1930); Follow the Dot Books: By the Sea (1927), More Rhymes and Riddles (1927), Easy Drawing Book (1927), The Three Bears (1928), Humpty Dumpty (1928), Jack and the Beanstalk (1929), Cinderella (1929)

Periodicals: Cassell's Annual, Playbox Annual

Nigel Lambourne (b. 1919)

Born in London. Studied at the Central School of Arts and Crafts and at the Royal College of Art, where he gained a diploma in engraving. Army service during World War II. Senior Lecturer in graphics at St Martin's School of Art (from 1948) and at Leicester Polytechnic and University (from 1971). Graphic artist, painter and printmaker. Figures, drawn naturalistically in an animated, sketchy style, play an important part in his illustrations. He works in chalk and pen, pastel and

lithography, and on copper plates. Published mainly by the Folio Society. Lives in Leicestershire. Elected RBA (1947).

Books illustrated include:

Anton Chekhov Short Stories (1974)
Guy de Maupassant Short Stories (1961)
Daniel Defoe Moll Flanders (1954)
Fyodor Dostoyevsky Brothers Karamazov (1964)
Franz Kafka (translation by Willa and Edwin Muir) The Trial (1967)
Nigel Lambourne People in Action (1961)
Liam O'Flaherty The Informer (1961)
Laurence Sterne A Sentimental Journey (1949)
Virgil (trans. K.R. Mackenzie) The Georgics (1969)

References: Johnson & Greutzner; Vollmer; Wa (1980); Waters; *The Studio* 148 (1954)

Osbert Lancaster (b. 1908)

Born in London, son of a publisher. Educated at Charterhouse and Lincoln College, Oxford. Studied art at the Byam Shaw School (1925-26), the Ruskin School of Drawing, Oxford (1929-30) and the Slade School of Fine Art (1931-32); also stage design under Victor Polunin. During World War II, he served with the News Department of the

Nigel Lambourne. Frontispiece from Virgil's *The Georgics* translated by K.R. Mackenzie (1969).

Osbert Lancaster. 'English Renaissance' from his *Pillar to Post* (John Murray, 1938).

Foreign Office, and at the Embassy in Athens. He works as a writer, theatrical designer and painter, book illustrator and cartoonist. Today he is widely known for his 'Pocket Cartoons' in the *Daily Express*, but his importance as an illustrator dates from the 1930s when he established his reputation with his own witty and authoritative books on architecture and design. Here, in lively pen and ink outline, he depicts buildings and interiors with an unerring instinct for the minutiae of stylistic change, and recreates with irrepressible humour the modes of existence of the original inhabitants. Edward Lucie-Smith has written, 'he has a strong claim to be considered the most accurate recorder of English life, at least in pictures, now living' (*Art and Artists* April 1980). He is also adept at stylistic pastiche. Awarded CBE (1953).

Books illustrated include:
Max Beerbohm Zuleika Dobson (1975)
N. Dennis An Essay on Malta (1972)
V. Graham Say Please (1951)
S. Lambert London Night and Day (1951)
Osbert Lancaster Our Sovereigns (1936), Progress at Pelvis Bay (1936), Pillar to Post (1938), Homes, Sweet Homes (1939), Classical Landscape with Figures (1947), Saracen's Head (1948), Drayneflete Revealed (1949), Façades and Faces (1950), Studies from Life

(1954), Tableaux Vivants (1955), Private Views (1956), The Year of the Comet (1957), Here, of all Places! (1959), With an Eye to the Future (1967), Temporary Diversions (1968), Sailing to Byzantium (1969), Recorded Live (1970), Meaningful Confrontations (1971), Theatre in the Flat (1972), The Littlehampton Bequest (1973), Scene Changes (1978)
Nancy Mitford The Water Beetle (1962), *(ed)*Noblesse Oblige (1973)
C.N. Parkinson Parkinson's Law for the Pursuit of Progress (1958), In-Laws and Outlaws (1962), The Law and the Profits (1965)
Nancy Quenell The Epicure's Anthology (1936)
Saki Short Stories (1976), The Unbearable Bassington (1978)
Anne Scott-James The Pleasure Garden (1977)

Periodicals: Daily Express, Isis, Scottish Country Life, The Weekend Review

References: Bénézit; Chamot, Farr & Butlin; ICB 2; Phaidon; Vollmer; Wa (1934); WaG; Waters; *Art and Artists* (April 1980); Osbert Lancaster *All Done From Memory* (John Murray 1963)

Eveline Lance (active 1891-1909)

Landscape painter and children's illustrator for The Religious Tract Society and Ernest Nister. *Happy Playmates* is a prime example of the lavish but slightly 'downmarket' popular sentimental book favoured by Nister (also Raphael Tuck) during the 1890s, in which the technical advances of Bavarian lithographic printers were used for 'chocolate-box' images in colour and sepia half-tone. However, her illustrations for the Religious Tract Society (reproduced by line block and 'process') were relatively restrained and unexceptional examples of their type.

Books illustrated include:
Evelyn Everett-Green Short Tales from Storyland (1902)
Eveline Lance Holiday Friends (1901), Happy Playtimes (1901)
Amy Le Feuvre A Puzzling Pair (1898), Bulbs and Blossoms (1898), His Birthday (1909)
My Seaside Story Book (with others, nd)

Reference: Johnson & Greutzner

David Langdon (b. 1914)

Born in London. Studied at the London School of Economics. Squadron leader in the Royal Air Force during World War II; travelled extensively in Europe, America and the Middle East. Regular contributor to *Punch* since 1937, and a member of the *Punch* 'table'; cartoonist for Mirror Group newspapers since 1948, and contributor to the *New Yorker* since 1957. He works in brush and ink for black and white cartoons, and in line and gouache for portrait caricatures. His easily recognised graphic shorthand has remained remarkably consistent throughout his career. Elected FRSA and FSIA.[Q]

Books illustrated include:
Basil Boothroyd Let's Move House (1977)
Cyril H.W. Jackson It's a Piece of Cake (1943)
George Mikes Little Cabbages (1955), The Best of Mikes (with Nicholas Bentley, 1962), Italy for Beginners (nd), Shakespeare and Myself (nd), Über Alles (nd)
Ted Ray My Slice of Life (nd)
Dennis Rooke Camper Beware! (1965)
Fred Trueman You Nearly Had Him That Time (1968)

John Lawrence. From his *Rabbit and Pork* (1974).

Against the Law (Reader's Digest 1979)
You and Your Rights (Reader's Digest 1980)

Periodicals: The New Yorker, Paris Match, Punch, Radio Times, Sunday Mirror

References: Price; Wa (1972); *The Twentieth Century* 178 (1970); Percy Bradshaw *They Make Us Smile* (Chapman & Hall 1942); William Hewison *The Cartoon Connection* (Elm Tree Books 1977); Frank E. Huggett *Cartoonists at War* (Windward 1968)

Edith Mary Lawrence

See Claude Flight

John Lawrence (b. 1933)

Born in Hastings, Sussex, son of a company representative. Educated at the Salesian College, Cowley, Oxford. Studied at Hastings School of Art (1951-53) and at the Central School of Arts and Crafts under Gertrude Hermes* (1955-57). Part-time lecturer at Maidstone College of Art (1958-60), Brighton College of Art (1960-69) and Camberwell School of Art (since 1960). Book illustrator, book plate and press mark designer (e.g. for the Basilisk Press and Julia Macrae Books), relief printmaker. He is well known for his wood engravings in which he uses a wide range of tools to create elaborate effects of pattern and texture, giving emphasis to his forms by means of varied multiple outlines in white and black. He also works in pen and ink or pencil, sometimes with colour washes. His work has mainly been published by the Folio Society, Hamish Hamilton and Kestrel Books. Prize winner in the Francis Williams Book Illustration Award for 1972 and 1977. [Q]

Books illustrated include:
Richard Adams Watership Down (1976)
Allan Ahlbery and John Lawrence A Pair of Sinners (1980)
Michele Brown Food by Appointment: Royal Recipes since 1066 (1977)
David and Kay Canter The Cranks Recipe Book (1982)
Daniel Defoe Colonel Jack (1967), Robinson Crusoe (1972)
Mrs Henry de la Pasture The Unlucky Family (1980)
Nicholas Freeling Kitchen Book (1970), Cook Book (1972)

Frederick Grice and Dora Saint The Lifeboat Haul and Elizabeth Woodcock (1965)
George and Weedon Grossmith The Diary of a Nobody (1969)
Susan Hill The Magic Apple Tree (1982)
Jacynth Hope-Simpson Tales in School (1971)
Arthur F. Kinney Rogues, Vagabonds and Sturdy Beggars (1973)
Andrew Lang The Blue Fairy Book (1975)
John Lawrence The Giant of Grabbist (1968), Pope Leo's Elephant (1970), Rabbit and Pork, Rhyming Talk (1974), Tongue Twisters (1976)
Penelope Lively Fanny's Sister (1977)
Sibyl Marshall Everyman's Book of English Folktales (1981)
Francisco Nunez The Happy Captive (1977)
James Reeves Maildun the Voyager (1971)
Siegfried Sassoon Sherston's Progress (1974)
Ian Seraillier The Road to Canterbury (1979)
Laurence Sterne Tristram Shandy (1970)
Rosemary Sutcliff A Saxon Settler (1965)
Paul Theroux A Christmas Card (1978), London Snow (1979)
Elfrida Vipont A Child of the Chapel Royal (1967)
Junior Encyclopaedia (2 vols, A. & C. Black)

References: Garrett BWE, HBWE; ICB; Illustrators 22 (1978), 33 (1980)

Carol Antell Lawson (b. 1946)

Born in Giggleswick, Yorkshire. Studied at Harrogate College of Art and at Brighton College of Art where she specialised in typography and illustration. Part-time lecturer at Brighton College of Art (1978). Her illustrations for children's books, in black and white, are careful and often closely worked.

Books illustrated include:
Tilla Brading Pirates (with others, 1976)
Griselda Gifford Jenny and the Sheep Thieves (1975)
Deborah Manley The Piccolo Holiday Book (1976)
Caroline Rush The Scarecrow (1968)
Philip Street Colour in Animals (1977), Poison in Animals (1978)
Joan Woodberry Little Black Swan (1970)

Reference: ICB 4

Frederick Lawson (b. 1888)

Born in Yeadon, near Leeds. Studied at Leeds

Fred Lawson. From *Folk Tales of Yorkshire* by H.L. Gee (Nelson, 1952).

School of Art. Painter of landscapes in water-colour, etcher and wood engraver. His pen and ink book illustrations are informal and sketchy, his illustrations in other media more deliberate in style. Lived in Yorkshire at Redmire and later at Leyburn.

Books illustrated include:
H.L. Gee Folk Tales of Yorkshire (1952)
Dorothy Ratcliffe Dale Dramas (1923), Shoeing by Jerry-go-Nimble (1926), Dale Folk (1927), Fairings (1928), Lillilows (1931), Lapwings and Laverocks (1934), Under T'Hawthorn (1946)

References: Vollmer; Wa (1934); Waters; *The Artist* 40 (1951)

Arthur Layard (active 1893-1907)

Watercolour painter and writer and illustrator of children's books in black and white and full colour. *Billy Mouse* and *Harriet Hare* were published by Nisbet in a small format obviously influenced by Warne's Beatrix Potter books. The inconsistency of line in his pen and ink illustrations (e.g. in *Sir John Maundevile* and *Adam Bede*) suggests that he may have had no formal artistic training.

Books illustrated include:
George Eliot Adam Bede (1901)
H. Rider Haggard The People of the Mist (1894)
Ha Sheen Kaf The Winged Wolf (1933)
Arthur Layard The Alphabet of Musical (with music by E. Saver, 1899), Billy Mouse (1906), Harriet Hare (1907)
Sir J. Mandeville The Marvellous Adventures of Sir John Maundevile (1895)

Periodical: The Pall Mall Magazine

References: Houfe; Johnson & Greutzner

Errol John Le Cain (b. 1941)

Works as Errol Le Cain. Born in Singapore, son of a member of the police force. During his child-hood, he travelled extensively in the Far East and lived for five years in India. He worked in Pearl & Dean advertising studios (1956-60), and on ani-mated films and titles in the Richard Williams Studio (1960-67). Since then he has worked free-lance as a film, television and exhibition designer. As a book illustrator, Le Cain has developed a distinctive graphic style in which outline and pattern are dominant elements. He aims to create bold, simple designs (retaining relevant detail) that can be dramatic or humorous, and adapts his style to the varying moods of the stories. He uses pen and ink, with gouache for colour work.[Q]

Books illustrated include:
Kathleen Abell King Orville and the Bullfrogs (1976)
Hans Andersen (retold by Naomi Lewis) The Snow Queen (1979)
Elaine Andrews Judge Pao (1975)
Sara and Stephin Corrin (retold by) Mrs Fox's Wedding (1980)
Helen Cresswell The Beachcombers (1972)
Samuel Taylor Coleridge The Rime of the Ancient Mariner (1972)
Anthea Davies Sir Orfeo (1970)
William Golding Wigger (1974)
Brothers Grimm Thorn Rose (1975), Briar Rose (1975), The Twelve Dancing Princesses (1978)

Rosemary Harris The Child in the Bamboo Grove (1971), The King's White Elephant (1973), The Lotus and the Grail (1974), The Flying Ship (1975), The Little Dog of Fo (1976), Beauty and the Beast (1979)
Andrew Lang Aladdin and the Wonderful Lamp (1981)
Errol Le Cain King Arthur's Sword (1968), The Cabbage Princess (1969), The White Cat (1973)
Thomas Lewis The Dragon Kite (1974)
Mitchell and Bliss (ed) The Faber Book of Children's Songs (1970)
Malcolm Neville Kammerer's Cave (1976)
Walter Pater Cupid and Psyche (1977)
Brian Patten The Sly Cormorant and the Fishes (1977)
Charles Perrault Cinderella (1972)
James Riorden The Three Magic Gifts (1980)
Idries Shah The Pleasanteries of the Incredible Mulla Nasrudin (with Richard Williams 1975)
Paulin Van Woerkom The Hat, the Ox and the Zodiac (1976)
The Collected Rhymes and Verses of Walter de la Mare (1970)

References: Contemporary Authors; ICB 4; *Books for your Children* (Winter 1979); *Daily Telegraph* (January 9th 1977); *Dorset Evening Echo* (November 10th 1977); *Mother* (May 1976); *Radio Times* (December 25th 1977)

Howard Leigh

See Alfred Sindall

Clare Veronica Hope Leighton (b. c.1901)

Works as Clare Leighton. Born in London. Stu-died at Brighton School of Art, the Slade School of Fine Art and the Central School of Arts and Crafts where she learned wood engraving under Noel Rooke*. During the late 1920s and 1930s, she became a noted wood engraver, winning first prize at the International Engravers' Exhibition at the Art Insitute of Chicago (1930). She emi-grated to the United States of America in 1939 and became an American citizen in 1946. She lectured for two years at Duke University and settled in a house of her own design in Connecti-cut. She designed stained glass windows (including 37 for St Paul's Cathedral, Worcester, Massa-chusetts) and also worked in mosaic. As a book illustrator, she worked mainly for commercial rather than private presses, and her engravings are, at their best, vigorous and striking. Her fig-ures, with pronounced tonal contrasts are often effectively offset by closely textured backgrounds of delicate grey; in this, as well as in her preference for rural figure subjects, her work is reminiscent of that of the mid-Victorian illustrator G.J. Pin-well. Author of *Wood Engravings and Woodcuts* (Studio, 1932) and *Wood Engravings of the 1930s* (Studio, 1936). Elected SWE (1928), ARE (1930), RE (1934); former Vice-President of the Society of American Graphic Art and Fellow of the Na-tional Academy of Design, New York.

Books illustrated include:
Emily Brontë Wuthering Heights (1931)
Eleanor Farjeon Perkin the Pedlar (1932), Pannychis (1933)
Thomas Hardy The Return of the Native (1929)
Clare Leighton The Farmer's Year (1933), The Wood That Came Back (1934), The Musical Box (1936), Country Matters (1937), Where Land Meets Sea (1954)
Alan Mulgan Home, a New Zealander's Adventure (1927)

Clare Leighton. Headpiece to 'Tramps' from her *Country Matters* (Gollancz, 1937).

Elinor Milnor Parker The Singing and the Gold (1962)
H.M. Tomlinson The Sea and the Jungle (1930)
Gilbert White The Natural History of Selborne (1941)
Thornton Wilder The Bridge of San Luis Rey (1929)

References: Balson EWE, WEMEB; Garrett BWE, HBWE; ICB 1, 2, 3, 4; Thieme & Becker; Vollmer and supp; Wa (1980); Waters; *The Print Collector's Quarterly* 22; *The Studio* 93 (1927), 98 (1929), 103 (1932), 113 (1937), special (Spring 1927, Spring 1930, Winter 1931, Autumn 1938); *Graven Images* (Scottish A.C. catalogue 1979); *Shall We Join the Ladies?* (Studio One Gallery Oxford 1979); Vera Brittain Testament of Youth (Gollancz 1933); A.C. Sewter *Modern British Woodcuts and Wood Engravings in the Collection of the Whitworth Art Gallery* (Manchester 1962)

Henriette Willebeek Le Mair (1889-1966)

Born in Rotterdam into a wealthy and cultured family. Illustrator of children's books and postcards, she is included here for her nursery rhyme illustrations commissioned and published in England by Augener, the music publishers. Her first book, *Premières Rondes Enfantines*, was published in France when she was 15. She later ran a small school for several years and used her young pupils as models for her drawings. In 1920, she married a leading Sufi, and, soon afterwards, joined the movement, assuming the name Saida. Her delicate, mannered watercolour drawings, mostly dating from before her marriage, were the outcome of extensive preparation and research, and became classics of nursery illustration.

Books illustrated include:
R.H. Elkin Little People (1913), The Children's Corner (1914), Old Dutch Nursery Rhymes (1917)
A.A. Milne A Gallery of Children (1925)
A. Moffat (arranged by) Little Songs of Long Ago (1912)
R.L. Stevenson A Child's Garden of Verses (1926)
Our Old Nursery Rhymes (1911)
Schumann's Album of Children's Pieces (1915)

References: Bénézit; Cope; Houfe; ICB 1; Vollmer; *The Studio* 62 (1914); *A Gallery of Children* (Bethnal Green Museum catalogue 1975)

Angela Jacqueline Lemaire (b. 1944)

Born in Burnham, Buckinghamshire, niece of Rosemary Grimble*. Partly educated in Australia; returned to London (1961). Studied at Chelsea College of Art (1963), Camberwell School

of Arts and Crafts (1964-67) and Morley College (1961), where she was taught etching. Self-taught wood engraver (1970). Her own books were privately published and are illustrated with etchings and wood engravings. Lives in Scotland. [Q]

Books illustrated include:
Graham Kerr The Complete Galloping Gourmet Cookbook (1972)
Angela Lemaire The Plague (1967), The Monk's Life (1970), Her Day (1973)

References: *The Art of the Wood Engraver* (catalogue Becket Centre, Pensford 1981)

Cecil Mary Leslie (1900-80)

Born Wimbledon, Surrey. Daughter of a shipbroker. Served as a Voluntary Aid Detachment nurse during World War I. Studied at Heatherley's School of Art (1919), at the London School of Photolithography and Engraving, and at the Central School of Arts and Crafts (c.1924). Taught etching at Iain Macnab's* Grosvenor School of Modern Art (1925). Ran a Red Cross detachment during World War II. From 1946 she lived at Blakeney, Norfolk, where she played an active part in local and church life. She was a still-life, flower and portrait painter (executing what is believed to be the only painted portrait of the 'Old Vic' director, Lilian Baylis, now in the National Portrait Gallery), an etcher (mainly dust-ground aquatints) and illustrator of children's books, principally for Hamish Hamilton, Faber and the Bodley Head. For illustration, she worked mainly in pen and ink, sometimes with added watercolour, crayon or chalk. She adhered conscientiously to her authors' texts, was assiduous in researching places and periods and always drew from life. Among earlier book illustrators,

Cecil Leslie. 'He was lying with his legs crossed full length along the back seat, pretending to puff a cigar.' from *The Country Bus* by Rosemary Garland (Hamish Hamilton, 1958).

she particularly admired the work of Charles Keene* and William Nicholson*. [Q]

Books illustrated include:

Helen Clare Five Dolls in a House (1953), Merlin's Magic (1953), Five Dolls and the Monkey (1956), Five Dolls in the Snow (1957), Five Dolls and their Friends (1959), Five Dolls and the Duke (1963)

Pauline Clarke The Pekinese Princess (1948), The Great Can (1952), Smith's Hoard (1955), Sandy the Sailor (1956), The Boy with the Erpingham Hood (1956), James the Policeman (1957), James and the Robbers (1959), Torolv the Fatherless (1959), The Lord of the Castle (1960), The Robin Hooders (1960), James and the Smugglers (1961), Keep the Pot Boiling (1961), The Twelve and the Genii (1962), James and the Black Van (1963), Crowds of Creatures (1964), The Bonfire Party (1966)

Rose Fyleman Jeremy Quince (1933), The Princess Dances (1933), Billy Monkey (1935)

Rosemary Garland The Country Bus (1958), The Little Forest (1959)

Elisabeth Kyle The Money Cat (1958)

E. Nesbit The Story of the Treasure Seekers (1958), The Wouldbegoods (1958), The Enchanted Castle (1964)

Johanna Spyri Heidi (1956)

Alison Uttley The Sam Pig Story Book (1965)

References: Fisher pp. 102, 137, 222; Johnson & Greutzner; Guichard; Vollmer; Wa (1980); Waters; *How to Distinguish Prints* (Print Society Publications no 3 1926); *Junior Bookshelf* vol 22 no 4 (1958)

Frederic George Lewin (d. 1933)

Humorous painter, occasional illustrator. His illustrative style was unusually varied. *Characters from Dickens* contains halftone reproductions of theatrical, slightly overstated, imaginary portraits. *An ABC Book* has large-scale woodcuts in a Joseph Crawhall-like, chapbook manner, while *Bristol* is recorded in neat, small, prosaic pen and ink drawings.

Books illustrated include:

F.G. Lewin An ABC Book for Good Boys and Girls (1911), Rhymes of ye Olde Sign Boards (1911)

B.W. Matz (intro) Characters from Dickens (1912)

Arthur L. Salmon Bristol (1922)

Periodical: Punch

References: Houfe; Vollmer; Wa (1929, Obituary 1934); Waters

Percy Wyndham Lewis (1882-1957)

Worked as Wyndham Lewis. Born in his father's yacht, somewhere off the coast of Nova Scotia. Educated at Rugby School and the Slade School of Fine Art. Worked with Roger Fry at the Omega Workshops and in 1913 was instrumental in forming the Rebel Art Centre. He was soon the dominant figure in the Vorticist group of artists. During World War I he was an Official War Artist. A decisive draughtsman, Lewis developed a strong, dynamic abstract style which was a personal extension of Cubism and Futurism. Though better known as a painter, novelist and satirist, he most ably illustrated some of his own works, notably *The Apes of God*. The 1914 series of drawings for *Timon of Athens* is also of remarkable quality. He was the designer of the Vorticist magazine *Blast*, contributing six strong abstract illustrations and

Wyndham Lewis. Frontispiece from his *Blasting and Bombardiering* (Eyre & Spottiswoode, 1937).

the cover illustration for its second (and last) issue (1915).

Books illustrated include:

Wyndham Lewis The Apes of God (1930), The Enemy of the Stars (1932), Thirty Personalities and a Self-Portrait (1932), Blasting and Bombardiering (1937)

N.M. Mitchison Beyond this Limit (1935)

William Shakespeare Timon of Athens (1914)

Periodicals: Blast, The Chapbook, The Enemy, The Tyro

References: Bénézit; Chamot, Farr & Butlin; Contemporary Artists; DNB (1951-60); Johnson & Greutzner; Phaidon; Rothenstein 2; Thieme & Becker; Vollmer and supp; Wa (1929); Waters; *Encounter* 213 (1963); *Word and Image* 1, 2 (National Book League 1971); Michael Ayrton Golden Sections (Methuen 1957); Richard Cork *Vorticism and Abstract Art in the First Machine Age* (2 vols, Gordon Fraser 1976); J. Gawsworth *Apes, Japes and Hitlerism* (Unicorn Press 1932); G. Grigson *A Master of Our Time: A Study of Wyndham Lewis* (Methuen 1951); C. Handley-Read and E. Newton *Art of Wyndham Lewis* (Faber 1951); H. Kenner *Wyndham Lewis* (Methuen 1954); Wyndham Lewis *Blasting and Bombardiering* (Eyre & Spottiswoode 1937), *Rude Assignment* (Hutchinson 1950); W. Michel *Wyndham Lewis: Paintings and Drawings* (Thames & Hudson 1971); W. Michel and C.J. Fox *Wyndham Lewis on Art* (Thames & Hudson 1969); H.G. Porteus *Wyndham Lewis: A Discursive Exposition* (Desmond Harmsworth 1932); E.W.F. Tomlin *Wyndham Lewis* (Longmans Green 1955); *Wyndham Lewis* (Methuen 1969); G. Wagner *Wyndham Lewis: A Portrait of the Artist as the Enemy* (Routledge 1957)

Jan Lewitt (b. 1907)

Born in Czestochowa, Poland. After leaving school he travelled for three years in Europe and the Middle East (1925-28), and then began work as a self-taught graphic artist and designer. He soon became well known in Poland as a pioneer of an experimental graphic style influenced by modernist painting, especially that of Paul Klee. In 1925, he designed the first modern Hebrew typeface *Chaim*. He met George Him* in 1933 and they formed the Lewitt-Him design partnership; they moved to London in 1937 and during World War II worked for various government departments including the Ministries of Information and Food, the Home Office and the G.P.O. They also designed commercial advertisements and illustrated books for children and adults. Their work was widely acclaimed and the partnership came to an end in 1954-55 only because Lewitt decided to devote himself full-time to painting. He had already been the subject of several one-man exhibitions and continued to exhibit abstract works.

During the 1940s and 1950s, the Lewitt-Him graphic style had a considerable impact on British illustration with its simplified, witty imagery and strong emphasis on page design. One of the partnership's best books, *The Little Red Engine Gets a Name* (1942), combines crisp stylisation and boldly inventive layouts with remarkable evocations of space and scale. The later books in this series were illustrated by Leslie Wood* in a style based on that of Lewitt-Him, but Wood's more decorative, whimsical approach is easily distinguishable from the Lewitt-Him geometrical tautness. Jan Lewitt's one solo venture into book illustration, *The Vegetabull* (1956), suggests that his personal interest lay in the direction of 'handwriting' and texture rather than in the more formal aspects of design.

Books illustrated include:
Alina Lewitt Blue Peter (with G. Him*, 1943), Five Silly Cats (with
   G. Him, 1944)
Jan Lewitt The Vegetabull (1956)
Jan Lewitt and George Him The Football's Revolt (1939)
Diana Ross The Little Red Engine Gets a Name (1942)
Julian Tuwim The Locomotive, the Turnip, the Birds' Broadcast (with
   G. Him, 1939)

References: Crouch; Hürlimann; ICB 1, 2; Lewis; Vollmer supp; WaG; William Feaver *When We Were Young* (Thames & Hudson 1977); Jan Lewitt *A Selection of Poems and Aphorisms from the Artist's Notebooks* (Routledge & Kegan Paul 1971)

Kenneth Arthur Lindley (b. 1928)

Born in Shepherd's Bush, London, son of a shopkeeper. Educated at St Clement Danes Grammar School (1938-43). Studied at Ealing School of Art (1943-49), and under Norman Janes* at Hornsey School of Art (1949-50). Lecturer at Loughborough School of Art (1950-57), and at Swindon School of Art (1957-65). Head of Wakefield School of Art (1966-71) and Principal of Herefordshire College of Art since 1971. Printmaker, painter, draughtsman, writer, and photographer. He has

Kenneth Lindley. From *The Kilpeck Anthology* edited by Glenn Storhaug (Five Seasons Press, 1981).

used a variety of processes for illustration including wood engraving, lino cut and relief etching. Much of his recent work has been for the Pointing Finger Press. He is the author of *The Woodblock Engravers* (David & Charles 1970).[Q]

Books illustrated include:
Baker Cottage by the Springs (1961)
David Burnett Shimabara (1970), Figures and Spaces (1978)
H.E. Carey One River (1952)
Gerald Manley Hopkins Selected Poems (1954)
Mackinlay Kantor But Look in the Morn (1950), Wicked Water (1950)
Kenneth A. Lindley A Sequence of Downs (1962), Town, Time and
   People (1962), Of Graves and Epitaphs (1965), Urns and Angels
   (1965), Coastline (1967), Figures in a Landscape (1967), Black
   Riding (1968), Chapels and Meeting Houses (1969), Townlook
   (1969), Coastwise (1970), Nostalgia (1970), Graves and Graveyards
   (1972), Landscape and Buildings (1972), Seaside Architecture
   (1973), Seamarks (1975), Seaside and the Seacoast (1975),
   Herefordshire Late Autumn (1977), A Hereford Window (1979),
   Border Incidents (1983)
J. Marshall Preparing for Marriage (1962)
William Nathan Gone Fishing (1961)
Reynolds The Farmer's Wife (1960)
Lionel T.C. Rolt G. & R. Stephenson (1960)
Glenn Storhaug (ed) The Kilpeck Anthology (1981)
St John Thomas Double Headed (1963)

Periodicals: Architectural Review, Country Life

References: Contemporary Authors; Garrett BWE, HBWE; Wa (1980)

Raymond George Lister (b. 1919)

Works as Raymond Lister. Born in Cambridge. As a schoolboy, he attended evening classes at the Cambridgeshire School of Art. He was apprenticed to the family firm of architectural metalworkers (1934-39), of which he became a director in 1940. He served in munitions during World War II (1939-45). Since 1958, he has been joint managing director of his own architectural metalwork company. His illustrated books have been published mainly by the Golden Head Press (which he founded in 1953) and the Windmill

House Press. His illustrative work has included small wood engravings, miniatures (reproduced in four colour, halftone blocks) and line drawings, sometimes hand-tinted in a manner derived from William Blake. Elected ARMS (1946), RMS (1948), PRMS (1970). President of the Private Libraries Association (1971-74) and of the Architectural Metalwork Association (1975). Governor of the Federation of British Artists (1972) and Fellow of Wolfson College Cambridge.

Books illustrated include:
Raymond Lister The First Book of Theodosius (1962), The Song of Theodosius (1963), Gabha (1964), Tao (1965), Inrey (1967), The Emblems of Theodosius or the Unity of Endymion and Prometheus (1969), A Title to Phoebe (1972), Apollo's Bird (1974), For Love of Leda (1976), Bergomask (1982), There Was a Star Danced (1983)
Thomas Moore The Song of Fionnuala and Nine Other Songs (1960)
Francis Warner Perennia (1962)
Virgil's Second Eclogue (1958)

References: Contemporary Authors; Wa (1980); Waters; *Apollo* (May 1948); Adrian Bury *The Art of Raymond Lister, RMS. A Miniaturist with a Mystical Message* (The Connoisseur Year Book 1959); C.R. Cammell, Peter Foster, Simon Lissim, L.G.G. Ramsay and Francis Warner *Raymond Lister: Five Essays* (Golden Head Press, Cambridge 1963); Simon Lissim *The Art of Raymond Lister* (John P. Gray & Son, Cambridge 1958)

Errol Lloyd (b. 1943)

Born in Jamaica. Studied at Monro College, Jamaica, then moved to London (1964) to study Law. Instead of pursuing a legal career, he became a professional painter; he taught painting at the Camden Arts Centre (1976-77) and was Resident Artist at the Kiskidee Arts Centre, Islington (1978). He began working as a book illustrator by chance when the children's book editor at The Bodley Head, who was looking for an illustrator for the 'Sean' series (intended particularly for children of West Indian origin living in Britain) saw some of his paintings. One of the books in the series, *My Brother Sean*, was highly commended in the 1973 Kate Greenaway competition for its illustrations. Recently, he has written his own stories. He works in full colour on a textured surface, often with freely drawn brush outlines, and concentrates on the painterly, spatial and compositional qualities of his designs.

Books illustrated include:
Petronella Breinburg My Brother Sean (1973), Doctor Sean (1974), Sean's Red Bike (1975)
Errol Lloyd Nini at Carnival (1978), Nini on Time (1981)
Hilary Sherlock and Dennis Craig New Caribbean Readers (1978)

References: Contemporary Authors; ICB 4

Grace Lodge (active 1920-65)

Illustrator and writer of children's books. Much of her early work was for cheaply printed girls' story anthologies such as those edited by 'Mrs Herbert Strang', and was typical of this genre.

Her later work was rather more individual, especially when she illustrated her own stories for children. *Lucy's Adventure* (1945), in which a child's drawings come to life in a dream, was one of her more imaginative illustrated books.

Books illustrated include:
Agnes Adams The Boy Next Door (1952)
Enid Blyton Just Time for a Story (1948), Brer Rabbit Books (8 vols 1948-58), A Story Party at Green Hedges (1949), Those Dreadful Children (1949), A Picnic Party (1951), Gay Street Book (1951), Tales of Toyland (1952), The Children at Green Meadows (1954), Bible Stories from the New Testament (1955), Bible Stories from the Old Testament (1955), Holiday House (1955), The Birthday Kitten (1958), Gulliver's Adventures (with others, 1960)
Grace Lodge Lucy's Adventure (1945), The Tiny Prince and Other stories (1946), The Little Men of the Mountains (1947), Puddleduck Farm (1947), The Hole in the Hedge (1948), Spring, Summer, Autumn, Winter (1948), The Marsh Princess (1949), Misty and the Magic Necklace (1954), My Picture Book of Animals (1961)
'Mrs Herbert Strang' The Golden Wonder Book (with others, 1921), The Golden Book for Girls (c. 1936)

Hugh Lofting (1886-1947)

Born Maidenhead, Berkshire. He showed an early interest in animals and natural history. He studied at Massachusetts Institute of Technology and the London Polytechnic. Working as an architect and civil engineer, he travelled in Canada, Africa and the West Indies. He married and settled in America (1912), but then enlisted in the British Army (1916). His famous creation Dr Dolittle, the man who could talk to animals, emerged from illustrated letters written to his children while he was at the Western front. *The Story of Dr Dolittle* (1920) was the first of this popular series; *The Voyages of Dr Dolittle* was awarded the Newbery Medal (1923). Lofting has been described by

Hugh Lofting. 'Nifty little party, I calls it!' from *Doctor Dolittle's Caravan* (Cape, 1927).

Frank Eyre as 'one of the truly great writers for children because his message of tolerance, generosity and unselfish helpfulness to others shines through so clearly' (*British Children's Books in the 20th Century* (1971). The stories are complemented by his own simplified outline drawings, which owe much of their charm to a consciously naive style of imagery.

Books illustrated include:
Hugh Lofting The Story of Dr Dolittle (1920), Dr Dolittle's Post Office (1923), The Story of Mrs Tubbs (1923), The Voyages of Dr Dolittle (1923), Dr Dolittle's Circus (1925), Porridge Poetry (1925), Dr Dolittle's Zoo (1926), Dr Dolittle's Caravan (1927), Dr Dolittle's Garden (1928), Dr Dolittle in the Moon (1929), Noisy Nora (1929), Gub Gub's Book (1932), Dr Dolittle's Return (1933), Tommy, Tilly and Mrs Tubbs (1937), Dr Dolittle and the Secret Lake (1949), Dr Dolittle and the Green Canary (1951)

References: Doyle CL; Eyre; Fisher p.87; ICB 1, 2; Kirkpatrick; Lewis; Thieme & Becker; Vollmer supp; *The Junior Bookshelf* vol 11 no 4 (1947); Edward Blishen *Hugh Lofting* (Bodley Head 1968); William Feaver *When We Were Young* (Thames & Hudson 1977)

John Vernon Lord (b. 1939)

Born in Glossop, Derbyshire. Studied at the School of Art, Royal College of Technology, Salford, Lancashire (1956-60) and at the Central School of Arts and Crafts (1960-61). Since 1961, he has worked freelance as an illustrator and visiting lecturer at various colleges of Art, and since 1970, he has been a full-time lecturer at Brighton Polytechnic. Illustrator of children's books, educational books, novels and technical books, and for magazines, newspapers and advertising. Many of his children's books have been translated into various languages and dramatised for television. He works in pen and ink, or, for colour drawings, in mixed media: often combining ink, gouache, crayon and pencil. His illustrations are humorous, detailed and tightly organised. He acknowledges the early influence of Ronald Searle*, Saul Steinberg and André François, and

John Vernon Lord. 'Then Bap the Baker leapt to his feet...' from *The Giant Jam Sandwich* with verses by Janet Burroway (Cape, 1972).

David Low. 'Max, Lord Beaverbrook' from his *Lions and Lambs* with interpretations by 'Lynx' [Rebecca West] (Cape, 1928).

the lasting influence of the Victorian steel engravers. Several of his children's picture books have been dramatised for television. [Q]

Books illustrated include:
Conrad Aiken Who's Zoo (1977)
Roy Brown Reynard the Fox (1969)
Janet Burroway The Truck on the Track (1970)
Joel Chandler-Harris The Adventures of Brer Rabbit (1972)
Ann Coates Dinosaurs Don't Die (1970)
Lena F. Hurlong Adventures of Jaboti on the Amazon (1968)
Edward Lear The Nonsense Verse of Edward Lear (1983)
John Vernon Lord (with verses by Janet Burroway) The Giant Jam Sandwich (1972), The Runaway Rollerskate (1973), Mr Mead and his Garden (1974), *(with verses by Fay Maschler)* Miserable Aunt Bertha (1980)

Periodicals: The Listener, New Society, The Observer, Punch, Radio Times, The Sunday Times, The Times and many others

References: Contemporary Authors; *Evening Argus* (Brighton 27th March 1980); *The West Sussex Gazette* (12th May 1977)

David Alexander Cecil Low (1891-1963)

Worked as David Low. Born at Dunedin, New Zealand. Brought up at Christchurch where he attended drawing classes at the School of Art. Began contributing drawings to the Christchurch *Spectator* at the age of 11 and became its political cartoonist in 1908. Moved to Australia (1911) and worked as a cartoonist for *The Sydney Bulletin*. Settled in London (1919); joined the staff of *The Star* (1919-27), the *Evening Standard* (1927-50), the *Daily Herald* (1950-53), *The Manchester Guardian* (1953-63), and also contributed to *New Statesman*. J. Geipel described him as 'undoubtedly the most outstanding British political cartoonist, an artist whose long and unchallenged reign straddled four decades... Low's conception was dramatically bold, simple and assertive, and his facile brushwork has been aptly likened to the techniques of oriental painting'. His graphic style was influenced early on by the work of Phil May* and remained consistently economical and effective. In his book illustration, as in his political cartoons, he concentrated on figure characterisation, suggesting background and settings with a few carefully selected lines. He was knighted in 1962.

Books illustrated include:
James Adderley Old Seed on New Ground (1920)
R.P. Fleming The Flying Visit (1940)
David Low Low's Annual (1908), Caricatures (1915), The Billy Book (1918), Man (1921), Lloyd George and Co. (1922), Low's Russian Sketch Book (1932), Ye Madde Designer (1935), Political Parade (1936), Low Again (1938), A Cartoon History of Our Times (1939), Europe at War (1939), Europe since Versailles (1939), The World at War (1942), C'est la Guerre (1943), Years of Wrath (1949), Low's Company (1952), Low Visibility (1953), The Fearful Fifties (1960)
Low and Lynx Lions and Lambs (1928)
G.F. Powell What is Democracy? (1940)
F.W. Thomas The Low and I Holiday Book (1925)
H.G. Wells The Autocracy of Mr Parham (1930)

Periodicals: Daily Herald, Evening Standard, The Manchester Guardian, New Statesman, Punch, The Saturday Book, The Spectator, The Star, The Sydney Bulletin

References: Chamot, Farr & Butlin; Houfe; Vollmer; WaG; Waters; *The Artist* 19 (1940); *The Strand Magazine* 72 (1926); *The Studio* special (Autumn 1928); Percy V. Bradshaw They Make Us Smile (Chapman & Hall 1942); John Geipel *The Cartoon* (David & Charles 1972); David Low *Low's Autobiography* (Michael Joseph 1956)

Thomas Esmond Lowinsky (1892-1947)

Born in London. Educated at Eton and Trinity College, Cambridge. Studied at the Slade School of Fine Art (1912-14). Served with the Scots Guards in France and Germany during World War I. He was a painter and book illustrator, and in 1926 held his first one-man exhibition at the Leicester Galleries. For illustration, he worked in pen and ink, sometimes with partial colour. His drawings are fastidious and precise, with hatched shading; his compositions are studied and often incorporate Renaissance motifs and devices. Douglas Percy Bliss* considered that 'his work is Pre-Raphaelite in its elaboration of detail, in its angular and somewhat grotesque types, and its bestowal of equal attention upon every inch of the surface'. (*The Penrose Annual* 31, 1929). His later illustration tends to be more economical in treatment. Member NEAC.

Books illustrated include:
M. Drayton Ballad of Agincourt (1926)
J. Laver Ladies' Mistakes (1933)
R. Lowinsky Lovely Food (1931), More Lovely Food (1935), What's Cooking (1945)
W. Meinhold Sidonia the Sorceress (1926)
John Milton Paradise Regained (1924)
R. Mortimer (intro) Modern Nymphs (1930)
William Shakespeare The Merchant of Venice (1923)
Richard Brinsley Sheridan The School for Scandal (1930)
Edith Sitwell Elegy on Dead Fashion (1926)
Sacheverell Sitwell Exalt the Eglantine and other poems (1926),

Doctor Donne and Gargantua Canto the Third (1926)
Voltaire The Princess of Babylon (1927)
Plutarch's Lives (1928)
Rubaiyat of Omar Khaiyam (1926)

References: Chamot, Farr & Butlin; Houfe; Johnson & Greutzner; Vollmer; Wa (1934); Waters; *The Penrose Annual* 31 (1929); *The Studio* special (Winter 1931)

Savile Lumley (active c.1910-c.1950)

Children's book illustrator and designer of the well-known World War I recruitment poster *'Daddy, What did YOU do in the Great War?'*. During the 1920s and 1930s, he contributed widely to children's annuals, anthologies and magazines. He was a competent illustrator in black and white and halftone who knew his market and was well

Thomas Lowinsky. 'A handsome VENETIAN, one among the twelve thousand girls registered in the great book of the Republic being appointed to carry on the most agreeable trade that ever enriched a nation' from *The Princess of Babylon* by M. de Voltaire (The Nonesuch Press, 1927).

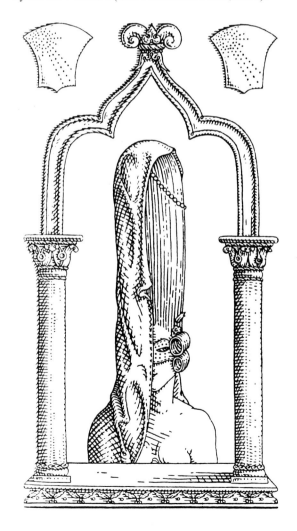

able to adapt his style for reproduction on cheap paper. He worked for both boys' and girls' publications, but in later years his subject treatment became increasingly static, and so less suited to action and adventure.

Books illustrated include:
Mary England (ed) Warne's Happy Book for Girls (with others, nd)
Evelyn Everett-Green A Disputed Heritage (1911)
Constance Heward Chappie and others (1926)
R.L. Stevenson The Black Arrow (1949)
Herbert Strang (ed) The Big Book for Boys (with others, nd)
Selfridge's Schoolboys' Story Book (with others, nd)

Periodicals: The Boy's Own Paper, The Champion Annual, Chatterbox, Chums, Little Folks, Nelson Lee, Printer's Pie, School Friend Annual, Schoolgirls' Own Annual, The Scout, Sketchy Bits, Young England

Reference: Doyle BWI

Ilbery Lynch (active 1909-16)

Painter and illustrator. His remarkable full-page pencil drawings for *The Transmutation of Ling* are oriental in inspiration, with echoes of the Rococo style and of Aubrey Beardsley's work.

Books illustrated include:
Ernest Bramah The Transmutation of Ling (1911)
Lord Dunsany Five Plays (1914)

References: Houfe; Johnson & Greutzner

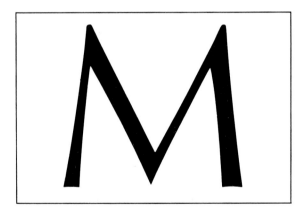

Molly MacArthur

See Florence Mary Anderson

Seaghan MacCathmhaoil

See John Patrick Campbell

Arthur David McCormick (1860-1943)

Born in Coleraine, Ireland. Studied at the South Kensington School of Art (1883-86). Artist on Sir Martin Conway's expedition to the Himalayas (1892) and Clinton T. Dent's expedition to the

A.D. McCormick. 'The little man whose voice you never hear' from *Drake's Drum and other Songs of the Sea* by Henry Newbolt (Hodder & Stoughton, 1914).

Caucasus (1894). Fellow of the Royal Geographical Society from 1895. His book illustrations consisted mainly of watercolour paintings, in which flickering brush strokes and subtle tints gave atmosphere to the scenes of action he often depicted. His work translated well into full colour plates but seldom reproduced well in halftone. For *An Artist in the Himalayas*, he used his rapid on-the-spot pencil sketches. He lived in London. Watercolourist, engraver and graphic designer; elected RBA (1897), ROI (1905) and RI (1906).

Books illustrated include:
R.F. Burton Wanderings in Three Continents (1901)
W.M. Conway Climbing and Exploration in the Karakoram-
   Himalayas (1894), The Alps from End to End (1895), The Alps
   (1904)
Sarah J. Cotes His Honor and a Lady (1896)
P.C. Faly Ninety-Eight (1897)
John Finnemore Switzerland (c.1908)
E.A. Fitzgerald Climbs in the New Zealand Alps (1896)
R.W. Frazer Silent Gods and Sun-Steeped Lands (1895)
Arnold Graves Prince Patrick (1898)
E.S. Gregan From Cape to Cairo (1900, 1902)
R. Horsley New Zealand (1908)
William Henry Hudson Birds in London (1898), Little Boy Lost (1905)
A.D. McCormick An Artist in the Himalayas (1895)
M. McGregor The Netherlands (1907)
C. Montague The Vigil (1896)
Henry Newbolt Drake's Drum (1914)
E.C. Oppenheim New Climbs in Norway (1898)
Edgar Allan Poe Arthur Gordon Pym (c.1898), Tales of Mystery and
   Imagination (1905)

E.L. Prescott A Small, Small Child (1898)
Morley Roberts The Western Avenues (1896)
G.S. Robertson The Kafirs of Hindu Kush (1896)
Richard Southey The Life of Nelson (1916)
The Arabian Nights Entertainment (with others, 1899)

Periodicals: The English Illustrated Magazine, Good Words, The Illustrated London News

References: Bénézit; Houfe; ICB 1; Johnson & Greutzner; Mallalieu; Thieme & Becker; Thorpe; Vollmer supp; Wa (1934); Waters; C. Wood

A.K. Macdonald (active 1898-1947)

Illustrator of magazines, books, and postcards in pen and ink or pencil and wash, whose early work clearly shows the influence of Claude Shepperson*; later there are echoes of Lewis Baumer* and E.H. Shepard*. Best known as a regular contributor to *The Tatler*.

Books illustrated include:
Anthony Armstrong The Naughty Princess (1945)
Lady Cynthia Asquith (ed) The Silver Ship (with others, 1926), The Treasure Ship (with others, 1926), Sails of Gold (with others, 1927), The Children's Cargo (with others, 1930)

Periodicals: Cassell's Magazine, Holly Leaves, The Illustrated London

R.J. Macdonald. 'In a moment more he was clambering out on the swaying, sagging branch' from *Billy Bunter the Bold* by Frank Richards (Cassell, 1954).

News, The London Magazine, The Longbow, Nash's Magazine, Pear's Annual, Pearson's Magazine, Printers' Pie, The Royal Magazine, The Sketch, The Strand Magazine, The Tatler

References: Houfe; Thorpe; G. Montague Ellwood *The Art of Pen Drawing* (Batsford 1927)

R.J. Macdonald (d. 1955)

Began illustrating boys' magazines during the 1890s and was a regular contributor to the *Gem*, 1909-1940; he was artist for the 'St Jim' stories from 1911, with a gap while he served in the Royal Air Force, 1914-18. He was the illustrator and jacket designer for the 'Billy Bunter' titles which started to appear as books in 1947, and continued until his death in 1955, when he was succeeded by C.H. Chapman* (an earlier 'Bunter' illustrator for *The Magnet*). According to Brian Doyle, Macdonald was a great admirer of Gordon Browne* and influenced by his style, although this is not evident in his later 'Bunter' illustrations.

Books illustrated include:
Frank Richards Billy Bunter of Greyfriars School (1947), Billy Bunter's Bailing Out (1948), Billy Bunter's Christmas Party (1949), Bessie Bunter of Cliff House School (1949), Billy Bunter among the Cannibals (1950), Billy Bunter's Benefit (1950), Billy Bunter Butts In (1951), Billy Bunter's Postal Order (1951), Billy Bunter and the Blue Mauritius (1952), Billy Bunter's Beanfeast (1952), Billy Bunter's Brain-Wave (1953), Billy Bunter's First Case (1953), Billy Bunter the Bold (1954), Bunter Does his Best (1954), Billy Bunter's Double (1955)

Periodicals: The Boys' Friend, The Gem, The Girls' Friend, The Magnet, The Marvel, Nelson Lee, Pluck, Wonderland Annual

References: Doyle BWI; Kirkpatrick (*See* under Frank Richards)

William Brown Macdougall (d. 1936)

Born in Glasgow. Studied at the Académie Julian in Paris. During the 1880s he became known for his oil and pastel landscapes. His main period of activity as an illustrator was during the 1890s, when he contributed to *The Yellow Book* and decorated a number of books in pen and ink in a more or less Art Nouveau style (influenced according to Houfe, by Beardsley), often with broad borders of twining, flattened foliage surrounding mannered drawings in outline and solid black. His illustrations seem to have been reasonably well received by contemporaries; James Caw, while not enthusiastic, considered that 'in a rather *outré* and artificial manner, his black and white possesses personality and is not without charm'. Today, however, it is easier to concur with John Russell Taylor who refers to 'a sadly deficient sense of form and a painfully limited repertoire of decorative motifs'. His drawing of figures was particularly inept, but he did produce some pleasant little watercolour landscapes which were reproduced in monochrome, entitled *The Home and Early Haunts of R.L. Stevenson*, and these perhaps give a clearer idea of his capacity as an artist. He was married to the poet and novelist Margaret Armour, and, in the later part of his life, lived in Essex.

Books illustrated include:
Margaret Armour The Home and Early Haunts of R.L. Stevenson (1895), Songs of Love and Death (1897), Thames Sonnets and Semblances (1897), The Shadow of Love (1898)
John Keats Isabella, or the Pot of Basil (1898)
A.M.F. Robinson The Fields of France (1905)
D.G. Rossetti The Blessed Damozel (1898)
The Book of Ruth (1896)
Chronicles of Strathearn (1896)
The Fall of the Nibelungs (1897)
Gudrun (1898)
Rubaiyat Of Omar Khayyam (1899)

Periodicals: The Evergreen, The Savoy, The Yellow Book

References: Baker; Houfe; Johnson & Greutzner; Sketchley; Taylor; Thorpe; Vollmer supp; Wa (1934); Waters; James L. Caw *Scottish Painting Past and Present* (T.C. & E.C. Jack, 1908)

Angusine Macgregor (active 1905-1915) and Angusine Jeanne Macgregor (active 1946-56)

It is not altogether certain whether there was one Angusine Macgregor or two members of the same family. Both favoured animal subjects drawn in outline and filled in with flat colour washes, and it is conceivable that the separate British Library catalogue entries represent different phases of work in the life of one long-lived artist. The books of A.J. Macgregor were all published by Ladybird.

Books illustrated by A. Macgregor include:
Olive Clarke Freddy Frizzlocks (1914)
Angusine Macgregor The Mysterious Disappearance of What and Why (1905), Flippity the Runaway (1915), Maxims for Alice and Others

Angusine Macgregor. From *The Bunny Book* by Jessie Pope (Blackie, 1909).

(1915), Mrs Bunny's Refugee (1915), The Bunty Books (1921), The Story of Snips (nd)
Jessie Pope The Bunny Book (1909), The Story of Fup and Fuzzy (1911), The Adventures of Silversuit (1912), Bobbity Flop (1912)

Books illustrated by A.J. Macgregor include:
W. Perring (verses) Danny Duckling (1946), Piggly Plays Truant (1946), Lost at the Fair (1948), The Runaway (1948), Mr Badger to the Rescue (1949), Bunny's First Birthday (1950), The Green Umbrella (1950), Pippety's Unlucky Day (1950), Five Little Kittens (1955), High Tide (1956)

Periodicals: Cassell's Annual, Little Folks

Norah McGuinness (1901-80)

Born in Derry, Ireland, daughter of a shipowner. Studied at the National College of Art, Dublin, at Chelsea School of Art, London, and in André Lhôte's studio, Paris. Married to poet Geoffrey Phibbs (1924-35). Designer of costumes and sets for the Abbey and Gate Theatres, Dublin; full-time painter since 1940, working in gouache and oil. For illustration, she worked mainly in black and white, adapting her style to her subject with considerable élan, and utilising sources as wide-ranging as Celtic manuscripts and Art Deco. [Q]

Books illustrated include:
Elizabeth Bowen The Shelbourne (1951)
Maria Edgeworth The Most Unfortunate Day of My Life (1931)
Eileen O'Faolain Miss Pennyfeather and the Pooka (1944)
Laurence Sterne A Sentimental Journey (1926)
W.B. Yeats Stories of Red Hanrahan (1927)

Periodical: The Golden Hind

References: Bénézit; Johnson & Greutzner; Vollmer; Wa (1950); Waters; *The Studio* 90 (1925), special (1927)

David John McKee (b. 1943)

Works as David McKee. Born in Calabria, Italy. Received no formal art training. Writer and illustrator of books for young children and creator of animated films including the 'Mr Benn' and 'King Rollo' series for television and others for the Save the Children Fund. As an illustrator he works in outline, sometimes with colour washes or crayon, manipulating superficially childlike images with humour and an instinct for unusual design. [Q]

Books illustrated include:
Merry Archard Cook for Your Kids! (1975)
Kurt Baumann Joseph the Border Guard (1972), Joachim the Dustman (1974), Joachim the Policeman (1975)
Rosemary Debnam A Book of Pig Tales (1979), A Book of Bears (1982)
Elizabeth Hull Froman Mr Crackle and His Dragons (1971)
David Gadsby and Beatrice Harrop Harlequin (1981)
Brothers Grimm Hans in Luck (1967)
Elizabeth Holt Kids' London (1972)
Walter Kreye The Poor Farmer and the Robber Knights (1969)
Heloise Lewis Vamos Amigos (1971)
David Mackay Fire (1973), The Day We Went to the Seaside (1973)
David McKee Bronto's Wings (1964), Two Can Toucan (1964), Mr Benn, Red Knight (1967), Hans in Luck (1967), Mark and the Monocycle (1968), Elmer: The Story of a Patchwork Elephant (1968), 123456789 Benn (1970), The Magician Who Lost his Magic (1970), Six Men (1972), Lord Rex (1973), The Magician and the

David McKee. From his *King Rollo and the new shoes* (Andersen Press, 1979).

Sorcerer (1974), Elmer Again and Again (1975), The Day the Tide Went Out… and Out… (1976), The Magician and the Petnapping (1976), Two Admirals (1977), Tusk Tusk (1978), The Magician and the Balloon (1978), The Magician and the Dragon (1979), Big Game Benn (1979), King Rollo and the New Shoes (1979), King Rollo and the Birthday (1979), King Rollo and the Bread (1979), Big Top Benn (1980), Not Now Bernard (1980), King Rollo and the Tree (1980), King Rollo and the Balloons (1980), King Rollo and the Dishes (1980), The Magician and the Balloon (1980), King Rollo and King Frank (1981), King Rollo and the Search (1981), King Rollo and the Bath (1981), The Magician and Double Trouble (1981), King Rollo's Playroom (1983)
Deborah Manley Piccolo Book of Parties and Party Games (1973)
Caroline Moorehead Helping (1975)
Sydney Paulden Yan and the Gold Mountain Robbers (1974), Yan and the Firemonsters (1976)
Christine Pullein-Thompson Follyfoot Pony Quiz Book (1974)
Alvin Schwartz Tomfoolery (1975), Witcracks (1975)
Liane Smith Bertha the Tanker (1969)
R.A. Smith Blue Bell Hill Games (1982)
Hazel Townson The Speckled Panic (1982)
Katie Wales (ed) A Book of Elephants (1977)
Ursula Moray Williams Jeffy, the Burglar's Cat (1981)
Forrest Wilson Super Gran (1980), Super Gran Rules OK (1981), Super Gran Superstar (1982)

Periodicals: Parents, Punch, Readers Digest, The Times, The Times Educational Supplement

Reference: Kirkpatrick

Thomas Blakeley Mackenzie (1887-1944)

Born in Bradford, Yorkshire. Studied at Bradford College of Art and afterwards on a scholarship at the Slade School of Fine Art. Worked as a painter, etcher and wood engraver and, rather spasmodically, as an illustrator during the 1920s. He moved to France in 1929 in the hope of establishing himself there as a painter, but soon returned to England, and during the 1930s produced topographical etchings of Oxford and hand-made

jewellery. He died in Cornwall. The British Library catalogues Mackenzie as two separate artists: T.B. and Thomas Mackenzie, and this perhaps reflects the fact that, in illustration at least, he never developed a consistent style. His published work falls into three distinct groups: smoothly executed, naturalistic drypoints; full colour plates with echoes of, among others, Edmund Dulac*, the Fauves, oriental art, medieval manuscripts and black and white illustrations (wood engravings, and pen and ink drawings) that were the most spontaneous among his productions. Despite his lack of consistency, or perhaps because of his continuing search for a personal language, he produced some interesting illustrative work.

Books illustrated include:
Christine Chaundler Arthur and his Knights (1920)
James Elroy Flecker Hassan (1924)
Walter Pater Marius the Epicurean (1929)
A.M. Ransome Aladdin and his Wonderful Lamp (1919)
E. Southwart Brontë Moors and Villages (1923)
James Stephens The Crock of Gold (1926)
Ali Baba and Aladdin (1918)

Periodical: The Sketch

References: Johnson; Johnson & Greutzner

Haydn Reynolds Mackey (b. 1883)

Studied at the Slade School of Fine Art and the Langham School of Art. Lived mainly in London. Taught life drawing at Walthamstow School of Art. Official war artist during World War I. As an illustrator, he was attracted by the portentous and sinister; though varied in medium (lithographs, wood engravings, pencil drawings), his designs share a mood of macabre theatricality. He worked entirely for the less-known private presses, e.g. The Mandrake Press, the Verona Press and Romney Press.

Books illustrated include:
G. Flaubert Salammbô (1930)
Haydn Mackey La Grande Ducasse Drolatique (1922)
Thomas Nash The Unfortunate Traveller (1930)

Periodicals: The Golden Hind

References: Johnson & Greutzner; Vollmer; Wa (1960); Waters.

George Mackley (b. 1900)

Born in Tonbridge, Kent. Studied etching at Goldsmith's College (1918-21) and wood engraving under Noel Rooke* at the Central School of Arts and Crafts. Mackley's favourite subject was the riverside and his engravings are characterised by firmness and precision. Elected ARE (1950), SWE (1952), RE (1961); member Art Workers' Guild (1959).

Books illustrated include:
Armida Colt Weeds and Wild Flowers (1965)

George Mackley Wood Engraving (1948), Engraved in the Wood
(1968)

References: Balston EWE, WEMEB; Garrett BWE, HBWE; Johnson
& Greutzner; Wa (1972); Waters; *Image* 8 (Summer 1952); *Graven
Images* (Scottish Arts Council catalogue 1979); Hugh Casson (intro)
George Mackley, Wood Engraver (Gresham Press 1981); George
Mackley *Confessions of a Woodpecker* (Gresham Press 1981)

Edward Rolland McLachlan (b. 1940)

Usually works as Edward McLachlan. Born in
Leicester and studied at Leicester College of Art
(1956-58). Cartoonist, film writer and designer
(for Tony Cuthbert Ltd and Beryl Stevens Associates), advertising designer, book illustrator for
O.U.P., Longmans, Corgi/Transworld, C.U.P.,
Hodder and Stoughton etc. Worked for Wintertons
(1958-61), Cadburys (1961-62), Gayton Advertising
(1962-65) and freelance since 1965. Political
cartoonist on the *Sunday Mirror* (1967-70) and
Punch (1969-71). His illustrations, in pen and inks
of various colours are in a lively cartoon style.
Lives in Leicestershire. Won the Illustrator of the
Year Award in 1980 with a London Transport
poster and has won many prizes and awards for
film design. [Q]

Books illustrated include:
Jean English Tippy the Tipper Wagon (1969)
Paul Groves Bangers and Mash Series 1-26 (1975-79)
Anita Hewett Fire Engine Speedy (1966)
Roger Kilroy Graffiti 1 (1979), Graffiti 2 (1980), Graffiti 3 (1981),
Limericks 1 (1981)
Edward McLachlan Simon Books (1969-74), The Dragon that only
Blew Smoke (1971)
Simon Webb Chess for Tigers (1978), The Changing of Claude (1979)

Periodicals: Interface, Playboy, Private Eye, Punch, Radio Times,
Readers Digest, Sunday Mirror, Sunday Telegraph, The Times

Iain Macnab of Barachastlain (1890-1967)

Worked as Iain Macnab. Born in the Philippines,
son of an official of the Hong Kong and Shanghai
Bank; childhood spent in Scotland. Studied chartered accountancy in Glasgow (1911-14), a training
that was later to prove valuable in administrative
posts. Served in France during World War I.
Wounded by a shell at the Battle of Loos (1916);
invalided out of the army and spent much time in
hospital. He studied at Glasgow College of Art
(1917), at Heatherley's School of Art (1918), and
in Paris; Joint Principal of Heatherley's (1919-
25). In 1925, he founded the Grosvenor School of
Modern Art and remained its Principal until it
closed in 1940. He was twice invalided out of
Royal Air Force during World War II. In 1946 he
rented part of the former premises of the Grosvenor School to Heatherley's School of Art and
became its Director of Art Studies until 1953.
Painter and draughtsman, wood engraver, etcher,
writer on art techniques. Apart from the pen and
ink drawings for *Introduction to Woodstock*, his

Edward McLachlan. Tippy the Tipper Wagon by
Jean English (BBC, 1969).

book illustrations consist of wood engravings.
They are capably executed, revealing an awareness of contemporary stylistic developments in
the medium. Governor of the Federation of British
Artists (1959-67). Elected ARE (1923), RE
(1932, Hon Sec 1940), PROI (1959), FRSA, NS,
SWE.

Books illustrated include:
Robert Browning Selected Poems (1937)
Robert Burns Tam O'Shanter (1934)
Walter Savage Landor The Sculptured Garland (1948)
Iain Macnab Figure Drawing (1936), Wood-Engraving (1938),
Introduction to Woodstock (1951)
Dr. A.W.W. Ramsey (selected by) Nicht at Eenie, The Bairn's
Parnassus (1932)
J.H. Whyte (ed) Towards a New Scotland (1935)

References: Balston EWE, WEMEB; Garrett BWE, HBWE;
Guichard; Johnson & Greutzner; Vollmer; Wa (1970); Waters; *The
Artist* (April 1937); *The Studio* 117 (1939), special (Spring 1930, Winter
1936, Autumn 1938); Albert Garrett *Wood Engravings and Drawings
of Iain Macnab of Barachastlain* (Midas 1973)

Iain Macnab. 'Pippa Passes' from *Selected Poems
of Robert Browning* (Penguin, 1937).

Colin McNaughton. 'How Doth the Little Crocodile' by Lewis Carroll from *The Springtime Book* by James Reeves (Heinemann, 1975).

Colin McNaughton (b. 1951)

Born at Wallsend-upon-Tyne, Northumberland, son of a pattern-maker father and ballet dancer mother. Studied graphic design at the Central School of Arts and Crafts and illustration at the Royal College of Art. Part-time lecturer at Cambridge School of Art, and illustrator and writer of children's books since 1975. For illustration, he draws in pen and ink or pencil with watercolour washes, in a restrained, descriptive style much appreciated by children, often depicting humorously caricatured animals in realistic human settings and situations. He admires and has been influenced by the early English caricaturists, especially James Gillray and Thomas Rowlandson, and also by the contemporary American cartoonist Robert Crumb. He lives in Covent Garden, London. [Q]

Books illustrated include:
Allan Ahlberg Mr and Mrs Hay the Horse (1981), Miss Brick the Builder's Baby (1981)
Hester Burton A Grenville Goes to Sea (1977)
Jenny Hawkesworth A Handbook of Family Monsters (1980)
Russell Hoban The Great Fruit Gum Robbery (1981), They Came From Aargh (1981)
Mary McCaffrey The Mighty Muddle (1979)
Colin McNaughton 123 and Things (1976), ABC and Things (1976), Walk Rabbit Walk (1977), The Great Zoo Escape (1978), The Rat Race (1978), The Pirats (1979), Football Crazy (1980), Fat Pig (1981), If Dinosaurs Were Cats and Dogs (1981), King Nonn the Wiser (1981), In Out, Hide Seek, Fat Thin, Long Short, Over Under (Board Books 1982)
Colin McNaughton and Elizabeth Attenborough Walk Rabbit Walk (1977)
Emil Pacholec A Ship to Sail the Seven Seas (1980)
James Reeves (ed) The Springtime Book (1975), Egg Time Stories (1975), The Autumn Book (1977)

Reference: *Contemporary Authors*

Kenneth Mahood (b. 1930)

Born in Belfast, Northern Ireland. After leaving school he worked for a lithographic designer, and painted and drew cartoons in his spare time. His first drawing appeared in *Punch* when he was 18, and since 1950 he has contributed regularly to *Punch, The New Yorker* and other magazines. He was art editor of *Punch* (1960-65) and political cartoonist for *The Times* (1966-69). His illustrations for children's books, in outline with full colour, are in the humorous and unmistakable style of his newspaper and magazine drawings.

Books illustrated include:
Roger Benedictus Fifty Million Sausages (1975)
Kenneth Mahood The Laughing Dragon (1970), Why Are There More Questions Than Answers, Grandad? (1974), Losing Willy (1977)

Reference: ICB 4

Antony Jasper Maitland (b. 1932)

Works as Antony Maitland. Born in Andover, Hampshire. Studied at West of England College of Art, Bristol. Won the Leverhulme Research Award and spent a year studying in Europe. Painter, mural designer, graphic artist, jacket and children's book illustrator in black and white and full colour. His work is characterised by a crisp outline and fine multi-directional shading. Won the Kate Greenaway award with *Mrs Cockle's Cat* (1961). Books published principally by Constable.

Books illustrated include:
Ruth Ainsworth The Ten Tales of Shellover (1963), More Tales of Shellover (1968), The Phantom Cyclist and Other Stories (1971), The Bear who Liked Hugging People (1976)
Margery Williams Bianco Poor Cecco (1975)
Charles Causley Dick Whittington (1976)
Joan Clarke The Happy Planet (1963)
Lettice Cooper Contadino (1964)
Eleanor Farjeon Invitation to a Mouse and other poems (1981)
Kathleen Fidler The Little Ship Dog (1963), Flash the Sheep Dog (1965)
Leon Garfield Jack Holborn (1964), Devil-in-the-Fog (1966), Smith (1967), Black Jack (1968), Mr Corbett's Ghost and Other Stories (1969), The Drummer Boy (1969), The Ghost Downstairs (1972), The Lamplighter's Funeral (1976), Mirror Mirror (1976), John Diamond (1980)
Leon Garfield and David Proctor Child O'War (1972)

Anthony Maitland. From *A Dog So Small* by Philippa Pearce (Constable, 1962).

Penelope Lively Astercote (1970), The Ghost of Thomas Kempe (1973)
Elsie Locke The Runaway Settlers (1966)
Antony Maitland The Secret of the Shed (1962), Ben Goes to the City (1964), James and the Roman Silver (1965), Idle Jack (1977)
Anne Molloy A Proper Place for Chip (1963)
Philippa Pearce Mrs Cockle's Hat (1961), A Dog So Small (1962)
Meta Mayne Reid Beyond the Wide World's End (1972)
Emma Smith Out of Hand (1963)
R. Weir The Loner (1966)
Barbara Willard To London! To London! (1968)

References: Contemporary Authors; Eyre; Fisher pp.39, 325; Hürlimann; ICB 3, 4

William Henry Margetson (1861-1940)

Educated at Dulwich College, London; studied at the South Kensington and Royal Academy Schools. Lived at Wallingford, Berkshire; taught drawing at the Central School of Arts and Crafts. Figure and portrait painter in oil and watercolour, illustrator; also a keen sailor, dancer and gardener. His early reputation was based largely on his black and white and halftone illustrations, which were competent but conventional; after the turn of the century, he concentrated increasingly on figure painting. Father of illustrator Hester Margetson. Elected RMS (1896), ROI (1901), RI (1909).

Books illustrated include:
F. Barrett A Missing Witness (1897)
R. Hatton The Village of Youth (1895)
G.A. Henty With Cochrane the Dauntless (1897), A March on London (1898), The Tiger of Mysore (nd)
E. Nesbit The Old Nursery Stories (1908)
Overton The King's Pardon (1894)
H. Strang Humphrey Bold (1909)
A. Sutro Aglavine and Selsysette (1897)
S.J. Weyman The Wild Geese (1908)

Periodicals: Black and White, Cassell's Family Magazine, The English Illustrated Magazine, The Girls' Realm, The Graphic, The Harmsworth Magazine, The Idler, The Jolly Book, The Pall Mall Magazine, The Penny Magazine, The Quiver, Sunday at Home, The Tatler

References: Bénézit; Houfe; Johnson & Greutzner; Mallalieu; Thieme & Becker; Thorpe; Vollmer supp; Wa (1934); Waters; C. Wood; *The Studio* special (1898-99)

Yoshio Markino (b. 1874)

Born Koromo, Japan. Attended an American missionary college (1887). Moved to San Francisco (1894), where he paid for lessons at the Hopkins Art School by working as a cook and houseboy. Borrowed the fare for his passage to England; settled in Chelsea, London, and attended evening classes at Goldsmith's Institute and the Central School of Arts and Crafts. Visited Paris (1907) and Italy (1910). He was entranced by the atmosphere of London 'whose greyness is built up of every colour of the rainbow, whose murkiness gives quality to the silvery greys...whose mists and moisture lend height and add dignity to the buildings' (*The Colour of London*, 1907). Fascinated by East-West contrasts, he painted from

memory, combining Japanese simplicity with a Western perspective.

Books illustrated include:
L. Descaves The Colour of Paris (1908)
Alfred H. Hyatt The Charm of London (1912)
W.J. Loftie (intro) The Colour of London (1907)
Yoshio Markino The Japanese Dumpy Book (1902, 1932), A Japanese Artist in London (1911), When I Was a Child (1912), My Recollections and Impressions (1913), My Forty Years in England (in Japanese, 1940)
Y. Noguchi The Story of Yone Noguchi (1914)
Olave M. Potter The Colour of Rome (1909), A Little Pilgrimage in Italy (1911, 1913)
H. de Sélincourt Oxford from Within (1910)
D.B.W. Sladen Twenty Years of My Life (1915)

Periodicals: Black and White, Cassell's Magazine

References: Johnson & Greutzner; Waters; *The Magazine of Art* (new series, 1903)

Patricia Marriott (b. 1920)

Works as Pat Marriott. Born in Cheshire; grew up in London. Studied at Westminster and Chelsea Schools of Art. Illustrator in black and white and occasionally full colour. Lives in Wales.

Books illustrated include:
Joan Aiken All You've Ever Wanted, and other stories (1953), More

Pat Marriott. From *The Grey Family* by Noel Streatfeild (Hamish Hamilton, 1956).

Than You Ever Bargained For, and other stories (1955), The Wolves of Willoughby Chase (1962), Black Hearts in Battersea (1963), The Whispering Mountain (1968), A Small Pinch of Weather, and other stories (1969), The Cuckoo Tree (1971), A Harp of Fishbones (1972), Midnight is a Place (1974), The Faithless Lollybird (1977)
Caroline Baxter The Stolen Telesm (1975)
Charles Causley Figgie Hobbin (1970)
Joan Clarke Foxon's Hole (1969)
T. Colson Rinkin of Dragon's Wood (1965)
Ronald Fuller Pilgrim (1980)
Grace Hogarth A Sister for Helen (1976)
Jacynth Hope-Simpson The Great Fire (1961), The Ice Fair (1963)
Willard Price Arctic Adventure (1980)
Ann Schlee The Strangers (1971)
Ian Serraillier Belinda and the Swans (1952)
Noel Streatfeild The Grey Family (1956)
Mary Treadgold The Polly Harris (1968)
Elfrida Vipont Larry Lopkins (1965), Michael and the Dogs (1969)
Ursula Moray Williams No Pomes for Mill Pobjoy (1975)

References: Fisher p.85; ICB 2,3,4

Constance Kay Marshall (b. 1918)

Born in Waterford, Ireland; grew up in Cheshire, England. Studied at Burslem School of Art, Staffordshire and at the Royal College of Art. She has worked as a book and commercial illustrator since 1952, undertaking a wide range of commissions, but particularly enjoying drawing and painting animals. During her career, her style has varied in response to changing graphic trends.

Books illustrated include:
Mabel Allan At School in Skye (1957)
Leila Berg A Newt for Roddy (1965)
Roy Brown Little Brown Mouse (1967)
Bruce Carter The Gannet's Nest (1966)
Dorothy Clewes Roller Skates, Scooter and Bike (1966)
Marie Hynds The Television Castle (1975)
Rosemary Manning Green Smoke (1957), Dragon in Danger (1959), The Dragon's Quest (1961)
Ruth Manning-Sanders Slippery Shiney (1965)
Diana Ross Nothing to Do (1966)
Jenny Seed To the Rescue (1966)
Noel Streatfeild Look at the Circus (1960)
Meriol Trevor The Treasure Hunt (1957)
Elfrida Vipont The China Dog (1967)
Barbara Willard The Pram Race (1961)

References: ICB 2,4

Frank Vernon Martin (b. 1921)

Works as Frank Martin. Born Dulwich, London; father a scientist, mother an actress. Read history at Hertford College, Oxford, then studied wood engraving under Gertrude Hermes* at St Martins School of Art, and etching privately with John Buckland-Wright*. Served in the Royal Artillery during World War II; a freelance artist since 1949. Taught engraving and etching at Camberwell School of Arts and Crafts (1953-76), head of Department of Graphic Arts there (1976-80). His book illustrations have been published mainly by the Folio Society, Burns & Oates and Hutchinson. They consist of wood engravings, sometimes in a deliberately archaic manner (as in *Jonathan Wilde*), at other times in a style particularly suited to reproduction, as though from pen and ink originals (as in *Scarlet and Black*). Around 1966, he

Frank Martin. From *The Bridge of San Luis Rey* by Thornton Wilder (Folio Society, 1956).

gave up book illustration in favour of limited edition printmaking, favouring pre-war theatre and cinema subjects. Member of the Graphic Design Board and of the Council for National Academic Awards (1977-81). Member SWE (Hon. Sec. 1952-59), SIA (1955-71); Fellow RE (1955-74, secretary 1955-56). Honorary Academician of the Accademia delle Arti del Disegno, Florence (1965).

Books illustrated include:
Thomas Balston (ed) The Housekeeping Book of Susanna Whatman (1956)
Henry Fielding The Life of Mr Jonathan Wild the Great (1966)
Norman Goodland My Father Before Me (1953)
William Hazlitt Essays (1964)
Magdalen King-Hall The Diary of a Young Lady of Fashion (1982)
Charles Lamb Essays (1963)
Mardrus and Mathers (trans) The Book of the Thousand Nights and One Night Vols II and IV (1958)
Marjorie Sisson The Cave (1957)
Tobias Smollett The Adventures of Roderick Random (1959)
Stendhal Scarlet and Black (1965)
Susanna Whatman The Housekeeping Book (1956)
Oscar Wilde Salome (1957)
Thornton Wilder The Bridge of San Luis Rey (1956)
The Bedside Book of the Art of Living (Readers Digest 1959)
The Manual of Catholic Prayer (1962)
The New Small Missal (1965)

References: Garrett BWE, HBWE; Wa (1972); Waters; *Arts Review* (14th August 1971); *Form und Technik* (Stuttgart, January 1958); *The Sphere* (25th August 1956); *Illustrated Exhibition Catalogues* (London Arts 1968, Editions Graphiques 1972, 1975); Brian North Lee, *British Bookplates* (David & Charles 1979)

Enid Crystal Dorothy Marx (b. 1902)

Works as Enid Marx. Born in London, daughter of a consulting engineer. Studied at the Central School of Arts and Crafts and at the Royal College of Art. Painter, printmaker (wood engravings, lithographs, and lino cuts), textile designer, author and illustrator of children's books, writer on art, designer of book jackets, trademarks and UK postage stamps (e.g. Accession 1952, Christmas 1970). She worked with the textile designers Barron and Larcher (1925-27), then set up her own studio designing and printing hand blockprinted textiles during the late 'twenties and 'thirties until World War II; she also designed for the Curwen Press, Chatto & Windus, Faber & Faber among others. For illustration she used wood engraving and lithography and drew in pen and ink, working in a freely decorative style that varied with her media but always reflected her interest in pattern and design. The first woman engraver to be appointed a Royal Designer for Industry (1944). Elected FSIA (1946), SWE (1955); Honorary FRCA (1982). [Q]

Books illustrated include:
Francesca Allinson A Childhood (1937)
Norman Douglas An Almanac (1945)
Margaret Lambert When Victoria Began to Reign (1937)
Enid Marx Book of Nursery Rhymes (1938), Bulgy the Barrage
    Balloon (1941), Nelson the Kite of the King's Navy (1942), The
    Little White Bear (1945), Quiz (1945), Tom Thumb (1945), A Book
    of Rigmaroles, or Jingle Rhymes (1946), The Pigeon Ace (1946), A
    Menagerie (1946), Slithery Sam (1947), Sam and Amy (1972)
English Popular and Traditional Art (with Margaret Lambert, 1946)
English Traditional Art (with Margaret Lambert, 1951)

References: Garrett BWE, HBWE; Wa (1980); Waters 2;
Architectural Review (1930 & 1934); *Designer* (November 1979); *The
G.B. Journal* (no 2 1979, no 5 1979, no 1 1980, no 2 1980); *Graphis* 10
(1954); *The Listener* (1932, 1938); *Signature* 4 (1936); *The Woodcut*
(1927); *Shall We Join the Ladies?* (Studio One Gallery, Oxford 1979);
Thirties (Hayward Gallery catalogue 1979)

Dodie Masterman (b. 1918)

Maiden name: Rhoda Helen Glass. Born Brixham, Devon, daughter of the director of a motor-car trading firm. While at boarding school, attended classes at Leicester School of Art. Studied at the Slade School of Fine Art (1934-39, Slade Scholar 1938-39), where she studied stage design and scene painting with Diaghilev's scene painter Vladimir Polunin. Served in the WVS until 1945, and during the 1940s, she worked as a model for *Vogue* magazine. Visiting lecturer in drawing and illustration at Camberwell School of Art (1945-65). Taught in European Summer School, Parsons School of Design, New York (1957-65). With three other members of the Tennyson Society, she publishes *The Enchanted Moan*, a magazine devoted to the poem *Maud*. Landscape and still-life painter; glass painter (mainly illustrations of 18th and 19th-century literature); expert on English and European Toy theatre prints and 19th-century colouring methods. Collector of 19th-century ephemera. As a book illustrator (mainly of classics) and jacket designer, she works in pen, chalk, etching (hard and soft ground), aquatint, lithography, line with adhesive tone ('zip-a-tone'), and monotype (favouring the latter for its tonal range and reproductive simplicity). Her choice of medium plays an important part in her work, and her range of techniques has resulted in unusual stylistic diversity. [Q]

Books illustrated include:
Louisa M. Alcott Little Women (1966)
Margaret Barker Jane and Peter Series of Readers (1956)
Lucy W. Bellhouse The Helicopter Children (1956), Carolina's

Enid Marx. From *Book of Nursery Rhymes* (1938, Zodiac 1949).

Holiday (c. 1957)
Betty Cavanna The Scarlet Sail (1962)
Jules Barbey D'Aurevilley Les Diaboliques (1947)
Honoré de Balzac Eugénie Grandet (1953)
Nichole de Buron Feed the Brute (c.1961), Say I'm in Conference
    (c.1961)
Fernando de Vilmorin Les Belles Amours (1956), Love Story (1957),
    The Letter in a Taxi (1960)
Fernando de Rojas (trans J.M. Cohen The Spanish Bawd (1973)
Eleanor Farjeon Perkin the Pedlar (1956)
James Joyce A Portrait of the Artist as a Young Man (1965)
D.H. Lawrence The Virgin and the Gypsy (1955)
Mikhail Lermontov A Hero of Our Time (1980)
W. Somerset Maugham Cakes and Ale (1970)
Henry Mürger (trans Norman Cameron) Vie de Bohème (1960)
Amoret Scott A Murmur of Bees (1980)
E.G. Thorpe Sad Little Star (1958)
Leo Tolstoy Anna Karenina (1975)
Jennifer Wayne The Day the Ceiling Fell Down (1961), The Night the
    Rain Came In (1963)

Periodicals: The Enchanted Moan, Envoy, Radio Times, Vogue

References: ICB 2; Jacques; Usherwood; *Illustration and Graphic
Design* (Phaidon 1980)

Jack Matthew (b. 1911)

Born in Oldham, Lancashire. Attended Oldham Art School and Goldsmith's College School of Art, London, where he studied illustration under Rowland Hilder*, wood engraving, and lithography. He was a prolific illustrator of adventure stories in a style influenced by E.J. Sullivan* and the German graphic artist Adolf Menzel, whose work he much admired. Though his draughtsmanship was conventional, his tonal transitions were often striking. He drew mainly in ink, sometimes combined with crayon on rough-textured paper to give the effect of lithography, and sometimes with flat colour washes.

Books illustrated include:
R.M. Ballantyne Coral Island (1952)
Lucy Evelyn Cheesman Marooned in Du-Bu Cove (1949)
Peter Dawlish Peg-Leg and the Invaders (1940)
Kathleen Fidler Tales of the North Country (1952)
Angus MacVicar Tider Mountain (1952)
Carola Oman Robin Hood (1942)
Monica Redlich Jam Tomorrow (1937)
Marjorie Sankey Chuckwaggon (1939)
R.L. Stevenson Catriona (1947), Treasure Island (1951)
L.G. Strong The Fifth of November (1937), Henry of Agincourt (1937)
Donald Suddaby Merry Jack Jugg, Highwayman (1954)
Tudur Watkins The Spanish Galleon (1945)
Percy Westerman Round the World in the 'Golden Gleaner' (1952),
    Bob Strickland's Log (1953)
Ursula Moray Williams Peter and the Wanderlust (1939)
J.R. Wyss Swiss Family Robinson (1949)

Periodical: Radio Times

Reference: ICB 2

Donald Maxwell (1877-1936)

Son of a schoolmaster. Studied at the Royal College of Art (1896), the Slade School of Fine

Jack Matthew. Frontispiece from *Jam Tomorrow* by Monica Redlich (Nelson, 1937).

Donald Maxwell. 'The Weavers, Canterbury' from *Adventures with a Sketch Book* (John Lane, 1914).

Art (1897) and Clapham Art School. Landscape and marine painter, graphic artist and author. Naval artist-correspondent to *The Graphic* for twenty years and official artist to the Admiralty during World War I; travelled widely, visiting Palestine and Mesopotamia (1918); accompanied the Prince of Wales on a tour of India. He illustrated his many travel and topographical books with skill and consistency, and was particularly successful at evoking achieving convincing effects of light and temperature.

Books illustrated include:
James Baker Austria (1913)
J.H.P. Belloc Hills and the Sea (1927)
Agnes Herbert The Isle of Man (1909)
Rudyard Kipling Sea and Sussex (1926), Songs of the Sea (1927), East
    of Suez (1931)
A.B. Laird This Way to Arcady (1926)
H.W. Longfellow The Building of the Ship (1904)
Donald Maxwell The Log of the Griffin (with C.W. Taylor, 1905), A
    Cruise across Europe (with C.W. Taylor, 1907), Adventures with a
    Sketch Book (1914), A Dweller in Mesopotamia (1920), Unknown
    Kent (1921), Unknown Sussex (1923), Unknown Surrey (1924),
    Unknown Essex (1925), Unknown Norfolk (1925), The New Lights
    o'London (1926), Unknown Suffolk (1926), History with a Sketch-
    Book (1926), The Book of the Clyde (1927), The Enchanted Road
    (1927), Unknown Dorset (1927), Unknown Somerset (1927),
    Adventures Among Churches (1928), A Detective in Kent (1929),
    More Adventures among Churches (1929), A Detective in Surrey
    (1932), A Detective in Sussex (1932), A Detective in Essex (1933),

Colour Sketching in Chalk (1934), Unknown Buckinghamshire
  (1935)
Gordon S. Maxwell The Motor Launch Patrol (1920), The Naval Front
  (1920), The Fringe of London (1925), Just Beyond London (1927),
  The Road to France (1928)
James Milne Travels in Hope (1928)
C.B. Mortlock Famous London Churches (1934)
W. Watson Wordsworth's Grave (1904)
William Wordsworth Lines Composed a Few Miles above Tintern
  Abbey (1904), Resolution and Independence (1904)

References: Houfe; Johnson & Greutzner; Vollmer supp; Wa (1970);
The Studio 34 (1905), special (1911, Autumn 1914).

F. Stocks May (active 1950s)

Children's book illustrator in full colour, halftone
and black and white, who produced bland, reasonably competent designs that were typical of their
type. The *Blackberry Farm* books were re-issued
in the late 1970s.

Books illustrated include:
Enid Blyton The Story of Our Queen (1953)
Monica Marsden The Mystery of the Blue Brethren (1950), The
  Mystery of Beacon Hill (1951)
Jane Pilgrim The Blackberry Farm Books (1949-67)
R.L. Stevenson Treasure Island (1958)

Philip William May (1864-1903)

Worked as Phil May. Born in Worthley, near
Leeds, son of an unsuccessful businessman. After
leaving school at an early age he worked as a
scene painter at the Grand Theatre, Leeds, and
toured the country playing small parts and drawing
caricatures for advertisements. He moved to
London in 1883 and worked sporadically for magazines, then travelled to Australia and spent three
years drawing for the *Sydney Bulletin*. He then
studied art briefly in Paris and returned penniless
to London in 1888. By that time the majority of
British magazines had switched to photomechanical
reproduction methods for their drawn illustrations (an exception was *Punch* which remained
with the wood engraving firm of Joseph Swain
until the early 1890s) and were looking for new
artists to supply the greater number of illustrations facilitated by the new process. In this climate
May achieved rapid success. He contributed to
many magazines and joined the staff of *The Graphic*
in 1891, *Punch* in 1893 and for twelve years produced a *Phil May Annual* (published 1892-1904).
Well known in London for his bohemian lifestyle,
he died of cirrhosis of the liver and consumption
in 1903. Although most of May's work was for the
magazines of the 1890s, he exerted an important
influence on 20th-century illustration through his
wide influence on artists of his generation, most
of whom outlived him and remained active until
well into the 1920s and 1930s. He pioneered a
vigorous economical style of pen and ink drawing
(sometimes combined with wash) which was particularly suited to reproduction. Though his

drawings had the appearance of spontaneous
reportage, they were in fact the outcome of detailed
preparatory sketches from which he extracted
only the essential lines; this awareness of the
importance of every line was a significant element
in his drawings, which were inherently funny,
even without their accompanying captions. He
was an acute observer and drew people as individuals rather than merely as types. May's work
formed a striking contrast with that of the other
remarkable but short-lived pen and ink draughtsman of the 1890s, Aubrey Beardsley, but both
artists partly owed their success to the new photographic process that for the first time enabled pen
drawings to be accurately reproduced. May was
elected RI (1896), RP (1896); member of NEAC
(1894-97) and the London Sketch Club.

Books illustrated include:
J.M. Barrie The Little Minister (1898)
C. Bertram Isn't It Wonderful (1896)
Sir Walter Besant East London (1901)
Sir F.C. Burnand The Zig Zag Guide (1897)
H.L. Grin Green on Rougemont (1898)
H.W. Lucy The Balfourian Parliament 1900-05 (1906)
Phil May Phil May's Gutter Snipes (1896), Phil May's ABC (1897)
H.H.S. Pearce The 'Comet' Coach (1895)
Revd Joseph Slapkins The Parson and the Painter (under pseudonym
  Charlie Summers, 1892)
M.H. Spielmann Littledom Castle (1903)
B. Webber Fun, Frolic and Fancy (1894)

Periodicals: Black and White, The Century Magazine, The Daily
Chronicle, The Daily Graphic, The English Illustrated Magazine,
Eureka, The Graphic, The Illustrated Londo News, The Pall Mall
Budget, The Penny Illustrated Paper, Phil May's Annual, Pick-Me-Up,
The Pictorial World, Punch, St Stephen's Review, The Savoy, The
Sketch, Society, The Sydney Bulletin, The Tatler, The Unicorn, The
Yorkshire Gossip

References: Bénézit; Bryan; Chamot, Farr & Butlin; Cuppleditch;
DNB (1901-11); Harper; Houfe; ICB 1; Johnson & Greutzner;
Mallalieu; Pennell PD; Price; Ray; Thieme & Becker; Thorpe; Waters;
C. Wood; *The Studio* 29 (1903), 30 (1904), special (1900-01, 1917,
Spring 1922, 1923-24, Autumn 1928); William Feaver *Masters of
Caricature* (Weidenfeld & Nicholson, 1981); Holbrook Jackson *The
1890s* (Grant Richards 1913); J. Thorpe *Phil May* (Harrap, 1932)

Thomas Maybank

See Hector Thomas Maybank Webb.

Robert Ashwin Maynard (1888-1966)

Born London. After studying at Westminster
School of Art and in Paris, he specialised in typography at the Central School of Arts and Crafts
under J.H. Manson. Painter, wood engraver,
typographer, designer. On his appointment as
first director of the Gregynog Press (1922), he
taught himself wood engraving, and later contributed illustrations and engravings to Gregynog
publications. He commissioned illustrations from
his wood-engraving pupil Horace Walter Bray*
and from David Jones*. He left the Gregynog
Press to start the Raven Press (1931-40) with
Bray, and was succeeded at the Gregynog by

Blair Hughes-Stanton*. In his later years, he worked as a designer and typographic advisor to several publishing houses. He was a member of the Arts and Crafts Exhibition Society.

Books illustrated include:
John Milton Samson Agonistes (1931)
Ernest Rhys The Life of Saint David (1927)
P.E. Thomas Chosen Essay (1926)
Henry Vaughan Poems (1924)
The Penillion Omar Khayyam (1928)
The Plays of Euripides (1931)

References: Balston WEMEB; Johnson & Greutzner; Vollmer; Wa (1934); *The Studio* special (Spring 1930, Autumn 1938)

Eileen Mayo (b. 1906)

Married name: Mrs Gainsborough. Educated in Yorkshire and Bristol; studied at the Slade School of Fine Art (1924-25), part-time at the Central School of Arts and Crafts under Noel Rooke* and John Farleigh*, at the Chelsea Polytechnic (1936), and at the Académie Montmartre, Paris, under Fernand Léger (1948-49). She was instructed in lino-cutting by telephone by Claude Flight* in 1927, and her resulting print, 'Turkish Bath', was included in the Redfern Gallery's first exhibition of lino-cuts and then bought by the Victoria and Albert Museum. She became well-known as an artists' model, working particularly for Laura Knight. Later she became a lecturer at St Martin's School of Art and Sir John Cass College, London (1950-53), at the National Art School, Sydney, Australia, (1957-62) and at the School of Fine Art, University of Canterbury, New Zealand (from 1967). Her work as a painter ranges from large-scale murals and travel posters to postage stamps (including the Australian Mammals and Barrier Reef series): her prints have been widely exhibited and she is a member of the SWE, Senefelder Club, Sydney Printmakers, and the Print Council of New Zealand. For economic reasons, since they entailed long periods of work without payment, most of her book illustrations date from the period of her marriage (1936-late 1940s), indeed *The Story of Living Things* took five years to complete. As an illustrator, she has used coloured crayon, pencil, chalk, pen and ink, designer colour, and wood engraving and wood cutting. Her work is dynamic and boldly drawn, with a lively sense of page design. She is best known for her animal illustrations, which combine accuracy with boldly decorative qualities. She has lived in Christchurch, New Zealand, since 1962. [Q]

Books illustrated include:
C.W. Beaumont Toys... (1930)
Edmund C. Blunden Japanese Garland (1928)
Sally Carrighar One Day on Beetle Rock (1946)
Sir William Jones (trans) The Poem of Amriolkais (1930)
Eileen Mayo Shells and How they Live (1944), The Story of Living Things (1944), Nature's A B C (1944), Little Animals of the Countryside (1945), Larger Animals of the Countryside (1949), Animals on the Farm (1950)

Mays. ' "Phew! That was frantic!" gasped Darbishire' from *Take Jennings for Instance* by Anthony Buckeridge (Collins, 1958).

Sacheverell Sitwell (trans) Serge Lifar (1928)

References: Hürlimann; Johnson & Greutzner; Wa (1980)

Douglas Lionel Mays (b. 1900)

Has sometimes worked as Mays. Studied at Goldsmith's School of Art (1920-23) under Harold Speed and E.J. Sullivan*. Painter and illustrator. For illustration he used pen, pencil and wash in various combinations, often on tinted paper with white highlights. He has lived in Buckinghamshire and Cornwall.

Books illustrated include:
Angela Brazil Three Terms at Uplands (nd)
Nancy Breary Junior Captain (1946), Rachel Changes Schools (1948),
Anthony Buckeridge Take Jennings for Instance (1958), Jennings, as Usual (1959), The Trouble with Jennings (1960), Just Like Jennings (1961), Leave it to Jennings (1963), Jennings, of Course! (1964), Especially Jennings! (1965), Jennings Abounding (1967), Jennings in Particular (1968), Trust Jennings! (1969), The Jennings Report (1970)
'Mrs Herbert Strang' (ed) The New Green Book for Girls, (with others, 1934)
Noel Streatfeild Tennis Shoes (1937), The House in Cornwall, (1940), Curtain Up (1944)
Percy Westerman The Disappearing Dhow (1933), Andy-All-Alone (1934), The Call of the Sea (1935), Midshipman Webb's Treasure (1937), His Unfinished Voyage (1937), Cadet Alan Car (1938)
My Book of Elves and Fairies (with others, nd)

Periodicals: The Big Budget, Holiday Annual, Punch

References: Johnson & Greutzner; Price; Waters

William Gordon Mein (active 1888-1925)

Worked as Will Mein. Figure painter and illustrator mainly of children's books. Lived in Edinburgh (1894) and London (1903). Much of his illustrative work is in pen and ink, drawn in a tight, formal, tidy style.

Books illustrated include:
W.E. Cule Mabel's Prince Wonderful (1899)

Christie Deas Pan-o'-the-Pipes (1915)
James J. Eaton The Worship of It (1915)
C.R. Gull From the Book Beautiful (1903)
P.W.D. Izzard Homeland (1918)
D.L.A. Jephson A Fragment... (1903)
Irene Osgood Where Pharaoh Dreams (1914)
C.W. Scott Some Notable Hamlets of the Present Time (1900)
N. Tourneur Hidden Witchery (1898)
The Indelicate Duellist (with others, 1914)

Periodical: The Dome

References: Houfe; Johnson & Greutzner

Roy Meldrum (active 1919-55)

A writer of children's fiction and a landscape painter, Meldrum also published books on Latin elegiac verse composition (1919) and on rowing techniques (1950-55). His children's books were all published by Basil Blackwell. His illustrations for these, normally in pen or brush, often attempted bold effects and were occasionally experimental in approach; but his sketchy style failed to conceal poor draughtsmanship.

Books illustrated include:
Laurence Housman Turn Again Tales (with others, 1930)
Roy Meldrum Col & Joy (1927), The Silver Ship (1927), Zed (1930)
    The Happy Cobbler (1932), Robin the Monk (1934), Susanna; also
    The Duckling (1936)

Periodical: Joy Street

Reference: Johnson & Greutzner

Mortimer Menpes (1860-1938)

Born in Australia. Educated at Port Adelaide. Landscape and portrait painter and etcher. After moving to London, he became a studio assistant to J.A. McNeill Whistler (c.1884). He later expressed the view that among the many followers of Whistler, only he and the painter W.R. Sickert were genuine pupils of 'The Master' and recalled 'I was almost a slave in his service, ready and only too anxious to help, and no matter in how small a way.' (*Whistler as I Knew Him*). He later studied in Japan under the master Kyô Sai. He was a 'special' artist in South Africa for *Black and White* (1900) and travelled widely, often as a press artist. His book illustrations consisted mainly of portraits, and topographical watercolours for travel books written by his daughter. He eventually settled in Berkshire as a fruit farmer, and there ran the Menpes Press. He was elected RE (1881), RBA (1885), NEAC (1886), RI (1897) and Fellow of the Royal Geographical Society.

Books illustrated include:
John Finnemore Delhi and the Durbar (1907), India (1912)
Pierre Loti Madame Prune (1919)
J. McCarthy and Mrs C. Praed The Grey River (nd)
Dorothy Menpes War Impressions (1901), Japan (1901), World
    Pictures (1902), The Durbar (1903), The World's Children (1903),
    Venice (1904), India (1905), Brittany (1905)
G.E. Mitton The Thames (1906), The People of India (1910)

Periodicals: Black and White, The Pall Mall Magazine

References: Bénézit; Guichard; Houfe; Johnson & Greutzner; Thieme & Becker; Vollmer supp.; Wa (1934); Waters; C. Wood; *The Art Journal* (1881); *The Magazine of Art* (1899); *The Studio* 6 (1896), 10 (1897), 17 (1899), special (1900-01, 1902); Mortimer Menpes *Whistler as I Knew Him* (A. & C. Black, 1904); Frederick Wedmore *Etching in England* (G. Bell, 1895).

Amy Joyce Mercer (1896-1965)

Worked as Joyce Mercer. Born in Sheffield, daughter of a solicitor. Studied at Sheffield School of Art and at Chelsea School of Art. Book illustrator, postcard designer and contributor of topical cartoons to several magazines. Naturally left-handed, she trained herself to draw with both hands simultaneously so as to be able to execute symmetrical designs. During World War II, she served with the Women's Voluntary Service, but was so appalled by her experiences in bombed-out London dockland that she retired to Penrith in the Lake District and lived there in solitude. Her illustrations are mainly in pen and ink, sometimes in full colour. She drew in a sharp, two-dimensional style in which pattern and decoration were of primary importance. Her work was distinctive and easily recognised, but hard to imitate effectively as her collaborator, Rosalind Turvey, demonstrated in the *Mister Meddle* books.

Books illustrated include:
Hans Christian Andersen Andersen's Fairy Tales (1935)
Enid Blyton Mister Meddle's Mischief (with Rosalind M. Turvey,
    1940), Mister Meddle's Muddles (with Rosalind M. Turvey, 1950),
    Merry Mister Meddle! (with Rosalind M. Turvey, 1954)
The Favourite Wonder Book (Odhams, 1938)
Grimm's Fairy Tales (1934)

Periodicals: The Bystander, The Girl's Own Paper, The Illustrated London News, London Opinion, The Prize, Punch, The Sketch

Reference: Cope

Norman Meredith (active from 1940s)

Born in Liverpool. Studied at Liverpool School of Art, won a scholarship at the Royal College of Art, and a travelling scholarship in Italy, France, Germany, and Holland. Lecturer in Art at University College, Aberystwyth (1935), technical illustrator for the Ministry of Aircraft Production, Farnborough (1940-46), part-time lecturer at St Martin's School of Art, London (1947-74). He has contributed humorous illustrations to a large number of magazines and newspapers, and a comic strip to the London *Evening Standard*. His career as a children's book illustrator began when Enid Blyton asked him to illustrate her stories at the end of World War II. Since then, he has illustrated over 100 books, using a pen and black ink in Normatone. In some of his working methods he was influenced by his friend Leslie Illingworth (fellow-contributor to the *Daily Mail* and *Punch*).

Norman Meredith. 'Romans defeating the Iceni' from *The Roman World* by Paul Titley (Mills & Boon, 1975).

Since 1978, he has concentrated on humorous full-colour paintings of anthropomorphised animals as decorations for textiles, chinaware, greetings cards, and nursery pictures. Lives in Surrey. [Q]

Books illustrated include:
Enid Blyton Rubbalong Tales (1950), Feefo, Tuppenny and Jinks (1951), The Queer Adventures (1952)
Grania Brandon Sangler's Circus (1948), Sangler's Sawdust Ring (1951), Sangler's Rising Star (1952), Sangler Comes to Town (1953), Sangler Buys Babette (1954)
C.A. Burland Montezuma, Lord of the Aztecs (1967)
Irene Byers Sea Sprite Adventure (1960), The Twins' Good Turn (1961)
Ralph F. Eagle Lively English (5 books 1965)
Eleanor Graham The Story of Charles Dickens (1952)
Adrian Johnson Peter the Great: Round the World Histories (1966)
V.S. Petheram Racing Car Mystery (1960), Sam Spanner Detective (1960), The Sea-Devil Divers (1960), The Moon Rocket (1960)
A.E. Smith Mr Tarr's Tale (1966)
C.F. Bricknell Smith Social English (4 books 1960)
Pamela Symonds Let's Speak French (1963)
Paul Titley Look and Remember History Series (6 books 1969-77), Look and Remember People and Events Series (4 books 1975-76)
Geoffrey Trease Fortune, My Foe (1949)
Children's Wonder Book of Colour (vol 2, 1948; vol 3, 1949)
The Modern Gift Book for Children (1948)

Periodicals: The Bystander, Daily Mail, Evening Standard, Punch, The Sketch, The Tatler

Reference: Wa (1980)

Gerald Fenwick Metcalfe
(active 1890-1930)

Born Landour, India, son of an army doctor. He studied at the South Kensington, Royal Academy, and St John's Wood Schools of Art and worked as a painter and miniaturist, and in clay and bronze. He lived in London and at Albury, Surrey. He was an enthusiastic gardener, and interested in amateur theatre and folk dance. At times, his graphic style revealed the influence of his better-known and more prolific contemporaries J. Byam Shaw* (with whom he shared a studio during the 1890s) and E.J. Sullivan*, but his drawings had considerable power and enough individuality to make it a matter for regret that he did so little work in black and white.

Book illustrated:
The Poems of Coleridge (1907)

Periodicals: Country Life, The Ladies' Field, Punch

References: Houfe; Johnson & Greutzner; Vollmer; Wa (1934); C. Wood; *The Studio* Special (1911, Autumn 1914)

Sydney Harold Meteyard (1868-1947)

Born Stourbridge, West Midlands. Studied at Birmingham School of Art. Painter (oil, water-colour and gouache) and designer of stained glass. As an illustrator, he is chiefly remembered for his 25 neatly-drawn colour plates for the expensively produced *Golden Legend* (Hodder and Stoughton 1910), which showed the influence of Sir Edward Burne-Jones.

Book illustrated:
H.W. Longfellow The Golden Legend (1910)

Periodicals: The Quest, The Yellow Book

Gerald Metcalfe. 'Alone, alone, all, all alone on a wide, wide sea!' from *The Poems of Coleridge* (John Lane, 1907).

References: Houfe; Johnson & Greutzner; Mallalieu; Vollmer supp; Wa (1952); Waters; C. Wood; *The Studio* 1 (1893) pp 237-40

Arthur C. Michael (active 1903-1928)

Lived at Bedford Park, London. Painter and etcher. A reliable descriptive illustrator, able to evoke atmosphere. He worked mainly in full colour (watercolour or body colour) in a style typical of his period.

Books illustrated include:
Charles Dickens A Christmas Carol (1911)
John Galsworthy The Forsyte Saga (1928)
H. Rider Haggard The Ghost King (1908), King Solomon's Mines (1912), Finished (1917)
H.E. Marshall A History of France (1912), A History of Germany (1913), The Story of the United States (1919)
A.C. Michael An Artist in Spain (1914)
R.L. Stevenson Catriona (1925)
H.G. Wells The War in the Air (1908)
Princess Mary's Gift Book (with others, nd)

Periodicals: The Girls' Realm, The Illustrated London News, Little Folks, The London Magazine, The Morning Star, Nash's Magazine, The Pall Mall Magazine, Pearson's Magazine, The Quiver, The Strand Magazine, Sunday at Home, The Windsor Magazine

References: Houfe; Johnson & Greutzner; *The Bookman* (Christmas Number 1928)

Robert Flavell Micklewright (b. 1923)

Usually works as Robert Micklewright. Born in Staffordshire, son of a doctor. Studied at Croydon School of Art (1939). After war service in

A.C. Michael. 'Presently the English Channel was bridged' from *The War in the Air* by H.G. Wells (Bell, 1908).

Algeria, Tunisia, Italy and Greece (1939-42), he attended Wimbledon School of Art (1947-49) and the Slade School of Fine Art (1949-52). His output as a freelance painter and designer in many media since 1952 has included paintings for the headquarters of Gulf Oil, designs for Shell calendars, posters for London Transport, stamp books for the Post Office, and illustrations for over 200 plays published by the BBC. In common with many book illustrations of the 1960s, Micklewright's pen and ink drawings tend to emphasise the page surface by means of such graphic devices as multiple outlines, dotted sequences, and sometimes spattered shading. Such mannerisms might easily become distracting, but in Micklewright's work they are used with a degree of academic restraint. FSIA, RWS. [Q]

Books illustrated include:
Michel-Aimé Boudray Mike and the Motorbike (1961)
Howard Agg A Cypress in Sicily (1967)
E.L. Almedingen Ellen (1971), Anna (1972)
Arthur C. Clarke A Fall of Moondust (1967), The Song Tree (1972)
Humphrey M. Dobinson Bird Count (with Roy Wiltshire, 1976)
John Escott Oddments Corner (1976)
Katherine Hudson The Story of Elizabethan Boy Actors (1971), The Story of Geoffrey Chaucer (1973)
Sita Rathnamal Beyond the Jungle (1968)
Malcolm Saville See How it Grows (1971), The Seashore Quiz (1981)
Noreen Shelley Family at the Lookout (1972)

Robert Micklewright. From *Mick and the Motorbike* by Michel-Aimé Boudray (Bodley Head, 1961).

R.L. Stevenson Treasure Island (1963), The Black Arrow (1968)
Rosemary Sutcliff Witches Brat (1970)
John Rowe Townsend Summer People (1972)
Jean Wills The Sawdust Secret (1973)

Periodical: Radio Times

References: Driver; Fisher p.189; ICB 4; Jacques; Ryder; Usherwood;
Wa (1980); Waters; *Designers in Britain* 5,6,7

John Guille Millais (1865-1931)

Born in London, youngest son of Sir John Everett
Millais, PRA. Educated at Marlborough College
and Trinity College Cambridge. Served 11 years
in the army. Travelled (mainly on hunting expeditions) to Iceland, Canada, the United States,
Alaska, the Arctic, the Carpathians, and South
Africa. Painter of animals, landscapes and portraits and a sculptor. His illustrations, mainly of
animal and bird subjects, were in pen and ink,
pencil or crayon, sometimes with halftone washes,
and occasionally in full colour. R.E.D. Sketchley
wrote, 'No-one else draws animals in action,
whether British deer or African wild beast, from
more intelligent or thorough observation... Birds
in flight, beasts in action, Mr Millais is indisputably
master of his subject. Many drawings show the
humour which is one of the charms of his work.'
Elected FZS. Lived at Horsham, Surrey.

Books illustrated include:
Earl of Berkshire (ed) Encyclopaedia of Sport (1898)
J. Harvie Brown and T.E. Buckley A Fauna of the Outer Hebrides
   (with others, 1888), A Fauna of Sutherland, Caithness & West
   Cromarty (with others, 1887), A Fauna of the Orkney Islands (with
   others, 1891), A Fauna of Argyll & the Inner Hebrides (with others,
   1892)
Sir R. Payne Gallwey Shooting (1887), Letters to Young Shooters
   (1896)
J.G. Millais Game Birds and Shooting Sketches (1892, frontispiece
   J.E. Millais), A Breath from the Veldt (1895, frontispiece J.E.
   Millais), British Deer and their Horns (1897), The Wildfowler in
   Scotland (1901, frontispiece J.E. Millais), Newfoundland and its
   Untrodden Ways (1907), The Natural History of British Game Birds
   (with Archibald Thorburn, 1909), American Big Game (1915), Far
   Away up the Nile (1924)
Arthur Newmann Elephant Hunting in East Equatorial Africa (1897)
H. Hesketh Pritchard Through the Heart of Patagonia (1902)
Henry Seebohm A Monograph of the Charadriidae (1888)
W.B. Tegetmeier Pheasants (1897)
Lord Walsingham and Sir R. Payne Gallwey Shooting (with others,
   1900)

Periodical: Pearson's Magazine

References: Baker; Bénézit; Houfe; Johnson & Greutzner; Mallalieu;
Sketchley; Thieme & Becker; Vollmer supp.; Waters; C. Wood; J.C.
Wood

Harold Robert Millar (1869-c.1940)

Worked as H.R. Millar. Born in Dumfriesshire,
Scotland. Studied at Birmingham School of Art.
He was a painter and prolific illustrator of books,
particularly for children, and of magazines. He
had a lively and distinctive graphic style, and a
strong sense of history, seen at its best in his black
and white illustrations for Rudyard Kipling's

H.R. Millar. The Giant Who Kept a School from
My Fairy Tale Book by Tetta Ward (Blackie,
c.1919).

Puck of Pooks Hill and *Rewards and Fairies*, and
in his work for E. Nesbit's children's stories. He
was a collector of Eastern works of art and ancient
weapons, and these interests are at times reflected in his work. In her biography of E. Nesbit,
(whose books Millar illustrated for 13 years),
Doris Langley Moore wrote, 'There will be few
ready to dispute H.R. Millar's pre-eminence as
the interpreter of her invention. He fulfilled to
something near perfection the exacting demands
she made upon him; one has only to compare the
books containing his pictures with those in which
the work of other draughtsmen was used, to
perceive at once how much more clearly than they
he understood her requirements. She herself
shared this view, and was so surprised at the skill
with which he had expressed the very essence of
her ideas that she frequently insisted that there
must be some sort of telepathy between them.
Mr. Millar was not of this opinion...'

Books illustrated include:
F. Anstey Only Toys! (1903)
Isabel Bellerby and others The Diamond Fairy Book (1897)
Sarah Bernhardt and others The Silver Fairy Book (1895)
Maria Louisa Charlesworth Ministering Children (with others, 1890),

Evelyn Everett-Green General John (1910)
Myra Hamilton Kingdom Curious (1905)
Newman Harding The Little Grey Peddlar (1914)
Beatrice Harraden Untold Tales of the Past (1897)
Anthony Hope Phroso (1897)
Victor Hugo The Story of the Bold Pecopin (1902)
A.W. Kinglake Eothen (1898)
Rudyard Kipling Puck of Pooks Hill (1906), Rewards & Fairies (1910),
    Land and Sea Tales (1925)
F. Marryat The Phantom Ship (1896), Frank Mildmay (1897),
    Snarleyyow (1897)
H.R. Millar The Dreamland Express (1927), Aly the Philosopher
    (1930)
Mrs Molesworth The Wood-Pigeons and Mary (1901), Peterkin (1902)
James Morier The Adventures of Hajji Baba (1895)
Geoffrey Mure The Boots and Josephine (1939)
E. Nesbit The Book of Dragons (1900), Nine Unlikely Tales for
    Children, Five Children and It (1902), The Phoenix and the Carpet
    (1904), Oswald Bastable and others (with C.E. Brock*, 1905), The
    Story of the Amulet (1906), The Enchanted Castle (1907), The
    House of Arden (1908), Harding's Luck (1909), The Magic City
    (1910), The Wonderful Garden (1911), The Magic World (with
    Spencer Pryse, 1912), Wet Magic (1913)
Thomas Love Peacock Headlong Hall and Nightmare Abbey (1896)
George Sand etc The Golden Fairy Book (1894)
R.L. Stevenson The Merry Men (1928), New Arabian Nights (1928)
Susan M. Taylor (ed) The Humour of Spain (1894)
Leo Tolstoi Booklets (1895-97)
C. Turley The Playmate (1907)
Edith I. Walker Joyous Stories (1935)
Tetta Ward My Fairy Tale Book (c.1919)
Fairy Tales Far and Near (1895)

Periodicals: Black and White, Cassell's Family Magazine, Chatterbox
Chums, Comus, Good Words, Eureka, The English Illustrated
Magazine, Fun, The Girl's Own Paper, The Idler, Judy, Little Folks,
The Ludgate Monthly, The Minster, Passing Show, Pick-me-up,
Pearson's Magazine, Punch, The Quiver, Scraps, The Strand
Magazine, The Tatler

References: Baker; Crouch; Doyle BWI, CL; Fisher pp.242, 293-94;
Houfe; Johnson & Greutzner; Peppin; Sketchley; Thorpe; Waters 2;
The Idler (Oct. 1895) pp 228-36; *The Junior Bookshelf* vol 22 no 4
(1958); G.M. Ellwood, *The Art of Pen Drawing* (Batsford 1927); Doris
Langley Moore, *E. Nesbit—A Biography* (Benn 1933)

Hilda T. Miller (1876-1939)

Grew up in Edgbaston, Birmingham, daughter of
a textile representative. Studied at Birmingham
School of Art, the Slade School of Fine Art, and
later at St Albans Art School. Settled at Harpenden, Herts. Through an introduction by her father,
she worked extensively for the London store,
Liberty and Co. (1910-18), designing calendars,
advertisements and cards in a somewhat diffident
style. Her later work was more assured and reflected the widespread influence of the Dutch
illustrator H. Willebeek Le Mair*.

Books illustrated include:
J.A. Bentham Shoes (1920)
Walter de la Mare Lucy (1927)
Phyllis Saunders The Flame Flower (1922)
The Pageant of Flowers
The Butterflies' Day
The Rose Fyleman Fairy Book

References: Cope; Johnson & Greutzner; Waters

Agnes Miller-Parker (1895-1980)

Born Ayrshire, Scotland, daughter of an ana-
lytical chemist. Studied at Glasgow School of Art

Agnes Miller-Parker. From *Through the Woods*
by H.E. Bates (Gollancz, 1936).

(1914-19); awarded a Haldane Scholarship. Later,
inspired by the style and techniques of early Renaissance Northern European copper engravings,
she began to teach herself to engrave on wood
(1926). She subsequently studied under Gertrude
Hermes* and Blair Hughes-Stanton*. She collaborated with her husband, the typographer and
sculptor William MacCance, on *The Fables of
Aesop* (Gregynog Press, 1931), the success of
which established her as a wood engraver. Further
book illustration commissions included a number
from the Gregynog and Golden Cockerel Presses.
She recorded landscapes and rural life with sensitivity and distinction, becoming known for her
subtle tonal modulations, achieved with layers of
very fine cross-hatching and minute white dots.
Lived in Glasgow and on the Isle of Arran, Scotland. Elected RE.

Books illustrated include:
H.E. Bates The House with the Apricot and two other tales (1933),
    Through the Woods (1936), Down the River (1937)
Caxton The Fables of Aesop (1931)
Adrien le Corbeau The Forest Giant (1935)
Rhys Davies Daisy Matthews and Three Other Tales (1932)
Herbert Furst Essays in Russet (1944)
Thomas Hardy The Return of the Native (1942), Tess of the
    D'Urbervilles (1956), Far from the Madding Crowd (1958)
A.E. Housman A Shropshire Lad (1940)
Richard Jefferies The Spring of the Year (1946), The Life of the Fields
    (1947), The Open Air (1948), The Old House at Coate (1948), Field
    and Hedgerow (1948)
Andrew McCormick The Gold Torque (1951)
T. Moult (ed) Best Poems of 1935 (with E. Montgomery), Best Poems
    of 1936 (with E. Montgomery)
Rhoda Power How it Happened (1930)
John Cowper Powys Lucifer (1956)
Aloysius Roche Animals under the Rainbow (1952)
J. Sampson Welsh Gypsy Folk Tales (1933)
William Shakespeare Richard II (1940)

Edmund Spenser The Faerie Queen (1953—prepared 1939—with John
   Austen)
Gray's Elegy (1938)

Periodical: The Saturday Book

References: Balston EWE, WEMEB; Garrett BWE, HBWE; Johnson
& Greutzner; Vollmer; Wa (1980); Waters; *The Studio* special (Winter
1931, Winter 1936, Autumn 1938); *Graven Images* (Scottish Arts
Council Catalogue 1979); *Shall We Join the Ladies?* (Studio One
Gallery Oxford 1979); A.C. Sewter, *Modern British Woodcut and
Wood Engravings in the Collection of the Whitworth Art Gallery*
(Manchester 1962); Christopher Sandford, *Bibliography of the Golden
Cockerel Press, 1921-36* (Dawson 1975)

A. Wallis Mills (1878-1940)

Born in Sussex. Studied at the South Kensington
School of Art. He served in the Royal Green
Jackets and Camouflage Corps during World War
I. Mills's lack of ability as a draughtsman did not
stand in the way of a successful career on the staff
of *Punch*, to which he contributed stereotyped
social anecdotes drawn in a cheerfully banal style
for many years. Lived in London and Lincolnshire.

Books illustrated include:
Andrew Lang The Red Book of Heroes (1909)
Archibald Williams Petrol Peter (1906)
The Works of Jane Austen (1908)

Periodicals: The Graphic, Judy, The Humorist, The Ludgate Monthly,
Printer's Pie, Punch, The Royal Magazine, The Strand Magazine

References: Houfe; Johnson & Greutzner; Price; Thorpe; Wa (1934)

Francis John Minton (1917-57)

Worked as John Minton. Born near Cambridge.
Studied at St John's Wood School of Art (1936-
38) and in Paris at Colarossi's (1938-39). A conscientious objector during World War II, he served
in the Pioneer Corps (1941-43). He then taught at
Camberwell School of Art (1943-47), the Central
School of Arts and Crafts (1947-48), and the
Royal College of Art (1948-56). He died from a
drug overdose. Minton was one of the neo-romantic
artists (others included Michael Ayrton* and
Felix Kelly*) whose work found a ready response
in the austerity of the post-war years. He became
well known and influential—the *Dictionary of
20th Century Art* comments that 'his graphic and
topographic mannerisms were rife in postwar
British art schools'. His book illustrations, though
stylised and varying in quality, were often remarkable for their intensity and sparkle, and for their
perceptive textual interpretations. They were
mainly drawn in pen and ink. He also worked as a
stage designer and designer of wallpapers. Elected
member of London Group (1949), RBA (1950).

Books illustrated include:
Odo Cross The Snail that Climbed the Eiffel Tower (1947)
Elizabeth David A Book of Mediterranean Food (1950), French
   Country Cooking (1951)
Alain Fournier The Wanderer (1947)
Alan Ross Time Was Away (1948)
R.L. Stevenson Treasure Island (1947)

George M. Whiley Leaves of Gold (1951)
William Shakespeare Macbeth (nd)

Periodical: Radio Times

References: Benezit; DNB (1951-60); Driver; Jacques; Phaidon;
Shone; Usherwood; Vollmer & supp; Wa (1952); Waters; Image 1
(Summer 1949); William Feaver *When We Were Young* (Thames &
Hudson 1977); Diana Klemin *The Illustrated Book* (Bramhall House,
New York 1970); John Lewis *A Handbook of Type and Illustration*
(Faber 1956); Michael Middleton *John Minton* (Arts Council
Catalogue 1959)

Elinor May Monsell (d. 1954)

Born Limerick, Ireland, sister of J.R. Monsell*.
Studied at the Slade School of Fine Art on a
scholarship (1896). Painter; decorator of silk and
fans. Balston relates that she was introduced to
wood engraving by the poet Laurence Binyon,
whose enthusiasm for Japanese prints she shared;
she worked briefly in the medium (1898) and later
taught the basic techniques to Gwen Raverat*,
first cousin of her husband, the writer and golfer
Bernard Darwin. Her own book illustrations were
in crayon or pen and ink, and her later black and
white figure drawings (e.g. in *Ishybushy and
Topknot* and *Every Idle Dream*) have some affinities with Gwen Raverat's work. Her coloured
illustrations for the *Mr Tootleoo* series were in a
simplified, deliberately childlike style.

John Minton. From *French Country Cooking* by
Elizabeth David (John Lehmann, 1951).

Books illustrated include:
Bernard R.M. Darwin The Tale of Mr. Tootleoo (1925), Tootleoo
   Two (1927), Mr. Tootleoo, One and Two (1932), Mr. Tootleoo
   and Co (1935), Oboli, Boboli and Little Joboli (1938), Ishybushy and
   Topknot (1946), Every Idle Dream (1948)
Walter de la Mare The Three Mulla Mulgars (1910)
Eva Eckersley Stories Barry Told Me (1927)
Roger Ingpen Nursery Rhymes for Certain Times (1946)
Alice M.C. Smith Tom Tug and Others (1898)

Periodicals: The Dome, The Venture

References: Balston WEMEB; ICB 1,2; Johnson & Greutzner;
Country Life (April 1921); *Drawing and Design* 13 (May 1921), 14
(June 1921)

John Robert Monsell (b. 1877)

Born in County Kerry, Ireland. After the early
death of his father (an Irish R.M.), he was brought
up in Limerick and educated in Dublin. When his
sister Elinor Monsell* won a scholarship to the
Slade School of Fine Art, the family moved to
London. He does not appear to have had any
formal art training. By 1900, he was working as a
magazine and book illustrator in a distinctly diffident style, but his draughtsmanship became
steadily more confident over the years. He wrote
and illustrated humorous books and books for
children, sometimes in verse, and composed
songs; he was interested in heraldry and designed
heraldic dust-wrappers for historical books by his
wife, Margaret Irwin, and contributed numerous
illustrations to the *Children's Encyclopaedia* by
Arthur Mee.

Books illustrated include:
B.R.M. Darwin Elves and Princes (1913)
Brothers Grimm Fairy Tales (1908)
M.C. Hime The Unlucky Golfer, His Handbook (1904)
L.E. Housman What-o'Clock Tales (1932)
Compton Mackenzie Kensington Rhymes (1912)
Arthur Mee The Children's Encyclopaedia (1908)
J.R. Monsell The Pink Knight (1901), Funny Foreigners (1905), The
   Jingle Book (1905), Notable Notions (1905), The Hooded Crow
   (1926), Balderdash Ballads (1934), Un-Natural History (1936)
W. Pulitzer My Motor Book (1911)
W.M. Thackeray The Rose and the Ring (1911)
Orlando C. Williams Three Naughty Children (1922)

Periodicals: Cassell's Magazine, The Girls' Realm, Joy Street, Little
Folks, The London Magazine, My Magazine, The Royal Magazine

References: Houfe; ICB 1

Norah Mary Montgomerie (b. 1913)

Studied at Putney School of Art. Worked freelance in London, and then joined the staff of a
publishing firm in Scotland in 1934. She married
William Montgomerie, poet, teacher and authority
on Scottish ballads and folk songs; Together they
compiled and edited anthologies of traditional
tales, rhymes, and games, which she then illustrated. Many of her drawings are based on studies
of their two children. She also worked as a child
portraitist and painter of nursery murals. Her

book illustrations were spontaneous and lively
and very well integrated with their texts.

Books illustrated include:
N.M. Montgomerie Poems and Pictures (1959), Twenty-Five Fables
   (1961)
N.M. and W. Montgomerie Sandy Candy (1948), The Well at World's
   End (1956), A Book of Scottish Nursery Rhymes (1965)

Periodical: The Scottish Education Journal

References: ICB 2,3

Elizabeth Montgomery (active 1920-40)

Painter, illustrator, and designer. Member of the
Chelsea Illustrators Club. Founder member, with
Audrey and Peggy Harris, of the firm of Motley
(stage design and later couture).

Books illustrated include:
Thomas Moult (ed) Best Poems of 1930 (1931), Best Poems of 1932
   (1933)

Reference: Johnson & Greutzner

Thomas Sturge Moore (1870-1944)

Born Hastings, son of a doctor. Educated at
Dulwich College; studied at Lambeth School of
Art. Dramatist, poet and critic; wood engraver
and designer. He became a lifelong friend of
Charles Ricketts* and Charles Shannon and contributed to *The Dial* (from 1893); worked for
Ricketts's Vale Press as an illustrator and engraver,
and for Lucien Pissarro's* Eragny Press. He was a
close friend of the poet W.B. Yeats for whom he
designed book covers, title pages, and a bookplate, as well as illustrations. Despite a relatively
small output, Sturge Moore played a significant
part in the rediscovery of autographic wood
engraving. David Bland makes the important
observation that he was 'perhaps the first engraver of his period to use wood as if it was his
natural medium'. He explored the possibilities of
using the incised line for positive drawing (the
'white-line' that Thomas Bewick used) instead of
merely reproducing the black line of a pen and
ink original. In his romantic, pastoral imagery
(frequently illuminated by the moon or setting
sun), he was influenced by the wood engravings
of William Blake and Edward Calvert, which he
held in profound regard. Founder member SWE
(1920).

Books illustrated include:
John Gawsworth New Poems (1939)
Maurice de Guérin The Centaur and the Bacchante (1899)
Villiers de l'Isle-Adam Axel (1925)
Thomas Sturge Moore Two Poems (1893), The Little School (1905), A
   Sicilian Idyll and Judith (1911), Poetry Bookshop Rhyme Sheet No 6
   (1925)
William Penn Some Fruits of Solitude (1901)
Charles Perrault Histoire de Peau d'Ane (with Lucien Pissarro*, 1902)
Frank Pearce Sturm Eternal Helen (1921)
W.B. Yeats Four Plays (1921)
Poems from Wordsworth (1902)

Periodicals: The Artist Engraver, Criterion, The Dial, Form, The Venture

References: Baker; Bland; Bliss; Garrett BWE, HBWE; Houfe; Johnson & Greutzner; Sketchley; Taylor; Thieme & Becker; Vollmer supp; Waters 2; *The Pageant* 2 (1897); *The Print Collector's Quarterly* 18; *The Studio* 66 (1915), special (1917, 1919, 1923-24); *Graven Images* (Scottish Arts Council catalogue 1979); *Thomas Sturge Moore* Short List 10 (Warrack & Perkins 1975); *T. Sturge Moore* University of Hull Catalogue 1970; Ursula Bridge *W.B. Yeats and T. Sturge Moore: Their Correspondence 1901-37* (Routledge 1953); David Chambers *A Check List of Books Illustrated by T. Sturge Moore*)The Private Library 2nd series vol 4 no 1 1971; Malcolm Easton *T. Sturge Moore Wood Engraver* (The Private Library 2nd series vol 4 no 1 1971); Cecil French, *Thomas Sturge Moore: Modern Woodcutters no 3* (Morland Press 1921); Basil Gray *The English Print* (A. & C. Black 1937); Frederick L. Gwynn *Sturge Moore and the Life of Art* (Richards Press 1952); T.S. Moore, *Art and Life* (Methuen 1910), *A Brief Account of the Origin of the Eragny Press* (Eragny Press 1903); John Rothenstein *The Artists of the 1890s* (Routledge 1928)

Albert George Morrow (1863-1927)

Worked as Albert Morrow. Born in Comber, County Down, elder brother of George Morrow*. Studied art at South Kensington School of Art. On the staff of *The English Illustrated Magazine* from 1884. He was a contributor to *Punch*, to numerous boys' magazines and to children's annuals and picture books. He drew in a sketchy, linear style, and was also a watercolour painter and poster designer. He lived in Sussex for many years.

Books illustrated include:
Charles Harold Avery Between Two Schools (c.1923)
Wilkie Collins No Name (c.1915)
Mary England (ed) Warne's Happy Book for Girls (with others, c.1920)
Eleanor Luisa Haverfield The Happy Comrade (1920)
Frederick Wicks The Stories of the Broadmoor Patient (1893), My Undiscovered Crimes (with H. Furniss*, 1909)

Periodicals: The Big Budget, The Boys' Friend, The Boys' Leader, Cassell's Magazine, Ching Ching's Own, Chums, The English Illustrated Magazine, The Girls' Friend, Good Words, Illustrated Bits, Little Folks, The London Magazine, Mrs Strang's Annual for Girls, Puck, Punch

References: Bénézit; Houfe; Johnson & Greutzner; Mallalieu; Thieme & Becker; Vollmer supp; Wa (1927); Waters; C. Wood; *The Poster* 7 (1899); G. Montague Ellwood *The Art of Pen Drawing* (Batsford 1927)

George Morrow (c.1869-1955)

Born Belfast, brother of artists Albert and Edwin Morrow. Studied art in Paris. Illustrated many boys' books for Seeley Service (1890-1908). He was a contributor to *Punch* for nearly 50 years (1906-54), joining the staff in 1924, and was Art Editor (1932-37). Morrow was best known for his humorous drawings, but his children's illustrations were descriptive and lively. He had an unpretentious and lucid graphic style, which was easily recognisable. He concentrated on depicting people rather than their settings, and gave particular emphasis to gesture and facial expression, often, for this purpose, enlarging the heads of his figures in his humorous illustrations. R.G.G. Price, who

Albert Morrow. 'Hearing no alarming sound, he cautiously proceeded' from *A Son o' the Sea* by E.R. Spencer in *Little Folks* Vol 102 edited by Herbert D. Williams (Cassell, 1925).

described him as a 'cheerful Bohemian Irishman' observed that 'Morrow in his prime, which lasted much longer than with most humorous artists, could draw a simple little figure with a face that was funny *per se*. Much of his work was straight-forward anachronism.' He also considered that 'his versatility and his variety make some of the later draughtsmen look tired and repetitive'. Lived in Richmond, London and later in Thaxted, Essex.

Books illustrated include:
Cynthia Asquith (ed) The Flying Carpet (with others, 1926)
Susan C. Buchan Jim and the Dragon (1929)
J.F.M. Carter Diana Polwarth Royalist (with others, 1905)
G. Chater Helmet and Spear (1901), The Crusaders (1904), Gown of Pine (1906), A Flutter in Feathers (1913)
A.J. Church Heroes of Chivalry and Romance (1898)
Franck Cowper The Island of the English (1899)
A.B. Cox Jugged Journalism (1925)
George S. Dickson A Nursery Geography (1916), My First Book of Geography (1919)
William M. Dickson Cinderella's Garden (1927)
F.G. Evans Puffin, Puma and Co. (1929), Here Be Dragons (1930)
Geoffrey C. Faber Elnovia (1925)
Hilda Finnemore Stories Of Course (1921)
Margaret L. Gower Chuckles (1927)
Lady Sybil M.C. Grant Founded on Fiction (1913)
C.L. Graves Musical Monstrosities (1909)
A.P. Herbert Light Articles Only (1921), The Wherefore and the Why

(1921), Tinker Tailor (1922), Laughing Ann (1925), Wisdom for the Wise (1930)
Agnes G. Herbertson Hurrah for the O-Pom-Pom (1931)
John Hilton and Joseph Thorp Change, The Beginning of a Chapter (with others, 1919)
H.W.G. Hyrst Adventures in the Great Deserts (with others, 1907)
John K. Kendall Odd Creatures (1915)
Edmund G.V. Knox 'Parodies Regained' (1921), Fiction as She Is Wrote (1923), I'll Tell the World (1927)
Dorothy M. Large Irish Airs (1932)
William J. Locke Morals for the Young (with others, 1915)
J.H.B. Lockhart A French Picture Gallery (1914)
E.V. Lucas Swollen-Headed William (1914), In Gentlest Germany (1915), You Know What People Are (1922)
E.V. Lucas and C.L. Graves Change for a Half Penny (1905), If (1908), Hustled History (with others, 1908)
Archibald Marshall Simple Stories (1927), Simple People (1928), The Birdikin Family (1932)
Mary Russell Mitford Country Stories (1896)
Taro Miyako and Yukio Tani The Game of Ju-Jitsu (with others, 1906)
George Morrow Podgy and I (1926), Some More (1928)
John B. Morton The Death of the Dragon (1934)
Elizabeth O'Neill My First Book of British History (1920)
L.M. Oyler The Children's Entente Cordiale (1915)
M. Rittenberg Potted Game (1908)
Noel Ross The House-Party Manual (1917)
Edith Seeley Under Cheddar Cliffs (1903)
E.A.W. Smith Some Pirates and Marmaduke (1921), The Marvellous Land of Snergs (1927)
R. Stead Adventures on the Great Rivers (with others, 1907)
Jonathan Swift Gulliver's Travels (1932)
Cecil W. Wilson Had You Lived in London Then (1937)
Richard Wilson A Picture History for Boys and Girls (nd)

Periodicals: The Bystander, The Captain, The Idler, The London Mercury, The Pall Mall Magazine, Pear's Annual, Pearson's Magazine, Pick-Me-Up, Printer's Pie, Punch, The Sphere, The Strand Magazine, The Tatler, Toc H Annual

References: Bénézit; Doyle BWI; Houfe; Johnson & Greutzner; Price; Thieme & Becker; Veth; Wa (1934); Waters; *The Artist* (October 1943); *The Studio* special (1911) Fougasse, *The Good Tempered Pencil* (Reinhardt 1956)

Edward Eugene Louis Mortlemans
(b. 1915)

Often works as Edward Mortlemans. Born in London. Studied at Upper Hornsey Road Evening Art Institute, the Central School of Arts and Crafts, and at the Slade School of Fine Art under Randolph Schwabe*. Mural painter, advertising artist and illustrator of historical books (for children and adults) and book jackets. He works in pen and ink or full colour in a naturalistic vein.

Books illustrated include:
Erik Abranson Ships of the High Seas (1976)
Enid Blyton Robin Hood and his Merry Men (1980)
H.G. Castle Spion Kop (1976)
Arthur Catherall Antlers of the King Moose (1970)
Gerald Durrell Catch me a Colobus (1972)
Kathleen Fidler The Boy with the Bronze Axe (1968)
Richard Garrett Great Sea Mysteries (1971)
John Gilbert Buccaneers and Pirates (1975), Prehistoric Man (1979)

Reference: ICB 4

John Morton-Sale (b. 1901) and Isobel Morton-Sale (b. 1904)

A husband and wife partnership. John was born in Kensington and studied at Putney School of Art and at the Central School of Arts and Crafts

Edward Mortlemans. 'Hobbs squeezed the trigger' from *Great Sea Mysteries* by Richard Garrett (Pan Books, 1971).

under A.S. Hartrick* and Spenser Pryse*. Isobel was born in Chelsea and studied at Ramsgate and Margate Schools of Art, and at the Central School under Hartrick, Pryse and Noel Rooke*. They settled in an isolated house on the edge of Dartmoor, working as artists in oil, watercolour, pastel, chalk and lithography, John concentrating on landscapes and Isobel on portraits. John devised a scientific theory of colour-camouflage which was widely used during World War II. Together, they founded and for many years directed the Parnassus Gallery, publishing high quality reproductions, initially of their own paintings and subsequently works by established masters. They often worked together as illustrators, most notably on poems by Eleanor Farjeon, to whom they were introduced by the publisher Robert Lusty. Their first major success with Eleanor Farjeon, *Martin Pippin*, was followed by several titles, including three called *Cherrystones*, *The Mulberry Bush*, and *The Starry Floor*, which were inspired by their drawings of childhood games, and were later republished in one volume as *Then There were Three* (1958). Their illustrative work combines graphic spontaneity with conscious charm. Their drawings are unsigned, and it is sometimes hard to distinguish between their individual styles. Their daughter, Roysia Romanelli, is also a book illustrator. [Q]

Books illustrated include:
J.M. Barrie Plays (nd)
Lewis Carroll Alice in Wonderland and Through the Looking Glass (John Morton-Sale only, 1933)
Columbus Good Afternoon Children (1932)
Eleanor Farjeon Martin Pippin in the Daisy Field (1937), Sing for Your Supper (1938), Cherrystones (1942), The Mulberry Bush (1945), The Starry Floor (1949), Then There Were Three... (1958)
Mary Grigs The Yellow Cat (1936)
Beverley Nichols The Tree that Sat Down (1945)
W.H. Ogilvie A Clean Wind Blowing (John Morton-Sale only, 1930)
Rosalind Ramirez and Ann Driver Something Particular (1955)

Periodicals: Good Housekeeping, Nash's Magazine, The Strand Magazine, Woman's Journal

References: Crouch; Doyle CL; Fisher p.209; ICB 1,2; Johnson & Greutzner; *The Junior Bookshelf* vol 5 no 2 (1941), vol 5 no 3 (1941).

Irene Mountfort (active 1934-39)

An illustrator who worked mainly for Basil Black-

John Morton-Sale. Watercolour from *The Old Wives' Tale* by Arnold Bennett (nd).

Charles Mozley. From *Ginger Over the Wall* by Prudence H. Andrew (Lutterworth, 1962).

well. Her drawings, in pen and ink, occasionally with colour washes, were pleasant and typical of their period.

Books illustrated include:
Lewis Carroll Alice in Wonderland and Through the Looking Glass (1939)
Eleanor Farjeon Jim at the Corner and other stories (1934), The Clumber Pup (1934), And I Dance My Own Child (1935)
Rose Fyleman (ed) Here We Come A'Piping (1936), A'Piping Again (1936), Bells Ringing (1938), Pipe and Drum (1939)

Charles Mozley (b. 1915)

Born in Sheffield. Studied at Sheffield School of Art and at the Royal College of Art (1933-37). Taught anatomy and life drawing at Camberwell School of Art (1938-39) before army service in World War II. His book illustrations are often drawn in pencil or crayon, sometimes on tinted paper with white painted highlights; he also uses pen or brush and ink. He concentrates on figures, which he presents with some panache, and has also produced some convincing caricatures (e.g. of Berthold Wolpe* in *Wolperania*). He has illustrated several books for the Folio Society and has designed book jackets, theatre and film posters, and advertisements; he was responsible for several murals for the Festival of Britain (1951).

Books illustrated include:
Prudence H. Andrew Ginger Over the Wall (1962), Ginger and Batty Bill (1963), Ginger and Number 10 (1964), Ginger Among the Pigeons (1966)

Erskine Childers The Riddle of the Sands (1970)
Stephen Crane The Red Badge of Courage (1971)
Guy de Maupassant The Tellier House (1964)
Charles Dickens The Bagman's Story (1953)
Denis Diderot The Nun (1972)
Pérez Galdós The Spendthrifts (nd), Torment (nd)
René Guillot Nicolette and the Mill (1960)
E. Hall Proverbs: A Selection (1970)
Charles Kingsley The Water Babies (1965)
Elisabeth Kyle Girl with an Easel (1962), Girl with a Pen (1963), Girl
    with a Song (1964), Girl with a Destiny (1965)
George Macdonald At the Back of the North Wind (1963)
Margaret Mahy The Procession (1969), The Little Witch (1970)
Charles Mozley The First Book of Tales of Ancient Egypt (1960),
    Arabian Nights – The First Book of Tales of Ancient Araby (1960),
    Wolperiana (1960), The State Funeral of Sir Winston Churchill
    (1965)
Bill Naughton A Dog Called Nelson (1976)
Cyril Ray Lickerish Limericks (1979)
Anna Sewell Black Beauty (1967)
P. Morton Shand Building (1954)
George Bernard Shaw Man and Superman (1962)
Edmund Spenser An Hymne of Heavenly Beautie (1963)
Joanna Spyri Heidi (1967)
R.L. Stevenson Treasure Island (1965)
Noel Streatfeild A Vicarage Family (1963), Gran-Nannie (1976), Far to
    Go (1976)
Elizabeth Stucley Springfield Home (1961)
Anthony Trollope The Duke's Children (nd)
Jean Ure Pacala and Tandala (1961)
Frank Waters The First ABC (1970)
Oscar Wilde Fairy Tales (1960)
The Gospel According to St Luke (1962)
Pacala and Tandala (1960)

References: Fisher p.66; ICB 3,4; Ryder; WaG

A. Fairfax Muckley (active 1892-1944)

It is not clear whether the book illustrator and children's author A. Fairfax Muckley is the same person as Angelo Fairfax Muckley (active 1886-95) who appears in Johnson & Greutzner. This A.F. Muckley lived in London and Buckinghamshire and did portrait and landscape paintings, and etchings. Alternatively, he could be the portrait painter Arthur Fairfax Muckley (active 1886-91) who is mentioned by C. Wood. His early plant and animal drawings are meticulous and refined, and his children's book illustrations, in the 'rabbits and mice' tradition that derived from Beatrix Potter* contained some well-depicted natural detail.

Books illustrated include:
A.E. Bonsor Cassell's Natural History for Young People (1905)
G.E.S. Boulger Familiar Trees (1906)
A.F. Muckley Widow Grizzles (1920), Sly Bill Again (1920, 1943), Sly
    Bill and Squeak Shrew (1943), Mr and Mrs Fuzzymops (1944),
    Sammy Sharpnose (1944), The Story of Bunnikins (1944), The Story
    of Teddy Toad (1944)
Selfridges Schoolboys' Book (nd)

References: Harper, Johnson & Greutzner; C. Wood

Louis Fairfax Muckley (active 1889-1914)

Born Stourbridge, Worcestershire. Studied at the Manchester School of Art and was associated with the Birmingham School of Handicraft. He exhibited genre and landscape paintings and did

Louis Fairfax Muckley. 'Like as a ship, whom cruel tempest drives upon a rocke' from the fifth book of *The Faerie Queene* by Edmund Spenser (Dent, 1897).

etchings and wood engravings. It would be tempting to assume a family relationship with A. Fairfax Muckley*, and perhaps with the well known Victorian painter William Jobez Muckley (1837-1905), but no information on this has so far come to light. His illustrations were highly accomplished products of the Arts and Crafts movement, and possessed a degree of self-confidence remarkable in an artist who published so little.

Books illustrated include:
R.D. Blackmore Fringilla (1895)
Edmund Spenser The Faerie Queene (1897)

Periodicals: Illustrated London News, The Graphic, The Quiver

References: Baker; Bénézit; Crane; Houfe; Johnson & Greutzner; Pennell MI; Peppin; Sketchley; Taylor; C. Wood

Alexander Hallam Murray (1854-1934)

Born in London, son of publisher John Murray III. Educated at Eton and Caius College, Cambridge. Studied at the Slade School of Fine Art. Joined the family firm where he planned and designed many publications including the early volumes of *The Letters of Queen Victoria*. Painter, illustrator, and garden designer. He travelled and painted in Europe, India (with Sir Ernest George), Australia, New Zealand, Egypt, Ceylon and Algeria. His book illustrations consist mainly of accomplished topographical water colour studies and black and white drawings; one of his authors, H.W. Nevinson, considered that in all his topographical paintings he achieved a 'sense of association'. Elected FRGS, FSA; member RWS.

Books illustrated include:
J. Cartwright The Pilgrim's Way from Winchester to Canterbury (1911)
L.J. Jennings Rambles among the Hills (1880)
A. Murray The High-Road of Empire (1905)
H.W. Nevinson Sketches on the Old Road through France to Florence (1904)
A.I. Shand Old-Time Travel (1903)

References: Bénézit; Johnson & Greutzner; Vollmer supp; Wa (1934); Waters, C. Wood

Donia Nachshen (b. 1903)

Born Ghitomir, Russia. Studied at the Slade School of Fine Art. Her illustrative work sometimes recalls that of John Austen* in style, but has an individual flavour: it is bold, animated, rather slapdash at times but with its own cheerful appeal. She was also a portrait painter. Lived in London.

Books illustrated include:
V. Bartlett Topsy Turvy (1927)
Enid Blyton Nature Lover's Book (1944)
Samuel Butler The Way of All Flesh (1936)
Anatole France The Works of Anatole France (1925), The Red Lily (1930)
Irina Odoevtseva Out of Childhood (1930)
A.M. Remizov On a Field of Azure (1946)
S.K. Schimanski Russian Literature Library (1945)
Arthur Schnitzler Rhapsody (1928), Fräulein Else (1929)
Geoffrey Trease Black Night, Red Morning (1944)
The Haggadah (1934)
The Works of Oscar Wilde (1931)

References: Johnson & Greutzner; Vollmer; Wa (1934); *The Studio* special (Winter 1931)

John Northcote Nash (1893-1977)

Worked as John Nash. Born Earl's Court, London, younger brother of Paul Nash*. Educated at Wellington College; on the advice of his brother

he avoided any formal art training. In 1914 he took up oil painting. Served with the Artists' Rifles (1916-18). Appointed an official war artist (1918). Taught at the Ruskin School of Drawing, Oxford (1924-29), the Royal College of Art (1934-40, 1945-57) and at the Colchester School of Art. During World War II, he was again appointed as an official war artist. He settled at Wormingford, Essex in 1944. Though best known as a landscape painter, John Nash was also an inspired illustrator. His first published illustrations were humorous drawings of theatrical subjects for the period *Far and Wide* (1919) and he continued intermittently to publish humorous illustrations, which were described by Douglas Percy Bliss* as 'the best comic drawings of today'. Figures, normally absent from his paintings, were quite often included in his illustrative work, and his subject range also embraced plants and rural landscapes. For reproduction he worked mainly in pen and ink, in a firm and responsive line, occasionally with watercolour washes, reproduced by the *pôchoir* process of hand stencilling (as in *The Shepheard's Calendar* and *Seven Short Stories*), in colour line, or in full colour. He also used wood engraving and experimented with autolithography. He considered that wood engravings were better suited to the intimacy of the printed page than to being framed for individual display, and used the medium up to 1935 for seven books, including the justly celebrated *Poisonous Plants*, and *Flowers and Faces* which he considered his best engraved book. His style of engraving was direct and lively, and his work showed a marked sensitivity towards the physical qualities of the wood block. D.P. Bliss, comparing his wood engravings with those of Paul Nash observed, 'John Nash's work is gentler and more reticent than that of his brother, not tortured by the same daemonic urge. He is more sensitive and whimsical, more interested in natural objects for their own sakes'. Founder member of the London Group (1914); elected NEAC (1919), SWE (c.1920), ARA (1940), RA (1951); awarded CBE (1964).

Books illustrated include:
H.E. Bates Flowers and Faces (1935)
Adrian Bell Men and the Fields (1939)
William Cobbett Rural Rides (3 vols 1930)
Desmond Coke The Nouveau Poor (1921)
W. Dallimore Poisonous Plants (1927)
Walter de la Mare Seven Short Stories (1931)
W.W. Gibson The Early Whistler (1927)
R. Gathorne Hardy Wild Flowers in Britain (1938), The Tranquil Gardener (1958), The Native Garden (1961)
Jason Hill The Curious Gardener (1932), The Contemplative Gardener (1940)
Trevor Housby The Art of Angling (1965)
'Stephen Hudson' Céleste (1930)
John Nash English Garden Flowers (1948)
Paul Nash The Sun's Calendar (1920)
T.F. Powys When Thou Wast Naked (1931)
J. Pudney Almanack of Hope (1944)

John Nash. 'The Tree' from *Seven Short Stories* by Walter de la Mare (Faber, 1931).

L. de G. Sieveking Dressing Gowns and Glue (1919), Bats in the
  Belfry (1926)
Edmund Spenser The Shepheard's Calendar (1930)
Jonathan Swift Directions to Servants (1925)
P. Synge Plants with Personalities (nd)
Gilbert White The Natural History of Selborne (1951, 1972)
Happy New Year (1959)
Ovid's Elegies *(trans Christopher Marlowe)* (1926)
Parnassian Molehill (1953)
Shell Guide to Bucks (1937)

Periodicals: The Apple, Art and Letters, The Countryman, Form, The
Golden Hind, Land and Water, The Listener, The London Mercury,
The Monthly Chapbook, The Owl, The Saturday Book

References: Balston EWE, WEMEB; Bénézit; Bliss; Chamot, Farr &
Butlin; Garrett BWE, HBWE; Gilmour; Hofer; Houfe; Johnson &
Greutzner; Phaidon; Rothenstein 2; Shone; Vollmer; Wa (1977);
Waters; *Alphabet and Image* 3 (1946); *The Art Bulletin* (Spring 1948);
The Artist (January 1945); *Country Life* (7th September 1967); *The
Countryman* 69 (1967); *Picture Post* (1st April 1939); *The Studio* 101
(1931), 109 (1935), special (Spring 1929, Autumn 1930, Winter 1936,
Autumn 1938); *The Sunday Times* colour supplement (31st August
1975); *The Woodcut* 3 (1929); John Lewis *John Nash, the Painter as
Illustrator* (Pendomer Press 1978); John Lewis *The Twentieth Century
Book* (Studio Vista 1967)

Paul Nash (1889-1946)

Born in London, son of a barrister and elder
brother of John Nash*. Educated at St Paul's
School. Studied art at Chelsea School of Art
(1906-08), the London County Council School at
Bolt Court (1908-10) and at the Slade School of
Fine Art (1910-11). Served in the Artists' Rifles
and Hampshire Regiment during World War I,
injured at Ypres. Appointed official war artist
(1917). Taught design at the Royal College of Art
(1924-25 and 1938-40), where his pupils included
Edward Bawden* and Eric Ravilious*. Co-founder
(with Henry Moore) of Unit One Group (1933);
contributed to the International Surrealist Exhibition, London (1936). Official war artist (1940-
45). Nash was an early participant in the wood-
engraving revival of the 1920s and illustrated
eight books in the medium; otherwise, he generally used pen and ink, sometimes with colour.
He took a detailed interest in the colour printing
of his work, and from that point of view was most
satisfied with *Urne Buriall* (1932) for which collotype with hand-stencilled colours was used. His
imagery in these illustrations reflected his growing
involvement with surrealist ideas. With only the
Shell Guide to Dorset to follow, this work represents the climax and almost the swan-song of his
illustrative career. Several of his books, notably
Genesis (1924) and *A Song about Tsar Ivan Vasilyevitch* (1929), both of which are illustrated with
wood engravings, are markedly abstract in approach, but he more often interpreted his texts
with associative and symbolic landscape imagery

Paul Nash. Lithograph from *Urne Buriall and the
Garden of Cyrus* by Sir Thomas Browne (Cassell,
1932).

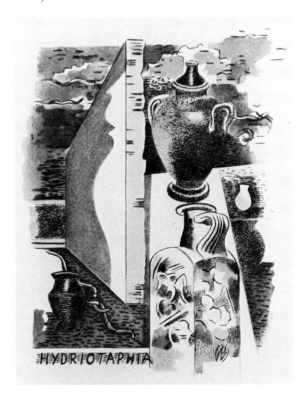

HYDRIOTAPHIA

and his illustrations thus form an illuminating pendant to his development as a painter during the same period. Interested in all aspects of the book, he also designed dust-wrappers and bindings. His work in other fields included designs for posters, fabrics, glassware and ceramics, the theatre and interior decoration. Member London Group (1914), NEAC (1919), SWE (1922).

Books illustrated include:
Richard Aldington Images of War (1919)
Martin Armstrong Saint Hercules and other stories (1927)
Sir Thomas Browne Urne Buriall and the Garden of Cyrus (1932)
John Drinkwater Loyalties (1918), Cotswold Characters (1921)
Ford M. Ford Mister Bosphorus and the Muses (1923)
Robert Graves Welchman's Hose (1926)
T.E. Lawrence Seven Pillars of Wisdom (privately published 1926)
M.Y. Lermontov A Song about Tsar Ivan Vasilyevitch (1929)
L. Archer Leroy Wagner's Music Drama of the Ring (1925)
Paul Nash The Sun Calendar (with John Nash*, 1920), Places (1922), Dark Weeping (1929), A Shell Guide to Dorset (1935)
M. Pitt Rivers Dorset (1936, 1966)
Siegfried Sassoon Nativity (1927)
William Shakespeare A Midsummer Night's Dream (1924), King Lear (1927)
Jules Tellier Abd-er-Rhaman in Paradise (1928)
Genesis (1924)

Periodicals: Form, Radio Times, The Woodcut

References: Balston EWE, WEMEB; Bénézit; Bland; Bliss; Chamot, Farr & Butlin; *Contemporary Artists*; DNB (1941-50); Driver; Garrett BWE, HBWE; Gilmour; Hofer; Houfe; Johnson & Greutzner; Lewis; Phaidon; Rothenstein 2; Shone; Vollmer & supp; Wa (1934); Waters; *Drawing and Design* vol 1 (1926); *The Print Collector's Quarterly* vol 15; *Signature* 2 (1936), 5 (1937); *The Studio* 96 (1928), 100 (1930), 104 (1932), 135 (1948), special (Spring 1927, 1927, Autumn 1930, Autumn 1938); *Graven Images* (Scottish Arts Council catalogue 1979); *Paul Nash, Paintings and Watercolours* (Tate Gallery catalogue 1975); Abbott *Poet and Painter* (Oxford University Press 1955); Anthony Bertram *Paul Nash, Portrait of an Artist* (Faber 1955); Margot Eates *Paul Nash* (Lund Humphries 1948, Royal Academy 1973); Basil Gray *The English Print* (A. & C. Black 1937); Rigby Graham *A Note on the Book Illustration of Paul Nash* (Brewhouse Press 1965); John Lewis *Graphic Design* (Routledge 1954); Paul Nash *Outline. An Autobiography* (Faber 1949), *Fertile Image* (Faber 1951); Alexander Postan *The Complete Graphic Works of Paul Nash* (Secker & Warburg 1973); Herbert Read *Paul Nash* (Penguin 1944); John Rothenstein *Paul Nash* (Beaverbrook Newspapers 1962); A.C. Sewter *Modern*

Harold Nelson. From *Early English Prose Romances* by W.H. Thoms (Otto Schulz, 1903).

British Woodcuts and Wood Engravings in the Collection of the Whitworth Art Gallery (Manchester 1962); Lance Sieveking *The Eye of the Beholder* (Hulton Press 1957)

Harry Bingham Neilson (1861-1941)

Worked at Claughton, Cheshire. Illustrator (principally of children's books) in black and white and and occasionally halftone. He was a mediocre draughtsman but developed a line in cheerful gnomes and humanised rabbits that was evidently popular.

Books illustrated include:
G.C. Bingham The Animal's Academy (1903)
W. Boyle Comic Capers (1903), Christmas at the Zoo (1904)
J. Brymer Games and Gambols (1902)
F.T. Buckland Curiosities of Natural History (1903)
S.H. Hamer Micky Magee's Menagerie (1897), Why and Other Whys (1898), Topsy-Turvy Tales (1901), The Ten Travellers (1902)
Baron Krakemsides The Careless Chicken (1924)
E.E. Millard Mr Skiddleywinks (1927)
H.B. Neilson The Adventures of Sam Pippins (1889), A Leap Year's Proposal (1889), Animal ABC (1901), Jolly Jumbo (1904), Jumbo's Jolly Tales (1908-10), 'Auld-Lang-Syne' (1935)
Life's Book of Animals (with others, 1898).

Periodicals: Cassell's Family Magazine, Little Folks, The Sketch

References: Houfe; ICB 1; Johnson & Greutzner; Mallett supp

Harold Edward Hughes Nelson (1871-1946)

Born in Dorchester, Dorset. Studied at Lambeth School of Art and at the Central School of Arts and Crafts. A designer, illustrator, etcher and engraver on copper, he also lectured on posters, decorative illustration and heraldry and became a well known designer of bookplates. His style was founded on a profound admiration for the work of Dürer, but also showed the influence of the Arts and Crafts Movement, with which, as a member of the Art Workers' Guild, he was closely involved. He lived in Clapham, South London, and later at Carshalton, Surrey.

Books illustrated include:
F.H.C. de la Motte Fouqué Undine and Aslauga's Knight (1901)
W.H. Thoms Early English Prose Romances (1903)

Periodicals: The Book-Lover's Magazine, The Bookplate, Cassell's Magazine, The Graphic, Ladies' Field, The Queen, The Sphere

References: Bénézit; Houfe; Johnson & Greutzner; Peppin; Thieme & Becker; Vollmer; Waters 1 and 2; C. Wood; *The Studio* special (1898-99, 1900-01, Spring 1914, Autumn 1914, 1923-24); *Harold Nelson: His Book of Bookplates* (Otto Schutze 1904); P. Hornung *Bookplates by Harold Nelson* (Caxton Press, New York 1929); Brian North Lee *British Bookplates* (David & Charles, 1979)

Edmund Hort New (1871-1931)

Born Evesham, Gloucestershire, son of a solicitor. Studied at the Birmingham School of Art under E.R. Taylor and A.J. Gaskin. Settled in Oxford. Painter, illustrator, bookplate designer and lecturer in art and architecture. His book illustrations

G.A. Payne Knutsford (1904)
E.M. Sympson Lincoln (1906)
A.H. Thompson Cambridge and its Colleges (1898)
H.W. Tomkins Hertfordshire (1904)
Izaac Walton The Compleat Angler (1896)
J. Wells Oxford and its Colleges (1897)
Gilbert White The Natural History of Selborne (1900)
Bertram C. Windle Shakespeare's Country (1899), The Malvern
   Country (1901), The Wessex of Thomas Hardy (1901), Chester
   (1903)
Poems by Wordsworth (1907)

Periodicals: The Daily Chronicle, The English Illustrated Magazine,
The London Mercury, The Pall Mall Magazine, The Quest, The
Yellow Book

References: Baker; Bénézit; Crane; Houfe; Johnson & Greutzner;
Mallalieu; Pennell PD; Ray; Sketchley; Thorpe; Wa (1929); Waters; C.
Wood; *The Print Collector's Quarterly* vol 18 (obituary); *The Studio* 64
(1915), 80 (1920)

Edmund H. New. From *The Compleat Angler* by
Izaac Walton (John Lane, 1896).

consist of quiet, well-considered and well-drawn
pen and ink drawings of architectural subjects.
Thorpe regarded him as the greatest of the illustrators of the Birmingham School and described
him as 'an artist whose work combined with a
strong personal line, the accuracy of the architect's drawing and great decorative charm. He
illustrated many books of topographical interest,
and always so truthfully and delightfully as to
make one wish to see the places he had drawn.'
Elected ARBSA (1909), Hon ARIBA.

Books illustrated include:
Matthew Arnold The Scholar-Gypsy and Thyrsis (1906)
A. Austin Haunts of Ancient Peace (1902)
F.G. Brabant Sussex (1900), The English Lakes (1902), Oxfordshire
   (1906), Berkshire (1911)
M. St. C. Byrne Somerville College (1922)
J.C. Cox Surrey (1910)
Mrs E.C. Gaskell Cranford (1914)
A. Gissing Broadway (1904), Ludlow and Stokesay (1905)
A. Harvey Bristol (1906)
T.S. Holmes Wells and Glastonbury (1908)
W.H. Hutton Highways and Byways in Shakespeare's Country (1914)
W.A. Knight Coleridge and Wordsworth in the West Country (1913)
F.A.H. Lambert Surrey (1903)
J.W. Mackail The Life of William Morris (1899)
Helen Milman In the Garden of Peace (1896), Outside the Garden
   (1900)
E.H. New Evesham (1904), The College Monographs (1906), The
   New Loggan Guide to Oxford Colleges (1932)

William Newzam Prior Nicholson
(1872-1949)

Usually worked as William Nicholson. Born
Newark-on-Trent, son of an ironworks proprietor and Member of Parliament. He attended
and was expelled from Hubert von Herkomer's
Art School at Bushey, Hertfordshire (1888-89)
and studied at the Académie Julian, Paris
(1889-90). He and his brother-in-law James Pryde*,
formed a partnership under the name: J. & W.
Beggarstaff and produced poster designs of revo-
lutionary boldness and simplicity, inspired by
French examples, notably those by Toulouse-
Lautrec had a great influence on the development
of British poster art. Nicholson was introduced by
J.A. McNeill Whistler to the publisher William
Heinemann (1896), who commissioned from him

William Nicholson. 'The Barmaid' from *London
Types* by W.E. Henley (Heinemann, 1898).

the design for the company's windmill trademark (still in use). *Alphabet* and *London Types* (both published by Heinemann in 1898) brought a completely new look to illustrated books, with forceful images in heavy black that resembled lino prints but were actually hand-coloured wood engravings printed by lithography. Designed as a whole, and closely resembling Beggarstaff posters with hand-drawn outline borders and hand-written captions, these influential books owed their straightforward handling of the printed page to the example of early chapbooks, which Nicholson much admired. For later book illustrations (e.g. *Characters of Romance*,(1900) and *Clever Bill*, (1926) he often used lithography alone. He pursued a successful career as a painter, though was often diverted from his *métier* of still life and landscape by the demands of portraiture. Member of Chelsea Arts Club and International Society; founder member of the NPS (1911). Elected RP (1909). Awarded Gold Medal (for woodcuts) at Exposition Universelle, Paris (1900). Trustee of the Tate Gallery (1934-39).

Books illustrated include:
W.H. Davies True Travellers (1923), Moss and Feather (1928)
John Gay Polly (1923)
W.E. Henley An Almanac of Twelve Sports (1898), London Types (1898)
William Nicholson An Alphabet (1898, reprinted in facsimile 1978), Characters of Romance (1900), Clever Bill (1926), The Book of Blokes (1929), The Pirate Twins (1929)
Edwin Pugh Tony Drum (with James Pryde, 1898)
Siegfried Sassoon Memoirs of a Fox-Hunting Man (1929)
A. Waugh The Square Book of Animals (1900)
Margery Williams The Velveteen Rabbit (1922)

Periodicals: The Dome, Form, St Pauls

References: Bénézit; Bland; Bliss; Chamot, Farr & Butlin; Crouch; DNB (1941-50); Fisher pp.71, 368; Garrett BWE, HBWE; Hofer; Houfe; ICB 1, 2, 4; Johnson & Greutzner; Lewis; Muir; Ray; Rothenstein 1; Shone; Thieme & Becker; Thorpe; Vollmer and supp; Wa (1934); Waters; C. Wood; *Penrose Annual* (1956); *The Studio* 12 (1898), 53 (1911), 74 (1918), special (1898-99, 1899-1900, 1917, 1919, 1923-24, Autumn 1930, Autumn 1933); Lilian Browse *William Nicholson* (Hart Davis 1956); William Feaver *When We Were Young* (Thames & Hudson 1977) *Masters of Caricature* (Weidenfeld & Nicholson 1981); Basil Gray *The English Print* (A. & C. Black 1937); Robert Nichols *William Nicholson* (Penguin 1948); S.K.N. *William Nicholson* (1923); Marguerite Steen *William Nicholson* (Penguin 1943); Frederick Wedmore *Some of the Moderns* (Virtue 1909)

Will Nickless (b. 1902)

Born in Essex. Started work at the age of fourteen. In 1920, he joined *The Motor* as a technical draughtsman, later moving on to general figure work and advertisement illustrations. He lived in London until 1958 when he moved to Rotherfield, Sussex. A poet and etcher, he acquired a private press on which he occasionally printed his own poems, which he illustrated, bound and issued in limited editions. His illustrations of his own poetry were economical and delicate, sometimes surrealistically combining disparate images

Will Nickless. 'Escaping to the rocket, they journey to earth' from *The Green Rays from Mars* in *The Children's Wonder Book* (Odhams, 1948).

drawn to different scales. His children's illustrations, much less formal and more animated in feeling, were stylishly drawn with multiple outlines and hatching. He also painted, made several violins and violas, and built a six-inch astronomical telescope and several locomotive models.

Books illustrated include:
M.W. Jennings The Story of the Golden Fleece (1954)
Frank Knight Stories of Famous Ships (1963), Stories of Famous Sea Fights (1963), Stories of Famous Explorers by Sea (1964), Stories of Famous Explorers by Land (1965), Stories of Famous Sea Adventures (1966), Stories of Famous Adventurers (1966)
Will Nickless A Guide to the Tower (1947), Aesop's Fables and Fables by others (1962), Owlglass (1964), Dotted Lines (1968)
Barbara Euphan Todd Worzel Gummidge and Saucy Nancy (1947), Worzel Gummidge Takes a Holiday (1949)
Henry Treece The Return of Robinson Crusoe (1958)
Percy Westerman Missing, Believed Lost (1949)
The Children's Wonder Book (1948)

Reference: ICB 3

Kay Rasmus Nielsen (1886-1957)

Worked as Kay Nielsen. Born in Copenhagen, Denmark, son of the Director of the Royal Danish Theatre. He studied art in Paris at the Académie Julian and at Colarossi's (1904-11), and then moved to London. An exhibition of his work in Bond Street (illustrations for a projected *Book of Death*) led to his first commission from Hodder and Stoughton, who were to publish his most important English books. Nielsen remained in England until about 1916 and then returned to Denmark, where he designed sets and costumes for the Royal Danish Theatre, including particularly spectacular productions of *Aladdin* and *Scaramouche*. He emigrated to America in 1926, and in 1939 moved to Hollywood, where one of his first jobs was working on Walt Disney's *Fantasia*. He later executed some mural paintings but was virtually forgotten as an artist by the end of his life.

Kay Nielsen. 'The Princess on the Glass Hill' from *East of the Sun, West of the Moon* by P.C. Asbjörnsen and J.I. Moe (Hodder & Stoughton, 1914).

Though he illustrated several books abroad, Nielsen's most remarkable illustrations were for the four lavishly produced limited editions published by Hodder and Stoughton (a fifth English book, *Red Magic*, was published in a trade edition by Jonathan Cape). Though influenced in style by the drawings of Aubrey Beardsley and by Oriental and Middle Eastern art, his work revealed above all his talent for theatrical design. His illustrations were formally dramatic in conception, the figures portrayed as actors posed against backdrops, their clothes depicted with all the elegance of costume designs. Within this essentially artificial context, he was able to introduce images that were sometimes strikingly imaginative or bizarre. He drew in pen and ink, often with watercolour washes, in a manner that was decorative, stylish and immaculate, and the gift books in which much of his work appeared were further embellished with his designs for endpapers, initial letters, friezes and other decorative motifs.

Books illustrated include:
Hans Christian Andersen Fairy Tales (1924)
P.C. Asbjörnsen & J.I. Moe East of the Sun, West of the Moon (1914)
Brothers Grimm Hansel and Gretel (1925)
Arthur Quiller-Couch In Powder and Crinoline (1913)
Romer Wilson Red Magic (1930)

References: Bénézit; Houfe; ICB 1; Johnson; Peppin; Ray; Thieme & Becker; Vollmer; Waters 2; *The Studio* 60 (1914); *The Studio Year Book of Decorative Art* (1923); William Feaver *When We Were Young*

(Thames & Hudson 1977); Keith Nicholson (introduction) *Kay Nielsen* (Coronet Books 1975)

Charles Thrupp Nightingale (b. 1878)

Born Kingston-on-Thames. Worked in London. Wood engraver and illustrator. He worked in a sketchy style often using areas of solid black shadow with contrasting highlights.

Books illustrated include:
Walter de la Mare Old Joe (1927), Readings (1928)
Laurence Housman Turn Again Tales (with others, 1930)
Madeleine Nightingale The Babe's Book of Verse (1918), Verses Wise and Otherwise (1918), Nursery Lays of Nursery Days (1919), Tony-o'-Dreams (1919), Farmyard Ditties (1920), Tinker, Tailor (1920), Ring a Ring o' Fairies (1921), Benedicamus Domino (1922), Adeste Fideles (1922), Boggarty Ballads (1923), Mostly Moonshine (1924), Roundabout Tabitha (1927), Poems (1929), The Magic Snuff Box (1936)
Bernard Sleigh Wood Engraving (19329

Periodical: Joy Street

References: Johnson & Greutzner; Campbell Dodgson Contemporary English Woodcuts (Duckworth 1922); A.C. Sewter *Modern British Woodcuts and Wood-engravings in the Collection of the Whitworth Art Gallery* (Manchester 1962); Bernard Sleigh *Wood Engraving Since 1890* (Pitman 1932)

Kathleen Irene Nixon (b. 1894)

Born in Woodside Park, North London. Studied at Camden School of Art and later taught there (1911), then studied illustration at Birmingham School of Art (1913). Flower, bird and animal

Edwin Noble. From *Aesop's Fables* (J. Coker, 1921).

painter. Her first book illustrations were published in 1922, and from 1924 to 1927, she illustrated and designed covers for numerous stories by Enid Blyton, published by George Newnes. She lived in India for 25 years (1927-53) and married there. She illustrated regularly for The Times of India Press, designed 30 nature posters for the Indian State Railways, painted horse portraits and a mural of wild ducks for the Bombay Natural History Museum, and designed costumes and scenery for three productions of the Bombay Operatic Society. After her return to England she wrote and illustrated a number of children's animal stories (some based on her own pet dog and cat) published by Warne, and worked as an animal portrait painter. Awarded numerous medals; made an 'academic of Italy with Gold Medal' 1980. She lives in East Sussex. Member SWA. [Q]

Books illustrated include:
Mortimer Batten Sentinels of the Wild (1938), Whispers in the
  Wilderness (1960)
Enid Blyton Heyo. Brer Rabbit (1938)
Maurice Burton Bird Families (1962)
Major Foran Animal Mothers and Babies (1960)
Kathleen Nixon Pushti (1955), Pindi Poo (1957), Poo and Pushti
  (1959), The Bushy Tail Family (1963), Animal Legends (1966),
  Strange Animal Friendships (1967), Animals and Birds in Folklore
  (1969)
Bird Studies in India (Oxford University Press 1928)
Nature Stories (Harrap 1922)
Poetry of Nature (5 books 1926)

Periodicals: Sunny Stories, The Times of India Press Annual and
Weekly Magazine

Reference: Cope

John Edwin Noble (1876-1941)

Worked as Edwin Noble, son of John Noble RBA. Studied at the Slade School of Fine Art, Lambeth School of Art, and the Royal Academy Schools. Subsequently instructor at Calderon's School of Animal Painting (1906-12), lecturer on animal drawing and anatomy at the Central School of Arts and Crafts and at the Camberwell School of Arts and Crafts. A sergeant in the Royal Army Veterinary Corps during World War I, he was employed as an official war artist, depicting horses and mules in charcoal and watercolour. He also designed posters. Noble seems to have worked exclusively as an animal artist, but his characteristically emphatic outline gives his work a strongly decorative quality. Some of his black and white illustrations recall the posters of the Beggarstaff Brothers (*see* William Nicholson) in their bold, simplified treatment. RBA (1907), FZS (1909-26).

Books illustrated include:
Ellen C. Davies Our Friends at the Farm (with Leonard Brightwell*,
  1920)
Carl Ewald The Twelve Sisters (1923)
E. Noble Animals at the Zoo (1910), The Dog Lover's Book (1910),
  Camp-Fire Tales (1912), Animal Drawing and Anatomy (1928)

W.P. Pycraft The Animal Why Book (1909), The British Museum of
  Natural History (1910), Pads, Paws and Claws (1911)
Aesop's Fables (1921)

References: Houfe; Wa (1958); Waters; C. Wood

A. Nobody

See Gordon Frederick Browne

Edwin Arthur Norbury (1849-1918)

Born Liverpool. He contributed to *The Illustrated London News* and to *The Illustrated Times,* and later he joined the staff of *The Graphic.* Lived in North Wales (1875-90). Took charge of Royal School of Arts, Siam (1892). Special artist to *The Graphic* during the Franco-Siamese war (1893). In 1896 he returned to London and founded the Norbury Sketching School. He also ran St James's Life School, Chelsea and was principal of the Henry Blackburn Studio. His book illustrations, in black and white, monochrome and full colour, are, considering his experience, somewhat naive in execution. Founder member of the Royal Cambrian Academy.

Edgar Norfield. From *The Small Miracle* by Paul Gallico (Michael Joseph, 1951).

Books illustrated include:
H. Coupin & J. Lea The Romance of Animal Arts and Crafts (with others, 1907)
Lucy M.J. Garnett Greek Wonder Tales (1913)
Ernest Young The Kingdom of the Yellow Robe (1898), Corsica (1909)

References: Houfe; Johnson & Greutzner; Waters; C. Wood

Edgar George Norfield (d. 1977)

Usually worked as Edgar Norfield. Studied art in Cambridge, London and Paris. Lived at Lewes, Sussex. Painter in oil and watercolour and humorous illustrator (mainly brush drawings). His illustrations for *Mother of Parliaments* are very much in the vein of those by John Reynolds* for *1066 and All That.*

Books illustrated include:
Charles R. Benstead Alma Mater (1944), Mother of Parliaments (1948)
Lewis Carroll Alice in Wonderland (nd)
Lewis Dutton 'Rags, M.D.' (1933)
Paul Gallico The Small Miracle (1951)
John Gibbons Roll on, Next War! (1935)

Periodical: Punch

References: Wa (1977); Wa (1980)

Graham Oakley (b. 1929)

Studied at Warrington School of Art. Worked as a stage designer for various repertory companies and spent two years with the Royal Opera House, Covent Garden. Television designer for the BBC (1962). Turning to book illustration relatively late, he immediately made his name with the *Church Mice* series in which fast-moving narrative is packed with detailed, brightly coloured images. *Magical Changes* (1979) explores and exploits subconscious association in wordless Magritte-like metamorphoses. Lives in Wiltshire.

Books illustrated include:
Charles Kevern White Horizons (1975)
Elisabeth MacDonald The Two Sisters (1975)
Graham Oakley The Church Mice Spread Their Wings (1975), The Church Mice Adrift (1976), The Church Mice at Bay (1978), The Church Mice and the Moon (1979), Magical Changes (1979), The Church Mice at Christmas (1980), Hetty and Hamlet (1981)

Reference: ICB 4

John Scorror O'Connor (b. 1913)

Born in Leicester. Studied at Leicester College of Art (1931-34) and at the Royal College of Art (1934-37) under Eric Ravilious*, John Nash* and R.S. Austin*. Lecturer in fine art at Birmingham College of Art (1937), and in graphics at Bristol College of Art (1938-41). Served in the Royal Air Force (1942-46). Head of Colchester School of Art (1948-64), visiting lecturer in St Martin's School of Art (1964-74); from 1975 he was visiting lecturer at Glasgow College of Art and Colchester Institute of Education. He is primarily a painter, and his book illustrations often have a painterly richness of surface. He has experimented with combining engraved wood with lino blocks (for coloured areas); he has also used lithography, pen and ink, and watercolour for illustration. His wood engravings are strikingly decorative in the tradition of Eric Ravilious, with tonal and textural contrast achieved through a wide variety of tooling. He has illustrated a number of books for the Golden Cockerel Press and the Dropmore Press. Lives in Kircudbrighthire, Scotland. Elected ARE, ARCA. [Q]

Books illustrated include:
E.H. Blakeney (trans) Funeral Oration of Pericles (1948)
John Clare The Wood is Sweet (1971)
H.B. Farnie The Golfers' Manual (1947)
Thomas Gray Elegy Written in a Country Churchyard (1955)
T.M. Hope Essex Pie (1951)
John O'Connor Canals, Barges and People (1950), An Essex Dozen (1953), A Patter of People (1959), Landscape Painting (1967), The Technique of Wood Engraving (1971), Introducing Relief Printing (1973), A View of Kilvert (1981)
Joan Rutter (compiled by) Here's Flowers (1937)
Owen Rutter (compiled by) We Happy Few (1946)
Christopher Sandeman Thyme and Bergamot (1947)
E.L. Grant Watson Departures (1948)
Christopher Whitfield Together and Alone (1945)
John Nyren Young Cricketer's Tutor (1948)
The Kynoch Press Notebook (1948)

Periodicals: Harper's Bazaar, Radio Times, The Saturday Book

References: Balston EWE; Bénézit; Garrett BWE, HBWE; Jacques; Johnson & Greutzner; Usherwood; Vollmer supp; Wa (1980); Waters; *Image* 1 (Summer 1949); Dorothea Braby *The Way of Wood Engraving* (Studio 1953); Christopher Sandford *Bibliography of the Golden Cockerel Press* (Dawson 1975)

Alan Elsden Odle (1888-1948)

Born Deptford, London, son of banker. Studied at the Sidney Cooper School of Art, Canterbury and St John's Wood School of Art. Art editor of *The Gypsy* (1915-16), a short-lived periodical that published a number of his drawings. An habitué of the Café Royal, London, alcoholic and consumptive, doctors had given him six months to live when he married the novelist Dorothy Richardson (1873-1957) in 1917. Living in near penury, they moved to Cornwall, visiting London each summer. Although he worked in relative isolation, Odle's pen and ink drawings were strongly

John O'Connor. From his *Canals, Barges and People* (Art & Technics, 1950).

surrealist in character, and, as though anticipating the 1960s, almost psychedelic in feeling. A recurring theme was the transmutability of one life form into another, often with slaughter, dismemberment, and saprophytic regeneration. He himself admitted to the influence of the artists of the children's comic *Chatterbox* and of William Hogarth in his treatment of crowds. In 1925 he shared an exhibition at the St George's Gallery with Harry Clarke*, A.O. Spare* and John Austen*; the latter, a close friend who considered Odle 'the supreme master of the pen', made repeated, though seldom successful efforts to find publishers and buyers for his work. Critical acclaim was not lacking: reviewing the 1925 exhibition, P.G. Konody asked 'Who else can approach him in the richness of quality which marks his pen work, in the vital power of his arabesque, in the exuberance of his baroque invention, in the exquisiteness of detail maintained through the commanding breadth and tempestuous flow of his line?' Nevertheless, only two of his drawings sold from the show to H.G. Wells (a friend and former lover of Dorothy Richardson), and the gallery proprietor disappeared with most of the rest. Recently, Odle has begun to be widely recognised as one of the masters of grotesque illustration, and ninety-seven of his previously unpublished illustrations for Rabelais and Balzac appeared in *Gargantua et Contes Drôlatiques de Balzac* published in Geneva in 1977.

Books illustrated include:
James Hanley The Last Voyage (1931)
Jack Lindsay The Miniambs of Herondas (1926)
Mark Twain 1601 (1936)
Voltaire (trans Henry Morley) Candide (1922)

Periodicals: The Golden Hind, The Gypsy, Radio Times, Vanity Fair

References: Houfe; Lewis; Vollmer; Wa (1954); *Antiquarian Book*

Monthly Review (October 1979); *Drawing and Design* (May 1925); *The Studio* 89 (1925), 95 (1928); John Austen *The ABC of Pen and Ink Rendering* (Pitman 1937); G. Montague Ellwood *The Art of Pen Drawing* (Batsford 1927); Rose Odle *Salt of Our Youth* (Wardens 1972); John Rosenberg *Dorothy Richardson, the Genius they Forgot* (Duckworth 1973)

Richard Bertram Ogle (active 1920-62)

Portrait painter, illustrator and writer of children's books. He generally worked in pen and ink; occasionally produced full-colour plates. His drawings of animal are invariably more successful than those of people.

Books illustrated include:
Charles Kingsley Hereward the Wake (1948)
A. Miles Brave Deeds by Brave Men (nd)
R.B. Ogle The Secret (1936), Seal Cove (1943), Albert the Ant (1946), Silent Terror (1947), Mystery of the Migrants (1947), Animals Strange and Rare (1951), Sailors of the Queen (1954), People of the Sun (1955), Pets and their Care (1955), Animals in the Service of Man (1957), Animals and their Camouflage (1958), Animals of the Past (1962)
Philip Rush He Sailed with Dampier (1947)
Percy Westerman Clinton's Quest (1925)
King Arthur and his Knights (1929)
Old English Fairy Tales (1930)
Stories from the Arabian Nights (1928)
Wild Life of the World (1944)

Periodicals: The Boy's Own Paper, The Graphic, Printer's Pie

Reference: Johnson & Greutzner

Olive F. Openshaw (active 1942-53)

The original illustrator of the *Mary Mouse* books. This series of picture-strip books, published by the Brockhampton Press, was produced on off-cuts of paper in a tiny oblong format, and printed in two colours. Olive Openshaw's restrained, sympathetic illustrations succeeded in bringing life to Enid Blyton's minimal texts. In 1954 the series lost its charm when Olive Openshaw was replaced by another (uncredited) illustrator who attempted, unsuccessfully, to imitate her style. The whole series was later re-illustrated in an updated mode.

Books illustrated include:
Enid Blyton Mary Mouse and the Doll's House (1942), More Adventures of Mary Mouse (1943), Little Mary Mouse Again (1944), Hallo, Little Mary Mouse (1945), Mary Mouse and Her Family (1946), Here Comes Mary Mouse Again (1947), How Do You Do, Mary Mouse (1948), We Do Love Mary Mouse (1950), Welcome Mary Mouse (1950), A Prize for Mary Mouse (1951), Mary Mouse and her Bicycle (1952), Mary Mouse and the Noah's Ark (1953)

Reference: Fisher p.216

Jack Orr (active 1904-44)

It seems virtually certain that Jack Orr was the brother of Monro and Stewart Orr*. Their styles and signatures were not dissimilar, all lived in Glasgow, and it is known that there were three Orr brothers.

Jack Orr. From *Nursery Rhymes* by Louey Chisholm (T.C. & E.C. Jack, c.1904).

Books illustrated include:
Louey Chisholm Nursery Rhymes told to the Children (with S.R. Praeger*, c.1904)
E.F. Sellar The Story of Lord Roberts (1909)
Old Nursery Rhymes (Nelson nd)
The Travels of Perrywinkle (1944)

Reference: Johnson & Greutzner

Monro Scott Orr (b. 1874)

Born Irvine, Scotland, son of a merchant, brother of Stewart Orr, and probably of Jack. Studied at Glasgow School of Art where he won a Queen's prize for anatomy. He lived in Glasgow and worked as a painter and etcher of figure subjects. His illustrations have bold outlines and bright colours and he was clearly influenced by William Nicholson* but lacked Nicholson's vigour and originality as a designer. Like Nicholson, he sometimes depicted 'types', but though these show a tendency towards caricature, the characterisations lack wit.

Books illustrated include:
R. Fergusson Scots Poems (1912)
G. Kobbé The Loves of the Great Composers (1912)
Frances Olcott The Arabian Nights (1913)
F.H. Pritchard The Children's Ali Baba (frontispiece with H.C. Appleton*, 1938)
Dante Gabriel Rossetti The Ballad of Jan van Hunks (1929)

R.L. Stevenson Treasure Island (1934)
L. Weirter The Story of Edinburgh Castle (1913)
The Alphabet (1931)
Grimm's Fairy Tales (1914)
Mother Goose (1915)
Twelve Drawings of Familiar Characters in Fiction and Romance (1903)
The World's Fairy Book (1930)

Periodicals: Holly Leaves, The Odd Volume

References Bénézit; Houfe; ICB 1; Johnson & Greutzner; Thieme & Becker; Vollmer; Wa (1934); Waters; C. Wood; *The Studio* 29 (1903), special (1911, Autumn 1914); James L. Carr *Scottish Painting Past and Present* (T.C. & E.C. Jack 1908).

Stewart Orr (1872-c.1945)

Born in Glasgow, brother of M.S. Orr*. Studied at Glasgow School of Art. Lived in Glasgow and on the Isle of Arran, and enjoyed hill and rock climbing. Landscape and animal painter. His book illustrations, in black and white, halftone and colour, depend for effect on their economical, controlled outlines. Malcolm Salaman praises his 'animal whimsicalities'. *The Studio* Special Autumn 1914).

Books illustrated include:
J. Brymer Gammon and Spinach (1901), Two Merry Mariners (1902)
Azubah J. Lee Tales and Tags (with C.H.L., 1921)

Monro S. Orr. From *The Arabian Nights* by Frances Olcott (Harrap, 1913).

Periodicals: Cassell's Magazine, Little Folks, The Odd Volume

References: Houfe; Johnson & Greutzner; Vollmer supp; Wa (1929); Waters; C. Wood; *The Studio* special (1911, Autumn 1914); Fred Gettings *Arthur Rackham* (Studio Vista 1975)

Edward Osmond (b. 1900)

Born in Suffolk. Studied art at the Regent Street Polytechnic. He was a painter and commercial artist, magazine illustrator, and also a writer, designer and illustrator of chidren's books, mainly on historical and ethnological subjects. A highly professional illustrator, particularly adept at historical reconstruction, he worked in full and partial colour, halftone and black and white. He lives in Sussex. He won the Carnegie Medal with *A Valley Grows Up* in 1953.

Books illustrated include:
Richard Armstrong The Lost Ship (1956)
Wendy Boorer Dog Care (1979)
Arthur Catherall Tenderfoot Trapper (1958), Lone Seal Pup (1964), A
    Zebra Came to Drink (1967)
Helen Griffiths Horse in the Clouds (1957), Wild and Free (1958),
    Moonlight (1959)
Cynthia Harnett Monasteries and Monks (1963)
Edward Osmond A Valley Grows Up (1953), Animals of the World
    (1956), Houses (1956), Villages (1957), Towns (1958), From
    Drumbeat to Tickertape (1960) The Artist in Britain (1961), People
    of the Jungle Forest (1963), People of the Desert (1963), People of
    the Arctic (1964), Kangaroos (1964), People of the Grasslands
    (1964), People of the High Mountains (1965), People of the Lonely
    Island (1965), Exploring Fashions and Fabrics (1967)
A.S. Playfair Modern First Aid (1973)
M.J. Robson Children of Africa (1970)
Percy Westerman Held in the Frozen North (1956), Jack Craddock's
    Commission (1958)

References: ICB 2, 4; Vollmer; Wa (1980)

Henry Ospovat (1877-1909)

Born in Russia. His family emigrated and settled in Manchester. In 1897, he enrolled at the Manchester School of Art, and afterwards studied at the National Art Training Schools at South Kensington, specialising in lithography. While at college, he designed a number of book plates described by Onions as 'thinly drawn'; also during this period, he became a friend of the painter, G.F. Watts. After leaving college he continued to live in London, but moved house frequently. He rapidly became known as an illustrator, caricaturist and portrait painter. He died after a few months' illness at the age of 31. Although, as a student, Ospovat had a great admiration for the work of the 1860s illustrators (e.g. Pinwell, Walker, Boyd Houghton), his own book illustrations are essentially 'fin-de-siècle' in mood, with echoes of the work of Laurence Housman and E.J. Sullivan*. They were characterised by strong chiaroscuro created with distinctive style of closely-worked hatching that does much to disguise his sometimes shaky grasp of form, and by an often intensely miasmatic feeling of atmosphere. His caricatures,

Stewart Orr. 'Weel Saipit is half shaven' from *The Studio Special* (1914).

on the other hand, were economically drawn with liveliness and panache and were often brilliantly convincing.

Books illustrated include:
Matthew Arnold Poems (1900)
Robert Browning Men and Women (1903)
C.E. Maud Heroines of Poetry (1903)
Shakespeare's Songs (1901)
Shakespeare's Sonnets (1899)
The Song of Songs (1906)

Periodical: The Idler

References: Baker; Bénézit; Chamot, Farr & Butlin; Houfe; Johnson & Greutzner; Mallalieu; Sketchley; Thieme & Becker; Waters; C. Wood; *Art Journal* (1909); *The Daily Telegraph* (12th February 1909); *The Studio* special (1898-99, Spring 1922, 1923-24); *The Work of Henry Ospovat with an appreciation by Oliver Onions* (St Catherine Press 1911); William Feaver *Masters of Caricature* (Weidenfeld & Nicolson 1981)

Will Owen (1869-1957)

Born Malta, son of a naval officer. Studied at Lambeth School of Art. Owen's work remained well within the stylistic parameters of Edwardian humorous illustration, and his drawings often contained echoes of his better known contemporaries Phil May*, Tom Browne* and John Hassall*. He tended to use heavy outlines and often experimented with spatter and other techniques to achieve tone. His full-page illustrations for magazines were very popular in their day and he enjoyed a long collaboration with the humorous writer W.W. Jacobs, but in many ways his

Helen Oxenbury. 'Its taste in costume is entirely absurd—/It is ages ahead of the fashion' from *The Hunting of the Snark* by Lewis Carroll (Heinemann, 1970).

style was best suited to the commercial and poster work that formed a large part of his output.

Books illustrated include:
Arthur E. Copping Jolly in Germany (1910)
W.W. Jacobs At Sunwich Port (1902), Sailor's Knots (1909), A Master of Craft (1910), Short Cruises (1920)
Jerome K. Jerome A Miscellany of Sense and Nonsense (1923)
B.T. Jones What's the Buzz? (1943)
D.I.B MacCulloch Gardening Guyed (1931)
Will Owen Alleged Humour (1917), Three Jolly Sailors and Me (1919), Old London Town (1921), Mr Peppercorn (1940), What's the Dope? (1944)

Periodicals: The Bystander, The Grand Magazine, The Graphic, The Humorist, The Idler, Pear's Annual, Pearson's Magazine, Pick-me-up, Printer's Pie, Punch, The Sketch, The Strand Magazine, The Tatler, The Temple Magazine

References: Doyle BWI; Houfe; Johnson & Greutzner; Lewis; Thorpe; Vollmer; Wa (1956); Waters; *The Girls' Realm Annual* (1910)

Helen Oxenbury (b. 1938)

Born in Ipswich, Suffolk, daughter of an architect. Attended Ipswich School of Art and then studied theatre design at the Central School of Arts and Crafts. She was assistant designer and then designer at Colchester Repertory Theatre

and spent three years in Israel as scene painter and designer for the Habinek Theatre, Tel-Aviv. On her return she worked for television at Teddington and on film sets at the Shepperton Studios. Her first book, *Numbers of Things*, was published in 1967 and in 1969 she won the Kate Greenaway Medal with *The Quangle Wangle's Hat* and *The Dragon of an Ordinary Family*. These and her subsequent picture books have been notable for their humour and freshness, and often for their conceptualised, deliberately childlike iconography. She generally works in pen and ink, coloured with crayon, watercolour washes or gouache. She married the children's illustrator and writer John Burningham*. [Q]

Books illustrated include:
Brian Anderson Cakes and Custard (1974)
Jill Bennett (ed) Tiny Tim: Verses for Children (1981)
Lewis Carroll The Hunting of the Snark (1970)
Ivor Cutler Meal One (1971), The Animal House (1976), Elephant Gild (1976)
Edward Lear The Quangle Wangle's Hat (1969)
Margaret Mafry The Dragon of an Ordinary Family (1969)
Helen Oxenbury Numbers of Things (1967), The Dragon of an Ordinary Family (1969), Letters of Thanks (1969), ABC of Things (1971), Pig Tale (1973), A Child's Book of Manners (1978), Rosie Randall (1978), The Queen and Rosie Randall (1978), Heads Bodies Legs (1980), 729 Animal Allsorts (1980), 729 Curious Creatures (1980), 729 Puzzle People (1980), Bill and Stanley (1981), Friends, Playing, Dressing, Working, Family (5 board books 1981)
Helen Oxenbury and Fay Maschler A Child's Book of Manners (1978)
Leo Tolstoy The Great Big Enormous Turnip (1968)

Reference: ICB 4

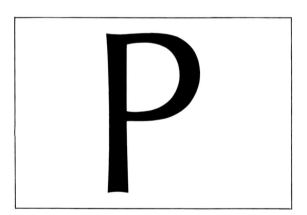

Henry Marriott Paget (1856-1936)

Often worked as H.M. Paget. Born in London, brother of Sidney and Walter Paget*. He entered the Royal Academy Schools in 1874. He travelled widely as a magazine illustrator in Europe, Canada and Turkey, covering the Balkan War (1912-13) as a special artist for *The Sphere*. During the late 1880s, he was a neighbour of Jack B. Yeats* in Bedford Park, and was described by Yeats's biographer Hilary Pyle, as 'rather pedestrian in his illustrations'. Thorpe considered him 'an efficient illustrator using black and white in the manner of

Sidney Paget. From *The Man with the Twisted Lip* in *The Adventures of Sherlock Holmes* by Arthur Conan Doyle (Smith, Elder, 1911).

the watercolour artist'. He was also a painter of portraits and classical and historical subjects, and a keen boxer. Elected RBA (1889).

Books illustrated include:
E.L.L. Arnold The Wonderful Adventures of Phra the Phoenician (1892)
E.T. Bradley Annals of Westminster Abbey (1895)
John Finnemore The Wolf Patrol (1908)
Oliver Goldsmith The Vicar of Wakefield (1898)
G.A. Henty Through the Fray (1886), The Bravest of the Brave (1887), Captain Bayley's Heir (1889), With Moore at Corunna (1898)
Walter Scott Kenilworth (1893), Quentin Durward (1894)
Robert Louis Stevenson The Black Arrow (1892)
Pictures from Dickens (1895)

Periodicals: The Boy's Own Paper, The Graphic, The Illustrated London News, Little Folks, The Quiver, The Windsor Magazine

References: Baker; Bénézit; Doyle BWI; Houfe; ICB 1; Johnson & Greutzner; Thieme & Becker; Thorpe; Vollmer supp; Waters; C. Wood; Hilary Pyle *Jack B. Yeats* (Routledge and Kegan Paul 1970); F.G. Kitton *Dickens and his Illustrators. Appendix 2.* (G. Redway 1899)

Sidney Edward Paget (1860-1908)

Worked as Sidney Paget. Born London, brother of H.M. Paget* and Walter Paget*. He studied art at the British Museum, Heatherley's School of Art, and the Royal Academy Schools. Genre, portrait and landscape painter; on the staff of *The Illustrated London News* and *The Sphere*. As the first illustrator of the *Sherlock Holmes* stories (published initially in *The Strand Magazine*), he created the visual archetype of the famous detective. Thorpe considered that he 'illustrated the

Sherlock Holmes series very literally but without much imaginative interest. Such themes as "he opened the door", "he sat down at the table", "she gazed out of the window", were drawn accurately enough but did not provoke much enthusiasm. Among a certain disrespectful group of art students of the period "illustrated by Sidney Paget" was synonymous with anything obvious and banal.'

Books illustrated include:
B.M. Croker Terence (1899)
Sir Arthur Conan Doyle Adventures of Sherlock Holmes (1892), The Hound of the Baskervilles (1892), The Memoirs of Sherlock Holmes (1894), Rodney Stone (1896), The Tragedy of the Korosko (1898), The Hound of the Baskervilles (1892), The Return of Sherlock Holmes (1905)
L.T. Meade and Robert Eustace The Sanctuary Club (1900)
Walter Scott Old Mortality (1898)

Periodicals: Cassell's Family Magazine, The Graphic, The Illustrated London News, The London Magazine, The Pall Mall Magazine, The Quiver, The Sphere, The Strand Magazine, The Windsor Magazine

References: Baker; Bénézit; DNB (1901-11); Doyle BWI; Houfe; Johnson & Greutzner; Lewis; Sketchley; Thieme & Becker; Thorpe; Waters; C. Wood

Walter Stanley Paget (1863-1935)

Worked as Walter Paget. Younger brother of H.M. Paget* and Sidney Paget*. Figure painter, magazine and book illustrator. As a war correspondent for *The Illustrated London News,* he covered the Gordon relief expedition (1884-85), and, like his brother Sidney, later became a staff artist on the newly founded periodical *The Sphere* (from 1900). As a book illustrator in colour, black and white, and halftone, he worked in a reliably conventional vein. He lived for many years in London and died at Bromsgrove, Worcestershire. He is said to have been used by his brother Sidney as the original model for Sherlock Holmes.

Books illustrated include:
F.S. Brereton With Our Russian Allies (1916)
Dorita Bruce Dimsie Moves Up (1921)
John Bunyan The Pilgrim's Progress (1906)
Daniel Defoe Robinson Crusoe (1896)
John Cryden Aeneid of Virgil (1910)
G.A. Henty Easter Dawn (1889), Condemned as a Nihilist (1893), At Agincourt (1897), With Moore at Corunna (1898), Under Wellington's Command (1899), At the Point of the Bayonet (1902), The Treasure of the Incas (1903), With the British Legion (1903), With the Allies to Pekin (1904)
Charles Kingsley The Heroes (1909), Hereward the Wake (nd)
Charles and Mary Lamb Tales from Shakespeare (1901)
F. Marryat The Children of the New Forest (1922)
Mrs L.T. Meade Out of Fashion (1894)
Walter Scott The Black Dwarf (1893), Castle Dangerous (1894), A Legend of Montrose (1895), The Talisman (1895),
R.L. Stevenson Treasure Island (1899), The Master of Ballantrae (1911)
Percy Westerman A Lively Bit of the Front (1918), The Arabian Nights (1907)
Christmastide in Prose and Poetry (1906)

Periodicals: Cassell's Magazine, The English Illustrated Magazine, The Graphic, Illustrated London News, Little Folks, The Pall Mall Magazine, The Quiver, The Sphere, The Strand Magazine, The Windsor Magazine, Young England

References: Baker; Doyle BWI; Houfe; Johnson & Greutzner; Lewis; Sketchley; Thieme & Becker; Thorpe; Waters 2; C. Wood; Pat Hodgson *The War Illustrators* (Osprey 1977)

Garrick S. Palmer (b. 1933)

Born in Portsmouth, Hampshire. Studied at Portsmouth College of Art and Design (1951-55) and at the Royal Academy Schools (1955-59); awarded David Murray landscape scholarships (1955-57), Leverhulme scholarship (1957), Royal Academy gold medal and the Edward Scott travelling scholarship (1958). Head of the Foundation department at Winchester School of Art since 1964. Painter, lithographer, wood engraver and photographer. For book illustration he uses wood engraving, sometimes with a second colour (as in *The Destruction of the Jews*, 1971) to create rich, dramatic effects. Elected ARE (1963), RE (1970).

Books illustrated include:
Flavius Josephus (trans G.A. Williamson) The Destruction of the Jews (1971)
Herman Melville Three Stories (1967), Benito Cereno (1972), Moby Dick (1974)
H.M. Tomlinson The Sea and the Jungle (1971)
Also works published by Imprint Society, Mass., USA

References: Garrett BWE, HBWE; Wa (1977); Kenneth Lindley *The Woodblock Engravers* (David & Charles 1970)

Harold Sutton Palmer (1854-1933)

Born in Plymouth. Studied at the South Kensington School of Art where he was awarded a gold medal. He was primarily a landscape watercolourist, and his book illustrations consisted of competent and detailed topographical paintings, reproduced in full colour. Martin Hardie observed that his was a 'pleasing but a conscious and sophisticated art, depending upon recipe and very skilful technique' (*Watercolour Painting in Britain*). Elected RBA (1892), RI (1920).

Books illustrated include:
Mary H. Austin California (1914)
V.C.C. Baddeley Devon (1925)
A.G. Bradley The Wye (1910); The Rivers and Streams of England (1920)
G.E. Mitton Buckinghamshire and Berkshire (1920)
A.R.H. Moncrieff Bonnie Scotland (1904), Surrey (1906), The Heart of Scotland (1909), Scotland (1922)
Scott Country (with W. Smith, 1920)

References: Bénézit; Houfe; Johnson & Greutzner; Mallalieu; Thieme & Becker; Vollmer; Wa (1929); Waters; C. Wood; Martin Hardie *Watercolour Painting in Britain* vol 2 (Batsford 1967)

Juliette Palmer (b. 1930)

Born at Romford, Essex. Studied at South East Essex School of Art (1946-50) and at the London University Institute of Education (1950-51). Art and craft teacher in Essex secondary modern schools (1952-57); display artist for the Metal Box Company, London (1957-58); representative for a commercial art studio (1958-59). Painter in watercolour and freelance illustrator of educational

books and children's stories since 1959. Initially her illustrations consisted of pen and ink drawings in a sketchy style; later, as her line became more precise, she added tone and texture in a variety of media. She works from life studies and photographs. Since 1973, she has been writing and illustrating picture information books published by Macmillan; she has also worked for Hamish Hamilton (early books), Abelard-Schumann, World's Work and Methuen, and has illustrated some 20 school books for Edward Arnold (1961-68). An illustrator with a strong sense of design she often creates varied effects with a limited colour range.

Books illustrated include:
Betty Baker The Sun's Promise (1962)
Laura Nelson Baker Torkel's Winter Friend (1961)
Bernagh Brims Runaway Riders (1963), Red Rosette (1965)
Irma Chilton The Witch (1979)
Dorothy Clewes All the Fun of the Fair (1961), The Birthday (1962), The Branch Line (1963)
Elizabeth Coatsworth Cricket and the Emperor's Son (1962)
Lois Dubkin Quiet Street (1963)
Dorothy Edwards (ed) Once, Twice, Thrice Upon a Time (1976), Once, Twice, Thrice Again (1976)
Eleanor Farjeon Jim and the Pirates (1967)
Rosemary Garland The Canary Shop (1960), The Umbrella Man (1962)
Jo Hatcher The Gasworks Alley Gang (1960)
Wilma Horsburgh Puppies to the Rescue (1966)
Helen Kay A Duck for Keeps (1962)
Celia Knowles Hippo, a Welsh Cob (1963)
Elizabeth Kyle Eagle's Nest (1960)
Patricia Lynch The Golden Caddy (1962)
Compton Mackenzie The Stairs that Kept Going Down (1967)
Pamela Mansbridge No Clues for Caroline (1966)

Juliette Palmer. 'The garden shed seemed a mile from the house...' from *The Penny Pony* by Barbara Willard (Hamish Hamilton, 1961).

William Papas. From *The Children Take Over* by Gilliam Avery in *Miscellany One* edited by Edward Blishen (Oxford University Press, 1964).

Jo Packer Pepper Leads the String (1965)
Juliette Palmer Cockles and Shrimps (1973), Mountain Wool (1974), Swan Upping (1974), Stow Horse Fair (1976), Barley Sow, Barley Grow (1978), Barley Ripe, Barley Reap (1979)
Jill Paton-Walsh The Butty Boy (1975)
Ann Thwaite (ed) Allsorts 6 & 7 (1974-75)
Viola Wahlstedt Come Back Jock (1961)
Abbie Phillips Walker Sandman's Fairy Stories (1962), Sandman's Moonlight Stories (1963),
Barbara Wilkinson Hambro (1961)
Barbara Willard The Penny Pony (1961)
Dorian Williams Wendy at Wembley (1960)
I Spy History (1961)
I Spy Churches (1962)

Periodical: The Elizabethan

References: Contemporary Authors

William Papas (b. 1927)

Born to Greek/German parents in the Transvaal, South Africa, and educated there. Studied at Beckenham School of Art, Kent, and at St Martin's School of Art, London. Staff artist on the *Cape Times* (1951-59); moved with his family to England (1959) and contributed political cartoons to *The Guardian, The Sunday Times,* and *Punch* (1959-70). Banned from South Africa since 1965. Since 1970, he has worked as a freelance cartoonist, illustrator, lithographic printmaker, painter and writer. For illustration, he draws mainly in pen and ink and wash in a very distinctive graphic

style influenced by Daumier and Goya. He now lives in Greece. [Q]

Books illustrated include:
Edward Blishen (ed) Miscellany One (1964)
H.F. Brinsmead Beat of the City (1968)
Charles Downing Tales of the Hodja (1964), Armenian Folk Tales (1972)
Frederick Grice A Severnside Story (1964)
René Guillot Guillot's African Folk Tales (1965)
C.S. Lewis The Screwtape Letters (1979)
Ruth Manning-Sanders Damien and the Dragon (1965)
G. Moorhouse The Church (1967)
Malcolm Muggeridge In a Valley of this Restless Mind (1978)
H.M. Namad The Peasant and the Donkey. Tales of the Near and Middle East (1967)
Walter Henry Nelson The Londoners (1975)
P.H. Nortje Dark Waters (1965)
Theodore Papas The Story of Mr Nero (1965)
William Papas Under the Tablecloth (1952), The Press (1964), Tasso (1966), No Mules (1967), A Letter from India (1968), A Letter from Israel (1968), Taresh the Tea Planter (1968), People of Old Jerusalem (1980),
Norman Shrapnel Parliament (1966)
J. Stone The Law (1966)
Philip Turner The Grange at High Force (1965)
Peter Walsh Freddy the Fell Engine (1966)

Periodicals: The Cape Times, The Guardian, The Sunday Times

References: Eyre; Fisher p.81; ICB 3,4; Hurlimann

Frank Cheyne Papé (1878-1972)

A well-known illustrator about whom little biographical information survives. His illustrations were rather old-fashioned for their period—decorative, with finely drawn shading and frequent use of the 'partial framing' device that was so popular in the late 1880s and 1890s. His best work, the illustrations to books by the American writer James Branch Cabell and the French writer Anatole France appeared in the 1920s and inspired something of a Papé cult; there are even references to him in the literature of the time for example this passage from Alec Waugh's novel *Kept*: (1925) 'For several minutes she remained bent over Papé's illustrated *Jurgen*."How good they are," she said. "I should doubt if an artist has ever entered more completely into the spirit of the writer..." ' *Jurgen,* widely regarded as Papé's finest book, sold out on the day of publication. *Figures of Earth* was another notable collaboration between Papé and Cabell, who, in the preface, described Papé's illustrations as 'opulent in conceits and burgeons and whimseys'. Papé's graphic work has undeniable charm, and he produced some striking images, but he lacked the graphic tautness, the imaginative range and the strongly personal viewpoint of the top-ranking illustrators of his generation such as Arthur Rackham* and Edmund Dulac*. However, he did have a redeeming sense of humour that manifested itself, sometimes unexpectedly, as grotesque characterisation, and in the pendants to his larger drawings. Papé married Agnes Stringer, a former Slade student whose illustrations to *Little Folks*

Frank C. Papé. From *Old Rowley* by Dennis Wheatley (Hutchinson, 1933).

(c.1910) are in her husband's early manner, and who did much of the colouring of his pictures. They lived for many years in Tunbridge Wells, Kent.

Books illustrated include:
R.D. Blackmore Picture Story of Lorna Doone (1933)
E.F. Buckley Children of the Dawn (1908)
John Bunyan The Pilgrim's Progress (1910)
James B. Cabell Jurgen (1921), The High Place (1923), Figures of
    Earth (1925), The Cream of the Jest (1927), The Silver Stallion
    (1928), Something about Eve (1929), The Way of Ecben (1929),
    Domnei (1930)
F.W. Carové The Story without an End (1912)
A. Clark As it is in Heaven (1912)
Alphonse Daudet Tartarin de Tarascon (1932)
R. Davies The Stars, The World and The Women (1930)
Daniel Defoe Picture Story of Robinson Crusoe (1933)
Bernard Falk The Naked Lady (1934), Rachel the Immortal (1935)
R.H. Foster Two Romances in Verse (1922)
Anatole France At the Sign of the Reine Pedauque (1922), The Revolt
    of the Angels (1924), Penguin Island (1925), Thais (1925), The Well
    of St Clare (1928), Mother of Pearl (1929)
G. Hodges When the King Came (1923)
Homer The Toils and Travels of Odysseus (1916)
Charles & Mary Lamb Tales from Shakespeare (nd)
F.C. Papé The Diamond Fairy Book (with H.R. Millar*, nd), The
    Golden Fairy Book (with H.R. Millar*, nd)
Ethel Reader The Story of the Little Merman (1909)
S. Rice Tales from the Mahabharata (1924)
M.C. Rowsell The Pedlar and his Dog (nd)
George Sand The Wings of Courage (1911)
M.M. Stawell The Fairy of Old Spain (1912)
R.D.K. Storer Hercules (1962)
Dennis Wheatley Old Rowley (1933)

Ella Wheeler Wilcox Poems of Pleasure (nd)
R. Wilson The Indian Story Book (1914), The Russian Story Book
    (1916)
Hans Andersen's Fairy Tales (1910)
The Book of Psalms (1913)
The Complete Works of Dr François Rabelais (1927)
The Gateway to Spenser (1912)
Siegfried and Kriemhild (1912)
Stories from Spenser (1912)
Suetonius's Lives of the Twelve Caesars (1930)
Tales from the Arabian Nights (1934)

Periodicals: The Boys' Herald, Cassell's Magazine, The Pall Mall
Magazine

References: Fisher pp.176, 177; Houfe; Johnson; Johnson &
Greutzner

Carton Moore Park (1877-1956)

Studied at Glasgow School of Art. He was active as a book and magazine illustrator in the early years of the century, working in pen and ink or pencil and wash. He became well known for his decorative animal illustrations which were drawn with simplicity and style. His most distinctive quality was a striking sense of design—retaining something of the flavour of Glasgow Art Nouveau —that informed even his least inspired drawings. Charles Hiatt wrote in *The Studio* 21 (1901), 'His treatment is refreshingly broad and invariably decorative. Sometimes he exaggerates in the interest of decoration, but he is never guilty of sentimentalising.' He also worked as a lithographer, muralist, portrait painter and caricaturist. Elected RBA (1899, resigned 1905). he emigrated to America (c.1910) and settled in New York.

Books illustrated include:
E. Bicknell A Dog Book (1902)
John Brown A Little Book of Dogs (1911)
H. Hendry A Child's London (1900)
S.P. Hyatt Biffel: A Trek Ox (1909)
C.J. Lever The Confessions of Harry Lorrequer (1900)

Carton Moore Park. From *An Alphabet of Animals* (Blackie, 1898).

A.T. Morris Old Friends and New Fables (nd)
'*Norman*' A Book of Elfin Rhymes (1900)
C.M. Park An Alphabet of Animals (1898), A Book of Birds (1900),
    The Child's Pictorial Natural History (1901), The King of the Beasts
    (1904)
Edmund Selous The Romance of Insect Life (with Lancelot Speed*
    1906)
M.H. Spielmann The Love Family (1908)
La Fontaine's Fables (with Rene Bull*, 1905)
The Lilliput Library for Children (1907)

References: Baker; Bénézit; Houfe; Johnson & Greutzner; Sketchley;
Thieme & Becker; Thorpe; Waters; *The Studio* 21 (1901), special
(1900-01, 1911, Autumn 1914)

Jacynth Parsons (b. 1911)

Child artist, daughter of stained-glass designer
and maker, Karl Parsons, whose close friend
Harry Clarke* helped to organise an exhibition of
her work at the Medici Galleries in 1927. Clarke
also introduced her to W.B. Yeats, who, in an
enthusiastic preface to *Songs of Innocence*, wrote,
'Jacynth Parsons is a genius of an amazing pre-
cocity, an accomplished artist and dreaming child'.
She lived with her family in Middlesex and was a
friend of the poet W.H. Davies from the age of
two. She does not appear to have published anything in adult life.

Books illustrated include:
William Blake (intro W.B. Yeats) Songs of Innocence (1927)
W.H. Davies Forty-nine Poems (1928)
J.E. Masefield South East (1929)
Karl Parsons Ann's Book (1929)

References: ICBI; *The Quiet Life* (Catalogue no 3, Potter Books);
Harry Clarke (The Douglas Hyde Gallery, Trinity College, Dublin
1979)

Marjorie Tulip Parsons (b. 1902)

Worked as Trekkie Ritchie. Married name, Mrs
Peter Brooker. Born in Natal, South Africa,
daughter of an architect. Studied at the Slade
School of Fine Art. Her illustrations consisted
mainly of freely-drawn lithographs in full colour.
Her own books were mainly published by Chatto
and Windus.

Books illustrated include:
M. Alice Gibbs Living Things (1957)
Norah and William Montgomery Scottish Nursery Rhymes (1946)
Trekkie Ritchie Midget Books (36 titles from 1942), Treasures of Li-Po
    (1948), A Junior Course in Nature Study: Come and See (1950),
    England Under Four Queens (1953)
Trekkie Ritchie and Lilla Healing Cooking for Mother (1958)
Bells Across the Sand (1944)

References: ICB 2; Johnson & Greutzner; Waters

John Bernard Partridge (1861-1945)

Often worked as Sir J. Bernard Patridge. Born in
London, son of Sir Richard Partridge, President
of the Royal College of Surgeons and Professor of
Anatomy at the Royal Academy. He started his
career as a stained glass artist and decorative
painter (1880-84), and then worked as an illustrator of magazines and books. He also acted for

Bernard Partridge. From *Rabbi Ben Ezra and
other poems* by Robert Browning (Hodder &
Stoughton, 1915).

a number of years, under the stage name of Bernard
Gould. He was introduced to *Punch* by George
Du Maurier in 1891, and joined the staff in the
following year, contributing 'socials' and theatrical
sketches. He was promoted to second cartoonist
in place of Linley Sambourne in 1901, on John
Tenniel's retirement, and principal cartoonist
from 1909-45, a task for which he considered
himself 'singularly ill-equipped' ('Bernard Partridge and Punch' in *Image* 8, 1952). He was an
occasional painter in oil and watercolour. His
reputation rested mainly on the political cartoons
which he produced with great consistency until
the time of his death. He often worked in a symbolic vein, evoking a sense of occasion through
the use of emblematic animals and figures, but he
also had a gift for capturing facial likeness and
expression. His book illustrations date mainly
from the earlier part of his career. Derek Pepys
Whiteley records in *Image* 8 that his 'sharp, clean
technique was deliberately adapted to the new
mechanical method [of reproduction]'; Though
distinctive, his style had much in common with

Lennox Paterson. From *The Roadmender and other writings* by Michael Fairless (Collins, 1950).

that of his *Punch* colleagues F.H. Townsend* and L. Raven-Hill*. His most highly praised book was *Proverbs.* He also occasionally worked in colour, as in the later *Rabbi Ben Ezra* (1915), in which he achieved a sense of atmosphere and drama. Elected NEAC (1893) and RI (1896, resigned 1906); knighted (1925).

Books illustrated include:
F. Anstey Voces Populi (1890-1892), The Travelling Companions (1892), The Man from Blankley's (1893), Mr Punch's Pocket Ibsen (1893), Under the Rose (1894), The Pocket Ibsen (1895), Baboo Jabberjee (1897), Puppets at Large (1897), The Tinted Venus (1898), Bayard from Bengal (1902)
J.M. Barrie Tommy and Grizel (1900)
H.D. Browne Papers from Punch (1898)
Robert Browning Rabbi Ben Ezra and other poems (1915)
Austin Dobson Proverbs in Porcelain (nd)
M.F. Guillemard The Kitchen Maid (1896)
L.A. Harker Wee Folk, Good Folk (1899)
Jerome K. Jerome Stage-Land (1889)
M.H. Spielman The Rainbow Book (with Arthur Rackham and others, 1909)
M. Wynman My Flirtations... (1892)
The Works of G.J. Whyte-Melville (with others, 1898)

Periodicals: Black and White, The Idler, The Illustrated London News, Illustrated Bits, Judy, The Lady's Pictorial, The New Budget, The Penny Illustrated Paper, Pick-Me-Up, Punch, The Quiver, The Sketch, The Sporting and Dramatic News.

References: Baker; Bénézit; Bradshaw; DNB (1941-50); Hammerton; Harper, Houfe; ICB 1; Johnson & Greutzner; Mallalieu; Pennell MI, PD; Price; Ray; Sketchley; Spielmann; Thieme & Becker; Thorpe; Vollmer supp; Wa (1934); Waters; C. Wood; *Image* 8 (Autumn 1952); *The Studio* special (1900-01, 1911); *The Times* (obituary 11th August, 1945); William Feaver; *Masters of Caricature* (Weidenfeld & Nicholson 1981); G. Montague Ellwood *The Art of Pen Drawing* (Batsford 1927).

G.W. Lennox Paterson (b. 1915)

Sometimes worked as Lennox Paterson. Studied at Glasgow School of Art, where he later taught graphic art and eventually became Deputy Director. Portrait painter and printmaker. His wood-engraved illustrations are poetic in feeling and show a command of the medium. He won the Guthrie Award (1946); elected ARE (1947).

Books illustrated include:
Robert Burns Poetical Works (1958)
Alastair M. Dunnett Land of Scotch (1953)
Michael Fairless The Roadmender... and other writings (1950)
G.W. Lennox Paterson Scraperboard (1960), Making a Colour Lino Cut (1963)
Naomi Mitchison A Fishing Village on the Clyde (1960)

References: Balston EWE; Johnson & Greutzner; Wa (1980); Waters.

Jane Elizabeth Paton (b. 1934)

Studied at St Martin's School of Art, and graphic design under Edward Ardizzone* at the Royal College of Art. In her final year (1957), she was commissioned to illustrate her first children's book, *The Twins in Ceylon.* She works in black and white and full colour.

Books illustrated include:
Honor Arundel The Amazing Mr Prothero (1968)
Claude Cenac Four Poems into Adventure (1965)
Mary Cockett Farthing Bundles (1970)
Dorothy Clewes Boys and Girls Come Out to Play (1964)
Evelyn Davies Little Bear's Father (1972)
Eleanor Farjeon Mr Garden (1966), Around the Seasons (1969)
René Guillot Three Girls and a Secret (1963)
George MacDonald The Princess and the Goblin (1960)
Janet McNeill I Didn't Invite You to my Party (1967), A Helping Hand (1971)
Naomi Mitchison The Fairy Who Couldn't Tell a Lie (1963)
James Reeves Ragged Robin (1961)
Bjorn Rongen Anna of the Bears (1967)
Elfrida Vipont Rescue for Mittens (1965)
Barbara Willard Surprise Island (1966), A Dog and a Half (1964), The Bridesmaid (1976)
Harry Williams The Twins in Ceylon (1958)
Ursula Moray Williams Beware of this Animal (1964)

References: ICB 3,4

Evelyn Paul (active 1910-22)

Studied at the South Kensington Schools and worked as an illustrator and illuminator. Her work as a conventional illustrator, in *Cranford* for example, was hampered by her shaky grasp of perspective. Where spatial recession was not needed, she could be much more convincing, as in her vaguely oriental colour illustrations for *Myths and Legends of Japan.* She was at her best with linear, Celtic-style illumination, seen in the title-page and decorative borders of *The Romance of Tristram of Lyones and La Belle Isoude.*

Books illustrated include:
Susan Cannington Stories from Dante (1910)
Dante The New Life (1916)
Frederick H. Davis Myths and Legends of Japan (1912)
Mrs Gaskell Cranford (1910)

W.J. Gorden (ed) Warne's Pleasure Book for Girls (1928)
W.D. Monro Stories of Indian Gods and Heroes (1911)
Charles Reade The Cloister and the Hearth (1922)
Estelle Ross The Birth of England (1910), From Conquest to Charter (1911)
James L.T.C. Spence Legends of Ancient Egypt (1915), Myths and Legends of Babylonia and Assyria (1916)
Michael P. West Clair de Lune, and other troubadour romances (1913)
The Romance of Tristram of Lyones and La Belle Isoude (1921)

Reference: Houfe

A. Wyndham Payne (active c.1920-30)

Decorative printmaker, draughtsman and water-colourist. He worked mainly for publisher Cyril Beaumont as a designer of book covers and end-papers and illustrator. His illustrations consisted of lino-cuts and woodcuts and pen and ink drawings, often hand-coloured. In 1927, Cyril Beaumont considered that 'as an artist Payne has not yet mastered all the techniques of his profession, but his work is possessed of a high decorative value... He has a vein of good humour and light-hearted fun which creeps in everywhere. In addition he is endowed with a fertile imagination and considerable powers of invention'... (preface to *Town and Country*).

Books illustrated include:
Basildon A Handful of Sovereigns (1930)
C.W. Beaumont A Burmese fire at Wembley (1924), The Mysterious Toyshop (1924), The Strange Adventures of a Toy Soldier (1926), The Wonderful Journey (1927), Sea Magic (1928)
Kenneth Grahame The Wind in the Willows (1927)
Wyndham Payne Town and Country (1927)
Ann Taylor Meddlesome Matty (1925)
Peter Piper's Practical Principles... (1926)

References: Fisher p.353; ICB 1

Charles Johnson Payne (active 1915-23)

Often worked under the pseudonym 'Snaffles'. A sporting painter and illustrator, he worked in watercolour, pen and ink, or crayon, or in combinations of these, in the sketchy style often favoured by sporting artists of the day. His work was often humorous, and he was adept at expressing movement.

Books illustrated include:
M.J. Farrell Red Letter Days (1933)
C.J. Payne My Sketch Book in the Shiny (1930), 'Osses and Obstacles (1935), More Bandobast (1936), A Half Century of Memories (1949), Four-Legged Friends and Acquaintances (1951), I've Heard the Revelly (1953)

References: Wa (1934); J.C. Wood

Irene Payne (active 1904-1913)

Illustrator, probably without formal training, who worked in pen and ink with colour washes. Some of her images—particularly in *Burbling Billy and the Bubble Bee*—were distinctly odd in character.

Books illustrated include:
Mary Garth What Happened to Hannah? (1913)

Irene Payne Baby Bunting and Co (1904), Burbling Billy and the Bubble Bee (nd)

Roger Payne (active from 1950s)

Illustrator of children's books in black and white and full colour, in a competent but not very individual manner.

Books illustrated include:
Richard Armstrong Greenhorn (1965), The Secret Sea (1966)
Enid Blyton Adventure of the Strange Ruby (1960)
Arthur Catherall Night of the Black Frost (1968)
Christopher Fagg Lost Cities (1980)
E.W. Hildick Jim Starling Stories (1958-63)
Alan Kendall Beethoven and his World (1979)
David Kent Escape from Egypt (1981)
Penelope Lively The Wild Hunt of Hagworthy (1975)
Mary E. Patchett Summer on Wild Horse Island (1975)
Henry Treece War Dog (1962)
Brian Williams Joan of Arc (1979)

Reference: Fisher p.157

Mervyn Lawrence Peake (1911-68)

Worked as Mervyn Peake. Born in Kuling, Central China, son of medical missionaries. Lived in Tientsing until the family returned to England (1923). Educated at Eltham College (1924-29); studied briefly at Croydon School of Art, and then at the Royal Academy Schools, where he won the Arthur Hacker Prize. He worked with a group of painters on Sark, Channel Islands (1933-35), and on his return, taught life drawing at Westminster School of Art (1935-38). His first illustrated book, *Captain Slaughterboard*, a humorous fantasy for children, was published in

Mervyn Peake. 'Elisabeth Francis with toad' from *Witchcraft in England* by Christina Hole (Batsford, 1945).

1939. During war service in an anti-aircraft regiment he started work on his epic cycle of *Titus* novels. After being invalided out of the forces in 1943, he was able to concentrate on writing, illustrating and painting. He visited Germany (1946) to record the devastation for *Leader* magazine and was sent to make drawings at Belsen—an experience that profoundly affected his later work. He returned to Sark with his family (1946-49) and there wrote *Gormenghast*; then taught drawing at the Central School of Arts and Crafts (1950-60) while continuing to write and illustrate. However, signs of illness appeared in 1955 and he became gradually incapacitated by Parkinson's Disease, spending his last four years in hospital. His final works were completed only with the support of his wife, artist Maeve Gilmore.

Peake's book illustrations were varied in approach. In *Craft of the Lead Pencil* he suggested that a draughtsman's primary concern should be expression, and in his own drawings he freely adapted his graphic style in response to the imaginative demands of his texts. He was at his best interpreting fantasy—his own and other writers'—and was one of the few successful illustrators of Lewis Carroll since Tenniel, replacing Tenniel's authoritative but sometimes static imagery with ephemeral and often whimsical designs expressing the mutability of a dream. The lively humour present in much of his work was matched by an equally strong instinct for the macabre and the grotesque, and these qualities were merged in the facial caricatures that were a recurring element in his illustrative drawing. Peake's *Titus* novels were first published without illustrations. However, the manuscripts were accompanied by numerous sketches, and some of these appeared as illustrations in later editions.

Books illustrated include:
Algernon Blackwood The Wendingo
Lewis Carroll The Hunting of the Snark (1941), Alice's Adventures in Wonderland and Through the Looking Glass (1954)
Samuel Taylor Coleridge The Rime of the Ancient Mariner (1943)
Maurice Collins Quest for Sita (1946)
Quentin Crisp All This and Bevin Too (1943)
Honoré de Balzac Droll Stories (1961)
H.B. Drake The Book of Lyonne (1952)
D.K. Haynes Thou Shalt Not Suffer a Witch (1949)
Christina Hole Witchcraft in England (1945)
C.E.M. Joad The Adventures of the Young Soldier in Search of a Better World (1943)
Aaron Judah The Pot of Gold and Two Other Tales (1959)
A.M. Laing Prayers and Graces (1944), More Prayers and Graces (1957)
E.C. Palmer The Young Blackbird (1953)
Mervyn Peake Captain Slaughterboard Drops Anchor (1939), Ride-a-Cock-Horse (1940), Rhymes without Reason (1944), The Craft of the Lead Pencil (1946), Letters from a Lost Uncle (1948), Drawings (1949), Mr Pye (1953), Figures of Speech (1954), The Rhyme of the Flying Bomb (1962), A Book of Nonsense (1972)
A. Sander Men: A Dialogue between Women (1955)
R.L. Stevenson Dr Jekyll and Mr Hyde (1948), Treasure Island (1949)
J.D. Wyss The Swiss Family Robinson (1950)
Grimm's Household Tales (1946)

Periodicals: The Ballet, Harvest, Lilliput, The London Mercury, Radio Times, Satire, The Transatlantic Review

References: Doyle CL; Driver; Eyre; ICB 2,4; Jacques; Johnson & Greutzner; Lewis; Thieme & Becker; Wa (1934); Waters; *Alphabet & Image* 1 (1946); *Picture Post* (21st December, 1946); *The Studio* 132 (1946); *Mervyn Peake* (National Book League 1972); 1 (1946); John Batchelor *Mervyn Peake* (Duckworth 1974); Maeve Gilmore *A World Away* (Gollancz 1970); *Mervyn Peake, Writings and Drawings* (Academy 1974); Pearse Hutchinson *Mervyn Peake* (Comham 1959); Michael Moorcock *Architect of the Extraordinary* (Vector 1960); Hilary Spurling *The Drawings of Mervyn Peake* (Davis Poynter, 1974); John Watney *Mervyn Peake* (Michael Joseph 1976)

Charles Pears (1873-1958)

Born in Pontefract, Yorkshire. Moved to London in 1897 and succeeded L. Raven-Hill* as theatrical caricaturist on *Pick-Me-Up* (1898-1902), initially working in a style somewhat influenced by Phil May. He also contributed drawings of 'social' and genre subjects to magazines, but became best known as a marine painter and draughtsman. During World War I, he was an Official War Artist to the Admiralty (1915-18), a position which he occupied again during World War II (1940-45). He also wrote extensively on sailing and yachts, and was founder and first president of the Society of Marine Artists. Though concentrating on marine subjects in his late years, Pears was an impressive all-round draughtsman with a strong, individual sense of compositional and linear style. For illustration, he worked in pencil, crayon, or pen and ink, sometimes with halftone washes or with one or two colours. Elected ROI (1913).

Books illustrated include:
Lewis Carroll Alice's Adventures in Wonderland (1922)
Richard Henry Dana Two Years Before the Mast (1911)
James Gilbert Toby and his Little Dog Tan (1903)
John Masefield Salt-Water Poems and Ballads (1911)
Charles Pears 'Men' (1902), Mr Punch's Book for Children (1902), From the Thames to the Seine (1910), From the Thames to the Netherlands (1914), South Coast Cruising from the Thames to Penzance (1931), Yachting on the Sunshine Coast (1932), Going Foreign (1933)
William Makepeace Thackeray Some Round-About Papers (1908)
Percy Westerman Sea Scouts All (1920)
Works of Charles Dickens (The Waverley Edition, with Fred Barnard, 1913)

Periodicals: The Bystander, Cassell's Magazine, The Dome, The Graphic, The Idler, The Illustrated London News, The London Magazine, The Longbow, The Ludgate Monthly, Nash's Magazine, The Odd Volume, Pear's Annual, Pearson's Magazine, Pick-Me-Up, Printer's Pie, Punch, The Quartier Latin, The Sketch, The Strand Magazine, The Tatler, The Windsor Magazine, The Yellow Book, The Yorkshireman.

References: Bénézit; Hammerton; Houfe; ICB 1; Johnson & Greutzner; Thieme & Becker; Thorpe; Vollmer supp; Wa (1934); Waters; C. Wood; Mrs Charles Pears *Who Hath Desired the Sea* (Arthur Barker, 1962)

Alfred Pearse (1856-1933)

Black and white artist, painter of figure subjects and portrait miniatures, wood engraver. Lived in London. Studied wood-engraving (1872-75);

worked as a 'special' artist for *Pictorial World* (1879-86) and for *The Sphere* on the Royal colonial tour (1901-03), and contributed to *The Boy's Own Paper* for 45 years (1878-1923). Thorpe describes his work as 'competent without showing much personality', and records that he was known as 'Punctual Pearse'. He contributed two miniature paintings to Queen Mary's doll's house.

Books illustrated include:
G.A. Henty By England's Aid (1891), Maori and Settler (1891), Redskin and Cow-Boy (1892)
Charles Herbert Robin Hood (nd)
R. Leighton The Thirsty Sword (1900)
Alfred Pearse Merrie England (c.1928)
Mrs E.R. Pitman My Governess Life (c.1900)
Talbot Baines Reed The Willoughby Captains (1887), Sir Ludor (1889)
Walter Scott Ivanhoe (frontispiece nd)
Gordon Stables Westward with Columbus (1894)
Wheaton's History Picture Books (1933)

Periodicals: The Boy's Own Paper, The Captain, Cassell's Magazine, The Girl's Own Paper, The Girls' Realm, Little Folks, The London Magazine, Pearson's Magazine, The Penny Magazine, Pictorial World, Punch, The Royal Magazine, The Sphere, The Strand Magazine, The Wide World Magazine, Young England

References: Doyle BWI; Houfe; Johnson & Greutzner; Lewis; Thorpe; Vollmer supp; Waters 1, 2; C.Wood

Susan Beatrice Pearse (1878-1980)

Often worked as S.B. Pearse. Born in Fair Oak, Hampshire, daughter of a journalist. Studied at the Royal College of Art. Married W.E. Webster, portrait painter and illustrator. Lived in London (1910) and at Blewbury in Oxfordshire (from 1926). A watercolour painter and illustrator of children's books, Susan Pearse had a distinctive and simple style of great charm. She became well known for her 'Ameliaranne' books which demonstrate her use of clear, delicate colour. She was the designer of the now famous poster for Start-Rite Shoes (c.1920).

Books illustrated include:
Charles Dickens The Magic Fishbone (1912)
Eleanor Farjeon Ameliaranne's Prize Packet (1933), Ameliaranne's Washing-Day (1934)
M. Gilmour Ameliaranne at the Circus (1931), Ameliaranne at the Seaside (1935)
Constance Howard Ameliaranne and the Green Umbrella (1920), The Twins and Tabiffa (1923), Ameliaranne at the Farm (1937), Ameliaranne Keeps School (1940)
N. Joan Howard Ameliaranne in Town (1930), Ameliaranne and the Big Treasure (1932)
Ethelberta Morris Ameliaranne Bridesmaid (1946)
E.M. Osborne Ameliaranne and the Jumble Sale (1943)
K.L. Thompson Ameliaranne at the Zoo (1936)

Periodicals: Little Folks, Playbox Annual

References: Cope; Fisher p.19; Houfe; ICB 1; Johnson & Greutzner; The Times (15th January 1980)

Frederick Pegram (1870-1937)

Born in London first cousin of the brothers C.E. and H.M. Brock*. Painter, etcher and black and white illustrator. His work appeared in numerous

magazines from the 1880s onwards; he joined the staff of *The Pall Mall Gazette* and contributed to *Punch* from 1894. As a book illustrator working on Macmillan's Illustrated Standard Novels, series and for Service Paton, he started off in the Hugh Thomson* tradition, but soon developed an individual pen style characterised by subtle gradations of finely drawn shading. James Thorpe described his illustrations of serials published in *Cassell's Family Magazine* as 'highly finished pen drawings conscientiously drawn but rather too suggestive of the posed model' and compared his illustrations to those of F.H. Townsend*. However, his later work lost much of the anxious tightness of the earlier examples. Pennell considered him an 'accomplished technician'. Member of the Chelsea Arts Club during the 1890s. Elected RI (1925).

Books illustrated include:
Sir Walter Besant The Orange Girl (1899)
George Bulwer-Lytton The Last of the Barons (1897)
Charles Dickens Martin Chuzzlewit (1900)
Benjamin Disraeli Sybil, or the Two Nations (1895)
Maria Edgeworth Ormond (1900)
Ellen Thorneycroft Fowler Concerning Isabel Carnaby (1900)
Captain Marryat Mr Midshipman Easy (1896), Masterman Ready 1897), Poor Jack (1897)
Frank Matthew At the Rising of the Moon (1898)
C.E. Pascoe London's World's Fair (1898)

S.B. Pearse. From *Ameliaranne in Town* by Natalie Joan [Howard] (Harrap, 1930).

Walter Scott The Bride of Lammermoor (1898)
Miss Wetherell The Wide, Wide World (1897)

Periodicals: Black and White, Cassell's Family Magazine, The Daily Chronicle, Fun, The Gentlewoman, The Girl's Own Annual, Home Chat, The Humorist, The Idler, The Illustrated London News, Judy, The Lady's Pictorial, The Minster, The New Budget, The Pall Mall Magazine, Pearson's Magazine, The Penny Magazine, Printer's Pie, Punch, The Queen, The Quiver, The Sporting and Dramatic News, The Windsor Magazine, Women at Home

References: Baker; Bénézit; Guichard; Houfe; ICB 1; Johnson & Greutzner; Pennell MI & PD; Price; Sketchley; Thieme & Becker; Thorpe; Vollmer supp; Waters; C. Wood; *Drawing and Design* (July 1924) p.69; G. Montague Ellwood *The Art of Pen Drawing* (Batsford 1927).

Peter Pendrey.
See Peter Strausfield.

Joseph Pennell (1860-1926)

Born in Philadelphia, USA into a Quaker family that disapproved of art. He attended evening classes at the Philadelphia Industrial Art School while working by day in a coal and iron company office, and subsequently at the Philadelphia Academy. He moved to London during the 1880s and became an admirer and then close friend of his compatriot J.A. McNeill Whistler. Like Whistler, he took up etching and was a writer on art; he also worked in pen and ink and made lithographs. In 1894 he organised the short-lived Society of Illustrators in an 'attempt to organise the profession and maintain its privileges and dignity' (Thorpe). During World War I he made some front-line drawings for the French Government but, a convinced pacifist, returned to America (1917), and settled in Brooklyn, New York. Pennell's early work was in pen and ink but he also became well known for his etchings and lithographs. His work was mainly topographical but very often contained figures to enliven the compositions and create scale. His graphic style showed the influence of the Spanish draughtsman Martin Rico who worked with a fragmented pen line well suited to photographic reproduction. As a critic, Pennell was one of the first to evaluate and promote the work of graphic artists, and to recognise the implications and possibilities of the photomechanical reproductive methods introduced during the 1880s and 1890s. However, the polemical tone of his articles and books sometimes made him unpopular. Member of the American Academy of Art and of the Chelsea Arts Club and first president of the Senefelder Club; elected RE (1882).

Books illustrated include:
Earl of Albermarle and G.L. Hillier Cycling (1894)
Sir Walter Besant East London (1901)
A.G. Bradley Highways and Byways in North Wales (1898), Highways and Byways in The Lake District (1901)
A.M. Caird Romantic Cities of Provence (1906)

F.M. Crawford Gleanings from Venetian History (1905)
S.R. Crockett Raiderland (1904)
S. Dark London (1924)
Percy Dearmer Highways and Byways in Normandy (1900)
Anna B. Dodd On the Broads (1896)
William A. Dutt Highways and Byways in East Anglia (1901)
J.C. van Dyke The New New York (1909)
E.A. Fitzgerald Climbs in the New Zealand Alps (1896)
Wickham Flower Aquitaine (1897)
P.G. Hamerton The Saône, a Summer Voyage (1897)
J.M. Hay Castilian Days (1903)
W.E. Henley (ed) A London Garland with others (1895), *M. Hewlett* The Road in Tuscany (1904)
W. Eden Hooper The Stock Exchange in 1900 (1900)
W.D. Howells Tuscan Cities (1886), Italian Journeys (1901)
Washington Irving The Alhambra (1896)
Henry James A Little Tour in France (1900), English Hours (1905), Italian Hours (1909)
Justin McCarthy Charing Cross to St Paul's (1891)
Benjamin E. Martin Old Chelsea (1889)
Arthur H. Norway Highways and Byways in Devon and Cornwall (1897), Highways and Byways in Yorkshire (1899)
Mrs Margaret Oliphant The Makers of Modern Rome (1895)
Elizabeth Robins Pennell A Canterbury Pilgrimage (1885), Two Pilgrims' Progress (1886), An Italian Pilgrimage (1887), Our Sentimental Journey Through France and Italy (1888), Our Journey to the Hebrides (1889), To Gypsyland (1893), Tantallon Castle (1895), Over the Alps on a Bicycle (1898), Our Philadelphia (1914)
M. Sabbe Christopher Plantin (1923)
Malcolm C. Salaman (intro) Joseph Pennell: 28 Modern Masters of Etching (The Studio, 1931)
F.R. Stockton Personally Conducted (1889)
Sir Frederick Treves Highways and Byways in Dorset (1906)

Periodicals: The Butterfly, The Daily Chronicle, The English Illustrated Magazine, The Graphic, Illustrated London News, The Neolith, The Pall Mall Budget, The Pall Mall Gazette, Pall Mall Magazine, The Portfolio, The Quarto, The Savoy, Yellow Book

References: Baker; Bénézit; Guichard; Houfe; ICB 1; Johnson & Greutzner; Pennell MI, PD; Sketchley; Thieme & Becker; Thorpe; Waters; *Burlington Magazine* (August 1903); *The Imprint* (January 1913); *Joseph Pennell* (Catalogue Memorial Exhibition Philadelphia 1926); *The Life and Letters of Joseph Pennell* (Ernest Benn 1930); G. Montague Ellwood *The Art of Pen Drawing* (Batsford 1927); Elizabeth Robins Pennell *Joseph Pennell* (Metropolitan Museum of Art, New York, 1926); Joseph Pennell *The Adventures of an Illustrator* (Fisher Unwin 1925); Malcolm Salaman *Joseph Pennell* (Studio 1931)

Rodney Peppé (b. 1934)

Born in Eastbourne, son of a naval commander. Lived in India (1935-41). Studied at Eastbourne School of Art (1951-53 and 1955-57, interrupted by National Service in Malaya) and at the Central School of Arts and Crafts in London (1957-59), where he specialised in illustration. Art director in advertising and for television (1959-65). He has practised as a freelance graphic artist and design consultant in London since 1965, and has written and illustrated children's books since 1968. He has also made moving toys since 1979. For illustration he used collage for his first 7 books (up to *Odd One Out,* 1975) and also for the pop-up book *Run Rabbit Run* (1982), bold black outline with colour washes for the *Henry* books, followed by pencil and watercolour. More recently, he has used fine ink line with watercolour on an emulsion base (as in *The Mice who Lived in a Shoe*) which he considers his most successful technique. He lives at Midhurst, West Sussex.[Q]

Books illustrated include:
R. & J. Marchant The Little Painter (1971)
Rodney Peppé The Alphabet Book (1968), Circus Numbers (1969), The House that Jack Built (1970), Hey Riddle Diddle! (1971), Simple Simon (1972), Cat and Mouse (1973), Odd One Out (1974), Humpty Dumpty (1975), Henry's Present (1975), Henry's Sunbathe (1975, expanded edition 1978), Henry's Garden (1975, expanded edition 1978), Henry's Exercises (1975, expanded edition 1978), Picture Stories (1976), Rodney Peppé's Puzzle Book (1977), Henry's Toy Cupboard (1978), Henry's Aeroplane (1978), Henry Eats Out (1978), Humphrey the Number Horse (1978), Ten Little Bad Boys (1978), Three Little Pigs (1979), Rodney Peppé's Moving Toys (1980), My Surprise Pull-Out Wordbook Indoors (1980), My Surprise Pull-Out Wordbook Outdoors (1980), The Mice who Lived in a Shoe (1981), Run Rabbit Run! A Pop-Up Book (1982), The Kettleship Pirates (1983)

Periodicals: Homes and Gardens, The Observer, Radio Times

References: Contemporary Authors; ICB 4; *Books for Your Children* vol 9, no 1 (Oct. 1973), vol 13, no 4 (Autumn 1978); Dorothy Butler *Cushla and her Books* (Hodder & Stoughton 1975), *Babies Need Books* (Bodley Head 1980)

Rosa C. Petherick (d. 1931)

Illustrator of children's books. Houfe surmises that she was the daughter of the illustrator H.W. Petherick. Her work was pleasing in appearance, though somewhat bland and was characterised by uniformly heavy outlines.

Books illustrated include:
Lillian D. Gask Little Folks of Many Lands (with Kate Fricero, nd)
Elsie Oxenham The Abbey Girls in Town (1925)
Mother Hubbard's Cupboard of Nursery Rhymes (1903)
Simple Composition Steps (1930)

Periodical: Little Folks

References: Houfe; Waters 2

Gladys Emma Peto (1890-1977)

Worked as Gladys Peto. Married name: Mrs C.L. Emmerson. Born Maidenhead, Berkshire. Studied at Maidenhead School of Art (1908) and in London. Subsequently worked as a black and white illustrator, watercolourist and designer of fabric, pottery, scenery and posters. She lived in Chelsea and (from 1939) in Northern Ireland. Her first book illustrations were for the works of Louisa M. Alcott (1914), and she contributed a satirical illustrated diary to *The Sketch* (1915-26). During the 1920s, she published light-hearted travel books (on Malta, Egypt and Cyprus) and, in the 1930s, a popular series of children's annuals.

She has been regarded as a follower of Beardsley. In *The Glass of Fashion* (1954), Beaton refers to her work as 'bastard Beardsley'. Certainly, she inherited from the Beardsley tradition a feeling for the decorative use of outline and for the value of areas of solid black in articulating a linear design. However, her drawings were strongly individual, and had a stylish ebullience that reflected more than anything, the Art Deco mood of the period. She made ingenious use of pattern and texture to create tonal greys, repeating the

Gladys Peto. 'Will you tell me why you are called Sweet William?' from her *The Peto Picture Book* (Sampson Low, Marston, nd).

motifs in the decorated borders and half-borders that often surrounded her drawings.

Books illustrated include:
Enid L. Hunt A Fine Lady Upon a White Horse (1929)
Gladys Peto Books for Children (4 vols, 1924-25), Malta and Cyprus (1928), Sojourner (1928), Children's Annuals (1930s), Bedtime Stories (1931), Twilight Stories (1932), Girl's Own Stories (1933), The Four-Leaved Clover and other stories (1937), Sunshine Tales (nd), The Peto Picture Book (nd)
Sewell Stokes The China Cow (1929)

Periodicals: The Bystander, Gladys Peto's Childrens Annual, Pearsons Magazine, Printer's Pie, The Sketch

References: Houfe; Johnson & Greutzner; Vollmer; Wa (1934, *see under* Emmerson); Waters 2; *The Times* (obituary, 7th June, 1977)

John Petts (b. 1914)

Born Hornsey, London, son of a tailor. Studied at Hornsey College of Art, Royal Academy Schools and the Central School of Arts and Crafts. Sculptor, engraver, stained glass artist. Worked freelance, mainly in Wales, 1935-40, 1947-51, and 1961 onwards. Set up the Caseg Press in North Wales (1937). Served in Israel, Egypt and Greece (1941-46). Assistant Director for Wales (Visual Arts), Arts Council of Great Britain (1958-61). Awarded a Churchill Fellowship (1966); travelled in USA and Mexico. A friend of David Jones*. His pen and brush drawings and wood engravings show the influence of early Christian art, notably Byzantine icons, the Ravenna mosaics and the sculpture and stained glass of Chartres. The bold outlines and rich textures ofhis colour wood engravings are clearly seen in his illustrations for *Against Women* (1953), printed from five successive blocks. Elected SWE (1953), ARE (1957). [Q]

Books illustrated include:
James Bramwell Sauna, a Narrative Poem (1949)
E. Curig Davies Storiau am Annibynwyr (1939), Y Morwr a'r Merthyr (1940)
John Dyer Grogar Hill (1977)
Cledwyn Hughes A Wanderer in North Wales (1949)
Gwyn Jones The Green Island (1946)
Alun Lewis Raider's Dawn (1942), In the Green Tree (1948)
Moelwyn Merchant Shakespeare and the Artist (1959)
Gwyn Williams (trans) Against Women (1953), In Defence of Woman (1960)
Apocrypha: Susanna and the Elders (1949)

Periodicals: The Caseg Broadsheets of Welsh Poetry, The Listener, The Welsh Review.

References: Garrett BWE, HBWE; Wa (1980); Waters; *International WW in Art and Antiques; WW in the World; The Anglo-Welsh Review* vol 19, no 44 (1971) pp.200-210; *Art Review* (1948); *Cinnamon* (30th July, 1965); *Country Fair* (January 1966); *Flamingo* 4, (December 1964); *The Observer* magazine (9th May, 1977); *The Tablet* vol 222, no 6673 (1968); *Western Mail* (5th February, 26th February, 19th March, 9th April, 1973); *Y Genhinen* (February 1977); *Catalogue of John Petts Retrospective Exhibition* (Glynn Vivian Art Gallery, 1975); Hugh Macdiarmid *Lucky Poet* (Methuen 1943); Meic Stephens *Artists in Wales* 3 (Welsh Arts Council and Gomer Press 1977); Brian Thomas (ed) *Directory of Master Glass-Painters* (Oriel Press 1972)

Douglas Phillips (b. 1925)

Born in Dundee, Scotland. Worked in an office, then served for three and a half years with the Royal Army Service Corps in India and Ceylon (1945-48). Joined the studio of D.C. Thomson Dundee and for 18 years illustrated boys' adventure magazines. Since 1966, he has worked freelance as a children's book illustrator. He draws in a loose, free style, sometimes with blotted shading or colour washes, and specialises in action subjects, often with horses. He also paints landscapes and seascapes. He lives in Dundee. [Q]

Books illustrated include:
Mary Cathcart Borer The Boer War (1971), American Civil War (1974)
Arthur Catherall The Big Tusker (1970)
Graeme Cook Air Adventures (1973), Sea Adventures (1974)
Joseph Edmundson Great Moments in Boxing (1974)
Kathleen Fidler Seal Story (1979)
Diana Finley The Rhine (1975)
Justine Furminger Bobbie Takes the Reins (1981)
Bernard Henry Heathrow Airport (1974)
Sir John Hunt My Favourite Mountaineering Stories (1978)
Marie Hynds Dolphin Boy (1975), Mumbo Jumbo (1976)
John Laurie Stories of Scotland (1978)
Donald MacIntyre Battle of the Atlantic (1970)
Reginald Ottley Brumbie Dust (1969)
Mary Patchet Roar of the Lion (1973)
Kathleen Sibley Adam and the Football Mystery (1979)
Joyce Stranger Jason (1970), The Honeywell Badger (1971)
Pamela Sykes Emma's Afternoon (1970)
Joan Tate The Runners (1974)
Geoffrey Trease Comrades for the Charter (1972), The Baron's Hostage (1973)

Peter Wenham York (1971)
John Williams Gallipoli (1969)

Periodicals: Adventure, Reader's Digest, Rover, Scots' Magazine, Scottish Field, Wizard

References: *Dundee Courier* (June 1979), *People's Journal* (March 1979)

W. Francis Phillipps (active 1960s)

Illustrator of children's books. He worked mainly in black and white, drawing with a pen or brush. He specialised in scenes of dramatic action, enlivened by shiny surfaces created with modulated cross-hatching. He occasionally worked in body colour for full colour reproduction.

Books illustrated include:
Lettice Cooper James Watt (1963), The Twig of Cyprus (1965)
Kathleen Fidler True Tales of Treasure (1962), Tales of the South Country (1962), True Tales of Escapes (1965)
Marjorie Sankey Holiday in Hiding (1960)
Rosemary Weir Little Lion's Real Island (1960)

Jan Michel Pieńkowski (b. 1936)

Born Warsaw, Poland; childhood spent in Austria, Germany and Italy; educated in England and Wales. Read Classics and English at King's

Jan Pieńkowski. From The Kingdom under the Sea and other stories by Joan Aiken (Cape, 1971).

College Cambridge. Founder director (1961) of Gallery Five Ltd, greetings card publishers. As an illustrator of children's books, he works in bold colours and simplified shapes, sometimes (as in the *Meg and Mog* series) adopting a childlike drawing style. Winner of the Kate Greenaway medal with Joan Aiken's *Kingdom under the Sea* (1971) and with his own pop-up book *The Haunted House* (1979). Also a graphic designer for advertising and television, designer of wallpaper, stage designer and art editor. [Q]

Books illustrated include:
Joan Aiken A Necklace of Raindrops (1968), The Kingdom under the
   Sea and other stories (1971), Tale of a One-Way Street (1978)
Edith Brill The Golden Bird (1970)
Jan Pieńkowski Colours (1973), Numbers (1973), Shapes (1973), Sizes
   (1973), Fairy Tale Library (1977), Haunted House (1979), Dinner
   Time (1980), Robot (1981)
Jan Pieńkowski and Helen Nicoll Meg and Mog (1972), Meg's Egg
   (1972), Meg at Sea (1973), Meg on the Moon (1973), Meg's Car
   (1975), Meg's Castle (1975), Quest for the Gloop (1980)
Dinah Storkey Ghosts and Bogles (1978)
Jessie Townsend Annie, Bridget and Charlie (1967)

References: Fisher p.223; ICB 4

Margaret Pilkington (1891-1974)

Born in Salford, Lancashire. Studied at the Slade School of Fine Art (1913) and Central School of Arts and Crafts (1914), where she had her first lesson in wood engraving from Lucien Pissarro* and continued under Noel Rooke*. She succeeded Robert Gibbings* as the first secretary of the Society of Wood Engravers (1924) and later became Chairman (1952). Director of the Whitworth Art Gallery, Manchester (1936-59), where she built up a collection of SWE members' work. Member of Art Workers' Guild, founder member of the Red Rose Guild of Craftsmen. Justice of the Peace; OBE (1954). Her book illustrations consist mainly of wood engravings. They are simple in style (showing Rooke's influence) with clear, vivacious imagery. Member of Art Workers' Guild, founder member of the Red Rose Guild of Craftsmen. Justice of the Peace; OBE (1954).

Books illustrated include:
Katherine Chorley Hills and Highways (1928)
Lawrence Pilkington An Alpine Valley & Other Poems (1924),
   Tattlefold (1926), The Chimneys of Tattleton (1928), Early Climbing
   Memories (cover, 1941)
Margaret Swanson Needlecraft for Older Girls (1920)

References: Balston WEMEB; Garrett BWE, HBWE; Johnson &
Greutzner; Wa (1974); *The Studio* special (1919); *Shall We Join the
Ladies?* (Studio One Gallery, Oxford 1979); Campbell Dodgson
Contemporary English Woodcuts (Duckworth 1922); A.C. Sewter
*Modern British Woodcuts and Wood-Engravings in the Collection of the
Whitworth Art Gallery* (Manchester 1962)

John Piper (b. 1903)

Born in Epsom, Surrey. Worked in the office of his solicitor father for five years, then studied at

John Piper. Lithograph of Rievaulx Abbey, Yorkshire from *English, Scottish and Welsh Landscape, 1700-c.1860* (Muller, 1944).

Richmond and Kingston Schools of Art and at the Royal College of Art. Member of the London Group (1933) and the Seven and Five Society (1934-35). Official war artist (1940-42). Later visiting lecturer at the Slade School of Fine Art. Painter, printmaker, designer of stained glass and textiles and for the theatre, writer on the arts, photographer, and one of the leading neo-romantic landscape painters of the post-war era. His book illustrations (of landscape and architectural subjects) share with his paintings a preoccupation with decorative and picturesque effects, achieved with dramatic lighting and bold, varied texture. [Q]

Books illustrated include:
John Betjeman Shell Guide to Shropshire (1951), First and Last Loves
   (1952), Poems in the Porch (1954), Collins' Pocket Guide to English
   Parish Churches (1958)
John Betjeman and Geoffrey Taylor English, Scottish and Welsh
   Landscape 1700—c.1860 (1944)
Walter de la Mare The Traveller (1946)
Ronald Duncan The Rape of Lucretia (1948), Judas... (1960)
John Hadfield (ed) Elizabethan Love Songs (1955)
Edwin Muir Prometheus (1954)
Charles Piper The Gaudy Saint and Other Poems (1924), Shell Guide
   to Oxfordshire (1938), Brighton Aquatints (1939), Buildings and
   Prospects (1948), Romney Marsh (1950)
J.M. Richards Castles on the Ground (1946)
Bertrand Russell The Wisdom of the West (1959)
George Sitwell On the Making of Gardens (1949)
Osbert Sitwell Left Hand, Right Hand (4 vols, 1945-49)
Adrian Stokes Venice (1965)
R.S. Thomas The Mountains (1969)
David Verney Shell Guide to Wiltshire (1935)
Gilbert White The Natural History of Selborne (1962)
Wordsworth Guide to the Lakes (1951)

Periodicals: The Ambassador Magazine, The Architectural Review,
Ark, Axis, The Cornhill Magazine, Curwen Press Newsletter, House
and Garden, London Mercury, New Leader, The Pavilion, Signature

References: Bénézit; Chamot, Farr & Butlin; Contemporary Artists;
Gilmour pp. 84-88; Johnson & Greutzner; Parry-Crooke; Phaidon;
Rothenstein 3; Shone; Vollmer; Wa (1980); Waters; *American Book
Collector* 21, no 3 (1971), 22, no 4 (1972); *Image* 2 (1949); *The Penrose
Annual* (1949); John Betjeman *John Piper* (Penguin Modern Painters,
1944); St John Woods *John Piper, Paintings, Drawings and Theatre
Designs 1932-1954* (Faber 1955); Anthony West *John Piper* (Secker &
Warburg 1979)

Gabriel Joseph Pippet (b. 1880)

Born in Solihull. Studied at Birmingham School of Art and then worked as assistant to his artist father, Raphael Pippet. After his father's death, he worked, with his brother Michael at Paul Woodroffe's* stained glass studio, but he was forced to leave through illness, and took up wood carving and illustration. After World War I, he visited Italy to study the Ravenna Mosaics, and after his return spent many years decorating a church in Droitwich, Worcestershire, with mosaics and carvings in marble, stone and wood. He spent five years in the Gold Coast (now Ghana) teaching painting and carving. After returning to settle in London, he was awarded a Civil List pension (1942). He was an illustrator in pen and ink outline of religious books for children and humorous verse for adults. He also made woodcuts and wood engravings for devotional works.

Books illustrated include:
Robert Benson A Child's Rule of Life (1912), Old Testament Rhymes (1913)
Guy Boas Domestic Ditties (1919), Traffic and Theatre Rhymes (1925), Lays of Learning (1926)
E. Hamilton Moore Fifteen Roses (1927)
Gabriel Pippet A Little Rosary (of woodcuts) (1930)
Richard Rolle The Stations of the Cross (1917)
G. Martinez Sierra Holy Night (1928)
More Old Rhymes with New Tunes (1925)
Old Rhymes with New Tunes (1912)
Still More Old Rhymes with New Tunes (1927)

Periodical: Joy Street

References: ICB 1; Johnson & Greutzner

Lucien Pissarro (1863-1944)

Born Paris, eldest child of the Impressionist painter Camille Pissarro. Learned the rudiments of wood engraving from Auguste Lepère; worked for the Parisian lithographic firm Manzi Joyant (1884). With his father, he was closely associated with the Neo-Impressionist group during the 1880s. He settled in London (1890) and became a member of Charles Ricketts's* circle, contributing to *The Dial*. He set up the Eragny Press (named after his father's farm in Normandy at his home in Epping (1894). The earlier Eragny Press books, distributed by the Vale Press, were mainly set in Ricketts's 'Vale' type, but after the closure of the press in closure (1904) Pissarro designed his own 'Brook' type, which he used for his 16 subsequent books. The illustrations were engraved on wood by Pissarro and his wife Esther, mainly from his own drawings but also from those of Camille Pissarro and friends including Thomas Sturge Moore*. The Eragny Press depended heavily on Continental sales (many of its books were in French), and was brought to an end by the outbreak of World War I. Pissarro continued to make prints (wood engravings, etchings, and

Lucien Pissarro. From *The Book of Ruth and the Book of Esther* (Eragny Press, 1896).

lithographs) until 1939, but concentrated on painting (always his primary concern). Through his work at the Eragny Press, Pissarro brought to the English Arts and Crafts tradition an Impressionist awareness of colour and surface, and his books, particularly late publications such as *Livre du Jade* (1911) and *La Charrue d'Erable* (1912), were outstanding for their perfectly adjusted colour harmonies. Sometimes working on tinted paper and mixing his own inks, he treated the page as a unified colour field, often printing borders and texts in greys, blues or greens, with illustrations using two to four colour blocks (overprinted to multiply the hues) an outline block in a darker tone or black. He also invented a method of printing in gold leaf.

In early life Pissarro was, with his father, a profound admirer of the *Punch* drawings of Charles Keene. In the development of modern wood engraving, he occupied a transitional place between the purely reproductive function of the craft in the 19th century and its 20th century emergence as an artist's autographic medium (as developed by his friend and pupil Noel Rooke*). Member NEAL (1906), founder member Camden Town Group (1911) and SWE (1920). He became a British subject (1920) and died in Somerset.

Books illustrated include:
R.L. Binyon Dream Come True (1905)
Samuel Taylor Coleridge Cristabel (1904)
Gustave Flaubert Hérodias (nd)
Judith Gautier Poèmes Tirés du Livre du Jade (1911)
Ben Jonson Songs (1906)
John Milton Areopagitica (1904)
Charles Perrault La Belle au Bois (1899), Histoire de Peau d'Ane (with T. Sturge Moore*, 1902), Riquet à la Houppe (1907)
M. Rust The Queen of the Fishes (1894)
The Book of Ruth and the Book of Esther (1896)
C'est d'Aucassin et de Nicolette (frontispiece, 1903)

Periodicals: The Dial, L'Image, The Venture

References: Balston EWE, WEMEB; Bénézit; Chamot, Farr & Butlin; DNB (1941-50); Garrett BWE, HBWE; Guichard; Hofer; Houfe; Johnson & Greutzner; Muir; Ray; Rothenstein 1; Taylor; Thieme & Becker; Wa (1934); Waters; C. Wood; *Signature* 6 (1948); *The Studio* 69 (1917), special (1919, 1923-24, Spring 1930); Alan Fern *Notes on the Eragny Press* (C.U.P. 1957); Colin Franklin *The Private Presses* (Studio Vista 1969); Basil Gray *The English Print* (A. & C. Black 1937); W.S. Meadmore *Lucien Pissarro, Un Coeur Simple* (Constable 1962); John Rewald *Camille Pissarro: Letters to his Son* (Kegan Paul 1943)

William Andrew Pogańy (1882-1955)

Worked as Willy Pogańy. Born in Szeged, Hungary. Studied engineering at Budapest University and then art briefly in Budapest and in Munich. He worked in Paris for two years and then moved to London (c.1905) for what was intended as a brief visit *en route* to America; instead he stayed for ten years, achieving a considerable reputation as a book illustrator. He eventually reached America in 1915 and settled in New York where he continued to illustrate books, and also designed hotel interiors and stage sets. He worked in Hollywood as an art director for Warner's First National Studios for several years during the 1930s.

Despite the considerable popularity of his work, Pogańy never really developed a distinctive style of his own during his years in England. His work contained echoes of many of the leading illustrators of the day—his friend Edmund Dulac*, Arthur Rackham*, Charles Robinson*, H.R. Millar*, Byam Shaw* and many others. His best illustrations were in pen and ink—a medium which he handled with fluency and confidence; his colour plates were seldom as successful. One of his best-known books was *The Rime of the Ancient Mariner* (1910) (published, like many of his books in England, by Harrap) which appeared in limited and trade editions; Pogańy was responsible for the hand-scripted text, green and mauve page decorations and borders, full-page black and white drawings and tipped-in plates in full colour; the effect was curious rather than artistically satisfying. Member of the London Sketch Club.

Books illustrated include:
S.C. Bryant Stories to Tell the Littlest Ones (1918)
Samuel Taylor Coleridge The Rime of the Ancient Mariner (1910)
Padraic Colum The King of Ireland's Son (1920), The Children of Odin (1922)
G.W. Dasent Norse Wonder Tales (1909)
Madalen G. Edgar A Treasury of Verse for Little Children (1908)
G.E. Farrow The Adventures of a Dodo (1907)
Edward FitGerald (trans) The Rubaiyat of Omar Khaiyam (1909)
Lilian Gask The Fairies and the Christmas Child (1912), Folk Tales from Many Lands (1916)
Nathaniel Hawthorne Tanglewood Tales (1909)
Heinrich Heine Atta Troll (1913)
Homer (ed Padraic Colum) The Adventures of Odysseus (1920)
Ignácz Kúnos Forty-Four Turkish Fairy Tales (1913)
Isadora Newman Fairy Flowers (1926)
Frances J. Ocott Tales of the Persian Genii (nd)
Nandor Pogańy The Hungarian Fairy Book (1913)
Jonathan Swift Gulliver's Travels (1919)
W. Jenkyn Thomas The Welsh Fairy Book (1907)
J.W. von Goethe Faust (1908)
Wagner (retold by T.W. Rolleston) Tannhäuser (1911), Parsifal (1912), The Tale of Lohengrin (1913)
Mary Augusta Ward Milly and Olly (1907)
Gerald Young The Witch's Kitchen (1910)

References: Bénézit; Cuppleditch; Houfe; Johnson; Thieme & Becker; William Feaver *When We Were Young* (Thames & Hudson, 1977); *Junior Book of Authors* (US, 1954)

Monica Mary Poole (b. 1921)

Married name: Mrs Small. Born in Canterbury, daughter of writer Charles Reginald Poole. Worked in an aircraft factory during World War II. Studied at Central School of Arts and Crafts (1946-49). Her early work consisted mainly of book jacket designs, but she has concentrated on wood engraving since 1955. Elected ARE (1967), RE (1975), member of the Art Workers' Guild (1970). Lives in Tonbridge, Kent. [Q]

Books illustrated include:
Elizabeth Jennings Winter Wind (1979)
Reginald Turner Kent (1950)
Open Air Anthology (Collins 1952)

Periodical: The Saturday Book 31 (1971)

References: Garrett BWE, HBWE; Wa (1980); Waters; *Shall We Join the Ladies?* (Studio One Gallery, Oxford 1979)

Alexander Potter (b. 1912)

Born in Derby, son of a master painter and decorator. Studied at the University of Sheffield. Worked in London as an architect's assistant (1934-37). Lecturer at the School of Architecture, University of Liverpool (1937-40 and 1946-48). Head of Department of Architecture, Regional College of Art, Hull (1948-57). Founder, Head of Department and Professor of Architecture at the University of Khartoum, Republic of Sudan (1957-64), and Professor of Architecture at Queens University of Belfast, Northern Ireland (1965-74). Emeritus Professor of Architecture, Queens University (1975). With his wife, Margaret Potter*, he has travelled widely in North Africa, the Middle East, Europe, India and and Pakistan. [Q]

For books illustrated *see* Margaret Potter.

*Margaret and Alexander Potter. From their
Interiors (Murray, 1957).*

Helen Beatrix Potter (1864-1943)

Worked as Beatrix Potter. Born Kensington,
London. Educated at home, she had a lonely and
repressed childhood in which her pencil and
paintbox became her chief resources. She filled
her notebooks with careful studies of her pets
(among them a mouse, a rabbit and a hedgehog),
and later with subjects gleaned from the Natural
History Museum at South Kensington. Holidays
in Scotland and in the Lake District gave her an
enduring love of the countryside, and provided
imagery which, with her visual memory, she was
able to recall and use many years later. Her first
book *Peter Rabbit,* grew out of letters written to a
child in 1893. It was printed privately in 1901, in
1902 a revised colour edition was published by
Warne and Co., and it was followed over the
years by more than twenty others. In these small
books, pages of simple text are faced by delicate
but sharply observed and visualised watercolour
vignettes. The meticulously painted animal subjects
(real animals, in spite of some human attributes)
in their rural North country settings, have become
part of English nursery folklore.

From 1905, with the proceeds of her first successful
books, Beatrix Potter began to acquire
land and farms at Sawrey in the Lake District.
She eventually settled there and turned her interests
to farming and sheep breeding. In 1913,
she married William Heelis, a local solicitor who
shared her farming interests. She bequeathed her
properties to the National Trust, which preserves
many of her original drawings at Hill Top Farm.

Books illustrated include:
Beatrix Potter The Tale of Peter Rabbit (privately 1901, 1902), The
Tailor of Gloucester (privately 1902, 1903), The Tale of Squirrel
Nutkin (1903), The Tale of Benjamin Bunny (1904), The Tale of
Two Bad Mice (1904), The Tale of Mrs Tiggy-Winkle (1905), The
Pie and the Patty-Pan (1905), The Tale of Mr Jeremy Fisher (1906),

The Story of a Fierce Bad Rabbit (1906), The Story of Miss Moppet
(1906), The Tale of Tom Kitten (1907), The Tale of Jemima Puddle-
Duck (1908), The Roly-Poly Pudding, *renamed* The Tale of Samuel
Whiskers (1908), The Tale of the Flopsy Bunnies (1909), Ginger and
Pickles (1909), The Tale of Mrs Tittlemouse (1910), The Tale of
Timmy Tiptoes (1911), The Tale of Mr Tod (1912), The Tale of
Pigling Bland (1913), Appley Dapply's Nursery Rhymes (1917), The
Tale of Johnny Town-Mouse (1918), Cecily Parsley's Nursery
Rhymes (1922), The Fairy Caravan (privately printed 1929,
published USA 1929, published UK 1952), The Tale of Little Pig
Robinson (1930)
F.E. Weatherly A Happy Pair (c.1893)

References: Bénézit; Bland; Chamot, Farr & Butlin; Crouch; DNB
(1941-50); Doyle CL; Fisher pp.119-20, 276-77; Houfe; ICB 1,2;
Johnson; Kirkpatrick; Lewis; Mallalieu; Ray; Waters; C. Wood; *The
Linder Collection of the Works and Drawings of Beatrix Potter*
(National Book League 1971); Marcus Crouch, *Beatrix Potter* (Bodley
Head 1960); Margaret Lane *The Tale of Beatrix Potter* (Warne, 1946),
The Writings of Beatrix Potter (Warne 1971), *The Magic Years of
Beatrix Potter* (Warne 1978); Leslie Linder *The Journal of Beatrix
Potter from 1881 to 1897* (Warne 1966), *A History of the Writings of
Beatrix Potter* (Warne 1971); Anne Carroll Moore *The Art of Beatrix
Potter* (Warne 1955)

Margaret Potter (b. 1916)

Born Margaret Whittington in Heathrow, Middlesex,
daughter of a farmer. Studied at Ealing
School of Art and Chelsea Polytechnic. Worked
in a commercial art studio in London (1932-36)
and as a travelling cookery demonstrator and
cartoonist (1936-39). Women students' warden at
the University of Khartoum, Sudan (1959-61).
Animal portrait painter (miniatures), writer,
lithographer and draughtsman in pen and pencil.
Margaret and Alexander Potter have collaborated
on writing and illustrating educational books
since 1944. Their aim is to bring the history of
architecture and design history to a wider public.
Their architectural drawings are scrupulous in
proportion and detail, and often enlivened with
humorously observed incident.

Books illustrated (with Alexander Potter*) include:
L.A. Dovey The Cotswold Village: Puffin Building Books (3 parts,
1950), A Half-Timbered Village: Puffin Building Books (3 parts,
1951)
Peter Hood Maps (1947)
Margaret and Alexander Potter A History of the Countryside (1943),
The Building of London (1946), Houses (1948), Interiors (1957)
The Modern Encyclopaedia for Children (1948)

References: William Feaver; *When We Were Young* (Thames &
Hudson 1977)

Tom L. Poulton (d. 1963)

Painter and illustrator. His pen and ink work
controlled and at times almost mechanical in
treatment. He took obvious pleasure in depicting
characters from literature and history, and in
recreating historical ornament and detail. Some
of his work for the Nonesuch Press was in colour,
and was reproduced at the Curwen Press by the
pôchoir process of hand stencilling. He lived in
London and was a member of the Double Crown
Club (the dining club founded 1924, for those
interested in good printing).

Books illustrated include:
James Boswell The Conversations of Dr Johnson (1930)
G.M. Boumphrey The Story of the Ship (1933)
Bernard de Fontanelle The Plurality of Words (1929)
Herodotus The History of Herodotus of Halicarnassus (1935)
Plutarch The Lives of the Noble Grecians and Romans (5 vols, 1929-30)
Izaak Walton The Compleat Angler (with Charles Sigrist, 1929)
   Kynoch Press Notebook (1930)
   The Week End Book (1930)

Periodicals: Over the Points (Southern Railway), Radio Times

References: Johnson & Greutzner; Herbert Simon *Songs and Words* (Allen & Unwin, 1973)

Sophia Rosamond Praeger (1867-1954)

Worked as Rosamond Praeger or S.R. Praeger. Born in Holywood, County Down, Ireland. Studied at the Belfast School of Art, the Slade School of Fine Art and in Paris. She became a well known sculptress specialising in studies of children, and exhibited sculptures and drawings fairly regularly at the Royal Academy. She was the sister of Dr. R.L. Praeger (President of the Royal Irish Academy), and illustrated two of his books on botany. She wrote and illustrated children's books of exceptional charm and quality and several of them *Three Bold Babes, Wee Tony* and *How They Went to/Came Back from School* remained popular for many years and were reprinted several times. She observed children with insight and affection, and much of her work had a touch of distinctive Irish humour. Elected HRHA (1927); awarded MBE (1939) and Hon. M.A., Queen's University, Belfast.

Books illustrated include:
Louey Chisholm(ed) Nursery Rhymes (with Jack Orr*, c.1904)
Lena Dalkeith Aesop's Fables Told to the Children (1906)
B. Inson A Sunshiny Holiday (1896)
E. Nesbit As Happy as a King (1896)
Brian O'Linn The Olde Irishe Rimes of Brian O'Linn (1901)
R.L. Praeger Open-Air Studies in Botany (1897), Weeds (1913)
Rosamond Praeger A Visit to Babyland (1896), The Adventures of The Three Bold Babes (1897), Further Doings of the Three Bold Babes (1898), The Tale of the Little Twin Dragons (1900), The

S.R. Praeger. From Aesop's Fables by Lena Dalkeith (T.C. & E.C. Jack, 1906).

Child's Picture Grammar (1900), How They Went to School (1903), How They Went to the Seaside (1909), How They Came Back from School (1911), Wee Tony. A Day in his Life (1913), Billy's Garden Plot (1918), The Fearful Land of Forgets (1921)

References: Johnson & Greutzner; Wa (1954); Waters; The Times (obituary April 19th, 1954)

Ernest Prater (active 1885-1937)

Born in London. He was an athlete and soldier, serving with the 3rd Middlesex Artillery, and embarked on a career in art only after working in commerce for some years. He became known as a painter, and magazine and book illustrator specialising in scenes of action. At various times he was on the staff of *Black and White, The Graphic,* and *The Sphere,* for which he covered the Boer War as a 'special' artist. His work for *The Sphere* was, however, generally re-drawn for publication by one of the other staff artists (e.g. A.S. Hartrick* or Reginald Cleaver*.

Books illustrated include:
E.C. Dawson Missionary Heroines of India (with others, 1909)
E. Gilliat Heroes of Modern Crusades (with others, 1910)
G.A. Henty The Lost Heir (1899)
Basil J. Matthews Livingstone the Pathfinder (1912)
W.P. Nairne Greatheart of Papua (1913)
E. Sanderson Heroes of Pioneering (with others, 1908)
G.F. Scott Elliot The Romance of Savage Life (with others, 1908)
Percy Westerman The Scouts of Seal Island (1913), Under Fire in Spain (1937)

Periodicals: Black and White, The Boy's Own Paper, Cassell's Magazine, Chums, The Graphic, Harmsworth's Magazine, The Idler, The Ludgate Monthly, Pearson's Magazine, The St James's Budget, The Sphere, The Strand Magazine

References: Doyle BWI; Houfe; Johnson & Greutzner; Thorpe; Vollmer; Wa (1934); C. Wood; *The Ludgate Monthly* 2 (1896); Pat Hodgson *The War Illustrators* (Osprey 1977)

Jean Logan Primrose (b. 1910)

Born in Glasgow into a family of musicians. Studied at Hammersmith and the City and Guilds Art Schools. Portrait painter in oil and watercolour; children's book illustrator. Runner-up for the Kate Greenaway medal with her illustrations for *Miss Happiness and Miss Flower* (1961).

Books illustrated include:
Bernos de Gasztold (trans Rumer Godden) The Beasts' Choice (1967)
Rumer Godden Miss Happiness and Miss Flower (1961), St Jerome and the Lion (1961), Home is the Sailor (1964), Little Plum (1963)

References: ICB 3; Wa (1966); Waters

Alison Prince (b. 1931)

Born in Beckenham, Kent. Studied at the Slade School of Fine Art and Goldsmith's College. Taught art until 1958. Designed B.B.C. television's Watch With Mother series 'Joe', and contributed to comics for the next ten years. She now runs a small farm in Suffolk and writes teenage novels. 'I like drawing silly people and fat ladies though I sometimes have to pull myself together and draw properly, if the author wants technical detail. Mostly I lend an air of mild fatuity to an otherwise solemn book.' She works in rapidograph, over careful pencil drawings. Has worked mainly for publishers Heinemann and Methuen.

Books illustrated include:
Jane Allen and Mary Danby Hello to Ponies (1979), Hello to Riding (1980)
Audrey Coppard Sending Secrets (1972), Don't Panic! (1975), Get Well Soon (1978)
Mary K. Harris Jessica on her Own (1968)
Richard Parker Keeping Time (1973)
Alison Prince One of the Family (1980)

Reference: Wa (1980)

Gerald Spencer Pryse (1882-1956)

Studied art in London and Paris, then worked as a landscape painter, lithographer, etcher and wood engraver. In 1907-1908, he was co-editor of *The Neolith* (a short-lived quarterly magazine publishing lithographs and original writing with a marked social conscience; another of the editors was the children's writer E. Nesbit). He served as a Captain in World War I and was awarded the Military Cross and the Croix de Guerre. As a specially employed war artist, he drew a number of lithographs on stone on location in the trenches. In 1928, he visited Nigeria and the Gold Coast. He lived in London until 1950, when he moved to Morocco. Many of his illustrations consisted of freely handled lithographs conveying considerable strength of feeling through dramatic simplification. His *Tom Jones* drawings in pen and wash, and brush and ink were effective in a deceptively rough-and-ready style.

Books illustrated include:
Henry Fielding The History of Tom Jones (1930)
E. Nesbit The Magic World (with H.R. Millar*, 1912), Jesus in London (1924)
G.S. Pryse The Pageant of Empire (1924)

Periodicals: The Graphic, The Neolith, Punch, The Strand Magazine

References: Bénézit; Bradshaw; Guichard; Houfe; Thieme & Becker; Vollmer; Waters; *The Junior Bookshelf* vol 22, no 4 (1958); *The Studio* 55 (1912), special (1917, 1919)

Roland Pym (b. 1920)

Born in Cheveley, Newmarket, son of Sir Charles Pym. Studied at the Slade School of Fine Art. Served in the Eighth Army in the desert during World War II. Principally a mural painter, he spent five years painting the grand saloon at Woburn Abbey, Bedfordshire, and also executed murals, for example, at Buckland Abbey, Devon, The Maritime Museum, London, the Guinness Brewery, Dublin and the Dorchester Hotel, London. He is also a stage designer (eight London productions during the 1960s), painter of

landscapes and conversation pieces, and designer of mosaics. As a book illustrator, mainly for children, he works in pen and ink and watercolour (black and white, two colours or full colour), reviving in a sketchy style the picturesque formality of early Victorian illustrations. His books include three peepshows (*Cinderella, Beauty and the Beast, Sleeping Beauty*) designed like model theatres. He has travelled widely in Europe, the Middle East and Africa and lives in Kent. [Q]

Books illustrated include:
Bryan W. Guinness The Story of Johnny and Jemima (1936), The Children in the Desert (1947), The Story of Catriona and the Grasshopper (1958), The Story of Priscilla and the Prawn (1960)
Christopher Tower A Distant Fluting (1977)

References: Johnson & Greutzner; Andrew Forge (ed), *The Townsend Journals* (Tate Gallery 1976)

Charles Henry Bourne Quennell (1872-1935) and Marjorie Quennell (b. 1883)

C.H.B. Quennell studied at the South Kensington Schools and practised successfully as an architect until World War I interrupted his career. From then on, he and his wife Marjorie, a trained artist, collaborated on writing and illustrating children's books on social history which, beginning with a series entitled *A History of Everyday Things in England* (1918-33), profoundly influenced school textbook production and history teaching. The admirably clear, mostly black and white illustrations were drawn by the Quennells working both individually and in collaboration, with Marjorie responsible for figures and landscapes, and C.H.B. for architectural subjects and machinery.

Books illustrated include:
C.H.B. Quennell The Cathedral Church of Norwich (1927)
C.H.B. Quennell and Peter Courtney Quennell Somerset: Shell Guide (1936)
Marjorie and C.H.B. Quennell A History of Everyday Things in England (4 vols, 1918-33), The Everyday Life Series (1921-26), The Good New Days (1935)
Modern Suburban Houses. A Series of Examples (1906)

References: Houfe; Johnson & Greutzner

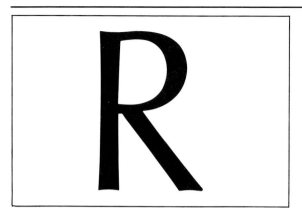

Arthur Rackham (1867-1939)

Born Lewisham, London, son of the Admiralty Marshal of the High Court of Justice. Educated at City of London School; visited Australia and, on his return, worked as a clerk in the Westminster Fire Insurance Office (1885-92). At the same time, he enrolled as an evening student at the Lambeth School of Art (where contemporaries included L. Raven-Hill*, F.H. Townsend* and Charles Ricketts*), and contributed drawings to some of the cheaper illustrated papers. With his graphic style still undistinguished and hesitant, he joined the staff of *The Westminster Budget* (1892) and began illustrating books (1893). As a pictorial journalist, he was only mediocre, but book illustration offered a field in which he could expand his imaginative gifts, and by the end of the decade he had evolved his characteristic style. With its roots in the early Victorian fairyland of Cruikshank and Richard Doyle, his imagery was pervaded by romantic *fin-de-siècle* moodiness and sharpened by naturalistically observed detail. He worked in black and white and watercolour, and the expressive linear quality of his drawing was enhanced by his perceptive use of a muted colour range that could be reproduced particularly well by use of the newly invented four-colour process (black with red, blue and yellow). For some 15 years, his only serious rival as a fairy story and gift book illustrator in colour was Edmund Dulac* who, though a more polished designer and ultimately a more inventive colourist, lacked Rackham's feeling for the bizarre, ominous and macabre faces of nature. The last 20 years of Rackham's career were something of an anti-climax, partly attributable to the decline in book printing and production standards during the years of the depression. Elected ARWS (1902), RWS (1908, vice-president 1910), Master of Art Workers' Guild (1919). Awarded Gold Medals at Milan (1906), Barcelona (1912), Paris (1912).

Books illustrated include:
R.H. Barham The Ingoldsby Legends (1898)
J.M. Barrie Peter Pan in Kensington Gardens (1906)

Mrs Alfred Berlyn Sunrise Land (1894)
Maggie Browne Two Old Ladies, Two Foolish Fairies, and a Tom Cat (1897), The Book of Betty Barber (1910)
Robert Browning The Pied Piper of Hamelin (1934)
Fanny Burney Evelina (1898)
Robert Burns The Cotter's Saturday Night (1908)
Lewis Carroll Alice's Adventures in Wonderland (1907)
Francis James Child Some British Ballads (1918)
F.H.C. de la Motte Fouqué Undine (1909)
Charles Dickens A Christmas Carol (1915), The Chimes (1931)
William Price Drury The Peradventures of Private Pagett (1904)
Charles S. Evans (retold by) Cinderella (1919)
S.J. Adair Fitzgerald The Zankiwank and the Bletherwitch (1896)
Julia E. Ford Snickerty Nick, Rhymes by Whitter Bynner (1919)
Oliver Goldsmith The Vicar of Wakefield (1929)
Kenneth Grahame The Wind in the Willows (1940)
Louisa Lilias Greene The Grey House on the Hill (1903)
Brothers Grimm (trans Mrs Lucas) Fairy Tales (1900), Little Brother and Little Sister (1917)
Edmund Gosse (intro) The Allies' Fairy Book (1916)
Myra Hamilton Kingdoms Curious (1905)
Nathaniel Hawthorne A Wonder Book (1922)
Arthur L. Haydon Stories of King Arthur (1910)
G.A. Henty Gallant Deeds (1905)
Anthony Hope The Dolly Dialogues (1894)
Henrik Ibsen Peer Gynt (1936)
Washington Irving Tales of a Traveller (1895), The Sketch Book (with others, 1895), Bracebridge Hall (2 vols, 1896), Rip Van Winkle (1905), The Legend of Sleepy Hollow (1928)
Charles Richard Kenyon The Argonauts of the Amazon (1901)
Rudyard Kipling Puck of Pook's Hill (1906)
Charles and Mary Lamb Tales from Shakespeare (1899)
Charles Lever Charles O'Malley (1897)
Harriet Martineau Feats on the Fjords (1899)
Henry Seton Merriman The Grey Lady (1897)
Henry Seton Merriman and S.G. Tallintyre The Money Spinner and other character notes (1896)
John Milton Comus (1921)
Clement C. Moore The Night before Christmas (1931)
Christopher Morley Where the Blue Begins (1925)
Barthold G. Niebuhr The Greek Heroes (1903)
Eden Phillpotts A Dish of Apples (1921)
Edgar Allan Poe Tales of Mystery and Imagination (1935)
Alfred Pollard (abridged from Thomas Malory) The Romance of King Arthur and his Knights of the Round Table (1917)
Christina Rossetti Goblin Market (1933)
John Ruskin The King of the Golden River (1932)
William Shakespeare Henry IV, Part II (1908), Macbeth (1908), A Midsummer-Night's Dream (1908), The Tempest (1926)
Flora Anne Steel English Fairy Tales (1918)
James Stephens Irish Fairy Tales (1920)
Jonathan Swift Gulliver's Travels (1900)
Algernon C. Swinburne The Springtide of Life, poems of childhood (1918)
Richard Wagner The Rhinegold and the Valkyrie (1910), Siegfried and the Twilight of the Gods (1911)
Izaak Walton The Compleat Angler (1931)
Margery Williams Poor Cecco (1925)

Arthur Rackham. 'The Cat and the Cock' from *Aesop's Fables* (Heinemann, 1912).

Aesop's Fables (1912)
Arthur Rackham's Book of Pictures (1913)
Hans Christian Andersen's Fairy Tales (1932)
Mother Goose, Old Nursery Rhymes (1913)

Periodicals: Cassell's Magazine, Chums, The Gentlewoman, The Graphic, The Harmsworth Magazine, Little Folks, Nash's Magazine, The Pall Mall Budget, The Pall Mall Gazette, Pearson's Magazine, Punch, St Nicholas, Scraps, The Strand Magazine, The Westminster Budget

References: Baker; Bénézit; Chamot, Farr & Butlin; DNB (1931-40); Doyle BWI, CL; Houfe; ICB 1,2; Johnson; Johnson & Greutzner; Mallalieu; Pennell PD; Peppin; Ray; Sketchley; Thieme & Becker; Thorpe; Vollmer; Wa (1934); Waters; C. Wood; *The Booklover's Magazine* 6 (1905); *The Bookman Christmas Number* (1933); *The Girls' Realm Annual* (1909); *The OWS Club Volume* 18; *The Studio* 34 (1905), special (Spring 1905, 1911, Autumn 1914, Spring 1922, 1923-24); F. Coykendall *Arthur Rackham. A List of Books* (New York 1922); Fred Gettings *Arthur Rackham* (Studio Vista 1975); Derek Hudson *Arthur Rackham* (Heinemann 1960); David Larkin *Arthur Rackham* (Pan 1975); S.B. Latimore and G.C. Haskell *Arthur Rackham* (Suttonhouse, Los Angeles 1936)

Walter George Raffé (b. 1888)

Born Bradford, Yorkshire. Studied at Halifax Technical College, Leeds School of Art and the Royal College of Art. Lecturer at the Northern Polytechnic; Principal of the Lucknow Government School of Art, lecturer at Calcutta University and at the City of London College. Published *Poster Design* (Chapman & Hall 1929), a survey of the field. His most successful book illustrations were woodcuts in which he used the essentially primitive qualities of the medium to achieve striking simplified effects. Elected FRSA (1919) and Institute of Decorators (1921); member of the Arts & Crafts exhibition society.

Books illustrated include:
C.J. Campbell The Children of Aries (1925)
Laurence Housman Turn Again Tales (with others, 1930)
W.G. Raffé Poems in Black and White (1922), Art and Labour (1927), Graphic Design (with others, 1927), Poster Design (1929)

References: Johnson & Greutzner; Vollmer; Wa (1929); *Artwork* 2 (1924)

Fanny Railton.
See Herbert Railton.

Herbert Railton (1858-1910)

Born Pleasington, Lancashire. Educated in Belgium and at Ampleforth School. Trained as an architect in Blackburn. Moved to London (1885) and built up a reputation for picturesque black and white drawings of architectural subjects in a style somewhat influenced by the Spanish graphic artist Martin Rico. Also an etcher. Joseph Pennell, who disliked his work, noted that the figures in his compositions were drawn in by John Jellicoe and continued '...when one finds that all his windows open in the same manner and all his trees grow in the same fashion one must regret that a man of his

cleverness and ability never draws from nature, or if he does, seems to care so little for what is about him. His mannerisms give his drawings, at first very pretty, an endless monotony.' In a similar vein, Charles Harper concluded that 'he has but one treatment and applies it to every subject,' and adds, 'A very characteristic feature of his drawings is the ruinous condition in which everything is represented, irrespective of its actual age or stability.' His wife, Fanny Railton, illustrated *A Midsummer Night's Dream* (1901) and several children's stories of her own, with amateur pen-and-ink drawings.

Books illustrated include:
William Benham Windsor Castle (1897)
James Boswell The Life of Samuel Johnson (3 vols 1901)
J.W. Brown The Builders of Florence (1907)
William Danks Ripon Cathedral (1899)
John L. Darby Chester Cathedral (1898)
P.H. Ditchfield The Cathedrals of Great Britain (1902)
G. Eyre-Todd The Book of Glasgow Cathedral (1898)
Frederick W. Farrar Westminster Abbey (1897)
R.J. Finch A Visit to Cambridge (1911)
Joseph T. Fowler Durham Cathedral (1898)
Frederick Gilliat-Smith The Story of Bruges (1901)
Oliver Goldsmith The Poems and Plays (1889), The Citizen of the World (1891)
C. Headlam The Story of Chartres (1902), Oxford and its Story (1904), The Story of Oxford (1907)
Thomas Hood The Haunted House (nd)
J.H.L. Hunt The Old Court Suburb (1902)
William H. Hutton Hampton Court (1897)
William C. Ingram Peterborough Cathedral (1898)
Charles Lamb The Essays of Elia (1888)
Walter Savage Landor Pericles and Aspasia (1890)
R. Le Gallienne Travels in England (1900)
John Leyland The Peak of Derbyshire (1891)
William J. Loftie Windsor (1886), Westminster Abbey (1890), The Inns of Court and Chancery (1893)
Anne Manning The Household of Sir Thomas More (1896), Cherry and Violet (1897), The Maiden and Married Life of Mary Pavell (1898), The Old Chelsea Bun Shop (1899)
William Outram Tristram Coaching Days (with Hugh Thomson*, 1888)
Gilbert White The Natural History and Antiquities of Selborne (1900)
M.G. Williamson Edinburgh (1906)
Collected Works of Thomas Love Peacock (1891)
Select Essays of Dr Johnson (1889)

Periodicals: Cassell's Magazine, The Daily Chronicle, The English Illustrated Magazine, Good Words, The Graphic, The Idler, The Illustrated London News, The Pall Mall Budget, The Portfolio, The Sketch, The Sporting and Dramatic News, The Temple Magazine, The Windsor Magazine

References: Baker; Bénézit; DNB supp 2 (1912); Harper; Houfe; Pennell PD; Sketchley; Thorpe; G. Montague Ellwood *The Art of Pen Drawing* (Batsford 1927)

William H. Rainey (1852-1936)

Born in London. Studied at South Kensington School of Art and at the Royal Academy Schools. Landscape and figure painter in watercolour, and author and illustrator of children's books published principally by Blackie. As a watercolourist, he won medals at the Chicago (1893) and Paris (1900) exhibitions. His delicate brush strokes reproduced well in both colour and halftone. Thorpe considered him a great but unrecognised illustrator who was 'never conventional in his designs, had a fine sense of character, and maintained the interest throughout the whole of the drawing.' Elected RI (1891), ROI (1932). Died at Eastbourne, Sussex.

Books illustrated include:
Charles Dickens David Copperfield (1900)
John Finnemore The Lone Patrol (1910)
G.A. Henty At Aboukir and Acre (1899), A Roving Commission (1900), Out with Garibaldi (1901), With Butler in Natal (1901), Grit and Go (1902), With Roberts in Pretoria (1902), With Kitchener in Sudan (1903), By Conduct and Courage (1905), The Final Reckoning (nd), The Bravest of Men (nd)
Charles Kingsley Westward Ho! (1903)
J. and J. Lang The Poetry of Empire (1900)
Amy Le Feuvre The Mender (1906)
Mary Macgregor The Story of France (1911), The Story of Rome (with others, 1913)
E.T. Meade Light o' the Morning (1899)
Mrs Molesworth Sweet Content (1891), White Turrets (1895), Meg Langholme (1897)
H.L.C. Pemberton Birdie: a tale (1888)
W.M. Thackeray The Newcomes (1903)
C.M. Trowbridge Satisfied (1882)
Percy Westerman The Buccaneers of Boya (1925)
J. Weston Stories and Pictures of Birds, Beasts, Fishes (1886)
Plutarch's Lives for Boys and Girls (1911)

Periodicals: Black and White, The Boy's Own Paper, The British Workman, Cassell's Family Magazine, Chatterbox, Chums, The Girl's Own Annual, Good Words, The Graphic, The Harmsworth Magazine, The Illustrated London News, Little Folks, The Ludgate Monthly, The Penny Magazine, Punch, The Quiver, The Strand Magazine, The Temple Magazine, The Windsor Magazine, Young England

References: Bénézit; Doyle BWI; Harper; Houfe; ICB 1; Johnson & Greutzner; Mallalieu; Pennell PD; Thorpe; Waters; C. Wood; *The Leisure Hour* (1901-02).

Arthur Ransome. 'Discovery', frontispiece from his *Swallowdale* (Cape, 1938).

William Ralston (1848-1911)

Born in Milton, Dumbartonshire. Humorous black and white illustrator and occasional writer. A photographer by profession, he learned to draw by watching his younger brother. He was introduced by the wood engraver Joseph Swain to Shirley Brooks, Editor of *Punch*, and contributed regularly to the magazine (1870-86); later he drew for *The Graphic*. He died in Glasgow. His work was cheerful and effective, if rather pedestrian in style.

Books illustrated include:
George Outram Legal and other Lyrics (with A.S. Boyd*, 1887)
William Ralston Sketches of Highland Character (1873), Kamdene, Barnesburie and D'Alston North Again, Golfing this time (1894), K.B. and D.A.'s Yachting Holiday (1896), Sport for Limited Purses, and the probable cost (1899), The Ubiquitous and His Portable Dark Tent (1899), The Story of the Jovial Elephant (1905), Letters from a Grandfather about Billy (1906)
W. Ralston and C.W. Cole Tippoo: A Tale of a Tiger (1886)
John S. Winter Houp-la (1889)

Periodicals: The Cornhill Magazine, The Daily Graphic, The Graphic, The Illustrated London News, Punch, The Sporting and Dramatic News

References: Bénézit; Hammerton; Houfe; Johnson & Greutzner; J.G. Reid; Spielmann; Thieme & Becker; Waters 2; C. Wood; J.G. Reid *At the Sign of the Brush and Pen* (Simpkin Marshall 1898)

Arthur Ransome (1884-1967)

Born in Leeds. After leaving Rugby School, he worked in the offices of publisher Grant Richards, writing articles and stories in his spare time. He travelled to Russia in 1913 and remained there through the Revolution, sending reports to the *Daily News*, *The Observer* and the *Manchester Guardian*. He later travelled widely, often sailing his own boat, in the Baltic and to China, Egypt, and the Sudan. After living in East Anglia, he settled in the Lake District, becoming an established children's writer. When *Swallows and Amazons* was first published in 1930, it had no illustrations; the second edition, and *Swallowdale* (1931) were illustrated by Clifford Webb*. The third title, *Peter Duck* (1932), for which Ransome provided his own drawings, was widely and enthusiastically reviewed, and he continued as illustrator of the series, re-drawing many of the earlier pictures in 1938 and illustrating *Swallows and Amazons* and *Swallowdale* at the same time. All the books in the series, with their detailed, practical approach to adventure, have remained widely popular and have been reprinted many times, retaining Ransome's clear, unpretentious and obviously amateur illustrations. Ransome was awarded an Honorary doctorate of Letters at Leeds University (where his father had been Professor of History) in 1952, and was made a CBE (1953).

Books illustrated include:
Arthur Ransome Peter Duck (1932), Winter Holiday (1933), Coot

Club (1934), Pigeon Post (1936), We Didn't Mean to go to Sea (1937), Swallowdale (1938), Secret Water (1939), The Big Six (1940), Missee Lee (1941), The Picts and the Martyrs (1943)

References: Doyle CL; Eyre; Kirkpatrick; Lewis; R.B. Shelley *Arthur Ransome* (Bodley Head 1968)

Leonard Raven-Hill (1867-1942)

Born Bath, Somerset. Studied at Lambeth School of Art (where his contemporaries included Charles Ricketts* and Arthur Rackham*) and at the Académie Julian, Paris (1885-87). On his return to Britain, he began working as an illustrator and humorous draughtsman in black and white, mainly for magazines. He was art editor of *Pick-Me-Up* (c.1890) and founded *The Butterfly* (1893, revived 1899) and the short-lived *The Unicorn* (1895). He contributed to *Punch*, joined the staff (1901), and succeeded Linley Sambourne (whom he had greatly admired) as junior political cartoonist under Bernard Partridge* (1910-35). He was commissioned by his friend Rudyard Kipling* to illustrate *Stalky and Co* when it appeared in *The Windsor Magazine*. Raven-Hill described himself as a punctual but irregular worker; he spent as much time as he could away from London, supervising the farm attached to his home in Wiltshire. Towards the end of his life his eyesight failed. Initially his work was very much in the tradition of Charles Keene, both in its social bias and its graphic freedom, but as time went on his draughtsmanship declined in sensitivity and was often stereotyped and cursory. His *Punch* cartoons often reflected his personal, strongly-held political views.

Books illustrated include:
Sir W. Besant East London (1901)
T. Coutts The Pottle Papers (1899)
J.H. Harris Cornish Saints and Sinners (1906)
K. Howard The Happy Vanners (1911)
J.C. Kernahan The Bow-Wow Book (1912)
Rudyard Kipling Stalky and Co (1929)
E.V. Lucas Slowcoach (1910)

Gwen Raverat. From *The Cambridge Book of Poetry for Children* chosen by Kenneth Grahame (Cambridge University Press, 1932).

Leonard Raven-Hill The Promenaders (1894), Our Battalion (1902) An Indian Sketch-Book (1903)
H.G. Wells Kipps (nd)

Periodicals: Black and White, The Butterfly, The Daily Chronicle, The Daily Graphic, The Flag, The Idler, Judy, The Ludgate Monthly, The Minster, The Neolith, The Nutshell, The Pall Mall Budget, The Pall Mall Magazine, Pear's Annual, Pick-Me-Up, Printer's Pie, Punch, Reveille, St Paul's, Scribner's Magazine, The Sketch, The Strand Magazine, The Unicorn, The Windsor Magazine

References: Bénézit; Chamot, Farr & Butlin; DNB (1941-50); Hammerton; Harper; Houfe; ICB 1; Johnson & Greutzner; Low; Pennell PD; Price; Sketchley; Thieme & Becker; Thorpe; Vollmer; Wa (1934); Waters; C. Wood; *The Art Journal* (1896); *Cassell's Magazine* 22 (1895-96); *The Idler* 8 (1896), 15 (1899); *The Magazine of Art* 19 (1896); *Pearson's Magazine* 22 (1906); *St. Paul's* (1895); *The Strand Magazine* 52 (1916); *The Studio* 1 (1893), special (1900-01), *The Windsor Magazine* 7 (1898); G. Montague Ellwood *The Art of Pen Drawing* (Batsford 1927); William Feaver *Masters of Caricature* (Weidenfeld & Nicolson 1981)

Gwendolen Mary Raverat (1885-1957)

Worked as Gwen Raverat. Born in Cambridge, daughter of Sir George Darwin, Professor of Astronomy, and granddaughter of Charles Darwin. She learned the rudiments of wood engraving from her cousin by marriage, Elinor Monsell*, but was mainly self-taught as an engraver. She studied painting at the Slade School of Fine Art (c.1908-10) and married fellow-artist Jacques Raverat (1911). They initially lived near Cambridge, but moved to France during World War I, settling eventually at Vence, Alpes-Maritimes (1920) where Jacques, suffering from disseminated sclerosis, died in 1925. She returned to England and lived for three years in London, where she designed sets and costumes for a new Vaughan Williams ballet *Masque for Dancing* (performed 1931), and then settled near Cambridge, eventually returning (1946) to live in an annexe of her childhood home. She was art critic for *Time and Tide* (1928-39) and worked during World War II as a draughtsman in the Naval Intelligence Office in Cambridge. A stroke in 1951 forced her to give up wood engraving, but she continued to paint until the end of her life.

An admirer since childhood of the work of Thomas Bewick, she began to engrave seriously soon after her marriage. In her earliest book illustrations, for her cousin's *Spring Morning* (1915), her work already showed the qualities of her mature style. Her underlying preoccupation was with the creation of solid forms and space through tonal change, but she also possessed to a rare degree an awareness of character and atmosphere which enlivened all her illustrative work. She developed her engraving skills to the point at which she could completely express her ideas, but (in contrast with some of the contemporaries of the 1930s) was uninterested in technique for its own sake. Her most ambitious book was *Bird Talisman* (1939), a Victorian fantasy for children, written by one of her ancestors, for which she made colour engravings using three or four blocks, a process little used for illustration since Lucien Pissarro's* Eragny Press publications. In these illustrations she succeeded in capturing the fairy-tale atmosphere of the story, while evoking something of the quality of hand-coloured children's books of the early 19th century. She also worked in pen and ink for *Countess Kate*, the *Bedside Barsetshire*, and notably for her own best-seller *Period Piece*, in which she described and drew her memories of life in Cambridge at the turn of the century with clarity, wit and humanity. Founder member SWE (1920); elected ARE (1920) and RE (1934).

Books illustrated include:
Frances Cornford Spring Morning (1915), Mountains and Molehills (1934)
Eleanor Farjeon Over the Garden Wall (1933)
Kenneth Grahame The Cambridge Book of Poetry for Children (1932), The Golden Age (1937)
Elizabeth Anna Hart The Runaway (1936)
E. Howe The London Bookbinders 1780-1806 (1950)
R.P. Keigwin (trans) Four Tales from Hans Anderson (1935)
Longus Les Amours Pastorales de Daphnis et Chlöe (1933)
Virginia Pye Red-letter Holiday (1940)
Gwen Raverat Period Piece (1952)
Laurence Sterne A Sentimental Journey (1932)
A.G. Street Farmer's Glory (1934)
Anthony Trollope The Bedside Barsetshire (1949)
Alison Uttley Mustard, Pepper and Salt (1938)
H.V. Wedgwood The Bird Talisman (1939)
Charlotte M. Yonge Countess Kate (1948)

Periodical: The Woodcut

References: Balston EWE, WEMEB; Bénézit; Bland; DNB (1951-60); Garrett BWE, HBWE; Houfe; ICB 1, 2; Johnson & Greutzner; Thieme & Becker; Vollmer; WW (1924); Waters; *Drawing & Design* (March 1926); *The Print Collector's Quarterly* vol 18; *The Studio* special (1917, 1919, Spring 1927, Spring 1930, Winter 1936, Autumn 1938) *Graven Images* (Scottish Arts Council catalogue 1979); Herbert Furst *Gwendolen Raverat: Modern Woodcutters no 1* (Morland Press 1920); Basil Gray *The English Print* (A. & C. Black 1937); Margaret Keynes *A House by the River* (Darwin College Cambridge, 1976); Gwen Raverat *Period Piece* (Faber 1952); Reynolds Stone *The Wood Engravings of Gwen Raverat* (Faber 1959)

Charles Raymond (active from 1955)

Book and magazine illustrator, botanical painter, book jacket designer, and designer of textiles and wallpapers for the Edinburgh Weavers, Hardy Amies and Sanderson; he has also done a certain amount of advertising work for international agencies. Many of his illustrations have been published by the Folio Society, Readers' Digest and the Sunday Times. He lives in Shropshire. [Q]

Books illustrated include:
Alexander Comfort The Joy of Sex (with Christopher Foss, 1972), More Joy of Sex (with Christopher Foss, 1974), The Joy of Lesbian Sex (1978)
F. Scott Fitzgerald The Great Gatsby (1968)
D.H. Lawrence The Rainbow (1981), Women in Love (1982)
British Trees in Colour (1973)
International Book of Trees (nd)
Old Garden Roses (1955)
Also books published in America

Periodicals: Esquire, Homes and Gardens, House and Garden, Mayfair, Men Only, The Observer, Radio Times, Reader's Digest, Sunday Times, T.V. Times, Woman, Woman's Realm, Women's Journal

Eric William Ravilious (1903-1942)

Born in London. His childhood was spent in Eastbourne, and he studied at the School of Art there before going on to the Royal College of Art, where he worked under Paul Nash* and was a contemporary of Edward Bawden* and Douglas Percy Bliss*. In 1925, he won a travelling scholarship to Italy. On his return Nash introduced him to the Society of Wood Engravers where he met Robert Gibbings* of the Golden Cockerel Press, for which he later made wood engravings. In 1929 he collaborated with Bawden on the murals at Morley College, and in the same year was appointed part-time teacher of design at the Royal College of Art, a post he held until 1938. As well as working as a wood engraver, Ravilious experimented with colour lithography (Curwen Press 1936-38), designed furniture, textiles, posters and advertisements, and became a designer of ceramic

Eric Ravilious. 'Chemist's Shop at Night' from *High Street* by J.M. Richards (Country Life, 1938).

decoration for the firm of Wedgwood in 1936. As a watercolourist, he had three one-man exhibitions in London. After 1940, as an official war artist, he depicted naval warfare off Norway, and also worked for the army and the Royal Air Force. In 1942, he was reported missing while on air patrol off Iceland. One of the most gifted and versatile artists of his generation, Ravilious was primarily a designer, infusing his work with energy and originality and also discipline which was reflected in his mastery of the craft of wood engraving. His work in this field is distinguished by bold contrasts of black and white, and by tones made with intricate patterns and textures. He treated his subjects with a lively wit which is particularly noticeable in some of his smaller illustrations and vignettes. A process of simplification that developed during the 1930s was undoubtedly due to the influence of Eric Gill*, though he never achieved a complete command of letter forms.

Books illustrated include:
Martin Armstrong Desert (1926), Fifty-Four Conceits (1933)
Nicholas Breton The Twelve Months (1927)
Ambrose Heath The Country Life Cookery Book (1937)
Thomas B. Hennell Poems (1936)
Christopher Marlowe The Rich Jew of Malta (1933)
Harold Munro Elm Angel (1930)
J.M. Richards High Street (1938)
William Shakespeare Twelfth Night (1932)
Aaron Smith The Atrocities of the Pirates (1929)
L.A.G. Strong The Hansom Cab and the Pigeons (1935)
Sir John Suckling A Ballad upon a Wedding (1927)
Gilbert White The Natural History of Selborne (2 vols, 1938)
Almanack for 1929: Ephemerides (1929)
The Apocrypha (with John Nash* and others, 1929)
English Wits (1941)
Kynoch Press Note Book (1932)
The Legion Book entitled Doctor Faustus conjuring Mephistophilis (with Edward Bawden* and others, 1929)

Periodicals: The Cornhill Magazine, Curwen Press Newsletter, Monotype Corporation Calendar, National Council of Social Science Journal, Wisden's Cricketer's Almanack, The Woodcut

References: Balston EWE, WEMEB; Bénézit; Bland; Chamot, Farr & Butlin; DNB (1941-50); Garrett BWE, HBWE; Gilmour; Johnson & Greutzner; Shone; Vollmer; Wa (1934); Waters; *Architectural Review* 94 (1943); *Artwork* 13 (1928); *Signature* 1 (1935); *The Studio* special (Spring 1927, Autumn 1928, Autumn 1930, Autumn 1938); *Memorial Exhibition Catalogue* (Arts Council 1948); Basil Gray *The English Print* (A. & C. Black 1937); Robert Harling *Notes on the Wood-engravings of Eric Ravilious* (Faber 1946); John Lewis and John Brinkley *Graphic Design* (Routledge & Kegan Paul 1954); J.M. Richards (intro) *The Wood Engravings of Eric Ravilious* (Lion & Unicorn Press 1972); Christopher Sandford *Bibliography of the Golden Cockerel Press* (Dawson 1975), *Cock-a-Hoop* (Private Libraries Association 1976)

Mary Rayner (b. 1933)

Maiden name: Mary Grigson. Born and brought up in Burma; when the Japanese invaded in 1942 she walked over the hills to India, where she spent the next three years, and eventually arrived in England in 1945. She studied English Literature at St Andrew's University, Scotland. Illustrator and writer of children's books, published mainly by Macmillan and Gollancz. In her own books about a family of pigs with human attributes, she

develops her plots with an obvious awareness of society's ambiguous relationship with animals that in real life are raised to be slaughtered for food. Her drawings, in a fine pen line, often with watercolour (which she prefers), are unpretentious and quietly humorous.

Books illustrated include:
Anthea Colbert Mr Weller's Long March (1983)
Daphne Ghose Harry (1973)
Griselda Gifford Because of Blunder (1977), Cass the Brave (1978), Silver's Day (1980)
Dick King-Smith Daggie Dogfoot (1980), Magnus Powermouse (1982)
Jan Mark The Dead Letter Box (1982)
Mary Rayner The Witch Finder (1975), Mr and Mrs Pig's Evening Out (1976), Garth Pig and the Icecream Lady (1977), The Rain Cloud (1980), Mrs Pig's Bulk Buy (1981)
Partap Sharma Dog Detective Ranjha (1978)
Emma Tennant The Boggart (1980)

Periodical: Cricket Magazine (US)

References: ICB 4; Nancy Chambers (ed) *The Signal Approach to Children's Books* (Kestrel 1980)

Rachel Reckitt (b. 1908)

Born in St Albans, Hertfordshire. Studied wood engraving at the Grosvenor School of Modern Art (1933-37) under Iain Macnab.* During World War II, she ran a branch of the Citizen's Advice Bureau at the Toynbee Hall, Whitechapel, East London, and a C.A.B. mobile unit touring bombed cities. In 1946, she moved to Somerset to run a small farm, and during the following years illustrated several books with well-executed, direct, unpretentious wood engravings based on observed subjects. After her last book illustrations, for *The Mill on the Floss* (commissioned by Paul Elek but unpublished) 1954, she did no further wood engraving until 1976, but since then has engraved three or four woodblocks a year, for individual prints. She makes sculpture in wood, stone and metal, carves inn-signs in relief, and designs church screens. Elected SWE (1950) and to the Somerset Guild of Craftsmen (1970).[Q]

Books illustrated include:
Mary Bosanquet People with Six Legs (1953)
Walter de la Mare and others English Country Short Stories (1949)
Sam Price Myers London South of the River (1949)
A.R.J. Wise and R.A. Smith (eds) Voices on the Green. Anthology of Poetry (1945)
Seven Psalms (1981)

References: Garrett BWE, HBWE; Johnson & Greutzner; Waters; *Shall We Join the Ladies?* (Studio One Gallery, Oxford 1979)

Peter George Reddick (b. 1924)

Works as Peter Reddick. Born Ilford, Essex, son of an insurance manager. Studied at the Slade School of Fine Art (1948-51). Visiting tutor at the Regent Street Polytechnic (1951-56), then studied at the London College of Printing (1959-60). Lecturer at Glasgow School of Art (1963-67). Since

Peter Reddick. 'Saul' from *The Poems of Robert Browning* (Limited Editions, New York, 1969).

1967, he has been a senior lecturer at Bristol Polytechnic. Founder/director of Artspace, Bristol and the Bristol Printmaking Workshop. Gregynog Arts Fellow (1979-80). As an illustrator (mainly for the Folio Society), he tends to focus on the physical qualities of his medium rather than on characterisation or background detail. For engraving, he uses a range of tools to create variegated effects of texture; his pen and ink drawings are looser, with a discursive line and freely-sketched areas of hatching. He illustrated the first major book of the revived Gregynog Press, *Cerddi Robert Williams Parry*, published in 1980. Prize winner in the Francis Williams Book Illustration Award for 1972. Elected SWE (1953), RE (1970), Fellow RE (1973). [Q]

Books illustrated include:
Thomas Hardy The Mayor of Casterbridge (1968), The Return of the Native (1971)
Thomas Love Peacock Crotchet Castle (1964)
Llewellyn Powys (letters of) So Wild a Thing (1972)
Anthony Trollope The Warden (1976), Barchester Towers (1977), Doctor Thorne (1978), Framley Parsonage (1979), The Last Chronicle of Barset (1980), The Small House at Allington (1980)
Cerddi [Poems of] Robert William Parry (1980)
The Poems of Robert Browning (1969)

References: Garrett BWE, HBEW; Wa (1980); Robin Jaques *Illustrators at Work* (Studio 1963); *Motif* 7 (1961); Brian North Lee *British Bookplates* (David & Charles 1979); Kenneth Lindley *The Woodblock Engravers* (David & Charles 1970)

Edward Tennyson Reed (1860-1933)

Born Greenwich, son of famous naval architect and Member of Parliament Sir Edward Reed. With his father, he visited Egypt and the Far East (1879-80), and on his return took up drawing and painting, becoming a friend of Sir Edward Burne-Jones*. He joined the staff of *Punch* in 1890, having first contributed a year earlier; from 1893,

he consolidated a growing reputation with his series 'Prehistoric Peeps', which launched a tradition of humorously anachronistic reconstructions of life in the past that was later developed by Lawson Wood*, George Morrow* and, more recently, in a cartoon series on American television, *The Flintstones*. He succeeded Harry Furniss* as parliamentary draughtsman on *Punch* after Furniss's precipitate resignation in 1894. In marked contrast to the facility and animation of Furniss's on-the-spot sketches, Reed's work was static, retaining some of the careful tidiness of a skilled amateur. His comparative weakness as a reporter was compensated for by a streak of whimsical inventiveness and an instinct for effective exaggeration which also proved valuable in book illustration. Though he often worked in pen and ink, he really preferred the more easily controlled and low-key medium of pencil. He left *Punch* in 1912 to work for other magazines.

Books illustrated include:
W.H. Burnet Quite So Stories (1918)
Elizabeth L.R. de la Pasture The Unlucky Family (1907)
J. Indermaur A Epitome of Leading Common Law Cases (1922)
R.C. Lehmann The Adventures of Picklock Holes (1901)
H.W. Lucy A Diary of the Unionist Parliament 1895-1900 (1901), The Balfourian Parliament 1900-05 (1906)
Montague H.M.T. Pigott The Beauties of Home Rule! (1914)
Ernest E. Spicer and E.C. Pegler De Mortuis Nil Nisis Bona (1914)
'The Belgian Hare': Tails with a Twist (1898)
Also collections of Punch cartoons: Prehistoric Peeps (1896), Animal Land (1898), Book of Arms (1899)

Periodicals: The Bystander, Cassell's Family Magazine, The English Illustrated Magazine, The Graphic, The Idler, The Pall Mall Magazine, Passing Show, Punch, The Sketch

References: DNB (1931-40); Hammerton; Houfe; Hillier; Johnson & Greutzner; Price; Spielmann; Thorpe; Waters 2; C. Wood; *Punch* (19th July 1933); *The Studio* special (1900-01, 1911); William Feaver *Masters of Caricature* (Weidenfeld & Nicolson 1981)

Gladys M. Rees. 'Primroses' from *The Children's Story Hour* by Christine Chaundler (Museum Press, 1939).

Gladys Mary Rees (b. 1898)

Usually worked as Gladys M. Rees. Married name: Gladys Mary Teesdale. Born in London. Studied and afterwards taught at Chelsea School of Art. Landscape painter, etcher, poster designer. A competent but variable illustrator, who sometimes achieved bold effects with scraperboard and partial colour. Elected ASWA (1927), SWA (1939).

Books illustrated include:
J.A. Bentham The City of Wishes (1922)
H.E. Chapman Barbara in Pixieland (1922)
Christine Chaundler The Children's Story Hour (1939)
F. Claremont The Book of the Cat Jeremiah (1929)
Elizabeth Clark Tales and How to tell them (nd)
B. Lovett The Princess who got out of bed on the wrong side (1945)
Gladys M. Rees Praise. A Book of Verse (1936), Loosey and Lankey (1945), A.B.C. and All That (1948), XYZ and after (1952)

References: Johnson & Greutzner; Vollmer; Wa (1980); Waters

Stephen Reid (1873-1948)

Born Aberdeen, Scotland. Studied at Gray's School of Art, Aberdeen, and at the Royal Scottish Academy Schools. Taught life drawing at King's College, Kensington, London. He painted historical subjects, landscapes and portraits in oil and watercolour. His illustrative work was mainly in pen and ink with colour washes, and was characterised by a graceful flowing line reminiscent of Rackham* in his lyrical vein. Elected RBA (c.1906).

Books illustrated include:
Oliver Goldsmith The Deserted Village (1907)
Eleanor Hull Cuchulain, the Hound of Ulster (1909)
Winifred M. Letts Helmet and Cowl (1913)
Dora F. Madeley The Heroic Life and Exploits of Siegfried the Dragon Slayer (1910)
T.W.H. Rolleston The High Deeds of Finn and other Bardic Romances of Northern Ireland (1910)
Estelle Ross Barons and Kings 1215-1485 (1912)
Netta Syrett The Castle of Four Towers (1909)

Periodicals: The Idler, The Strand Magazine, The Temple Magazine, The Windsor Magazine

References: Bénézit; Houfe; ICB 1; Johnson & Greutzner; Sketchley; Thieme & Becker; Thorpe; Vollmer supp; Wa (1948); Waters; *Art Journal* (1898)

Douglas Relf (active 1935-66)

Painter and illustrator, who exhibited paintings in London from addresses in London and Essex. As a book illustrator, he worked in a sketchy style in pen or brush and ink, sometimes with partial colour.

Books illustrated include:
A.G. Allbury Bamboo and Bushido (1955)
Kathleen Fidler Tales of London (1953), Tales of the Midlands (1954), Tales of Scotland (1956), Tales of the Island (1959)
Elisabeth Kyle Girl with a Lantern (1961)
Eric Leyland Indian Range (1953)
Angus MacVicar The High Cliffs of Kersevay (1964), The Kersevay Kraken (1966)

Reginald Maddock The Lost Horizon (1961)
John Pudney Saturday Adventure (2 vols 1950-51, 5 vols 1952-56), Spring Adventure (4 vols 1961-65)

Reference: Johnson & Greutzner

Frank Reynolds (1876-1953)

Born in London, son of an artist. Studied at Heatherley's School of Art. On the staff of *The Illustrated London News* and *The Sketch*, and later *Punch* on which he succeeded F.H. Townsend* as Art Editor (1920-30). He worked mainly from memory, in pencil, pen and ink, or watercolour, and was noted for his confident figure drawing and characterisation, though his interest was in generalised 'types' rather than in individuals. His succinct *Humorous Drawing for the Press* (1947) emphasises pictorial and spatial clarity, and demonstrates his straightforward drawing style, unembellished and untouched by aesthetic distractions. R.G.G. Price suggests that the ugliness of Reynolds drawing may have developed in reaction against 'the prettification of Punch', and quotes Fougasse's opinion that the freedom and energy of Reynolds' work made it a forerunner of the free-style drawing of the 1950s. Today, it seems easier to view it in the context of

Frank Reynolds. 'To the Re-Seeing!' from *Pictures of Paris and some Parisians* by J.N. Raphael (A. & C. Black, 1908).

John Reynolds. From *1066 And All That* by W.C. Sellar and R.J. Yeatman (Methuen, 1930).

the realist graphic tradition of the 1890s. Elected RI (1903, resigned 1933). Member of the London Sketch Club.

Books illustrated include:
Charles Dickens The Adventures of Mr Pickwick (1910), David
   Copperfield (1911), The Pickwick Papers (1912), The Old Curiosity
   Shop (1913), The Buchanan Portfolio of Characters from... (1925)
Keble Howard The Smiths of Surbiton (1906)
J.N. Raphael Pictures of Paris and some Parisians (1908)
Frank Reynolds Golf Book (1932), Off to the Pictures (1937), Hamish
   McDuff (1937), Humorous Drawing for the Press (1947)
William Sapte By the Way Ballads (1901)

Periodicals: Cassell's Magazine, The Flag, The Grand Magazine, The
Illustrated London News, Judy, The London Magazine, The Longbow,
The Odd Volume, Passing Show, Pears Annual, Pearson's Magazine,
Pick-Me-Up, The Playgoer, Printer's Pie, Punch, The Sketch, Sketchy
Bits, The Windsor Magazine

References: Bénézit; Bradshaw; Cuppleditch; Houfe; ICB 1; Johnson
& Greutzner; Mallalieu; Price; Thieme & Becker; Thorpe; Wa (1950);
Waters; *Drawing and Design* 3 (1923); *The Strand Magazine* 51 (1916);
The Studio 89 (1925), special (Autumn 1914); Percy Bradshaw *They
Make Us Smile* (Chapman & Hall 1942); A.E. Johnson *Frank Reynolds
RI* (A. & C. Black 1907); E.V. Lucas (intro) *Punch Pictures by Frank
Reynolds* (Cassell 1922)

John Patrick Reynolds (1909-1935)

Worked as John Reynolds, son of Frank Reynolds*. Book illustrator and cartoonist best known for his sketchy, cartoon-like drawings for *1066 and All That*. Committed suicide at the age of 26.

Books illustrated include:
Harry J.C. Graham Adam's Apples (1930)
Rose H. Heaton The Perfect Cruise and other holidays (1935)
Walter C. Sellar and R.J. Yeatman 1066 And All That (1930), And
   Now All This (1932)

R.J. Yeatman Horse Nonsense (1933)

References: Lewis; Waters 2

Warwick Reynolds (1880-1926)

Born in Islington, London; his father, who was an artist, was also named Warwick Reynolds. Warwick Reynolds the younger was an animal illustrator and etcher who showed early promise and was granted an artist's ticket to the Zoological Gardens at the age of 13. He supported himself while studying art at the Grosvenor Studio in Vauxhall Bridge Road by selling drawings to magazines. He was on the staff of *The Weekly Record* (Glasgow) for several years before studying at the Académie Julian, Paris. Guichard considered him one of the best animal etchers of his day, observing that he was 'more interested in the physical character before him than in some impending drama of tooth and claw'. For his illustrative work, he drew from memory, often in Conté crayon with the addition of pen and ink and occasionally wash.

Books illustrated include:
H.E. Barns Naju of the Nile (1924)
H. Mortimer Batten Habits and Chracters of British Wild Animals
   (1920), Romances of the Wild (1922)
G. Casserly Dwellers in the Jungle (1925)
C. Ewald The Pond (1922)
E. Glanville Claw and Fang (1923)
Donald A. Mackenzie Old-Time Tales (nd)
Warwick Reynolds Animal Drawing (1936)
C.G.D. Roberts Babes in the Wild (1912)
F. Saint-Mars The Prowlers (1913)
J. Arthur Thomson The New Natural History (nd)
J.M. Thomson Forest Dwellers (1922), Wild Kindred (1922), Wings
   and Pads (1922)

Periodicals: Ally Sloper's Half Holiday, The Bystander, The Daily
Record, The Dreadnought, The Gem, The Golden Hind, Hutchinsons
Magazine, Little Folks, The London Magazine, Nash's Magazine,
Passing Show, Pear's Annual, Pearson's Magazine, The Popular, Puck,
The Quiver, The Royal Magazine, The Strand Magazine, The Tatler,
Weekly Record, The Wide World Magazine, The Windsor Magazine

References: Bénézit; Bradshaw; Doyle BWI; Guichard; Houfe;
Johnson & Greutzner; Mallalieu; Thieme & Becker; Thorpe; Waters;
WW (1924); *The Studio* 93 (obituary, 1927)

George Woolliscroft Rhead (1855-1920)

Studied in London under Alphonse Legros and Ford Madox Brown*. Painter, etcher, graphic, stained-glass and ceramic designer, critic, and writer on ceramics, costume, etching and design. Elder brother of Frederick and Louis Rhead*, with whom he collaborated as an illustrator. He was a teacher at Putney School of Art (from 1896) and later director of Southwark Polytechnic Institute. In 1914 he married the decorative artist and occasional illustrator Annie French. Rhead belonged to the mainstream of the Arts and Crafts movement, and his graphic work has affinities with that of Walter Crane* and artists of the Birmingham School. He was a better draughtsman than either of his brothers, and his compositions have much greater clarity. Elected RE (1883), Hon ARCA. Member of the Art Workers' Guild.

Books illustrated include:
John Bunyan The Pilgrim's Progress (with L. and F. Rhead, 1898), The Life and Death of Mr Badman (with L. Rhead, 1900)
G.W. Rhead Modern Practical Design (1912), The Principles of Design (1913)
Alfred, Lord Tennyson Idylls of the King (with L. Rhead, 1898)

References: Bénézit; Harper; Houfe, ICB 1; Johnson & Greutzner; Thieme & Becker; Waters; C. Wood; *Art Journal* (1903); *The Studio* special (1898-99)

Louis John Rhead (1857-1926)

Born in England, brother of G.W. Rhead*. Studied art in Paris and London, then emigrated to America where he lived in Brooklyn and on Long Island, New York. Portrait painter, poster designer, lithographer, ceramic designer, watercolour and black-and-white illustrator. His early black and white style superficially resembled that of his elder brother, but his figure drawing was poor, his sense of proportion shaky, and his attempts to combine three-dimensional form with elaborate surface decoration generally came to

Louis Rhead. 'They were the most mortifying sight I ever beheld' from *Gulliver's Travels* by Jonathan Swift (Harper & Brothers, 1913).

grief. However he was responsible for some pleasant decorative borders based on plant forms. In America, he illustrated a large number of children's stories for Harpers, adopting a more conventional style, but showing little improvement as a draughtsman. More successful were his unpretentious fish drawings for *The Speckled Brook Trout* (New York, 1902). An exhibition of his poster designs was held in London in 1897. A third brother, Frederick, can be identified with reasonable certainty, as the F.A. Rhead listed by Houfe as a *Punch* contributor in 1914. He collaborated on *The Pilgrim's Progress* and *Robinson Crusoe* but does not appear to have illustrated any books without his brothers.

Books illustrated include:
John Bunyan The Pilgrim's Progress (with F. and G. Rhead, 1898), The Life and Death of Mr Badman (with G.W. Rhead*, 1900)
Daniel Defoe Robinson Crusoe (with F. Rhead, 1900)
N.D. Hillis David, the Poet and King (1901)
Thomas Hughes Tom Brown's Schooldays (1911)
Charles and Mary Lamb Tales from Shakespeare (1918)
D.M. Mulock The Fairy Book (1922)
Louis J. Rhead Bold Robin Hood and his Outlaw Band (1923)
Robert Louis Stevenson Kidnapped (1925), Treasure Island (1928)
Jonathan Swift Gulliver's Travels (1913)
Alfred, Lord Tennyson Idylls of the King (with G.W. Rhead, 1898)
J.R. Wyss Swiss Family Robinson (1923)
Aesop's Fables (1927)
Hans Andersen's Fairy Tales and Wonder Stories (1914)
Grimm's Fairy Tales (1923)
The Psalms of David (with others, 1923)

References: ICB 1; Thieme & Becker; *The Studio* 8 (1896), special (1899-1900)

Harold Ian Ribbons (b. 1924)

Works as Ian Ribbons. Born in London, son of a journalist. Studied at Beckenham School of Art, then served in the Royal Artillery. Studied at the Royal College of Art (1947-51). Part-time lecturer at Guildford School of Art (1952-65), Brighton College of Art (1965-66), Hornsey College of Art (1966-76) and St Martin's School of Art (from 1976). Ribbons bases his illustrations on pencil studies from life. For reproduction, he works with pens of all kinds, wood sticks, cane, and a fine brush used like a pen; he uses gouache for colour work and wash for halftone. He draws freely, creating texture with a variety of techniques, including hatching, spatter, frottage and collage. [Q]

Books illustrated include:
Alain-Fournier Le Grand Meaulnes (1979)
E.M. Almedingen Fanny (1970)
R. Burch Skiving (1964)
A. de Selincourt Nansen (1957)
L. de Vilmorin Madame De... (1952)
Penelope Farmer The Sea Gull (1964)
E.M. Forster A Passage to India (1983)
Elizabeth Goudge Linnets and Valerians (1964)
Roger Lancelyn Green Ten Tales of Detection (1967)
Frederick Grice The Luckless Apple (1966), Young Tom Sawbones (1972)
Jerome K. Jerome Three Men in a Boat (1964)

Ceri Richards. 'If Sir Alfred Butt lost his head and went "Expressionist" ' from *Review of Revues* edited by C.B.C. (Cape, 1930).

Rudyard Kipling Tales (1972)
Robert Leeson Beyond the Dragon Prow (1973)
W. Lichtman Blew and the Mag (1977)
Laurence Meynell Under the Hollies (1954)
P. Power Kangaroo County (1961)
A. Pushkin An Amateur Peasant Girl (1955)
Ian Ribbons Monday 21 October 1805 (1968), Tuesday 4 August 1914
    (1970), The Island (1971), The Battle of Gettysburg (1974), Mr
    McKenzie Painted Me (1975), Waterloo, 1815 (1982)
J. Ridgeway Gino Watkins (1974)
Cicely Fox Smith Knave-Go-By (1951)
Ivan Southall The Fox Hole (1967), Let the Balloon Go (1968), Over
    the Top (1972)
R.L. Stevenson The Wrong Box (1961), Treasure Island (1974)
Philip Turner Sea Peril (1966)
Elfrida Vipont The Secret Passage (1967)
Rosemary Weir High Courage (1967)
Ronald Welsh Bowman of Crecy (1966)
H.G. Wells The History of Mr. Polly (1957)

References: ICB 2,3,4; Jacques; Usherwood; Wa (1966); Culpan and Waite *Variety is King* (School Library Association 1977)

Ceri Geraldus Richards (1903-71)

Worked as Ceri Richards. Born at Dunvant, near Swansea, Wales. He was an electrical apprentice, then studied at Swansea School of Art (1921-24)

and the Royal College of Art (1924-27). Illustrator for the London Press Association (1927-28). Taught at Cardiff School of Art (1940-44), Chelsea Polytechnic (1947-57), the Slade School of Fine Art (1955-58) and the Royal College of Art (1958-60). Tate Gallery Trustee (1958-65). Painter, lithographer, muralist and designer for the theatre. As an illustrator, he sometimes worked in crayon, using outline with attached shading and a limited colour range to create the effect of lithographs as in *The Magic Horse*; he also, on occasion, used lithography to create exotic yet subtle colour and tonal gradations. Member of the Surrealist Group (1936) and London Group (1937); awarded CBE (1960). [Q]

Books illustrated include:
Dylan Thomas Under Milk Wood (1972)
Roberto Semesi (trans) Journey Towards the North (1971)
The Magic Horse (1930)
The Psalms (1969)

Periodical: Poetry London

References: Bénézit; Chamot, Farr & Butlin; Contemporary Artists; Johnson & Greutzner; Rothenstein vol 3; Vollmer; Wa (1970); Waters; David Thompson *Ceri Richards* (Methuen, 1963)

Frances Richards (b. 1901)

Maiden name: Frances Clayton. Born in Burslem, Stoke-on-Trent, Staffordshire, daughter of a fireman. Designer for Paragon China, Stoke-on-Trent (1918-24). Studied at Burslem School of Art (1919-24) and the Royal College of Art (1924-27). Married Ceri Richards* (1929). Teacher at Camberwell and Chelsea Schools of Art (1929-58). Painter, influenced by early Italian art; book and magazine illustrator. [Q]

Books illustrated include:
Richard Burns Some Poems (1977)
Arthur Rimbaud Les Illuminations (1975)
Acts of the Apostles (1930)
The Book of Revelation (1931)
Juliet and her Nurse (1976)
Lamentations (1969)
Poems of Experience (1981)

Periodicals: The Sunday Times, The Times

References: Bénézit; Chamot, Farr & Butlin; Wa (1980); Waters

Agnes Richardson (1885-1951)

Born in Wimbledon, daughter of a printer. Studied at Lambeth School of Art; lived at Wimbledon. Her stylised 'chubby child' drawings found a ready market, and she became a popular illustrator of children's stories, annuals, and picture postcards published by Raphael Tuck, C.W. Faulkner, Valentine, and other firms.

Books illustrated include:
Lewis Carroll Alice in Wonderland (1920)
A.G. Herbertson The Cosy Corner Book (1923)
Charles Perrault Fairy Stories from the French (1920)

Charles de Sousy Ricketts (1866-1931)

Born in Geneva, son of a naval officer. Studied wood engraving at Lambeth School of Art and there met his lifelong partner, the painter Charles Haselwood Shannon. During the early 1890s he contributed pen and ink drawings to illustrated magazines, and with Shannon, produced *The Dial,* an occasional magazine devoted to art and literature which was decorated with their own wood-engraved and lithographed designs. Ricketts also worked as a book cover designer and illustrator for publishers Osgood McIlvane (until 1892) and Elkin Mathews & John Lane. He designed covers for a number of books written by his friend Oscar Wilde, including *The Sphinx* (Mathews & Lane 1894): one of the earliest books for which he designed the cover, page layouts and illustrations. In partnership with Llewellyn Hacon (who provided financial backing) he set up the Vale Press (1896-1903), assuming complete responsibility for editorial policy and design. He created three new typefaces for the press; the *Vale,* its smaller version the *Avon,* and the *King's Fount,* and also engraved many border decorations and initials. Most of the illustrations were

Charles Ricketts. 'The Defeat of Glory' from *Poems Dramatic and Lyrical* by John Leicester Warren, Lord de Tabley (Elkin Mathews & John Lane, The Bodley Head, 1893).

also his, though some were engraved by others including his close friend Thomas Sturge Moore*. In 1899, many of the Vale's decorative woodblocks were destroyed in a disastrous fire at the Ballantyne press (where Vale books were printed), and from then on its publications were simpler and more austere. After 1904, Ricketts concentrated increasingly on painting, sculpture, and stage design, and on an art collection, formed with Shannon and eventually bequeathed to the Fitzwilliam Museum, Cambridge. However, he continued to design books for friends, including Gordon Bottomley and 'Michael Field' (Katherine Bradley and Edith Cooper). Near the end of his life, he illustrated his own *Beyond the Threshold* (1929, under the pseudonym John Paul Raymond) and *Unrecorded Histories* (1933, published posthumously).

Ricketts was one of the most important book designers of his generation. He believed that the visual element in a book (cover, format, page design and illustrations) should enhance and illuminate the textual content. He therefore approached each book as a separate entity rather than adopting a consistent 'house style'. An unrepentant eclectic, he looked to many sources to augment his decorative and ideographic range, notably Celtic and Japanese art, 16th century Venetian books, and contemporary French symbolism, while perfecting a style of his own that was finely-tuned, elegant and inventive. With Shannon he was a pioneer in the wood engraving revival and was one of the first illustrators to use wood engraving as an autographic medium. Though his engravings retained strong affinities with the pen drawings on which they were initially based, they helped to inspire a new consciousness of the aesthetic possibilities of wood engraving as a medium in its own right. Among the many friends who were influenced by his ideas were Laurence Housman, Thomas Sturge Moore, Lucien Pissarro* and William Strang*. Ricketts was offered (but refused) the directorship of the National Gallery, London, (1915), but later became adviser to the National Gallery of Canada. Elected ARA (1922), RA (1928).

Books illustrated include:
Lucius Apuleius The Excellent Narration of the Marriage of Cupid and
  Psyche (1897), De Cupidinis et Psyche Amoribus (1901)
William Blake The Book of Thel, Songs of Innocence, Songs of
  Experience (1897), Poetical Sketches (1899)
Lord de Tabley Poems Dramatic and Lyrical (1893)
Michael Drayton Nymphidia and the Muses Elizium (1896)
'Michael Field' The World at Auction (1898), The Race of Leaves
  (1901), Julia Domna (1903)
Edward Fitzgerald (trans) The Rubaiyat of Omar Khayyam (1901)
John Gray Spiritual Poems (1896)
Christopher Marlowe and G. Chapman Hero and Leander (with
  Charles Shannon, 1894)
John Milton Early Poems (1896)
Thomas Sturge Moore Danaë (1903)
Charles Ricketts A Bibliography of the Books published by Hacon and

Ricketts (1904), Beyond the Threshold (1929), Unrecorded Histories (1933)
G. Thornley (trans) Daphnis and Chloë (with C. Shannon, 1893)
Henry Vaughan Sacred Poems (1897)
Oscar Wilde A House of Pomegranates (with C. Shannon, 1891), The Sphinx (1894)
William Shakespeare The Passionate Pilgrim (1896)
The Parables from the Gospels (1903)

Periodicals: Black and White, The Dial, Form, Magazine of Art, The Pageant

References: Baker; Bénézit; Chamot, Farr & Butlin; Crane; DNB (1931-40); Garrett BWE, HBWE; Harper; Houfe; ICB 1; Johnson; Johnson & Greutzner; Muir; Peppin; Phaidon; Ray; Taylor; Thieme & Becker; Thorpe; Waters; C. Wood; *The Connoisseur* (August 1978); *The Print Collector's Quarterly* vols 14, 19; *The Studio* 48 (1910), 92 (1926), special (1917, 1919, 1927, Spring 1930, Autumn 1930); *A Collection of Books Designed by Charles Ricketts* (L'Art Ancien, Zurich 1972); Stephen Calloway *Charles Ricketts: Subtle and Fantastic Decorator* (Thames & Hudson 1979); Joseph Darracott *The World of Charles Ricketts* (Eyre Methuen 1980); Thomas Sturge Moore *Charles Ricketts RA* (Cassell 1933), *Self Portrait taken from the Letters and Journals of Charles Ricketts* (Peter Davies 1939); Charles Ricketts *A Defence of the Revival of Printing* (Hacon & Ricketts 1899), *Pages on Art* (Constable 1913)

Trevor Ridley (b. 1942)

Born in York and grew up in Northumberland. Worked as a teacher (1966-68), in advertising (1969-72), and from 1972 as a freelance painter, printmaker, ceramic designer, and illustrator (books and advertising). For illustration, he works in a pen line of varying weight, contrasted with black textured shading. He considers his draughtsmanship to have been influenced by Dürer and Rembrandt, and his treatment of spatial perspective by the masters of the Japanese woodcut. He lives in Essex. [Q]

Books illustrated include:
Roy Brown The Saturday Man (1969)
Hester Burton Five August Days (1981)
Kathleen Fidler Treasure of Ebba (1968)
Leon Garfield The Boy and the Monkey (1969), The Captain's Watch (1972), Lucifer Wilkins (1973)
Margaret Greaves The Night of the Goat (1976)
Frederick Grice The Oak and the Ash (1968)
Denise Hill The Castle Grey Pony (1976)
Mollie Hunter The Haunted Mountain (1972)
Ruth Manning-Sanders Stories from the English and Scottish Ballads (1968)
Sheila McCullagh When the Clouds Come Down (1976)
Michael Morpurgo Thatcher Jones (1975)
Victor E. Newbury History Hunter (1979)
Richard Parker Spell Seven (1971)
John Pelling Alfred at Athelney (1977), Alfred the Great (1977), 1812 (1978), The Emperor Napoleon (1978), Paris (1978)
Philip Saurain Imagining the Past (3 vols, 1979)
Philip Turner Steam on the Line (1968)
Hugh Walters School on the Moon (1981)

Periodicals: Continental Modeller, Cruising world, In Britain, Motorboat and Yachting, Punch, Radio Times, Speed and Power, TV Times, Yachting Monthly, Yachting World

Trekkie Ritchie

See Marjorie Tulip Parsons

Elizabeth Joyce Rivers (b. 1903)

Works as Elizabeth Rivers. Painter and wood

Elizabeth Rivers. From *The Valley of Graneon* by Sean Dorman (Peter Davies, 1944).

engraver. Studied at Goldsmith's College under E.J. Sullivan* (1921-24), at the Royal Academy Schools (1925-30) and in Paris (1931-34). For book illustration, she uses wood engraving, or pen and ink, combining creative draughtsmanship with a strong sense of relevance and drama. Elected SWA (1940).

Books illustrated include:
Walter de la Mare On the Edge (1930)
Sean Dorman Valley of Graneon (1944)
Patricia Lynch The Mad O'Haras (1948)
E.E. Mannin Connemara Journal (1947)
F. O'Connor A Picture Book (1943)
Elizabeth Rivers This Man (1939), Out of Bondage: Israel (1957)
C.C. Rogers Our Cornwall (1948)
C. Smart Out of Bedlam (1956)
Alfred, Lord Tennyson The Day-Dream (1928)
Theocritus (trans Charles Stuart Calverley) The Second and Seventh Idylls (1927)

References: Johnson & Greutzner; Waters

Brian Robb (1913-79)

Born in Scarborough, Yorkshire, son of a minister of the Church of Scotland. Educated at Malvern College (1926-30). Studied at Chelsea School of Art (1930-40) and part-time at the Slade School of Fine Art for a year. Illustrator, painter in oil and watercolour. During the 1930s, he contributed humorous drawings to *Punch* and designed advertisements for Shell. Lecturer at Chelsea School of Art (1936-39 and 1946-62); Head of the Illustration Department at the Royal College of Art (1963-78). Member of the London Group (c.1954). As an illustrator, he worked in pen and ink, sometimes with watercolour or wash, adapting his graphic style with ingenuity and sensitivity to suit his varying texts. Quentin Blake* wrote of his 'irrepressible quirkiness of drawing and outlook that seemed to express instinctively the comedy of human dilemmas' and commented that 'the diversity of his activities and his deep-seated modesty about his work meant that as an artist he never became celebrated or continuously commercially successful'. (*Illustrators*). Writing in

1950, Edward Ardizzone* considered him 'a born illustrator in the great tradition of the nineteenth century' (*Signature*).

Books illustrated include:
L.N. Andreyev Judas Iscariot (1947)
Aywyos Hints on Etiquette (c.1946)
G. Barkas The Camouflage Story (1952)
J. Roose Evans The Adventures of Odd and Elsewhere (1971), The Secret of the Seven Bright Shiners (1972), Odd and the Great Bear (1973), Elsewhere and the Gathering of the Clowns (1974), The Return of the Great Bear (1975)
Henry Fielding Tom Jones (1953)
E. Nesbit Fairy Stories (1977)
Brian Robb My Middle East Campaigns (1944), 12 Adventures of the Celebrated Baron Munchausen (1947), My Grandmother's Djinn (1976), The Last of the Centaurs (1978)
Laurence Sterne A Sentimental Journey (1948), Tristram Shandy (1949)
Aesop's Fables (1954)
The Golden Ass of Apuleius (1947)
Oxford Illustrated Old Testament (1965)

Periodicals: The Compleat Imbiber, Night and Day, Punch, The Saturday Book

References: Jacques; Vollmer; Wa (1980); Waters; *Illustrators* 23 (1978), 31 (1979); *Signature* new series 11 (1950); William Feaver *When We Were Young* (Thames & Hudson 1977); Diana Klemin *The Illustrated Book* (Bramhall House, New York 1970)

Doreen Roberts (b. 1922)

Born in Walthamstow, London. Served in the Women's Land Army during World War II. Studied at South West Essex Technical College (1945-47) and at the Slade School of Fine Art (1947-50). Head of art department at a secondary school (1952-73); part-time lecturer at Whitelands College, London (1973); lecturer at the College of All Saints (1974) and at Middlesex Polytechnic (from 1978); evening lecturer for Haringey Council and peripatetic lecturer on children's book illustration. Freelance illustrator and writer of children's books (often for Oxford University Press) since 1968, painter and photographer. For illustration, she works both in black and white and in colour, using waterproof inks, gouache or oil pastels. She enjoys working in a fairly loose style, and uses texture with vigour and freedom to animate the printed page. [Q]

Books illustrated include:
E.M. Almedingen A Candle at Dusk (1969)
Gillian Avery The Hole in the Wall (1968)
Margaret Baker The Last Straw (1971)
Alan Boucher The Sword of the Raven (1969)
Winifred Cawley Feast of the Serpent (1969)
Helen Cresswell The Outlanders (1970)
Marcus Crouch Canterbury (1970)
Roger Lancelyn Green Stories of Ancient Greece (1967)
Thomas Johnston The Fight for Arkenwald (1970)
Sheena Porter The Scapegoat (1968), The Valley of Carreg-Wen (1971)
Doreen Roberts Joe at the Fair (1972), Joe's Day at the Market (1973), Harry by the Sea (1974), The Charley Car (1975), Jem in the Park (1975), The Other Side of the Day (1976), Teaching Art (1978)
Frederick Grice The Black Hand Gang (1971)
R.C. Scriven The Prospect of Whitby (1971)
Eleanor Spence Jamberoo Road (1969)
Margaret Storey A Quarrel of Witches (1970)
Philip Turner War on the Darnel (1969)
Ronald Welch Sun of York (1970)
Barbara Willard Priscilla Pentecost (1970)

Brian Robb. From his *12 Adventures of the Celebrated Baron Munchausen* (Peter Lunn, 1947).

Periodicals: Birmingham Post, Child Education, Pictorial Education

References: ICB 3,4

Lunt Roberts (active 1913-54)

Illustrator of magazines, children's books and annuals. He drew freely in a conventional manner, often with vigorous hatching, in pen, brush, and crayon. Cuppleditch records that he first attended the London Sketch Club with John Hassall* in 1913, that he became a member of the Club in 1921 and its president in 1936. He lived in South London and every year drew a portrait of the new Captain of the Coombe Wood Golf Club.

Books illustrated include:
Mary England (ed) Warne's Happy Book for Girls (c.1938)
Kathleen Fidler Pete, Pam and Jim (1954)
Trevor Henley Let's Find Hidden Treasure (1947)
Angus MacVicar Stubby Sees it Through (1950)
John N. More Dugout Doggerels from Palestine (1922)
Malcolm Saville The Riddle of the Painted Box (1947), Redshank's Warning (1948), Two Fair Plaits (1948), The Flying Fish Adventure (1950), The Secret of the Hidden Pool (1953), Young Johnnie Bimbo (1956), The Fourth Key (1957)
R.L. Stevenson Two Stories (1964)

Periodicals: Cassell's Children's Annual, Daily Mail Annual, The Humorist, Punch

References: Cuppleditch; Doyle BWI

Graham Walford Robertson (1866-1948)

Worked as Walford Graham Robertson. Born in London. Educated at Eton. Studied art under Albert Moore. Through family introductions, he moved in prominent artistic circles from an early age and numbered among his friends many leading artists, writers and actors including Walter Crane*, James Abbott McNeill Whistler, Sir Edward Burne-Jones, John Singer Sargent, Oscar Wilde, Ellen Terry and Sarah Bernhardt. He achieved some success as a portrait, landscape and subject-painter, and during the 1890s designed theatre sets, costumes and posters for contemporary symbolist and Shakespearean productions. He

W. Graham Robertson. From his *Pan's Garden* (Macmillan, nd).

wrote fairy stories, children's verse, and plays (which he also produced), and in later life was responsible for a number of village pageants, often turning for inspiration to Surrey folklore. His early (unpublished) graphic work owed much to the Aesthetic movement and the example of Walter Crane and Dante Gabriel Rossetti, and he was also profoundly influenced by the illuminated poems of William Blake (of which he was an important collector), and by the work of Arthur Hughes*, Aubrey Beardsley, and Edward Gordon Craig*. For his published illustrations (1902-24), he evolved a simplified, but distinctive manner to express muted rustic fantasies. Elected NEAC (1891), RBA (1896), ROI (1910), RP (1912).

Books illustrated include:
E.R. Chapman A Little Child's Wreath (1904)
G.K. Chesterton Napoleon of Notting Hill (1904)
Juliana Horatia Ewing Old Fashioned Fairy Tales (1920)
Kenneth Grahame The Wind in the Willows (1908)
Maurice Maeterlinck The Bluebird (1915)
A. Ollivant Redcoat Captain (1907)
Petrarch Love's Crucifix (1902)
W. Graham Robertson A Masque of May Morning (1904), A Year of Songs for a Baby in a Garden (1905), Gold, Frankincense and Myrrh (1906), A Baby's Day Book for a Woman of Four (1907), Pinkie and the Fairies (1908), The Slippers of Cinderella (1919), Archibald (1924), Pan's Garden (nd)
Alfred, Lord Tennyson Maud (1906)
French Songs of Old Canada (1904)
Old English Songs and Dances (1902)

Periodical: The English Illustrated Magazine

References: Bénézit; Houfe; ICB 1; Johnson & Greutzner; Ray; Vollmer; Waters; C. Wood; *Art Chronicle* (December 1909) pp.77-78; *Cassell's Magazine* (November 1980); *The Illustrated London News* (Christmas 1979) pp.91-95; *Magazine of Art* (December 1899); *The Observer* (5th July 1931); *The Studio* 36 (1906) pp.99-107, special (1911, Autumn 1914, 1923-24); *The Lyle Official Arts Review* (1978); Percy Bate *The English Pre-Raphaelite Painters; Their Associates and Successors* (G. Bell 1899); Kerrison Preston (intro) *The Blake Collection of W. Graham Robertson* (Faber 1952), *Letters from Graham Robertson* (Hamish Hamilton 1958); W. Graham Robertson *Time Was* (Hamish Hamilton 1931); Alfred Sutro *Celebrities and Simple Souls* (Duckworth 1933)

Bay Robinson (b. 1898)

Born in Hampstead, London, daughter of Charles Robinson*. Educated by a governess and at the North London Collegiate School, and later taught at various schools. Landscape painter in watercolour, sketched in black and white; also a lithographer. As a book illustrator, she inherited her father's immaculate pen and ink line, and something of his decorative flair. [Q]

Books illustrated include:
Barbara Ellis Browne Sampa the Baby Seal (1948)
Frances Hodgson Burnett The Secret Garden (nd)
R.L. Stevenson A Child's Garden of Verses (nd)
Pedlar's Progress (1949)

References: Wa (1980); Waters 2

Charles Robinson (1870-1937)

Born in Camden Town, son of wood engraver and

Charles Robinson. 'The little boy he had loved' from *The Happy Prince and other stories* by Oscar Wilde (1913).

magazine illustrator Thomas Robinson, and brother of W. Heath Robinson* and T. Heath Robinson*. Apprenticed to the lithographers, Waterlow and Son. Inadequate funds prevented him from studying at the Royal Academy Schools, where he had obtained a place, but he was able to attend evening classes at the West London Art School and at Heatherley's School of Art. From 1892, he worked as a freelance illustrator, based on his father's studio in the Strand. He joined the very talented group of young artists then working for John Lane at The Bodley Head, and his black and white illustrated edition of R.L. Stevenson's *A Child's Garden of Verses* (1895) had an immediate success; he subsequently illustrated well over 100 books mostly for children.

He was basically a self-trained illustrator, and his work has freedom and originality linked with a real feeling for book design that makes it outstanding. His black and white illustration reflects the influence of Beardsley and Walter Crane*, and his watercolour illustrations have delicacy and sensitivity, greatly helped by the introduction of the four colour process early in the century as the alternative to lithography. By incorporating lettering into the page design, and in his planning of the book as a whole, he developed the Arts and Crafts tradition of the book as a work of art.

Books illustrated include:

Ruth Arkwright Brownikins and Other Fancies (1910)
P. Austin The Goldfish Bowl (1922)
Mrs Arthur Bell Dobbies' Little Master (1897)
J.J. Bell The New Noah's Ark (1899), Jack of All Trades (1900)
William Blake Songs of Innocence (with Mary Robinson, 1912)
Clare Bridgeman A Book of Days for Little Ones (1901), The Bairn's Coronation Book (1902), The Shopping Day (1902)
J.H. Burn The Mother's Book of Song (1902)
Frances Hodgson Burnett The Secret Garden (1911)
William Canton (ed) The True Annals of Fairyland: The Reign of King Herla (1900)
E. Carrington Animals in Wrong Places (1896)
Lewis Carroll Alice's Adventures in Wonderland (1907)
Agnes and E. Castle Our Sentimental Garden (1914)
E. Martinengo Cesaresco The Fairies' Fountain (1908)
C.R. Coleridge Minstrel Duck (1896)
W. Copeland The Farm Book (1901), The Book of the Zoo (1902), The Book of Ducks and Dutchies (1905), The Book of the Dutch Dolls (1905), The Book of the Fan (1905), The Book of the Little Dutch Dolls (1905), The Book of the Little J.D.s (1905), The Book of the Mandarinfants (1905), The Black Cat Book (1905), A Bookful of Fun (1905), The Book of Dolly's House (1906), The Book of Dolly-Land (1906), Bouncing Babies (1906), Mad Motor (1906), The Silly Submarine (1906), Awful Airship (1906), The Book of Dolly's Doings (1906), The Cake Shop (1907), The Sweet Shop (1907), The Toy Shop (1907), The Book of Other People (1908), The Book of Sailors (1908), The Book of Soldiers (1908), Babes and Blossoms (1908)
W.E. Cule Child Voices (1900)
F.H.C. de la Motte Fouqué Sintram and his Companions (1900)
Henry de Vere Stacpoole Pierrette (1899)
Rev. P. Dearmer The Little Lives of the Saints (1900)
J. Dunbar Young Hopeful (1932)
Eugene Field Lullaby Land (1897)
H. Fielding-Hall Margaret's Book (1913)
Edward FitzGerald (trans) The Rubaiyat of Omar Khayyam (1928)
F.H.C. de la Motte Fouqué Sintram and his Companions (1900)
Anatole France Bee: The Princess of the Dwarves (1912)
N. Garotin The Suitors of Aprille (1899)
J.M. Gibbon (ed) The True Annals of Fairyland: The Reign of Old King Cole (1901)
B. Girvan and M. Cosens Wee Men (1923)
S. Baring Gould Siegfried (1904)
M.E. Gullick Teddy's Year with the Fairies (1920)
Handasyde The Four Gardens (1912)
Robert Herrick Selections (1915)
Homer The Adventures of Odysseus (1900)
Washington Irving Rip Van Winkle (1915)
C. Jerrold Road, Rail and Sea (1906)
Douglas W. Jerrold Fireside Saints (1903)
Walter C. Jerrold Nonsense! Nonsense! (1902), The True Annals of Fairyland: The Reign of Oberon (1902), The Big Book of Nursery Rhymes (1903), The Big Book of Fairy Tales (1911), The Big Book of Fables (1912)
Charles and Mary Lamb Stories for Children (with Winifred Green, 1902)
H.D. Lowry Make Believe (1896)
B. MacGregor King Longbeard (1898)
M. MacLeod Longfellow (1912)
S.B. Macy In the Beginning (1910)
E. Marc Doris and David All Alone (1922)
L. Marsh (ed) Old Time Tales (1912)
Annie Matheson Songs of Love and Praise (1907)
I. Maunder Songs of Happy Childhood (1908)
A.A. Milne Once on a Time (1925)
W.J. Minnion Topsy Turvy (1913)
Alice T. Morris A Child's Book of Empire (1913)
'Netta' Baby Town Ballads (1906), Prince Babillon (1907)
L.N. Parker Richard Wagner and the Ring of the Nibelungs (with P. Billinghurst*, 1898)
Charles Perrault Tales of Past Times (1900), Fairy Tales (1913)
Jessie Pope Babes and Birds (1909), The Baby Scouts (1911), Babes and Beasts (1912)
Winifred Radcliffe The Saint's Garden (1927)
W.D. Rands Lilliput Lyrics (1898)
Grace Rhys The Children's Garland of Verses (1921)
Charles Robinson The Ten Little Babies (1905), Fanciful Fowls (1906), Peculiar Piggies (1906), Black Bunnies (1907), Black Doggies (1907), Black Sambos (1907)
George Sand The Master Mosaic-Workers (1900)

Gabriel Setoun The Child World (1896)
Evelyn Sharp The Child's Christmas (1906), The Story of the
   Weathercock (1907), What Happened at Christmas (1915)
Percy Bysshe Shelley The Sensitive Plant (1911)
M. Dykes Spicer Rainbows (1913)
John G. Stevenson Father Time Stories (1921)
Margaret Stevenson Bridget's Fairies (1919)
R.L. Stevenson A Child's Garden of Verses (1895)
Netta Syrett The Vanishing Princess (1909)
Ernest Temple Thurston The Open Window (1913)
K. Tynan A Little Book of Courtesies (1906)
I.H. Wallis The Cloud Kingdom (1905)
'Awfly Wierdly' Christmas Dreams (1896)
Oscar Wilde The Happy Prince and other stories (1913)
Aesop's Fables (1895)
Arabian Nights. The Story of Prince Ahmed and the Fairy Perie
   Banou (1915)
The Coronation Autograph Book (1902)
Fairy Tales from Hans Christian Andersen (with T.H. and W.H.
   Robinson*, 1899)
Granny's Book of Fairy Stories (1930)
Grimm's Fairy Tales (1910)
The Infant Reader (1895)
Mother Goose Nursery Rhymes (1928)
The New Testament of Our Lord and Saviour Jesus Christ (1903)
The First Primer (1895)
The Second Primer (1895)
The Songs and Sonnets of William Shakespeare (1915)

Periodicals: Black and White, The Graphic, The Illustrated London
News, Pan, Puck, The Queen, The Sunday Annual, The Wonderland
Annual

References: Baker; Bénézit; Crane; Doyle CL; Houfe; Johnson;
Johnson & Greutzner; Peppin; Sketchley; Thieme & Becker; Waters;
C. Wood; *The Studio* 5 (1895), 66 (1916), special (1897-98, 1899-1900,
Autumn 1914, Autumn 1928); Leo de Freitas *Charles Robinson*
(Academy 1976); David Larkin *Charles and William Heath Robinson*
(Constable 1976)

Frederick Cayley Robinson (1862-1927)

Often worked as Cayley Robinson. Born at
Brentford-on-Thames, Middlesex. Studied at St
John's Wood School of Art and the Royal Ac-
ademy Schools. After living on a yacht for two
years, he studied at the Académie Julian, Paris
(1891-94). Lived in Florence (1898-1902). Visiting
Professor of Figure Composition and Drawing at
Glasgow School of Art (1914-24). He painted
murals at Dublin Art Gallery and the Middlesex
Hospital, London, and designed costumes and
sets for the first production of Maeterlinck's *The
Blue Bird*, Haymarket Theatre, London (1909),
and posters for the London Midland Scottish
Railway. His quiet but distinctive style was influenced by Fra Angelico's frescos and by the
paintings of the French Symbolist painter Puvis
de Chavannes. As an illustrator he worked
mainly in watercolour washes bounded by delicate outlines. Elected RBA (1888), ROI (1906),
ARWS (1911), NEAC (1912), RWS (1918, Vice
President 1920-23), ARA (1921); Member of the
Tempera Society.

Books illustrated include:
G.K. Chesterton St Francis of Assisi (1926)
L.V. Hodgkin A Book of Quaker Saints (1907)
Maurice Maeterlinck The Blue Bird (1911)
Cardinal Manning (trans) Little Flowers of St Francis of Assisi (1915)
Ralph W. Trine In Tune with the Infinite (1926)
Peggy Webling Saints and their Stories (1922)
The Book of Genesis (1914)

Periodical: The Venture

References: Bénézit; Chamot, Farr & Butlin; Houfe; Johnson;
Johnson & Greutzner; Mallalieu; Thieme & Becker; Waters; C. Wood;
The Connoisseur (September 1977); *The OWS Club Volume* 5; *The
Magazine of Art* (1899); *The Studio* 31 (1904), 49 (1910), 83 (1922);
Fine Art Society Exhibition Catalogue (October - November 1977)

Geoffrey Favatt Robinson (b. 1910)

Works as Geoffrey Robinson. Born in London,
youngest child of Charles Robinson*. Studied at
Hornsey School of Art (1927-30) under Norman
Janes* and Robert Lyon, but was unable, through
lack of money, to continue his studies. Assistant
Art Editor of *Good Housekeeping* (1930-34),
Editor of the *Art Trade Journal*, *World of Art
Illustrated*, *Art Prices Current* and *Who's Who in
Art* (1935-38). He continued as a publishing ex-
ecutive until 1977. Landscape painter in oil and
watercolour (always working out of doors); book
designer, typographer, and illustrator in pen and
ink. Trustee of the Stanley Spencer Memorial
Gallery at Cookham. [Q]

Books illustrated include:
Hockley Clarke The Unfolding Year (1947)
A.J. Talbot Aesop's Fables (1936)

Cayley Robinson. 'St Christopher' from *Saints
and their Stories* by Peggy Webling (Nisbet,
1922).

Periodical: The Countryman

Reference: Johnson & Greutzner

Gordon Robinson (active 1905-19)

Illustrator of children's books and annuals in full colour, halftone and black and white. Houfe notes that he contributed to *The Illustrated London News* in the style of John Hassall*. His post-war coloured book illustrations are also rather reminiscent of Hassall's work, but without his exuberance.

Books illustrated include:
Hans Christian Andersen Fairy Tales (1917)
Daniel Defoe Robinson Crusoe (1915)
Charles Dickens The Cricket on the Hearth (1917)
Charles Kingsley The Water Babies (1919)

Periodicals: Cassell's Annual, Herbert Strang's Annual, The Illustrated London News, Tiny Tots, Tuck's Annual

Reference: Houfe

Joan Gale Robinson (b. 1910)

Worked as Joan G. Robinson and also under her maiden name, Joan Gale Thomas. Born at Gerrard's Cross, Buckinghamshire. An illustrator of children's books, she worked mostly with line blocks, sometimes introducing one or two colours, and occasionally in full colour. Her work is characterised by an easy natural line, producing simple illustrations of a consistent quality and charm. For a time, she collaborated with her husband, Richard Gavin Robinson in illustration and design. Member Chelsea Illustrators' Studio (1929). [Q]

Books illustrated include:
Enid Blyton Tales of Betsy-May (1940)

Joan G. Robinson. From her Dear Teddy Robinson (Harrap, 1956).

"Three cheers for me at the top of the tree."

Mary Cockett Jonathan on the Farm (1954), Jonathan and Felicity (1955)
Madeleine Collier Beryl's Wonderful Week (1944)
Jennifer Ford The House Under the Tree (1954), The House in Hyde Park (1956)
Dorothy Ann Lovell The Dip Bucket (1941), Lift up the Latch (1942), When the Fire Burns Blue (1944), Shadows on the Stairs (1946)
Irene Pearl Janey (1953), Janey and her Friends (1953)
Joan G. Robinson Debbie Robbie's Day Nursery (1950), Susie at Home (1953), Teddy Robinson series (1953-64), Mary Mary series (1957-60)
Joan Gale Thomas A Stands for Angel (1939), Our Father (1940), If Jesus Came to my House (1941), My Book about Christmas (1946), My Garden Book (1947), God of all Things (1947), One Little Baby (1950), Ten Little Angels (1951), If I'd Been Born in Bethleham (1952), The Happy Year (1953), I Ask a Blessing (1955), Where is God? (1957), The Christmas Angel (1961), Seven Days (1964)

References: Doyle CL; Fisher p.342; Kirkpatrick

Thomas Heath Robinson (c.1869-1950)

Born in Islington, London. Elder brother of Charles and William Heath Robinson.* Worked initially as assistant to his father, a magazine illustrator. Early in his career he collaborated with his brothers on books published by J.M. Dent. In middle age, he moved to Pinner, Middlesex where, with his brothers, he founded a walking club 'The Frothfinders' Federation', and painted the inn sign of the local pub, 'The Queen's Head'. He lacked his brothers' flair for fantasy and decoration, but was a competent and prolific illustrator in a conventional, realistic vein. In his later years he specialised in religious subjects and boys' adventure stories in anthologies and magazines.

Books illustrated include:
G. Aguilar Tales (1902)
G. C. Allen (trans) The Song of Frithiof (1912)
K. F. Boult Heroes of the Norselands (1903)
William Canton A Child's Book of Saints (1898)
Lewis Carroll Alice in Wonderland (1922)
M. D. Coxhead Mexico (1909)
P. Creswick Robin Hood and his adventures (1902)
John Crossland and J. M. Parrish (ed) The Children's Wonder Book (with others, 1933)
George Eliot The Mill on the Floss (1924)
Mrs Gaskell Cranford (1896)
Henry Gilbert King Arthur's Knights (nd)
Wilhelm Hauff Lichtenstein (1900)
Nathaniel Hawthorne The Scarlet Letter (1897)
Arthur L. Haydon The Book of Robin Hood (1931)
Thomas Hughes Tom Brown's Schooldays (1903)
M. D. Kelly The Story of Sir Walter Raleigh (1906)
Charles Kingsley The Heroes (1899)
George R. Lees The Life of Christ (1920)
S. B. Macy The Master Builders (1911), The Book of the Kingdom (1912)
F. T. Meade Stories from the Old Old Bible (1903)
John Milton Hymn on the Morning of Christ's Nativity (1897)
Bernard Minssen A Book of French Songs for the Young (1899)
Elsie Oxenham Goblin Island (1907)
Jane Porter The Scottish Chiefs (1900)
Frank Rinder Old-World Japan, Legends of the Land of the Gods (1895)
Edmund Spencer Una and the Red Cross Knight (1905)
Laurence Sterne A Sentimental Journey through France and Italy (1897)
Carmen Sylva Legends from River and Mountain (1896)
William Makepeace Thackeray The History of Henry Esmond (1896)
J.R. Wyss Swiss Family Robinson (1913)
Fairy Tales from the Arabian Nights (with Dora Curtis*, 1899)
The Child's Bible (1928)

Fairy Tales from Hans Christian Anderson (with C. and W.H.
  Robinson*, 1899)
The Ruba'iyat of Omar Khayyam (1907)
The Story Bible (1930)
Tales and Talks from History (1911)

Periodicals: The Captain, Cassell's Family Magazine, The Champion
Annual, Chums, The Girls' Realm, Herbert Strang's Annuals, Holiday
Annual, Ladies' Realm, Little Folks, The Pall Mall Magazine,
Pearson's Magazine, The Quiver, The Strand Magazine, The Sunday at
Home, The Windsor Magazine

References: Baker; Doyle BWI, CL; Houfe; Sketchley; Waters 2; *The
Studio* 8 special (1898-99); Langston Day *The Life and Art of W. Heath
Robinson* (Herbert Joseph 1974); Iona and Peter Opie *The Classic
Fairy Tales* (Oxford University Press 1974)

William Heath Robinson (1872-1944)

Worked as W. Heath Robinson. Born in Hornsey
Rise, North London, son of illustrator and wood
engraver Thomas Robinson and brother of Charles
Robinson* and Thomas Heath Robinson*. Studied
at Islington School of Art (1887) and, briefly, at the
Royal Academy Schools (1890). First attempted
landscape painting but soon turned to illustration
(his first book appearing in 1897) and established
himself with the 'Art Nouveau' drawings for *The
Poems of Edgar Allan Poe* (1900). He subsequently
illustrated many other books, in a variety of styles
and sometimes in colour, including two fantastic
children's books of his own, *The Adventures of
Uncle Lubin* (1902) and *Bill the Minder* (1912).
He also contributed humorous drawings to many
magazines before 1914. During World War I, he
began to emerge as the greatest comic artist of his
time, whose name was assimilated into the language
to describe dotty and makeshift contraptions.
Between the wars, he was occupied mostly with
humorous drawings for such magazines as *The
Bystander, The Humorist* and *The Sketch*, but he
also illustrated short stories in *Nash's Magazine*,
fairy tales in *The Strand Magazine* and undertook
many advertising commissions, as well as exhibiting a mural for the liner *Empress of Britain*.

Heath Robinson was certainly the most versatile of the major British illustrators, as much at
home with Rabelais, Shakespeare, Andersen and
de la Mare as with the authors of the comic 'How
to...' series. He was an original and witty draughtsman, with a highly developed eye for nuances of
character and detail. 'He simply cannot draw a
single *object* sword, coffee-pot, candlestick or
what you will – without endowing it with some
crazy personality of its own' (R. Furneaux-Jordan).
As a satirist of the machine age, he reconstituted
20th century technological dreams as home-
handyman contrivances in wood, nails, and string.
Sir Kenneth Clarke wrote, 'Heath Robinson lived
in the age of science triumphant, when machinery
had become a tyrant; and, as we all know, the
man who ridicules tyrants is a champion of humanity' (quoted by Langston Day). Like his brother

W. Heath Robinson. 'Intelligent Co-operation
among Turtles in their Search for Food' from
How to Run a Communal Home by W. Heath
Robinson and Cecil Hunt (Hutchinson, 1943).

Charles, he had an exceptional gift for page design.
He worked in black and white (sometimes with
wash), and watercolour.

Books illustrated include:
John Bunyan The Pilgrim's Progress (1897)
Roland Carse The Monarchs of Merrie England (1908)
Cervantes Don Quixote (1897)
Lillian M.C. Clopet Once Upon a Time (1944)
William Crooke The Talking Thrush (1899)
Walter de la Mare Peacock Pie (1916)
G.L. Gomme (ed) The Queen's Story Book (1902)
Norman Hunter The Incredible Adventures of Professor Branestawm
  (1933)
H. H. Kennedy The Merry Multifleet and Mounting Multicorps (1904)
Charles Kingsley The Water Babies (1915)
Rudyard Kipling A Song of the English (1909), Collected Verse (1910)
Charles and Mary Lamb Tales from Shakespeare (1902)
Elsie S. Munro Topsy-Turvy Tales (1923)
Richard F. Patterson Mein Rant (1940)
Charles Perrault Old-Time Stories (1921)
Edgar Allan Poe Poems (1900)
William Heath Robinson A Child's Book of Saints (1898), The
  Adventures of Uncle Lubin (1902), Bill the Minder (1912), Some
  Frightful War Pictures (1915), Hunlikely! (1916), The Saintly Hun
  (1917), Get On With It (1920), Fly Papers (1921), The Home Made
  Car (1921), Then and Now (1921), Peter Quip in Search of a Friend
  (1922), The Humours of Golf (1923), Wonders of Wilmington
  (1925), Absurdities (1934), Railway Ribaldry (1935), Lets Laugh!
  (1939), Heath Robinson at War (1942)
William Heath Robinson and K.R.G. Browne How to Live in a Flat
  (1936), How to Be a Perfect Husband (1937), How to Make a
  Garden Grow (1938), How to Be a Motorist (1939)
William Heath Robinson and H. Cecil Hunt How to Make the Best of
  Things (1940), How to Build a New World (1941), How to Run a
  Communal Home (1943)
W.H.D. Rouse The Giant Crab (1897), The Talking Thrush (1899)
T.H.E. Schuck Mediaeval Stories (1902)
William Shakespeare Twelfth Night (1908), A Midsummer Night's
  Dream (1914)
Elsie Smenton Topsy Turvy Tales (1923)
The Arabian Nights' Entertainments (with others, 1899)
Danish Fairy Tales and Legends of Hans Andersen (1897)
Fairy Tales from Hans Christian Andersen (with C. and T.H.
  Robinson*, 1899)

Hans Andersen's Fairy Tales (1913)
The Works of Rabelais (1904)

Periodicals: The Bystander, Good Housekeeping, The Graphic, Holly Leaves, The Humorist, Hutchinson's Magazine, The Ladies' Realm, Little Folks, London Opinion, Nash's Magazine, The Odd Volume, Out and Away, The Pall Mall Magazine, Passing Show, Pearson's Magazine, Playbox Annual, Printer's Pie, Punch, The Quiver, Radio Times, The Royal Magazine, The Sketch, The Strand Magazine, The Sunday Magazine, Tit Bits, The Toc H Annual

References: Baker; Bénézit; Bradshaw; Crouch; Cuppleditch; DNB (1941-50); Doyle BWI, CL; Driver; Houfe; ICB 1; Johnson; Johnson & Greutzner; Peppin; Ray; Sketchley; Thieme & Becker; Vollmer; Wa (1934); Waters; *The Daily Telegraph Magazine* (17th May 1974); *The Sketch* (4th January 1911); *The Strand Magazine* 36 (1908); *The Studio* 67 (1916), 89 (1925), special (1911, Autumn 1914); *The Sunday Times Magazine* (4th June 1972); Langston Day *Life and Art of Heath Robinson* (Herbert Joseph 1947); R. Furneaux-Jordan (intro) *The Penguin Heath Robinson* (1966); A. E. Johnson *W. Heath Robinson* (A. & C. Black 1913); David Larkin *Charles and William Heath Robinson* (Constable 1976); John Lewis *Heath Robinson: Artist and Comic Genius* (Constable 1973); W. Heath Robinson *My Line of Life* (Blackie 1938)

Maureen Roffey (b. 1936)

Studied at Hornsey College of Art and at the Royal College of Art. Worked in industry as a graphic designer and designer of cardboard toys for export. Illustrator since 1970 of magazines and of children's books published by The Bodley Head. Her work is boldly designed and executed in pen and ink with wash or cut-out coloured paper. She is married to designer Bernard Lodge with whom she often collaborates.

Books illustrated include:
Jill Bennett (ed) Roger was a Razor Fish (1980), Days Are Where We Live (1980)
Bernard Lodge Tinker, Tailor, Soldier, Sailor (1976), Rhyming Nell (1979), Door to Door (1980)
Maureen Roffey Who Killed Cock Robin? (1971), Indoors (1973)
Maureen Roffey and Bernard Lodge The Grand Old Duke of York (1975)

Reference: ICB 4

Stanley Reginald Harry Rogers (d. 1961)

Born in Nottingham. Studied at Goldsmith's College School of Art and at the Antwerp Acadèmie des Beaux Arts. Marine painter in oil and watercolour; writer and illustrator in pen and ink of books about ships and life at sea. Member of the Society of Marine Artists.

Books illustrated include:
Stanley Rogers Ships and Sailors (1928), Sea-Love (1929), Aboard the Bonaventure (1930), The Atlantic (1930), The Book of the Sailing Ship (1931), The Pacific (1931), Crusoes and Castaways (1932), Twelve on the Beaufort Scale (1932), The Indian Ocean (1932), Enchanted Isles (1933), Tales of a Traveller (1934), Tales of the Fore-an-Aft (1935), Freak Ships (1936), Derelicts of the Sea (1937), Let's Make Something (1938), Modern Pirates (1939), The Atlantic Buccaneers (1939), The Barbary Pirates (1939), Indian Ocean Rovers (1939), The Old Wild West (1940), More Gallant Deeds of the War (1942), The Sailing Ship (1950), Great Discoverers (1950)
Selfridge's Schoolboys' Story Book (with others, nd)

Reference: Waters

Noel Rooke (1881-1953)

Son of portrait painter T.M. Rooke. Educated in France. Studied at the Slade School of Fine Art (1899-1903) and at the Central School of Arts and Crafts under Edward Johnstone, with Eric Gill* as a fellow pupil. He took up wood engraving in 1904 and taught book illustration at the Central School from 1905, wood engraving from 1912, and was head of Book Production (1930-46). He also worked as a landscape painter and poster designer.

Through his teaching at the Central School of Arts and Crafts, Rooke had a profound influence on the modern movement in wood engraving. Looking back to Thomas Bewick, he saw wood engraving as a medium for autographic expression rather than as the reproductive process that it had become during the 19th century. He drew directly on to the wood block and worked in both black and white line; he also experimented with 'graduated' printing, wood cutting (into the side grain), and, following Lucien Pissaro*, colour printing. His book illustrations, however, were often in black line, perhaps because of his deep concern with balance and visual relationship between engraved illustration and letterpress. His ideas were developed by many of his pupils, who included John Farleigh*, Robert Gibbings*, Vivien Gribble* and Clare Leighton*. Founder member SWE (1920), ARE (1920), Governor of the British Institute of Industrial Art (1926-34).

Books illustrated include:
Rupert Brooke The Old Vicarage, Granchester (1916)
John Hilton and Joseph Thorp (ed) Change, the Beginning of a Chapter (with others, 1919)
R.L. Stevenson Travels with a Donkey (1909), An Inland Voyage (1913)
Iolo A. Williams Flowers of Marsh and Stream (1946)
The Birth of Christ, from the Gospel According to Saint Luke (1925)

Periodical: The Impact

References: Balston EWE, WEMEB; Bliss; Garrett BWE, HBWE; Houfe; Vollmer supp; Wa (1934); WW (1950); Waters; *Drawing and Design* (December 1924); *The Studio* 123 (1942), special (1919, Spring 1927, Spring 1930); Campbell Dodgson *Contemporary English Woodcuts* (Duckworth 1922); Noel Rooke *Woodcuts and Wood Engravings* (lecture delivered to the Print Collector's Club 20th January 1925); H.C. Sewter *Modern British Woodcuts and Wood Engravings in the Collection of the Whitworth Art Gallery* (Manchester 1962)

Francis Cyril Stanley Rose (1909-79)

Born Farnham, Surrey. Lived mainly abroad, moving in colourful international circles and numbering Gertrude Stein, Jean Cocteau, Serge Lifar, Tyrone Power and Francis Picabia among his friends. Painter, designer for ballets, artistic consultant to various textile firms, wallpaper designer. Served in the Royal Air Force during World War II. As an illustrator, he worked in

pencil, pen and wash, sometimes succeeding in making a virtue of unsophisticated techniques.

Books illustrated include:
Lord Byron Childe Harold's Pilgrimage (1931)
Julian Common or Garden (1946)
Sir Francis Rose Etoile de Mer (1927), The White Cow, and other Chinese Fairy Tales (1945), The Shadowy Pine Tree (1946), Your Home (1947)
Gertrude Stein The World is Round (1939), Paris, France (1940)
Emma Tollemache In the Light (1948)

References: Bénézit; Wa (1972); Waters; *Who Was Who* (1971-80); Sir Francis Rose *Saying Life* (Cassell 1961)

Gerald Rose (b. 1935)

Born Hong Kong, son of an engineer. Studied at the Royal Academy Schools (1956-59). Lecturer at Blackpool College of Art (1960-64) and Maidstone College of Art (since 1965). Children's illustrator and writer, poster designer. In his illustrative work, he makes effective use of a wide range of media, including oil, watercolour, and acrylic paint. Awarded the Kate Greenaway Medal (1960) for *Old Winkle and the Seagulls,* and the Premio Critici in Erba (Bologna 1979) for *Ahh said Stork.* [Q]

Books illustrated include:
Linda Allen Birds of a Feather (1975), When the Wind Blows (1976), The Flight of Fancy (1977)
Eva Bexell Christmas with Grandfather (1979), The Minister's Naughty Children (1979)
Léonce Bourliaguet The Giant who Drank from his Shoe (1966), A Sword to Slice Through Mountains (1967)
Lewis Carroll Jabberwocky (1968)
Irmengarde Eberle Pete and the Mouse (1964)
Wilma Horsburgh The Bold Bad Bus (1973)
Peter Hughes The Oblong Pancake (1961), The King who Loved Candy (1962)
Ted Hughes Nessie the Mannerless Monster (1964)
Barbara Ireson The Gingerbread Man (1964), The Pied Piper (1968)
Paul Jennings The Great Jelly of London (1967)
James Joyce The Cat and the Devil (1964)
Jeremy Kingston The Bird who Saved the Jungle (1973)
Edward Lear The Dong with the Luminous Nose (1969)
Carol Odell Mark and his Pictures (1962)

Gerald Rose. 'He built a larger hutch and bought the best hay, oats and bran. Still the rabbit grew bigger.' From his *Rabbit Pie* (1980).

Linda Pender Dan McDougall and the Bulldozer (1963)
Elizabeth Rose Wuffles Goes to Town (1959), How St Francis Tamed the Wolf (1959), Old Winkle and the Seagulls (1960), Charlie on the Run (1961), The Big River (1962), Punch and Judy Carry On (1963), St George and the Fiery Dragon (1963), Good King Wenceslas (1964), The Magic Suit (1966), The Great Oak (1967), Alexander's Flycycle (1967), The Giant Marrow (1970), Androcles and the Lion (1971), Albert and the Green Bottle (1972), Lucky Hans (1976), The Sorcerer's Apprentice (1977)
Gerald Rose Ironhead (1970), Trouble in the Ark (1975), Watch Out (1977), Ahhh Said Stork (1978), The Tiger Skin Rug (1979), Polar Bear Takes a Holiday (1980), Rabbit Pie (1980)
Rosemary Weir Albert and the Dragonettes (1977)

References: Eyre; Hürlimann; ICB 3, 4

Robert Traill Rose (1863-1942)

Born Newcastle-on-Tyne, son of a book and stationery wholesaler. Studied at Edinburgh School of Art. He was deaf from childhood; work on munitions during World War I caused a serious breakdown in his health: he began to lose his sight in 1925 and was blind by 1933. Watercolourist, commercial engraver, lithographer, designer of bookjackets and lettering, illuminator. His lettering and calligraphy could be confident and effective, but his figure drawing was generally hesitant. His best work was in pen and ink (e.g. *The Book of Job,* 1902). John Russell Taylor described him as 'an uneven artist with mystical aspirations and an unreliable colour sense'.

Sheila Rose. From *Seraphina* by Mary K. Harris (Faber, 1960).

Books illustrated include:
Cardinal Newman The Dream of Gerontius (1910)
Grace Warrack Isles to the West of Bethlehem (nd)
The Book of Job (1902)
A Child's Dante (nd)
Edinburgh Vignettes (nd)
The Rubaiyat of Omar Khayyam (nd)
Old Testament Stories (nd)
Yuletide (nd)

References: Houfe; Johnson & Greutzner; Taylor; Wa (1929); Waters 1, 2; C. Wood; *The Studio* special (1911, Autumn 1914); James L. Carr *Scottish Painting Past and Present* (T.C. & E.C. Jack 1908); Mary T.S. Rose *Alexander Rose, Geologist, and his Grandson Robert Traill Rose* (C.J. Cousland, 1953)

Sheila Rose (active from 1955)

Illustrator of children's books in pen and brush in the sketchy style of the 1950s.

Books illustrated include:
Mabel Allan The House by the Marsh (1958)
M.E. Atkinson Riders and Raids (1955), Unexpected Adventure (1955), Horseshoes and Handle Bars (1958)
Roy Brown The Children's Pinocchio (1960)
Monica Edwards Killer Dog (1959)
Kathleen Fidler Police Dog (1966)
Mary K. Harris Emily and the Headmistress (1958), Seraphina (1960), Penny's Way (1963)
Margaret MacPherson Ponies for Hire (1967)
Joyce Stranger Circus All Alone (1965)
Ruth Tomalin The Sea Mice (1962)
Lorna Wood Holiday on Hot Bricks (1958)

Reference: Fisher p.322

Leonard Rosoman (b. 1913)

Born Hampstead, London, son of a company director. Educated at Deacon's School, Peterborough and at Durham University. Studied at the Royal Academy Schools (1935-36) and the Central School of Arts and Crafts (1936-37). He was in the Fire Service (1939-41), and was illustrator of the Home Office Fire Service Manual (1941-43), then official war artist to the Admiralty (1943-46). On the staff of Camberwell School of Art (1946-48), Edinburgh College of Art (Head of the Mural Painting Department 1948-56) and tutor at the Royal College of Art (since 1957). He has worked in Europe, North Africa, America, and the Far East. Rosoman regards his illustrative work as inseparable from his activity as a painter, and his work shows a consistent concern with the underlying problems of draughtsmanship. His controlled outlines are often supplemented with points or dotted lines to suggest surface variations or directional changes. His simplified line drawings for *My Friend Mr Leakey* are more decorative and humorously inconsequential in approach than his work for adult books. Elected ARA (1960), RA (1970). Awarded the OBE (1981). [Q]

Books illustrated include:
Michael Baldwin Grandad with Snails (1960)
J.B.S. Haldane My Friend Mr Leakey (1937)
Aldous Huxley Point Counter Point (1958), Brave New World (1971)
Laurie Lee As I Walked Out One Midsummer Morning (1969)

L.H. Rosoman. From *My Friend Mr Leakey* by J.B.S. Haldane (1937).

Wolf Mankowitz Make Me an Offer (1952)
Charles Louis Philippe Bubu of Montparnasse (1952)
Ian Serraillier Everest Climbed (1955)
R. L. Stevenson A Child's Garden of Verse (1960)
Donald Suddaby The Moon of Snowshoes (1956)
The Oxford Illustrated Old Testament (with others, 1968)

Periodical: Radio Times

References: Bénézit; Chamot, Farr & Butlin; Driver; Jacques; Parry-Crooke; Ryder; Usherwood; Vollmer; Wa (1980); Waters; *Art News* 45 (1946); *Emporium* 104 (1946); *Image* 3 (1949); *The Studio* 135 (1948), 155 (1958)

Gunther Victor Ross (1899-1963)

Born Gunther Victor Russ in Berlin, son of a shoe factory owner. Worked as Victor Ross. He studied art at the Munich Academy (1920-23). In 1938, he moved to England where he settled. During World War II, he was in the Pioneer Corps (attached to the Royal Engineers Camouflage) and served in England and Brittany. He subseqently worked as a freelance illustrator and designer, and whenever possible painted portraits, landscapes and miniatures. As an illustrator, he used lithography, crayon, pen and ink, and wash in work that often sympathetically and humorously recalled *la belle époque*. [Q]

Books illustrated include:
Margaret Black Two Young Explorers (1947)
C.G. Dobson A Century and a Quarter (1951)

John Mortimer English Fashion (1947)
J. Taylor Page Field Guide to British Deer (1959)
Powell Perry Three Perry Colour Books (1949)
Peter Pirbright Off the Beeton Track (1949)
George Augustus Sala Paris Herself Again (1948)
Mary Schroeder Open Your Eyes Series: First Family Tree (Book 2
    Part 1, 1958), Families Nearer Home (Book 2 Part 2, 1958),
    Messengers of Man (Book 4 Part 2, 1954)

Periodicals: Country Fair, Eagle, F.A. Annual, Girl, Lilliput, The
Strand Magazine

Reference: Wa (1966)

Tony Ross (b. 1938)

Born in London, son of a conjurer. Studied at
Liverpool College of Art (1956-61). Worked in
advertising (1961-65); lecturer at Manchester
Polytechnic since 1965. Illustrator and writer of
children's books, mainly published by the Andersen Press. His illustrations are composed with
care and wit; they are freely drawn in pen and ink
with washes of transparent colour. He also makes
animated films. He lives in Macclesfield, Cheshire.
[Q]

Books illustrated include:
Philip Curtis Mr Browser and the Brain Sharpeners (1979), Mr
    Browser Meets the Burrowers (1980), Mr Browser and the Comet
    Crisis (1981), Mr Browser and the Mini Meteorites (1982)
Patricia Gray and David Mackay The Monkeys and the Moon (1979),
    The Monkeys and the Gardener (1979)
Iris Grender Did I Ever Tell You...? (1977), The Second 'Did I Ever
    Tell You?' Book (1978), The Third 'Did I Ever Tell You?' Book
    (1980), Did I Ever Tell You About My Ir (1981), Did I Ever Tell
    You About My Birthday (1983)
J.K. Hooper Kaspar Klotz (1982)
Naomi Lewis Hare and the Badger Go to the City (1981)
Eric Morcambe The Reluctant Vampire (1982)
Tony Ross Mr Toffy series (6 titles 1973), Goldilocks and the Three
    Bears (1976), Hugo and the Man Who Stole Colours (1977), Pied
    Piper of Hamelin (1977), Norman and Flop Meet the Toy Bandit
    (1977), Hugo and the Wicked Winter (1977), Hugo and Oddsock
    (1978), The Greedy Little Cobbler (1979), Little Red Riding Hood
    (1979), Mother Goose (1979), Hugo and the Ministry of Holidays
    (1980), Jack and the Beanstalk (1980), Hare and Badger Go to the
    City (1981), Puss in Boots (1981), The Enchanted Pig (1982),
    Naughty Nigel (1982)
Jean Russell (ed) The Magnet Book of Strange Tales (1980), Book of
    Sinister Stories (1982)

Tony Ross. From *Fantastique Maître Renard* by
Roald Dahl (Gallimard, 1981).

Bernard Stone The Charge of the Mouse Brigade (1979), The Tale of
    Admiral Mouse (1981)

Periodicals: Esquire, Punch, Storyteller, Time and Tide, Town

Albert Daniel Rothenstein (1881-1953)

Worked as Albert Rutherston. Born in Bradford,
Yorkshire, brother of the painter William Rothenstein. Studied at the Slade School of Fine Art
(1898-1902). Initially an easel painter, he concentrated increasingly on the decorative arts,
working as a muralist, painter on silk, stage,
poster and card designer. He took up watercolour
painting in 1906 and etching in 1924. He changed
his name to Rutherston in 1914 and served in
Palestine during World War I. He became a close
friend of Claud Lovat Fraser* and collaborated
with him on a London Underground poster (1921).
Editor of *Contemporary British Artists* (1923-27).
Visiting lecturer in painting and drawing at Camberwell School of Art and Master of Ruskin School
of Drawing, Oxford (1929-48). Died in Switzerland. As an illustrator, he worked mainly for the
Curwen, Cresset, and Nonesuch Presses, using
pen and ink line with cross hatching, often adding

Albert Rutherston (Rothenstein). From *A Box of
Paints* by Geoffrey Scott (The Bookman's
Journal, 1923).

partial or linear colour in the manner pioneered by Claud Lovat Fraser. With this deceptively simple technique, he moved away from illusion towards a more purely decorative approach, reflecting a modernist concern for relationship between image, line and picture surface in drawings that were nevertheless notable for their light-hearted panache. Member NEAC (1905), ARWS (1934), RWS (c.1942).

Books illustrated include:
Thomas Balston (ed) Sitwelliana 1915-27 (1928)
Edmund Blunden Winter Nights (1928)
Pauline Chase Peter Pan's Postbag (1909)
Kathleen Colville Mr Marionette (1925), Jason and the Princess (1926)
F.J. Harvey Darton The London Review (1923)
Jean-Galli de Bibiena The Fairy Doll (1926-27)
Walter de la Mare To Lucy (1931)
Anne-Claude-Philippe de Tubières The Coachman's Story (1926-27)
Joseph Durey de Sauroy The Masked Lady (1926-27)
John Drinkwater Collected Poems (frontispiece, 2 vols 1923)
Ronald Firbank Inclination (frontispiece and tailpiece 1916)
Thomas Hardy Yuletide in a Younger World (1927)
Laurence E. Housman Angels and Ministers (1922)
Aldous Huxley Holy Face and Other Essays (1929)
Georgette Leblanc The Children's Blue Bird (1913)
Vera Mendel and F. Meynell The Week-End Book (1928)
Peter Quennell Inscription on a Fountain Head (1929)
Geoffrey Scott A Box of Paints (1923)
William Shakespeare The Tragedie of Cymbeline (1923)
Edith Sitwell Poor Young People (1925)
Humbert Wolfe Cursory Rhymes (1927)
Haggadah (Soncino Press, 1930)
Poetical Works of Robert Herrick (1928)

Periodicals: The Chapbook, The Gypsy, The New Broadside

References: Bénézit; Chamot, Farr & Butlin; Gilmour; Houfe; Johnson & Greutzner; Lewis; Thieme & Becker; Vollmer; Waters; *The Fleuron* 3 (1924); *The Studio* 86 (1923), 147 (1954), special (1927, Winter 1931); Stanley Casson *Artists at Work* (Harrap 1933); R.M.Y. Gleadowe *Albert Rutherston* (Ernest Benn 1935)

Harry Rountree (1878-1950)

Born Auckland, New Zealand, son of a banker. Worked as a lithographer in a commercial studio. Attracted by British illustration, he moved to London in 1910, where his work was noticed by S.H. Hamer, the editor of *Little Folks*. Working for books as well as magazines, he became known for his drawings of animals, which he drew with a keen eye for humorous detail. His distinctive style had a faintly *fin-de-siècle* flavour, with densely worked areas of deep shadow contrasting with 'bleached out' areas of light, creating an insistent surface pattern. He was a member of the London Sketch Club, and a friend of Harold Earnshaw*, with whom he played golf. He seems to have out-lived his popularity as an illustrator, and died in relative poverty at St Ives, Cornwall, where he is commemorated by a plaque on the harbour jetty.

Books illustrated include:
Charles Avery The Little Robinson Crusoes (1908)
Ross Balfour Animal Rhymes (1931)
Harry M. Batten Dramas of the Wild Folk (1924)
Charles S. Bayne My Book of Best Fairy Tales (1915)
Enid Blyton The Children of Cherry-Tree Farm (1940), The Children

of Willow Farm (1942)
Olwen Bowen Beetles and Things (1931)
A.D. Bright The Fortunate Princeling (1909)
Lewis Carroll Alice's Adventures in Wonderland (1908), Through the Looking Glass (1928)
John R. Crossland and J.M. Parrish The Children's Wonder Book (with others, 1933)
Bernard Darwin The Golf Courses of the British Isles (1910)
Gladys Davidson Tales from the Woods and Fields (1911)
Harold Dearden A Wonderful Adventure (1929)
Arthur Conan Doyle The Poison Belt (1913)
Alexandre Dumas The Dumas Fairy Tale Book (1924)
H. Fonhus The Trail of the Elk (1922)
S.H. Hamer Quackles, Junior (1903), Cheepy the Chicken (1904), Archibald's Amazing Adventure (1905), The Transformations of the Truefitts (1908), The Wonderful Isles (1908), The Enchanted Wood (1909), The Forest Foundling (1909), The Dolomites (1910), Four Glass Balls (1911), The Adventures of Spider & Co (1912), Peter Pink-Eye (1923)
Joel Harris Uncle Remus (1906)
Baldwin S. Harvey The Magic Dragon (1911)
Winifred Humphries Wog and Wig (1947)
J.R. Jefferies Bevis (1913)
J.H. Machair Animal Tales from Africa (1914)
L.G. Mainland True Zoo Stories (1924)
Olga Morgan Mr. Punch's Book of Birthdays (1906)
E. Nesbit Pug Tree (1905)
Albert B. Paine The Arkansaw Bear (1919)
Gwynedd Rae All Mary (1931)
Harry Rountree The Child's Book of Knowledge (1903), Birds, Beasts and Fishes (1929), Jungle Tales (1934), Rabbit Rhymes (1934)
Lynda Rountree Me and Jimmy (1929), Ronald, Rupert and Reg (1930), Dicky Duck and Wonderful Walter (1931)
Richard P. Russ Caesar: the Life Story of a Panda Leopard (1930)
F. Saint-Mars Pinion and Paw (1919)
Marjorie F. Seymour The Misadventures of Tootles and Timothy (1922)
Mabel H. Spielmann The Rainbow Book (1909)
A.J. Talbot The Pond Mermaid (1929)
Aesop's Fables (1924))

Periodicals: The Boy's Own Paper, The Bystander, The Captain, Cassell's Magazine, The Flag, The Girls' Realm, The Graphic, The Humorist, The Jolly Book, Little Folks, The London Magazine, London Opinion, The Odd Volume, The Pall Mall Magazine, Pearson's Magazine, Playtime, Printer's Pie, Punch, Radio Times, The Royal Magazine, The Sketch, The Strand Magazine, The Tatler, Toc H Annual, The Windsor Magazine, The Wonderland Annual

References: Bradshaw; Cuppleditch; Doyle BWI, CL; Driver; Houfe; ICB 1; Waters; *The Strand Magazine* 60 (1920); *The Studio* special (1911, Autumn 1914)

Gavin Richard Rowe (b. 1929)

Works as Gavin Rowe. Born in Portsmouth. Worked as an insurance clerk (1946-47) before studying at Croydon School of Art (1948-51) and at the Royal College of Art (1951-54). He taught at a Secondary Modern School in West Bromwich (1954-55), and has been Art Director at a large advertising agency since 1955 and part-time lecturer in illustration at Medway College of Design since 1970. Landscape painter, children's book and television illustrator (BBC *Jackanory* programme), book jacket designer. For colour work, he uses watercolour or gouache; for black and white, he draws in pen and ink, sometimes with washed-in or blotted black, or small patches of hatching to give texture or emphasis. He is interested in period subjects for illustration, and

Harry Rountree. From *Alice's Adventures in Wonderland* by Lewis Carroll (Odhams, 1933).

has illustrated over 60 books, including many educational titles for Edward Arnold, Oxford University Press, Ward Lock and Rupert Hart-Davis. [Q]

Books illustrated include:
Margaret Baker Prickets Way (1973)
Pamela Brown Family Playbill (1980)
Elizabeth Coatsworth The Sailing Hatrack (1972)
Mary Cockett Shadow at Applegarth (1981)
Vera Cumberledge Trapped by the Tide (1977)
Judith Drazin The Midsummer Picnic (1981)
Maureen Duffy Inherit the Earth (1980)
Frank Dunne Wexford Road (1979)
Winifred Finlay Ghosts, Ghouls and Spectres (1976), Spies and Secret
    Agents (1977), Clever and Courageous Dogs (1980), Children in
    in Peril (1981), Secret Rooms and Hiding Places (1982)
Nina Warner Hooke The Snow Kitten (1978)
Margaret Macpherson The Battle of the Braes (1972)
Christobel Mattingly Emu Kite (1972), The Jetty (1978)
Heather Moon Winkle Picker (1980), Winkle Picker Goes South
    (1982)
Freda Nicholls Back to the Blitz (1978)
E. Palmer Houdini Come Home (1981)
Richard Parker Paul and Elta (1972)
Joan Phipson Polly's Tiger (1973)
David Rees Landslip (1977)
Elizabeth Renier The Light Keepers (1977), The Stone People (1978),
    Dangerous Journey (1979), The Post Rider (1980)
Colin Thiele Albatross Two (1975)
Ruth Tomalin A Green Wishbone (1975)
Alison Uttley Stories for Christmas (1977)
*Ursula Moray Williams** Mrs Townsend's Robber (1971), Out of the
    Shadows (1971)

Periodical: Reader's Digest

Florence M. Rudland (active c.1895-1905)

Studied at the Birmingham School of Art during the mid-1890s and her work has featured in *The Studio* (volume 2) and in *The Yellow Book* (April 1896) in articles on the Birmingham School. Her illustrations for *Undine* (1897) were thoroughly 'Birmingham' in manner, but her later books also showed the influence of Kate Greenaway and Charles Robinson*. She was a talented illustrator whose output was regrettably meagre.

Books illustrated include:
F.H.C. de La Motte Fouqué Undine (1897)
Mrs Sherwood The Fairchild Family (1902)
The Old Oak Chest (1905)

Periodical: The Quest

References: Fisher pp.192-3; Houfe pp.166, 170

Jim Russell (b. 1933)

Born in Walsall, Staffordshire. Studied at Birmingham College of Art and then did National Service in Singapore. Painter, freelance illustrator, especially of books by James Webster for Hart Davis Educational. He works in full colour, using watercolour applied wet with painted-in white, and in black and white in fluid outline in pen or brush, sometimes with texture off-printed with fabric or white over-painting.

Books illustrated include:
William H. Armstrong Sounder (1973)
Petronella Breinburg What Happened at Rita's Party (1976)
Robert Leeson The Demon Bike Rider (1976)
Margaret Mahy David's Witch Doctor (1976)

Jim Russell. From *Sounder* by William H. Armstrong (Puffin, 1973).

Jan Mark Thunder and Lightning (1976)
Helen Morgan The Sketchbook Crime (1980)
J. P. Rutland Kites and Gliders (1977)
James Webster Beauty and the Bus (1978), The Letter (1978), Missing (1978), A Real Beauty (1978), The Secret Wish (1978), Beauty Bess and Bottle (1979), Copper (1979), The Man in the West (1979), Poached Eggs (1979), Pups! (1979)

Reference: ICB 4

Mary Georgina Russon (b. 1937)

Born in Birmingham. Trained as a nurse (1956-60) and then studied at Birmingham College of Art (1960-63). Book illustrator (1964-70), full-time art teacher in Birmingham (1971-79), and since then an occasional illustrator and advertising designer. As a book illustrator, she worked mainly for Hamish Hamilton and developed a particular admiration for the writing of William Mayne. She uses pen and ink for black and white illustration; for colour work, various combinations of gouache, inks, wax and gum are used. She lives in Birmingham. [Q]

Books illustrated include:
Prudence Andrew The Christmas Card (1966)
Margaret J. Baker The Gift Horse (1982)
Irene Dark World Dolls Series: Scotland
Kathleen Fidler Mountain Rescue Dog (1969)
Jacynth Hope-Simpson Escape to the Castle (1967)
Lace Kendall The Mud Ponies (1965)
Gillian Lindsay The Dormice Who Didn't (1980)
Margaret Lowe Tales of the Black and White Pig (1965)
Janet McNeill Tom's Tower (1965), The Battle of St George Without (1966), Goodbye Dove Square (1969)
William Mayne Pig in the Middle (1965), Rooftops (1966), The Battlefield (1967)
Christine Pullein Thompson Boys from the Cafe (1965)
Jenny Seed Peter the Gardener (1966), Stop Those Children (1966)
Joan Tate Letters to Chris (1967)
Mary Treadgold This Summer Last Summer (1968)
Geoffrey Trease The Runaway Serf (1968)
Henry Treece Bronze Sword (1965)
Barbara Willard The Pocket Mouse (1969)

References: ICB 3; *The Times Literary Supplement* (17th June 1965, 24th November 1966)

Anne Margaret Rutherford (b. 1932)

Works as Meg Rutherford. Married name: Mrs A.S. Goldingham. Born in Bathurst, New South Wales, Australia; grew up on her parents' farm. Studied sculpture at the East Sydney Technical College (1954) and at the Slade School of Fine Art, London (1958-61). Since then she has remained in England, initially supporting herself by mending antiques—particularly articulated toys and figures, as well as Japanese screens. She made and exhibited sculptures for eight years, then began illustrating and writing. Her work is usually in black and white, using a fine pen or scraperboard, but she now works increasingly in watercolour. For her first book, *The Beautiful Island* (1969), she used collage; this book was chosen as one of the fifty best books of 1970 by

Mary Russon. From *Pig in the Middle* by William Mayne (Hamish Hamilton, 1965).

the American Institute of Graphic Art. More recently *Tokoloshi* (1980) won the American Parents' Choice Award for the Best Illustration.

Books illustrated include:
Chaim Bermant Belshazzar (1979)
Paul Dinnage The Book of Fruit and Fruit Cookery (1981)
Roger Grounds The Private Life of Plants (1980)
Arthur Hellyer Practical Gardening Illustrated (1976)
Gladys Hutcheson The Flower Book (1979)
Marghanita Laski Ferry, the Jerusalem Cat (1983)
Yann Lovelock The Vegetable Book (1972)
Fiona Macdonald Little Bird, I Have Heard (1980)
Brian Patten The Elephant and the Flower (1970)
Diana Pitcher Tokoloshi (1980)
Roslyn Poignant Myths and Legends of the South Seas (1970)
Meg Rutherford The Beautiful Island (1969), A Pattern of Herbs (1975)
Percy Thrower Guide to Colour in Your Garden (1976)
Raymond Wilson Times Delights (1977)
Your Microwave Cookbook (1980)

Periodicals: Herbal Review, Sunday Times

Reference: Contemporary Authors

Albert Rutherston

See Albert Daniel Rothenstein.

Meg Rutherford. From her *The Beautiful Island* (Allen & Unwin, 1969)

John Gerald Christopher Ryan (b. 1921)

Works as John Ryan. Born in Edinburgh, son of a diplomat. Educated at Ampleforth College, York. Served in Burma during World War II. Studied at Regent Street Polytechnic (1945-48). Assistant art master at Harrow School (1948-55). Illustrator and writer of children's books, television cartoon designer, playwright. In his black and white strip-cartoon *Harris Tweed* in *Eagle*, he anticipated the *Captain Pugwash* scenario of an inept but conceited adult who unknowingly owes his success to the actions of a quick-witted and unselfish boy hero. He works in pen and ink outline, usually with the addition of one or more colours. [Q]

Books illustrated include:
John Ryan Captain Pugwash (1955), Pugwash Aloft (1958), Pugwash and the Ghost Ship (1962), Pugwash in the Pacific (1973), Pugwash and the Sea Monster (1976), Pugwash the Smuggler (1976), The Story of Tiger-Pig (1977), Dodo's Delight (1977), Doodle's Homework (1978), Tiger-Pig at the Circus (1978), All Aboard (1979), Crockle Saves the Ark (1979), Pugwash and the Buried Treasure (1980), Crockle Takes a Swim (1980), The Haunted Ark (1980), Roll-call on the Ark (1980), The Weather Forecast (1980), All Aboard (and twelve other Noah's Ark stories, 1980-82), Crockle Adrift (1981), Crockle and the Kite (1981), The Floating Jungle (1981), Mr Noah's Birthday (1981), Action Stations! (1982), The Frozen Ark (1982), Pugwash and the Fancy Dress Party (1982), Pugwash and the Mutiny (1982), Pugwash—The Quest of the Golden Handshake (1983)

Periodicals: The Catholic Herald, Eagle, Girl, Radio Times

References: Driver; Fisher p.59; ICB 4; Wa (1980)

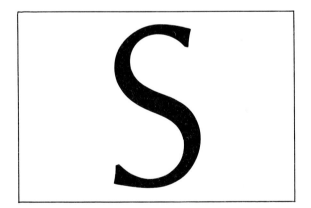

Hester Sainsbury (active 1920s)

Second wife of the Vorticist painter, architect, and publisher Frederick Etchells, for whom she often worked, sometimes as an illustrator. She was a wood and copper engraver and pen and ink draughtsman. Her delicate pen and ink drawings for *Hans Andersen's Tales* (1929), with their use of cross-hatching and hand-tinted partial colour, suggest the influence of Albert Rutherston*, while her white-line wood engravings, which are consciously primitive in approach and often

John Ryan. 'Captain Pugwash was still clinging on, quite safe...' from his *Pugwash Aloft* (Bodley Head, 1958).

executed with the use of the multiple graver, anticipated the work of Mary Groom*. Member SWE.

Books illustrated include:
Hans Christian Andersen Hans Andersen's Tales (1929)
Hilaire Belloc Mrs Markham's New History of England
A.F. The Ladies' Hand Book of Etiquette
Lord Holland Eve's Legend (1928)
A. Johnson Lucina Sine Concubitu (1930)
E.P. Mathers Eastern Love (1927)
P. Morand Earth Girdled (1928)
Ovid The Heroycall Epistles (1928)
Hester Sainsbury Holy Women, and other poems (1921), Meander Lane (1925), Noah's Ark (1926)
G. Saville The Lady's New-Year's-Gift (1927)
John Taylor A Dog of War (1927), Tales from the Brothers Grimm (1930)

Periodical: The Woodcut

References: Waters 2; *The Woodcut* 2 (1928); *The Studio* special (Spring 1927, Spring 1930, Winter 1931)

Balliol Salmon (1868-1953)

Studied at the West London School of Art, and for a year, under Fred Brown, at the Westminster School of Art, where fellow pupils included F.H. Townsend* and Fred Pegram*. With Pegram he afterwards spent 6 months working in Paris *ateliers*. He joined the staff of *The Pall Mall Budget*, where he worked on news illustrations in wash and pen and ink with E.J. Sullivan* and A.S. Hartrick*. Later he contributed theatrical drawings to *The Sporting and Dramatic News*, and society subjects to *The Graphic* (1899-1930). Percy Bradshaw recorded that he was particularly known for his 'Pretty Girl and Handsome Man' pictures. He

Balliol Salmon. 'Left alone, the two girls were not slow in discussing the wonderful news' from *The Jolliest Term on Record* by Angela Brazil (Blackie, 1915).

considered that Salmon possessed two particular claims to distinction as an artist—he popularised a new subject type 'the young lady of fifteen', and worked in a new medium, Russian charcoal which could only be used by artists without perspiring hands. Young ladies of fifteen figured prominently in Salmon's illustrations for Angela Brazil. He also frequently drew the popular, though slightly older, actresses Zena and Phyllis Dare.

Books illustrated include:
Angela Brazil The Jolliest Term on Record (1915), The Luckiest
Girl in the School (1916), The Madcap of the School (1917),
A Patriotic Schoolgirl (1918), For the School Colours (1918), The
Head Girl at the Gables (1919), A Popular Schoolgirl (1920)

Periodicals: Cassell's Family Magazine, The Graphic, The London
Magazine, The Ludgate Monthly, The New Budget, The Pall Mall
Budget, The Pall Mall Magazine, The Quiver, The Sporting and
Dramatic News, The Windsor Magazine

References: Bradshaw; Houfe; Thorpe; Waters; *The Artist* vol 4 nos 1-
4 (September-December 1932)

Lettice Sandford (b. 1902)

Born in St Albans, Hertfordshire. Studied at Chelsea School of Art (1926-29). She provided

wood, copper or zinc engravings for a number of books published by the Boar's Head Press and by the Golden Cockerel Press, of which her husband, Christopher Sandford, was director. Her wood engraving style varies from book to book, sometimes showing the influence of other engravers such as Blair Hughes-Stanton*, and Eric Ravilious*, but in spite of this, her work always had individual qualities, and was unpretentious and appealing. She wrote two children's books, *Roo Coo and Panessa* (1938) and *Coo My Doo* (1943) and illustrated them with flat colour and simplified outlines. She was also the author of a carefully researched book *Decorative Straw Work and Corn Dollies* (1964). [Q]

Books illustrated include:
Lucius Apuleius Cupid and Psyche (1934)
Barbara Bingley Tales of the Torquoise (1933), The Painted Cup
(1935)
Digby Haworth Booth Kleinias (1932)
E.M. Cox (trans) Sappho (1932)

Lettice Sandford. From *Sappho* translated by E.M. Cox (1932).

L. Cranmer-Byng Tomorrow's Star (1938)
Gérard de Nerval (trans V. Holland) Dreams and Life (1933)
Vadne Lascaris The Golden Bed of Kyno (1935)
F.L. Lucas (ed) The Golden Cockerel Greek Anthology (1937)
Marius Lyle The Virgin (1932)
Christopher Marlowe Hero and Leander (1933)
W.O.E. Oesterley (intro) Salome before the Head of St. John (1933),
   The Song of Songs (1936)
Christopher Sandford The Magic Forest (1931), Clervis and Belamie
   (1932)
Lettice Sandford Roo Coo and Panessa (1938), Coo my Doo (1943)
Walter Sidney Scott (ed) Letters of Maria Edgeware and Anna Letitia
   Barbauld (1933)
Edmund Spencer Thalamos (1932)
Christopher Whitfield Lady from Yesterday (1939)

References: Garrett BWE, HBWE; *Shall We Join the Ladies?* (Studio
One Gallery, Oxford, 1971); Christopher Sandford, *Bibliography of
Golden Cockerel Press* (Dawson 1975), *Cock-a-Hoop* (Private
Libraries Association 1976)

Reginald Savage (active 1898-1932)

Painter, graphic artist and wood engraver. He
was a member of Charles Ricketts's* circle, and
worked with C.R. Ashbee* at the Essex House
Press, designing and often engraving frontispieces
for volumes of poetry. According to C.J. Holmes
he 'displayed exceptional talent' but 'could not
remain content with the meagre rewards which
attend original design and scrupulous workman-
ship. To Ricketts's regret, he drifted off to make a
living as an illustrator in a manner much less
exacting and much better paid'. This profitable
later work has not yet been identified, but Savage
is recorded as teaching at Camberwell Art School
c.1910. Ashbee considered that Savage's style was
'peculiarly adapted to typographic illustration.
He has in his work that feeling of tapestry and
stained glass without colour which the wood-cut
designer is ever searching for; he has also a very
subtle and delicate sense of humour.' This was
particularly evident in his lively outline engravings
for *Miss Kilmansegg and her Precious Leg* (1904),
published by the Essex House Press.

Books illustrated include:
C.R. Ashbee The Abbots Court Papers (1932)
John Bunyan The Pilgrim's Progress (1899)
John Dryden Alexander's Feast (1904)
Robert Herrick Hesperides etc (1903)
Thomas Hood the Elder Miss Kilmansegg and her Precious Leg
   (1904)
John Keats The Eve of St Agnes (1900)
John Milton Comus (1902)
R.F. Sharp Wagner's Drama Der Ring des Nibelungen (1898)
Edmund Spenser The Epithalamion (1901),
A Book of Romantic Ballads (1901)
A Journal of the Life and Travels of John Woolman in the Service of
   the Gospels (1901)
Venus and Adonis (nd)

Periodicals: Black and White, The Butterfly, The Dial, Form, Fun,
The Golden Hind, The Ludgate Monthly, The Pageant, St Paul's, The
Venture

References: Houfe; Johnson & Greutzner; Pennell MI; Sketchley;
Thorpe; C. Wood; *The Studio* special (Spring 1930, Autumn 1914,
1923-24); C.R. Ashbee *The Private Press* (Essex House 1909); C.J.
Holmes *Self and Partners—Mostly Self* (Constable 1936)

Edith M.S. Scannell (active 1870-1921)

Painter of figures and portraits of children, whose
book illustrations consisted of idealised sketches,
mainly in crayon and wash.

Books illustrated include:
S.K. Cowan Play, a picture-book (1884)
E.M. Green The Child of the Caravan (1889)
E. Keary Pets and Playmates (1887)
Edith Scannell The Cousin from India (1919)
Edith Scannell and Florence Scannell The Highwaymen (1888)
Florence Scannell Sylvia's Daughters (1886), Cinderella's Sisters
   (1914)
M. Thornhill Indian Fairy Tales (1889)

References: Houfe; Johnson & Greutzner; Waters; C. Wood

Laurence Scarfe (b. 1914)

Born in Idle, Yorkshire. Studied at the Royal
College of Art (1933-37). Lecturer at Bromley
School of Art (1937-39), and at the Central School
of Arts and Crafts (1945-70). Mural painter, lithographer, commercial and graphic designer, art
editor of *The Saturday Book*; author of *Alphabets*,
a book on letter forms and typographic design.
Regular illustrator for the *Radio Times* and his
own books on Rome and Venice in pen and ink—
Rome with tautly drawn drawn detail, *Venice* in a
looser, less finished style. Member of the Senefelder Club and the Society of Mural Painters;
elected FSIA.

Books illustrated include:
Laurence Scarfe Rome, Fragments in the Sun (1950), Venice, the Lion
   and the Peacock (1952)

Periodical: Radio Times

References: Driver; Jacques; Johnson & Greutzner; Usherwood; Wa
(1980); Waters

Randolph Schwabe (1885-1948)

Born in Manchester, son of a cotton merchant.
Studied at the Royal College of Art, the Slade
School of Fine Art (1900-05) and the Académie Julian in Paris (1906). Official war artist during World
War I. Taught at Camberwell and Westminster
Schools of Art and the Royal College of Art. He
was Slade Professor from 1930 to 1948. As a book
illustrator he worked principally for the Beaumont Press. His draughtsmanship was based on
the example of the early Renaissance and he
handled pen and ink with sensitivity and precision. Writing about his work in 1924, R.H.
Wilenski observed, 'when he draws from nature,
he never falls into the vulgar habit of depicting
phenomena by copying the accidental shapes and
sizes of the shadows. He is not content to record
the appearances of things in light. Casual appearance is corrected and adjusted by the mind.
Schwabe's outlook is equable and surely poised.
He eschews the fantastic, the exotic, the bizarre.'

Died in Helensburgh, Scotland. Elected member of the London Group (1915), NEAC (1917), ARWS (1938), RWS (1942).

Books illustrated include:
H.E. Bates The Tinkers of Elstow (1946)
C.W. Beaumont Theory and Practice of Allegro in Classical Ballet (1930)
C.W. Beaumont and S. Idzikowski A Manual of the Theory and Practice of Classical Theatrical Dancing (1922)
Edmund Blunden To Nature (1923), Masks of Time (1925), A Summer's Fancy (1930), To Themis (1931)
John Clare Madrigals and Chronicles (1924)
Walter de la Mare Crossings (1921)
Robert Lloyd The Actor (1926)
W.S. Maugham Of Human Bondage (1936)
Arthur Symons The Café Royal and other essays (1929)
Henry Williamson The Wet Flanders Plain (1929)
The Curwen Press Almanack (1926)

Periodicals: The Apple, Fanfare

References: Bénézit; Chamot, Farr & Butlin; DNB (1901-50); Houfe; ICB 1; Johnson & Greutzner; Thieme & Becker; Vollmer Wa (1934); Waters; *Drawing and Design* (January 1925); *The Studio* 105 (1933), special (1923-24, 1927, Winter 1931, Autumn 1938); R.H.W. [Wilenski] *Draughtsmen* (Benn 1924)

Allen William Seaby (1867-1953)

Born in London, son of a cabinet maker. Studied under F. Morley Fletcher at Reading University School of Art, where he later became Professor of Fine Art (1920-33). Writer and illustrator of books on art techniques and art history (mainly published by Batsford), of historical stories for children and books about animals; also an illustrator of ornithological subjects. His illustration work is mainly in pen and ink in a competent but surprisingly run-of-the-mill style considering his professional status. He was well known for his colour wood engravings, lino cuts and painting in watercolour. Member of the Society of Animal Painters, the Society of Graver Printers in Colour and the Colour Woodcut Society. He lived in Reading.

Books illustrated include:
Primrose Cumming Doney (1934)
F.B.B. Kirkman British Birds (1913)
A.W. Seaby Art in the Life of Mankind (4 vols 1928-31), Exmoor Lass (1928), The Birds of the Air (1931), Omrig and Nerla (1934), Dinah, the Dartmoor Pony (1935), British Ponies (1936), Sons of Skewbald (1937), Sheltie (1939), The White Buck (1939), The Ninth Legion (1943), Purkess the Charcoal Burner (1946), Alfred's Jewel (1947), Mona, the Welsh Pony (1948), Pattern without Pain (1948), Blondel the Minstrel (1951)
Sir William Thomas and A.K. Collett The English Year (1913)

References: Bénézit; Johnson & Greutzner; Mallalieu; Thieme & Becker; Vollmer; Waters; Allen Seaby *Colour Printing with Linoleum and Wood Blocks* (Dryad 1928)

Edward Brian Seago (1910-74)

Worked as Edward Seago. Born in Norwich. Suffered from a mysterious, intermittent heart complaint for most of his life and, confined to bed for much of his childhood, had little formal education. However, he won a Royal Drawing Society

Edward Seago. From *The Rabbit Skin Cap* by George Baldry (Boydell, 1939).

Prize at the age of 14 and later studied privately under the landscape painter Bernard Priestman RA. He spent several years travelling with circuses in Britain and abroad (1928-33), exhibiting circus drawings and paintings, but subsequently became known as a landscape, portrait and animal painter. Many of his book illustrations were in fact reproductions of his drawings and paintings with accompanying texts. Elected RBA (1946), and RWS (1959).

Books illustrated include:
George Baldry The Rabbit Skin Cap (1939)
H. Rider Haggard (ed) I Walked by Night (1935)
John Masefield The Country Scene (1937), Tribute to Ballet (1938), A Generation Risen (1942)
Edward Seago Circus Company (1933), Sons of Sawdust (1934), Peace in War (1943), High Endeavour (1944), With Capricorn to Paris (1956)

References: Bénézit; Johnson & Greutzner; Vollmer; Wa (1972); Waters; J.C. Wood; *The Studio* 148 (1954); Jean Goodman *Edward Seago* (Collins 1978); Edward Seago *A Canvas to Cover* (Collins 1947), *A Review of the Years 1953-1964* (Collins 1965)

Ronald William Fordham Searle (b. 1920)

Works as Ronald Searle. Born in Cambridge. Studied at Cambridge School of Art (1936-39). Served in the army during World War II and was interned in Japanese PoW camps in Siam and Malaysia for three and a half years. On his release, he settled in London and began working as a humorous illustrator and caricaturist for books and magazines, including *Punch* and *Lilliput*. In 1959, at the invitation of the United Nations' High Commissioner for Refugees, he visited camps in Austria, Italy and Greece, and published a book illustrating his impressions. The following year he settled in France, where he still lives. Searle has illustrated over 60 books. *Hurrah for St. Trinian's!* (1948) was among the first of many giving a mock-horrific view of private schools and their denizens; in these and many of his other books, the predominant mood of effervescent humour is offset by sinister or macabre overtones.

He early developed a fanciful and strikingly individual graphic manner, subjecting the human form to grotesque distortions (bristling brows, hunched shoulders, matchstick legs and stiletto feet) and by the mid 1950s had become virtually a household name in Britain. He succeeds both at character-invention (favouring a number of well-defined 'types') and at caricature. He is also a painter in watercolour and gouache, etcher and lithographer and has worked on several films including *Those Magnificent Men in Their Flying Machines* (1965).

Books illustrated include:
A. Atkinson and R. Searle The Big City (1958), U.S.A. for Beginners (1959), Russia for Beginners (1960), Escape from the Amazon (1964)
I. Barnett Exploring London (1965)
L. Beebe The Savoy of London (1964)
R. Braddon The Piddingtons (1950), The Naked Island (1952)
W. Henry Brown Co-Operation in a University Town (1939)
Patrick Campbell A Long Drink of Cold Water (1949), An Irishman's Diary (1950), A Short Trot with a Cultured Mind (1950), Life in Thin Slices (1951), Patrick Campbell's Omnibus (1954)
F. Carpenter Six Animal Plays (1953)
William Cowper John Gilpin (1952)
Charles Dickens A Christmas Carol (1961), Great Expectations (1962), Oliver Twist (1962)
Kildare Dobbs The Great Fur Opera (1970)
Winifred Ellis London so help me! (1952)
Christopher Fry An Experience of Critics (1952), A Phoenix Too Frequent (1959)
Douglas Goldring Life Interests (1948)
G. Gorer Modern Types (1955)
Robert Graves The Anger of Achilles (1959)
Ronald Hastain White Coolie (1947)
R. Haydn The Journal of Edwin Carp (1954)
H. Hearson and J. Trewin An Evening at the Larches (1951)
Audrey Hilton (ed) This England: 1946-1949 (1949)
W.E. Stanton Hope Tanker Fleet (1948)
Heinz Huber Haven't we met somewhere before? (1966)

Ronald Searle. 'molesworth 2 zoom down with his rotors whirring' from *Molesworth's Guide to the Atommic Age* by Geoffrey Willans (Vanguard Press, 1956).

Noel Langley The Inconstant Moon (1949)
Mass Observation Meet Yourself at the Doctor's (1949), Meet Yourself on Sunday (1949)
Gillian Oliver Turn but a Stone (1949)
Denys Parsons It Must Be True (1953)
O. Philpot Stolen Journey (1950)
G. Rainbird The Subtle Alchemist (1973)
B. Richardson and A. Andrews Those Magnificent Men in their Flying Machines (1965)
Ronald Searle Forty Drawings (1946), Hurrah for St. Trinian's! (1948), The Female Approach (1949), Back to the Slaughterhouse (1951), Souls in Torment (1953), The Rake's Progress (1955), Merry England etc. (1955), Which Way Did He Go? (1961), From Frozen North to Filthy Lucre (1964), Searle's Cats (1967), The Square Egg (1968), Hello—where did all the people go? (1969), Secret Sketchbook (1970), The Addict (1971), More Cats (1975), Drawings from Gilbert & Sullivan (1975), Searle's Zodiac (1977), Ronald Searle (Monograph, 1978), The King of the Beasts (1980), The Big Fat Cat Book (1982)
Irwin Shaw Paris! Paris! (1977)
Reuben Ship The Investigator (1956)
W.M. Thackeray Mr. Robert Brown at the Club (1953)
James Thurber The thirteen Clocks and the Wonderful O (1962)
Kaye Webb and R. Searle Paris Sketchbook (1950), Looking at London (1953), The St Trinians Story (1959), Refugees (1960)
Geoffrey Willans Down with Skool (1953), How to be Topp (1954), Whizz for Atomms (1956), The Compleat Molesworth (1958), The Dog's Ear Book (1958), Back in the Jug agane (1959)
D.B. Wyndham Lewis and R. Searle The Terror of St. Trinian's (1952), Take One Toad (Dobson 1968)

Periodicals: Ark, Ballet, Le Canard Enchaîné (France), Fortune, Holiday Magazine, Jours de France, Life, Lilliput, The New Yorker, New York Times, Punch, Réalités, The Saturday Book, The Strand Magazine

References: Bénézit; Driver; ICB 2; Jacques; Price; Usherwood; Vollmer; Wa (1980); WaG; Waters; *Art News* (3 June 1950); *Studio International* 165 (1963); *Ronald Searle. 100 Blätter aus den Jahren 1965-1975* (Catalogue Staatliche Museum, Berlin 1976); *The Penguin Ronald Searle* (1960); *Searle in the 'Sixties* (Penguin 1964); Henning Bock (intro) *Ronald Searle* (Deutsch 1978); William Feaver *Masters of Caricature* (Weidenfeld & Nicolson 1981)

Mark Fernand Severin (b. 1906)

Often works as Mark Severin. Born Brussels, son of the poet F. Severin. During World War I, he lived as an exile in Oxford. Studied at Ghent University. Art Director at Messrs Carron Ltd, London (1932-37). Subsequently worked as a freelance painter, advertising and bookplate designer, and book illustrator for Belgian and English publishers including the Golden Cockerel Press. He took up copper and wood engraving in 1940 and illustrated many books in these media. P.R. Gauguin commends 'his unerring instinct for the fertile beauty of the naked human body' in his treatment of erotic motifs. Professor at the Institut Supérieur des Beaux Arts, Antwerp (1948-72) and at the Institut des Hautes Etudes Typographiques Plantin (from 1956). Member of the National Registry of Designers and the Belgian Royal Academy, Grand Officer of the Order of Leopold, and Officer of the Order of Leopold II, and Grand Officer of the Order of the Crown. [Q]

Books illustrated include:
William Browne Circe and Ulysses (1954)
Théophile Gautier (trans R.& E. Powys Mathers) Mademoiselle de Maupin (1948)
Herodotus (trans Paul Turner) Apollonius of Tyre (1956)

F.L. Lucas (ed) The Homeric Hymn to Aphrodite (1948)
Patrick Miller Woman in Detail (1947)
Ihara Saikaku (trans William Theodore de Burg) Five Japanese Love
    Stories (1958)
Ian Serraillier Thomas and the Sparrow (1946) The Tale of the
    Monster Horse (1950), The Ballad of Kon Tiki and other verses
    (1952), Beowulf the Warrior (1954)
Mark Severin The Month of Venus (nd)
Mark Severin and A. Reid Engraved Bookplates (1972)

Periodicals: The Bystander, The Sketch

References: ICB 2; Vollmer; Wa (1980); *Book Design and Production*
33 (1960); *The Studio* 131 (1946); P.R. Gauguin *Mark F. Severin* (Dan
and Ery, Copenhagen 1952); Christopher Sandford *Bibliography of the
Golden Cockerel Press* (Dawson 1975); *Cock-a-Hoop* (Private
Libraries Association 1976)

Prudence Eaton Seward (b. 1926)

Born in London, daughter of a wine merchant.
Studied at Harrow School of Art (1945-46) and
the Royal College of Art (1947-49). Rome Scholarship in engraving (1949-51). Etcher, watercolourist,
freelance illustrator of children's and educational
books (1952-75). Since 1975 she has been working
on paper conservation. She was awarded the
Diploma in Conservation of Prints and Drawings
at Camberwell School of Arts and Crafts (1979).
Her book illustrations, in pen and ink, sometimes
with colour, are in the free, sketchy style that
became popular during the 1950s, and are often
boldly decorative in treatment. Elected ARWS,
ARE (1949). [Q]

Books illustrated include:
Ruth Ainsworth Three's Company (1974)
Eileen Bell Tales from End Cottage (1970), More Tales from the End
    Cottage (1972)
Bruce Carter Tricycle Time (1957), The Night of the Flood (1959),
    Ballooning Boy (1960), The Playground (1964)
John Cunliffe The Farmer, the Books and the Cherry Tree (1974)
Lavinia Derwent Song of Sula (1976)
Joyce Donoghue Playtime Stories (1974)
Dorothy Edwards Listen and Play Rhymes I and II (1973), Look,
    Look my Garden Book (1973), Look, Look a Cookery Book (1973)
Penelope Farmer Saturday Shillings (1965)
Rumer Godden Candy Floss and Impunity Jane (1975)
Jacynth Hope-Simpson The Stranger in the Train (1960)

Prudence Seward. From *Tales from the End
Cottage* by Eileen Bell (Penguin, 1970).

Marie Hynds The Golden Apple (1976)
William Mayne The Man from the North Pole (1963), On the Stepping
    Stones (1963)
Richard Parker The Three Pebbles (1954), New Home South (1961),
    The House that Guilda Built (1963), The Boy who Wasn't Lonely
    (1964)
Elizabeth Roberts All About Simon and his Grandmother (1973)
Joan Gale Robinson Charley (1969)
Diana Ross The Dreadful Boy (1959)
Ian Serraillier Thomas and the Sparrow (1946), The Ballad of Kon-
    Tiki and Other Verses (1952), The Windmill Book of Ballads (with
    Mark Severin*, 1962)
David Severn The Green-Eyed Gryphon (1958)
David Taylor Zoovet: The World of a Wildlife Vet (1976)
Barbara Euphan Todd The Wizard and the Unicorn (1957)
Nancy Tuft Scruff's New Home (1978)
Elfrida Vipont The Pavillion (1969)
Priscilla Warner The Paradise Summer (1963)
Ursula Moray Williams High Adventure (1965)

Periodical: Radio Times

References: Fisher p.65; ICB 4; Wa (1980); Waters

John Byam Liston Shaw (1872-1919)

Often worked as Byam Shaw. Born Madras,
India, son of a High Court Registrar; the family
returned to England in 1878. Studied at St John's
Wood School of Art and at the Royal Academy
Schools (1890-93), then shared a studio with
former fellow-student Gerald Metcalfe*. He contributed to magazines from the early 1890s and
was active as a book illustrator from 1895, and
from early in his career he adopted the practice of
devoting every evening to black and white graphic
work. He joined the staff of King's College London (1903), and as co-founder of the Byam Shaw
and Vicat Cole School of Art in Kensington, London (1910). As a painter, illustrator and designer
he was industrious, prolific and showed great
technical assurance, and his essentially bourgeois
viewpoint ensured a steady flow of commissions.
A contemporary, Charles Holmes, wrote that
Shaw was admirably equipped as an illustrator 'by
the breadth of his sympathies and his happy in-
tuitions for character and for the romantic and
dramatic elements in any situation or story...'
(*Modern Pen Drawings. The Studio Special* 1900-
01.) More recently, John Russell Taylor has referred to his 'rather vulgar panache', while Houfe
points out that his strength lay in his page arrange-
ments rather than in his imaginative capabilities.
Elected RI (1898), ROI (1899), ARWS (1913).

Books illustrated include:
E.T. Atkinson A Garden of Shadows (1907)
Robert Browning Poems (1897)
John Bunyan The Pilgrim's Progress (1904)
Sir H.F. Burke Coronation Book (c.1902), Garter King of Arms
    (1904)
Benjamin Disraeli Young England (1904)
Prof. H.J.C. Grierson Tennyson, Selected Poems (1907)
J.C. Hadden The Operas of Wagner (1908), Favourite Operas from
    Mozart to Mascagni (1910)
Hippocrates Junior The Predicted Plague (1899)
Lawrence Hope The Garden of Kama (1914)
Joseph Jacobs Tales from Boccaccio (1899)
Charles and Mary Lamb Tales from Shakespeare (1903)

Byam Shaw. From *King Cole's Book of Nursery Rhymes* (nd).

Edgar Allan Poe Selected Tales of Mystery (1909)
Charles Reade The Cloister and the Hearth (1909)
Dante Gabriel Rossetti The Blessed Damozel (1906)
William Shakespeare The Chiswick Shakespeare (1899), Bell's
   Shakespeare for Schools (1914)
Byam Shaw Life's Ironies (1912)
F. Sidgwick Ballads and Lyrics of Love (1908), Legendary Ballads
   (1908)
Flora Steel The Adventures of Akbar (1913)
King Cole's Book of Nursery Rhymes (nd)
Stories from Wagner (1909)

Periodicals: Black and White, Cassell's Family Magazine, Comic Cuts,
The Connoisseur, Country Life, The Dome, The Field, The Flag, The
Graphic, The Idler, Illustrated Bits, The Ladies' Field, Moonshine,
The Pall Mall Magazine, Punch, The Sphere

References: Bénézit; DNB (1912-21); Houfe; ICB 1; Johnson &
Greutzner; Mallalieu; Peppin; Ray; Taylor; Thieme & Becker;
Thorpe; Waters; C. Wood; *The OWS Club Volume* 22; *The Studio* 10
(1897), 76 (1919), special (1898-99, 1900-01, Autumn 1914, 1923-24);
R.V. Cole *The Art and Life of Byam Shaw* (Seeley, Service & Co.
1932)

Ernest Howard Shepard (1879-1976)

Worked as E.H. Shepard. Born St. John's Wood,
London, son of an architect. Educated at St
Paul's School. Studied at Heatherley's Art School
(1896-97) and at the Royal Academy Schools
(1897-1902) where he won two scholarships. In
1907, the acceptance of two drawings by Punch
marked the beginning of a nearly 50-year association with the magazine; he was elected to the
table in 1921, becoming second cartoonist in 1935
and principal cartoonist, 1945-49. During World
War I he served in France, Belgium and Italy. A
highly successful and prolific book illustrator,
mainly in black and white, his collaboration
with A.A. Milne resulted in a series of children's
classics; in the words of his obituary in *The Times*
'the Pooh drawings were his greatest triumph,
perhaps because his own human and unassuming
genius was so much in harmony with the tender
facetiousness of his fellow-contributor to *Punch...*
He was perhaps the best-loved illustrator of children's books since Sir John Tenniel.

Shepard was an inveterate sketcher, and although his finished drawings were usually the
outcome of numerous pencil sketches, they always
retained an appearance of spontaneity. He used
pen and ink with exceptional flexibility, varying
the weight and quality of his line for emphasis and
expression. He excelled at depicting movement,
and had a fine instinct for characterisation.
Although best known for his association with
A.A. Milne, Shepard successfully illustrated a
wide range of books. His drawings for *The Wind
in the Willows* were the only ones that the author,
Kenneth Grahame, ever liked, while his illustrations for *Everybody's Pepys* and *Everybody's
Boswell* demonstrated that he could handle adult
historical subjects with aplomb. Late in life he
illustrated his own autobiographical reminiscenses
Drawn from Memory (1957) and *Drawn from
Life* (1961) with undiminished liveliness and
humour. Bevis Hillier described Shepard as 'the
perfect illustrator... He never allows his personality to obtrude. He translates, never transmutes'
(*The Work of E.H. Shepard,* ed. Rawle Knox).
His daughter, Mary Shepard* also became an
illustrator. Awarded OBE (1972).

Books illustrated include:
Georgette Agnew Let's Pretend (1927)
Hans Andersen Fairy Tales (1961)
F.H. Burnett The Secret Garden (1956)
Patrick Chalmers The Cricket in the Cage (1933)
Susan Colling Frogmorton (1955)
Charles Dickens The Holly Tree and other Stories (1926)
John Drinkwater Christmas Poems (1931)
J.H. Ewing The Brownies (1954)
Eleanor Farjeon The Silver Curlew (1953), The Glass Slipper (1955)
Winifred Fortescue Perfume from Provence (1935)
Kenneth Grahame The Golden Age (1928), Dream Days (1930), The
   Wind in the Willows (1931), The Reluctant Dragon (1938), Bertie's
   Escapade (1945)
Roger Lancelyn Green Modern Fairy Stories (1955), Old Greek Fairy
   Tales (1958)
Laurence Housman The Goblin Market (1933), Victoria Regina
   (1934), The Golden Sovereign (1937), The Gracious Majesty (1941)
Thomas Hughes Tom Brown's Schooldays (c.1904)
E.V. Isaacs The Little One's Log (1927)
Richard Jefferies Bevis (1932)
Dr Johnson The Great Charm (1933)
E.V. Lucas As the Bee Sucks (1937)
George MacDonald At the Back of the North Wind (1956)
A.A. Milne When We Were Very Young (1924), Winnie-the-Pooh
   (1926), Now We Are Six (1927), The House at Pooh Corner (1928)
F.V. Morley (ed) Everybody's Boswell (1930)
Mrs Molesworth The Cuckoo Clock (1954)
O.F. Morshead (ed) Everybody's Pepys (1927)

E.H. Shepard. From *When We Were Very Young* by A.A. Milne (Methuen, 1924).

Roland Pertwee The Islanders (1950)
E.V. Rieu The Flattered Flying Fish (1962)
Malcolm Saville Susan and Bill Books (1954-56)
E.H. Shepard Ben and Brock (1965), Betsy and Joe (1966)
Sir J.C. Squire Cheddar Gorge (1937)
Jan Struther Sycamore Square and other verses (1932), The Modern Struwwelpeter (1936)
Hugh Walpole Jeremy (1919)
A.C. Ward (ed) Everybody's Lamb (1933)

Periodicals: The Graphic, The Illustrated London News, Nash's Magazine, The Odd Volume, Pear's Annual, Printer's Pie, Punch, The Sketch

References: Crouch; Doyle CL; Eyre; Fisher pp.43, 352, 375, 381; Houfe; ICB 1,2,3,4; Johnson; Johnson & Greutzner; Price; Vollmer; Wa (1934); Waters 1&2; C. Wood; *The Artist* (May 1941); *The Studio* special (Autumn 1938) *The Times* (obituary 26th March 1976); Rawle Knox (ed) *The Work of E.H. Shepard* (Methuen 1979); R.G.G. Price *A History of Punch* (1957); E.H. Shepard, *Drawn from Memory* (Methuen 1957), *Drawn from Life* (Methuen 1961)

Mary Eleanor Shepard (b. 1909)

Born in Surrey, daughter of E.H. Shepard*. She studied at the Slade School of Fine Art under Professor Tonks and Randolph Schwabe*. In 1937 she married E.V. Knox ('Evoe'), editor of *Punch*. Etcher and illustrator, best known for her lively pen and ink drawings for the *Mary Poppins* books (several of which were first published in New York). Her style has some affinities with that of her father.

Books illustrated include:
Ruth Manning-Sanders Adventure Maybe Anywhere (1938), Children by the Sea (1938)
A.A. Milne Prince Rabbit (1966)
P.L. Travers Mary Poppins (1934), Mary Poppins Comes Back (1935), Mary Poppins Opens the Door (1944), Mary Poppins in the Park (1952), Mary Poppins from A-Z (1963)

References: Fisher p.217; ICB 2, 3; Rawle Knox (ed) *The Work of E.H. Shepard* (Methuen 1979)

James Affleck Shepherd (1867-1946)

Born London. Studied and worked for two years under Alfred Bryan, cartoonist of the magazine *Moonshine*. He was an animal painter and a writer, but was best known for his humorous black and white line drawings of animals with human clothing and personalities. He first made his name with his popular series of *Zig Zag Fables*, published in the *The Strand Magazine,* and immediately afterwards (in 1893), joined the staff of *Punch*, continuing as a contributor for the next forty years. At their best his drawings, which were often in outline, displayed remarkable style and wit. Thorpe considered that 'Shepherd's drawings of animals are the best and funniest that have ever been made'. In later years he worked at Charlwood, Surrey.

Books illustrated include:
A.S.M. Chester Tommy at the Zoo (1895)
E.W.D. Cumming Wonders in Monsterland (1901), The Three Jovial Puppies (1908), The Bodley Head Natural History (1913), Idlings in Arcadia (1934)
E.W.D. Cumming and J.A. Shepherd The Arcadian Calendar (1903)
W. Garstang Songs of the Birds (1922)
J.C. Harris Uncle Remus (1901), Nights with Uncle Remus (1907)
J. Mills The Life of a Foxhound (1910)
A. Morrison Zig-Zags at the Zoo (1895)
E. Rostand The Story of Chanticleer (1913)
E. Selous Jack's Insects (1910), The Zoo Conversation Book (1911), Jack's Other Insects (1920)
J.A. Shepherd Zig-Zag Fables (1897), A Frog He Would A-Wooing Go (1900), Who Killed Cock Robin! (1900), The Donkey Book (1903), Funny Animals and Stories About Them (1904), A Frolic Round the Zoo (1926), Animal Caricature (1936)

Raymond Sheppard. From *The Old Man and the Sea* by Ernest Hemingway (Cape, 1952).

Claude A. Shepperson. 'We'd hunt down love together...' from *The Open Road* by E.V. Lucas (1899).

S. Townsend A Throrough-Bred Mongrel (1900)
A.O. Vaughan Old Hendrick's Tales (1904)

Periodicals: Black and White, The Boy's Own Paper, Cassell's Family Magazine, Chums, Good Words, Holly Leaves, Judy, Moonshine, Punch, The Strand Magazine

References: Bénézit; Hammerton; Houfe; ICB 1; Spielmann; Thieme & Becker; Thorpe; Waters; *Cassell's Family Magazine* 22 (1895-96); *The Ludgate* 2 (1897); *The Strand Magazine* 54 (1917); *The Studio* special (1900-01, 1911, Autumn 1928)

Raymond Sheppard (1913-58)

Born London, studied at Bolt Court. Painter in watercolour and oil, draughtsman in pastel, pencil and pen and ink. His book illustrations in pencil or pen and ink, demonstrated his ability as a confident representational draughtsman. Elected SGA (1947), PS (1948), RI (1949). Lived in Middlesex.

Books illustrated include:
Joseph Chipperfield Beyond the Timber Trail (1951)
J. Corbett Tree Tops (1955)
M. Edwin Round the Year Stories (1942)
Ernest Hemingway The Old Man and the Sea (with C. Tunnicliffe*, 1952)
Laurence Meynell Animal Doctor (1956)
Raymond Sheppard How to Draw Birds (1940), Drawing at the Zoo (1949), More Birds to Draw (1956)

References: ICB 2; Wa (1958); Waters

Claude Allin Shepperson (1867-1921)

Born Beckenham, Kent. Initially a law student, he studied art at Heatherley's School of Art and

in Paris. Painter in oil and watercolour, lithographer, etcher, draughtsman in pastel and black and white. His early book illustrations were accomplished and realistic in the manner of his *Punch* colleagues Fred Pegram* and F.H. Townsend*. Later, and especially in the pages of *Punch*, he specialised in Society Scenes based on sketches from life in Kensington Gardens and elsewhere in the West End), drawn with great elegance in a hazy and slightly elongated manner and often featuring the 'Shepperson Girl' who embodied every contemporary notion of aristocratic refinement. Elected ARWS (1910), ARA (1919), ARE (1921), RI (1900-05), RMS (1900), member of the London Sketch Club.

Books illustrated include:
George Borrow Lavengro (1899 or 1900)
Robert Burns Poetical Works (1909)
Benjamin Disraeli Coningsby (1900)
G. Goodchild Caravan Days (1916)
J.M. Leigh Hunt The Old Court Suburb (1902)
John Keats Poetical Works (1916)
E.V. Lucas The Open Road (1899)
E. Nesbit Nine Unlikely Tales for Children (with H.R. Millar*, 1901)
E. Phillpotts Up-Along and Down-Along (1905)
Walter Scott The Heart of Mid Lothian (1900)
William Shakespeare As You Like it (1900), The Merchant of Venice (1899), The Swan Shakespeare (1900)
Stanley J. Weyman Shrewsbury (1898)
Kate D. Wiggin The Diary of a Goose-Girl (1902)

Periodicals: Black and White, Cassell's Family Magazine, The English Illustrated Magazine, Harmsworth's Magazine, The Idler, Illustrated Bits, The Illustrated London News, The Pall Mall Magazine, Pear's Annual, Pick-Me-Up, Punch, The Queen, St Paul's, The Sketch, The Sphere, The Strand Magazine, The Tatler, The Wide World Magazine The Windsor Magazine

References: Baker; Bénézit; Bradshaw; Cuppleditch; Guichard; Houfe; Johnson & Greutzner; Mallalieu; Price; Sketchley; Thieme & Becker; Thorpe; Waters; C. Wood; *Art Journal* (1898); *Drawing and Design* 18 (October 1921); *The Ludgate* 2 (1897); *The Print Collector's Quarterly* 10; *The Studio* 76 (1919), special (1917, 1919, Spring 1922); G. Montague Ellwood *The Art of Pen Drawing* (Batsford 1927)

George Sheringham (1884-1937)

Born in London. Educated at the King's School, Gloucester; studied at the Slade School of Fine Art (1899-1901) and in Paris (1904-06). Designer of posters and textiles, stage designer, muralist, landscape painter, and decorator of fans. Awarded The Grand Prix at the Paris Salon (1925) for mural and theatrical design. Though his illustrative work was varied in style and technique with echoes of Art Nouveau, the Beggarstaff Brothers (*see* William Nicholson and James Pryde), and oriental art it often reflected his fascination with stage design and the theatre. He often worked in crayon, pen and chalk, pen and wash, and in brush alone, to create decorative, stylised effects.

Books illustrated include:
Max Beerbohm The Happy Hypocrite (1918)
G. Macmillan Canadian Wonder Tales (1918)
Edmond Rostand La Princesse Lointaine (nd)
Richard Brinsley Sheridan The Duenna (1925)
H.T. Sheringham and J.C. Moore The Book of Fly-Rod (1931)

References: Bénézit; Chamot, Farr & Butlin; Houfe; Johnson; Johnson & Greutzner; Lewis; Mallalieu; Thieme & Becker; Vollmer; Wa (1934); Waters; *Art Journal* (1911); *Drawing and Design* new series 3 (1923); *The Studio* 61 (1914), 68 (1916), 89 (1925), 115 (1938), 130 (1945), special (1927)

Robert Stewart Sherriffs (b. 1907)

Born in Edinburgh. Educated at Arbroath High School. Studied at Edinburgh School of Art, specialising in heraldic design. Contributed drawings to the *Radio Times* from 1927, and caricatures of celebrities and full-page theatre illustrations to the *Sketch* (c. 1933-40). He was widely tipped to succeed Will Dyson* on *The Daily Herald* (1938) but was passed over in favour of George Whitelaw. He served in the Royal Armoured Corps during World War II. In 1948, he succeeded J.H. Dowd* on *Punch* as film caricaturist and continued to contribute to the paper until his death. He was a draughtsman of outstanding panache with a remarkable instinct for caricature. Initially, he worked mainly with a pen and and his early illustrations for *Tamburlaine the Great* (1930) incorporated stylistic allusions to the work of Aubrey Beardsley, Kay Neilsen*, and Harry Clarke*, in a *tour-de-force* of graphic ingenuity. By the mid 1930s, he had developed his mature manner; often brush-drawn, always immaculately stylish, and somewhat influenced by fellow Punch artist Thomas Derrick* whose work he much admired. He was also a noted cricketer.

Books illustrated include:
Charles Dickens Captain Boldheart (1948), Mrs Orange (1948)
Edward FitzGerald Rubaiyat of Omar Khayyam (1947)
Christopher Marlowe The Life and Death of Tamburlaine the Great (1930)
R.S. Sherriffs Salute if You Must (1945)

Periodicals: The Bystander, The Daily Herald, Punch, Radio Times, The Sketch, The Tatler

References: Driver; Price; *The Artist* (June 1943); *Punch* (obituary, 4th January 1961); *Weekly Scotsman* (12th October 1961); William Feaver *Masters of Caricature* (Weidenfeld & Nicolson 1981)

Mary Shillabeer (b. 1904)

Maiden name: Mary Eleanor Wright. Born and grew up at Downton, near Salisbury. Studied at the Central School of Arts and Crafts, where she won two scholarships. She subsequently worked as a painter and children's book illustrator. For illustration she worked in lithography or in pen and ink, sometimes with colour overlays. [Q]

Books illustrated include:
Mary Cockett Jasper Club (1959)
Lettice Cooper Blackberry's Kitten (1961)
Roger Lancelyn Green (ed) The Book of Verse for Children (1962)
Elisabeth Kyle Run to Earth (1957)
Patricia Lynch Holiday at Rosquin (1964), Mona of the Isle (1965)
Mary Shillabeer My Animal ABC (1938), My Farmyard Counting Book (1940), We Visit the Zoo (1946), At First (1947)
Barbara Sleigh Patchwork Quilt (1956)

R.L. Stevenson A Child's Garden of Verses (1960)
Ursula Moray Williams Adventures of Puffin (1939)

References: ICB 3; Johnson & Greutzner

Ellis Silas (b. 1883)

Born in London, son of flower painter Louis Silas. Studied under his father and under W.R. Sickert. Official war artist for the Australian Government in World War I; *Crusading in Anzac* is based on his front-line sketchbooks. He afterwards spent three years living Gauguin-style, among the natives of Papua, recording his impressions in pencil sketches and watercolours. Painter of landscapes and seascapes in oil and watercolour, designer of stained glass windows, murals, posters, cards and souvenirs. President of the London Sketch Club (1930).

Books illustrated include:
Charles Kingsley Westward Ho! (1927)
Ellis Silas Crusading in Anzac Anno Domini 1915 (1916), A Primitive Arcadia: being the impressions of an artist in Papua (1926)
Percy Westerman One of the Many (1945), First Over! (1948), Mystery of the Key (1948), Held to Ransom (1951), Working Their Passage (1951), Sabotage! (1952)
Harold F.B. Wheeler The Story of the British Navy (1922)

Periodicals: The Boy's Own Paper, The Illustrated London News, Little Folks

References: Cuppleditch; Wa (1966); Waters

Sara Lesley Silcock (b. 1947)

Studied at Southampton College of Art and Hornsey College of Art. Printmaker and etcher: illustrator, mainly of children's books, in pen and ink, sometimes with colour washes. She lives in Surrey.

Books illustrated include:
Edward Barnes and Dorothy Smith 'Blue Peter' Special Assignment Venice and Brussels (1974)
Gyles Brandreth Here Comes Golly! (1979), Hey Diddle Diddle (1979), The Story of Humpty Dumpty (1979)
John Fitzgerald Me and My Little Brain (1974)
Susan McGibbon Party Food (1975)
Albert Murfy Anyone Can Draw (1981)
Geoffrey Palmer and Noel Lloyd Ghosts Go Haunting (1975)
Juliet Piggott Myth and Moonshine (1973)
Peter Seabrook Book of the Garden (with others, 1979)
Sara Silcock Going to Hospital (1980)
Noel Streatfeild Christmas Holiday Book Series (5 vols, 1973-77)
Geoffrey Trease A Voice in the Night (1973)

Reference: ICB 4

William Augustus Sillince (1906-1974)

Usually worked as Sillince. Born in Battersea, London, son of a naval commander. Studied at the Regent Street Polytechnic and School of Art and at the Central School of Arts and Crafts. Worked in advertising (1928-36). Part-time lecturer at Brighton College of Art (1949-52), and in graphic design at Hull Regional College of Art

(1952-71); painter and cartoonist. Contributed regularly to *Punch* for many years. For his illustrative work, he drew in soft pencil or pen and ink, sometimes on textured paper, in a humorous cartoon-like style. Elected RWS, RBA (1949).

Books illustrated include:
Leila Berg The Story of the Little Car (1955)
Dorothy L. Sayers Euen the Parrot (1944)
W.A. Sillince We're All In It (1941), We're Still In It (1942), Wine, Water and Song (1943), This Merrie English (1954), Basic British (1956)
Henry Treece The Jet Beads (1961)

Periodicals: Oxford Annual, Punch

References: Johnson & Greutzner; Price; Vollmer supp; Wa (1972); Waters; The Times (obituary 17th January 1974); W.A. Sillince *Comic Drawings* (Pitman 1950)

Sidney Herbert Sime (1867-1941)

Worked as Sidney Sime or S.H. Sime. Born in Manchester. Worked in a mine as a child then for a draper, a barber and a signwriter, and then studied at Liverpool School of Art. During the 1890s, he contributed to numerous periodicals and was editor of the magazine *Eureka* and co-editor of *The Idler*. In the 1900s, he withdrew to

Sidney Sime. 'Snide' from *Bogey Beasts, Jingles, etc.* by S.H. Sime, music by Holbrooke (Goodwin & Tabb, 1923).

the village of Worplesdon in Surrey where he worked in increasing isolation, though as something of a local celebrity. He painted in watercolour and sometimes in oil, etched, and produced numerous portrait caricatures, often of theatrical figures. His later paintings often showed the influence of the Japanese print. Many of Sime's magazine illustrations were published without any text, their mysterious imagery apparently inspired by a private mythological world. Some of his early black and white drawings clearly showed the influence of Aubrey Beardsley, a contributor to *The Idler*. His later work, often in halftone, was entirely individual in style and combined earthy but macabre humour with hauntingly eerie atmospheric effects. His best book illustrations were inspired by the fantasies of Lord Dunsany, in whom he found a kindred spirit; his designs for *Time and the Gods*, in particular were among the outstanding imaginative achievements of graphic art of the period. A collection of his work is preserved in a small museum at Worplesdon, Surrey.

Books illustrated include:
Lord Dunsany The Gods of Pegana (1905), Time and the Gods (1906), The Sword of Welleran (1908), A Dreamer's Tales (1910), The Book of Wonder (1912), Tales of Wonder (1916), The Chronicles of Rodriguez (frontispiece 1922), The King of Elfland's Daughter (frontispiece, 1924), The Blessing of Pan (frontispiece, 1927), My Talks with Dean Stanley (frontispiece, 1936)
William Hope Hodgson The Ghost Pirates (frontispiece, 1909)
Joseph Holbrooke and S.H. Sime Bogey Beasts (1923)
Arthur Machen The House of Souls (frontispiece, 1906), The Hill of Dreams, (frontispiece 1907)
Eden Phillpotts Fancy Free (with others, 1901)

Periodicals: Black and White, The Boy's Own Paper; The Butterfly, Eureka, Form, The Graphic, The Idler, The Illustrated London News, The Ludgate Monthly, The Minster, The Pall Mall Magazine, Pick-Me-Up, Punch, The Sketch, The Strand Magazine, The Tatler, The Unicorn

References: Bénézit; Houfe; Johnson; Johnson & Greutzner; Peppin; Ray; Thieme & Becker; Thorpe; Waters; *The Fortnightly Review* (August 1942); *The Graphic* (November 1922); *The Idler* 12 (1898-98); *The Illustrated London News* (November 1922); *The Magazine of Art* (1904); *The Saturday Book* 34 (1975); *The Strand Magazine* 36 (1908); *The Studio* special (1900-01, 1911, Spring 1922, 1927); *The Windsor Magazine* 7 (1898); Mark Amory *Lord Dunsany* (Collins 1972); Desmond Coke *Confessions of an Incurable Collector* (Chapman & Hall 1928); Lord Dunsany *Patches of Sunlight* (Heinemann 1938); William Feaver *Masters of Caricature* (Weidenfeld & Nicolson 1981); Simon Heneage and Henry Ford *Sidney Sime* (Thames & Hudson 1980); Holbrook Jackson *The 1890s* (Grant Richards 1913); George Locke *From an Ultimate Dim Thule* (Ferret Fantasy 1973), *The Land of Dreams* (Ferret Fantasy 1975); Bernard Muddiman *The Men of the Nineties* (Henry Danielson 1920); Paul W. Skeeters *Sidney H. Sime* (Ward Ritchie 1978).

Charles Walter Simpson (1885-1971)

Born in Camberley, Surrey, son of a Major-General. Studied at the Académie Julian in Paris. Painter of landscapes, hunting schenes, and marine birds; illustrator and writer. Won gold medals at the Panama Exposition in San Francisco (1915) and the Paris Olympia Exhibition (1924). Guy Paget considered him 'undoubtedly

Charles Simpson. From *Manners and Mannerisms* by Crascredo (Country Life, 1929).

the best bird painter living.' As a sporting illustrator and animal artist, he often had the benefit of lavish, expensively-printed productions, as in his own *The Harboro' Country* (1927), illustrated with sketchy but attractive pen and pencil drawings, and plates in full colour. Less typical of his work, but more original, were his 12 full-page woodcuts for *A Pastorale* (1922), which he published in a limited edition from his home at St Ives, Cornwall. These decorative and simple white line blocks, printed in colour on grey hand-made paper, were described by F.L. Emanuel as 'equal in merit to the best of much of such work at present being produced' (*The Jewish Guardian*, 10th March 1922). He later lived in Hampshire and London. Elected RBA (1914), RI (1914), ROI (1923).

Books illustrated include:
J.L.M. Barrett Practical Jumping (1930)
Crascredo Manners and Mannerisms (1929)
W.V. Faber Wit and Wisdom of the Shires (1932)
S.G. Goldschmidt The Fellowship of the Horse (1930)
D.U. Ratcliffe The Gone Away (1930)
C.W. Simpson A Pastorale (1922), El Rodeo (1924), The Harboro'
    Country (1926), Leicestershire and its Hunts (1926), Trencher and
    Kennel (1927), The Fields of Home (1948)
Charles R. Simpson The History of the Lincolnshire Regiment (1931)
C.E. Vulliamy Unknown Cornwall (1925)

References: Bénézit; Johnson & Greutzner; Thieme & Becker; Vollmer; Wa (1934); Waters; C. Wood; J.C. Wood; *Drawing and Design* (September 1924); Guy Paget *Sporting Pictures of England* (Collins 1945)

Joseph Simpson (1879-1939)

Born and educated in Carlisle. Various sources claim that he studied art in Carlisle (*The Studio* 35), Glasgow (Waters) or Edinburgh (Houfe). He worked as a designer for a Carlisle printer, and in Edinburgh, and early in his career received encouragement from D.Y. Cameron*. He later moved to London where he occupied a studio next door to his friend Frank Brangwyn*; he also worked in Kirkcudbright. He taught at the London School of Art, and in 1918 he served as an official war artist to the Royal Air Force in France Simpson established an early reputation as a designer of bookplates, in a style that had echoes of James Pryde*, and was also a gifted caricaturist working with a bold, economical brush line. His book illustrations were varied in approach; those for *Ibsen* resembled his caricatures, while *A Gallery of Heroes and Heroines* was illustrated with full colour plates. *Edinburgh Today* was illustrated with landscape sketches in pencil, chalk and watercolour, reproduced in halftone.

Books illustrated include:
Sir H.H. Johnston A Gallery of Heroes and Heroines (1915)
A. Keith Edinburgh Today (1915)
P. Kennedy Soldiers of Labour (1917)
Haldane Macfall Ibsen (1907)
H. Macpherson History of Fowling (nd)
Joseph Simpson and T.R. Dewar Great Scots (1914)
W. Whitten Twelve Masters of Prose and Verse (1909)
War Poems from The Times (1915)

References: Bénézit; Guichard; Houfe; Johnson & Greutzner; Taylor; Thieme & Becker; Waters; *The Studio* 35 (1905), special (Spring 1929); *Joseph W. Simpson, his Books* (Otto Schulze 1900)

James R. Sinclair (active from 1896)

Lived in Edinburgh. His later illustrations are markedly better than his earlier ones which are poorly drawn and scratchy. He worked in black and white, and in colour.

Books illustrated include:
Lewis Carroll Alice in Wonderland (1909)
John Finnemore Fairy Stories from the Little Mountain (1899)
J. Lea Queerie at the Pole (1911)
W.H. Stacpole The Victorian Picture Book (1897)
H.G. Wells Floor Games (1911), Little Wars (1913)

Reference: Johnson & Greutzner

Alfred Sindall (active 1910-41)

The most effective illustrator of the *Biggles* books. While Howard Leigh contributed bland full-colour frontispieces between 1935 and 1941, Sindall was responsible for full-page black and white illustrations in the text. Working with bold brush strokes, and sometimes adding flat halftone, he created vigorous action drawings that reproduced excellently on the cheap, absorbent paper used for the series.

Alfred J. Sindall. 'Mee-Kit moved unseen as he hunted in the tree-tops' from *Mee-Kit and the Elephant King* by H. Mortimer Batten in *The Children's Wonder Book* (Odhams, 1948).

Books illustrated include:
Eleanor Graham Six in a Family (1935)
W. E. Johns (with Howard Leigh) Biggles Flies East (1935), Biggles Hits the Trail (1935), Biggles in Africa (1936), Biggles & Co (1936), Biggles Air Commodore (1937), Biggles Flies West (1937), The Rescue Flight (1939), Biggles in the Baltic (1940), Biggles Secret Agent (1940), Biggles Sees it Through (1941), Biggles Defies the Swastika (1941)
Geoffrey Trease The Christmas Holiday Mystery (1937), Mystery on the Moors (1937)

Periodicals: The Captain, The Children's Wonder Book, Union Jack, The Wide World Magazine

Joseph Ratcliffe Skelton
(active 1888-1927)

Born in Newcastle-on-Tyne. Painter and draughtsman. During an apparently brief period as a book illustrator, he seems to have worked for only one publisher, T.C. & E.C. Jack, for whom he provided highly competent detailed watercolour paintings of heroic action. *The Child's English Literature* is mistakenly attributed on the title page to John R. Skelton. Elected RWA.

Books illustrated include:
John Lang Outposts of Empire (1908)
H. E. Marshall Our Empire Story (c.1908), The Child's English Literature (1909), Scotland's Story (with others, c.1909)

Periodicals: The Bystander, The Graphic, The Illustrated London News, The Sketch

References: Houfe; Johnson & Greutzner; Waters; C. Wood

Bernard Barnay Sleigh (1872-1954)

Worked as Bernard Sleigh. Born Birmingham. Apprenticed there to a commercial wood engraver, a regular part of his work consisting of engraving pictures of bicycles. He attended evening classes at Birmingham School of Art. He broke off his apprenticeship to teach wood engraving at the school and to carry out a commission from the publisher George Allen to engrave illustrations by A.J. Gaskin for an edition of Hans Christian Andersen. Later he engraved for the Essex House

John [Joseph] Skelton. 'Caedmon, sing some song to me' from *The Child's English Literature* by H.E. Marshall (T.C. & E.C. Jack, 1909).

Press, making the blocks for some of William Strang's* illustrations. His own illustrations tended to be restrained and low-key in feeling. Through his work as an engraver and teacher, Sleigh made a valuable contribution to the transformation of wood engraving from a medium of reproduction into one of expression. He also painted figure subjects in oil and watercolour and did murals, made stained glass designs, and was an occasional map-maker and writer. Elected ARBSA (1923), RBSA (1928).

Books illustrated include:
R. K. Dent A Picture Map of Birmngham in the Year 1730 (1924)
A. J. Gaskin A Book of Pictured Carols (1893)
Amy Mark The Sea King's Daughter (1895)
Bernard Sleigh Ancient Mappe of Fairyland (1918), A Faerie Calendar (1920), A Faerie Pageant (1924), Gates of Horn (1926), Handbook of Elementary Design (1930), Wood Engraving since Eighteen-Ninety (1932)
The Song of Songs as a Drama (1937)

Periodicals: The Dome, The Yellow Book

References: Baker; Bénézit; Houfe; Johnson & Greutzner; Sketchley; Taylor; Thieme & Becker; Wa (1934); Waters; *The Studio* special (1917); Colin Franklin *The Private Presses* (Studio Vista 1969)

David Charles Smee (b. 1937)

Born in Cambridge. Studied at Cambridge School

of Art (until 1956). After National Service in Cyprus, he worked in London advertising agencies until 1964, when he won the Shell Poster Competition and became a freelance illustrator and designer. His book illustrations, in pen or brush, are varied in manner and highly professional in execution. He lives in South Devon.

Books illustrated include:
Peter Dickinson Chance, Luck and Destiny (with Victor Ambrus*
    1975), The Blue Hawk (1976), The Dancing Bear (1976)
Geoffrey Trease The Seas of Morning (1976)
Jill Paton Walsh The Walls of Athens (1977)

Periodical: Punch

Reference: ICB 4

Lavinia Smiley (b. 1919)

Maiden name: Lavinia Pearson, a grand-daughter of the first Viscount Cowdray. She grew up in London and Sussex and was educated in London and Paris. The discomforts of her affluent childhood were recalled in *A Nice Clean Plate* (1981). She illustrated her own humorous stories for children with cheerful cartoon-like drawings in outline.

Books illustrated include:
Lavinia Smiley Come Shopping (1955), Hugh the Dragon Killer
    (1956), Robin in Danger (1956), Mr Snodgrass's Holiday (1958),
    Clive to the Rescue (1975), William and the Wolf (1975)

References: ICB 2; *A Nice Clean Plate (Recollections 1919-31)*
(Michael Russell 1981)

Lesley S.J. Smith (b. 1951)

Born in London. Studied at Cambridge School of Art (1969-71) and at St Martin's School of Art (1971-74). Freelance illustrator, since 1974, of children's books in black and white and colour, preferring subjects that involve animal characterisation.

Books illustrated include:
Mabel Esther Allan Strangers in Wood Street (1981)
Lavinia Derwent Macpherson's Mystery Adventure (1982)
Barbara Ireson The Beaver Book of Funny Rhymes (1980)
Pamela Oldfield The Gumby Gang Strikes Again (1980), More About
    the Gumby Gang (1979)
Tom Tully Little Ed (1979), Ed at Large (1980), Look Out—It's Little
    Ed (1981)

Richard Francis Shirley Smith (b. 1935)

Works as Richard Shirley Smith. Born in London. Educated at Harrow School. Studied at the Slade School of Fine Art (1956-60) under Anthony Gross* and in Rome for two years. Lecturer at St Alban's School of Art (1963); head of art department at Marlborough School (1966-70). For book illustrations (mainly of poetry and limited editions), he has worked in pen and ink and made lino cuts, however, he is best known for his wood

Richard Shirley Smith. From *Letters to his Son* by Philip Dormer Stanhope, 4th Earl of Chesterfield, edited by J. Harding (1973).

engravings which are in a very individual style with patches of hatched shading incised with a multiple graver. He also engraves bookplates and house portraits, and is active as a painter, collagist, and mural and furniture decorator. He has been greatly influenced by David Jones* whom he often visited between 1956 and 1966. [Q]

Books illustrated include:
J. Addison, Sir R. Steele and E. Budgell Sir Roger de Coverly (1967)
R. Bannister Prospect: the Schweppes Book of the New Generation
    (1962)
D. Bartrum The Gourmet's Garden (1964)
J.C. Bretherton The Prince and the Puppeteer (1969)
A.D. Burnett Hero and Leander (1975)
M. Claridge Margaret Clitherow (1966)
E. Clarke The Darkening Green (1964)
Joyce Finzi A Point of Departure (1967)
J. Heath-Stubbs Buzz Buzz; ten insect poems (1981)
R.H. Horne (trans. R. Hague) Memoirs of a London Doll (1967)
J. Reeves The Closed Door (1977)
F.E. Reynolds The Trial of S. Thomas More (1964)
S. Spender (ed) Poems of P.B. Shelley (1971)
Philip Dormer Stanhope; 4th Earl of Chesterfield (ed J. Harding)
    Letters to his Son (1973)

References: Fisher p.201; Garrett BWE, HBWE; *Architectural Review*
961 (March 1977); *The Private Library* vol 10 no.2 (Summer 1977); *The
Sunday Telegraph Magazine* (7th September 1980); *British Bookplates*
(David & Charles 1979)

Snaffles

See Charles Johnson Payne.

The Snark

See Starr Wood.

Edith Oenone Somerville (1858-1949)

Born in Corfu, daughter of an Anglo-Irish army officer. Brought up at Castletownshend, Co. Cork, Ireland. Studied art in London (1884) and later in Düsseldorf (1889) and Paris (1894); she returned to Paris in the winter of 1899 and there helped Cyrus Cuneo* set up an afternoon illustration class; her work was influenced by Cuneo's use of crayons. From 1886 she collaborated with her second cousin Violet Martin (pseudonym Martin Ross) in writing novels. They jointly published fourteen, including *Some Experiences of an Irish R.M.* (1890). After Violet's death (1915) her name continued to appear as author on the title pages of Edith's books. As an illustrator, she worked in a naturalistic vein in pen and ink, crayon, watercolour, and half-tone washes. She lived for many years at Skibbereen, Co. Cork. Edith was awarded an Hon. D.Litt. at Trinity College Dublin (1932), and Gregory gold medals by the Irish Academy of Letters (1941). She was the first woman Master of Fox Hunts.

Books illustrated include:
Martin Ross and Edith Somerville Beggars on Horseback (1895), Some Experiences of an Irish R.M. (1900), All on the Irish Shore (1903), Some Irish Yesterdays (1906), Further Experiences of an Irish R.M. (1908), In Mr. Knox's Country (1915), Irish Memories (1917), The Smile and the Tear (1933), Notions in Garrison (1941), Maria and some other dogs (1949)
Edith Somerville The Story of the Discontented Little Elephant (1912), Stray-Aways (1920), Wheel Trades (1923), The States Through Irish Eyes (1931), The Sweet Cry of Hounds (1936)

Periodicals: The Graphic, The Strand Magazine

References: DNB (1941-50); Houfe; Johnson & Greutzner; Vollmer; Wa (1934); Waters 2; Geraldine Cummins *Dr E. OE. Somerville: A Biography, with a Bibliography of 1st Editions by Robert Vaughan* (Andrew Dakers 1952); Hilary Robinson *Somerville and Ross: a Critical Appreciation* (Gill & Macmillan, Dublin 1980)

Eileen Alice Soper (b. 1905)

Daughter of George Soper* under whom she studied; first exhibited at the Royal Academy at the early age of 15. She has derived much of her subject matter from her father's garden in Hertfordshire, which she and her sister have maintained and preserved as a nature sanctuary. A painter of wildlife, children, portraits and miniatures, and engraver. Founder-member of the Society of Wildlife Artists, elected RMS (1972). [Q]

Books illustrated include:
Enid Blyton Merry Story Book (1943), Five Run Away Together (1944), Polly Piglet (1944), Jolly Story Book (1944), Tales from the Bible (1944), The Toys Come to Life (1944), The Runaway Kitten (1945), The Teddy Bear's Party (1945), The Blue Story Book (1945), The Twins Go to Nursery Rhyme Land (1945), Gay Story Book (1946), The Little White Duck and other stories (1946), The Train

That Lost its Way (1946), The Bad Little Monkey (1946), The Green Story Book (1947), Lucky Story Book (1947), At Seaside Cottage (1947), Secret of the Old Mill (1948), Tale of the Twins (1948), Five Get into Trouble (1949), Five Fall into Adventure (1950), The Three Naughty Children (1950), Tucky the Goblin (1950), The Astonishing Ladder (1950), Book of the Year (1950), My First Nature Book (1950), Bright Story Book (1952), Five Have a Wonderful Time (1952), Five Go Down to the Sea (1953), Five on a Secret Trail (1956), Five Go to Billycock Hill (1957), Five Get into a Fix (1958), Five Go to Demon's Rocks (1961), Five Have a Mystery to Solve (1962), Five All Together Again (1968)
Lewis Carroll Alice in Wonderland (1947)
Mazo de la Roche Bill and Coo (nd)
Phil Drabble No Badgers in my Wood (1979)
M. Kent The Children's Nature Series (1944)
Maxwell Knight How to Observe Wild Mammals (1957)
Wickham Malin Bully and the Badger (1974)
Eileen A. Soper Happy Rabbit (1947), Dormouse Awake (1948), Sail Away Shrew (1949), When Badgers Wake (1955), Wild Encounters (1957), Wanderers of the Field (1959), Wild Favours (1963), Muntjac (1969)
Ursula Moray Williams A Castle for John-Peter (1941)
The Song of Lambert (1955)

Periodicals: Christian Science Monitor, Country Life, The Countryman, Sunday Times, Wildlife

References: Fisher p.107; Guichard; ICB 1,2; Johnson & Greutzner; Vollmer; Wa (1980); Waters; *Fine Prints of the Year* (1923-25) *The Studio* 85 (1923)

George Soper (1870-1942)

Born Devon. Studied etching under Sir Frank Short. A keen amateur naturalist, he cultivated rare plants in his large, semi-wild garden in Hertfordshire. For watercolours, wood engravings

George Soper. From *Tales from Shakespeare* by Charles and Mary Lamb (Allen & Unwin, 1909).

and etchings, his subjects were the countryside and farm work before mechanisation. Elected ARE (1918), RE (1920). [Q]

Books illustrated include:
Lewis Carroll Alice's Adventures in Wonderland (1911)
M. England (ed) Warne's Happy Book for Girls (with others, c. 1935)
Reginald Farrer Among the Hills (nd)
Nathaniel Hawthorne Tanglewood Tales (1912)
Charles Kingsley The Water Babies (1908), The Heroes (1910)
Charles and Mary Lamb Tales from Shakespeare (1909)
Gladys Williams The Arabian Nights (1913), Little Gardens (1938), Grimm's Fairy Tales (1916)

Periodicals: The Boy's Own Paper, The Captain, Cassell's Magazine, Chums, Country Life, The Graphic, The Illustrated London News, The Strand Magazine, The Wide World Magazine, Young England

References: Bénézit; Guichard; Doyle BWI; Houfe; Johnson & Greutzner; Thieme & Becker; Thorpe; Wa (1934); Waters; C. Wood; *The Charm of the Etcher's Art, The Studio Graphic Arts Folios* Nos 2 & 3 (1920); *Fine Prints of the Year* (1923, 1927, 1928, 1935); *The Studio* 80 (1920), special (1919, Spring 1930); Eileen Soper *Muntjac* (Longmans 1969)

Amy Millicent Sowerby (1878-1967)

Worked as Millicent Sowerby. Daughter of designer and illustrator J.G. Sowerby. For several years she was a prolific and popular children's book and postcard illustrator. She was brought up in an Aesthetic milieu, but was largely self-taught as an artist, developing her style from the close study of other illustrators' work. Her long collaboration with her sister Githa on children's books began in response to their father's thriftlessness and the financial needs of his large family. Her earlier drawings have firm outlines with flat colour areas and often incorporated lettering; the looser handling of her later work was not always successfully reproduced.

Books illustrated include:
Lewis Carroll Alice in Wonderland (1907)
Rose Fyleman The Sunny Book (1918)
N. Joan The Glad Book (1921), The Darling Book (1922), The Joyous Book (1923)
Githa Sowerby The Wise Book (1906), The Bumbletoes (1907), Childhood (1907), Yesterday's Children (1908), The Happy Book (1909), Little Plays for Little People (1910), The Merry Book (1911), My Birthday (1911), Poems of Childhood (1912), The Gay Book (1915), The Pretty Book (1915), Cinderella (1915), The Dainty Book (1915), The Bright Book (1915), The Bonny Book (1918)
R.L. Stevenson A Child's Garden of Verses (1908), Cinderella's Playbook (1927), Grimm's Fairy Tales (1909), Little Stories for Little People (1910)

Periodicals: The Illustrated London News, The Pall Mall Magazine, The Tatler, The Windsor Magazine

References: Cope; Houfe; ICB 1; Johnson & Greutzner; Vollmer; Wa (1934); Waters

Austin Osman Spare (1888-1956)

Born in Smithfield, London, son of a city policeman. He first attracted attention at the age of 14, when one of his drawings was exhibited at the Royal Academy and he was acclaimed as a boy genius. He studied at Lambeth School of Art and

the Royal College of Art. Appointed editor of *Form* (1916-17), a short-lived magazine financed by John Lane, who hoped it would prove a successor to The *Yellow Book*. During army service (1917-18), he illustrated, designed and wrote for the Royal Army Medical Corps magazine. He later co-edited *The Golden Hind* (1922-24) with Clifford Bax. He eventually became a recluse living in poverty, and during World War II was injured by a bomb blast and lost the use of both his arms.

Spare was a painter (portraits and figure compositions), etcher and draughtsman and designed book plates. He was widely respected in his day as a draughtsman, but his obsession with the supernatural and the occult, his esoteric symbolism and often grotesque imagery limited his popularity. During the early 1920s he experimented (with Frederick Carter*) with automatic drawing, which he hoped might prove to be a means of releasing suppressed associations and images from the subconscious. He was a friend of Alastair (Hans Henning Voight*), who shared his interest in self-exploration and mysticism and who had been similarly influenced by the drawings of Aubrey Beardsley.

Books illustrated include:
J. Bertram and R. Wilkinson The Starlit Mine (1911)
C.J. Darling On the Oxford Circuit and other verses (1909)
Austin Osman Spare A Book of Automatic Drawings (1972), Earth, Inferno (1905), A Book of Satyrs (1909), The Book of Pleasure (1913), The Focus of Life: the muttering of Aäos (1920)
J.C. Squire Twelve Poems (1916), The Gold Tree (1917)
Ethel R. Wheeler Behind the Veil (1906)

Periodicals: Apple Form, The Golden Hind

References: Bénézit; DNB (1951-60); Houfe; Johnson & Greutzner; Thieme & Becker; Wa (1934); Waters; *Art Journal* (1980); *Artwork* 2 (1925); *Drawing and Design* (July 1925); Victor Arwas *Alastair* (Thames & Hudson 1979); Kenneth Grant *Images and Oracles of Austin Osman Spare* (Müller 1975); Brian North Lee *British Bookplates* (David & Charles 1979); Brian Reade *Catalogue of the Beardsley Exhibition* (Victoria and Albert Museum 1966)

Lancelot Speed (1860-1931)

Born in London, educated at Rugby and at Cambridge when he was a friend and contemporary of J.D. Batten* and H.J. Ford*. He had no formal art training, but became an illustrator, mainly in black and white. He was one of the earliest illustrators to benefit from process engraving, which particularly suited his fine-lined style. His work is straight-forward and accurate in detail, but his themes are rarely developed with much imagination or sense of design. However in *The Limbersnigs*, written for children in collaboration with his wife Flora, his illustrations show a greater sense of fantasy.

Books illustrated include:
A. and E. Castle 'If Youth but knew!' (1906)
C.J. Cornish Wild England of To-day, and the Wild Life in it (c.1899)

A. Coupin and J. Lea The Romance of Animal Arts and Crafts (1907)
W.J. Courthope The Paradise of Birds (1889)
M. Cunningham Until the Day I Declare It (1899)
H. Rider Haggard Eric Brighteyes (1895)
G.A. Henty In Battle and Breeze (frontispiece c.1896)
G.B.N. Hill Footsteps of Dr Johnson (1890)
S.K. Hocking When Life is Young (1900)
Thomas Hughes Tom Brown's School Days (1911)
Charles Kingsley Hypatia (frontispiece 1897)
H.R. Knipe Nebula to Man (1905)
Sir J. Knowles Legends of King Arthur and his Knights (1912)
J. Lambert The Romance of Missionary Heroism (1907)
Andrew Lang (ed) Old Friends Among the Fairies (with H.J. Ford* and G.P. Jacomb Hood,* c.1890), The Red Fairy Book (with H.J. Ford*, 1890), The Blue Poetry Book (with H.J. Ford, 1891)
J. Lea The Romance of Bird Life (1909)
Bulwer Lytton The Last Days of Pompeii (1897)
J.A. Savage The One Great Voyage of Life (1896)
G.F. Scott Elliott The Romance of Plant Life (1907), The Romance of Early British Life (1907), The Romance of Savage Life (1908)
Sir O. Seaman Oedipus the Wreck (1888)
E. Selous The Romance of the Animal World (1905), The Romance of Insect Life (1906)
Sophocles The Oedipus Tyrannus (1888)
Lancelot Speed The Limbersnigs (nd)
A.F. Wilson Carmen Pooleviense (1886)

Periodicals: The English Illustrated Magazine, Good Words, The Graphic, The Illustrated London News, Portfolio, Punch, The Sphere, The Sporting and Dramatic News, The Windsor Magazine, Young England

References: Houfe; ICB 1; Mallalieu; Thorpe; Vollmer; Wa (1929); Waters; C. Wood; *The Ludgate* 2 (1897); *The Studio* special (1897-98); Henry Blackburn *The Art of Illustration* (John Grant 1901)

Geraldine Spence (b. 1931)

Born in Esher, Surrey. Studied at Wimbledon School of Art (1947-52) and under John Nash* and Edward Bawden* at the Royal College of Art (1953-56). Freelance illustrator of children's books and jackets since 1966, working in a confident sketchy style typical of the period.

Books illustrated include:
Paul Berna Threshold of the Stars (1958)
Nan Chauncy Devil's Hill (1958)

Geraldine Spence. From *Mulbridge Manor* by James Reeves (Heinemann, 1958).

Anita Hewett The Bull Beneath the Walnut Tree and other stories (1966)
Lorna Hinds Crockery (1976)
Norman Hunter The Frantic Phantom (1973)
Barbara Lee The Five Wishes (nd)
Janet McNeill The Nest Spotters (1972)
William Mayne The Blue Boat (1957)
James Reeves Mulbridge Manor (1958)
Betty Roland The Forbidden Bridge (1961)
Eleanor Spence The Green Laurel (1963), The Nothing Place (1972)
Noel Streatfeild Lisa Goes to Russia (1963)

Periodical: Radio Times

References: ICB 3,4; Ryder; Usherwood; Vollmer supp

Gilbert Spencer (1892-1979)

Born at Cookham-on-Thames, Berkshire, brother of the painter Stanley Spencer. Studied at Camberwell School of Arts and Crafts, the Royal College of Art (1911-12) and at the Slade School of Fine Art (1913-15 and 1919-20). Served with the Royal Army Medical Corps (1915-1919). Professor of painting at the Royal College of Art (1932-48). Official War Artist (1940-43). Head of Department of Painting and Drawing at Glasgow School of Art (1948-50); head of Painting Department at Camberwell (1950-57). Spencer worked mainly as an easel painter and muralist, but he was also a distinguished book illustrator in pen and ink (with the addition of two colours in *Yeats' Three Things* in the Ariel Poems Series published by Faber) using line and cross hatching with directness and economy. Elected NEAC (1919), ARWS (1943), RWS (1949), ARA (1950), RA (1960).

Books illustrated include:
T.F. Powys Fables (1929)
Gilbert Spencer Stanley Spencer (1961)
W.B. Yeats Three Things (1929)

References: Bénézit; Chamot, Farr & Butlin; Johnson & Greutzner; Rothenstein II; Shone; Thieme & Becker; Vollmer; Wa (1934); Waters; *The Studio* special (Autumn 1930); *British Artists of Today; Gilbert Spencer* (The Fleuron 1926); Gilbert Spencer, *Memoirs of a Painter* (Chatto & Windus 1974)

Steven Spurrier (1878-1961)

Born in London. Educated at the City of London School. At seventeen, he was apprenticed to a silversmith. He studied art at the Lambeth School of Art and at Heatherley's School of Art. For many years, he worked as a freelance illustrator, in particular for *The Illustrated London News*. He also wrote, painted in oil and watercolour and designed posters. He lived in West Wittering, Sussex and died in London. His book illustrations were very much the work of a professional—'modern' in character, stylish, fluent and with a light touch. He usually depicted figures in motion which sometimes gave a feeling of restlessness to his compositions. Elected ROI (1912), RBA (c.1933), ARA (1945), RA (1952).

Books illustrated include:
Kitty Barne We'll Meet in England (1942), Three and a Pigeon (1944)
Charles Dickens The Life and Adventures of Nicholas Nickleby (1940)
Elizabeth Goudge The Valley of Song (1951)
William Shakespeare The Sonnets (1950)
Noel Streatfeild The Circus is Coming (1938)
William Wycherley The Country Wife (1934)
The Modern Gift Book for Children (1948)

Periodicals: The Graphic, The Illustrated London News, Radio Times

References: Bénézit; Chamot, Farr & Butlin; Driver; Houfe; Johnson & Greutzner; Thieme & Becker; Vollmer; Wa (1934); Waters

Walter Sydney Stacey (1846-1929)

Usually worked as W.S. Stacey. Born in London. Studied at the Royal Academy Schools. Painter of landscape in watercolour, and figure subjects in oils; decorative designer; illustrator of magazines and books. Stacey was a workmanlike illustrator who never tried to dominate or distract from the narrative. His illustrations, mainly in pen and ink or halftone, were animated and clear. Thorpe considered him a 'deft and graceful artist with the pen'. Elected RBA (1881), ROI (1883).

Books illustrated include:
G.A. Henty In Greek Waters (1893)

G.L. Stampa. 'That dash Toby Dog' from *Thy Servant a Dog* told by Boots, edited by Rudyard Kipling (Macmillan, 1930).

W.S. Stacey. 'But he was smashed at last' from *Courage, True Hearts* by Gordon Stables (Blackie, 1899).

Kirk Monroe The White Conquerors of Mexico (1894)
Edgar T. Pickering In Press Gang Days (1894)
Talbot Baines Reed Follow My Leader (1885)
E. Sanderson Heroes of Pioneering (with others, 1908)
Gordon Stables Courage, True Hearts (1899)
L.L. Weedon Bible Pictures (with W.J. Morgan, 1890), The Child 'Wonderful' (1903), Bible Stories (1911)

Periodicals: Black and White, The Boy's Own Paper; Cassell's Magazine, Chums, Cornhill Magazine, The Girl's Own Paper, Good Works, Quiver, Strand Magazine, Temple Magazine, Wide World Magazine, Young England

References: Bénézit; Houfe; Johnson & Greutzner; Mallalieu; Thorpe; Waters; C. Wood

George Loraine Stampa (1875-1951)

Usually worked as G.L. Stampa. Born in Constantinople, son of an architect. He studied at Heatherley's School of Art (c.1892) and the Royal Academy Schools (1895-1900), where fellow-students included W. Heath Robinson* and Lewis Baumer*. Painter in oil and watercolour, black-and-white artist. He contributed to Punch from 1895 to 1950, specialising in dogs and street urchins (his drawings of respectable citizens

Diana Stanley. From *The Borrowers Aloft* by
Mary Norton (Dent, 1961).

are inclined to be stilted). Price described him as
'Roué, bohemian, raconteur, link with the days
of Phil May* and tremendous evenings in hansom
cabs...' In early subject matter he was influenced by
Phil May and he has preserved the appearance of
the Gaiety chorus-girl and the Bohemian life of
the time; in method the influence of May on him
was small.' His drawings are unmistakable, not so
much for their graphic style as for the types he
depicts. Member of the Langham Sketch Club.

Books illustrated include:
B. Atkey Easy Money (1908)
S.L. Cummins Plays for Children (1922)
B.M. Hastings Memoirs of a Child (1926)
Rudyard Kipling Supplications of the Black Aberdeen (1927), Thy
    Servant a Dog (1930)
G.L. Stampa Loud Laughter (1907), Ragamuffins (1916), Humours of
    the Streets (1921), In Praise of Dogs (1948)
Joe Walker My Dog and Yours (1929), That Dog of Mine (1930),
    Come Out to Play (1937)

Periodicals: The Bystander, Cassell's Magazine, The Graphic, The
Homeland Annual, The Humourist, London Opinion, Moonshine,
The Odd Volume, The Pall Mall Magazine, Punch, The Sketch, The
Strand Magazine, The Tatler, Toc H Annual, The Windsor Magazine

References: Bénézit; Houfe; Johnson & Greutzner; Price; Thieme &
Becker; Wa (1934); Waters; *The Artist* (February 1943)

Edward Cyril Standon (b. 1929)

Born in London, son of an artist. Studied at St
Martin's School of Art. Painter of mammals and
birds, illustrator of children's books (often written
by his wife, Anna), cartoonist and designer of
graphics for children's television programmes
(e.g. *Blue Peter, Rainbow, Playschool*). He works
in pen and ink, and sometimes in colour, with wax
resist and sprayed texture. His books are published mainly by Constable.

Books illustrated include:
Leila Berg How John Caught the Sea Horse and other stories (1966),
    Penny Bell (1970)
Anna Standon The Singing Rhinoceros (1963), A Flower for Ambrose
    (1964), The Hippo Had Hiccoughs (1964), Three Little Cats (1964),
    The Tin Can Tortoise (1965), Little Duck Lost (1965), Bridie the
    Bantam (1967)
Edward Standon The Porridge Pot and the Big Turnip (1970)
Keith Chatfield Issi Pandemonium (1975), Issi's Magic Tonic (1976)

References: ICB 3,4

Diana Stanley (b. 1909)

Married name: Mrs Pannett. Born in London.
Studied at the Regent Street Polytechnic and
Byam Shaw School of Art (1929-34). Landscape
and animal painter, illustrator of children's books.
Author of *Anatomy for Artists* (Faber & Faber
1951). Best known for her entirely apposite pen
and ink illustrations for *The Borrowers* which, in
the book's many editions, have never been sup-
planted.

Books illustrated include:
Lewis Carroll Alice in Wonderland (1954)
Mary Cockett Bridges (1963), Ash Dry, Ash Green (1966)
Mary Norton The Borrowers (1952), The Borrowers Afield (1955),
    The Borrowers Afloat (1959), The Borrowers Aloft (1961), Poor
    Stainless (1971)

References: Doyle CL; Fisher pp. 284-85; ICB 2; Johnson &
Greutzner; Wa (1977); Waters

Percy Angelo Staynes (1875-1953)

Studied at Manchester School of Art, Royal College of Art and in Paris at the Académie Julian.
Lived in London. Painter in oil and watercolour,
and occasional illustrator. Elected ROI (1916),
RI (1935).

Books illustrated include:
Jonathan Swift Gulliver's Voyages to Lilliput and Brobdingnag (1912)
F. Wolfe The Orange Cat and other verses (1910), Roundabout Ways
    (1912)

Periodical: Little Folks

References: Houfe; Johnson & Greutzner; Waters

Leslie Leonard Stead (1899-1966)

Often worked as Stead. He trained under the
artist and designer Eugene Haskin, who was one

Stead. 'He splashed more water on the thin face' from *Another Job for Biggles* by Captain W.E. Johns (Hodder & Stoughton, 1951).

of Hodder & Stoughton's illustrators. His own association with Hodder & Stoughton began in March 1916, and he later illustrated many of the *Biggles*, *Worrals* and *Gimlet* books written by Captain Johns and published by Hodder & Stoughton and the Brockhampton Press. He specialised in figures in action (generally treating settings and props in a cursory fashion), and worked in black and white (pen or brush), halftone (crayon or pen and wash), and full colour. He served in the army (probably ARP), 1943-46.

Books illustrated include:
W. E. Johns Biggles Fails to Return (1943), Biggles King of the Commandos (1943), King of the Commandoes (1943), Biggles in the Orient (1944), Gimlet Goes Again (1944), Worrals Goes East (1944), Biggles Delivers the Goods (1946), Sergeant Bigglesworth CID (1946), Worrals in the Wilds (1947), Gimlet Mops Up (1947), Biggles' Second Case (1948), Biggles' Special Case (1948), Biggles Breaks the Silence (1949), Biggles Takes a Holiday (1949), Gimlet Lends a Hand (1949), Biggles Gets his Man (1950), Gimlet Bores in (1950), Another Job for Biggles (1951), Biggles Works it Out (1951), Gimlet Off the Map (1951), Biggles Follows on (1952), Biggles Takes the Case (1952), Gimlet Gets the Answer (1952), Biggles and the Black Raider (1953), Biggles in the Blue (1953), Biggles in the Gobi (1953), Biggles and the Pirate Treasure (1954), Biggles Foreign Legionnaire (1954), Gimlet Takes a Job (1954), Kings of Space (1954), Biggles in Australia (1955), Biggles Learns to Fly (1955), The Edge of Beyond (1955), Return to Mars (1955), Biggles' Chinese Puzzle (1955), Biggles Takes Charge (1956), Biggles Makes Ends

Meet (1957), Biggles of the Interpol (1957), Biggles on the Home Front (1957), To Outer Space (1957), The Death Rays of Ardilla (1959), Biggles Buries a Hatchet (1958), Biggles on Mystery Island (1958), Biggles at World's End (1959), Biggles' Combined Operation (1959), Biggles in Mexico (1959), Biggles and the Leopards of Zinn (1960), Biggles Goes Home (1960), To Worlds Unknown (1960), Biggles and the Missing Millionaire (1961), Biggles Forms a Syndicate (1961), Biggles Goes Alone (1962), Biggles Sets a Trap (1962), Orchids for Biggles (1962), Biggles and the Plane that Disappeared (1963), Biggles Takes a Hand (1963), Gimlet's Oriental Quest (1963), Biggles and the Black Mask (1964), Biggles Hunts Big Game (1965), Biggles Looks Back (1965)

Ralph Steadman (b. 1936)

Born in Wallasey, near Liverpool. Educated at Abergele Grammar School, North Wales. Apprentice engineer with the De Havilland Aircraft Company. Served in the Royal Air Force (1954-56). Studied at the London College of Printing (1958-62). Caricaturist, sculptor, painter, printmaker; also writer of music and songs. Contributor to *Punch, Private Eye, The Times,* and *The Daily Telegraph* (1961-69), to *Rolling Stone* (1970-79), and the *New Statesman* (since 1979). A winner of the Francis Williams Illustrations Award (1972) with *Alice in Wonderland* (1967). Has travelled extensively in America, Canada, Europe and the Orient.

As a caricaturist, Steadman has been influenced by the German expressionist George Grosz and the American Saul Steinberg. he was one of the artists (another was Gerald Scarfe) who during the 1960s broke away from the tradition of gentlemanly realism established in the 19th century by John Tenniel to explore the realms of passion, fantasy and nightmare. Significantly, perhaps, he took up the challenge of illustrating *Alice in Wonderland* and *Through the Looking Glass,* (first illustrated by Tenniel) and proved to be the only 'Alice' illustrator since Arthur Rackham* to succeed in creating convincing images that owed nothing to Tenniel's authoritative iconography. His more recent illustrations to *Sigmund Freud* have been described as 'the mature work of an artist in sympathy with a genius and through that sympathy finding new reaches in his own abilities'. (Michael McNay *The Guardian* 6th July 1982). [Q]

Books illustrated include:
Daisy Ashford Love and Marriage (1965), Where Love Lies Deepest (1966)
R. Carrickford This is Television (1958)
Lewis Carroll Alice in Wonderland (1967), Alice through the Looking Glass (1972), The Hunting of the Snark (1975)
Mischa Damjan The Big Squirrel and the Little Rhinoceros (1965), The False Flamingoes (1967)
Frank Dickens Fly Away Peter (1967)
Ted Hughes The Threshold (1979)
Richard Ingrams The Tale of Driver Grope (1969)
Ralph Steadman Ralph Steadman's Jelly Book (1967), Still Life with Raspberries (1969), Dogs Bodies (1970), Ralph Steadman's The Bumper to Bumper Book for Children (1972), Cherrywood Cannon (1978), Sigmund Freud (1979)
Barnard Stone Emergency Mouse (1978)
Dr Hunter S. Thompson Fear and Loathing in Las Vegas (1972), Fear and Loathing on the Campaign Trail (1974), America (1977)

Periodicals: Ambit, The Daily Telegraph, New Statesman, Private Eye, Punch, Radio Times, Rolling Stone, The Times

References: Doyle CL; Driver; *The Guardian* (6th July 1982); *Illustrators* 30 (1980); *The New Review* (March 1977); *View* (Spring-Summer 1979); *Viz* 5 (1979); William Feaver *Masters of Caricature* (Weidenfeld & Nicolson 1981)

Lorna R. Steele (active 1944-50)

Writer of children's books and illustrator in a generally bland style.

Books illustrated include:
Elisabeth Goudge Henrietta's House (1942)
Lorna R. Steele The Adventures of Andy and Ann (1944), Further Adventures of Andy and Ann (1947), Lucy Lambkin (1950), Three Little Elves (1950)
Lorna R. Steele and Margaret Lawson Miranda Mouse (1950)

Simon Stern (b. 1943)

Born in London. Studied at the London College of Printing and then worked in publishing. Freelance illustrator and writer of children's books since 1969. His simplified humorous drawings have heavy outlines with washes of bright colour, and in style are slightly reminiscent of the work of John Ryan* (especially in the comic *Captain Ketchup* series).

Books illustrated include:
Sylvia Caveney Inside Mum (1976), Little Zip's Dressing-Up Book (1977), Little Zip's Zoo Counting Book (1977), Little Zip's Night-Time Book (1978), Little Zip's Water Book (1978)
Doreen Coates Jacko and Delilah (1978)
Brian Earnshaw Dragonfall 5 and the Royal Beast (1972), Dragonfall 5 and the Space Cowboys (1972)
Eva Ibbotson The Great Ghost Rescue (1975)
Derek Sampson Grump and that Mammoth Again! (1981)
Ian Serraillier The Ballad of St Simeon (1970), The Bishop and the Devil (1971)
Simon Stern Astonishing Adventures of Captain Ketchup Series (1972-76), The Hobyahs: an old story (1977)

References: Contemporary Authors; ICB 4

Charles William Stewart (b. 1915)

Born at Ilo-Ilo, the Philippine Islands, son of a merchant. Brought up in Scotland and Sussex. Studied art at the Byam Shaw School (1932-38). A conscientious objector, he worked in London as an ARP stretcher bearer during World War II (1940-46). He taught drawing and illustration at the Byam Shaw School (1950-58), and became co-principal (1956-58). Returned to Scotland (1960) and settled in his family estate at New Abbey, Dumfries (1962). As an illustrator, Stewart has been influenced mainly by early black and white artists, in particular Thomas Bewick, George Cruikshank, and 'Phiz'; and in many of his drawings, successfully evokes the atmosphere of vanished times. He usually works in pen and ink or pencil, sometimes with watercolour washes, achieving subtle tonal modulations through the use of closely hatched and layered shading. He is

Charles W. Stewart. From *The Lady of the Linden Tree* by Barbara Leonie Picard (Oxford University Press, 1954).

also a painter of landscapes, flowers and antique costumes. [Q]

Books illustrated include:
William Beckford Vathek (1953)
Jocelyn Brooke The Flower in Season (1952)
Pigeon Crowle Come to the Ballet (1957)
Eric Crozier Noah Gives Thanks (1952)
Edward FitzGerald (trans) The Rubaiyat of Omar Khayyam (1955)
Jean Forbes-Robertson Chowry (1953)
Celia Furse The Visiting Moon (1956)
Rose Fyleman Hob and Bob (1944)
Nicholas Stuart Gray Grimbold's Other World (1963), Mainly in Moonlight (1965), The Edge of Evening (1975)
Barbara Leonie Picard The Faun and the Woodcutter's Daughter (1951), The Lady of the Linden Tree (1954), The Story of the Pándavas (1968), The Story of Ráma and Sitá (1960)
Arthur Ransome The Soldier and Death (1962)
Herbert Read (poetry selected by) This Way Delight (1957)
John Ruskin The King of the Golden River (1958)
Bertrand Russell Nightmares (1954)
Margaret Storey Timothy and the Two Witches (1966), The Dragon's Sister and Timothy Travels (1967), The Stone Sorcerer (1967)
William Makepeace Thackeray Pendennis (1961)
C. Henry Warren A Boy in Kent (1944)
Barbara Ker Wilson Path-Through-The-Woods (1958)

Reference: Wa (1980)

William Stobbs (b. 1914)

Born in South Shields, County Durham. Read history at Durham University. Head of design at the London College of Printing (1950-58). Principal of Maidstone College of Art (from 1958). He has been a prolific illustrator since the early 1950s, and in much of his work combines striking decoration with convincing imagery. In 1959, he won the Kate Greenaway Medal with *Kashtanka* and *A Bundle of Ballads*. He works in black and white (particularly in illustrations to children's novels) and full colour, and has also made particularly effective use of restricted colour (e.g. red

William Stobbs. From *The Boy and the Grandmother* by Frederick Grice in *Miscellany One* edited by Edward Blishen (Oxford University Press, 1964).

and black printing from halftone plates) a development perhaps from the 1940s Puffin book tradition of two-colour lithographs. Stobbs's work paved the way for the exuberant textural experiments of the next generation of illustrators, such as Brian Wildsmith*. Married to the illustrator Joanna Stubbs*.

Books illustrated include:

Edward Blishen (ed) Miscellany One (with others, 1964)
Christopher R. Brown Kentish Tales (1976)
Joan Cass The Cat Thief (1962), The Cat's Adventure with Car Thieves (1980)
N. Cavanagh Night Cargoes (1946), Sister to the Mermaid (1946)
Winifred Cawley Down the Long Stairs (1964), Silver Everything (1976)
Anton Chekhov Kashtanka (1959)
Marcus Crouch Six Against the World and other stories from Grimm (1978), The Ivory City (1980), Rainbow Warrior (1982)
John Cunliffe Mr Gosling and the Great Art Robbery (1979), Mr Gosling and the Runaway Chair (1978)
R.L. Dangerfield Adventure of Ben Gunn (1956)
D.S. Daniel Hunt Royal (1962)
Peter Dawlish The Boy Jacko (1962), Martin Frobisher (1956)
Nicholas Stuart Gray The Apple-Stone (1965)
Frederick Grice Aidan and the Strollers (1960), Rebels and Fugitives (1963)
Anita Hewett The Little White Hen (1962)
Joseph Jacobs Old Mother Wiggle-Woggle (1975)
Josephine Kamm Return to Freedom (1962)
Frank Knight The Last of the Lallows (1961), Clemency Draper (1963)
Hilda Lewis Here Comes Harry (1960)
David Wilson MacArthur Traders North (1951)
Edward Mackenzie Achilles (1972), Jason (1972), Perseus (1972), Theseus (1972)
Reginald Maddock The Big Ditch (1971)
Ruth Manning-Sanders A Bundle of Ballads (1959), The Smugglers (1962), The Three Witch Maidens (1972), Sir Green Hat and the Wizard (1974), Scottish Folk Tales (1976)
William Mayne Summer Visitors (1961)
Naomi Mitchison African Heroes (1968)
G. Pengelly The Grand Escapade (1947)
Madeleine Polland Beorn the Proud (1961), The White Twilight (1962), The Queen's Blessing (1963), Queen without Crown (1965)
Ian Serraillier The Ivory Horn (1960), The Gorgon's Head (1961), The Way of Danger (1962), A Fall from the Sky (1966)
William Stobbs Lilybelle (1946), The Story of the Three Bears (1964), The Story of the Three Little Pigs (1965), Jack and the Beanstalk (1965), The Three Billy Goats Gruff (1967), Life in England (1970), Dilly Dally (1974), Little Tiger (1974), Sophie (1974), The Derby Ram (1975), A Car Called Beetle (1976), The Country Mouse and the Town Mouse (1976), A Gaping Wide-Mouthed Frog (1977), Old Mother Goose and the Golden Egg (1977), The Hare and the Frogs (1978), Chanticleer: Chaucer's Story (1979), The Grape That Ran Away (1980), This Little Piggy (1981), Animal Pictures (1981)
Ronald Storer King Arthur and his Knights (1977)

Donald Suddaby The Death of Metal (1952), Fresh News from Sherwood (1959), Crowned with Wild Olive (1961)
Rosemary Sutcliff Houses and History (1960)
Ronald Syme That Must Be Julian (1947), Cortez, Conqueror of Mexico (1952), Columbus (1952), Magellan (1953), Gipsy Michael (1954), Henry Hudson (1955), They Came to an Island (1955), Balboa (1956), Isle of Revolt (1956), Ice Fighter (1956), The Forest Fighters (1958), River of no Return (1958), The Spaniards Came at Dawn (1959), Thunder Knoll (1960), The Buccaneer Explorer (1960)
Geoffrey Trease The White Nights of St Petersburg (1967)
Henry Treece The Golden One (1961), Man with a Sword (1962), Vinland the Good (1967)
Rosemary Weir The Star and the Flame (1962)
Ronald Welch Knight Crusader (1954), Captain of the Dragoons (1956), Mohawk Valley (1958), Captain of the Foot (1959), Escape from France (1960), For the King (1961), Nicholas Carey (1963)
Amabel Williams-Ellis Round the World Fairy Tales (1966)

References: Crouch; Doyle CL; Eyre; Hürlimann; ICB 2,3,4; Ryder

Alan Reynolds Stone (1909-79)

Worked as Reynolds Stone. Son and grandson of Eton housemasters; born and educated at Eton. Read history at Magdalene College Cambridge. Worked for the Cambridge University Press as an unofficial apprentice (1930-32). There, inspired by F.G. Nobbs (head of the composing department) and Stanley Morrison, he developed an interest in letter forms. He was also an admirer of Eric Gill* and visited him for two weeks at Pigotts. He worked for two years for a small commercial printer in Taunton, Somerset (1932-34), and then set up as an independent wood engraver and (from 1939) letter-cutter in stone. Visiting lecturer in typography and lettering at the Royal College of Art (c.1948-58). At various times he designed and engraved postage stamps, a £5 banknote (c.1961), heraldic devices, (including the Royal Arms for H.M. Stationery Office), and executed a number of monuments and memorial inscriptions. He also formed an important collection of early printing presses at his home in Litton Cheney, Dorset. His wood engraving technique was learned by studying the work of masters, particularly Thomas Bewick, and from a book *Wood Engraving: a Manual of Instruction* (1884) by W.J. Linton, one of the best of the Victorian (reproductive) engravers. Among contemporary engravers, he especially admired the work of Gwen Raverat*. His own engravings

Reynolds Stone. From *The Open Air* by Adrian Bell (Faber, 1936).

were usually of the quiet rural landscapes with which he was familiar; Sir Kenneth Clark described his view of nature as 'limited but optimistic'. His engravings inspired Sylvia Warner to write the collection of poems published as *Boxwood* (1957-60). His daughter is the illustrator Phillida Gili*. Elected member of Art Workers' Guild (1940), SWE (1948), RDI (1956); appointed RDI (1956), awarded CBE. [Q]

Books illustrated include:
Adrian Bell The Open Air (1936)
Benjamin Britten Tit for Tat (1969)
Elizabeth Barrett Browning Sonnets from the Portuguese (1962)
Kenneth Clark Moments of Vision (1973), The Other Side of the Alde (1968)
Anthony Gishford (ed) Tribute to Benjamin Britten on his Birthday (1963)
A.S.B. Glover Rousseau's Confessions (1938)
Antonio de Guevara The Praise and Happiness of the Country Life (1938)
Ralph Hodgson The Skylark (1958)
Philip James (ed) The Butler's Recipe Book (1935)
Eric Linklater A Social Plover (1957)
Herman Melville Omoo (1961)
Leslie Paul The Living Hedge (1946)
Forrest Reid Apostate (1947)
Siegfried Sassoon Siegfried's Journey (1945)
William Shakespeare Anthology (1935), Complete Works (1953), The Sonnets (1948)
John Sparrow Lapidaria (7 vols 1943-1976)
Freya Stark Perseus in the Wind (1949)
Algernon Swinburne Lucretia Borgia (1942)
Sylvia Townsend Warner Boxwood (1957, 1960)

References: Balston EWE, WEMEB; Bénézit; Garrett BWE, HBWE; Vollmer supp; Wa (1977); WaG; *Alphabet and Image* 7 (1948); *The Connoisseur* (September 1963); *Crafts Magazine* (March 1978); *House and Garden* (January 1978); *The Illustrated London News* (March 1978); *Signature* 2 (March 1936); *The Studio* special (Autumn 1938); *Vogue* (July 1977); Kenneth Clark *Reynolds Stone* (John Murray 1977); J.W. Goodison *Reynolds Stone* (Cambridge University Press 1947); Myfanwy Piper *Reynolds Stone* (Art & Technics 1951)

Simonette Strachey (b. 1915)

Born in London. Illustrator in pen and ink sometimes with watercolour washes, of children's books written by her husband.

Books illustrated include:
Richard Strachey Little Reuben's Island (1946), Little Reuben at the North Pole (1947), Buttercup Trail (1948), Moonshine (1953), Midsummer Moonshine (1956)

Periodicals: The Christian Science Monitor. The Oxford Mail

William Strang (1859-1921)

Born in Dumbarton, Scotland. Studied at the Slade School of Fine Art under the painter and etcher Alphonse Legros (1876-80), and then worked as assistant in Legros' etching class (1880-81). During the 1880s he concentrated on etching. His earliest illustrations—for *Death and the Ploughman's Wife* and *The Pilgrim's Progress* consisted of sets of etchings, and dated from the late 1880s though they were not published until some years later. He also worked in

pen and ink, contributing to *Lucian's True History* with Aubrey Beardsley and J.B. Clark (a former fellow-student at the Slade). He and Clark went on to share the illustration work for *Baron Munchausen* and *Sinbad*, in a decorative outline style, superficially influenced by Beardsley: the drawings that Strang contributed were outstanding for their fine draughtsmanship and compositional coherence. His wood engravings for his sinister *Book of Giants* (1898) led to commissions from C.R. Ashbee* (founder of the Essex House Press) for *The Doings of Death* and Erasmus's *The Praise of Folie* (in which his designs were engraved on wood by Bernard Sleigh*.) He also started work on the *Essex House Bible* for which 200 illustrations were planned, but the project was undersubscribed and eventually had to be abandoned. A friend of Ricketts* and Shannon as well as of Ashbee, Strang was fully in touch with the ideas and aims of the private press movement. However, in his etched illustrations he tended to adopt the more traditional approach in which illustrations were present in the book as individual works of art, rather than being subsumed into an overall decorative scheme. And indeed,

William Strang. From Sinbad the Sailor, and Ali Baba and the Forty Thieves (Lawrence & Bullen, 1896).

his etchings were strong, independent creations, often with suggestions of the macabre, or of the inescapably grim aspects of existence. To all his illustrations he brought the same qualities of seriousness and depth of feeling that were evident in his easel paintings, drawings and individual prints. He did little illustration after 1902, concentrating instead on portrait and genre painting and printmaking. By the end of his life he had completed 747 prints, mainly etchings. Elected member of the AA Workers' Guild (1895), RP (1904), ARA and RA as an etcher (1906 and 1921), and was President of the International Society of Sculptors, Painters and Gravers (1918-21). Founder member RE (1881, resigned 1902).

Books illustrated include:
Laurence Binyon Western Flanders (1899)
John Bunyan The Pilgrim's Progress (1895)
Robert Burns Tam O'Shanter (1902)
Cervantes Series of 30 etchings illustrating Don Quixote (1903)
Samuel Taylor Coleridge The Ancient Mariner (1896)
Desiderius Erasmus The Praise of Folie (1901)
Ian Hamilton The Ballad of Hadji (1894)
F. Hickes (trans) Lucian's True History (with others, 1894)
G.E. Lessing Nathan the Wise (1894)
John Milton Paradise Lost (1896)
Cosmo Monkhouse The Christ Upon the Hill (1895)
R.E. Raspe The Surprising Adventures of Baron Munchausen (with J.B. Clark, 1895)
(1892), Death and the Ploughman's
    Wife (1894), A Book of Giants (1898), The Doings of Death (1902)
Izaak Walton The Compleat Angler (1902)
Series of 30 etchings illustrating subjects from the writings of
    Rudyard Kipling (1901)
Sinbad the Sailor, and Ali Baba and the Forty Thieves (with J.B.
    Clark, 1896)

Periodicals: The Dome, The English Illustrated Magazine, The Hobby Horse, The Portfolio, The Yellow Book

References: Baker; Bénézit; Chamot, Farr & Butlin; Crane; DNB (1912-21); Guichard; Houfe; Johnson & Greutzner; Muir; Peppin; Ray; Shone; Sketchley; Thieme & Becker; Waters; C. Wood; *The Print Collector's Quarterly* vols 8, 24; *William Strang RA* (Sheffield City Art Gallery 1980); Laurence Binyon *William Strang: Catalogue of his Etched Work* (James MacLehose & Son 1906); James L. Carr *Scottish Painting Past and Present* (T.C. & E.C. Jack, 1908); Campbell Dodgson *The Etchings of William Strang and Sir Charles Holroyd* (Print Collector's Club 1933); Frank Newbolt *Etchings of William Strang* (George Newnes 1907)

Helen Stratton (active 1892-1924)

An illustrator who used her imaginative powers and strong decorative sense to the full in her black and white and colour work for books of legends and fairy tales. Her work reflects the Art Nouveau style of the period.

Books illustrated include:
Lady E.C. Barnes As the Water Flows (1920)
Walter D. Campbell Beyond the Border (1898)
Norman Gale Songs for Little People (1896)
A.C. Herbertson Heroic Legends (1908)
J. Lang A Book of Myths (1915)
George Macdonald The Prince and the Goblin (nd), The Princess and Curdie (1912)
Edmund Spenser Tales from the Faerie Queene (1902)
The Arabian Nights Entertainments (with others, 1899)
The Fairy Tales of Hans Christian Andersen (1899)
Grimm's Fairy Tales (1903)

Helen Stratton. From *Roland and the May-Bird* in *Grimm's Fairy Tales* (Blackie, 1903).

Selections from Le Morte d'Arthur (1902)
Stories from Grimm (1921)
Tales from Hans Christian Andersen (1896)

Periodical: Little Folks

References: Baker; Houfe; ICB 1; Johnson & Greutzner; Sketchley; C. Wood

Peter Strausfield (1910-80)

Worked as Peter Pendry. Born in Cologne, Germany, son of a civil servant. He studied at Cologne Art College, then worked as a stained glass designer, muralist and illustrator. He moved to England (1939), was interned (1940), released, served in the British army (1941-42), and subsequently made colour films for the Ministry of Information. From the 1940s until his death, he was responsible for the distinctive and widely acclaimed wood and lino-cut posters for George Hoellering's Academy Cinema, London. He was art director of George Hoellering's film *Murder in the Cathedral* (1951), for which he received the Art Director prize at the Venice Film Festival. He was also lecturer in graphic art and design at Brighton Polytechnic (1957-80). As an illustrator for the Folio Society, his work was vigorous and forceful. [Q]

Books illustrated include:
Karen Blixen Out of Africa (nd)
Samuel Taylor Coleridge Poems (1963)
Daniel Defoe A Journal of the Plague Year (1960)
Maxim Gorki The Artamonovs (1955)
Federico Garcia Lorca Three Tragedies (nd)
Francis Parkman The Laxdaela Saga (nd), The Oregon Trail (nd)
Peter Pendrey All is not Gold that Glitters (1944)

Helen Strickland (active 1927-30)

Studied at the Westminster School of Art under
Walter Bayes. A flower painter in watercolour. In
Shadow Birds, published by Blackwell and printed
at the Trinity Press, Worcester, she made striking
use of the *pôchoir* (colour stencil) process. This
effective but laborious technique was also em-
ployed, at about the same time at the Curwen
Press for books illustrated by by E. McKnight
Kauffer* and John Nash*. She lived at Dartford,
Kent, and was a member of the South London
Group.

Books illustrated include:
Helen Strickland The Bargerys (nd)
M. Strickland Shadow Birds (1930)

References: Johnson & Greutzner; Wa (1934); Waters; *The Studio*
special (Winter 1931)

Joanna Stubbs (b. 1940)

Born in London but spent much of her childhood
abroad. Studied at St Martin's School of Art and
Maidstone College of Art. Illustrator of children's
books in black and white (chalk) or full colour.
Married to the illustrator William Stobbs*.

Books illustrated include:
Peggy Appiah Why the Hyena Does not Care for Fish (1977)
Roy Brown The Million Pound Mouse (1975)
Margaret Donaldson The Moon's on Fire (1980)
Helen East Sara by the Seashore (1981)
Eva Figes Scribble Sam (1971)
Geraldine Kaye Koto and the Lagoon (1967)
Naomi Mitchison The Family at Ditlabeng (1969)
Joanna Stubbs The Tree House (1974), Weather Witch (1975),
   Hannah (1976), Happy Bears Day (1978)

Reference: ICB 4

Trevor Hugh Stubley (b. 1932)

Works as Trevor Stubley. Born in Leeds, Yorkshire. Studied at Leeds College of Art (1949-51)
and at Edinburgh College of Art (1951-53 and
1953-54 on a post-diploma scholarship); visited
France, Spain, Italy and Sicily on a travelling
scholarship (1954-55). National Service in Cyprus
(1955-57). Part time lecturer at Keighley, Harrogate, and Huddersfield Schools of Art (1957-58);
assistant lecturer at Huddersfield School of Art
(1958-60). Illustrator since 1960 of over 400 children's books. He works on board in black or
coloured ink, sometimes with spattered or off-

printed texture using washes of gouache, watercolour or acrylic paint and/or pastel or crayon to
give richness of colour and surface variety. In his
illustrative work, he tries to subordinate and
adapt his own ideas and point of view to those of
the author. He is also a painter of landscapes
based on the hill towns of the Yorkshire Pen-
nines. He lives near Huddersfield. Member RP
(1974), SIA (1976), Association of Illustrators
(1979); founder-member and first chairman of the
Kirklees Art Action group. Lives in Huddersfield, Yorkshire. [Q]

Books illustrated include:
Prudence Andrew Dog! (1968)
Agnes Ashton Saints and Changelings (1975)
Elizabeth Beresford The Four of Us (1980)
Gordon Boshell Capt Cobwebb and the Crustaks (1974), Capt
   Cobwebb and the Chinese Unicorn (1975), Capt Cobwebb and the
   Mischiefman (1976), Capt Cobwebb and the Quogs (1977), Capt
   Cobwebb and the Red Transistor (1979)
E.R. Braithwaite To Sir with Love (1974)
Marie Burg Salt and Gold (1975)
Bruce Carter The Perilous Descent (1975)
Dick Cate Flying Free (1975), A Funny Kind of Christmas (1976), Old
   Dog, New Tricks (1978), A Nice Day Out? (1979)
Aidan Chambers Flyers and Flying (1975), Funny Folk (1976)
Mary Cockett Drowning Valley (1978)
Clare Cooper The Black Horn (1980)
Alan Dale Portrait of Jesus (1977)
Nicholas Fisk Little Green Spacemen (1974), The High Way Home
   (1975), The Witches of Wimmering (1975)
Sheila Haigh Watch for Smoke (1978)
Michael Hardcastle Away from Home (1974), Saturday Horse (1976),
   Half a Team (1980)
John Harris A Tale of a Tail (1934)
Hans Eric Hellberg Maria (1974), Maria and Martin (1974), Ian and
   Maria (1977)
J. Holliday The Bus Boggart (1976)
Tim Hopkins Striker (1976)
Delia Huddy Tom Bates (1977), Hush-a-bye Baby (1977),
   Gatecrashers (1977), Blow Up (1977)
Geraldine Kaye In the New Forest (1975)
Benjamin Lee Paganini Strikes Again (1970), The Man in Fifteen
   (1972)
Frances Leigh The Lost Boy (1975)
George Macdonald The Princess and the Goblin (1974)
Sarah McNeill Whizz-Kid (1982)
Margaret Mahy Clancy's Cabin (1974), Bus Under the Leaves (1974)
Christobel Mattingley New Patches for Old (1977)
William Mayne The Yellow Airplane (1968), The Incline (1972)
Naomi Mitchison When the Bough Breaks (1974)
Alison Morgan Pete (1974), At Willie Tucker's Place (1975)
Michael Morpurgo Friend or Foe? (1976)
Richard Parker The Fire Curse (1974), Hugo Takes Off (1975),
   Digging for Treasure (1976), Sausages on the Shore (1976), Flood
   (1976), Sunday Papers (1976)
Madeleine Pollard A Family Affair (1971)
William Purcell Pilgrim's England (1980)
David Rees The Spectrum (1976)
K.P. Roadley Travellers (1976), Questing (1977)
Raj. Sacranie Charlie Chaplin (1980)
Jenny Seed The Voice of the Great Elephant (1968), The Prince of the
   Bay (1970), Kulumi the Brave (1970), The Great Thirst (1971), The
   Broken Spear (1972, Strangers in the Land (1977)
Ursula Synge Andrin and the Bear (1974)
Joan Tate Wild Boy (1972), Luke's Garden (1976)
Frank Walker Vipers & Co (1976)
T.H. White The Book of Merlyn (1977)
Also numerous educational books for Ginn, Macmillan Educational
and Schofield & Sims.

Periodical: Yorkshire Life

References: ICB 4; Wa (1980); *Growing Point* (November 1976);
Yorkshire Life (November 1976)

George Ernest Studdy (1878-1948)

Worked as G.E. Studdy. Born in Devon. Educated at Dulwich College, London. Attended evening classes in art at Heatherley's School of Art. Best known for his comic puppy 'Bonzo', who featured in animated films directed by Studdy but drawn by others, in picture books, and in his own *Bonzo Annual*. In contrast with his humorous canine creations, Studdy's humans were often stilted and stereotyped. He worked in black and white, half-tone and colour. Member of the London Sketch Club (President 1921-22).

Books illustrated include:
H.T. Sheringham Fishing: a diagnosis (1914)
G.E. Studdy Uncle's Animal Book, Bonzo and Us (1925), The Bonzo Book (1925), The New Bonzo Book (1927), The Bonzooloo Book (1929), Bonzo. The Great Big Midget book (1934), Jeek (1940)

Periodicals: The Big Budget, Bonzo Annual, The Graphic, The Humorist, Little Folks, The London Magazine, Punch, The Sketch, The Windsor Magazine

References: Cuppleditch; Doyle BWI; Houfe; Wa (1934); *Early Pioneers* (Cambridge Animation Festival Programme, November 1979)

Edmund Joseph Sullivan (1869-1933)

Worked as E.J. Sullivan. Born in London, brother of illustrator James Frank Sullivan. Studied under his father, artist Michael Sullivan, in Hastings. Recognition came early with his appointment (1889) to the staff of the newly-founded *Daily Graphic*, but was fired in 1892 (Thorpe suggests that his work was 'too artistic and unconventional' for the paper's proprietor). Indeed Sullivan was one of the most innovative and original of the black and white artists of the 1890s—the generation whose early careers coincided with the introduction of the photographic line block and halftone reproductive processes. His distinctive style was based on a freely drawn and very expressive linear 'handwriting', and he used shading both to describe form, and to generate a dynamic over the whole area of the drawing. He always worked within a defined rectangular format that served to compress and intensify the energy of his compositions. His inventive and often bizarre imagery could be simultaneously witty and macabre.

Sullivan's earliest book commissions came in the mid-1890s from publishers Macmillan and George Bell, and with *Sartor Resartus* (1898) his reputation became firmly established. He was particularly widely respected by his fellow-artists, many of whom apparently also envied his capacity to consume very large quantities of alcohol with no apparent ill-effects. During the 1890s he shared a studio with A.S. Hartrick*. He lectured in book illustration and lithography at Goldsmith's College, and was an examiner for the Board of Education and the Joint Matriculation Board in Manchester. Elected ARWS (1903), ARE (1925);

E.J. Sullivan. 'Dancing partners' from his *The Kaiser's Garland* (Heinemann, 1915).

President of the Art Workers' Guild (1931) and member of the Council of the International Society of Sculptors, Painters and Gravers. His brother James Frank Sullivan (1853-1936) was a humorous graphic artist of note, whose book illustrations were almost entirely published during the 19th century.

Books illustrated include:
Richard Barr A Prince of Good Fellows (1902)
George Borrow Lavengro (1896)
John Bunyan The Pilgrim's Progress (1901)
Thomas Carlyle Sartor Resartus (1898), The French Revolution (1910)
Edward FitzGerald (trans) The Rubaiyat of Omar Khayyam (1913)
F.H.C. de la Motte Fouqué Sintram and his Companions (1908)
Oliver Goldsmith A Citizen of the World (1904), The Vicar of Wakefield (1914)
Thomas Hughes Tom Brown's SchoolDays (1896)
J.H.L. Hunt The Old Court Suburb (1902)
Washington Irving The Sketch Book (1902), Poems of Keats (1910)
T. Lodge Rosalynde (1902)
Capt F. Marryat Newton Forster (1897), The Pirate and the Three Cutters (1897)
George Outram Legal and other Lyrics (1916)
Walter Scott The Pirate (1898),
Richard Brinsley Sheridan The Rivals and The School for Scandal (1896)
E.J. Sullivan The Kaiser's Garland (1915)
Alfred, Lord Tennyson A Dream of Fair Women (1900), Maud (1922)
Izaak Walton The Compleat Angler (1896)
H.G. Wells A Modern Utopia (1905)
Gilbert White A Garden Kalendar (with others, 1900), The Natural History of Selbourne (with others, 1900)

Poems by Robert Burns (1901)
Poems by Keats (1910)
Shakespeare's Works (1911)

Periodicals: Black and White, The Daily Chronicle, The Daily
Graphic, The English Illustrated Magazine, The Gentlewoman, Good
Words, The Graphic, The Lady Pictorial, The Ludgate Monthly, The
New Budget, The Pall Mall Budget, Pearson's Magazine, The Penny
Illustrated Paper, Punch, The Windsor Magazine, The Yellow Book

References: Baker; Bénézit; Bradshaw; Guichard; Houfe; ICB 1;
Johnson; Johnson & Greutzner; Mallalieu; Muir; Pennell MI, PD;
Peppin; Ray; Thieme & Becker; Thorpe; Wa (1929); Waters; C.
Wood; Drawing and Design (June 1924); Form vol 1 no 1 (April 1916);
The Print Collector's Quarterly obituary vol 20; The Studio 88 (1924),
special (1900-01, Autumn 1914, 1917, 1919, Spring 1922, 1923-24); G.
Montague Ellwood The Art of Pen Drawing (Batsford 1927); William
Feaver Masters of Caricature (Weidenfeld and Nicolson 1981); A.S.
Hartrick A Painter's Pilgrimage Through Fifty Years (Cambridge
University Press 1939); Holbrook Jackson The 1890s (Grant Richards
1913); J.G. Reid At the Sign of the Brush and Pen (Simpkin Marshall
1898); E.J. Sullivan The Art of Illustration (Chapman & Hall 1921),
Line (Chapman & Hall 1922); James Thorpe E.J. Sullivan (Art &
Technics 1948)

George Heywood Maunoir Sumner (1853-1940)

Worked as Heywood Sumner. Born in Arlesford,
Hampshire into a prominent clerical family. Educated at Eton and Christ Church, Oxford and
qualified as a barrister at Lincoln's Inn. A leading
member of the Arts and Crafts Movement during
the 1880s, he was organiser of the first Arts and
Crafts exhibition (1886) with Walter Crane* and
others; also a co-founder of the Fitzroy Picture
Society, which published inexpensive decorative
prints for schools, hospitals and mission halls. In
the late 1880s, he withdrew to rural Hampshire
due to ill health and later settled there in a house
of his own design, devoting much of his time to
archaeology and local history. During the 1880s,
he mainly illustrated works of fiction in a style
that was influenced by William Blake and anticipated Art Nouveau. His later illustrations, for his
own books, were of landscape and archaeological
subjects drawn with a straightforward but decorative pen line, slightly reminiscent of the work of
E.H. New*. He was also an etcher, designer of
stained glass and wallpaper and church decorator
in sgraffito. Member of the Century Guild and at
one time Master of the Art Workers' Guild.

Books illustrated include:
F.H.C. de la Motte Fouqué Sintram and His Companions (1883),
    Undine (1888)
J.R. de C. Wise The New Forest (with Walter Crane* 1883)
H.S. Leigh Cinderella, a Fairy Opera (1882)
F.M. Peard Jacob and the Raven (1896)
Heywood Sumner The Itchen Valley (1881), The Avon from Naxbury
    to Tewkesbury (1882), The Besom Maker (1888), The Book of
    Gorley (1910), The Ancient Earthworks of Cranbourne Chase
    (1913), Excavations on Rockbourne Down, Hampshire (1917), The
    Ancient Earthworks of the New Forest (1917), A Descriptive
    Account of the Roman Pottery made at Ashley Rails (1919), A
    Descriptive Account of Roman Pottery Sites at Sloden (1921), A
    Guide to the New Forest (1923), Excavations at East Grinstead,
    Wiltshire (1924)

Periodicals: Atalanta, The English Illustrated Magazine, The Hobby
Horse

References: Bénézit; Crane; Harper; Houfe; ICB 1; Johnson &
Greutzner; Pennell MI, PD; Sketchley; Taylor; C. Wood; Country Life
(September 28th, 1978); The Studio 13 (1898), special (1897-98, 1900-01)

Graham Vivian Sutherland (1903-80)

Born in London, son of a lawyer. Studied etching
and engraving at Goldsmith's College of Art
(1920-25) and drawing at Chelsea School of Art.
He taught engraving, then book illustration and
composition, at Chelsea School of Art (1928-32),
and designed posters, ceramics and fabrics during
the early 1930s. He took up painting (c.1935), and
contributed to the International Surrealist Exhibition, London (1936). Official war artist (1941-
44). After World War II, he worked mainly as a
portrait and landscape painter and exhibited extensively in Britain and abroad; he also made
lithographs and designed the tapestry for the new
Coventry Cathedral (completed 1962). He lived
mainly in France from 1956. His book illustrations
have marked affinities with his earlier landscape
paintings, particularly in their use of leaf and
tunnel-like motifs. Elected ARE (1925), RE
(1926-33); member London Group (1936-37).

Books illustrated include:
David Gascoyne Poems 1937-42 (1943)
Somerset Maugham Cakes and Ale (1954)
William Shakespeare The Comedies, Histories and Tragedies of
    (1939), Henry VI, Part One (1940)
V.M. Sackville West Invitation to Cast Out Care (1931)

Periodical: Signature

References: Bénézit; Chamot, Farr & Butlin; Contemporary Artists;
Gilmour; Guichard; Hofer; Johnson & Greutzner; Parry-Crooke;
Phaidon; Shone; Rothenstein 3; Thieme & Becker; Vollmer; Wa
(1980); Waters; The Print Collector's Quarterly vol 16; The Studio 146
(1953), special (Spring 1929); Douglas Cooper The Work of Graham
Sutherland (Lund Humphries 1961); John Hayes The Art of Graham
Sutherland (Phaidon 1980); Robert Melville (intro) Graham Sutherland
(Penguin 1943); Edward Sackville-West Graham Sutherland (Penguin
1943); R. Tassi The Complete Graphic Work of Graham Sutherland
(Thames & Hudson 1978)

Betty Swanwick (b. 1915)

Born in London, daughter of marine artist H.G.
Swanwick. Studied at Goldsmith's College School
of Art, the Royal College of Art and the Central
School of Arts and Crafts. Senior Lecturer at
Goldsmith's College (1948-69). Occasionally
taught at the Royal Academy Schools and the
Royal College of Art. Designer, mural painter
(e.g. for the Festival of Britain and Great Ormond
Street Hospital), animal painter, writer and illustrator. Her pen and ink illustrations, which often
accompany her own humorous novelettes, have
considerable sparkle. Elected ARA (1970), RA
(1980); member RWS. [Q]

Books illustrated include:
Ursula Hounhane Little Pig Finnigan (1958)
Richard Runcan Jan's Journal (1949)

Betty Swanwick The Cross Purposes (1945), Lord Olly's Bay (1946), Ella's Birthday (1946), Hoodwinked (1957), Beauty and the Burglar (1958), Guide to Character (1970)

Periodicals: Country Fair, Midox Message, The Strand Magazine

References: Jacques; Vollmer

Lindsay D. Symington (active 1891-1903)

Painter of landscapes and coastal scenes who lived in London and Buckfastleigh, Devon. Many of his book illustrations often consist of simplified but decorative line drawings. He worked mainly for the publishers Burns & Oates.

Books illustrated include:
A.P. Graves Father O'Flynn (1908)
Margaret M. Kennedy The Holy Child Seen by his Saints (1913)
A. Macquarie The Uffizi A.B.C (1908)
E.F. Nugent The Ship of Peter (1920)
Richard Southey The Inchape Rock (1907)
L.D. Symington As Stars for Ever (1908)
K. Tynan The Rhymed Life of St Patrick (1907)
Alphabet of Saints (1907)

Reference: Johnson & Greutzner

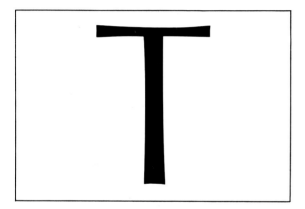

Margaret W. Tarrant (1888-1959)

Daughter of artist Percy Tarrant*. Studied at Clapham School of Art and Heatherley's School of Art. She started her career by designing cards and calendars, working almost exclusively for the Medici Society. She illustrated many children's books in black and white, and in colour. Her easy, naturalistic illustrations were widely known and very popular, particularly in the 1920s and 1930s. She was a close friend of Cicely Mary Barker*.

Books illustrated include:
M. St J. Adcock The Littlest One (1914)
M.A. Bigham Merry Animal Tales (1913)
Robert Browning The Pied Piper of Hamelin (1912)
Lewis Carroll Alice's Adventures in Wonderland (1916)
F. Cole A Picture Birthday Book for Boys and Girls (1915)
F.E. Crompton The Gentle Heritage (1920)
G. Davidson All about the Man in the Moon (nd)
D.S.N. The Songs the Letters Sing (1910), Simple Composition Steps (1930)
G.A.B. Dewar The Book of Seasons (1910)
Eleanor Farjeon An Alphabet of Magic (1928)
M. Gann Dreamland Fairies (1936)

H. Golding Verses for Children (1918), Zoo Days (1919), Fairy Tales (1930), Our Animal Friends (1930)
N.M. Hayes The Book of Games (with Nina K. Brisley*, 1920)
A.G. Herbertson Lucy-Mary or The Cobweb Cloak (nd)
K. Howard The Little God (1918)
Charles Kingsley The Water-Babies (1908)
E. Mackenzie Simple Reading Steps (1930)
J. Oxenham The Hidden Years (1931)
Charles Perrault Contes (1910)
G. Rhys In Wheelabout and Cockalone (with Megan Rhys, 1918)
R. Rudolph The Tookey and Alice Mary Tales (1919)
F.J. Snell The Girlhoods of Famous Women (1915)
M.W. Tarrant Autumn Gleanings from the Poets (1910), Our Day (1923), The Margaret Tarrant Birthday Book (1932), Joan in Flowerland (1935), The Margaret Tarrant Nursey Rhyme Book (1944), The Margaret Tarrant Story Book (nd)
B. Todd Magic Flowers (1933)
M. St J. Webb Knock Three Times! (1917), Eliz'beth, Phil and Me (1919), The Forest Fairies (1925), The House Fairies (1925), The Insect Fairies (1925), The Pond Fairies (1925), The Sea Shore Fairies (1925), The Wild-Fruit Fairies (1925), The Magic Lamplighter (1926), The Orchard Fairies (1928), The Littlest One's Third Book (1928), The Twilight Fairies (1928), The Little One In Between (1929), The Littlest One (with K. Nixon*, nd)
S. Wilman Games for Playtime and Parties (1914)
Fairy Stories from Hans Christian Andersen (1910)
Flowers of the Countryside (with others, 1943)
Mother Goose: Nursery Rhymes (1929)
Nursery Rhymes (1914)
Rhymes of Old Times (1925)
The Rose Fyleman Birthday Book (with Muriel Dawson, 1932)
The Tales the Letters Tell (with others, 1932)

Periodicals: Little Folks, Wonder Annual

References: Cope; Johnson & Greutzner; Wa (1958); Waters

Percy Tarrant (active 1880-1930)

Painter; book and magazine illustrator. Many of his illustrations consisted of oil paintings reproduced in full colour or halftone. They were quiet in feeling—temperamentally, he was better suited to *Little Women* than to *Wuthering Heights*. He was Margaret Tarrant's father and encouraged her to take up illustration; later, she supported him in his old age. He lived in London and in Surrey.

Books illustrated include:
Louisa M. Alcott Little Women (1926)
Emily Brontë Wuthering Heights (1924)
Amy le Feuvre A Bit of Rough Road (1908)
E.T. Meade Turquoise and Ruby (1906), The Princess of the Revels (1909), Pretty-Girl and the Others (1910), Three Girls from School (1913), The Girls of Abinger Close (1913)
M.L. Molesworth Greying Towers (1898)
Elsie Oxenham The Captain of the Fifth (1922), The Troubles of Tazy (1926), The Crisis in Camp Keema (1928)
Walter Scott Quentin Durward (1923)
Tales of all Time (1926)

Periodicals: Black and White, Cassell's Family Magazine, The Girl's Own Paper, The Penny Magazine, The Quiver, The Sunday Magazine

References Cope; Houfe; Johnson & Greutzner; Thorpe; C. Wood

Sibyl Tawse (active 1900-40)

Studied at Lambeth School of Art and at the Royal College of Art, where she won the King's Prize Scholarship and various medals. Portrait painter, poster designer and illustrator. Her illustrative work was often in pen and ink with wash, in a style sometimes reminiscent of E.J. Sullivan*. She lived in London and Hythe, Kent.

Books illustrated include:
M.M. Butt The Fairchild Family (1913)
William J. Clover Tales from the Poets (1915)
Alexandre Dumas The Count of Monte Cristo (1920)
Mrs Gaskell Cranford (1914)
Lizzie A. Harker Miss Esperance and Mr Wycherly (1926)
Charles Kingsley The Heroes (1915)
Charles Lamb The Essays of Elia (1910)
Captain Marryat Mr Midshipman Easy (1921)
Lucy Maud Montgomery Anne of Green Gables (1933)

References: ICB 1; Johnson & Greutzner; Wa (1934)

Norman Tealby (active 1927-31)

An able illustrator who clearly worked hard to adapt his style to the theme of each of his books. However, in his introduction to *Joseph Andrews*, J.B. Priestley, describing him as 'an artist who points a shrewd and humorous pencil', considered his work 'a shade too fantastic and too charmingly decorative to be absolutely in key with his subject.'

Books illustrated include:
P.A. de Alarcón The Three Cornered Hat (1927)
Eleanor Farjeon The Tale of Tom Tidler (1929)
Henry Fielding The History of the Adventures of Joseph Andrews (1929)
Leo Tolstoi Ivań the Fool and other tales (1931)

Margaret W. Tarrant. From *Verses for Children* edited by Hans Golding (Ward Lock, 1918).

Voltaire (trans Richard Aldington) Candide and other romances (1928)

Reference: ICB 1

Denis Tegetmeier (b. 1896)

Born in London. Studied at Lambeth School of Art under Eric Gill* whose daughter Petra he married in 1930. Gill, introducing Tegetmeier's *The Seven Deadly Virtues* alluded to the blamelessness of his home life (so far as anyone has heard)'. He was an etcher, pen and ink draughtsman and woodcut artist who used outline with precision and wit. He lived in High Wycombe, Buckinghamshire.

Books illustrated include:
Henry Fielding A Journey from this World to the Next (1930), The Life of Mr Jonathan Wild the Great (1932)
Eric Gill The Seven Deadly Virtues (c.1933), Money and Morals (1934), Unholy Trinity (1938), Sacred and Secular (1940)
William Langland A Version of Donald Attwater of the Vision of William Concerning Piers Plowman (1930)
Laurence Sterne A Sentimental Journey (1936)

Norman Tealby. From *The Old Woman's Story* in Voltaire's *Candide and Other Romances* with an introduction by Richard Aldington (The Abbey Library, 1928).

Denis Tegetmeier. 'Modes and Manners for the Theatre' from *Review of Revues* edited by C.B.C. (Cape 1930).

J. Taylor The Mysteriousness of Marriage (1928)

References: Johnson & Greutzner; Vollmer; *The Studio* special (Autumn 1938); Eric Gill *The Seven Deadly Virtues* (Lovat Dickson 1933)

Margaret Mary Tempest (1892-1982)

Worked as Margaret Tempest. Married name: Lady Mears. First studied in Ipswich, and later with the Royal Drawing Society (Queen Anne's Gate) and at the Westminster School of Art. In 1912, she founded the Chelsea Illustrators Club* (an association of freelance illustrators) with Muriel Goulden, and was Honorary Secretary of the club until its dissolution in 1939. Exclusively an illustrator of books for children, she was best known for her popular *Little Grey Rabbit* series, published by Collins from 1929. Later, she both wrote and illustrated a number of little books, including the 'Pinkie Mouse' series. Her meticulous and delicate small-scale watercolour drawings

Margaret Tempest. From *Little Grey Rabbit Goes to the Sea* by Alison Uttley (Collins, 1954).

have little depth but are full of charm, and the kind of minute factual detail that small children. She was also an accomplished calligrapher in the Edward Johnston tradition, designing covers and title pages, and sometimes the text of her smaller books.

Books illustrated include:
Rose Fyleman The Doll's House (1930)
P. Sage Katinka's Travels to the Himalayas (1926)
Margaret Tempest My Little Grey Rabbit Painting Book (1939), Pinkie Mouse and the Balloons (1944), Pinkie Mouse and the Elves (1944), A Belief for Children (1945), Pinkie Mouse and Christmas Day (1946), Pinkie Mouse and the Rainbow (1946), Pinkie Mouse and Koko (1947), An ABC for You and Me (1948), Curly Cobbler and the Fairy Shoe (1948), Curly Cobbler and the Snowfall (1948), Curly Cobbler and the Happy Return (1949), Curly Cobbler and the Cuckoo Clock (1950), A Sunday Book for Children (1954), Stories from the Old Testament (1955), The Little Lamb of Bethlehem (1957)
Alison Uttley The Squirrel, the Hare and the Little Grey Rabbit (1929), How Little Grey Rabbit Got Back Her Tail (1930), The Great Adventure of Hare (1931), The Story of Fuzzypeg the Hedgehog (1932), Squirrel Goes Skating (1934), Wise Owl's Story (1935), Little Grey Rabbit's Party (1936), The Knot Squirrel Tied (1937), Fuzzypeg Goes to School (1938), Little Grey Rabbit's Christmas (1939), Moldy Warp the Mole (1940), Hare Joins the Home Guard (1942), Little Grey Rabbit's Washing Day (1942), Water-Rat's Picnic (1943), Little Grey Rabbit's Birthday (1944), Little Grey Rabbit to the Rescue (1945), Little Grey Rabbit and the Weasels (1947), Grey Rabbit and the Wandering Hedgehog (1948), Little Grey Rabbit Makes Lace (1950), Hare and the Easter Eggs (1952), Little Grey Rabbit Goes to the Sea (1954), Hare and Guy Fawkes (1956), Little Grey Rabbit's Paint-Box (1958), Grey Rabbit Finds a Shoe (1960), Grey Rabbit and the Circus (1961), Grey Rabbit's May Day (1963), Hare Goes Shopping (1965), Little Grey Rabbit's Pancake Day (1967)

References: Cope; Johnson & Greutzner; Waters; *The Times* (obit 28th July 1982)

Nell Marion Tenison (1867-1953)

Born in London. Studied art in London, and

worked as a freelance illustrator before studying in Paris at Colarossi's where she met Cyrus Cuneo*; they were married in 1903 and settled in London. After his death (1916), she led a peripatetic life for many years, living in London, Devon and Cornwall. She was a capable illustrator, often working in full colour or halftone in a style that had much in common with that of her husband. Elected SWA (c.1917).

Books illustrated include:
Deborah Alcock The Spanish Brothers (1903)
Angela Brazil A Terrible Tomboy (1915)
A. Lucas The City and the Castle (c.1910)

Periodicals: Black and White, The Girl's Own Annual, The Girls' Realm, The Ladies' Realm, The Ludgate Monthly, Woman at Home

References: Houfe; Johnson & Greutzner; Vollmer; Wa (1934); Waters; Terence Cuneo The Mouse and his Master (New Cavendish Books, 1977)

C. Dudley Tennant (active 1898-1918)

Painter and illustrator in full colour, halftone and black and white. His work was typical of its period. The sculptor Dudley Trevor Tennant (born c.1900) was his son.

Books illustrated include:
Gilbert Barnett V.C.s of the Air (1918)

Harry G. Theaker. 'One night, when all the other children were asleep… he crept away among the rocks' from *The Water Babies* by Charles Kingsley (Ward Lock, 1922).

Periodicals: The Girls' Friend, The Girls' Realm, The Graphic, The Idler, The Penny Pictorial Magazine, Punch, The Royal Magazine, The Windsor Magazine

References: Houfe; Johnson & Greutzner; Thorpe

Lance Thackeray (d. 1916)

Sporting and genre painter in watercolour, and illustrator. A founder member of the London Sketch Club (1898) and a close friend of Cecil Aldin* with whom he explored Kent in a donkey cart. Like Aldin, he lived in Bedford Park, Chiswick during the 1890s. He later travelled in the Middle East, and held several one-man exhibitions in London. On the outbreak of World War I he enlisted with the Artists' Rifles, but died in Brighton two years later. Elected RBA (1899).

Books illustrated include:
G. Frankau The XYZ of Bridge (1906)
G. Holme (intro) The People of Egypt (1910)
Lance Thackeray The Light Side of Egypt (1908)

Periodicals: The Graphic, Printer's Pie, Punch, The Sketch, Sketchy Bits, The Sphere, The Tatler

References: Bénézit; Cuppleditch; Houfe; Johnson & Greutzner; Thieme & Becker; Waters WW (1914); Who Was Who (1916-28); C. Wood

Harry George Theaker (1873-1954)

Born in Wolstanton, Staffordshire, son of artist George Theaker. Studied at Burslem School of Art, the Royal College of Art, and in Italy. Painter, designer and illustrator. He was principal of Regent Street Polytechnic School of Art (1931-38). Lived in London for many years. His children's book illustrations tended to be banal and uninspired, but were often pleasantly coloured. Elected ARBA (1919), RBA (1920); member Art Workers' Guild.

Books illustrated include:
R.H. Barham The Ingoldsby Legends (1911)
D. Belgrave and H. Hart Children's Stories from Old British Legends (nd), Tales and Legends from India (nd)
Cervantes The Adventures of Don Quixote (1929)
Washington Irving Tales of the Alhambra (with others, nd)
N. Kato Children's Stories from Japanese Fairy Tales (1918)
Charles Kingsley The Water Babies (1922)
Oram Once Upon a Time (1923)
Jonathan Swift Gulliver's Travels (1928)
E.C.H. Vivian Robin Hood (1927)
Blanche Winder Stories of King Arthur (1925)
Children's Stories from the Arabian Nights (1914)
Grimm's Fairy Tales (1930)

Periodical: Holly Leaves

References: Johnson & Greutzner; Wa (1952); Waters; C. Wood

Norman Thelwell (b. 1923)

Born in Birkenhead, near Liverpool. Served in the East Yorkshire Regiment during World War II. Art editor of army publications in New Delhi (1945-47). Studied at Liverpool College of Art (1947-50). Lecturer at Wolverhampton College of Art (1950-55). He began contributing to *Punch* in 1952, and since 1955 has worked freelance as a book, magazine and commercial illustrator. His subjects are taken mainly from the countryside and rural pursuits - he is best known for his humorously depicted shaggy ponies with diminutive but irrepressible girl riders, but he is also a dedicated landscape watercolourist and draughtsman, and in his comic drawings the cartoon-style humans and animals are generally set against naturalistic landscape backgrounds. He has produced more than 20 humorous books (many of which have also been published abroad) and his cartoon characters have been used to decorate a wide range of products including tee shirts and crockery. [Q]

Books illustrated include:
M.J. Baker Away Went Galloper (1962)
C. Ramsden Racing Without Tears (1964)

Norman Thelwell. From *Away Went Galloper* by Margaret J. Baker (Methuen, 1962).

Norman Thelwell Angels on Horseback (1957), Thelwell Country (1959), Thelwell in Orbit (1961), A Leg at each Corner (1962), A Place of your own (1963), Top Dog (1964), Thelwell's Riding Academy (1965), The Compleat Tangler (1967), Up the Garden Path (1967), Thelwell's Book of Leisure (1968), This Desirable Plot (1970), The Effluent Society (1971), Penelope (1972), Three Sheets in the Wind (1973), Belt Up (1974), Thelwell Goes West (1975), Thelwell's Boat Race (1977), A Plank Bridge by a Pool (1978), Thelwell's Gymkhana (1979), A Millstone Round my Neck (1981)
Colin Willock Rod, Pole or Perch (1978)

Periodicals: New Chronicle, Punch, The Sunday Dispatch, Sunday Express

References: Hillier; Price; Wa (1980); William Hewison The Cartoon Connection (Elm Tree Books 1977); Norman Thelwell *A Plank Bridge by a Pool* (1978)

Franciszka Themerson (b. 1907)

Born in Warsaw, Poland, daughter of artist Jacob Weinles. Studied at the Warsaw Academy of Music and then at the Warsaw Academy of Fine Art. During the 1930s, she illustrated a number of children's books, and with her husband, Stefan Themerson, made the first avant-garde films in Poland, first independently and then within the Co-operative of Film Authors of which they were founders. They moved to Paris (1938) and London (1940) where they worked in the Film Unit of the Polish Ministry of Information and made their last films, *Calling Mr Smith* (1943) and *The Eye and the Ear* (1945). They founded their own publishing house—the Gaberbocchus Press (Latin for Jabberwock) in 1948. Franciszka Themerson illustrated the first English edition of Jarry's *Ubu Roi* (1950), produced a set of masks for a reading of the play at the ICA (1952) and sets and costumes for a production by the Stockholm Marioneteatrem (1964); she also designed *The Threepenny Opera* for the same company in 1966.

By establishing their own press, the Themersons were able to avoid normal publishing restraints and produce independent works of art. Franciszka Themerson's images bear little resemblance to conventional book illustrations but rather have their roots in Dada and concrete poetry. Introducing *Traces of Living*, Edward Lucie-Smith observed, 'Franciszka Themerson does not just *make* lines on a sheet of paper, she enters into collaboration—or should I say a conspiracy—with the line and waits to see what the result will be. The result is an extraordinary fertility of invention...'

Books illustrated include:
Aesop The Fox and the Eagle (1949)
Alfred Jarry Ubu Roi (1950)
Harold Lang and Kenneth Tynan The Quest of Corbett (1960)
Bertrand Russell The Good Citizen's Alphabet (1953), History of the World in Epitome (1962)
Franciszka Themerson Forty Drawings for Friends (1943), The Way it Walks (1956), Traces of Living (1959)
Stefan Themerson Bayamus (1949), Mr Rouse Builds his House (1950), The Adventures of Peddy Bottom (1951), Wooff Wooff, or Who Killed Richard Wagner? (1951), Professor Mmaa's Lecture

(1953), St Francis and the Wolf of Gubbio, or Brother Francis's Lamb Chop (1972)

References: Vollmer supp; Wa 1980; *Books and Bookmen* vol 12, no 6 (1967); *Studio International* (August 1966); *Typographica* 14 (1958); *Franciszka Themerson* (Whitechapel Art Gallery catalogue 1975); Stefan i Franciszka Themerson Visual Researches (Museum Sztuki w Lodzi 1981); Gerald Woods, Philip Thompson and John Williams *Art Without Boundaries* (Thames & Hudson 1972)

Bert Thomas (1883-1966)

Born Newport, Monmouthshire, son of a sculptor. Apprenticed (c.1897) to a commercial metal engraver and while there he specialised in the design and engraving of brass door plates. He contributed to magazines and newspapers from c.1900. A commission from Albert Chevalier for a large-scale theatre poster led to an introduction to Louis Meyer who appointed him to the staff of *London Opinion* (c.1913). He was a member of the London Sketch Club and close friend of fellow member of W. Heath Robinson*. He served as a private in the Artists' Rifles (World War I), and became known nationally for his 'Arf a mo', Kaiser' cartoon, drawn to advertise a tobacco

fund for soldiers (it raised £250,000). Thomas was one of the many artists to be influenced in style and subject by Phil May*. He worked rapidly 'Arf a mo', Kaiser' was dashed off in ten minutes. He seldom drew from models, using instead a large mirror in his studio, and referred to photographs for detail. He worked in pen, pencil, chalk, charcoal and wash with varied textural effects such as spatter, on many kinds of surface. His later work was often drawn directly with a brush.

Books illustrated include:
T.R. Arkell Meet these People (1928)
C. Graves and H.C. Longhurst Candid Caddies (1935)
W.W. Jacobs Sea Whispers (1926)
H. Simpson Nazty Nursery Rhymes (1940)
Bert Thomas In Red and Black. A Book of Drawings (1928), Cartoons and Character Drawing (1936), Fun at the Seaside (1944), Fun on the Farm (1944), A Mixed Bag (1945), Fun in the Country (1946), Fun in the Town (1946), A Trip on a Barge (1947)
Bert Thomas and A. Reubens Podgy the Pup (1945)

Periodicals: The Bystander, Fun, The Graphic, London Opinion, The Odd Volume, Passing Show, Punch, Radio Times, The Sketch, The World

References: Bradshaw; Cuppleditch; Driver; Houfe; Johnson & Greutzner; Price; Veth; Wa (1934); Waters; *Drawing and Design* no 2 (June 1920) p.33; Percy Bradshaw *They Make Us Smile* (Chapman & Hall 1942); William Feaver *Masters of Caricature* (Weidenfeld & Nicolson 1981)

Martin Thomas (active 1955-58)

Illustrator in pen and ink of books published principally by Collins. He worked without shading, initially in a diffident, fragmented line. Later his style developed greater fluency, though his drawings retained their reticent character.

Books illustrated include:
Naomi Mitchison The Far Harbour (1957)
Philip Rush The Minstrel Knight (1955), King of the Castle (1956)
Meriol Trevor The Other Side of the Moon (1956), Merlin's Ring (1957), Four Odd Ones (1958), The Sparrow Child (1958)

Hugh Thomson (1860-1920)

Born Coleraine, Co. Derry, Ireland, son of a tea merchant. Worked briefly for a linen manufacturer before being employed in Belfast by Messrs Marcus Ward, chromo-lithographic printers and Christmas card publishers. There he was helped and advised by the designer John Vinycomb, and also attended a handful of evening classes at Belfast School of Art; basically, however, he was self-taught as an artist. He moved to London in 1883, and was enlisted by *The English Illustrated Magazine* (1884); for the next eight years his drawings formed the magazine's main artistic attraction. From the late 1880s, he was in constant demand as a book illustrator, particularly for the classics with their opportunities for historical subject treatment. He also illustrated some modern authors such as J.M. Barrie and Austin Dobson (who had given him valuable help

Bert Thomas. 'Stand up', ses Alf, pulling 'im by the collar. Stand up and take wot's coming to you' from *Sea Whispers* by W.W. Jacobs (Hodder & Stoughton, 1926).

Hugh Thomson. From *Scenes from Clerical Life* by George Eliot (Macmillan, 1906).

and encouragement at the outset of his career), and a number of volumes in Macmillan's *Highways and Byways* series. He was awarded a civil list pension in 1918. One of the most popular and influential illustrators of his generation, Thomson specialised in atmospheric evocations of the 18th and early 19th centuries. His work in this vein was delicate and individual, although indebted to a considerable extent to the earlier artists E.A. Abbey and Randolph Caldecott who were the real pioneers in this field. In many ways he was Caldecott's natural successor; he shared Caldecott's charm, ease of manner and lighthearted approach to period themes, although as Sketchley points out he went further than Caldecott in exploring the forms and customs of bygone times. On the other hand his draughtsmanship, though more elaborate, was generally less assured than Caldecott's, and his use of colour much less positive. His *Days with Sir Roger de Coverley* (published in the year of Caldecott's death 1886) in one sense marked a new beginning; it was one of the first British books to have photomechanically reproduced illustrations instead of the then standard wood engravings, and Thomson's sensitive pen line proved extremely well suited to this new process. His *Cranford* illustrations (1891) were even more typical of his work, and gave their name to his nostalgic, affectionate and slightly whimsical

approach to historical themes. The 'Cranford School' numbered among its followers such prominent 1890s illustrators as C.E. Brock*, Chris Hammond and Fred Pegram*. Member of the London Sketch Club; elected RI (1897, resigned 1907).

Books illustrated include:
J.L. Allan A Kentucky Cardinal and Aftermath (1901)
Jane Austen Pride and Prejudice (1894), Emma (1896), Mansfield Park (1897), Northanger Abbey and Persuasion (1897)
J.M. Barrie Quality Street (1913), The Admirable Crichton (1914)
A.G. Bradley Highways and Byways in North Wales (1898)
Robert Buchanan The Piper of Hamlin (1893)
Fanny Burney Evelina (1903)
E.C. Cook Highways and Byways of London (1902)
F.J.H. Darton (retold by) Tales of the Canterbury Pilgrims (1904)
C.H. Dick Highways and Byways in Galloway and Carrick (1916)
Charles Dickens The Chimes (1913), The Cricket on the Hearth (1933)
Austin Dobson The Ballad of Beau Brocade and other poems (1892), Coridon's Song and other verses (1894), The Story of Rosina and other verses (1895)
George Eliot Scenes of Clerical Life (1906), Silas Marner (1907)
Mrs Gaskell Cranford (1891, new ed 1898)
Oliver Goldsmith The Vicar to Wakefield (1891), She Stoops to Conquer (1912)
P.A. Graham Highways and Byways in Northumbria (1920)
Stephen Gwynn Highways and Byways in Donegal and Antrim (1899), The Fair Hills of Ireland (1906), The Famous Cities of Ireland (1915)
Nathaniel Hawthorne The Scarlet Letter (1920)
Thomas Hughes Tom Brown's School Days (1918)
E. Hutton Highways and Byways in Gloucestershire (1932)
W.C. Jerrold Highways and Byways in Kent (1907), Highways and Byways in Middlesex (1909)
A. and J. Lang Highways and Byways in the Borders (1913)
Mary R. Mitford Our Village (1893)
John Moffat and Ernest Druce Ray Farley (1901)
Mrs Molesworth This and That (1899)
Arthur Norway Highways and Byways in Devon and Cornwall (1897), Highways and Byways in Yorkshire (1899)
Charles Reade Peg Woffington (1899)
Walter Scott St Ronan's Well (1894)
William Shakespeare As You Like It (1909), The Merry Wives of Windsor (1910)
Richard Brinsley Sheridan The School for Scandal (1911)
W. Somerville The Chase (1896)
Sir Isidore Spielmann Germany's Impending Doom (1918)
Mrs M.H. Spielmann Littledom Castle and other tales (with others, 1903), My Son and I (1908), The Rainbow Book (with A. Rackham*, 1909)
William Makepeace Thackeray The History of Samuel Titmarsh (1902), The History of Henry Esmond (1905)
H. Thomson Days with Sir Roger de Coverley (1886), The Poor in Great Cities (1896), Jack the Giant Killer (1898)
W.O. Tristram Coaching Days and Coaching Ways (with H. Railton*, 1888)
G.J. Whyte-Melville Riding Recollections (1898)

Periodicals: Black and White, The Boy's Own Paper, Chatterbox, The English Illustrated Magazine, The Girls' Realm, The Graphic, Little Folks, The New Budget, The Pall Mall Budget, The Pall Mall Magazine, The Sunday Magazine

References: Baker; Bénézit; Cuppleditch; DNB (1912-21); Doyle BWI; Harper; Houfe; ICB 1; Johnson & Greutzner; Mallalieu; Muir; Pennell MI, PD; Ray; Sketchley; Thieme & Becker; Thorpe; Waters; C. Wood; The Studio 70 (1917), special (1900-01, Autumn 1914, 1923-24); M.H. Spielmann and W. Jerrold *Hugh Thomson* (A. & C. Black 1931)

Archibald Thorburn (1860-1935)

Son of miniature painter Robert Thorburn. Educated in Dalkeith and Edinburgh. Moved to London in 1885; settled at Hascombe, Surrey in 1902. He was a celebrated painter and illustrator of birds and mammals. Many of his illustrations consisted of full colour vignettes of different species, often with landscape backgrounds; he also sometimes depicted landscapes on their own, usually shooting or fishing venues. He developed a distinctive style working in graduated water-colour washes with superimposed detail in gouache or bodycolour; he also made pen and ink drawings. Many of his books were published by Longmans, including the monumental and lavishly produced *British Birds* (1915-18), and *British Mammals* (1920). He was a close friend of John Guille Millais* and collaborated with him on several books. Elected Fellow of the Royal Zoological Society.

Books illustrated include:
Sir G.F. Archer and E.M. Godman The Birds of British Somaliland and the Gulf of Aden (1937)
S.C. Buxton Fishing and Shooting (1902)
T.F. Dale The Fox (1906)
G.A.B. Dewar Life and Sport in Hampshire (1908)
Gathorne-Hardy Autumns in Argyleshire with Dog and Gun (1900)
Augustus Grimble Highland Sport (1894), The Deer Forests of Scotland (1896), Deer-Stalking and Deer Forests of Scotland (1901), The Salmon Rivers of Scotland (1902), Shooting and Salmon Fishing and Highland Sport (1902)
J.E. Harting The Rabbit (1898)
W.H. Hudson British Birds (1895)
H.A. Macpherson The Hare (1896), Red Deer (1896)
J.G. Millais The Mammals of Great Britain and Ireland (1904), The Natural History of British Game Birds (1909), British Diving Ducks (1913)
H. Peek The Poetry of Sport (1898)
T.L. Powys Notes on the Birds of Northamptonshire (1895), Lord Milford on Birds (1903)
H.E. Stewart The Birds of Our Country (1897)
W. Swaysland Familiar Wild Birds (1901)
A. Thorburn The Pheasant (1895), British Birds (4 vols 1915-18), A Naturalist's Sketchbook (1919), British Mammals (2 vols, 1920), Game Birds and Wild Fowl of Great Britain and Ireland (1923)

Periodicals: The English Illustrated Magazine, The Illustrated London News, The Pall Mall Magazine, The Sporting and Dramatic News, Young England

References: Bénézit; Houfe; Johnson & Greutzner; Mallalieu; Thieme & Becker; Thorpe; Wa (1927); Waters; C. Wood; WW (1936); *The Studio* 91 (1926), p.79; James L. Caw *Scottish Painting Past and Present* (T.C. & E.C. Jack 1908); Robert Dougall (intro) *Thorburn's Naturalist's Sketchbook* (Michael Joseph, 1977); James Fisher *Thorburn's Birds* (Michael Joseph 1967); John Southern *Thorburn's Landscape* (Elm Tree Books 1981)

Rosalind Thornycroft (b. 1891)

Born Surrey, daughter of the eminent sculptor Sir Hamo Thornycroft. Studied at the London School of Economics, the Slade School of Fine Art and the Académie Julian, Paris. Her husband, A.E. Popham, was Keeper of Prints and Drawings at the British Museum (1945-54). An occasional book illustrator, she acknowledged the formative influence on her work of Pre-Raphaelite painting and the coloured picture books of Walter Crane*. Her admiration for Diaghilev's Russian Ballet found expression in the striking costumes and theatrical figure-poses in her coloured pen and ink illustrations for *Kings and Queens of*

England (written by her relatives Eleanor and Herbert Farjeon). She also made hand-printed textiles.

Books illustrated include:
Eleanor Farjeon Nuts in May (1926), Italian Peepshow and other tales (1926)
Eleanor and Herbert Farjeon Kings and Queens (1932), Heroes and Heroines (1933)

Reference: ICB 1

James H. Thorpe (1876-1949)

Born in Homerton, East London. Attended a local board school, then Bancroft's School on a scholarship. He unwillingly became a school-master until 1902. Studied at evening classes at Heatherley's School of Art (1897) and under Alec Carruthers Gould*. Founder member of the London Sketch Club, where he acquired a wide circle of friends, including Starr Wood* and fellow cricket enthusiast Frank Reynolds*. Designer of pictorial advertisements for the London Press Exchange (1902-22), and responsible for Three Nuns Tobacco posters for many years. He contributed theatrical drawings to *The Bystander*.

Rosalind Thornycroft. 'Charles I' from *Kings and Queens* by Eleanor and Herbert Farjeon (Dent, 1932).

Hans Tisdall. 'The Wheelwright' from *Wheels* by Oliver Hill and Hans Tisdall (Pleiades Books, 1946).

Served in the Artists' Rifles (1914-19), and afterwards settled in rural Hertfordshire. Author of valuable monographs on Phil May* and E.J. Sullivan*, and the exhaustive *English Illustration —the 'Nineties*. His own book illustrations were not particularly distinctive.

Books illustrated include:
G. Howe Happy Days (1933)
James Thorpe Jane Hollybrand (1932), Come for a Walk (1940)
Izaak Walton The Compleat Angler (1911)
Wells and Gardner A Cricket Bag (1929)

Periodicals: The Bystander, The Graphic, London Opinion, Nash's Illustrated Weekly, Punch, The Sketch, The Tatler, The Windmill, The Windsor Magazine

References: Bénézit; Cuppleditch; Houfe; Johnson & Greutzner; Thieme & Becker; Wa (1934); James Thorpe *Happy Days, Recollections of an Unrepentant Victorian* (Gerald Howe 1933)

Frederick Colin Tilney (1870-1951)

Studied at Westminster (c.1908) and St Martin's School of Art. Painter of landscapes and figures in oil and watercolour, writer on the arts, and editor of *Art and Reason*. The majority of his book illustrations seem to have been executed before he attended Art School, and are somewhat amateur in appearance.

Books illustrated include:
Elizabeth Barrett Browning Sonnets from the Portugese (1894)

Mrs. Craig John Halifax, Gentleman (1898)
Aesop's Fables (1913)
The Original Fables of La Fontaine (1913)
The Story of Wagner's 'Lohengrin' (1901)

Periodicals: The Leisure Hour, The Penny Magazine

References: Johnson & Greutzner; Vollmer; Wa (1950); *Art Digest* 25 (1951); *The Leisure Hour* (1901-20)

Hans Tisdall (b. 1910)

Born Hans Aufseeser in Munich, Germany. Studied at the Munich Academy of Fine Art, then worked in Ascona and Paris before settling in London (1930). Painter, and designer of murals, textiles and tapestries. Lecturer in Fine Art at the Central School of Arts and Crafts, London, the Dartington Summer School and in Venice. As a designer of book jackets and illustrations, his work was decorative, decisive and always up-to-date.

Books illustrated include:
F.S. Boas Songs and lyrics from the English Playbooks (1945)
Oliver Hill and Hans Tisdall Balbus: A Picture of Building (1944), Wheels (1946)
E.R.R. Linklater Position at Noon (1958)

References: Bénézit; Hürlimann; Lewis; Vollmer; Wa (1980); Waters; *Thirties* (Hayward Gallery Catalogue October 1979)

Michael Justin Todd (b. 1932)

Works as Justin Todd. Born in New Malden, Surrey, son of a Post Office engineer. Studied painting at Wimbledon College of Art (1949-53) and, after army service, illustration at the Royal College of Art (1955-58). He assisted Edward Bawden* on murals for Morley College, London (1958-59). Part-time lecturer in graphics at Tunbridge Wells School of Art (1963-64), and in illustration at Brighton Polytechnic (from 1964). He has worked as a freelance illustrator and designer since 1960. Since 1972 he has concentrated on cover illustrations for paperback books specialising in mysticism and horror (including the *Fontana Tales of Terror* series from 1974). Among these have been many striking images of dream and fantasy, often symbolist or surrealist in feeling and sometimes incorporating allusions from art history. He avoids direct references to nature whenever possible, and instead manipulates his component images into tightly structured yet freely imaginative designs. He works in black and white and full colour. [Q]

Books illustrated include:
Angela Carter Moonshadow (1982)
D. & J. Parker The Compleat Astrologer (1971)
H. Grant Scarfe As We Were (24 vols 1960-67)
David Smith and Derek Newton Wonders of the World (1969)
D. Taylor Pompeii and Vesuvius (1967)
Jules Verne Around the World in Eighty Days (1966)

References: *Observer* magazine (21st March 1982); M. Dempsey *The Magical Paintings of Justin Todd* (Fontana 1978)

Feliks Topolski (b. 1907)

Born Warsaw, Poland, son of an actor. Studied at the Warsaw Academy of Fine Art, and in Paris and Italy. Settled in London (1935). Official war artist to the Polish Forces (1940-45); a British subject since 1947. Since then he has received many public and large-scale commissions for easel paintings and murals, including 20 pictures of English writers for the University of Texas (1961-62), and of the Coronation for Buckingham Palace. His graphic work in pen and ink or pencil, sometimes with added colour or halftone washes, is linear and expressionist and has close affinities with his painting. He has contributed to many BBC television programmes and has designed theatrical costumes and sets. Awarded the Gold Medal of Honour by the International Fine Arts Council and Doctorate Honoris Causa of Jagiellonian University, Cracow, Poland (1974). [Q]

Books illustrated include:
Harold Acton Prince Isidore (1950)
H. Ainley In Order to Die (1965)
H. Burnett Face to Face (1964)
M.S. Collis Lord of the Three Worlds (1947)
John Elsom Post-War British Theatre Criticism (1980)
D.C.C. O'Brien The United Nations Sacred Drama (1968)
Tony Palmer The Trials of Oz (1971)
George Bernard Shaw Geneva (1939), In Good King Charles' Golden Days (1939), Pygmalion (1941)
Leo Tolstoy War and Peace (1971)
Feliks Topolski The London Spectacle (1935), Britain in Peace and War (1941), Russia in War (1942), Portrait of G.B.S. (1946), Three Continents 1944-45 (1946), Confessions of a Congress Delegate (1949), 88 Pictures (1951), Coronation (1953), Sketches of Gandhi (1954), The Blue Conventions (1956), Holy China (1968), Topolski's Legal London (1961), Topolski's Chronicle for Students of World Affairs (1958), Shem, Ham & Japheth Inc. (1971), Paris Lost (1973), Topolski's Buckingham Palace Panoramas (1981), Travels with my

Feliks Topolski. From his *Art for All* (Art & Technics, 1949).

Mary Tourtel. From *Rupert. Three Stories of the Little Bear's Adventures* (Marks & Spencer, nd).

Father, a South American Journey (with Daniel Topolski, 1983)
Richard Whalen A City Destroying Itself (1964)

Periodicals: Fortune, Harper's Bazaar, The Illustrated London News, Literary Review, Look, News Chronicle, Night and Day, Picture Post, The Sketch, The Tatler, Topolski's Chronicle, Vogue

References: *The Architectural Review* (March 1978); *Art and Artists* (October 1981); *Arts Review* (18th July 1980); Bénézit; Chamot, Farr & Butlin; *The Guardian* (17th April 1982); ICB 2; *New Yorker* (24th April 1965); Phaidon; Thieme & Becker; Vollmer; Wa (1980); WaG; Waters; *The Artist* (March 1944); *Typography* 2 (1937)

Mary Tourtel (1897-1940)

Wife of H.B. Tourtel, sub-editor of the *Daily Express*, she became well-known as the creator of the little bear Rupert, much-loved hero of a two-frame cartoon that has appeared in the paper daily since November 8th 1920. H.B. Tourtel wrote Rupert captions until his death in 1931 but Mary Tourtel continued to draw the strip until prevented by failing eyesight in 1935. It was then taken on by A.E. Bestall*. She worked in an outline technique that reproduced exceptionally well in newsprint and Margaret Blount has observed that her drawing 'was characterised by its great clarity and simplicity, allied to attention to detail'. Rupert has appeared regularly in books and annuals published by the *Daily Express* and drawn by Mary Tourtel and her successors.

Books illustrated include:
E.V. Lucas A Horse Book: Dumpy Books for Children no 10 (1897), The Three Little Foxes: Dumpy Books for Children no 21 (1897)
Mary Tourtel Humpty Dumpty Book (1902), The Adventures of the Little Lost Bear (1921), The Little Bear and the Fairy Child (1922), The Little Bear and the Ogress (1922), Rupert. Little Bear's Adventures (1924), Little Bear Library (1928-36), The Monster Rupert series (1929-35), The Rupert Story Book (1938), Rupert Little Bear. More Stories (1939), Rupert Again (1940)

Periodicals: Daily Express, The Girls' Realm

References: Doyle CL; Fisher p.314; Margaret Blount *Animal Land* (Hutchinson 1974); William Feaver *When We Were Young* (Thames & Hudson 1977); George Perry and Alan Aldridge *The Penguin Book of Comics* (1967)

Jack Townend (b. 1918)

Lithographer, wood engraver and illustrator. Studied at Bradford College of Art and under Randolph Schwabe at the Slade School of Fine Art. Lecturer in printmaking at Ruskin School of Drawing, Oxford. Elected FRSA (1948).

Books illustrated include:
Jack Townend A Railway ABC (1942), Jenny the Jeep (1944), A Story about Ducks (1945), The Clothes We Wear (1947), Ben (nd)

Reference: Wa (1972)

Frederick Henry Linton Jehne Townsend (1868-1920)

Worked as F.H. Townsend. Born in London. Studied at Lambeth School of Art where contemporaries included Leonard Raven-Hill*, Reginald Savage*, and Charles Ricketts*. By the age of nineteen, he had built up a reputation as a versatile illustrator and pictorial journalist who enjoyed the challenge of difficult commissions. He contributed to many magazines during the 1890s and in 1905 became the first Art Editor of *Punch*. Bernard Partridge*, a *Punch* colleague, introducing a posthumous collection of Townsend's work, described it in these terms '...unconquerable gaiety, joyousness, sanity and sureness of his power...no hesitancy anywhere nor affectation: the theme is set down firmly and with conviction: the witty line, now crisp and decisive, now blond and rippling, flickers in an out of it...suffusing the page with that silvery sparkle of which he held the secret.' However Partridge also recorded 'From... early days I watched Townsend's progress and it is curious to note, while his powers of observation ripened and his style shed something of formality, how little of the slick dexterity of his essential method changed; it was crystallised from the outset'. ('*Punch*' Drawings by F.H. Townsend, 1921). Townsend was also a painter and in later life became interested in etching. G.P. Jacomb-Hood* recorded that he died suddenly on a golf course. Member of the Chelsea Arts Club during the 1890s; elected ARE (1915).

Books illustrated include:
Florence L. Barclay The Following of the Star (1911)
Charlotte Brontë Jane Eyre (1896), Shirley (1897)
G. Campbell The Joneses and the Asterisks (1895)
V.C. Cotes Two Girls on a Barge (1891)
Charles Dickens A Tale of Two Cities (1897)
S.J. Duncan A Social Departure (1890), An American Girl in London (1891), The Simple Adventures of a Memsahib (1893), The Path of a Star (1899)
S. Baring Gould Gladys of the Stewponey (1897)
Henry Harland The Cardinal's Snuffbox (1900)
Nathaniel Hawthorne The House of the Seven Gables (1897), The Scarlet Letter (1897), The Blithdale Romance (1898), Works (1899)
Mrs E. Hohler For Peggy's Sake (1898)
Rudyard Kipling 'They' (1905), The Brushwood Boy (1907)
E.J. Lysaght Grannie (1892)
F. Marryat The King's Own (1896)

Thomas Love Peacock Crotchet Castle (1895), Maid Marian (1895), Gryll Grange (1896), Melincourt (1896), The Misfortunes of Elphin and Rhododaphne (1897)
Walter Scott Rob Roy (1897)
L. Thompson Gladys Anstruther (nd)
I. Zangwill The Old Maids' Club (1896)

Periodicals: Black and White, Cassell's Family Magazine, The Daily Chronicle, Fun, The Gentlewoman, Good Words, The Graphic, The Idler, The Illustrated London News, The Lady's Pictorial, The Longbow, The New Budget, The Pall Mall Magazine, Pick-me-up, Printer's Pie, Punch, The Queen, The Quiver, The Royal Magazine, The Sketch, The Sphere, The Tatler, The Unicorn, The Windsor Magazine

References Bénézit; Bradshaw; Guichard; Harper; Houfe; Johnson & Greutzner; Mallalieu; Price; Sketchley; Thieme & Becker; Thorpe; Waters; C. Wood; *The Studio* 68 (1916), special (1900-01); G. Montague Ellwood *The Art of Pen Drawing* (Batsford 1927); G.P. Jacomb-Hood *With Brush and Pencil* (John Murray 1925); J. Bernard Partridge (intro) '*Punch' Drawings by F.H. Townsend* (Cassell 1921)

Katharine Tozer (active 1936-55)

Children's writer and illustrator, best known for her books about Mumfie (a toy elephant) published by John Murray. They were illustrated with

Katharine Tozer. 'The last toy was chosen an hour ago' from *The Wanderings of Mumfie* (1935).

stylish, decorative outline drawings that more than hold their own among the productions of a very line-conscious age. Using a fine pen she contrasted passages of precisely patterned texture with areas of solid black, sometimes adding one or two flat colours.

Books illustrated include:
Eleanor Farjeon Paladins in Spain (1937)
Katharine Tozer The Wanderings of Mumfie (1935), Here Comes Mumfie (1936), Mumfie the Admiral (1937), Mumfie's Magic Box (1938), Mumfie's Uncle Samuel (1939), Noah. The Story of Another Ark (1940), Adventures of Alfie (1941), Mumfie Marches On (1942), Mumfie's Picture Book (1947)

References: Margaret Blount *Animal Land* (Hutchinson 1974)

Mary Christine Tozer (b. 1947)

Born in London. Studied at Reigate College of Art and Design (1963-65). Worked as technical illustrator (1965-69), a textile consultant (1970-74) and as a freelance journalist (1966-74). Author and illustrator of children's books published by World's Work since 1975. Influenced by the early 20th century Russian artist Bilibin, her illustrations, in pen outline with colour washes, are peopled with bold fairytale characters. [Q]

Books illustrated include:
Mary Tozer Sing a Song of Sixpence (1975), Old Mother Hubbard (1977), The King's Beard (1978), Peter Pipkin and his Very Best Boots (1979), The Grannies Three (1980), Queen Yesno (1981), The Nightingale and other Tales from Hans Andersen (1981)

References: *Arts Review XXIX no 1 (7th January 1977), XXX no 25 (22nd December 1978); Book Window* (Summer 1979); *The Designer* New York 21 no 259 (4th August 1978); *The Essex Review of Children's Literature* (Summer 1981); *New Zealand Farmer* (28th August 1978)

Cecil Stuart Tresilian (b. 1891)

Worked as Stuart Tresilian. Born in Bristol; spent some of his early life in Liverpool where he became interested in ships. Studied art at the Regent Street Polytechnic, taught there as a pupil-teacher, then won a scholarship to the Royal College of Art. During army service (1914), he was wounded and taken prisoner. After the war he returned to Regent Street as a teacher. Retired to Winslow, Buckinghamshire. As a children's illustrator he worked in pen, brush and crayon, producing conventional, rapid-looking 'adventure style' drawings with strong tonal contrasts and plenty of action, but often a lack of facial differentiation between individual characters. Master of the Art Workers' Guild (1960); President of the SGA (1962-65). [Q]

Books illustrated include:
M.E. Atkinson Challenge to Adventure (1942), The Monster of Widgeon Weir (1943), The Nest of the Scarecrow (1944), Problem Party (1945)
Enid Blyton The Castle of Adventure (1946), The Valley of Adventure (1947), The Sea of Adventure (1948), The Mountain of Adventure (1949), The Circus of Adventure (1952), The River of Adventure (1955)

Joseph Chipperfield Petrus, Dog of Hill Country (1960), The Grey Dog from Galtymore (1961)
Eilis Dillon Midsummer Magic (1949)
Rose Fyleman Bears (1935)
Michael Gaunt Brim's Boat (1964), Brim Sails Out (1966)
Rudyard Kipling Animal Stories (1932), All the Mowgli Stories (1937)
Ian Serraillier The Cave of Death (1965)
Mary Treadgold We Couldn't Leave Dinah (1941)

References: Fisher pp.61, 244-45; ICB 1, 2, 3; Johnson & Greutzner

Walter Trier (1890-1951)

Born in Prague. Studied at the Munich Academy. From 1910 he worked in Berlin, contributing to a number of magazines including *Simplizissimus*, and as an advertising artist, stage designer, and cartographer. In 1936, he moved to England. He died in Canada. His work, in pen and ink, sometimes with added halftone or colour, is freely drawn, humorous and forceful.

Books illustrated include:
K. Barclay The Story of Frisky (1945)
E. Kästner Annaluise and Anton (1932)
D. Morgan My Sex Right or Wrong (1947)
C. Nelson and Walter Trier The Jolly Picnic   (1944)
D.S. Smith Jolly Families (1946)
Walter Trier Toys (1923), 10 Little Negroes, a new version (1944), 8192 Quite Crazy People (1949), 8192 Crazy Costumes in One Book (1950) Book (1950)

Periodical: Lilliput

References: Fisher p.103; Hillier; Hurlimann; ICB 1, 2; Thieme & Becker; Vollmer; William Feaver *When We Were Young* (Thames & Hudson 1977), *Masters of Caricature* (Weidenfeld & Nicolson 1981)

Elisabeth Trimby (b. 1948)

Worked as Elisabeth Trimby for her earliest books, and as Elisa Trimby later. Born in Reigate, Surrey. Studied at the Froebel Institute (1967-68) and then at Brighton College of Art where she specialised in graphics. Part-time lecturer at Thames Polytechnic School of Architecture (1973-77) and Southend College of Art (1975-76); part-time art therapist at St Thomas's Hospital London (1975-77). Since 1971 she has worked freelance as an illustrator and graphic designer. She works in pen and ink or occasionally pencil, sometimes with watercolour washes, and also makes wood engravings. Her lively, unassuming illustrations have considerable individuality.

Books illustrated include:
Charlotte Bronte Shirley (1972)
Ruth Craft The King's Collection (1978)
Mary Curran The Country Ones (1978)
Arthur Conan Doyle The Lost World (1977)
Ruth Harris The Cornerstone (1976)
Trevor Honsby Big Fish (1973)
Ann Lawrence Mr Robertson's 100 (1976)
Ann Monsarrat And the Bride Wore (1973)
Clement Clarke Moore The Night before Christmas (1977)
Fiona Satow You (1975)
Elisa Trimby Mr Plum's Paradise (1976), Mr Plum's Oasis
J. Wyatt The Shining Levels (1973)

References: *The Daily Telegraph* (11th December 1976); *The Evening Standard* (24th February 1977); *Woman* (19th February 1977)

Joanna Margaret Troughton (b. 1947)

Born in London. Studied graphics at Hornsey College of Art. Part-time lecturer at Harrow School of Art (1975-81) and at Barnet College of Art (since 1979). Freelance illustrator and writer of children's books since 1969, working in pen and ink, watercolour and gouache and sometimes crayon. [Q]

Books illustrated include:
Richard Blythe Fabulous Beasts (with Fiona French*, 1977)
Wendy Body Clayhorses (1979)
Kevin Crossley-Holland The Sea-Stranger (1973), The Fire-Brother (1974), The Earth-Father (1975)
Julia Dobson The Smallest Man in England (1977)
Adèle Geras A Thousand Yards of Sea (1979)
Elisabeth Kyle The Key of the Castle (1976)
J.D. Lincoln Montezuma (1977), The Fair-Skinned Strangers (1977)
Sheila McCullagh The Kingdom Under the Sea (1976)
Robert Nye Out of the World and Back Again (1977)
Michael Pollard My World (1979)
James Reeves Quest and Conquest (1976)
Gail Robinson Raven the Trickster (1981)
Anna Sproule Warriors (1980), Villains (1980)
Jenny Taylor and Terry Ingleby Ganpat's Long Ride (1979)
Geoffrey Trease Days to Remember (1973)
Joanna Troughton The Little Mohee (1971), Sir Gawain and the Loathly Damsel (1972), Spotted Horse (1972), Why Flies Buzz (1974), The Story of Rama and Sita (1975), How the Birds Changed their Feathers (1976), What Made Tiddalik Laugh (1977), How Rabbit Stole the Fire (1979), Tortoise's Dream (1980), The Magic Mill (1981), The Wizard Punchkin (1982), Blue-Jay and Robin (1983)
Gillian Wrobel Ali Baba and the Forty Thieves (1979)

References: ICB 4; *Children's Books of the Year* (catalogues 1971, 1972, 1974, 1975, 1977)

Charles Frederick Tunnicliffe (1901-79)

Born in Langley, near Macclesfield, Cheshire where he grew up on his parent's small farm. Studied on scholarships at Macclesfield School of Art (1915-21) and the Royal College of Art (1921-25) where he was taught etching by Sir Frank Short. After leaving college he shared lodgings with Eric Ravilious*. Taught part-time at Woolwich Polytechnic (1925-29); returned to Macclesfield and from then on (apart from a short period teaching at Manchester Grammar School during

C.F. Tunnicliffe. 'Treading the onion' from *Green Tide* by Richard Church (Country Life, 1945).

the 1940s) worked full time as a freelance painter, printmaker and draughtsman in pencil, pen and ink and scraperboard. He specialised in birds, animals and rural landscapes, and initially much of his work consisted of advertisements for veterinary products and animal feeds, but he soon made his name as a more serious illustrator with wood engravings for Henry Williamson's *Tarka the Otter* (1932). He subsequently illustrated six of Williamson's other books, but eventually found it impossible to remain on friendly terms with the author. Altogether he worked on over 90 books by nearly 40 different authors and editors. His biographer, Ian Niall, observed that 'what Tunnicliffe had above all was a determination to succeed at whatever he took on. He had the undoubted talent of being able to illustrate what he knew about and what the customer asked for.' During his later years, pressure of work led to his increasing use of scraperboard for illustration, and, although he used the medium with sensitivity, his scraperboard drawings lacked the authority and subtlety of his engravings on wood. He lived in Anglesey from 1947. Elected ARE (1929), RE (1934), RA (1954); awarded the OBE (1978).

Books illustrated include:
H.E. Bates The Seasons and the Gardener (1940), In the Heart of the Country (1942), O More than a Happy Countryman (1943)
Charles S. Bayne The Call of the Birds (1944), Exploring England (1944)
Nellie Brocklehurst Up with the Country Park (1978)
D.H. Chapman The Seasons and the Woodman (1941)
Richard Church Green Tide (1945)
F. Fraser Darling The Seasons and the Farmer (1939), The Seasons and the Fishermen (1941), The Care of Farm Animals (1944)
C.D. Dimsdale Come Out of Doors (1951)
Norman Ellison Wandering with Nomad (1946), Out of Doors with Nomad (1947), Over the Hills with Nomad (1948), Roving with Nomad (1949)
George Ewart Evans The Horse in the Furrow (1967)
Negley Farson Going Fishing (1942)
R.L. Haig-Brown Pool and Rapid (1936)
Ernest Hemingway The Old Man and the Sea (1953)
Kit Higson The Dull House (1934)
Terence Horsley Fishing and Flying (1947), The Long Flight (1947)
A.J. Huxley Wild Flowers of the Countryside (1962)
John R. Jefferies Wild Life in a Southern County (1949)
Ronald M. Lockley Letter from Stockholm (1947), The Cinnamon Bird (1948), Puffins (1953), The Island (1969), Orielton (1977)
Ian Niall The Way of a Countryman (1965), A Galloway Childhood (1967), A Fowler's World (1968), To Speed the Plough (1977)
Mary O'Hara My Friend Flicka (1943)
Mary Priestley A Book of Birds (1937)
W.F.R. Reynolds Angling Conclusions (1947)
Sidney Rogerson and C.F. Tunnicliffe Our Bird Book (1947), Both Sides of the Road (1949)
Richard Patrick Russ Beasts Royal (1934)
C.F. Tunnicliffe My Country Book (1942), Bird Portraiture (1945), How to Draw Farm Animals (1947), Mereside Chronicle (1948), Shorelands Summer Diary (1952), Birds of the Estuary (1952), Wild Birds in Britain (1974), A Sketchbook of Birds (1979)
Alison Uttley Country Hoard (1943), The Country Child (1945), Country Things (1946), Carts and Candlesticks (1948), The Farm on the Hill (1949), Ambush of Young Days (1951), Plowmen's Clocks (1952), Here's a New Day (1956), Something for Nothing (1960), Wild Honey (1962), Cuckoo in June (1964), A Peck of Gold (1966), The Button Box and other essays (1968), A Ten O'Clock Scholar (1970), Secret Places (1972)
Brian Vesey-Fitzgerald Rivermouth (1949)

Clarence Henry Warren Happy Countryman (1946)
E.L. Grant Watson Nature Abounding (1941), Walking with Fancy (1943), The Leaves Return (1947), Profitable Wonders (1949), What to Look for in Winter (1959), What to Look for in Autumn (1960), What to Look for in Summer (1960), What to Look for in Spring (1961)
E.G. Harcourt Williams Tales from Ebony (1934)
Henry Williamson Tarka the Otter (1932), The Lone Swallows (1933), The Old Stag (1933), The Star Born (1933), The Peregrine's Saga (1934), Salar the Salmon (1935)
Kenneth Williamson The Sky's Their Highway (1937)

Periodical: Radio Times

References: Balston EWE; Bénézit; Crouch; Driver; Guichard; ICB 2; Johnson & Greutzner; Thieme & Becker; Usherwood; Vollmer; Wa (1977); Waters; J.C. Wood; *The Junior Bookshelf* vol 5 no 2 (1941); Ian Niall *Portrait of a Country Artist* (Gollancz 1980), *A Sketchbook of Birds* (Gollancz 1979)

Krystyna Zofia Turska (b. 1933)

Born in Poland. At the outbreak of war in 1939, she escaped through Russia to the Middle East and eventually arrived in England. She studied at Hammersmith School of Art. Illustrator of children's books and winner of the Kate Greenaway Medal for 1972 with *The Woodcutter's Duck*. She often works in pen and ink with multiple outlines supplemented by hatched, stippled or offprinted shading for ambient atmospheric effects.

Books illustrated include:
Honor Arundel The High House School (1976)
Gillian Avery Ellen's Birthday (1971), Red Letter Days (1971), Ellen and the Queen (1972), Freddie's Feet (1976)
Helen Cooper Great Grandmother Goose (1978)
Alan Garner (ed) The Hamish Hamilton Book of Goblins (1969)
Roger Lancelyn Green (ed) The Hamish Hamilton Book of Dragons (1970)
Moira Heritage The Happy Little King (1979)
Kathleen Killip Saint Bridget's Night (1975)
Janet McNeill A Snow-Clean Pinny (1973)
William Mayne A Year and a Day (1976), The Mouse and the Egg (1980), *(ed)* The Hamish Hamilton Book of Heroes (1967)
Robert Nye The Bird of the Golden Land (1980)
James Reeves The Trojan Horse (1968), The Path of Gold (1972)
James Riordan Tales from Central Russia (1976)
Geoffrey Trease A Masque for the Queen (1970)
Krystyna Turska Pegasus (1970), Tamara and the Sea Witch (1971), The Woodcutter's Duck (1972), The Magician of Cracow (1975)
Barbara Willard (ed) Happy Families (1974)
Ruzena Wood The Palace of the Moon (1981)

Reference: ICB 4

Twym

See Alexander Stuart Boyd.

Walter Frederick Roofe Tyndale (c.1855-1943)

Born in Bruges, Belgium, of English parents. Studied at Antwerp Academy where he won a silver medal, and in Paris. From around 1890, he concentrated on watercolour painting, working in a detailed style based on that of the watercolourist and illustrator Helen Allingham. He toured the Continent, the Middle East and Japan, making topographical watercolour studies to illustrate his popular travel books. During World War I, he was Head Censor at Boulogne with the rank of Captain. Elected RI (1911).

Books illustrated include:
H.R.E. Brown Dalmatia (1925)
D. Hann Somerset (1927)
C. Holland Wessex (1906)
H.G. Hutchison The New Forest (1904)
H. Taylor Japanese Gardens (1912)
Walter Tyndale Below the Cataracts (1907), Japan and the Japanese (1910), An Artist in Egypt (1912), An Artist in Italy (1913), An Artist on the Riviera (1916), Dorset Watercolours (reprinted from *Wessex*, with A. Heaton Cooper, 1936), Somerset Watercolours (with A. Heaton Cooper, 1936)

References: Bénézit; Johnson & Greutzner; Houfe; Mallalieu; Thieme & Becker; Wa (1934); Waters; C. Wood; *The Studio* 38 (1906)

George Claude Leon Underwood (1890-1977)

Worked as Leon Underwood. Born in London, son of an impoverished antique dealer. Studied at the Regent Street Polytechnic (1907-10) and the Royal College of Art (1910-13) on a scholarship. Served in the Royal Horse Artillery and the Camouflage Section of the Royal Engineers in France (1914-18). Studied at the Slade School of Fine Art (1919-20) and there met Ralph Chubb*, with whom he explored gipsy life and culture. Taught part-time at the Royal College of Art (1920-23) and St Martin's School of Art (1929). Founded and ran his own art school, the Brook Green School of Art (1921-38) for postgraduate students of promise; drawing was the main subject, but wood engraving and etching were also introduced. Students included Blair Hughes-Stanton*, Gertrude Hermes*, Mary Groom* and Nora Unwin*. He visited America (1926-27), where he illustrated for the New York publisher Brentano's and executed a number of title page drawings for *Vanity Fair*. He spent some time in Mexico (1928) and was profoundly influenced by pre-Columbian art. Also travelled (at various times) to Poland and Russia, Iceland, Western Europe, Canada and West Africa.

Painter, sculptor, printmaker and writer, Underwood was influential both through his teaching and through his early insistence on the importance of 'primitive' art. His encounters with paleolithic cave paintings and the sculpture of Mexico and Africa confirmed his belief in the primacy of subject in art, and in the necessity for a close functional relationship between a work of art and the society that produced it. These ideas ran counter to the modernist emphasis on formal exploration and language development, and contributed to the relative critical neglect of his later work. His published illustrations all dated from the period 1925-30 (apart from the cover of the Victory issue of *The Listener* in 1945). They consist mainly of woodcuts and engravings of outstanding technical fluency combined with a highly distinctive brand of vigorous and witty imagery.

Books illustrated include:
Joseph Bard (ed) The Island (1931)
James Branch Cabell Music from Behind the Moon (1926)
Philip Russell The Red Tiger (New York, 1929)
Leon Underwood Animalia; or Fibs about Beasts (New York, 1926),
  · The Siamese Cat (New York, 1928), Art for Heaven's Sake (1934),
  Figures in Wood of West Africa (1947), Masks of West Africa
  (1948), Bronzes of West Africa (1949)

Periodicals: The Island, The Woodcut

References: Balston EWE, WEMEB; Bénézit, Chamot, Farr & Butlin; Garrett BWE, HBWE; Guichard; ICB 1; Johnson & Greutzner; Thieme & Becker; Vollmer; Wa (1934); Waters 1 and 2; *The Studio* special (Spring 1927, Winter 1936); *Annual Report of the Royal Society of British Sculptors* (1961); *Exhibition Catalogues, Beaux Arts Gallery* (1953), *Kaplan Gallery* (1963), *Leicester Galleries* (1934); *Thirties* (Arts Council catalogue 1979); *Leon Underwood Mexico and After* (National Museum of Wales, Cardiff 1979); Christopher Neve *Leon Underwood* (Thames & Hudson 1974); A.C. Sewter *Modern British Woodcuts and Wood-Engravings in the Collection of the Whitworth Art Gallery* (Manchester 1962); R.H. Wilenski *Draughtsmen* (Ernest Benn 1924)

Nora Spicer Unwin (1907-82)

Born in Tolworth, Surrey, daughter of a master printer. Studied at Leon Underwood's* School (1924-26), Kingston School of Art (1926-28) and the Royal College of Art (1928-32). Painter, wood engraver and illustrator of her own and other authors' books. She worked with children during World War II, and then encouraged by her friend Elizabeth McGreal Yates, for whom she illustrated a number of books, emigrated in 1946 to the United States where some of her work had already been published. There she worked as a lecturer and teacher, gained a considerable reputation as a watercolourist and was elected Associate of the American National Academy (1954). Her illustrations are intimate in feeling and drawn with care, mainly in pen or brush, sometimes with one or two colour line blocks or halftone washes. For *The Christmas Story* she used wood engraving. Her drawings for *The Doll who Came Alive* are based on her collection of wooden-jointed dolls.

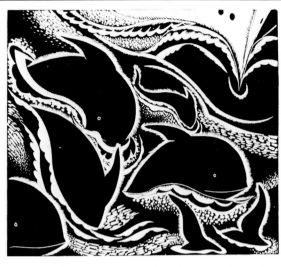

Leon Underwood. 'Dolphins' from his *Animalia* (1926).

She died in Massachusetts. Elected ARE (1935), RE (1946), and SWE (1963). [Q]

Books illustrated include:
Cécile de Banke Tabby Magic (1959), More Tabby Magic (1961)
Hetty Bennett First Alphabet and Jingle Book (1946)
Enid Blyton Rainy Day Stories (1944), Round the Clock Stories
  (1945), Rambles with Uncle Nat (1947)
Gwendy Caroe Lucy and the Fairy Feasts (1943), Mrs Mouse and
  Family (1948)
Charles Elton Exploring the Animal World (1933)
George MacDonald Gathered Grace (1939), The Princess and the
  Goblin (1951)
E. Nesbit Five of Us and Madeline (1925)
Beverley Nichols How Does Your Garden Grow? (1935)
Dorothy Una Ratcliffe Rosemary Isle (1944)
Antonia Ridge Leave it to Brooks! (1950)
Enys Tregarthen The Doll who Came Alive (1944)
Nora S. Unwin Round the Year (1939), My Own Picture Prayer Book
  (1946), Lucy and the Little Red Horse (1948), The Christmas Story
  (1949), Doughnuts for Lin (1950), Proud Pumpkin (1953), Jack and
  Jill Books (8 vols, 1955-56), Poquito, the Little Mexican Duck
  (1961), The Way of the Shepherd (1964), Two Too Many (1965)
Elizabeth Yates Hans and Frieda (1939), Under the Little Fir (1942),
  Mountain Born (1943), Carolina and the Indian Doll (1965)

References: Garrett BWE, HBWE; ICB 1,2,3,4; Johnson & Greutzner; Kirkpatrick; Wa (1980); Waters; *The Times* (obituary 18th January, 1982); *Shall We Join the Ladies* (Studio One Gallery Oxford 1979); A.C. Sewter *Modern British Woodcuts and Wood-Engravings in the Collection of the Whitworth Art Gallery* (Manchester 1962)

Florence Kate Upton (1873-1922)

Born in New York of English parents. Studied Art in New York, Paris and Holland. Mainly a portrait painter, she is more widely known as the originator of the *Golliwogg*; a series of picture books with simple rhymes written by her mother, Bertha, and lively full page illustrations in colour of Golliwogg and Dutch Doll escapades. The original 'nigger doll' and Dutch dolls which she used as models for her drawings are now in the Long Gallery in the British Prime Minister's official country house, Chequers.

Florence Upton. 'But even wooden limbs get tired/And want a change of play...' from *Adventures of Two Dutch Dolls and a Golliwogg* by Florence K. Upton (Longmans Green, 1895).

Books illustrated include:
E. Beckman Pax and Carlino (1894)
Bertha Upton The Adventures of Two Dutch Dolls and a Golliwogg (1895), The Golliwogg's Bicycle Club (1896), Little Hearts (1897), The Vege-Man's Revenge (1897), The Golliwogg at the Sea-Side (1898), The Golliwogg in War! (1899), The Golliwogg's Polar Adventures (1900), The Golliwogg's 'Auto-Go-Cart' (1901), The Golliwogg's Airship (1902), The Golliwogg's Circus (1903), The Golliwogg in Holland (1904), The Golliwogg's Fox-Hunt (1905), The Adventures of Barbee and the Wisp (1905), The Golliwogg's Desert Island (1906), The Golliwogg's Christmas (1907), Golliwogg in the African Jungle (1908)

Periodicals: The Idler, Punch, The Strand Magazine

References: Cope; Doyle CL; Fisher p. 122; Houfe; Johnson & Greutzner; Lewis; Thieme & Becker; Waters; *The Junior Bookshelf 8 vol 12 no 4 (1948); The Studio* special (Autumn 1933); William Feaver *When We Were Young* (Thames & Hudson 1977); Edith Lyttleton *Florence Upton, Painter* (Longmans 1926); Eric Quayle *The Collector's Book of Children's Books* (Studio Vista 1971)

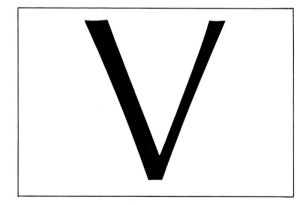

Denys Gathorne Valentine (active 1959-75)

An illustrator who worked in black and white and in full colour, in a consistently sketchy style. His illustrations were published mainly by Heinemann.

Books illustrated include:
Ruth Ainsworth Rufty Tufty Flies High (1959), Rufty Tufty's Island (1960), Rufty Tufty and Hattie (1962), Rufty Tufty Makes a House (1965)
Richard Armstrong The Lame Duck (1959), Horseshoe Reef (1960), Out of the Shallows (1961), Trial Trip (1962)
Cyril Barnes William Booth and his Army of Peace (1975)
T.V. Bulpin The Great Trek (1975)
Patricia Lynch The Longest Way Round (1961)
Pamela Mansbridge The Seventh Summer (1959)

Judith Valpy (b. 1940)

Married name: Mrs Aspinall. Born in Malaysia where her father was working in the Malayan Police Force. Studied at the Regent Street Polytechnic (1959-62) and at the Central School of Arts and Crafts (1962-64). Freelance illustrator and jacket designer since 1964; wood engraver, collagist and pen and ink draughtsman. Lives in Reigate, Surrey. [Q]

Books illustrated include:
Elisabeth Beresford Awkward Magic (1964), Travelling Magic (1965)
Kevin Crossley-Holland Running to Paradise (1967)
Joseph Edmundson Pan Book of Health (1963), Pan Book of Party Games (1963)
David Ross Letters from Foxy (1966)
Under the Sun (with others, 1964)

Periodical: Busy Bee's News

Salomon Van Abbé (1883-1955)

Born in Amsterdam, son of a diamond dealer, and brother of Joseph Van Abbé, later known as Joseph Abbey*. He moved to England with his family at the age of five, and later became a British subject. Sources differ as to exactly where he studied art but it seems that he attended a school in Kennington, the People's Palace at Bow, the London County Council School at Bolt Court and the Central School of Arts and Crafts. He worked initially as a newspaper illustrator, but later became known for his portrait paintings, book illustrations and drypoint etchings of the British legal system at all levels of operation. All these gave him the opportunity to explore people's attitudes, gestures and facial expressions—his main artistic preoccupation. He drew in a conventional style, usually with finely-hatched shading. According to an interview in the *Print Collectors' Quarterly*, he sometimes illustrated books for the publisher Herbert Jenkins under the pseudonym 'C. Morse' because of complications with a rival publishing house. He also designed book covers for the publisher Ward Lock. He was a member of the London Sketch Club and the Art Workers' Guild (President 1941); elected ARE (1928), RBA (1933).

Books illustrated include:
Louisa M. Alcott Little Women (1948), Good Wives (1953)
John Galsworthy Loyalties (1930)
Nathaniel Hawthorne The Wonder Book (1949), Tanglewood Tales (1950)
Thomas Hughes Tom Brown's Schooldays (1951)
W.R.G. Kent My Lord Mayor (1947)

S. Van Abbé. 'Joe thrashing away with his whip and I flourishing the demijohn' from *Grandma's Story* by Louisa M. Alcott in *The Modern Gift Book for Children* (Odhams, 1948).

Charles Kingsley The Heroes (1955)
Carola Oman Robin Hood (1939)
Percy Westerman With the Commandos (1943)
The Modern Gift Book for Children (1948)

Periodicals: The Christian Science Monitor, Colour, The Illustrated London News, The Londoner, Sporting and Dramatic News, The Strand Magazine

References: Cuppleditch; Guichard; ICB 2; Johnson & Greutzner; Wa (1972); Waters; The Print Collector's Quarterly vol 26

John Verney (b. 1913)

Born London, son of Ralph Verney, secretary to the Speaker of the House of Commons. Educated at Eton, Oxford and the Architectural Association, London, then worked in films. After army service (1939-45), he became a full-time painter in oil, gouache and watercolour; illustrator and author, and more recently a decorator of furniture. He lived for thirty years at Farnham, Surrey where he was founder of the Farnham Trust (for building conservation); he now lives at Clare in Suffolk. His book illustrations (mostly in pen and ink) are sketchy and humorous in a style that sometimes recalls the work of Edward Ardizzone*. In the early 1950s, he drew the very effective and popular covers for *Collins Magazine* (later *The Young Elizabethan*), and in 1965 he invented the Dodo-Pad, an amusing diary published by Collins, which has appeared every year since. [Q]

Books illustrated include:
Gillian Avery James Without Thomas (1959), The Elephant War (1960), To Tame a Sister (1961), The Greatest Gresham (1962), The Peacock House (1963), The Italian Spring (1964), Unforgettable Journeys (1965), School Remembered (1967)
C.I. Bermant Diary of an Old Man (1966)
Wilfred Blunt Omar (1966)
George Brennand Walton's Delight (1961)
Anthony Buckeridge Our Friend Jennings (1958), Jennings Goes to School (1965)
Susan Chitty My Life and Horses (1966)
George Kerr (trans) The Odyssey (1947)
Geoffrey Lincoln No Moaning of the Bar (1957)
Richard G. Robinson My Uncle's Strange Voyages (1964)
Gordon Shepherd Where the Lion Trod (1960)

John Verney Verney Abroad (1954), Look at Houses (1959), Friday's Tunnel (1959), February's Road (1961), Ismo (1964), The Mad King of Chichiboo (1964)

Periodical: Collins Magazine for Boys and Girls

References: ICB 3,4; Kirkpatrick; Vollmer supp; Wa (1977); Waters

Frederic Villiers (1851-1922)

Born in London. Studied art in the British Museum, at South Kensington Schools and at the Royal Academy Schools. Painter, writer and illustrator of military subjects. As a war artist and correspondent for *The Graphic* and *The Illustrated London News*, he devoted his life to a relentless pursuit of combat, travelling extensively in most parts of the world. His work is essentially journalistic in character.

Books illustrated include:
A.M. Broadley How We Defended Arabi (1884)
P.H. Colomb The Great War of 189- ??? (1893)
Frederic Villiers Pictures of Many Wars (1902), Port Arthur (1905), Peaceful Personalities and Warriors Bold (1907)

Periodicals: Black and White, The English Illustrated Magazine, The Graphic, Harpers Magazine, The Idler, The Illustrated London News, The Sphere, The Windsor Magazine

References: Houfe; Johnson & Greutzner; Waters; C. Wood; Pat Hodgson *The War Illustrators* (Osprey 1977); Frederic Villiers *Villiers: His First Five Decades of Adventure* (Harper 1920)

Hans Henning Voight (1887-1969)

Worked as 'Alastair'. Born Karlsruhe, Germany. Studied philosophy briefly at the University of Marburg and (for a year) anatomy and life drawing, after which he repudiated academic disciplines of draughtsmanship. He was a dancer and mime artist, pianist, writer and illustrator, but the real focus of his creative impulse was the cultivation of

John Verney. From *The Odyssey* by Homer translated by George P. Kerr (Warne, 1947).

an exquisite, decadent and mysterious *persona* and lifestyle. He was launched as a graphic artist in 1914 by the publication of *43 Drawings by Alastair* by John Lane, who went on to publish several of his illustrated books. During the 1920s his work was also published in Switzerland, Germany, France, Austria and the United States. His drawings, in black and sometimes coloured ink, or pencil, were inspired by the 1890s (his favourite period) and particularly by the work of Aubrey Beardsley. They combine decorative elegance with a fascination with the perverse, sinister and satanic. He led a peripatetic life supported by a few patrons; his numerous friends included (for a time) A.O. Spare*.

Books illustrated include:
Walter Pater Sebastian van Storck (1927)
Abbé Prévost d'Exiles Manon Lescaut (with others, 1928)
Oscar Wilde The Sphinx (1920)

Periodical: The Golden Hind

References: Houfe; Johnson; Peppin; *Fifty Drawings by Alastair* (Alfred A. Knopf, New York 1925); Victor Arwas *Alastair* (Thames & Hudson 1979); Philippe Jullian *Dreamers of Decadence* (Phaidon 1971); Robert Ross *Forty-Three Drawings by Alastair* (John Lane 1914)

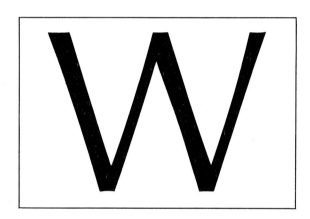

Edward Alexander Wadsworth (1889-1949)

Born Cleckheaton, Yorkshire. Educated at Fettes School, Edinburgh. Studied engineering in Munich (1906-07), then art at Bradford School of Art and at the Slade School of Fine Art (1907-12). Painter and draughtsman, wood-cutter and copper engraver. Associated with Roger Fry's Omega Workshop and then with Wyndham Lewis* at the Rebel Arts Centre; signatory of the Vorticist Manifesto published in *Blast* (1914). Served with the RNVR (1914-17) and worked on dazzle camouflage for ships (1917-18). His later paintings, in tempera and often of marine subjects, were influenced by Surrealism. Immediately after World War I, Wadsworth had a considerable impact as a wood-cutter on the newly revived school of wood engraving, with his angular, boldly

facetted prints of ships and machinery. His drawings for *The Black Country* (1920), had a comparable boldness, in striking contrast to his delicate (and later hand-coloured) copper engravings for *Sailing Ships and Barges* (1930). He also designed striking black and white initial letters for T.E. Lawrence's *Seven Pillars of Wisdom* Member of Unit One (1933) and Group X.

Books illustrated include:
Arnold Bennett (intro) The Black Country (1920)
Edward Wadsworth Antwerp (1933)
Bernard Windeler (intro) Sailing Ships and Barges of the Western Mediterranean and Adriatic Seas (1926)

Periodicals: Blast, Form

References: Balston EWE; Bénézit, Chamot, Farr & Butlin; DNB (1941-50); Garrett BWE, HBWE; Lewis; Phaidon; Rothenstein 2; Thieme & Becker; Vollmer; Wa (1934); Waters; *Alphabet and Image* 8 (Winter 1948); *Apollo* 9 (1929); *The Egoist* (15th August, 1914); *The Studio* 97 (1929), 106 (1933), 115 (1938), 125 (1943); *Abstract Art in England 1913-15* (D'Offay Couper Gallery 1969); *Vorticism and its Allies* (Arts Council Hayward Gallery 1974); Richard Cork *Vorticism and Abstract Art in the First Machine Age* (2 vols, Gordon Fraser 1976); O. Raymond Drey *Edward Wadsworth: Modern Woodcutters no 4* (Morland Press 1921); Herbert Read *Unit One: The Modern Movement in English Architecture, Painting and Sculpture* (Cassell, 1934); Waldemar George et al *Edward Wadsworth* (Anvers 1933)

Louis Wain (1860-1939)

Born in London. His father was a traveller in textiles and his mother a designer of carpets and ecclesiastical fabrics. He studied music privately and attended the West London School of Art (1877-80), remaining there as an assistant teacher until 1883. He began contributing black and white drawings to various magazines in 1881 and joined the staff of the *The Illustrated Dramatic and Sporting News* in 1882. In 1886 he moved to *The Illustrated London News,* where he produced his pictures in the mildly humorous genre of stylised cats in human costumes and situations for which he was to become so famous. By the turn of the century, his name was synonymous with humorous cat drawings and he was producing some 600 a year for books, magazines, postcards and for private patrons, enabling him to support his mother and five unmarried sisters in relative comfort (his father had died in 1880 and his wife in 1887). He worked in New York on the staff of the *New York American* (1907-10), but lost most of his savings in a business speculation and thereafter lived in increasing poverty. His cat pictures remained saleable but by then had been joined by a whole range of anthropomorphised animals of every description in children's literature and illustration. He experimented with animated film-making in 1917 and continued drawing regularly for annuals and magazines until 1924, when he became insane. He spent the rest of his life in asylums and hospitals, cared for with funds raised by a public appeal. He was a longstanding member

Louis Wain. 'The Turkish Bath' from *All Sorts of Comical Cats* with verses by Clifton Bingham (Ernest Nister, nd).

of most of the animal protection societies of the day including Our Dumb Friends League and the Society for the Protection of Cats, and was for many years President of the National Cat Club, doing much to promote the development and exhibition of pedigree varieties.

Wain's obsessive fondness for cats has been traced back to the time of his wife's terminal illness (1885-87), when he frequently sketched their pet kitten at her bedside; he continued to keep cats and draw them from life throughout his career. While he faithfully transferred alterations in human costume and manners to his feline subjects, there was no essential development in his work, either in range or in graphic style, during his long career. Thanks to this predictability, the 'Louis Wain Cat' became a universally-known element in popular and nursery culture for more than a generation. Although he was by no means the first to depict animals clothed and walking erect (Lear, Tenniel, Tom Hood and Griset were among the many who had already done so), he was the first to work consistently within the convention, making it a speciality.

Books illustrated include:
W.L. Alden Cat Tales (1905)
G.C. Bingham Kittenland (1903), Ping-Pong as seen by Louis Wain (1903), Claws and Paws (1908), Full of Fun (1908), All Sorts of Comical Cats (nd)
C.J. Cornish The Living Animals of the World (1901)

May Crommelin Little Soldiers (1916)
M.C. Gillington Cat's Cradle (1908)
J. Hannon The Kings and the Cats (1908)
M.I. Hurrell The Adventures of Friskers and his Friends (1907)
Kari Madame Tabby's Establishment (1886)
Kittycat The Story of Tabbykin Town (1920)
R. Leander Dreams of French Firesides (1890)
C. Morley Peter, a Cat o' One Tail (1892)
E. Nesbit Our New Story Book (with Elsie Wood*, 1913)
M.A. Owen Old Rabbit the Voodoo (1893)
F.W. Pattenden Our Farm (1888)
J. Pope The Cat Scouts (1912)
A.W. Riddler Holidays in Animal Land (1909), The Merry Animal Picture Book (1910), Animal Happyland (1913)
C.M. Rutley Valentine's Rocker Books (1921)
C.Y. Stephenson 'Mephistopheles' (1907)
Father Tuck Pa Cats, Ma Cats and their Kittens (1902)
E. Vredenburg 'Tinker, Tailor' (1914)
Louis Wain Puppy Dog's Tales (1896), Pussies and Puppies (1899), Nursery Book (1902), Baby's Picture Book (1903), Big Dogs, Little Dogs, Cats and Kittens (1903), Kitten Book (1903), Summer Book for 1903 (1903), In Animal Land (1904), Animal Show (1905), Cats about Town (1907-10), Grimalkin (1907-10), A Cat Alphabet (1914), Daddy Cat (1915), Pussy Land (1920), Children's Book (1923), Animal Book (1928)
L. Wain and G.C. Bingham The Dandy Lion (1900), Fun and Frolic (1902)
S.C. Woodhouse Cats at Large (1910), Two Cats at Large (1911), Cinderella and other Fairy Tales (1917)
Little Red Riding Hood and other tales (1917)

Periodicals: The Captain, The English Illustrated Magazine, Father Tuck's Annual, The Illustrated London News, The Illustrated Sporting and Dramatic News, Little Folks, Louis Wain's Annual, New York American, The Pall Mall Budget, Playbox Annual, The Sketch, Stock Keeper

References: DNB (1931-40); Doyle BWI, CL; Houfe; ICB 1; Johnson & Greutzner; Vollmer; Waters; C. Wood; J.C. Wood; *The Idler* 8 (January 1896); *The Times* (7th July 1939); Rodney Dale *Louis Wain. The Man Who Drew Cats* (William Kimber 1968); Brian Reade *Louis Wain* (Victoria & Albert Museum 1972)

Albert Wainwright (active 1920-27)

Decorative illustrator in line. Exhibited between 1921 and 1924.

Books illustrated include:
S. Matthewson Poems (1927)
Osbert Sitwell and others Seven (1922)
Algernon Swinburne Cleopatra (1924)
Theocritus Hylas (1929)
A. Vickridge The Forsaken Princess (1924), The Mountain of Glass (1924)
Albert Wainwright Café Noir (1926)

References: Johnson & Greutzner; *Drawing and Design* 19 (November 1921); *The Studio* special (Christmas 1894)

Geoffrey Wales (b. 1912)

Born Margate, Kent, son of a master-builder. Studied at Thanet School of Art (1929-33) and at the Royal College of Art (1933-37) under Eric Ravilious*. Taught at the East Kent Group of Art Schools (1937-40). Married the painter Marjorie Skeeles, 1940. Served in the Royal Air Force during World War II, afterwards returning to teach in Kent. Lecturer at Norwich School of Art (1953-77). Exhibited widely in England and abroad since the 1930s. Wales uses wood engraving as a medium for book illustration and for prints; he also works in collage and in water-colour. His concern is with landscapes, coastlines and objects in space. His engravings have been published as illustrations by the Golden Cockerel Press, the Kynoch Press and the Folio Society. Albert Garrett writes in *A History of British Wood Engraving*: '...he is an artist who has evolved through engraving and has found that the aesthetics of form and the disciplines of wood-engraving run in parallel'. Elected SWE (1946), ARE (1948), RE (1961). [Q]

Books illustrated include:
Theodore Besterman The Pilgrim Fathers (1939)
Janet and John Hampden Sir Francis Drake's Raid on the Treasure Trains (1954)
Geoffrey Rawson (ed) Nelson's Letters (1954)
The Kynoch Press Diary for 1950

References: Balston EWE; Garrett BWE, HBWE; Vollmer supp; Wa (1980); Waters; *The Artist* 59 (April 1960); *Prints and Collages by Geoffrey Wales RE* (catalogue, Norwich School of Art Gallery, April 1978); John Buckland Wright *Etching and Engraving* (Studio 1953); Christopher Sandford *Bibliography of the Golden Cockerel Press* (Dawson 1975); *Cock-a-Hoop* (Private Libraries Association 1976)

Arthur George Walker (1861-1939)

Born in Hackney, London. From 1883, he studied at the Royal Academy Schools where he won several awards. He subsequently worked as a sculptor, painter, book illuminator and illustrator, and designer of mosaics. He taught sculpture at the Goldsmith's Institute, and often appeared on the title pages of the books he illustrated as 'A.G. Walker, Sculptor'. His pen drawings were characterised by fine, careful shading, rather in the manner of E.A. Abbey; he also worked in full colour. He exhibited internationally and was elected ARA (1925) and RA (1936).

Books illustrated include:
F.J.H. Darton A Wonder Book of Old Romance (1907)
George MacDonald The Lost Princess (1895)
Mary Macleod A Book of Ballad Stories (1906), Robin Hood and his Merry Men (1909), Tales from Old Ballads (1910)
Sir Thomas Malory (adapted by Mary Macleod) The Book of King Arthur and his Noble Knights (1900)
Edmund Spenser (adapted by Mary Macleod) Stories from the Faerie Queene (1897)
G.I. Witham Captive Royal Children (1911)

References: Baker; Bénézit; Chamot, Farr & Butlin; Houfe; Johnson & Greutzner; Sketchley; Thieme & Becker; Vollmer; Wa (1934); Waters; C. Wood

Pickford Waller (1873-1927)

Connoisseur, designer of book-plates, book covers and stationery; book decorator associated with James Guthrie* at the Pear Tree Press. Lived in London and later at Boscombe, Devon.

Books illustrated include:
Edmund Waller Some Songs and Verses (1902), Songs and Verses (1926)
Sybil Waller A Song of Thanksgiving (1950)

References: Houfe; *Type and Talent* (November 1915); Brian North Lee *British Bookplates* (David & Charles 1979); W.G. Blaikie Murdoch *Pickford Waller's Bookplates* (Morland Press 1922)

Cecile Walton (1891-1956)

Born in Glasgow, daughter of painter E.A. Walton (one of the 'Glasgow Boys', a group of artists and designers active in Glasgow at the turn of the century). Studied in London, Edinburgh, Paris and Florence. Decorative illustrator in black and white and full colour, mainly of children's books; painter and sculptor. Married artist Eric H.M. Robertson (and thus sometimes appears as Robertson in books of reference).

Books illustrated include:
Hans Christian Andersen Fairy Tales (1911)
A.J. Clinski Polish Fairy Tales (1920)
A. Priestman Child Verses and Poems (1926)
Dorothy Una Ratcliffe Nightlights (1929)
Cecile Walton The Children's Theatre Book for Young Dancers and Actors (with Edward W. Robertson, 1949)

Periodical: Vogue

References: Bénézit; ICB 1; Johnson & Greutzner; Taylor; Thieme & Becker; Vollmer (under Eric Robertson); Waters; Wa (1934) (under Mrs C. Robertson)

Bryan Ward (b. 1925)

Born in Leicester, son of a photo-lithographer. Studied for a year at Leicester Art College and worked for a year with the David Hand Film Company at Cookham, Berkshire. Served in the army (1943-47). Since then he has worked as a portrait draughtsman, adult education lecturer, children's book illustrator and designer of badges. At the age of 16, he produced several children's books with his own very polished cartoon-like full-colour drawings, but he is best known for his simple but appropriate *Ant and Bee* illustrations

Bryan Ward. 'At the door, a solider bee looked at George's ticket' from his *George the Snail Bee* (Spectrum, 1975).

in outline and flat colour, which undoubtedly contributed to the success of the series. His early books were for the Leicester publisher Edmund Ward, and later ones for Kaye & Ward. Lives in Leicester and is secretary of the Leicester Sketch Club. [Q]

Books illustrated include:
Angela Banner Ant and Bee (1951), More Ant and Bee (1956), Mr Fork and Curly Fork (1956), One, Two, Three with Ant and Bee (1958), Around the World with Ant and Bee (1960), Happy Birthday with Ant and Bee (1960), Ant and Bee and the Rainbow (1962), Ant and Bee and the Kind Dog (1963)
H.E. Todd Bobby Brewster and the Winkers' Club (1949)
Bryan Ward The Leaping Match (1940), Elfin Mount (1941), Sindibad's First Voyage (1942), George the Snail Bee (1975)

References: Fisher pp.24, 77; *After Alice* (Museum of Childhood Catalogue, 1977)

John Stanton Ward (b. 1917)

Born in Hereford, son of an antique dealer. Studied at Hereford School of Art (1933-36) and

John Ward. 'Peter Apps, the gamekeeper' from *The White Doe* by Richard Church (Heinemann, 1968).

the Royal College of Art (1936-39). Served in the Royal Engineers (1939-46). Royal College of Art travelling scholarship (1947). Part-time lecturer at Wimbledon School of Art while under contract to *Vogue* magazine (1948-52). Since 1952, he has worked as a freelance portrait and architectural painter and draughtsman; book, advertising and fashion illustrator. For his illustrative work, he draws directly from the model in pen and ink without pencil guidelines, allowing the drawing to develop spontaneously. Elected ARA (1956), RA (1965). [Q]

Books illustrated include:
H.E. Bates Autobiography (3 vols, 1969-72)
Cynon Beaton-Jones The Adventures of So-Hi (1955)
Henry Bosco The Adventures of Pascalet (1976)
Katherine M. Briggs Nine Lives (1980)
Richard Church The Little Kingdom (1964), The White Doe (1968)
Joyce Grenfell George, Don't Do That (1977), Stately as a Galleon (1978)
Laurie Lee Cider with Rosie (1959), Poetry for Pleasure: Over the Hill, The Brave Days of Old, Falling Splendour (1958)
T.F Powys Rosie Plum (1966)
A.L. Rowse Brown Buck: A Californian Fantasy (1976)
G. Taylor Creative Writing in English (5 vols, 1960)
George Ward Alphonse

Periodical: Vogue

References: ICB 2; Jacques; Parry-Crooke; Vollmer; Wa (1980); Waters

Peter Warner (b. 1939)

Studied at Wimbledon School of Art and the Royal Academy Schools. Painter, animal draughtsman, children's book illustrator. He works in colour and in pen and ink in a characteristically 1960s style with freely drawn outline, augmented with patches of hatched and dotted texture.

Peter Warner. From *Let's Go Coaching* by Noel Streatfeild (Hamish Hamilton, 1965).

Books illustrated include:
Sidney Charles George The Happy Fisherman (1965)
Jacynth Hope-Simpson The Edge of the World (1966)
Rosemary Elizabeth Jackson The Witch of Castle Kerry (1966), Aunt
    Eleanor (1969)
William Mayne No More School (1965)
Noel Streatfeild Let's Go Coaching (1965)
Hugh Sturton Zomo the Rabbit (1966)

Reference: ICB 3

Priscilla Mary Warner (b. 1905)

Born in London. Studied at the Royal College of Art. Taught art at various girls' schools but gave up due to ill health and became a freelance illustrator and writer of children's books and books on embroidery. As an illustrator, she sometimes worked on white scraperboard, using closely textured hatching (black on white/white on black) to create an embroidered effect. She also worked in full colour, sometimes using decorative flat shapes without outlines.

Books illustrated include:
Priscilla Warner Biddy Christmas (1948), Embroidery Mary (1948),
    Picture Come True (1951), Tessie Growing Up (1952), Tessie's
    Caravan (1953), Mr and Mrs Cherry (1954)

Reference: ICB 2

Dudley Dexter Watkins (1907-69)

Born Manchester, son of a lithographer. Brought up in Nottingham, and attended evening classes at Nottingham School of Art before entering as a full-time student on a scholarship (1924). Subsequently worked as a cartoonist and illustrator for the newspaper and magazine publisher D.C. Thomson and Co., Dundee (1925-69). He was a lay preacher and drew calendars and cartoons in support of missionary work. He also taught life drawing and illustration at evening classes at Dundee School of Art. For D.C. Thomson he largely created and entirely drew such strip-cartoon classics as *Oor Wullie* and *the Broons (The Sunday Post), Biffo the Bear* and *Lord Snooty and his Pals (Beano)*, and *Desperate Dan (Dandy)*. He worked in black and white, offsetting fluent economical outlines with small areas of hatching and solid black (any wash work was done by Thomson): a style that reproduced admirably on newsprint. Beneath his simplification lay confident draughtsmanship, a capacity for effective frame compositions and an instinct for well-selected detail. Since his death, his cartoon strips have been continued in a clumsy paraphrase of his style, but originals are still sometimes republished in the various Thomson comics and annuals. Though book illustration formed a very minor part of his work, he is included here for his important contribution to a humorous graphic tradition that goes back to W.G. Baxter and Tom Browne*. [Q]

Books illustrated include:
Daniel Defoe The Story of Robinson Crusoe (1952)
Charles Dickens The Story of Oliver Twist (1949)
Robert Louis Stevenson The Story of Kidnapped (1948), The Story of
    Treasure Island (1950)

Periodicals: Beano, Beezer, Dandy, The Sunday Post, Topper

References: *The Glasgow Herald* (27th January 1979); *Nottingham
Evening Post Centenary Supplement* (1978); *The Scotsman* (15th
January 1979); *The Sunday Times Magazine* (29th July 1973); *The
Times* (20th March 1976); *The Weekend Scotsman* (14th June 1975);
The Dudley Watkins Exhibition (Dundee Museums and Art Gallery
Catalogue January-February 1979); Maurice Horn (ed); *World
Encyclopaedia of Comics* (Chelsea House, New York 1976)

Denys James Watkins-Pitchford (b. 1905)

Born Northampton, son of a clergyman. Studied art in Paris and at the Royal College of Art. Art teacher at Rugby School. Landscape painter in watercolour and oils; an expert field sportsman and amateur naturalist. Served in the Territorials before World War II and as a Captain in the Home Guard. As an author he worked under the pseudonym 'BB', after the size of the shot used for shooting wild geese). He illustrated over 40 of his own books in black and white and colour, as well as many works by other writers. Many of his illustrations are in scraperboard and are often very sympathetic to the text, especially where natural history or sporting subjects are concerned. *The Little Grey Men* was awarded the Carnegie Medal in 1942 and ran to many editions, but its white-line scraperboard drawings are perfunctory and insubstantial (perhaps reflecting wartime difficulties) in comparison with the more varied texture and tonal counterpoint of scraperboard illustrations in earlier and later books. Elected Fellow of the Royal Society of Arts. [Q]

Books illustrated include:
Gerald D. Adams Red Vagabond (1946)
Arthur Applin Philandering Angler (1948)
Eric Barfield The Southern English (1942)
BB The Sportsman's Bedside Book (1937), Wild Lone. The Story of a
    Pytchley Fox (1938), Sky Gypsy (1939), The Countryman's Bedside
    Book (1941), The Little Grey Men (1942), The Idle Countryman
    (1943), Brendon Chase (1944), The Wayfaring Tree (1945), The
    Fisherman's Bedside Book (1945), BB's Fairy Book (1948), Down
    the Bright Stream (1948), The Shooting Man's Bedside Book (1948),
    A Stream in Your Garden (1948), Confessions of a Carp Fisher
    (1950), Letters from Compton Deverell (1950), Tide's Ending
    (1950), The Wind in the Wood (1952), Dark Estuary (1953), The
    Forest of Boland Light Railway (1955), Alexander (1957), Ben the
    Bullfinch (1957), Five More Stories (1957), Monty Woodpig's
    Caravan (1957), Wandering Wind (1957), A Carp Water: Wood Pool
    and How to Fish it (1958), Monty Woodpig and his Bubblebuzz Car
    (1958), Mr Burnstead (1958), The Autumn Road to the Isles (1959),
    Bill Badger's Winter Cruise (1959), The Wizard of Boland (1959),
    Bill Badger and the Pirates (1960), The Badgers of Bearshanks
    (1961), Bill Badger's Finest Hour (1961), The White Road
    Westwards (1961), Bill Badger's Whispering Reeds Adventure
    (1962), Lepus, the Brown Hare (1962), September Road to
    Caithness and the Western Sea 1962), Bill Badger's Big Mistake
    (1963), The Pegasus Book of the Countryside (1964), The Summer
    Road to Wales (1964), A Summer on the Nene (1967), The Whopper
    (1967), The Tyger Tray (1971), Lord of the Forest (1975), Ramblings
    of a Sportsman-Naturalist (1979)
Norah Burke King Todd (1963)
Mabel C. Carey (ed) Fairy Tales of Long Ago (1952)
J.B. Drought A Sportsman Looks at Eire (1949)

D.J. Watkins-Pitchford. 'Over the Sands', frontispiece from *The Wayfaring Tree* by 'B.B.' (Hollis & Carter, 1945).

Brian Vesey Fitzgerald It's my Delight (1947)
William Mayne The Long Night (1958), Thirteen o'Clock (1960)
Hesketh Prichard Sport in Wildest Britain (1936)
Arthur Richards Vix. The Story of a Fox Cub (1960), Birds of the Lonely Lake (1961)
L.T.C. Rolt Narrow Boat (1944)
A.G. Street Landmarks (1949)
Henry S. Tegner Beasts of the North Country (1961)
M. Traherne Be Quiet and Go a-Angling (1949)
Elfrida Vipont The Secret of Orra (1957)
R.G. Walmsley Winged Company (1940)
G.H. Warren England is a Village (1940)

References: Crouch; Doyle CL; Fisher pp.34, 305; Guichard; ICB 2; Kirkpatrick; Waters 2; WW (1979); *A Child Alone: the Memoirs of BB* (Michael Joseph 1978)

A.H. Watson (active 1924-58)

Children's book illustrator. She worked in a decorative and sometimes sketchy graphic style that at times shows the influence of Arthur Rackham* and E.H. Shepard*.

Books illustrated include:
Cynthia Asquith Everything Easy (1926), The Treasure Ship (with others, 1926), Sails of Gold (with others, 1927), The Children's Cargo (with others, 1930), The Silver Ship (1932)
Herbert Asquith Pillicock Hill (1926)
Esther Boumphrey The Hoojibahs (1929)
C. Brahms Curiouser and Curiouser (1932)
Lewis Carroll Alice's Adventures in Wonderland (1939)

Charles Collodi (foreword by Sir Compton Mackenzie) The Adventures of Pinocchio (1958)
Walter de la Mare Told Again (1927)
Kathleen Fidler The Brydons Go Camping (1948), The Brydons Do Battle (1949), The Brydons in Summer (1949), The White-Starred Hare and Other Stories (1951)
Rose Fyleman The Adventure Club (1925)
Pixie Gann Martyn Manyfeather (1942)
Mary Gervaise The Farthinglale Fête (1959)
Laurence Housman Turn Again Tales (with others, 1930)
A.S.M. Hutchinson The Book of Simon (1930)
Elisabeth Kyle The Reiver's Road (1953)
M.B. Lodge A Fairy to Stay (1928), The Wishing Wood (1930)
Compton Mackenzie Santa Claus in Summer (1924), The Adventures of Two Chairs (1929), The Dining-Room Battle (1933)
D. Mariford The Dragon who Would Be Good (1929)
R.L. Stevenson A Child's Garden of Verses (1946)
'Mrs Herbert Strang' Our Old Fairy Stories (1939)
A.H. Watson Nursery Rhymes (1958)
M. StJ. Webb The Littlest One: his Book (1927), John and Me and the Dickery Dog (1930)
My Book of Elves and Fairies (with others, nd)
The Princess Elizabeth Gift Book (with others, nd)

Periodical: The Wonder Book

Arthur George Watts (1883-1935)

Born Chatham, Kent, son of a Deputy Surgeon-General in the Indian Medical Service. Educated at Dulwich College; studied at the Slade School of Fine Art and in Antwerp, Paris, Moscow and Madrid. Served in World War I, and was awarded a DSO. Magazine and book illustrator, poster designer. Though well within the graphic conventions of its time, his work was distinctive and witty; its economical outlines and crisp directional

A.H. Watson. 'On the Spanish main in the days of the buccaneers' from *The Silver Ship* by Lady Cynthia Asquith (Putnam, 1932).

shading helped to set a style that later included the cartoonist Leslie Illingworth among its exponents. He also had a tendency to elongate figures or to view them from unusual overhead angles. His early colour work was distinctly reminiscent of Edmund Dulac*. He died in an air crash. Elected ARBA (1923).

Books illustrated include:
E.M. Delafield Diary of a Provincial Lady (1930), The Provincial Lady Goes Further (1932)
H.F. Ellis So this is Science! (1932)
G.B. Hartford Commander, R.N. (1927)
E.G.V. Knox Poems of Impudence (1926)
I.M. Parsons Shades of Albany (with others, 1930)
A.R. Thorndike and R. Arkell The Tragedy of Mr Punch (1923)
A Little Pilgrim's Peeps at Parnassus (1927)

Periodicals: The Bystander, The Humorist, Life, The London Magazine, London Opinion, Nash's Magazine, Pear's Annual, Pearson's Magazine, Punch, Radio Times, The Sketch

References: Bénézit; Driver; Houfe; Johnson & Greutzner; Price; Thieme & Becker; Vollmer; Wa (1934); Waters; *The Studio* special (Autumn 1928); *Thirties* (Arts Council Catalogue 1979); John Geipel *The Cartoon* (David & Charles 1972)

Bernardette Watts (b. 1942)

Born in Northampton. Studied at Maidstone College of Art. Illustrator and occasional writer of children's books, sometimes working as 'Bernardette'. She draws in pen and ink, often with watercolour or gouache, in a childlike manner that aims to recreate the innocence of a child's vision by avoiding conventional graphic disciplines.

Books illustrated include:
Ruth Ainsworth Look, Do and Listen (1969)
Patricia Crompton (retold by) Aesop's Fables (1980)
Reinhold Ehrhardt Kikeri (1970)
Brothers Grimm Rapunzel (1975), Cinderella (1979)
Gwen Marsh (trans) Chibby: the Little Fish (1980)
Juli Phillips Hwyl cyn Noswylio (1977)
James Reeves One's None (1968)
Margaret Rogers Green is Beautiful
Arthur Scholey Sallinka and the Golden Bird (1978)
Bernadette Watts David's Waiting Day (1975), The Little Flute Player (1975)

Reference: ICB 4

Marjorie-Ann Watts (active from 1955)

Born in London, daughter of Arthur Watts*. Studied illustration and painting under Edward Ardizzone* and Brian Robb* and lithography under Harold Jones* at the Chelsea School of Art. After leaving college, she worked as a teacher for five years and then briefly for a publisher. Landscape painter, writer and illustrator of children's books, etcher and lithographer. She generally uses pen and ink for illustration but occasionally works in colour. [Q]

Books illustrated include:
Margaret Baker The Magic Sea Shell (1959)
Catherine Storr Clever Polly and the Stupid Wolf (1955), Polly the Giant's Bride (1956), The Adventures of Polly and the Wolf (1957), Marianne Dreams (1958), Marianne and Mark (1960)

Archibald Webb. 'The lion sprang upon Rover and with one blow knocked him off the saddle' from *Masterman Ready* by Captain Marryat (Ernest Nister, nd).

Marjorie-Ann Watts Tea Shop by the Water (1960), Mulroy's Magic (1971), The Dragon Clock (1974), Crocodile Medicine (1977), Crocodile Plaster (1978), The Mill House Cat (1978), Zebra Goes to School (1981), Tall Stories for Mr Tidyman (1983)

Reference: Fisher p.202

Archibald Bertram Webb (b. 1887)

Born in Ashford, Kent. Studied at St Martin's School of Art, and later taught art at Perth Technical College, Western Australia. Landscape painter (frequently exhibiting at the Fine Art Society), wood engraver, poster and commercial artist and competent illustrator, particularly of boys' adventure stories in full colour or halftone.

Books illustrated include:
R.M. Ballantyne Deep Down (c.1937)
James Fenimore Cooper The Last of the Mohicans (c.1923)
Charles Kingsley Westward Ho! (1910)
W.G. Kingston Roger Willoughby (c.1910), Paddy Finn (1910), The Three Lieutenants (c.1910), The Rural Crusoes (1911), The Three Admirals (1912), The Missing Ship (1913), John Deane (1921), From Powder Monkey to Admiral (1923)
Captain Marryat Masterman Ready (nd)
R.L. Stevenson New Arabian Nights (1926)
Herbert Strang One of Rupert's Horses (nd), Roger the Scout (nd)
Charlotte M. Young The Little Duke (nd)
My Seaside Story Book (with others, nd)

Princess Mary's Gift Book (with others, nd)
The Queen's Gift Book (with others, nd)

Periodicals: The Captain, Chums, The Empire Annual, The Girls' Realm, Herbert Strang's Annuals, Little Folks, The Quiver, Sunday at Home

Reference: Johnson & Greutzner

Clifford Cyril Webb (1895-1972)

Worked as Clifford Webb. Born London. Educated at Chigwell Grammar School, Essex. Apprenticed to a London firm of lithographers. After service in Europe and the Near and Far East during World War I, he studied at Westminster School of Art (1919-22) and taught himself wood-engraving (c.1921). Painter in oil and water-colour, draughtsman and printmaker. On the staff of Birmingham School of Art (1923-26), Westminster School of Art (1934-39), and St Martin's School of Art (1945-65). Worked free-lance in London (1927-33); spent World War II in Newcastle as controller of petrol for the North of England (1939-45). His illustrative work is notable for its sense of pattern and design, and for its decorative but sympathetic treatment of animals. Balston described his engraved illustrations for the Golden Cockerel Press as 'works of great distinction'. He made subtle and effective use of colour in wood engravings and prints (and some-times a combination of the two); this colour work was generally reproduced by lithography. For his early books, he also used scraperboard, and for his later titles a mixture of watercolour, chalk and spatter-work. Lived in Surrey for many years; elected RBA (1934), SWE (1935), ARE (1937), RE (1948).

Books illustrated include:
M. Alleyne The Pig Who Was Too Thin (1946)
Ivor Bannet The Amazons (1948)

Fritz Wegner. From A Picnic with the Aunts by Ursula Moray Williams in Bad Boys edited by Eileen Colwell (Penguin, 1972).

V. Garcia Calderon The White Llama (1938)
Somerset de Chair The First Crusade (1945), The Story of a Lifetime (1954)
M. Dixey Words, Beasts and Fishes (1936)
Patrick Miller Ana the Runner (1937),
Ella Monckton For the Moon... (1932), The Boy and the Mountain (1961)
Arthur Ransome Swallows and Amazons (1931), Swallowdale (1931)
E.B. Vesey The Hill Fox (1937)
Eurof Walters The Serpent's Presence (1954)
Clifford Webb Butterwick Farm (1933), A Jungle Picnic (1934), The North Pole Before Lunch (1936), Animals from Everywhere (1938), The Story of Noah (1949), Magic Island (1956), More Animals from Everywhere (1959), The Friendly Place (1962), Strange Creatures (1965), The Thirteenth Pig (1965), A Visit to the Zoo
H.G. Wells The Country of the Blind (1939)
M. Woodward A Key to the Countryside (1935)
Julius Caesar's Commentaries (1959)
Four Parables from the Holy Bible (1927)

References: Balston EWE; Bénézit; Garrett BWE, HBWE; Guichard; ICB 1,2,3; Johnson & Greutzner; Thieme & Becker; Vollmer; Wa (1934); Waters; The Studio 92 (1926), 101 (1931), 138 (1949), special (Spring 1927, Spring 1930, Winter 1936); Dorothea Braby The Way of Wood Engraving (Studio 1953); Christopher Sandford Bibliography of the Golden Cockerel Press (Dawson 1975), Cock-a-Hoop (Private Libraries Association 1976); A.C. Sewter Modern British Woodcuts and Wood Engravings in the Collection of the Whitworth Art Gallery (Manchester 1962)

Fritz Wegner (b. 1924)

Born in Vienna, but moved to England when he was fourteen. Studied at St Martin's School of Art. Since 1946, he has worked freelance as a book illustrator for British and American publishers, for magazines, and in advertising, and has developed a wiry, controlled pen line and a stylised, often humorous manner. Visiting lecturer at St Martin's School of Art. Lives in London.

Books illustrated include:
Janet Barber The Voyage of Jim (1973)
Eileen Colwell The Bad Boys (1972)
John D. Fitzgerald The Great Brain (1976)
Sid Fleischman The Ghost in the Noonday Sun (1966)
Leon Garfield The Strange Affair of Adelaide Harris (1971), The Pleasure Garden (1976)
Brothers Grimm Snow White and the Seven Dwarves (1973)
Norman Hunter The Home-Made Dragon (1971), Dust up at the Royal Disco (1975)
Joseph Jacobs Jack the Giant Killer (1970)
Sally Patrick Johnson Hamish Hamilton Book of Princesses (1963)
William Mayne The House on Fairmount (1968)
André Maurois Fattypuffs and Thinifers (1971)
Mordecai Richler Jacob Two-Two Meets the Hooded Fang (1975)
Ian Serraillier The Robin and the Wren (1974)
Christopher Sinclair-Stevenson Hamish Hamilton Book of Princes (1964)
Carolyn Sloan Carter is a Painter's Cat (1971)
Johann von Grimmelshausen Mother Courage (1965)
Barbara Willard (ed) Hullabaloo! (1969)
Amabel Williams-Ellis (retold by) More Grimm's Fairy Tales (1976)

Periodicals: Cricket, Everywoman, Farmer's Weekly

References: Eyre; Fisher pp.50, 100; ICB 2,4; Jacques; Usherwood; Vollmer supp; Wa (1980)

Hellmuth Weissenborn (1898-1982)

Born in Leipzig, Saxony, son of a Professor of Art. Studied at the Schiller Gymnasium and at

Hellmuth Weissenborn. From *Simplex Simplicissimus* (John Calder, 1964).

the Academy of Art in Leipzig. Lecturer at Leipzig Academy of Art (1926-38). Moved to England and became a part-time lecturer at Ravensbourne College of Art, London (1941-70). Co-owner, with his wife Lesley Macdonald, of the Acorn Press, publishing limited editions of finely produced, hand-set and hand-printed illustrated books. He has worked as a book illustrator for some thirty London publishers, making wood engravings, lino-cuts and drawings in pen and ink and occasionally crayon. Recently he has made wood and perspex engravings for portfolios of *Beasts, Insects, Flora, Hortus Fabulae* He also paints landscapes (oil, gouache, watercolour, watercolour and pastel), depicting greatly enlarged insects (oil on Japan paper), and makes monoprints. [Q]

Books illustrated include:
H.K. Adam German Cookery (1967)
V.B. Carter Billy the Bumblebee (1946), A Posie of Wildflowers (1946)
Jacqueline Forget Vingt Poèmes (1978)
R. Friedenthal Goethe Chronicle (1949)
Grimmelshausen Simplicissimus (1964)
Heinrich Heine Doktor Faust (1952)
M. Home Autumn Fields (1944), Spring Sowing (1946)

D'Arcy Kaye Masks and Unmasks (1978), Columbus (1978)
R.C. Kenedy Grotesques (1975), Cretan Picture Postcards (1981)
Gotthold Ephraim Lessing Fables in English and German (1979)
J. Lied Return to Happiness (1941)
Lucian True History of Lucius or the Ass (1958)
A. Marston London: Some Aspects (1968)
S. Read The Poetical Ark (1946)
William Shakespeare Sonnets (1982)
Helena Swann Eleven Poems (1978)
E. Thomas Diary (1977)
Ian Warren (trans) Aesop's Fables (1982)
Florian Weissenborn Roads, Rails, Bridges (1979)
Hellmuth Weissenborn Simplex Simplicissimus (1964), Picture Alphabet (1975), Ruins (1977), Fantasy (1978), Signs of the Zodiac (1978), A Collection of Proverbs from all Nations (1979), ABC of Names (c.1980)
H. White The Singing Stream (1950)
Aesop's Fables (trans. Ian Warren, 1982)

References: Vollmer suppl; Wa (1980); *Art International* (January 1969); *Illustration 63: Journal for Book Illustration* vol 3 (1977); *Hellmuth Weissenborn: Painter and Graphic Artist* (Bachman and Turner 1976)

Maurice Denton Welch (active 1915-48)

Worked as Denton Welch. Born in Shanghai, China. Studied art at Goldsmith's College London. From 1935 he was a permanent invalid following a bicycle accident. His writings (many of them published posthumously) are largely autobiographical; some are decorated with his scratchy but evocative pen and ink designs, and with some appealing endpapers.

Books illustrated include:
Denton Welch Maiden Voyage (1943), In Youth is Pleasure (1944), A Voice through a Cloud (1950), A Last Sheaf (1951), Dumb Instrument (1976)

Periodical: Words 11-16 (1975)

References Johnson & Greutzner; Jocelyn Brooke (ed) *Denton Welch* (Chapman & Hall 1963), *The Denton Welch Journals* (Hamish Hamilton 1952)

Dorothy M. Wheeler (1891-1966)

Studied at Blackheath School of Art. Lived at Esher, Surrey. Her sister Millicent was also an artist. A watercolour painter, postcard designer and children's book illustrator, she was one of Enid Blyton's most regular illustrators during the 1940s and 1950s, often working in the early comic strip format of pictures accompanied by text. Within the limitations of this field, and working in black and white, she used a crisp, dextrous outline, and produced varied frame-by-frame compositions. Dawn and Peter Cope record that she 'at one time based a lot of her work on the patterns seen in soap bubbles, and used a special soap bubble making machine so that she could study them in detail.'

Books illustrated include:
Enid Blyton The Little Tree House (1940), Six O'Clock Tales (1942), Dame Slap and her School (1943), Eight O'Clock Tales (1944), Josie, Click and Bun Again (1946), The Magic Faraway Tree (1946), More About Josie, Click and Bun (1947), Bumpy and his Bus (1949), Mr Tumpy and his Caravan (1949), The Rockingdown Mystery (1949), Further Adventures of Josie, Click and Bun (1950), Mr Pink-Whistle

Intervenes (1950), The Adventures of Mr Pink-Whistle (1951), Josie, Click and Bun and the Little Tree House (1951), Up the Faraway Tree (1951), Welcome Josie, Click and Bun! (1952), Mr Pink-Whistle's Party (1955), The Ring O' Bells Mystery (1965)
Dorothy Wheeler The Three Little Pigs (1955)
English Nursery Rhymes (1915)

Periodical: The Strand Magazine

References: Cope; Houfe; Waters

Edward J. Wheeler (c.1848-1933)

Painter and black and white artist. Introduced by the wood engraver Joseph Swain to the editor of *Punch*, to which he contributed small drawings and decorations from 1880. As early as 1896, M.H. Spielmann described his drawings as rather old fashioned in method. Some of his later figure work shows the influence of Bernard Partridge*.

Books illustrated include:
St. J. Hankin Mr Punch's Dramatic Sequels (1901)
R.C. Lehmann The Adventures of Picklock (1901)
The Works of Laurence Sterne (1894)
Tales from Pickwick (1888)

Periodicals: The Cornhill Magazine, Punch

References: Bénézit; Houfe; Price; Spielmann; Thieme & Becker; Veth; Waters 2; C. Wood

Mary V. Wheelhouse (active 1895-1947)

Born in Yorkshire. Studied in Paris for three years. Painter and illustrator of children's books in pen and ink with colour washes. One of her earliest books, *The Adventures of Merrywink*, written by a friend, won a competition in *The Bookman*. Most of her illustrative work was commissioned by the publisher George Bell. She lived in London, and later moved to Cambridge where she ran a small shop.

Books illustrated include:
Louisa M. Alcott Little Women (1909), Good Wives (1911)
May Baldwin Holly House and Ridges Row (1908)
Charlotte Bronte Jane Eyre (1911)
George Eliot Silas Marner (1910)
Juliana H. Ewing Six to Sixteen (1908), Jan of the Windmill (1909), We and the World (1910), A Great Emergency (1911), Mary's Meadow (1915)
Mrs Gaskell Cousin Phillis (1908), Cranford (1909), Sylvia's Lovers (1910), Wives and Daughters (1912)
E.V. Lucas The Slowcoach (1910)
Mrs Molesworth 'Carrots' (1920)
F.M Peard Mother Molly (1914)
Mary E. Phillips Tommy Tregennis (1914)
George Sand Les Maitres Sonneurs (1908)
Johann C. von Schmidt Easter Eggs (1908)
Amy Steadman The Story of Florence Nightingale (1915)
Christina Wyte The Adventures of Merrywink (1906)

References: Houfe; ICB 1; Johnson & Greutzner; C. Wood

Rowland Wheelwright (1870-1955)

Born Queensland, Australia. Studied in England a Hubert van Herkomer's Art School at Bushey, Hertfordshire. Painter of historical and classical subjects, illustrator in black and white, and in colour. For his colour illustrations, he seems to have used oils rather than the more usual watercolour or gouache, creating impasto effects that are not always very successful in reproduction. Elected RBA (1906).

Books illustrated include:
R.D. Blackmore Lorna Doone (with others, 1931)
Charles Dickens The Old Curiosity Shop (1930), A Tale of Two Cities (1926)
Alexandre Dumas The Three Musketeers (1920), Twenty Years After (1923)
Henry Fielding The History of Tom Jones (1925)
W. Killingworth Matsya (1905)
Eleanor Price (ed) The Adventures of King Arthur (with others, 1931)
M.N. Roberts Young Masters of Music (1932)
Walter Scott The Talisman (1929)
Laurence Sterne The Life and Opinions of Tristram Shandy (1926)

References: Bénézit; ICB 1; Johnson & Greutzner; Thieme & Becker; Wa (1934); Waters; C. Wood; *The Connoisseur* 74 (1926) p.59

Reginald John Whistler (1905-1944)

Worked as Rex Whistler. Born at Eltham, Kent, elder brother of glass engraver Laurence Whistler. His gifts were evident early; he studied for a year at the Royal Academy Schools, then moved to the Slade School of Fine Art (1922-26), where Professor Tonks admired and encouraged

M.V. Wheelhouse. Title page from *Mary's Meadow* by Juliana Horatia Ewing (Bell, 1915).

Rex Whistler. From *New Keepsake* (Cobden-Sanderson, 1931).

his work. After some small commissions, his chance came in 1926 when he was invited to design and paint mural decorations in the Tate Gallery Refreshment Room. '*The Pursuit of Rare Meats*', a lively Rococo architectural fantasy (inspired by the Temple Gardens of Stowe and Wilton), epitomises the style he was to make his own. Their success brought work and social popularity, and he became a prolific illustrator and designer. His most important book is *Gulliver's Travels* (Cresset Press 1935), illustrated with full plates, maps and head and tail pieces in fine pen and ink with colour washes on the larger plates applied by hand. The full-page illustrations have elaborate Baroque borders, at times almost overwhelming the inset drawings. The effect is superb, and Whistler's *Gulliver* remains one of the great illustrated books of this century. Other notable works include the much acclaimed *New Forget-Me-Not* (1929) and *Fairy Tales* (1935). All his work reflects his own personal charm and lively wit.

As well as being one of the outstanding illustrators of his generation, Whistler promised to be a great and original stage designer; his work for ballet, plays and opera included *The Rake's Progress*, Laurence Housman's *Victoria Regina*, *Fidelio* and *The Marriage of Figaro*. In 1940, he volunteered for the Welsh Guards; he was killed on active service in 1944.

Books illustrated include:
James Agate Kingdoms for Horses (1936)
Hans Andersen Fairy Tales and Legends (1935)
P. and M. Bloomfield The Traveller's Companion (1931)
Walter de la Mare Desert Islands (1930), The Lord Fish and other tales (1933)
Elizabeth Godley Green Outside (1931)
John Hadfield (ed) Restoration Love Songs (1950), Georgian Love Songs (1955)
Simon Harcourt-Smith The Last of Uptake (1942)
Edward James The Next Volume (1932)
Beverley Nichols Down the Golden Path (1932), A Thatched Roof (1933), A Village in a Valley (1934)
Edith Olivier Night Thoughts of a Country Landlady (1943)

F. Swettenham Arabella in Africa (1925)
Jonathan Swift Gulliver's Travels (1930)
Laurence Whistler Children of Hertha (1929), Armed October (1932), The Emperor Heart (1936), Oho! (1946)
Constance Wright Silver Collar (1934)
The New Forget-Me-Not (1934)

Periodical: Radio Times

References: Bénézit; Chamot, Farr & Butlin; Crouch; DNB (1941-50); Driver; Eyre; ICB 1; Johnson & Greutzner; Lewis; Vollmer; Wa (1934); Waters; *The Studio* special (Autumn 1930, Winter 1931, Autumn 1938); *Rex Whistler* (Arts Council Catalogue 1960); Laurence Whistler *Rex Whistler, His Life and His Drawings* (Art & Technics, 1948); Laurence Whistler and R. Fuller *The Work of Rex Whistler* (Batsford 1960)

Ethelbert White (1891-1972)

Born at Isleworth, Middlesex, and studied at the St John's School of Art under Leonard Walker (1911-12). He subsequently worked as a painter in oil and watercolour, illustrator and self-taught wood-engraver and poster designer. Between 1919 and 1921, he designed and sometimes engraved covers, text decorations and endpapers for the Beaumont Press, and in 1921 held his first one-man exhibition of painting at the Carfax Gallery. On the recommendation of Robert Gibbings*, he was appointed art editor of the Penguin Modern Classics series in 1938. He worked mainly in England, but exhibited internationally, and made frequent jouneys around France, Spain and North Africa in a gypsy caravan, collecting folk songs. White produced some of the earliest book illustrations in the 'modern' wood-engraving style of the 1920s (exemplified in *The Story of My Heart* 1923). His work was characterised by bold contrasts of black and white, with texture achieved with clearly incised tool marks. He was also one of the first British artists of his generation to use lino-cuts. Member of the London Group (1916), NEAC (1921), ARWS (1933), RWS (1939).

Books illustrated include:
Carlo Goldoni The Good-Humoured Ladies (1922)
Richard Jefferies The Story of My Heart (1923)
R.M.B. Nichols The Smile of the Sphinx (1920)
The Wedding Songs of Edmund Spenser (1923)

References: Balston EWE, WEMEB; Bénézit; Chamot, Farr & Butlin; Garrett BWE, HBWE; Thieme & Becker; Vollmer; Wa (1934); Waters; *Drawing and Design* 1 (1926); *Image* 3 (1949-50); *The Studio* 100 (1930), 103 (1932), special (Spring 1927, Winter 1936, Autumn 1938); *Letters from Ethelbert White to G.H.B. Holland* (Victoria and Albert Museum, 1935-36, 1958); Herbert Furst *The Modern Woodcut* (John Lane 1924); Charles Johnson *English Painting* (G. Bell 1932); A.C. Sewter *Modern British Woodcuts and Wood Engravings in the Collection of the Whitworth Art Gallery* (Manchester 1962)

Gwendolen Beatrice White (b. 1903)

Works as Gwen White. Born Exeter, Devon, daughter of a master coach-builder. Studied at Bournemouth School of Art and the Royal College of Art, and taught book illustration and perspective part time at Farnham and St Alban's Schools of Art. She married the painter and stained-glass artist C. Rupert Moore. Writer, illustrator and designer of books, landscape and mural painter, designer of children's programmes and annuals for the BBC and of catalogues for the National Book League; also a writer on the subject of toys. Her book illustrations are clearly drawn with a strong sense of design, in black and white (pen and ink or scraperboard), sometimes with colour added for colourline reproduction. [Q]

Books illustrated include:
Enid Blyton Tales of Green Hedges (1946)
Rhoda Power Ten Minute Tales and Dialogue Stories (1943)
Gwen White Ancient and Modern Dolls (1928), The Toys' Adventures at the Zoo (1929), Ladybird, Ladybird (1938), A Book of Toys (1946), Eight Little Frogs (1947), A Book of Pictorial Perspective (1955), A Book of Dolls (1956), A World of Pattern (1957), Dolls of the World (1962), European and American Dolls (1966), Perspective for Artists, Architects and Designers (1968), Antique toys and their Background (1971)

References: Johnson & Greutzner; Wa (1980); Waters 2; *The Studio* special (Winter 1931)

Geoffrey Whittam (b. 1916)

Born in Woolston, Southampton, son of a pattern maker. Studied at Southampton School of Art (1932-33). Worked in the Post Office (1935-39) and served in the Royal Navy during World War II before studying at the Central School of Arts and Crafts (1946-49) and then worked freelance as an illustrator, designer and landscape painter. His output has included illustrations for children's adventure stories, educational books (mostly for African countries book jackets and comic strips (including *Mandy*, and *Victor* for D.C. Thomson newspapers). He also makes graphic visualisations of buildings from plans, and designs posters. For illustration, he works in pen, brush and indian ink, and in gouache for full colour. [Q]

Books illustrated include:
Alec Adrian He Wore a Red Jersey (1975)
Judith M. Berrisford Skipper and Son (1975), Skipper and the Runaway Boy (1975), Jackie and the Misfit Pony (1975), Jackie and the Pony Thieves (1978), Jackie and the Phantom Ponies (1979), Jackie and the Moonlight Ponies (1980), Jackie and the Pony Rivals (1981)
Emily Brontë Wuthering Heights (1956)
Arthur Catherall Ten Fathoms Deep (1954), Jackals of the Sea (1955), Forgotten Submarine (1956), Land Under the White Rose (1956), Java Sea Duel (1957), Sea Wolves (1959), Dangerous Cargo (1960), China Sea Jigsaw (1961), Prisoners Under the Sea (1963), Death of an Oil Rig (1967), Island of Forgotten Men (1968), The Unwilling Smuggler (1971)
Lucy Evelyn Cheesman Sealskins for Silk (1952)
Richard Church The Cave (1950)
Monica Edwards The White Riders (1950), Black Hunting Whip (1950), Cargo of Horses (1951), Hidden in a Dream (1952), Storm Ahead (1953), No Entry (1954), The Nightbird (1955), Frenchman's Secret (1956), Strangers to the Marsh (1957), Operation Seabird (1957), The Cownappers (1958), No Going Back (1960), The Outsider (1961), The Hoodwinkers (1962), Dolphin Summer (1963), Five in the Punchbowl (1965), The Wild One (1967)
Kathleen Fidler The Droving Lad (1955), Escape in Darkness (1961)

Geoffrey Whittam. 'The Lydia shot down the starboard side of the Natividad' from *Hornblower Takes Command* by C.S. Forester (Michael Joseph, 1954).

C.S. Forester Cadet Edition of Hornblower Stories (1954)
Frank Knight Family on the Tide (1956)
Meta Mayne Reid All Because of Danks (1955), Danks Does it Again (1956), Danks on Robbers' Mountain (1957), Storm on Kildoney (1961)
L. Todd Tortoise and the Trickster (1979)
Geoffrey Trease Word to Caesar (1956)
Geoffrey Whittam The Whale Hunters (1954), Fur Hunting and Fur Farming (1957), Lumbering in Canada (1957), Farming on the Canadian Prairies (1959), The Zambezi (1961), The Rhine (1962), Canals and Waterways (1968)

Periodicals: Mandy, Radio Times, Victor

References: Fisher p.160, 339, 345; ICB 2

Charles Whymper (1853-1941)

Born in London, into a family of artists and wood engravers; brother of the illustrator and alpine climber Edward J. Whymper (1840-1911). Studied under the animal painter Joseph Wolf. He was a painter of landscapes, sporting subjects, mammals and birds; also a wood engraver, etcher and illustrator in line, halftone and full colour. He was a capable watercolourist whose work was held in considerable regard by naturalists and sportsmen.

Books illustrated include:
F.G. Alfalo Fisherman's Weather (1906)
John Brown The Pilgrim Fathers (1895)
Abel Chapman The Art of Wildfowling (with the author, 1896), Wild
    Norway (with others, 1897)
Charles Dixon Our Rarer Birds (1888), Lost and Vanishing Birds
    (1898), Bird Life in a Southern Country (1899), Among the Birds in
    Northern Shires (1900), Game Birds and Wild Fowl of the British
    Islands (1900), Open-Air Studies in Bird Life (1903)
Evelyn Everett-Green A Child Without a Name (1887)
Sir R. Payne Gallwey The Fowler in Ireland (1882), Letters to Young
    Shooters (with J.G. Millais*, 1896)
A.St.H. Gibbons Exploration and Hunting in Central Africa (1898)
T. de Grey Shooting...Field and Covert (1900)
F.H.H. Guillemard The Cruise of the Marchesa (1886)
A.E. Gathorn Hardy The Salmon (1898)
James E. Harting The Rabbit (with others, 1898)
J.M. Heathcote and C.G. Tebbutt Skating (with others, 1902)
J.S. Jameson Story of the Rear Guard of Emin Pasha Relief
    Expedition (1890)
Richard Jefferies The Gamekeeper at Home (1880)
Frederick V. Kirby In Haunts of Wild Game (1896)
H.R. Knipe Nebula to Man (with others, 1905)
Alexander Mackennal Homes and Haunts of the Pilgrim Fathers
    (1899)
H.A. MacPherson The Hare (with others, 1896)
G. Malcolm and A. Maxwell Grouse and Grouse Moors (1910)
Frank Oates Marabele Land and Victoria Falls (with others, 1889)
J. Macdonald Oxley On the World's Roof (1896)
E.L. Peel A Highland Gathering (1885)
Clive Phillipps-Wolley and others Big-Game Shooting (with others,
    1895)
Lt. Col. Pollock Sporting Days in India (1894)
P. Robinson Birds of the Wave and Moorland (with others, 1894)
Charles St. John Wild Sport in the Highlands (1878)
Henry Seeboh Siberia in Europe (1880), Siberia in Asia (1882)
Francis C. Selous Sunshine and Storm in Rhodesia (with others, 1896),
    Travel and Adventure in South Africa (with others, 1893)
Percy Selous Travel and Big Game (1897)
Gordon Stables Off to Klondyke (1898)
S.J. Stones In and Beyond the Himalayas (1896)
A. Trevor-Battye Icebound in Kolgue (with others, 1895)
Lord Walsingham and Sir R. Payne Gallwey Shooting (with others,
    1900)
C.P. Wolley Big-Game Shooting (1895)

Periodicals: The English Illustrated Magazine, Good Words, The
Illustrated London News, The Leisure Hour

References: Baker; Bénézit; Houfe; Johnson & Greutzner; Mallalieu;
Sketchley; Thieme & Becker; Vollmer; Wa (1929); Waters; C. Wood;
J.C. Wood; *The Connoisseur* 65 (1923) p.238

W. Edward Wigfull (active 1890-1939)

Magazine and book illustrator, specialising in
adventure stories and the sea, and one of Percy
Westerman's most regular illustrators. He worked
mainly in halftone, in a style that became more
linear as his career progressed, but which generally
lacked distinguishing features.

Books illustrated include:
Percy Westerman The Sea-Girt Fortress (1914), The Thick of the Fray
    at Zeebruge (1919), The Wireless Officer (1922), A Cadet of the
    Mercantile Marine (1923), The Good Ship 'Golden Effort' (1924),
    On the Wings of the Wind (1928), Captain Scarlet (1929), The Secret
    of the Plateau (1931), The Amir's Ruby (1932), The Westar
    Talisman (1934), Standish Gets his Man (1938), Standish Loses his
    Man (1939)

Periodicals: The English Illustrated Magazine, The Girls' Realm,
Herbert Strang's Annuals, The Idler, The Longbow, Oxford Annual,
The Quartier Latin

Reference: Thorpe

Katherine Wigglesworth (b. 1901)

Maiden name: Katherine Semple. Born in India,
daughter of the Director of the Pasteur Institute
at Kasauli. Studied at the Slade School of Fine
Art (1921-23). After working briefly in a commercial studio, she joined Liberty and Co. as a
designer of children's clothes, fabrics, china,
embroidery and smocking, and also did line
drawings of children and animals for Liberty's
advertisements. As an illustrator of books by
Alison Uttley for 30 years, she was responsible
for the *Little Brown Mouse* series (Heinemann)
and the *Little Red Fox* series (Puffin Books). She
took over the *Little Grey Rabbit* series (Collins)
when Margaret Tempest* was unable to continue
through ill health, and illustrated the last five
books Alison Uttley wrote before she died.
Working in pen and ink or in full colour, she created lively pictures of little animals, endearingly
humanised. Although Alison Uttley disliked her
illustrators working for other authors, she agreed
to Katherine Wigglesworth making drawings for
books on insects by her husband Sir Vincent
Wigglesworth, Quick Professor at Cambridge,
and illustrating scientific papers with specimens
viewed through a microscope. [Q]

Books illustrated include:
Emma Smith Emily (1959)
Alison Uttley The Little Brown Mouse Books (13 vols, 1950-57), Little
    Red Fox and the Wicked Uncle (1954), Little Red Fox and
    Cinderella (1956), Little Red Fox and the Magic Moon (1958), Snug
    and Serena Count Twelve (1959), Snug and Serena Go to Town
    (1961), Little Red Fox and the Unicorn (1962), Little Grey Rabbit
    Goes to the North Pole (1970), The Brown Mouse Book (1971),
    Fuzzypeg's Brother (1971), Little Grey Rabbit's Spring Cleaning
    Party (1972), Little Grey Rabbit and the Snow-Baby (1973), Hare
    and the Rainbow (1975)
The Modern Gift Book for Children (with others, 1948)

Reference: Fisher p.179

Jocelyn Wild (b. 1941)

Maiden name: Jocelyn van Ingen. Born in Mysore,
India. Educated in India and England, and studied
Spanish at King's College, London. Writer and
illustrator of children's books in collaboration
with her husband, Robin Wild. She works mostly
in pen and ink, with crayon or gouache with
acrylic medium. [Q]

Books illustrated include:
Robin and Jocelyn Wild The Tiger Tree (1976), The Bears' ABC Book
    (1977), The Bears' Counting Book (1978), Spot's Dogs and the Alley
    Cats (1979), Spot's Dogs and the Kidnappers (1981)

Periodicals: Cricket, The Egg, Pomme d'Api

Brian Lawrence Wildsmith (b. 1930)

Works as Brian Wildsmith. Born at Penistone,
Yorkshire. Won a chemistry scholarship to the
De La Salle College at Sheffield, but turned to art

and studied at Barnsley School of Art and the Slade School of Fine Art. He later taught at Maidstone College of Art under William Stobbs*. He began working freelance in 1957. As an illustrator in black and white, and in full colour, he rapidly became known for the striking effects of texture and surface decoration which were achieved by combining widely varied media and application techniques within single designs. He won the Kate Greenaway Medal with *ABC*, (1962) and his work remained highly influential throughout the 1960s. He now lives in France.

Books illustrated include:
Paul Berna The Knights of King Midas (1961)
Edward Blishen (ed) The Oxford Book of Poetry for Children (1960)
Nan Chauncy The Secret Friends (1960), Tangara (1960)
Kevin Crossley-Holland Havelock the Dane (1964)
Jean de la Fontaine The Hare and the Tortoise (1966), the Lion and the
    Rat (1963), The North Wind and the Sun (1964), The Rich Man and
    the Shoemaker (1965)
Eleanor Graham The Story of Jesus (1959)
Roger Lancelyn Green The Saga of Asgard (1960), Myths of the
    Norsemen (1962)
Frederick Grice The Bonny Pit Laddie (1960)
R.J. MacGregor Indian Delight (1958), The Warrior's Treasure (1962)
Maurice Maeterlinck The Blue Bird (1977)

Frank Wiles. 'Stella and the Great Dane' from *Stella Maris* (John Lane, 1914).

Brian Wildsmith. From *The Knights of King Midas* by Paul Berna (Bodley Head, 1961).

Madeleine Polland A Town across the Water (1961)
Ian Serraillier Happily Ever After (1963)
R.L. Stevenson A Child's Garden of Verses (1966)
Ruth Tomalin The Daffodil Bird (1959)
Geoffrey Trease Follow My Black Plume (1963), A Thousand for Sicily
    (1964)
Philip Turner The Bible Story (1968)
Brian Wildsmith ABC (1962), Mother Goose (1964), 1 2 3 (1965),
    Birds (1967), Wild Animals (1967), Fishes (1968), Circus (1970),
    Puzzles (1970), The Owl and the Woodpecker (1972), The Twelve
    Days of Christmas (1972), Python's Party (1974), What the Moon
    Saw (1978), Hunter and his Dog (1979), Professor Noah's Spaceship
    (1980), Bears' Adventure (1981)

References: Bland; Doyle CL; Eyre; Hürlimann; ICB 3,4; Jacques;
Ryder; *The Junior Bookshelf* vol 27 no 3 (1963); *Library Journal* (15th
November 1965)

Frank Wiles (active 1912-30)

Portrait painter and magazine and book illustrator, mainly of girls' school stories. He drew very much in the accepted manner for books of this type, working in pen or pencil with halftone washes or occasionally in colour, and aiming at dashing, polished effects.

Books illustrated include:
Angela Brazil A Fourth Form Friendship (1912), The Princess of the
    School (1920), St Catherine's College (1929), Jean's Golden Term
    (1934)
Percy Westerman The Quest of the 'Golden Hope' (1912)
Frank Wiles Stella Maris (1914)

Periodicals: Blackie's Annuals, The Strand Magazine

References: Houfe; Johnson & Greutzner; *The Studio* special
(Autumn 1914)

Barry Wilkinson (b. 1923)

Born in Dewsbury, Yorkshire. Studied at Dewsbury Art School, then, after serving in the Royal Air Force (1942-47), at the Royal College of Art (1947-49). He worked in a stained glass studio, then taught at Wimbledon School of Art where he became head of the Graphics Department. Since

1961, he has worked freelance, designing transparent murals, street Christmas decorations, advertisements (e.g. for Whitbread beer), Christmas cards and book jackets. He has illustrated a number of children's stories and educational books, and has provided illustrations for the BBC TV children's programme *Jackanory*.He succeeded Peggy Fortnum* as an illustrator of the Paddington Bear series in 1976. For book illustration he mainly uses watercolour; for magazines and periodicals, pen and ink. His television illustrations are in designer's gouache. [Q]

Books illustrated include:
Michael Bond Paddington at the Station (1976), Paddington Goes to the Sales (1976), Paddington Takes a Bath (1976), Paddington's New Room (1976), Paddington's Counting Book (1977)
Mary Cockett As Big as the Ark (1974)
Marjorie Darke What Can I Do? (1975)
Charles Dickens A Tale of Two Cities (1973)
Sheila Haigh Watch for the Champion (1980)
Joseph Jacobs Lazy Jack (1968)
Naomi Lewis (ed) The Story of Aladdin (1970)
David Mackay Sally Go Round the Sun (1970)
William MacKellar Davie's Wee Dog (1965)
Sybil Marshall Seafarer's Quest to Colchis (1981)
Naomi Mitchison Sun and Moon (1970)
Ursula Moray-Williams The Line (1974)
Felicity Sen My Family (1975)
Ruth Silcock Albert John Out Hunting (1980), Albert John in Disgrace (1981)
Noel Streatfeild Old Chairs to Mend (1966)
Walter Scott Kenilworth (1970)
R.L. Stevenson Kidnapped (1973)
Barry Wilkinson The Diverting Adventures of Tom Thumb (1967), Lazy Jack (1968), Puss in Boots (1968), What can you do with a Dithery-Doo? (1971), Jonathan Just (1971)
Ursula Moray Williams The Line (1974)

Periodicals: Honey, New Society, Punch, Radio Times, TV Times,

References: ICB 4; *Graphis* 131

Barry Wilkinson. 'Albert John sang a little song of homecoming...' from *Albert John in Disgrace* by Ruth Silcock (Kestrel, 1981).

Norman Wilkinson (1878-1971)

Born in Cambridge. Studied at Portsmouth and Southsea School of Art, Hampshire, and worked there as a pupil-teacher. Studied painting under Louis Grier at St Ives, Cornwall (1899), then figure painting in Paris. Settled in London and worked consistently (1901-15) on *The Illustrated London News*, where his colleagues included Russell Flint*, and R. Caton Woodville* During World War I, he invented and developed the first effective form of dazzle camouflage for ships; during World War II, he worked on the aerial camouflage of important land sites. Between the wars, he established a considerable reputation as a marine painter in oil and watercolour, and as an etcher. He was a pioneer in the design of 'artistic' railway posters in full colour. He published his autobiography in 1969, and continued painting into his nineties. His book illustrations sometimes consist of dramatised representations of naval and similar subjects in pen and ink or full colour, and fluent, well-composed dry points of landscape and angling subjects. Member of the St John's Wood Art Club, Honorary Marine Painter to the Royal Yacht Squadron (1919); elected RBA (1902), RI (1906), PRI (1937), ROI (1908). Awarded CBE (1948).

Books illustrated include:
A.B. Austin An Angler's Anthology (1913)
J.Baikie Peeps at the Royal Navy (1913)
P.R. Chalmers A Fisherman's Angles (1931)
J.W. Hills A Summer on the Test (1924)
Sir Henry Newbolt The Book of the Blue Sea (1914), Tales of the Great War (1916), Submarine and Anti-Submarine (1918)
L. Swinburne The Royal Navy (1907)
Norman Wilkinson The Dardanelles: Colour Sketches from Gallipoli (1915), Landscapes and Seascapes (1929), Ships in Pictures (1944), Watercolour Sketching out-of-doors (1953), A Brush with Life (1969)

Periodicals: The Graphic, The Harmsworth Magazine, The Illustrated London News, The Illustrated Mail, Young England

References: Bénézit; Guichard; Houfe; Johnson & Greutzner; Thieme & Becker; Wa (1929); Waters; A.L. Baldry *British Marine Painting* (Studio special 1919); B. Heckstall Smith *Yachts and Yachting in Contemporary Art* (Studio special 1925); C. King *Rule Britannia* (Studio special 1941); *The War* (Studio special 1918); *Fine Prints of the Year* (1925, 1926, 1927); Norman Wilkinson *A Brush with Life* (Seeley Service 1969)

Norman Wilkinson of Four Oaks (1882-1934)

Studied at Birmingham School of Art and in Paris. Painter of historical subjects and later of landscapes; stage-designer admired for his work for Shakespearean productions. As a book illustrator, he adopted the suffix 'of Four Oaks' to distinguish himself from the marine artist of the same name. Despite this precaution, confusion persists; even Houfe attributes the illustrations for *Virginibus Puerisque* to the other Wilkinson. The illustrations for this book are typical of

Wilkinson of Four Oaks's work: meticulous in execution with echoes of *fin-de-siècle* symbolism in their pale colour and studied figure postures. He was a close friend of Maxwell Armfield*.

Books illustrated include:
Geoffrey Chaucer The Romaunt of the Rose (with Keith Henderson*, 1911)
William Shakespeare Love's Labour Lost (1924)
R.L. Stevenson Virginibus Puerisque and other papers (1910)

References: Johnson & Greutzner; Waters 2; *The Studio* 35 (1905) pp.290-94, 40 (1907) pp.230-61, 61 (1914) pp.301-07, special (1927)

Jenny Williams (b. 1939)

Born in London. Studied at Wimbledon School of Art. Freelance illustrator and writer of children's books, book jacket designer and commercial artist. She works in pen and coloured inks, body-colour and transparent washes. For her highly effective page layouts, she collaborates with her husband, a typographic and graphic designer.

Books illustrated include:
Dorothy Edwards A Wet Monday (1975), The Read-Me-Another-Story Book (1976)
John Gilbert Evans Llyfr hwiangerddi y Dref wen (1981)
David Grant Favourite Fairy Tales (1976)
Douglas Kirby The Silver Wood (1966)
Margaret Mahy A Lion in the Meadow (1969), The Boy with Two Shadows (1971), The Witch in the Cherry Tree (1974), Leaf Magic (1976)
Sheila Parsons My First Reading and Writing Book (1979)
Martha and Charles Shapp Let's Find out about Babies (1977)
Jenny Williams On Holiday (1975), First-Fourth Fairy Story Books (1977-79), Alphabet Adventures (1978), The Poor Man's Kingdom/The Snake Prince (1980), The Fisherman and the Mermaid/The Brothers (1980), The King of the Fishes/The Magic Lime Tree (1980), The Magic Kettle/The Golden Fish/The Fairy Hill (1980)
Helen Young Wide Awake Jake (1974)

Reference: ICB 3, 4

Morris Meredith Williams (b. 1881)

Born in Cowbridge, Glamorgan, Wales. Studied at the Slade School of Fine Art, in Florence and in Paris. Landscape painter; stained glass designer. As an illustrator, he was particularly known for his detailed penwork. His compositions are also distinctive, often with densely packed figures giving an effect of overall pattern. He lived in Edinburgh.

Books illustrated include:
T.B. Franklin Tactics and the Landscape (1914)
Elizabeth W. Grierson The Scottish Fairy Book (1910)
Eleanor Hull The Northmen in Britain (1913)
Anne MacDonnell The Italian Fairy Book (1911)
Robert L. Mackie The Story of King Robert the Bruce (1913)
William Platt Stories of the Scottish Border (1911)
E.M. Tappan Heroes of the Middle Ages (1918)
Ethelreda M. Wilmot-Buxton The Story of the Crusades (1911), Anselm (1915), A Book of English Martyrs (1915)
The Boy's Froissart (1912)

Periodical: Punch

References: Bénézit; Houfe; ICB 1; Johnson & Greutzner; Thieme & Becker; Wa (1929)

M. Meredith Williams. 'The Vision of Mohammed' from *Heroes of the Middle Ages* by E.M. Tappan (Harrap, 1918).

Ursula Moray Williams (b. 1911)

Married name: Mrs John. Born in Petersfield, Hampshire. Educated at home, then in France; studied art for a year at Winchester School of Art. She now lives in Gloucestershire. Since 1931 she has written some 70 children's books, of which she has illustrated about a third herself. She draws mainly in pen and ink, although during the 1930s she occasionally used simple lino prints; later, she sometimes worked with brightly coloured paper shapes, as in *The House of Happiness* (1946).

Books illustrated include:
Ursula Moray Williams Jean-Pierre (1931), For Brownies (1932), The Pettabomination (1933), Grandfather (1933), More for Brownies (1934), Kelpie (1934), Anders and Marta (1935), Adventures of Anne (1935), The Twins and Their Ponies (1936), Sandy-on-the-Shore (1936), Tales for the Sixes and Sevens (1936), Dumpling (1937), Elaine of La Signe (with Barbara Moray Williams, 1937), Gobbolino the Witch's Cat (1942), The Good Little Christmas Tree (1942), The Three Toymakers (1945), The House of Happiness (1946), Malkin's Mountain (1948), The Story of the Laughing Dandino (1948), The Binklebys at Home (1951), The Binklebys on the Farm (1953), The Secrets of the Wood (1955), Grumpa (1955), Goodbody's Puppet Show (1956), Golden Horse with a Silver Tail (1957), Hobbie (1958), The Moonball (1958), O for a Mouseless House (1964)

References: Contemporary Authors; Kirkpatrick

Irene G. Williamson (active 1932-65)

Although not the original illustrator of Mary Plain (*Mostly Mary* and *All Mary* were illustrated respectively by Audrey Harris and Harry Rountree* in their first editions of 1930 and 1931), Irene Williamson was the artist who created the image of this self-possessed bear character who was in many ways the forerunner of 'Paddington'. She drew in pen and ink in a style that became more elaborate in later books in the series. She was credited as Irene Williamson in the Mary Plain books and as I.G. Williamson elsewhere, but stylistic comparison of the drawings confirms their common authorship.

Books illustrated include:
Gwynedd Rae Mary Plain in Town (1935), Mary Plain on Holiday (1937), Mostly Mary (1938), All Mary (1938), Mary Plain in Trouble (1940), Mary Plain Home Again (1941), Mary Plain's Big Adventure (1944), Mary Plain to the Rescue (1950), Mary Plain and the Twins (1952), Mary Plain Goes Bob-a-Jobbing (1954), Mary Plain Goes to America (1957), Mary Plain V.I.P. (1961), Mary Plain's Whodunit (1965)
B.G. Williamson The Dragon Farm (1932), The Polar Piggy (1932)
I.G. Williamson The Adventures of Griselda (1938)

Althea Willoughby (active 1930s)

Book illustrator and decorator, wood engraver, and painter of ceramic tiles. She illustrated three books in the *Ariel* series of individual poems published by Faber and Faber in the characteristic format of a small black and white title-page drawing and one full-page drawing and one full-page line block illustration in black and three

Althea Willoughby. 'Masquerade at Ranelagh, 1751' from *Review of Revues* edited by C.B.C. (Cape, 1930).

individually printed colours. Her graphic style was restrained, and her works possessed quiet imaginative conviction.

Books illustrated include:
C.B.C. (ed) Review of Revues (1930)
D.H. Lawrence The Triumph of the Machine (1930)
Christopher Morley Rudolph and Amina (1931)
Sir Henry Newbolt A Child is Born (1931)
J. Stephens The Outcast (1929)
The Glades of Glenbella (frontispiece, nd)

Periodicals: The Book Collector's Quarterly, The Woodcut

References: Johnson & Greutzner; *The Studio* 100 (1930) p 464, special (Spring 1930)

Ursula Moray Williams. '...the Pettabomination plunged out, seized the calf of the Governess's left leg in his claws and bit it, with twenty-four crunchy baby-dragon double-teeth' from her *The Pettabomination* (Denis Archer, 1933).

Vera Willoughby (active 1905-39)

Born in Hungary. Studied at the Slade School of Fine Art under Legros. Initially a watercolour painter working at Slindon, Sussex (1911) and in London (1913), she achieved sudden renown as an illustrator in the late 1920s, with books published by Peter Davies. She worked in a distinctive style, usually in pencil (sometimes edged with watercolour), becoming best known for her decorative treatment of elegant 'period' (especially

18th-century) subjects. James Laver praised her 'power of decorating her book without overloading it' and her 'exquisite sense of the appropriate style'. Her illustrations for *The Four Gospels*, with their somewhat Byzantine formality, show her facility for a more sombre approach. She also designed advertisements and costumes for the theatre.

Books illustrated include:
Jane Austen Pride and Prejudice (1929)
Benjamin Disraeli Popanilla and other tales (nd)
J.M. Edmonds (trans) Some Greek Love Poems (1929)
George Farquhar The Recruiting Officer (1926)
E.E. Frisk (ed) Lovely Laughter (1932)
L. Frank Carl and Anna and Breath (1931)
William Shakespeare Henry V (c.1939)
Laurence Sterne A Sentimental Journey (1927)
F.A. Vane (ed) Memoirs of a Lady of Quality (1925)
Vera Willoughby A Vision of Greece (1925)
The Four Gospels (1927)
Horati Carminum Libri IV (1926)
The Poems of Catullus (1929)
Sappho Revocata (1928)

Periodical: The Bystander

References: Houfe; Johnson & Greutzner; Vollmer; Wa (1934); *The Artist* 12 (1936); *The Studio* 94 (1927), special (1927, 1928, Winter 1931); James Laver *Vera Willoughby: Illustrator of Books* (J. & E. Bumpus 1929)

Mary G.W. Wilson (active 1882-1936)

Born Bantaskine, Falkirk. Studied in Edinburgh and Paris. She sketched landscapes, gardens and flowers in watercolour and pastel. Her book illustrations, consisting of colour plates of gardens, are very uniform in subject and style but the quality of both artwork and printing declines after *Scottish Gardens* (1908). Member of the Pastel Society and the Royal Scottish Academy.

Books illustrated include:
Handasyde Four Gardens (1924)
Sir Herbert Maxwell Scottish Gardens (1908)
M.G.W. Wilson Garden Memories (1912), Enchantment of Gardens (1924), The Book of Dovecots (nd)

References: Johnson & Greutzner; Vollmer; Wa (1934)

Maurice Wilson (b. 1914)

Born in London. Studied at Hastings School of Art and at the Royal Academy Schools. Lecturer at Bromley School of Art and the Royal School of Needlework. An animal painter of distinction; also a marine artist and occasional portrait painter. Much of his output is for reproduction. He works in watercolour, acrylic paint or in oils for colour plates, and in pen or brush and ink for black and white illustrations. Member RI; Vice President of the Society of Wildlife Artists. [Q]

Books illustrated include:
E.G. Boulenger Zoo Animals (1948)
Richard Carrington A Guide to Earth History (1958)
John Cunliffe Our Sam (1980)
J.M.M. Fisher Birds and Beasts (with Rowland Hilder*, 1956)

Margery Fisher A World of Animals (1962)
Helen Griffiths Patar (1970)
James Reeves (retold by) Fables from Aesop (1961)
D. Tovey Donkey Work (1962)
Maurice Wilson Just Monkeys (1937), Dogs (1946), Coastal Craft (1947), Animals We Know (1959), Animals (1964), Birds (1965)

Periodical: Radio Times

References: Jacques; Usherwood; Wa (1980)

Oscar Wilson (1867-1930)

Born in London. Studied at the South Kensington School of Art and at the Antwerp Academy. Genre painter and illustrator of books, magazines and newspapers, particularly known for his pictures of pretty women. Elected RMS (1896), ARBA (1926).

Books illustrated include:
Elizabeth Grierson Bishop Patteson of the Cannibal Islands (1927)
G.I. Witham The Last of the Whitecoats (1906), Adventures of a Cavalier (1914)

Periodicals: Black and White, Cassell's Magazine, The Idler, The Illustrated London News, The Lady's Realm, Madame, Pick-me-Up, St Paul's, The Sketch

References: Houfe; Johnson & Greutzner; Mallalieu; Thorpe; Vollmer; Waters; C. Wood; *The Ludgate* 2 (1897)

Patten Wilson (1868-1928)

Born Cleobury Mortimer, Shropshire. Studied briefly at Kidderminster School of Art but left to devote himself to the study of Albrecht Dürer. Spent a year as director's secretary at a Liverpool gymnasium and a year as assistant to a London wall-paper manufacturer. Designed textiles and some of the first stencilled friezes. Became a freelance designer and studied under Fred Brown at evening classes at the Westminster School of Art. He was introduced by John Lane to black and white illustration and was employed by him on dust wrappers, title pages and designing the Keynote series; he also worked on *The Yellow Book*. His early illustrations have densely textured linear detail and were described by *The Studio* as 'alive with imaginative and wild strangeness'. His later work is less individual and less complex, revealing an erratic sense of proportion, but is finely shaded and shows a continuing concern with animal and plant life.

Books illustrated include:
Ernest Fitzroy Ames The Tremendous Twins (with Mrs Ames, 1900)
Sara Cone Bryant Stories to Tell Children (1912)
Samuel Taylor Coleridge Selections (1898)
H.B. Cotterill (trans) Homer's Odyssey (1911)
T.W.H. Crosland The Coronation Dumpy Book (1902)
Charles Dickens A Child's History Book (1902)
J.S. Fletcher Life in Arcadia (1896)
W.S. Furneaux Field and Woodland Plants (1909)
Lillian Gask In the 'Once Upon a Time' (1913)
J.H. Harris Phyllis in Piskie-Land (1913)
C.G. Hartley Stories of Early British Heroes (1902)
M.D. Haviland Wild Life on the Wing (1913)
A. Herbert The Moose (1913)

Katherine T. Hinkson Miracle Plays (1895)
A. Klein Anatole (1904)
V. Phillips Trip to Santa Claus Land (1905)
Walter C. Rhoades A Houseful of Rebels (1897)
William Shakespeare King John (1899)
Patten Wilson Nature Round the House (1907), The Book of the Zoo (1913)
The Gospel Story of Jesus Christ (1901)
The Sunday Dumpy Book for Children (from 1903)

Periodicals: The Keepsake, The Pall Mall Magazine, The Yellow Book

References: Baker; Bénézit; Crane; Houfe; ICB 1; Johnson; Johnson & Greutzner; Sketchley; Thieme & Becker; Thorpe; Waters 2; C. Wood; *The Studio* 23 (1901), special (1900-01); Holbrook Jackson *The 1890s* (Grant Richards 1913)

Edward Wolfe (b. 1897)

Born Johannesburg, South Africa. He was a child actor in South Africa, then emigrated to England and studied art at Regent St Polytechnic (1916) and the Slade School of Fine Art (1917-18). Worked at Roger Fry's Omega Workshops (1917-19). He subsequently painted in S. Africa, France, Italy, Morocco, Spain, USA and Mexico as well as in England and Wales. His few book illustrations shared the relaxed Matisse-like simplification and elegance of his easel paintings. Member London Group (1923), the Seven and Five Society (1926-31), and the London Artists' Association; elected ARA (1967), RA (1972).

Books illustrated include:
John Garratt The Dancing Beggar (1946)
Michael Joyce Peregrine Pieram (1936)

References Bénézit; Chamot, Farr & Butlin; Johnson & Greutzner; Shone; Thieme & Becker; Waters; *Apollo* 14 (1931) p.168

Berthold Ludwig Wolpe (b. 1905)

Born in Offenbach, Germany. Served an apprenticeship with a firm of metal workers (gold, silver and copper) and studied at the Offenbach Kunstgewerbeschule (1924-28) under Rudolf Koch, who had a profound influence on his early work as a typographic designer. He taught at the Frankfurt and Offenbach School of Art (1929-33), then moved to England in 1935 and worked for the Fanfare Press for four years. He joined Faber & Faber in 1941 and remained with the company until his retirement in 1975. He also taught part-time at Camberwell School of Arts and Crafts (1948-52) and was tutor and visiting lecturer at the School of Graphic Design at the Royal College of Art. He now teaches at the City and Guilds of London School of Art. An outstanding and internationally known designer of printing type, his typefaces have included *Hyperion* (designed while still in Germany), *Albertus* (for the Monotype corporation), *Tempest* (1936), *Sachsenwald* (1937), *Pegasus* (1938) and *Decorata* (1955). He was responsible for over 1500 book jackets for Faber & Faber, often with distinctive hand-drawn

lettering. He has also designed memorial inscriptions (e.g. for Walter de la Mare in St Paul's Cathedral), trade marks, advertisements, tapestries and jewellery, and has written extensively on typography and handwriting. Between 1938 and 1951, he illustrated several books with small, lively pen and ink decorations and drawings. Elected RDI; awarded Honorary Doctorate at the Royal College of Art (1968); a member of the Double Crown Club. [Q]

Books illustrated include:
Walter de la Mare Collected Poems (1942), Collected Rhymes and Verses (1944)
Nell Heaton Traditional Recipes of the British Isles (with Margaret Wolpe 1951)
F. le Mesurier Sauces, French and English (1947)
Kenneth M. Moir Some Adventures of a Cornet of Horse in the Crimean War (1938)
N. Denholm Young Magna Carta and other Charters of English Liberties (1938)

References: Lewis; WaG; WW (1980); *Art and Industry* vol 28 no 167 (1940); *Signature* 15 (1940); *Berthold Wolpe, A Retrospective Survey* (Victoria and Albert Museum/Faber & Faber, 1980); James Laver, *Adventures in Monochrome* (Studio 1941); [J. Moran] *Wolpe, Book Designer* (Printing World Supplement, Book Design and Production, 1974); Charles Mozley* *Wolperiana* (Merrion Press, 1960)

Clarence Lawson Wood (1878-1957)

Worked as Lawson Wood. Born in Highgate, London, into an artistic family. Spent his early life at Shere, Surrey. Studied at the Slade School of Fine Art, Heatherley's School of Art and at Frank Calderon's School of Animal Painting. From 1896 to 1902, he was employed as principal artist by the publishing house, Arthur Pearson. Member of the London Sketch Club and a close friend of Tom Browne*. During World War I, he served in the Royal Flying Corps as a balloonist, and was decorated by the French. Later, he set up a factory to make wooden toys to his own designs. Towards the end of his life, he lived as something of a recluse in a medieval manor house that he had earlier discovered in Sussex and rebuilt on a new site in Kent. Wood's wide reputation as a humorous illustrator and commercial artist was based on astute management; he retained copyrights in all his work and sold many of his pictures in Britain and abroad for posters, postcards, etc. He was especially well known for his drawings of monkeys, comic policemen and Stone Age characters, often seen performing absurd antics against immaculate, dead-pan backgrounds. P.V. Bradshaw commented that he had a 'breadth, ease and fluency which many an infinitely more serious artist must envy'. He worked in pen and ink, pencil, chalk and watercolour. Elected RI.

Books illustrated include:
John Finnemore The Red Men of the Dusk (1899)
J.C. Kernahan The Bow-Wow Book (1912)
Lawson Wood The 'Mr' Books (1916), The 'Mrs' Books (1920), Rummy Tales (1920), The Noo-Zoo Tales (1922), Colour Book

Series (from 1925), The Scot 'Scotched' (1927), Fun Fair (1931), A
Bedtime Picture Book (1943), Meddlesome Monkeys (1946),
Mischief Makers (1946)
R. Wylett A Basket of Plums (with others, 1916), Box of Crackers
(with others, 1916)
Jolly Rhymes (with others, 1926)
The Old Nursery Rhymes (1933)

Periodicals: The Boy's Own Paper, The Bystander, The Captain,
Cassell's Magazine, Chums, The Flag, The Graphic, Holly Leaves, The
Humorist, The Illustrated London News, Little Folks, The London
Magazine, The Odd Volume, Pearson's Magazine, Printer's Pie, The
Royal Magazine, The Sketch, The Strand Magazine, The Windsor
Magazine

References: Bénézit; Bradshaw; Crouch; Cuppleditch; Doyle BWI;
Houfe; ICB 1; Johnson & Greutzner; Thieme & Becker; Waters; *The
Strand Magazine* 55 (1918); *The Studio* 63 (1915); Percy Bradshaw
They Make Us Smile (Chapman & Hall 1942); A.E. Johnson *Lawson
Wood* (A. & C. Black 1910)

Elsie Anna Wood (active 1921-50)

Illustrator in black and white, and in full colour,
mainly of bible stories for children.

Books illustrated include:
Muriel J. Chalmers Bible Books for Small People (1932)
Mary Entwhistle Musa: Son of Egypt (1927)
J.M.M. Ferguson Jesus, Friend of Birds and Beasts (1932)
Dorothy S. Forester Fumiko's Happy New Year (1922)
William H.T. Gairdner Joseph and his Brothers (1921)
E. Nesbit Our New Story Book (with Louis Wain*, 1913)
Elsie Oxenham The Abbey Girls Go Back to School (1923), The New
Abbey Girls (1923), The Abbey Girls Again (1924)
Constance E. Padwick The Boy by the River (1921)
Henry T. Vodden Govind (1923)
Elsie Anna Wood Ayo and her Brother (1927), The Big World Picture
Book (1927), The Elsie Anna Wood Scripture Picture Books (1929-
31), Gospel Picture Books (1938)
Mwana Mpotevu (Bible selections in Swahili, 1929)
SPCK Giant Picture Books (with N.K. Brisley*, 1950)

Periodical: The Girls' Realm

Reference: *After Alice* (Museum of Childhood Exhibition Catalogue
1977)

Leslie Wood (b. 1920)

Born Stockport, Cheshire, son of a master-
craftsman. Studied at Manchester School of Art.
Since 1946, he has worked freelance as a landscape painter, lithographer, book illustrator and
designer for advertising. Part-time lecturer at
Epsom and Ewell School of Art (1965-68) and
associate lecturer at Bristol Polytechnic Faculty of
Art and Design since 1964. He became known as
an illustrator when he took over as illustrator of
the *Little Red Engine* series of children's stories
from Lewitt-Him*, working in full colour and
halftone wash. He taught himself wood engraving
and his illustrations in this medium for the Cresset
Press's *Baron Munchausen* (1948) were also well
received. He describes his work as 'versatile—
sometimes whimsical, sometimes serious, but
endeavouring to produce lively and vigorous
work which "lives" '. [Q]

Books illustrated include:
Margaret Baker Hi-Jinks Joins the Bears (1968), Teabag and the Bears
(1970), Boots and the Ginger Bears (1972)

Leila Berg The Little Red Car Has a Day Out (1970)
Michael Bond Thursday Ahoy (1969), Thursday in Paris (1971)
Carver and Stowasser Oxford Colour Readers and Workbooks (1963)
Helen Cresswell Jumbo Back to Nature (1965), Jumbo Afloat (1966),
Jumbo and the Big Dog (1968)
E.M. Hatt Callers at our House (1945), The Cat with a Guinea to
Spend (1947)
Geraldine Kaye The Rotten Old Car (1973)
William Mayne Dormouse Tales (5 vols 1966)
Johnny Morris Delilah (1964)
R.E. Raspe The Adventures of Baron Munchausen (1948)
Antonia Ridge and Mies Bouhuys Melodia (1969)
Diana Ross The Story of The Little Red Engine (1945), Whoo, Whoo
The Wind Blew (1946), The Little Red Engine Goes to Market
(1946), The Little Red Engine Goes to Town (1952), Ebenezer the
Big Balloon (1952), The Little Red Engine Goes Travelling (1955),
The Little Red Engine and Rocket (1956), The Little Red Engine
Goes Home (1958), The Little Red Engine Goes to be Mended
(1966), The Little Red Engine and the Taddlecombe Outing (1968),
The Little Red Engine Gets a Name (1968), The Little Red Engine
Goes Carolling (1971)
Diana Ross and Leslie Wood I love my love with an 'A' where is he:
Wih! (1972)
Joan Tate Little Sister Bee (1973)
Leslie Wood Six Silly Cyclists (1979)
Leslie Wood and Roy Burden The Big Red Bus, an introduction to
maths for infants (9 titles, 1978-81)

References: Balston EWE; Fisher p.323; ICB 2; William Feaver *When
We Were Young* (Thames & Hudson 1977)

Stanley L. Wood (1866-1928)

Born in Monmouthshire. Spent his childhood in
America; worked in London and the USA. Subject painter and illustrator of adventure stories,
best known for his 'Captain Kettle' drawings
which appeared in magazines and later books.
Most of Wood's illustrations are wash drawings;
his emphatic tonal contrasts reproduced well in
the halftone process and he was noted for his
vigorous, dramatic style and for the authenticity
of his American 'frontier' backgrounds.

Books illustrated include:
G. Boothby Doctor Nikola (1896), The Phantom Stockman (1897)
F.N. Connell How Soldiers Fight (with others, 1899)
H.N. Crellin Romances of the Old Seraglio (1894)
T.R. Dewar A Ramble round the Globe (1894)
Bret Harte A Wait of the Plains (1890)
G.A. Henty Riyub, the Juggler (1893), No Surrender (1900),
H. Herman Lady Turpin (1895)
C.J.W. Hyne Further Adventures of Captain Kettle (1899)
S.J. Mackenna Brave Men in Action (1899)
B. Mitford The King's Assegai (1894)
J.E. Muddock Maid Marian and Robin Hood (1892)
Stanley Wood Ten Little Sausages (1915)
The Arabian Nights Entertainments (with others, 1890)
The Arabian Nights Entertainments (1901)

Periodicals: Black and White, The Boy's Own Paper, Cassell's
Magazine, Chums, The Graphic, The Harmsworth Magazine, The
Idler, The Illustrated London News, The London Magazine, The Pall
Mall Magazine, Pearson's Magazine, The Penny Magazine, The
Sporting and Dramatic News, The Strand Magazine, The Wide World
Magazine, The Windsor Magazine, Young England

References: Doyle BWI; Houfe; Johnson & Greutzner; Thorpe;
Waters 2; C. Wood; *The Ludgate* 2 (1897)

Starr Wood (1870-1944)

Born London, son of a customs officer. Entered
the office of a chartered accountant in 1887, but

from 1890 worked full-time as a humorous artist and caricaturist, contributing to many magazines and often using the pseudonym 'The Snark'. A self-taught draughtsman, he developed a slick, animated and always up-to-date style which, with his very down-to-earth sense of humour, won him lasting popularity. He produced a quarterly, *The Windmill*, and (from 1910) *Starr Wood's Magazine*. He lived in Hertfordshire, was an early member of the London Sketch Club and a close friend of James Thorpe* (with whom he went on hiking expeditions).

Books illustrated include:
H.I. MacCourt Women as Pets (1938)
Starr Wood Cocktail Time (1896), Dances You have Never Seen (1921), P.T.O. A Collection of 94 Humorous Drawings (1934)
Starr Wood and H. Simpson (dished up by) Woman en Casserole (1936)
The Snark's Annual (1910)
Woman (1919)

Periodicals: Ariel, The Bystander, The Captain, Chums, The English Illustrated Magazine, Fun, The Humorist, The Idler, Judy, London Opinion, Moonshine, The Odd Volume, Passing Show, Pick-Me-Up, Printer's Pie, Punch, The Royal Magazine, St Paul's, The Sketch, Starr Wood's Magazine, The Tatler, The Windmill, The Windsor Magazine

References: Bénézit; Cuppleditch; Hammerton; Houfe; Johnson & Greutzner; Thieme & Becker; Thorpe; Vollmer; Wa (1934); Waters 2; *Who Was Who* (1941-50); *The Strand Magazine* 53 (1917)

Paul Vincent Woodroffe (1875-1954)

Born in Madras, India, son of a judge. Educated in England at Stonyhurst School. Studied at the Slade School of Fine Art, where he won a prize for life drawing. During the late 1890s he worked for the stained glass designer Chrisopher Whall, and in 1904 set up his own stained glass workshop at Chipping Campden, Gloucestershire, in loose association with the Chipping Campden Guild of Handicraft. His most important commission in stained glass was for windows for St Patrick's Cathedral in New York (1912-34). He was also a landscape painter, heraldic draughtsman, poster designer, book illustrator, and book cover designer, the latter mainly for the publishing firm of T.C. & E.C. Jack. As an illustrator, he collaborated with his brother-in-law, composer Joseph Moorat, on books of songs for which he wrote out words and song settings; he also worked with his friends Laurence and Clemence Housman. Laurence Housman was forced to give up book illustration in 1900 because of failing sight, and Woodroffe illustrated several of his later books of verse with drawings that were engraved on wood by Clemence Housman. Woodroffe belonged to the transitional period in the wood engraving revival when artists who were not necessarily engravers themselves began to rediscover the aesthetic possibilities of the medium. Woodroffe's later book illustrations include some evocative full colour plates for *The Tempest*, as well as more conventional work, including religious illustrations for children. He also designed the first unicorn pressmark (c.1916) and music punches for the Curwen Press and decorations commissioned for the Shakespeare Head Press by his friend Bernard Newdigate. Elected to the Art Workers' Guild (1902) and the Society of Master Glass Painters.

Books illustrated include:
Robert Browning The Flight of the Duchess (1905)
Lena Dalkeith Stories from Roman History (1907)
Laurence Housman Aucassin and Nicolette (1902), The Snow Lay on the Ground (1902), Noel (1903), The World is Old Tonight (1903) (all engraved by Clemence Housman)
Ethelwyn Lemon Stories from Greek History (1907)
Mark Lemon The Enchanted Doll (1915)
Joseph Moorat (music), Ye Booke of Nursery Rhymes (1895), Second Booke of Nursery Rhymes (1896), Humpty Dumpty and Other Songs* (1905), A Country Garland of Ten Songs Gathered from the Hesperides of Robert Herrick (1897), Thirty Old Time Nursery Songs (1907)
William Shakespeare Songs from the Plays of William Shakespeare (1898), The Tempest (1908)
Amy Steedman A Little Child's Life of Jesus (1906)
C.M. Steedman The Child's Life of Jesus (1906)
Alfred, Lord Tennyson The Princess and other Poems (1904)
The Confessions of Saint Augustine (with Laurence Housman, engraved by Clemence Housman 1900)
Froissart's Cronycles (Shakespeare Head Press edition 1927-28)
The Little Flowers of Saint Benet
The Little Flowers of Saint Francis of Assisi (1899)

Periodicals: The Illustrated London News, The Quarto

References: Baker; Crane; Houfe; ICB 1; Johnson; Johnson & Greutzner; Sketchley; Taylor; Thieme & Becker; Wa (1934); C. Wood; *The Studio* special (1897-98, 1898-99, 1899-1900, 1923-24, Autumn 1938); *Paul Woodroffe 1875-1954* (William Morris Gallery, Walthamstow 1982); Herbert Simon *Song and Words* (Allen & Unwin 1973)

Richard Caton Woodville (1856-1927)

Born in London, son of an American painter of the same name. Brought up in Russia and Germany; studied art at Düsseldorf under Eduard von Gebhert and in Paris under Jean-Léon Gérôme (1824-1904). Early on, he achieved a European reputation as a painter of battle scenes, and in *Random Recollections* expresses mild surprise that the British public should have only sporadic enthusiasm for paintings of such subjects. As a correspondent for *The Illustrated London News*, he covered a number of military campaigns, including the Russo-Turkish war (1878) and the Egyptian rebellion (1882), and he also depicted the Boer War and World War I. He was a successful portrait painter, with Edward VII among his sitters. Woodville was one of the most popular of the late 19th-century war correspondents, and was admired for the panache of his style and the accuracy of his detail. He was skilful at conveying the excitement of battles and at overlooking the depressing realities of such encounters. His book illustrations are mostly of military subjects. However, when his work as a reporter called for drawings of civilian hardship and poverty, he was able to respond with sympathy, as demonstrated by his pictures of Ireland for *The Illustrated London News* (1880), which were admired by Vincent Van Gogh. His early illustrations are sometimes in black and white, his later ones in halftone or full colour.

Books illustrated include:
P. Bigelow History of the German Struggle for Liberty (with others, 1896), White Man's Africa (with others, 1898)
F.N. Connell How Soldiers Fight (with others, 1899)
H. Rider Haggard Cleopatra (1889)
M.L. Molesworth A Charge Fulfilled (1886)
W. Richards His Majesty's Territorial Army (1910)
E. Sanderson The Fight for the Flag in South Africa (1900)
H.F.B. Wheeler Makers of the British Empire (1927
R.C. Woodville The Dawn of Waterloo: a Sketch in One Scene (1913), Random Reminiscences (1913), The Romance of India (1913)
Social Life in the British Army (1900)

Periodicals: The Captain, Cassell's Magazine, Chums, The Cornhill Magazine, The English Illustrated Magazine, Harper's Magazine, The Illustrated London News, Pearson's Magazine, The Sketch, The Sporting and Dramatic News, The Strand Magazine, The Tatler, The Windsor Magazine

References: Chamot, Farr & Butlin; Doyle BWI; Harper; Houfe; Johnson & Greutzner; Pennell MI; Thieme & Becker; Thorpe; Waters; C. Wood; *The Idler* 10 (1897); *The Ludgate* 2 (1897); Pat Hodgson *The War Illustrators* (Osprey 1977); R.C. Woodville *Random Reminiscences* (Everleigh Nash 1914)

Alice Bolingbroke Woodward (1862-1911)

Born in London, daughter of Dr Henry Woodward, Keeper of Geology at the British Museum. As a child she drew in the Greek and Roman galleries of the museum and made diagrams and scientific drawings for her father. Studied at the South Kensington and Westminster Schools of Art and in Paris at the Académie Julian. Watercolour painter and an accomplished illustrator of children's books in pen and ink, or pencil and wash, with a graceful, economical line, who often brought a refreshing sense of humour to her work. Some of her earlier drawings are in the manner of Charles Robinson*.

Books illustrated include:
W.B. Allen Forty Fables for Fireside Reflection (1904)
Sheila E. Braine The Princess of Hearts (1899), To Tell the King the Sky is Falling (1896),
Lewis Carroll Alice's Adventures in Wonderland (1913)
Mary S. Clark Lost Legends of the Nursery Songs (1921)
M.I. Cole The Story of Santa Claus for Little People (1920)
Euie Jock and the Fairy Robin (1902), To Fairyland on a Swing (1904)
Juliana H. Ewing Lob Lie-by-the-Fire (1909), Brownies and other Tales (1910)
Mrs M. Gatty Parables from Nature (1910)
W.S. Gilbert The Pinafore Picture Book (1908), The Story of the Mikado (1921)
Countess of Jersey Eric, Prince of Lorlonia (1895)
Edith King Hall Adventures in Toyland (1897, The Flowers of Fairyland (1910)
Hamish Hendry Red Apple and Silver Bells (1897)
Edith Howes Rainbow Children (1912)
W.C. Jerrold Bon-Mots of the Eighteenth Century (1897), Bon-Mots of the Nineteenth Century (1897)
Charles Kingsley The Water Babies (1909)
H.R. Knipe Nebula to Man (1905), Evolution in the Past (1912)
Mrs. Molesworth The Horse That Grew (1900)
Alice Talwin Morris The Elephant's Apology (1899), The Troubles of Tatters and other stories (1898)

Daniel S. O'Connor The Peter Paul Picture Book (1907), The Story of Peter Pan (1914)
Alice Sargeant The Brownies (1897)
E. Sharp Round the World to Wympland (1902)
G.C. Young Bimbo (1896)
Banbury Cross and other Nursery Rhymes (1895)
The Cat and the Mouse (1899)
The Golden Ship and other tales (with others, 1900), The History of Little Goody Two Shoes (1924)

Periodicals: Blackie's Annuals, Cassell's Magazine, The Daily Chronicle, The Daily Graphic, The Illustrated London News, The Quarto

References: Baker; Bénézit; Houfe; ICB 1; Johnson & Greutzner; Sketchley; Thieme & Becker; C. Wood; *The Studio* special Christmas 1894, 1897-98, 1900-01); Walter Shaw Sparrow *Women Painters of the World* (Hodder and Stoughton 1905)

Guy Worsdell (1908-78)

Born in York. Studied at the Central School of Arts and Crafts (1930-33) under Noel Rooke* and John Farleigh*, and had further instruction in wood engraving from John Beedham. As a painter and wood engraver, he specialised in landscape and railway subjects, often depicting locomotives designed by his grandfather, T.W. Worsdell, for the North Eastern Railway. His book illustrations were published by the Caravel and Batchworth Presses. [Q]

Books illustrated include:
Anna Gordon Keown Collected Poems (1952)
Leslie Paul Heron Lake (1948), Exile and Other Poems (1951)
Rondel's Poems from the French (1951)

References: Garrett BWE, HBWE

John Worsley (b. 1919)

Born in Liverpool, son of a naval commander and sometime Kenya coffee farmer. Studied art at Goldsmith's College (1934-37) and subsequently worked freelance. Served in the RNVR (1939-46), and was an official Naval War Artist (1943-46). As a prisoner of war (from 1943), he helped a fellow prisoner to escape by constructing a dummy officer, 'Albert', an exploit later commemorated in a feature film *Albert R N* (1953), which was made with his assistance. During the 1950s, he became known as a children's illustrator through his halftone drawings for the comic strip *P.C. 49* (which was based on a radio series) in the boys' magazine *Eagle* (Hulton Press). A portrait and marine painter, children's book illustrator, sculptor and designer of television programmes using multiple still pictures, he works in most media. He has made wood engravings for the Dropmore Press. Lives and works in Putney. Vice-President of the RSMA.

Books illustrated include:
Jane Carruthers (retold by) Purnell Colour Classics: Robinson Crusoe (1975), Treasure Island (1975), The Three Musketeers (1976), Tom Sawyer (1977), Lorna Doone (1979)
Thomas Cubbin The Wreck of the Serica (1950)

John Fernald Destroyer from America (1942)
Kenneth Grahame The Wind in the Willows (1983)
Robert Harling The Steep Atlantick Stream (1946), Amateur Sailor
   (1947)
Macdonald Hastings Sydney the Sparrow (1971), Mary Celeste (1972)
Guy Morgan Only Ghosts Can Live (1945)

Periodicals: Eagle, Girl

References: Vollmer supp; Wa (1972); Waters; *John Worsley*
(catalogue, Anglia Television August 1972); *John Worsley* (catalogue,
Mall Galleries December 1971)

Arthur Wragg (b. 1903)

Born near Manchester, studied at Sheffield
School of Art from 1916. In 1923, he moved to
London and worked initially for magazines. His
book illustrations had a *succès d'estime* in the
1930s, being valued for their political and spiritual
message as well as for their powerful designs. His
versatility as a draughtsman is seen by comparing
the stark black and white imagery of *Jesus Wept*,
with the surrealist complexity of his pencil drawings for *Seven Words*, or the lighthearted ease of
his fine pen and ink sketches for *Cranford* and
Three Husbands Hoaxed. In subject matter, *Jesus*

Arthur Wragg. 'To-morrow—and To-morrow'
from his *Jesus Wept* with an introduction by
Vernon Bartlett (Selwyn Blount, 1935).

Wept is somewhat reminiscent of the work of the
radical Belgian woodcut artist Frans Masereel
(1889-1972).

Books illustrated include:
Daniel Defoe Moll Flanders (1948)
R.M. Freeman Samuel Pepys Looks at Life (1931)
Mrs Gaskell Cranford (1947)
W. Greenwood The Cleft Stick (1937)
W. Holt I was a Prisoner (1935)
G. Téllez Three Husbands Hoaxed (1954)
Oscar Wilde The Ballad of Reading Gad (1948)
Arthur Wragg The Psalms for Modern Life (1933), Jesus Wept (1935),
   Seven Words (1939), Thy Kingdom Come (1939), Alice Through
   the Paper-Mill (with others, 1940), The Song of Songs (1952)
The Lord's Prayer in Black and White (1946)

Periodicals: Nash's Magazine, The Sunday Magazine, Woman's
Journal, Woman's Pictorial

References: Waters 2; *The Artist* 11 (1936)

Alan Wright (1864-1927)

Lived as a child at Chard, Somerset, and later in
London. Studied at St John's Wood School of
Art. He shared rooms with Gleeson White, art
critic and first editor of *The Studio*. In 1912, he
married the illustrator Anne Anderson*, and
sometimes collaborated with her on books — even
at times working on the same drawings, which
they signed jointly. He was a painter, children's
writer and illustrator, and postcard designer. As
an illustrator he was particularly known for his
drawings for G.E. Farrar's *Wallypug* series. He
worked in black and white and full colour, initially
without much expertise, in a style that became
increasingly like Anne Anderson's in his later
books.

Books illustrated include:
Anne Anderson and Alan Wright The Cuddly Kitty, etc. (1926)
W.S.W. Anson The Christmas Book of Carols and Songs (with others
   1905)
A. Corkran The Life of Queen Victoria (1910)
G.E. Farrow Adventures in Wallypug Land (1897), The Wallypug in
   London (1897), The Little Panjandrum's Dodo (1899), The
   Mandarin's Kite (1900), Baker Minor and the Dragon (1902), The
   New Panjandrum (1902), In Search of the Wallypug (1903), The
   Cinematograph Train (1904), Professor Philandapan (1904), The
   Wallypug Birthday Book (1904), The Wallypug in Fog-Land (1904),
   The Wallypug in the Moon (1905)
A.G. Herbertson Sing-Song Stories (1922)
Washington Irving Rural Life in England (with Vernon Stokes, 1906),
   Rip Van Winkle (1921)
Mark Lemon The Enchanted Doll (1921)
Frances H. Low Queen Victoria's Dolls (1894)
Alan Wright Comic Sport and Pastime (with E.V. Stokes, 1904), Mrs
   Bunnykins' Busy Day (1919), Bingo and Babs (1919), Mrs
   Bunnykins Builds an Igloo (1920), The Story of the Saucy Squirrel
   (1924), Tony Twiddler, His Tale (1924), The Wonderful Tale of the
   Trail of a Snail (1924), The Cuddly Kitty (with Anne Anderson*,
   1926), The Podgy Puppy (with Anne Anderson*, 1927), The Book of
   Baby Birds (with C. Englefield, 1936), Little Teddy Bear (nd)

Periodicals: Atalanta, The Dome, The Girl's Own Paper, The Idler,
The Pall Mall Magazine, The Parade, The Strand Magazine, The
Sunday Pictorial, The Wide World Magazine, The Windmill

References: Baker; Becker; Bénézit; Houfe; Johnson & Greutzner;
Sketchley; Thieme & Becker; Thorpe; *The Book Collector* (Winter
1979)

John Buckland Wright (1897-1954)

Born Dunedin, New Zealand. Educated in England at Clifton and Rugby. Awarded the Croix de Guerre for gallantry during World War I. Studied history at Oxford and architecture at the Bartlett School in London University; then, inspired by Gordon Craig's* *Woodcuts and Some Words* (1924) and by the wood engraving display at the Victoria & Albert Museum, he taught himself to engrave on wood. Moved to Brussels and rapidly gained a European reputation as a printmaker and book illustrator. He joined Stanley William Hayter's printmaking studio in Paris (1929), afterwards becoming a director; there he met and worked with artists of international stature, including Picasso, Matisse, Brancusi and Miró, as well as British printmakers such as Leon Underwood* and Anthony Gross*. His work reached a British public in 1936 when he illustrated the first of 15 books for the Golden Cockerel Press. During World War II, he worked in England in a camouflage unit and later as censor-in-charge at Reuter's. He was on the staff of Camberwell School of Art (1948) and, on the recommendation of John Piper*, of the Slade School of Fine Art (1950 until his death). Buckland Wright is widely regarded as one of the most polished and technically brilliant engravers of the 20th century. Hayter suggested that the 'meticulous organisation acquired in his architectural training gave him special access to the techniques of wood engraving and etching', and gave him credit for many technical innovations in printmaking that subsequently passed into general use. He drew from life regularly, and female nudes (uniformly statuesque and voluptuous) became almost a leitmotiv of his work. He illustrated some 75 books, many of which many were published in France, Belgium and Holland; however, his *magnum opus* was undoubtedly Keats's *Endymion* (Golden Cockerel Press, 1947), for which he made 58 wood engravings. Member of the London Group and SWE.

Books illustrated include:
Richard Aldington (trans) The Decameron of Giovanni Boccaccio (2 vols, 1954-55)
Leonid Andreyev The Seven Who Were Hanged (1947)
F. Beaumont (attributed to) Salmacis and Hermaphroditus (1951)
Marie Bonaparte Flyda of the Seas (1950)
Rupert Brooke Poems (1948)
Adrian Bury Syon House (with others, 1955)
James B. Cabell Jurgen (1949)
Paul Claudel (trans) Two Poems of Coventry Patmore (1931)
Somerset de Chair (trans) Napoleon's Memoirs (1945)
Edward FitzGerald (trans) The Golden Cockerel Rubaiyat of Omar Khayyam ┊ (1938)
Théophile Gautier Mademoiselle de Maupin (1938)
Phyllis Hartnoll The Grecian Enchanted (1952)
Frances Hume (trans) The Story of the Circle of Chalk (1953)
Gwyn Jones (ed) Poems and Sonnets of William Shakespeare (1960)
John Keats Sonnets (1930), Endymion (1947)
F.L. Lucas (trans) Pervigilium Veneris (1939), The Odyssey of Homer (1948), Hero and Leander (1949), The Iliad of Homer (1950)

John Buckland Wright. Headpiece from *Hymn to Proserpine* by Algernon Swinburne (Golden Cockerel Press, 1944).

Stephen Mallarmé L'Après-Midi d'un Faune (1956)
Powys Mathers Love Night (1936)
G. Rawson Matthew Flinders' Narrative of the Voyage of the Schooner Francis: 1798 (1946)
George Reavey Quixotic Perquisitions (1939)
Percy Bysshe Shelley Poems (1949)
Algernon Swinburne Dolores (1933), Hymn to Proserpine (1944), Laus Veneris (1948), Pasiphae (1950)
Mary Waddington Cassell's Picture Dictionary (1952)
Cupid's Pastime (1935)

Periodical: The Woodcut

References: Balston EWE, WEMEB; Bénézit; Garrett BWE, HBWE; Guichard; Johnson & Greutzner; Thieme & Becker; Vollmer; Wa (1954); Waters; *Apollo* 16 (1932) pp.298-99; *Image* 4 (1950); *The Studio* 134 (1947), special (Winter 1936, Autumn 1938); *John Buckland Wright's Engravings* (University of Florida Libraries 1964); Anthony Reid *A Check-List of the Book Illustrations of John Buckland Wright* (Private Libraries Association 1968); Christopher Sandford *Bibliography of the Golden Cockerel Press* (Dawson 1975), *Cock-a-Hoop* (Private Libraries Association, 1976); John Buckland Wright (intro) *Christopher Buckland Wright* (Catalogue, Anthony Blond 1981)

Matvyn Wright (active from 1954)

Illustrator of Maria Bird's *Andy Pandy* series (after Irene Hawkins*, who illustrated the first title), and other books originating from the *Watch with Mother* television series.

Books illustrated include:
Ruth Ainsworth Five 'Listen with Mother Tales' about Charles (1957)
Maria Bird Andy Pandy, Teddy and Looby Loo (1954), The Flowerpot Men and the Bush Baby (1954), The Flowerpot Men and the Weathercock (1954), Jenny Penny and the Flowerpot Men (1955), Andy Pandy and the Queen of Hearts (1955), Andy Pandy Builds a House for Looby Loo (1956), Andy Pandy and the Woolly Lamb (1959), Andy Pandy's Adventures (1959), Andy Pandy and the Teddy Dog (1960), Andy Pandy's Tea Party (1960), Andy Pandy and the Baby Pigs (1961), Andy Pandy's Little Goat (1961), Andy Pandy and the Patchwork Cat (1962), Andy Pandy and the Snowman (1962), Andy Pandy's New Pet (1963), Andy Pandy's Weather House (1963), Andy Pandy and the Green Puppy (1965)

References: Fisher p.6

William Lionel Leonard Wyllie (1851-1931)

Born in London, son of painter W.M. Wyllie, brought up at Wimereux on the north coast of France. Marine painter in watercolour and oil. Studied art at Heatherley's School of Art and at the Royal Academy Schools, where he won the

Turner Gold Medal (1869). A marine painter in watercolour and oil, he became well known through engravings and reproductions of his paintings and through illustrations for *The Graphic*, for well-informed and convincing descriptions of the life and atmosphere of ships and the sea. He won gold (1889) and silver (1900) medals at Paris Exhibitions. His patrons included the Royal Victoria Yacht Club (of which he was an honorary member), the Royal Navy and the White Star Shipping Line. He published a monograph on J.M.W. Turner (whom he greatly admired) in 1905. Though by then elderly, he served in the Royal Navy during World War I. Elected RBA (1875), RI (1882-94 and 1917-31), NEAC (1887), ARA (1889), and RA (1907), ARE and RE (1903).

Books illustrated include:
C.G.B. Allen The Tidal Thames (1892)
F.T. Jane The British Battle Fleet (1912)
E.R. Pennell Tantallon Castle (with others, 1895)
M.A. Wyllie London to the Nore (1905), Norway and its Fjords (1907)
W.L.L. Wyllie Nature's Laws and the Making of Pictures (1903),
    Marine Painting in Watercolour (1905), Sketch-Book (with M.F.
    Wren 1908), Sea Fights of the Great War (1918), The Old
    Portsmouth and the New Southsea (1931)

Periodicals: The Graphic, The Windsor Magazine

References: Bénézit; Chamot, Farr & Butlin; DNB (1931-40);
Guichard; Harper; Houfe; Johnson & Greutzner; Mallalieu; Pennell
MI, PD; Thieme & Becker; Thorpe; Wa (1929); Waters; C. Wood; *Art
Journal* (1889); *The Studio* special (Christmas 1949); *Great Victorian
Pictures* (Arts Council catalogue 1978); M.A. Wyllie *We Were One. A
Life of W.L. Wyllie* (G. Bell 1935)

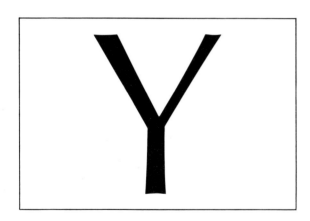

Jack Butler Yeats (1871-1957)

Contributed regularly to *Punch* (1910-41) under the pseudonym W. Bird. Born in London, son of the Irish figure and portrait painter John Butler Yeats, and brother of the poet W.B. Yeats. Educated in County Sligo where he lived with his grandparents. Studied art at South Kensington and Chiswick Art Schools and under Frederick Brown* at Westminster School of Art. He wrote and illustrated stories and plays for books and magazines, edited and largely illustrated two monthly publications *A Broadsheet* (1902-03)

Jack B. Yeats. 'Singing a Political Ballad' from his *Life in the West of Ireland* (Maunsel & Co., 1912).

and *A Broadside* (1908-15), and produced prints, Christmas cards and calendars for the Cuala Press. He lived in Devon from 1897 to 1910 and then in Ireland; he died in Dublin.

From around 1905, Yeats devoted much of his energy to oil paintings of Irish life and landscape, and it is for these that he is now best known. Nevertheless, his drawings an illustrations form an important part of his work. They are bold and spirited, recalling in their directness and informality, the graphic work of Manet, but drawn in a wholly individual manner. The simplicity and throwaway humour of his *Punch* drawings compare very favourably with the more laboured efforts of many of the other contributors. Elected ARHA (1915), RHA (1916), Hon. Member of the London Group (1940), Governor and Guardian of the National Gallery of Ireland.

Books illustrated include:
G.A. Birmingham Irishmen All (1913)
T. Bodkin My Uncle Frank (1940)
Norma Borthwick Ceachta Beag a Gaelige (1902)
Padraic Colum A Boy in Erinn (1913), The Big Tree of Bunlahy
    (1933), The Jackdaw (nd)
M. Cregan Sean-Eoin (1938)
G.C. Duggan The Stage Irishman (1937)

O.St.J. Gogarty The Ship and Other Poems (1918)
Patricia Lynch The Turfcutter's Donkey (with others, 1934)
John Masefield A Mainsail Haul (1905)
S. Mitchell Frankincense and Myrrh (1912)
S. O'Beirn Paistidheacht (1910)
F. O'Connell A Lament for Art O'Leary (1940)
S. O'Kelley Ranns and Ballads (1918), The Weaver's Grave (1922)
J.H. Reynolds The Fancy (1906)
E. Rhys The Great Cockney Tragedy (1891), The Prince of Lisnover (1904)
G.W. Russell (ed) New Songs (1904)
J.M. Synge The Aran Islands (1907), In Wicklow, West Kerry and Connemara (1911)
J.B. Yeats James Flaunty of the Terror of the Western Seas (1901), The Scourge of the Gulph (1903), The Treasure of the Garden (1903), The Bosun and the Bob-Tailed Comet (1904), A Little Fleet (1909), Life in the West of Ireland (1912), Sligo (1930), Three Plays: Apparitions, The Old Sea Road, Rattle (1933), Sailing, Sailing Swiftly (1933), The Amaranthers (1936), Ah Well (1938), The Charmed Life (1938), And To You Also (1944), The Careless Flower (1947), In Sand (1964)
W.B. Yeats Irish Fairy Tales (1892), A London Garland (1895) Reveries over Childhood and Youth (1917), On the Boiler (1939) Outriders (1943)
The Book of St Ultain (1920)

Periodicals: Ariel, The Big Budget, The Boy's Own Paper, A Broadsheet, A Broadside, Celtic Christmas, Chips, Chums, Comic Cuts, The Daily Graphic, Dundrum, Fun, The Golden Hind, Illustrated Chips, The Jester, Judy, Lika Joko, Manchester Guardian, New Budget, The New Leader Book, Paddock Life, Punch, Shanachie, The Sketch, Sporting Sketches, Vegetarian

References: Bénézit; Chamot, Farr & Butlin; DNB (1951-60); Doyle BWI; Houfe; ICB 1,2; Johnson & Greutzner; Phaidon; Price; Shone; Thieme & Becker; Vollmer; Wa (1956); Waters; *The Bookplate (1926); The Studio* special (Autumn 1914); *T.P.'s Weekly* (18th July 1914); *Westminster Gazette* (21st December 1921); T. Macgreevy *Jack B. Yeats* (Waddington, Dublin 1945); Ernest B. Marriott *Jack B. Yeats* (Routledge & Kegan Paul 1970); T.G. Rosenthal *Jack B. Yeats 1871-1957* (Knowledge Publications 1966)

Anna K. Zinkeisen. From *The Complete Hostess* by Quaglino, edited by Charles Graves (Hamish Hamilton, 1935).

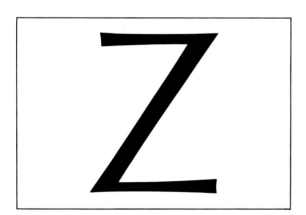

Anna Katrina Zinkeisen (1901-76)

Worked as Anna Zinkeisen. Married name: Mrs Heseltine. Born Kilcreggan, Scotland, daughter of a research chemist and sister of the theatrical designer Doris Zinkeisen. At 15, she was awarded a scholarship to the Royal Academy Schools, where she won bronze and silver medals. Best known for society portraits, she also painted flowers, executed murals (including commissions for the liners *Queen Mary* and *Queen Elizabeth*), made sculptures and designed book jackets and magazine covers. As a nurse in St Mary's Hospital, Paddington during World War II, she worked in a former operating theatre, making detailed paintings of wounds for the benefit of the medical profession. In 1953, she exhibited in the *Art in Medicine* show in London. Her book illustrations, mostly in black and white, are lively and stylish, often with fringes of shading in the manner of the later work of John Austen* and other 1930s illustrators. Elected ROI (1928).

Books illustrated include:
C.H. Abrahall Prelude (1947)
C. Brahms The Moon on my Left (1930)
B.H. Buergel Oolo-Boola's Wonder Book (1932)
Herbert Farjeon Nine Sharp and Earlier (1938)
A.P. Herbert She-Shanties (1926), Plain Jane (1927)
J. Phoenice A Rainbow of Paths (1965)
Quaglino (ed Charles Graves) The Complete Hostess (1935)
M. Sharp The Nymph and the Nobleman (1932)
Noel Streatfeild Party Frock (1946)

Periodicals: Nash's Magazine, The Sketch, The Tatler

References: Bénézit; Johnson & Greutzner; Thieme & Becker; Vollmer; Wa (1934); Waters; *The Artist* 14 (1938); *The Studio* 109 (1935), 147 (1954)